Managerial Accounting

Managerial Accounting

Fifth Edition

Belverd E. Needles, Jr. Ph.D., C.P.A., C.M.A.
DePaul University

Marian Powers Ph.D.
Northwestern University

Sherry K. Mills Ph.D., C.P.A.
New Mexico State University

Henry R. Anderson Ph.D., C.P.A., C.M.A.
Professor Emeritus, University of Central Florida

CONSULTING AUTHOR
James C. Caldwell Ph.D., C.P.A.
Andersen Consulting

CONTRIBUTING EDITOR
Susan V. Crosson M.S. Accounting, C.P.A.
Santa Fe Community College, Florida

Houghton Mifflin Company   Boston   New York

To Professor Reginald R. Rushing, Texas Tech University (Deceased)
To Professor Joseph Goodman, Chicago State University
To Professor James H. Bullock, New Mexico State University
To Professor S. James Galley, Augustana College, Illinois (Deceased)
To Professor W. Baker Flowers, University of Alabama (Deceased)

SENIOR SPONSORING EDITOR: Anne Kelly
ASSOCIATE SPONSORING EDITOR: Margaret E. Monahan
SENIOR PROJECT EDITOR: Margaret M. Kearney
SENIOR PRODUCTION/DESIGN COORDINATOR: Sarah L. Ambrose
SENIOR MANUFACTURING COORDINATOR: Priscilla J. Abreu
MARKETING MANAGER: Juli Bliss

COVER DESIGN: Diana Coe
COVER IMAGE: Spiral Staircase–Spain by Joao Paulo—The Image Bank
PHOTO CREDITS: page 1, © Mark Wagner/Tony Stone Images; page 40, © Peter Johansky/Envision; page 86, © Palma Allen; page 118, © Ian Shaw/Tony Stone Images; page 158, © Frank Edson/Tony Stone Images; page 198, © Gary Gladstone/The Image Bank; page 234, © C. Van Der Lende/The Image Bank; page 286, © David Gould/The Image Bank; page 328, © Eric Kamp/Index Stock; page 366, © TEK Image/Science Photo Library/Photo Researchers; page 396, © Gabriel Covian/The Image Bank; page 434, © Zigy Kaluzny/Tony Stone Images; page 472, © Bill Ellzey/Comstock, Inc.; page 485, © Don Carstens/Folio; page 528, © Thierry Dosogne/The Image Bank; page 532, © David Swanson/Gamma Liaison.

The Toys "R" Us Annual Report (excerpts and complete) for the year ended February 1, 1997, which appears at the end of Chapter 1, pages 57–83, is reprinted by permission. The cartoon characters in the margins of the Supplement to Chapter 1: How to Read an Annual Report, pages 48–54, are reprinted by permission from the Toys "R" Us Annual Report for the year ended January 28, 1995.

This book is written to provide accurate and authoritative information concerning the covered topics. It is not meant to take the place of professional advice.

Printed in the U.S.A.

Library of Congress Catalog Card No.: 98-72068

ISBN: 0-395-92099-X

123456789-VH-02 01 00 99 98

Contents in Brief

Contents

PART ONE **Fundamentals of Management Accounting**

CHAPTER 1 **Introduction to Management Accounting**   **1**

CHAPTER 8

Cost Control Using Standard Costing and Variance Analysis   287

PART FOUR   Information and Analysis for Management Decision Making

CHAPTER 9

Short-Run Decision Analysis   329

About the Authors

Belverd E. Needles, Jr., Ph.D., C.P.A., C.M.A.

Belverd E. Needles, Jr. received his BBA and MBA degrees from Texas Tech University and his Ph.D. degree from the University of Illinois. Dr. Needles teaches auditing and financial accounting at DePaul University, where he is the Arthur Andersen LLP Alumni Distinguished Professor and is an internationally known expert in international auditing and accounting education. He has published in leading journals in these fields and is the author or editor of more than twenty books and monographs.

Dr. Needles is active in many academic and professional organizations. He is president of the International Association for Accounting Education and Research and past president of the Federation of Schools of Accountancy. He has served as the elected U.S. representative to the European Accounting Association and chair of the International Accounting Section of the American Accounting Association. He has served as director of Continuing Education of the American Accounting Association. He serves on the Information Technology Executive Committee of the American Institute of CPAs. For the past five years he has served as the U.S. representative on the Education Committee of the International Federation of Accountants.

Dr. Needles has received the Distinguished Alumni Award from Texas Tech University, the Illinois CPA Society Outstanding Educator Award, the Joseph A. Silvoso Faculty Award of Merit from the Federation of Schools and Accountancy, the Ledger & Quill Award of Merit, and the Ledger & Quill Teaching Excellence Award. In 1992, he was named Educator of the Year by the national honorary society Beta Alpha Psi. In 1996, he received from the American Accounting Association the award of Outstanding International Accounting Educator.

Marian Powers, Ph.D.

Marian Powers earned her Ph.D. in accounting from the University of Illinois at Urbana. She has served on the accounting faculty of the Kellogg Graduate School of Management at Northwestern University, the University of Illinois at Chicago, and the Lake Forest Graduate School of Management. Since 1987, she has been a professor of accounting at the Allen Center for Executive Education at Northwestern University, specializing in teaching financial reporting and analysis to executives. She is co-author of several successful in-depth cases on financial analysis, and her research has been published in *The Accounting Review; The International Journal of Accounting; Issues in Accounting Education; The Journal of Accountancy; The Journal of Business, Finance, and Accounting;* and *Financial Management,* among others. Dr. Powers has received recognition and awards for her teaching.

Dr. Powers has been active in several professional organizations, including the Illinois CPA Society, the American Accounting Association, the European Accounting Association, the International Association of Accounting Education and Research, the American Society of Women Accountants, and the Education Foundation for Women in Accounting. She is currently serving as secretary of the Education Foundation for Women in Accounting. She is past president of the Chicago chapter and past national officer of the American Society of Women Accountants.

Sherry K. Mills, Ph.D., C.P.A.

Sherry K. Mills is Associate Professor of Accounting at New Mexico State University, where she received the Outstanding Teaching Award in the College of Business Administration and Economics and the Burlington Northern Foundation Faculty Achievement Award at the university level in 1993. She also has been recognized for teaching innovations as a runner-up for the Boeing Award in 1993 and winner of the 1996 American Accounting Association's Innovation in Accounting Education Award. Dr. Mills has made presentations about accounting innovations at conferences held by the American Accounting Association, the Institute of Management Accountants, the International Association for Accounting Education, and the Accounting Education Change Commission. She currently is designing courses for the Manufacturing Engineering and Management curriculum, a joint project between the College of Business Administration and the College of Engineering at New Mexico State University. She received her Ph.D. from Texas Tech University.

Henry R. Anderson, Ph.D., C.P.A., C.M.A.

Henry R. Anderson is KPMG Peat Marwick Professor Emeritus of Accounting at the University of Central Florida. He served as Director of UCF's School of Accounting for seven years; is the former Dean of the School of Business Administration & Economics at California State University, Fullerton; and was Assistant Director of the research staff of the Cost Accounting Standards Board, Washington, D.C. Dr. Anderson was National President of Beta Alpha Psi, 1981–82, and won the California CPA Society's 1981 Faculty Excellence Award and the 1987 Florida Excellence in Teaching Award from the College of Business at the University of Central Florida. He has been very active in the Institute of Management Accountants and has served on many committees of the American Accounting Association, the American Institute of Certified Public Accountants, and the Florida Institute of CPAs. Dr. Anderson is a graduate of Augustana College and the University of Missouri at Columbia.

Goals for MANAGERIAL ACCOUNTING, Fifth Edition

Our goal is for all students to become intelligent users of accounting information and to understand that financial information and related nonfinancial information, when interpreted and analyzed, will be useful to them in making critical business decisions throughout their careers.

Our goal is to provide the opportunity for the development in students of a wide skill set essential to success in business and management today.

Our goal, beginning with the Fourth Edition and continuing with the Fifth Edition, is to place more emphasis throughout the book on the use and analysis of accounting information by management and on the decisions that management makes regarding accounting information, including performance measurement.

Our goal is to make a significant improvement in all content coverage.

Our goal is to reflect business practice as it is today in a context that is relevant and exciting to students.

Our goal is to provide exactly the right balance between conceptual understanding and technical application and analysis.

Our goal is to provide the most comprehensive and flexible set of assignments available involving real companies.

Our goal is to provide a complete supplemental learning system— including manual and technology applications for computer, CD-ROM, video tape, and Internet support—that directly facilitates student learning.

Our goal is to provide a complete support system for the instructor.

Preface

MANAGERIAL ACCOUNTING, Fifth Edition, is a first course in accounting for students with no previous training in accounting or business. This textbook is intended for use at the undergraduate or graduate level and is designed for both business and accounting majors. It is part of a well-integrated package for students and instructors that includes several manual and computer ancillaries. It has proven successful in a variety of quarter or semester sequences.

Decision Making and the Uses of Accounting Information

MANAGERIAL ACCOUNTING recognizes that a majority of the students in the first accounting course are business and management majors who will read, analyze, and interpret accounting information throughout their careers. We believe the fundamental purpose of accounting is to provide information for decision making, and while not neglecting topics important for accounting majors,

> Our goal is for all students to become intelligent users of accounting information and to understand that financial information and related nonfinancial information, when interpreted and analyzed, will be useful to them in making critical business decisions throughout their careers.

Essential to MANAGERIAL ACCOUNTING is our conviction that the use of integrated learning objectives can significantly improve the teaching and learning of accounting. This system of learning by objectives enhances the role of the overall package, particularly the textbook, by achieving complete and thorough communication between instructor and student. Basic to this approach are the following objectives, which we have accomplished in this new revision:

- To write for business and management students as well as accounting majors
- To emphasize the role of accounting in decision making
- To make the content authoritative, practical, and contemporary
- To integrate the learning-by-objectives approach throughout the text, assignment material, and ancillaries
- To develop the most complete and flexible teaching-learning system available
- To adhere to a strict system of quality control

The success of the first four editions of MANAGERIAL ACCOUNTING has justified our confidence in this fundamental approach.

New Authors

The addition of two new authors, Dr. Marian Powers and Dr. Sherry K. Mills, over the past two editions strengthens the author team's expertise in the areas of (1) teaching business executives the latest tools of financial analysis and (2) the most current thinking on management's use of accounting information. With more than fifteen years of teaching experience at the undergraduate and graduate levels in both large and small classes, Marian Powers is an accomplished instructor who brings various instructional strategies to her financial accounting classes to develop critical thinking, group interaction, communication, and other broadening skills in students. In addition, she has taught thousands of executives how to read, interpret, and analyze corporate financial statements.

Sherry Mills, now contributing to MANAGERIAL ACCOUNTING for a second edition, has a reputation as an outstanding teacher and innovator in management accounting education. She has won the American Accounting Association's Innovation in Accounting Education Award and has taught contemporary management accounting topics in executive training. She brings a new approach to the managerial accounting chapters.

Essential Student Skills

The Fifth Edition of MANAGERIAL ACCOUNTING represents a major expansion of the decision-making approach and extends significantly the changes implemented in the Fourth Edition. The pedagogical system underlying MANAGERIAL ACCOUNTING is based on a model that encompasses a growing group of instructional strategies designed to develop and strengthen a broad skill set in students. This model, which includes learning objectives, the teaching-learning cycle, cognitive levels of learning, and output skills, is described in detail in the Course Manual that accompanies this text.

> Our goal is to provide the opportunity for the development in students of a wide skill set essential to success in business and management today.

Applying this model, the Fifth Edition achieves (1) a stronger decision-making approach with emphasis on performance measurement; (2) improved content coverage, including integrated, contemporary discussions of state-of-the-art topics; (3) maximized real-world coverage; (4) reduction of procedural detail; and (5) reorganized and expanded assignment material to increase flexibility and to concentrate on developing students' critical thinking, group and team-building, communication, and financial statement analysis skills.

Stronger Decision-Making Approach with Emphasis on Performance Measurement

MANAGERIAL ACCOUNTING continues to emphasize the use of accounting information in decision making with a new focus on the importance this information plays in performance measurement.

> Our goal, beginning with the Fourth Edition and continuing with the Fifth Edition, is to place more emphasis throughout the book on the use and analysis of accounting information by management and on the decisions that management makes regarding accounting information, including performance measurement.

To give greater prominence to decision making and performance measurement, we have made several major changes in the organization and presentation of chapter topics. Part One fully integrates the contemporary topics of activity-based costing, just-in-time, and total quality management. In Part Two, Chapter 5, *Activity-Based Systems: Activity-Based Management and Just-in-Time,* is a new chapter that caps the first two parts. We have moved cost-volume-profit analysis (in Chapter 6) to the beginning of Part Three to provide a smoother introduction to the budgeting process. We have revised Chapter 7, *The Budgeting Process,* substantially to fully integrate the master budget and to closely tie the problem material to the examples in the text. To deemphasize the procedural aspect of standard costing, in Chapter 8 we now focus on managerial uses of standard costing in the new business environment. Part Four provides both strong coverage of information and analysis for management decision making, including target costing, and a capstone chapter on total quality management and performance measurement.

Improved Content Coverage Including Integrated, Contemporary Discussions of State-of-the-Art Topics

This edition represents a major revision in terms of both structure and content.

Our goal is to make a significant improvement in all content coverage.

There are three major themes to the content of this revision.

Consistent Approach   All chapters are now fully consistent with our focus on decision making, performance measurement, and the management issues associated with various topics. We define accounting as an information system that provides information for making the critical decisions needed to operate a business successfully. We carry this idea forward by beginning each chapter with a learning objective linked to the management cycle. Also, we emphasize that costing systems can apply to both service businesses and manufacturing concerns. We use service companies as the focal point of all major examples and illustrations.

Contemporary Coverage   We have mainstreamed contemporary topics such as activity-based costing, just-in time, total quality management, and target costing from the beginning of the introductory chapter and have integrated them at appropriate points throughout the chapters. This book presents state-of-the art techniques and shows how they are used to add value to a company's operations. Decision Points and Business Bulletins emphasize these techniques and other current trends—for example, the need to assign costs to such areas as research and development, legal activities, and human resources.

Systematic Improvement   Every chapter has been thoroughly revised in a systematic way with the assistance of an experienced developmental editor to achieve a concise, clear, understandable presentation. The result is shorter chapters, with simplified examples and greater congruence between chapters and substantially revised and improved assignment material.

Maximized Real-World Coverage

We have taken many steps to increase the real-world emphasis of the text.

Our goal is to reflect business practice as it is today in a context that is relevant and exciting to students.

Decision Points   Every chapter contains at least one Decision Point. Based on excerpts from real companies' annual reports or from articles in the business press, Decision Points present a situation requiring a decision by management or other users of accounting information and then demonstrate how the decision can be made using accounting information.

Business Bulletins   We have added more Business Bulletins to each chapter of this edition. Business Bulletins are short items related to the chapter topics that show the relevance of accounting in four areas:

- Business Practice
- International Practice
- Technology in Practice
- Ethics in Practice

Real Companies in Assignments   We have substantially increased the number of real companies appearing in the assignment materials.

International Accounting   In recognition of the global economy in which all businesses operate today, we introduce international accounting examples in Chapter 1 and integrate them throughout the text. A small sampling of foreign companies mentioned in the text and assignments includes Skandia (Sweden), Wattie Frozen Foods Limited (New Zealand), and Daihatsu Motor Company (Japan).

Governmental and Not-for-Profit Organizations   Acknowledging the importance of governmental and not-for-profit organizations in our society, we include discussions and examples of government and not-for-profit organizations at appropriate points.

Reduction of Procedural Detail

This edition furthers our efforts to reduce the procedural detail in the chapters and to decrease the amount of "pencil pushing" on the part of students completing the assignments.

> Our goal is to provide exactly the right balance between conceptual understanding and technical application and analysis.

Because our focus is on the application of concepts, we have substantially revised many chapters to reduce procedural detail. We have accomplished this goal by deleting unnecessary topics or by placing procedures that are not essential to conceptual understanding in supplemental objectives at the end of chapters. In the end-of-chapter assignments, we have scrutinized all exercises and problems with a view to reducing the number of journal entries and the amount of posting required, and we now employ T accounts more frequently as a form of analysis. Consistent with the emphasis on decision making and performance measurement, we have eliminated all journal entries from the managerial accounting chapters. The most significantly revised chapters in this regard are:

Chapter 2   Operating Costs and Cost Allocation, Including Activity-Based Costing

Chapter 3   Costing Systems: Job Order Costing

Chapter 4   Costing Systems: Process Costing

Chapter 8   Cost Control Using Standard Costing and Variance Analysis

Chapter 11   Pricing Decisions and Target Costing

Chapter 13   The Statement of Cash Flows

Reorganized and Expanded Assignment Material

In answer to the demand for a more sophisticated skill set in students, coupled with greater pedagogical choice for faculty members, we have reorganized and expanded the end-of-chapter assignments and accompanying materials.

> Our goal is to provide the most comprehensive and flexible set of assignments available involving real companies.

In recognition of the fact that our students need to be better prepared to communicate clearly, both in written and oral formats, we provide ample assignments to enhance student writing and interpersonal skills, including the writing of good business memorandums and working effectively in groups and teams.

NEW! **Video Cases** Two new 5-minute video vignettes, each accompanied by an in-text case, provide more real-world opportunities to reinforce key concepts and techniques. The cases work equally well as individual or group assignments, and both include a written critical thinking component. Each video case serves as an introduction to the chapter in which it is found:

- *UPS* (Chapter 1) introduces management accounting, presents it in the context of the management cycle, and examines the concept of performance measures.
- *Enterprise Rent-A-Car* (Chapter 7) presents the budgeting process in the management cycle and describes the master budget process for a service company.

Building Your Knowledge Foundation This section consists of a variety of questions, exercises, and problems designed to develop basic knowledge, comprehension, and application of the concepts and techniques in the chapter.

Questions (Q) Fifteen to twenty-four review questions that cover the essential topics of the chapter.

Short Exercises (SE) Approximately ten very brief exercises suitable for classroom use.

Problems At least five extensive applications of chapter topics, often covering more than one learning objective, and often containing writing components. All problems may be worked on our Excel Templates software.

Alternate Problems An alternative set of the most popular problems, which we have selected based on feedback from our study of users' syllabi.

Chapter Assignments: Critical Thinking, Communication, and Interpersonal Skills
This section consists of ten or more Skills Development (SD) cases and Managerial Reporting and Analysis (MRA) cases, usually based on real companies. All of these cases require critical thinking and communication skills in the form of writing. At least one assignment in each chapter requires students to practice good business communication skills by writing a memorandum reporting results and explaining recommendations. In addition, all cases are suitable for development of interpersonal skills through group activities: for selected cases that we have designated as especially appropriate for group activities, we provide specific instructions for applying a suggested group methodology. We also identify Internet assignments. To

provide guidance in the best use of these assignments, we display the following icons in the margins:

- International
- Ethics
- Communication
- Video
- Internet
- Critical Thinking
- Group Activity
- Memo *M*
- Spreadsheet
- Managerial Technology

Each Skills Development assignment has a specific purpose:

Conceptual Analysis Designed so a written solution is appropriate, but which may be used in other communication modes, these short cases address conceptual accounting issues and are based on real companies and situations.

Ethical Dilemma In recognition of the need for accounting and business students to be exposed in all their courses to ethical considerations, every chapter has a short case, often based on a real company, in which students must address an ethical dilemma directly related to the chapter content.

Research Activity These exercises enhance student learning and participation in the classroom by acquainting students with business periodicals, the use of annual reports and business references, and resources in the library and on the Internet. Some are designed to improve students' interviewing and observation skills through field activities at actual businesses. An icon in the margin indicates which activities can be researched on the Internet.

Decision-Making Practice In the role of decision maker, students are asked to extract relevant data from a case, make computations as necessary, and arrive at a decision. The decision maker may be a manager, an investor, an analyst, or a creditor.

Managerial Reporting and Analysis cases sharpen students' ability to comprehend and analyze financial and nonfinancial data:

Interpreting Management Reports These short, specially designed internal management scenarios require students to extract relevant data, make computations, and interpret the results.

Formulating Management Reports Students strengthen analytical, critical thinking, and written communication skills with these assignments. They teach students how to examine, synthesize, and organize information with the object of preparing reports such as a memo to a company president identifying sources of waste, outlining performance measures to account for waste, and estimating the current costs associated with the waste.

International Company These exercises involve a company from another country that has had an accounting experience compatible with chapter content.

NEW! *Excel Spreadsheet Analysis* New to the Fifth Edition, these assignments in the managerial accounting chapters require the use of a spreadsheet to conduct an analysis and include a written component for interpretation and decision making. Excel Spreadsheet Analysis: Cases for Management Reporting and Analysis, a software program containing all the cases, is available for student use.

Readable, Accessible Text

Growing numbers of students who take the introductory accounting course are from foreign countries, and English is a second language for them. To meet their needs fully, we as instructors must be aware of how the complexities and nuances of English, particularly business English, might hinder these students' understanding.

Each chapter of MANAGERIAL ACCOUNTING has been reviewed by business instructors who teach English As a Second Language (ESL) courses and English for Special Purposes courses, as well as by students taking these classes. With their assistance and advice, we have taken the following measures to ensure that the text is accessible.

- Word Choice: We replaced words and phrases that were unfamiliar to ESL students with ones they more readily recognize and understand. For instance, we substituted "raise" for "bolster," "require" for "call for," and "available" for "on hand."
- Length: Because short, direct sentences are more easily comprehended than sentences containing multiple clauses, we paid strict attention to the length and grammatical complexity of our sentences.
- Examples: Examples reinforce concepts discussed and help to make the abstract concrete. We have added examples that are simple and straightforward for further clarity.

Supplementary Support Materials

Supplementary Learning Aids

Our goal is to provide a complete supplemental learning system—including manual and technology applications for computer, CD-ROM, videotape, and Internet support—that directly facilitates student learning.

Working Papers for Exercises and Problems

Study Guide

Accounting Transaction Tutor

Excel Templates

NEW! **Excel Spreadsheet Analysis: Cases for Managerial Reporting and Analysis**

NEW! **Internet Web Site**

NEW! **Houghton Mifflin Brief Accounting Dictionary**

Managerial Decision Cases

Aspen Food Products Company

McHenry Hotels, Inc., Second Edition

The Windham Company, Second Edition

Callson Industries, Inc.

Instructor's Support Materials

Our goal is to provide a complete support system for the instructor.

Instructor's Solutions Manual

`NEW!` **Electronic Solutions**

Course Manual

Test Bank with Achievement Test Masters and Answers

Computerized Test Bank

Teaching Transparencies

Solutions Transparencies

`NEW!` **Powerpoint Classroom Presentation Software**

`NEW!` **Video Cases**

`NEW!` **Presentation Videos**

Master Teacher Videos

Business Bulletin Videos

`NEW!` **Internet Web Site**

Acknowledgments

Preparing an accounting text is a long and demanding project that cannot really succeed without the help of one's colleagues. We are grateful to a large number of professors, other professional colleagues, and students for their many constructive comments on the text. Unfortunately, any attempt to list those who have helped means that some who have contributed would be slighted by omission. Some attempt, however, must be made to mention those who have been so helpful.

We wish to express our deep appreciation to our colleagues at DePaul University who have been extremely supportive and encouraging.

The thoughtful and meticulous work of Edward H. Julius (California Lutheran University) is reflected not only in the Study Guide but also in many other ways. We would also like to thank Paul J. Robertson (New Mexico State University) for his contribution to the Study Guide, Marion Taube (University of Pittsburgh) for her contribution to the Test Bank and the Working Papers, and Dick D. Wasson (Southwestern College) for his contribution to the Test Bank.

Also very important to the quality of this book is the supportive collaboration of our senior sponsoring editor, Anne Kelly. We further benefited from the ideas and guidance of our associate sponsoring editor, Peggy Monahan.

Others who have been supportive and have had an impact on this book throughout their reviews, suggestions, and class testing are:

Kym Anderson

Gregory D. Barnes — Clarion University

Charles M. Betts — Delaware Technical & Community College

Michael C. Blue — Bloomsburg University

Cynthia Bolt-Lee
Gary R. Bower
Lee Cannell
Lloyd Carroll

Naranjan Chipalkatti
Stanley Chu

John D. Cunha
Mark W. Dawson
Patricia A. Doherty
Lizabeth England
David Fetyko
Roxanne Gooch
Christine Uber Grosse

Dennis A. Gutting
Edward H. Julius
Howard A. Kanter
Kevin McClure
George McGowan
Anita R. McKie
Gail A. Mestas
Michael F. Monahan
Janette Moody
Jenine Moscove
Glenn Owen
Debra Parker-Fleming
Beth Brooks Patel
Yvonne Phangi-Hatami

LaVonda Ramey
Roberta Rettner
Donald Shannon
S. Murray Simons
Ellen L. Sweatt
Marion Taube
Rita Taylor
Robert G. Unterman
Stan Weikert
Kay Westerfield
Carol Yacht
Glenn Allen Young
Marilyn J. Young

The Citadel
Community College of Rhode Island
El Paso Community College
The Borough of Manhattan
  Community College
Ohio Northern University
The Borough of Manhattan
  Community College
University of California—Berkeley
Duquesne University
Boston University
American Language Academy
Kent State University
Cameron University
The American Graduate School of
  International Management
Orange County Community College
California Lutheran University
DePaul University
ESL Language Center

University of South Carolina—Aiken

The Citadel

Alan Hancock College
Ohio Dominican College
University of California—Berkeley
The Borough of Manhattan
  Community College
Schoolcraft College
American Ways
DePaul University
Northeastern University
DeKalb College—Dunwoody
University of Pittsburgh
University of Cincinnati
Glendale Community College
College of the Canyons
University of Oregon

Tulsa Junior College
Tulsa Junior College

To the Student

How to Study Accounting Successfully

Whether you are majoring in accounting or in another business discipline, your introductory accounting course is one of the most important classes you will take, because it is fundamental to the business curriculum and to your success in the business world beyond college. The course has multiple purposes because its students have diverse interests, backgrounds, and purposes for taking it. What are your goals in studying accounting? Being clear about your goals can contribute to your success in this course.

Success in this class also depends on your desire to learn and your willingness to work hard. And it depends on your understanding of how the text complements the way your instructor teaches and the way you learn. A familiarity with how this text is structured will help you to study more efficiently, make better use of classroom time, and improve your performance on examinations and other assignments.

To be successful in the business world after you graduate, you will need a broad set of skills, which may be summarized as follows:

Technical/Analytical Skills   A major objective of your accounting course is to give you a firm grasp of the essential business and accounting terminology and techniques that you will need to succeed in a business environment. With this foundation, you then can begin to develop the higher-level perception skills that will help you to acquire further knowledge on your own.

An even more crucial objective of this course is to help you develop analytical skills that will allow you to evaluate data. Well-developed analytical and decision-making skills are among the professional skills most highly valued by employers, and will serve you well throughout your academic and professional careers.

Communication Skills   Another skill highly prized by employers is the ability to express oneself in a manner that is understood correctly by others. This can include writing skills, speaking skills, and presentation skills. Communication skills are developed through particular tasks and assignments and are improved through constructive criticism. Reading skills and listening skills support the direct communication skills.

Interpersonal Skills   Effective interaction between two people requires a solid foundation of interpersonal skills. The success of such interaction depends on empathy, or the ability to identify with and understand the problems, concerns, and motives of others. Leadership, supervision, and interviewing skills also facilitate a professional's interaction with others.

Personal/Self Skills   Personal/self skills form the foundation for growth in the use of all other skills. To succeed, a professional must take initiative, possess self-confidence, show independence, and be ethical in all areas of life. Personal/self skills can be enhanced significantly by the formal learning process and by peers and mentors who provide models upon which you can build. Accounting is just one course in your entire curriculum, but it can play an important role in your development of the above skills. Your instructor is interested in helping you gain both a knowledge of accounting and the more general skills you will need to succeed in the business world. The following sections describe how you can get the most out of this course.

The Teaching/Learning Cycle™

Both teaching and learning have natural, parallel, and mutually compatible cycles. This teaching/learning cycle, as shown in Figure 1, interacts with the basic structure of learning objectives in this text.

The Teaching Cycle The inner (tan) circle in Figure 1 shows the steps an instructor takes in teaching a chapter. Your teacher *assigns* material, *presents* the subject in lecture, *explains* by going over assignments and answering questions, *reviews* the subject prior to an exam, and *tests* your knowledge and understanding using examinations and other means of evaluation.

The Learning Cycle Moving outward, the next circle (green) in Figure 1 shows the steps you take in studying a chapter. You should *preview* the material, *read* the chapter, *apply* your understanding by working the assignments, *review* the chapter, and *recall* and *demonstrate* your knowledge and understanding of the material on examinations and other assessments.

Integrated Learning Objectives Your textbook supports the teaching/learning cycle through the use of integrated learning objectives. Learning objectives are simply statements of what you should be able to do after you have completed a chapter. In Figure 1, the outside (blue) circle shows how learning objectives are integrated into your text and other study aids and how they interact with the teaching/learning cycle.

1. Learning objectives appear at the beginning of the chapter, as an aid to your teacher in making assignments and as a preview of the chapter for you.
2. Each learning objective is repeated in the text at the point where that subject is covered to assist your teacher in presenting the material and to help you organize your thoughts as you read the material.
3. Every exercise, problem, and case in the chapter assignments shows the applicable learning objective(s) so you can refer to the text if you need help.
4. A summary of the key points for each learning objective, a list of new concepts and terms referenced by learning objectives, and a review problem covering key learning objectives assist you in reviewing each chapter. Your Study Guide, also organized by learning objectives, provides for additional review.

Why Students Succeed Students succeed in their accounting course when they coordinate their personal learning cycle with their instructor's cycle. Students who do a good job of previewing their assignments, reading the chapters before the instructor is ready to present them, preparing homework assignments before they are discussed in class, and reviewing carefully will ultimately achieve their potential on exams. Those who get out of phase with their instructor, for whatever reason, will do poorly or fail. To ensure that your learning cycle is synchronized with your instructor's teaching cycle, check your study habits against these suggestions.

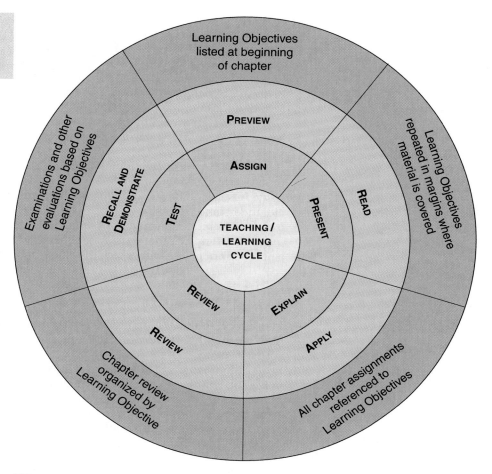

**Figure 1
The Teaching/Learning Cycle™
with Integrated Learning
Objectives**

▪ **TEACHING CYCLE**

▪ **LEARNING CYCLE**

▪ **LEARNING OBJECTIVES STRUCTURE**

Previewing the Chapter

1. Read the learning objectives at the beginning of the chapter. These learning objectives specifically describe what you should be able to do after completing the chapter.
2. Study your syllabus. Know where you are in the course and where you are going. Know the rules of the course.
3. Realize that in an accounting course, each assignment builds on previous ones. If you do poorly in Chapter 1, you may have difficulty in Chapter 2 and be lost in Chapter 3.

Reading the Chapter

1. As you read each chapter, be aware of the learning objectives in the margins. They will tell you why the material is relevant.
2. Allow yourself plenty of time to read the text. Accounting is a technical subject. Accounting books are so full of information that almost every sentence is important.

3. Strive to understand why as well as how each procedure is done. Accounting is logical and requires reasoning. If you understand why something is done in accounting, there is little need to memorize.
4. Relate each new topic to its learning objective and be able to explain it in your own words.
5. Be aware of colors as you read. They are designed to help you understand the text. (See the chart on the back of your textbook.)
   Orange: All source documents and inputs are in orange.
   Aqua: All accounting forms, working papers, and accounting processes are shown in aqua.
   Purple: All financial statements, the output or final product of the accounting process, are shown in purple.
   Gray: In selected tables and illustrations, gray is used to heighten contrasts and aid understanding.
6. If there is something you do not understand, prepare specific questions for your instructor. Pinpoint the topic or concept that confuses you. Some students keep a notebook of points with which they have difficulty.

Applying the Chapter

1. In addition to understanding why each procedure is done, you must be able to do it yourself by working exercises, problems, and cases. Accounting is a "do-it-yourself" course.
2. Read assignments and instructions carefully. Each assignment has a specific purpose. The wording is precise, and a clear understanding of it will save time and improve your performance. Acquaint yourself with the end-of-chapter assignment materials in this text by reading the description of them in the Preface.
3. Try to work exercises, problems, and cases without referring to their discussions in the chapter. If you cannot work an assignment without looking in the chapter, you will not be able to work a similar problem on an exam. After you have tried on your own, refer to the chapter (based on the learning objective reference) and check your answer. Try to understand any mistakes you may have made.
4. Be neat and orderly. Sloppy calculations, messy papers, and general carelessness cause most errors on accounting assignments.
5. Allow plenty of time to work the chapter assignments. You will find that assignments seem harder and that you make more errors when you are feeling pressed for time.
6. Keep up with your class. Check your work against the solutions presented in class. Find your mistakes. Be sure you understand the correct solutions.
7. Note the part of each exercise, problem, or case that causes you difficulty so you can ask for help.
8. Attend class. Most instructors design classes to help you and to answer your questions. Absence from even one class can hurt your performance.

Reviewing the Chapter

1. Read the summary of learning objectives in the chapter review. Be sure you know the definitions of all the words in the review of concepts and terminology.
2. Review all assigned exercises, problems, and cases. Know them cold. Be sure you can work the assignments without the aid of the book.
3. Determine the learning objectives for which most of the problems were assigned. They refer to topics that your instructor is most likely to emphasize on an exam. Scan the text for such learning objectives and pay particular attention to the examples and illustrations.

4. Look for and scan other similar assignments that cover the same learning objectives. They may be helpful on an exam.
5. Review quizzes. Similar material will often appear on longer exams.
6. Attend any labs or visit any tutors your school provides, or see your instructor during office hours to get assistance. Be sure to have specific questions ready.

Taking Examinations

1. Arrive at class early so you can get the feel of the room and make a last-minute review of your notes.
2. Have plenty of sharp pencils and your calculator (if allowed) ready.
3. Review the exam quickly when it is handed out to get an overview of your task. Start with a part you know. It will give you confidence and save time.
4. Allocate your time to the various parts of the exam, and stick to your schedule. Every exam has time constraints. You need to move ahead and make sure you attempt all parts of the exam.
5. Read the questions carefully. Some may not be exactly like your homework assignments. They may approach the material from a slightly different angle to test your understanding and ability to reason, rather than your ability to memorize.
6. To avoid unnecessary errors, be neat, use good form, and show calculations.
7. Relax. If you have followed the above guidelines, your effort will be rewarded.

Preparing Other Assignments

1. Understand the assignment. Written assignments, term papers, computer projects, oral presentations, case studies, group activities, individual field trips, video critiques, and other activities are designed to enhance skills beyond your technical knowledge. It is essential to know exactly what your instructor expects. Know the purpose, audience, scope, and expected end product.
2. Allow plenty of time. "Murphy's Law" applies to such assignments: If anything can go wrong, it will.
3. Prepare an outline of each report, paper, or presentation. A project that is done well always has a logical structure.
4. Write a rough draft of each paper and report, and practice each presentation. Professionals always try out their ideas in advance and thoroughly rehearse their presentations. Good results are not accomplished by accident.
5. Make sure that each paper, report, or presentation is of professional quality. Instructors appreciate attention to detail and polish. A good rule of thumb is to ask yourself: Would I give this work to my boss?

Check Figures

Chapter 1
P 1. No check figure
P 2. Cutting/Lining, average hours per pair on Monday: .25 hours
P 3. No check figure
P 4. 2.a. Gross Margin: $181,200
2.d. Cost of Goods Manufactured: $253,500
P 5. 1.a. $4
1.e. $10
1.n. $10
P 6. Molding, Week 1, First Shift, hours per board: 3.50
P 7. No check figure
P 8. 2.a. Gross margin $191,800
2.d. Cost of Goods Manufactured: $312,100

Chapter 2
P 1. 2. Total unit cost: $6.86
P 2. Cost of Goods Manufactured: $1,171,150
P 3. a. $2
f. $4
P 4. 2. Overhead applied to Job 2214: $29,717
P 5. 2. $69,280.40 Total costs assigned to Holstrum order, activity based costing approach
P 6. 1. Predetermined overhead rate for year 20x3: $5.014 per machine hour
P 7. 2. $41,805.60 Total costs assigned to Hines order, activity-based costing approach
P 8. 1.c. Rigger II: $10,665
BioScout: $13,940

Chapter 3
P 1. b. $58,512
h. $65,448
P 2. 1. Manufacturing overhead applied, January 15: $108,000
P 3. 2. $185,073
P 4. Contract revenue, Job Order P-12: $28,990
P 5. No check figure
P 6. Manufacturing overhead applied, April 15: $75,480
P 7. 3. $89,647
P 8. 1. Audit revenue, Brodahl Bakeries: $37,163

Chapter 4
P 1. 1.b. Unit Cost: $2.00
1.c Cost of Ending Work in Process Inventory: $18,900
P 2. 1.b. Unit Cost: $1.20
1.c Cost of Ending Work in Process Inventory: $1,530
P 3. 1.b. Unit Cost: $1.25
1.c Cost of Ending Work in Process Inventory: $5,512
P 4. 2. Total ABC overhead assigned: $46,090
3.b. Unit Cost: $10.70
3.c Cost of Ending Work in Process Inventory: $5,880
P 5. 1.b. Unit Cost: $7.00
1.c Cost of Ending Work in Process Inventory: $37,200
P 6. 1.b. Unit Cost: $2.12

1.c Cost of Ending Work in Process Inventory: $5,644
P 7. 1.b. Unit Cost: $3.80
1.c Cost of Ending Work in Process Inventory: $9,672
P 8. 1.b. Unit Cost: $4.25
1.c Cost of Ending Work in Process Inventory: $30,250

Chapter 5
P 1. No check figure
P 2. 1. Product unit cost: $270.00
4. Product unit cost: $279.53
P 3. 1a. Total materials handling cost: $20,286
P 4. No check figure 30%
$8.80
P 5. 1. Product unit cost: $878.25
P 6. No check figure
4. Product unit cost: $863.90

Chapter 6
P 1. 4. Cost per job: $81.56
P 2. 1. 7,500 billable hours
P 3. 3. $255
P 4. 2. 190,000 units
P 5. 1. 740 systems
P 6. 1.a. 3,500 units

Chapter 7
P 1. 1. Total manufacturing costs budgeted for November: $578,500
P 2. 7. Income from Operations = $3,086
P 3. 1. Ending Cash Balance, August: $3,600
P 4. 1. Projected Net Income: $101,812
P 5. Ending Cash Balance, February: $919,400
P 6. 1. Net Income: $930,415
P 7. 1. Ending Cash Balance, February: ($1,450)
P 8. 1. Net Income: $52,404

Chapter 8
P 1. 2. Total standard cost of front entrance, Year 20x0: $8,510
P 2. 1. Direct materials quantity variance—metal: $792 (U)
2. Direct labor efficiency variance—molding: $1,290 (U)
P 3. 2. Flexible budget formula = ($.35 × units produced) + $10,500
P 4. 1.a. Direct materials price variance, chemicals: $12,200 (F)
1.e. Controllable overhead variance: $3,100 (U)
P 5. c. $11.50
P 6. 1. Total standard direct materials cost per unit $169.62
P 7. 1. Direct materials price variance—liquid plastic: $386 (F)
2. Direct labor rate variance—Trimming/Packing: $56 (U)
P 8. 2. Direct materials quantity variance: $3,720 (U)
6. Manufacturing Overhead volume variance: $320 (F)

Chapter 9
P 1. 1. Cost to make: $3,147,200
P 2. 2. $68.20
P 3. 1. Segment margin for Nieto: $223,560
P 4. 2. Contribution margin per machine hour for WR3: $4.50
P 5. 1. Contribution margin per hour for phone calls: $130
P 6. 3. Net income from further processing; bagel sandwich: $.50
P 7. 1. Net loss if Baseball line is dropped: ($50,000)
P 8. 1. Net income from special order: $6,180

Chapter 10
P 1. 1. 11.1%
P 2. 2. Coupe Machine: 25.46%
      3. Coupe Machine: 4.348 years
P 3. 1. $72,536.50
P 4. 2. Negative net present value: ($7,080)
P 5. 1.c. Negative net present value: ($26,895)
P 6. 1. Kypros Machine: $40,670
      3. Darcy Machine: 5.482 years
P 7. 1. $99,672
P 8. 1. Positive net present value: $35,540

Chapter 11
P 1. 1. $22.80
P 2. 1. Regular Blend: $4.44 per pound
P 3. 2. Total billing: $9,593.55
P 4. 1. Speed-Calc 4: $78.40
      2. Speed-Calc 5: $84.84
P 5. 1. $19.20
P 6. 1. $276.80
P 7. 1. Product Y14: $520.00
      2. Product Z33: $623.40
P 8. 1. $34.08

Chapter 12
P 1. 1. East Division, total costs of conformance: $348,500
      2. East Division, percentage of nonconformance costs: 9.50%
P 2. 1. Anchor Division is first, Carter Division is last.
P 3. 1. Total product delivery performance, weekly average delivery cycle time: 58.04 hours
      Inventory control performance, weekly average inventory turnover; 2.16 times

P 4. 3. Assembly B4, contribution margin: $1,349,300
      4. Assembly B4, full cost profit margin: $1,817,480
P 5. 1. Currence Company, total costs of conformance: $533,600
      2. Currence Company, percentage of nonconformance costs: 10.30%
P 6. 1. Total product delivery performance, weekly average delivery cycle time: 73.43 hours
      Inventory control performance, weekly average inventory turnover: 3.73 times

Chapter 13:
P 1. No check figure
P 2. 1. Net Cash Flows from: Operating Activities, $46,800; Investing Activities, ($14,400); Financing Activities, $102,000
P 3. 1. Net Cash Flows from: Operating Activities, ($106,000); Investing Activities, $34,000; Financing Activities, $44,000
P 4. 2. Same as P 3
P 5. Net Cash Flows from Operating Activities: $47,600
P 6. 1. Net Cash Flows from: Operating Activities, $548,000; Investing Activities: $6,000; Financing Activities, ($260,000)
P 7. No check figure
P 8. Net Cash Flows from: Operating Activities, $63,300; Investing Activities, ($12,900); Financing Activities, $7,000
P 9. 2. Same as P 8

Chapter 14:
P 1. No check figure
P 2. Increase: a, b, e, f, l, m
P 3. 1.c. Receivable turnover, 20x2: 14.1 times; 20x1: 14.4 times
P 4. 1.b. Quick ratio, Allison: 1.5 times; Marker: 1.2 times; 2.d. Return on equity, Allison: 8.8%; Marker, 4.9%
P 5. Increase: d, h, i
P 6. 1.a. Current ratio, 20x6: 1.9 times; 20x5: 1.0 times; 2.c. Return on assets, 20x6: 8.4%; 20x5: 6.6%
P 7. 1.b. Quick ratio, Emax: 0.4 times; Savlow: 1.0 times; 2.d. Return on equity, Emax: 11.8%; Savlow 8.8%

CHAPTER 1

Introduction to Management Accounting

LEARNING OBJECTIVES

1. Define *management accounting* and distinguish between management accounting and financial accounting.
2. Explain the management cycle and its connection to management accounting.
3. Identify the new management philosophies for continuous improvement and discuss the role of management accounting in implementing these philosophies.
4. Define *performance measures,* recognize the uses of these measures in the management cycle, and prepare an analysis of nonfinancial data.
5. Identify the important questions a manager must consider before requesting or preparing a management report.
6. Compare accounting for inventories and cost of goods sold in merchandising and manufacturing organizations.
7. Identify various approaches managers use to classify costs and show how the purpose of a manager's cost analysis can change the classification of a single cost item.
8. Identify the standards of ethical conduct for management accountants.

DECISION POINT

GENERAL MOTORS

Prosperous organizations identify key success factors, such as satisfying customer needs, developing excellent manufacturing processes, leading the market with innovative products, and developing technological advances. General Motors Corp. (GM) has all of these key success factors in mind as it leads the market with the introduction of EV1, the first electric vehicle to be mass-produced in the United States.[1] This vehicle is an alternative to fossil-fueled cars and uses rechargeable batteries. Lightweight aluminum frames (chassis), magnesium seat frames, and special exterior panels made of a lightweight composite material are some examples of the technological advances in materials used in the EV1. Less weight yields better battery efficiency, a feature customers want.

Workers put aluminum car parts together with an adhesive and then bake the frame in an oven, rather than welding the parts. Suppliers deliver premade parts to the factory floor, thus reducing the number of workers and machines used in production. After the tires are mounted, a worker drives the car to other stations, thus eliminating the conveyors traditionally used

VIDEOCASE

UPS

OBJECTIVES

- To define management accounting.
- To describe the management cycle and its connection to management accounting
- To recognize performance measures.

BACKGROUND FOR THE CASE

UPS, one of the largest package distribution companies in the world, transports more than three billion parcels and documents annually. UPS supports its commitment to serving the needs of customers throughout the world with more than 500 airplanes, 147,000 vehicles, and 2,400 facilities in over 200 countries. Like many other companies, UPS relies on management accounting information to plan, execute, review, and report its business activities. Management accounting helps managers at UPS make better decisions about embracing new technology, managing environmental issues, and improving fuel efficiency.

 For more information about UPS, visit the company's web site through the Needles Accounting Resource Center at
http://www.hmco.com/college/needles/home.html

REQUIRED

 View the video on UPS that accompanies this book. As you are watching the video, take notes related to the following questions:

1. In your words, how would you define management accounting?
2. Describe the management cycle and explain how management accounting information helps managers at UPS move through each stage of the management cycle.
3. Define the term "performance measures" and give examples of some performance measures used by UPS.

to transport heavier cars. A robot installs windshields that contain an invisible electronic film to defrost the glass, and portable "stations" allow assembly to be expanded from 2,000 cars per year to 10,000 or more. The $34,000 cars are leased for $480 to $680 per month.

All of these changes demonstrate GM's desire to reestablish its reputation as a technology leader. The company has invested more than $1.5 billion in the EV1 electric car project and has earned 30 patents from developing the EV1. Now General Motors needs objective, quantifiable performance measures for the key success factors mentioned above. What is management accounting's role in the design and production of a vehicle like the EV1? What performance measures would you suggest for developing excellent manufacturing processes and satisfying customer needs related to the EV1?

Management accounting has provided and will continue to provide General Motors with relevant, useful information for making decisions about the selling and leasing prices for the car and the cost of new materials, new production processes, outsourcing premade parts assemblies through suppliers, and leasing cars. Management accounting uses tools such as budgets and performance measures to help GM managers develop, manufacture, sell, and distribute the EV1 using limited resources. Budgets influence daily operating goals for the workers and provide benchmarks for evaluating the workers' performance. Performance measures for the production process at GM include the time to complete one cycle of the production process, number of setups, and time to rework errors in the production process. Number of customer complaints, number of service change notices, and number of customer referrals are potential performance measures of customer satisfaction. As GM continues to improve the EV1 by introducing new materials, such as a nickel-metal hybrid battery to increase by more than 180 miles the miles driven before recharge, management accounting will provide quantifiable information to support GM's achievement of its strategic key success factors.

What Is Management Accounting?

OBJECTIVE 1

Define management accounting *and distinguish between management accounting and financial accounting*

Management accounting consists of accounting techniques and procedures for gathering and reporting financial, production, and distribution data to meet management's information needs. The management accountant is expected to provide timely, accurate information—including budgets, standard costs, variance analyses, support for day-to-day operating decisions, and analyses of capital expenditures. The Institute of Management Accountants defines management accounting as

> the process of identification, measurement, accumulation, analysis, preparation, interpretation, and communication of financial [as well as nonfinancial] information used by management to plan, evaluate, and control within the organization and to assure appropriate use and accountability for its resources.[2]

The information that management accountants gather and analyze is used to support the actions of management. All business managers need accurate and timely information to support pricing, planning, operating, and many other types of decisions. Managers of manufacturing, merchandising, government, and service

Table 1. Comparison of Management and Financial Accounting

Areas of Comparison	Management Accounting	Financial Accounting
Report format	Flexible format, driven by user's needs	Based on generally accepted accounting principles
Purpose of reports	Provide information for planning, control, performance measurement, and decision making	Report on past performance
Primary users	Employees, managers, suppliers	Owners, lenders, customers, government agencies
Units of measure	Historical or future dollar; physical measure in time or number of objects	Historical dollar
Nature of information	Future-oriented; objective for decision making; more subjective for planning; rely on estimates	Historical, objective
Frequency of reports	Prepared as needed; may or may not be on a regular basis	Prepared on a regular basis (minimum of once a year)

organizations all depend on management accounting information. Multidivisional corporations need large amounts of information and more complex accounting and reporting systems than do small businesses. But small- and medium-sized businesses make use of certain types of financial and operating information as well. The types of data needed to ensure efficient operating conditions do not depend entirely on an organization's size.

Management accounting information helps organizations make better decisions. Such decisions make all organizations become more cost-effective and help manufacturing, retail, and service organizations become more profitable. Financial accounting takes the results of management decisions about the actual operating, investing, and financing activities and prepares reports for external parties (investors, creditors, and governmental agencies).

Both management accounting and financial accounting (1) provide an information system crucial to reporting and analysis, (2) provide reports used by individuals to analyze and make decisions, and (3) develop relevant, objective product cost information for valuing inventories included on the balance sheet.

Table 1 compares management accounting to financial accounting. Management of accounting data is essential for management planning, control, performance measurement, and decision making. Employees and managers need accounting information to handle daily operations efficiently and effectively to achieve the organization's goals. Management reports are very flexible. Either historical or future information may be reported without any formal guidelines or restrictions. The information may communicate dollar amounts or physical measures of time or objects, such as number of hours worked or number of inspections. The information may be relevant and objective for decision-making purposes or may be more subjective for estimating future activities. Management accounting reports can be prepared monthly, quarterly, or annually. Management may also request reports daily or for special purposes.

In contrast, financial accounting communicates economic information to external parties. In profit-generating organizations, such as manufacturing, retail, and service organizations, owners and creditors contribute money to assist managers in investing in resources and generating profits from operating activities. Government agencies, such as the Internal Revenue Service and the Securities and Exchange Commission, also require reports. Managers must distribute financial reports to those parties to show the organization's actual performance. The reports are historical and measured in dollars. Generally accepted accounting principles require that specific standards and procedures be followed in the preparation of these reports. Financial reports include objective information that is prepared and distributed regularly, usually on an annual basis.

Connecting Management Accounting to the Management Cycle

OBJECTIVE 2

Explain the management cycle and its connection to management accounting

To better understand the relationship between management and management accounting, let's take a look at the management cycle and the connections between it and management accounting.

The Management Cycle

Management is expected to use resources wisely, operate profitably, pay debts, and abide by laws and regulations. These expectations motivate managers to establish the objectives, goals, and strategic plans of the organization and to guide and control operating, investing, and financing activities to reach those goals. The management process differs from organization to organization, but traditionally management operates in four stages: (1) planning, (2) executing, (3) reviewing, and (4) reporting. Figure 1 illustrates these stages as an overall management cycle. Each stage of the cycle is discussed below.

Planning   Management needs to plan the future operating, investing, and financing activities of the organization. Appropriate objectives and goals must be established and organizational policies enacted. Strategic planning represents the formulation of long-term strategies and related goals, objectives, and organizational policies. Management strives to complement the organization's strategic plans with annual operating plans. The development of strategic and operating plans requires managers to make decisions concerning various alternatives. These plans often include expectations about the performance of individuals, working teams, products, or services.

Executing   Planning alone does not guarantee satisfactory operating results. Management must implement the strategic and operating plans by executing activities, or tasks, in a way that maximizes the use of available resources. Smooth operations require one or more of the following: (1) hiring and training of personnel, (2) properly matching human and technical resources to the work that must be done, (3) purchasing or leasing facilities, (4) maintaining an inventory of products for sale,

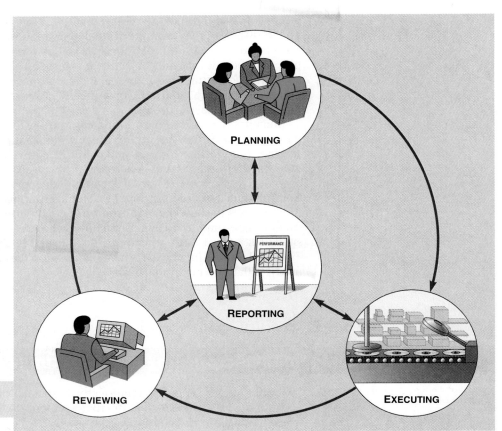

Figure 1
The Management Cycle

and (5) identifying operating activities, or tasks, that minimize waste and improve the quality of the products or services.

Management executes the plan by overseeing the daily operations of the organization. In small organizations, managers often have much direct contact with their employees. They supervise their employees and interact with them to help them learn or complete a task or to improve their performance. In larger, more complex organizations, there may be less direct contact between managers and employees. Instead of directly watching employees, management monitors performance by measuring the actual time taken to complete an activity (for example, number of inspection hours) or the frequency of an activity (such as number of inspections).

Reviewing In many organizations, financial rewards are given to those managers who follow the plan and manage their resources well. Thus, control of operations becomes very important to managers. Often managers compare actual performance to the expected performance established at the planning stage. Any significant differences are then identified for further analysis. Problems that arise may be corrected, or the original plans may be revised as a result of changes in the organization's operating environment. Ideally, the adjustments made in the review stage will improve the performance of future activities.

Reporting Because managers have an obligation to use resources wisely, management is responsible for reporting the results of operations to external parties. Periodic summaries of past performance are sent to stockholders, creditors, and other people and groups who are interested in the organization's operations. Also, internal reports about plans and reviews of past performance provide useful information for management decision making.

Management Accounting Connections to the Management Cycle

Management accounting serves the multiple information needs of managers by (1) developing plans and analyzing alternatives; (2) communicating plans to key personnel; (3) evaluating performance; (4) reporting the results of activities; and (5) accumulating, maintaining, and processing an organization's financial and nonfinancial information. These management accounting activities complement the management cycle.

For example, let's suppose that Abbie Awani is about to open her own retail business, Sweet Treasures Candy Store. She plans to purchase candy and other confections from various candy manufacturers and to sell them after some repackaging. What types of information does Abbie need before she opens the doors of her new store? Her first need is for a business plan so that she can apply for a start-up loan from a local bank. This plan includes a full description of the business as well as a complete budget for the first two years of operations. The budget includes a forecasted income statement, a forecasted statement of cash flows, and a forecasted balance sheet at the end of the second year.

Since Abbie does not have a financial background, she will consult a local accounting firm to help her with this project. But she can provide relevant input into the business plan. She needs to decide (1) the types of candy she wants to sell; (2) the volume of sales she anticipates; (3) the selling price for each product; (4) the monthly costs of leasing or purchasing facilities, employing personnel, and maintaining the facilities; and (5) the number of display counters, storage units, and cash registers that she will need.

Once she obtains the loan and opens the business, Abbie's information needs continue. She must now measure how well her business is doing. She also needs budgeted information as her guide to evaluate the store's performance. Spending on advertising campaigns, pricing for special sales, and hiring temporary versus full-time personnel are decisions that are also linked to her business plan. Actual revenues and expenses must be compared to the planned amounts and any differences explained. Reasons for such differences may lead Abbie to change parts of her original business plan.

Abbie may also want to measure and evaluate the past performance of employees. This information will help her to develop new strategies or goals. For example, keeping a record of the number of complaints about poor customer service can help her improve quality by finding better ways to train personnel or change the service-delivery process.

Thus Sweet Treasures Candy Store needs management accounting information about the purchase of display counters and office equipment; the selection, training, and rewarding of employees; and the marketing, production, and distribution of its products. Abbie can use this information to plan operations, organize resources, execute business activities, and review the performance of her employees and her business.

This example illustrates the connection between management accounting and the management cycle. Management accounting can provide a constant source of relevant information. Compare Abbie's activities and informational needs with the management cycle shown in Figure 1. She started with a business plan, organized her thoughts, planned actions, executed those actions, and reviewed the results. Accounting information helped her to develop her business plan, communicate that plan to the banker and employees, evaluate the performance of employees, and report the results of operations for a period of time. As you can see, accounting plays a critical role in managing the operations of an organization.

Meeting the Demands of Global Competition

During the 1970s and 1980s, the United States lost its dominance in the world marketplace. Countries such as Japan, Germany, Great Britain, and Korea successfully entered many product markets with high-quality, low-cost goods. Customers around the world were pleased with the quality of the new products and purchased them in large numbers. Most affected by the emergence of foreign competition were the automobile, television and VCR equipment, appliance, steel, and audio equipment industries. These industries represented a significant portion of the United States' manufacturing sector, and hundreds of companies were affected. American management had to develop the means to cope with this world-class competition.

New Management Philosophies and Management Accounting

> **OBJECTIVE 3**
>
> *Identify the new management philosophies for continuous improvement and discuss the role of management accounting in implementing these philosophies*

Three significant new management philosophies evolved in the United States to deal with expanding global competition: just-in-time operating techniques, total quality management, and activity-based management. In addition, flexible manufacturing systems have been developed to assist in improving quality and reducing manufacturing time.

The just-in-time (JIT) operating environment is an organizational environment in which personnel are hired and raw materials and facilities are purchased and used only as needed; emphasis is on the elimination of waste. Workers are trained to be multiskilled, and production processes are consolidated to allow workers to operate several different machines or processes. Raw materials and parts are scheduled to be delivered when they are needed in the production process, so materials inventories are reduced significantly. Products are produced continuously, so work in process inventories are very small. Goods are usually produced only when an order is received and are shipped when completed, so inventories of finished goods are reduced. Adopting the JIT operating environment results in reduced production time, reduced investment in raw materials inventory, reduced materials waste, higher-quality goods, and reduced production costs. Funds that are no longer invested in high inventory levels can be redirected according to the goals of the strategic plan. The accounting system responds to the new environment by tracking the costs of the product differently. JIT processes help management accountants assign more accurate costs to the product and identify costs of waste and inefficient manufacturing activities.

Total quality management (TQM), is an environment in which all functions work together to build quality into the organization's product or service. TQM has many of the same characteristics as the JIT operating philosophy. Workers function as team members and are empowered to make operating decisions that improve both the product or service and the work environment. TQM focuses on improved product quality by identifying and reducing or eliminating the waste of resources caused by poor product or service quality. Emphasis is placed on using resources efficiently and effectively to prevent poor quality and on examining current operations to spot possible causes of poor quality. Improved quality of both the work environment and the product or service is the goal of TQM. Like JIT, TQM results in reduced waste of materials, higher-quality goods, and lower production costs in a manufacturing environment and time savings and higher-quality services in service organizations.

To determine the impact of poor quality on profits, management uses accounting information about the magnitude and classification of the costs of quality. The costs of quality include both the costs of achieving quality (such as training costs and inspection costs) and the costs of poor quality (such as rework costs and costs of handling customer complaints). Managers use cost of quality information to (1) connect strategic goals of the organization with daily operating activities, (2) stimulate improvement by involving everyone, (3) identify opportunities for reducing customer dissatisfaction, (4) identify major opportunities for cost reduction, and (5) determine the costs of quality relative to net income.

Activity-based management (ABM) is an approach to managing an organization that identifies all major operating activities, determines what resources are consumed by each activity, identifies what causes resource usage of each activity, and categorizes the activities as either adding value to a product or service or being non-value-adding. ABM includes a management accounting practice called activity-based costing. Activity-based costing (ABC) is a system that identifies all of an organization's major operating activities (both production and nonproduction), traces costs to those activities, and then determines which products or services use the resources and services supplied by those activities. Activities that add value to a product or service, as perceived by the customer, are known as value-adding activities. Such activities are enhanced to improve product or service quality and customer satisfaction. All other activities are called nonvalue-adding activities. Nonvalue-adding activities that are needed because they support the organization are focal points for cost reduction. Nonvalue-adding activities that do not support the organization are eliminated. ABM results in reduced costs, reduced waste of resources, increased efficiency, and increased customer satisfaction.

Activity-based costing is most often used to improve the assignment of overhead costs to products or services. More accurate costs allow managers to make better product or service pricing decisions and decisions about expanding or contracting certain market segments.

The Goal: Continuous Improvement

One of the most valuable lessons to be gained from the emergence of stiff global competition is that management cannot afford to become complacent. While the United States rested on its laurels as the world's most productive nation, countries around the globe were perfecting their productive capabilities. Because our industry had been lulled into self-satisfaction, other countries equaled and surpassed our levels of quality and productivity. What followed was a period of catch-up by American companies. The concept of continuous improvement evolved during this period. Organizations that adhere to continuous improvement are never satisfied with what is; they constantly seek a better method, product, service, process, or resource. Their goal is perfection in everything they do.

JIT, TQM, and ABM all have perfection by means of continuous improvement as their goal. Figure 2 shows how each approach tries to accomplish its goal. In the just-in-time operating environment, management wages a relentless war on waste:

BUSINESS BULLETIN: **BUSINESS PRACTICE**

The Internal Revenue Service (IRS) wants to continually improve the quality of its services and reduce the costs of collecting tax revenues from individuals who fail to submit tax returns or who file tax returns but do not pay their taxes. The Field Collection function is responsible for this service. The IRS measures the performance of IRS Field Collection offices and revenue officers based on (1) total dollars collected, (2) number of delinquent taxpayer accounts closed (in total and in subtotals of taxpayers who paid in full, agreed to pay in installments, etc.), and (3) number of delinquent taxpayer investigations. The IRS believes these measures will guide its employees to increase revenue collection, reduce costs of collection, increase job satisfaction, and improve the productivity of the Field Collection function within the organization.[3]

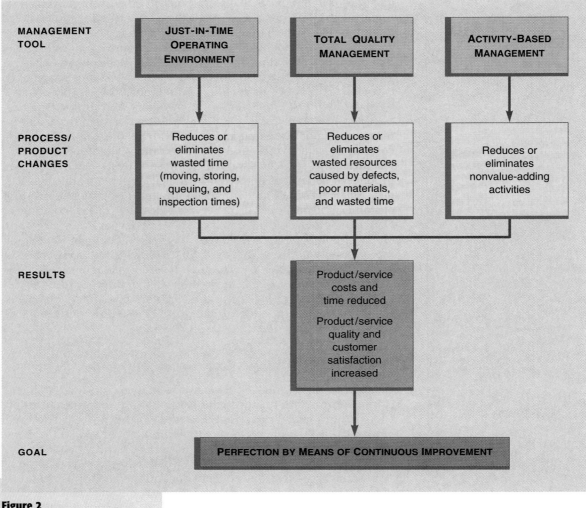

**Figure 2
The Continuous Improvement Environment**

wasted time, wasted space, and wasted use of materials. All employees are encouraged to continuously look for ways to improve processes and save time. Total quality management focuses on improving the quality of the product or service and the work environment. It pursues continuous improvement by reducing the number of defective products and the amount of wasted time to complete a task or provide a service. Activity-based management focuses on the ongoing reduction or elimination of nonvalue-adding activities as its way of seeking continuous improvement.

Each of these management tools can be used as an individual system, or parts of them can be combined to create a new operating environment. Some aspects of them can be employed in service industries, such as banking, as well as in manufacturing. By continuously trying to improve and fine-tune operations, these new management tools contribute to the same basic results for any organization: Product or service costs and delivery time are reduced, and the quality of the product or service and customer satisfaction are increased. If American organizations continuously improve upon all these results, the United States will catch up with and then surpass its competition.

Performance Measures and the Analysis of Nonfinancial Data

Performance measures are quantitative tools that provide an indication of an organization's performance in relation to a specific process, activity, or task or to an expected outcome. Performance measures may be financial or nonfinancial. Financial performance measures include return on investment, net income as a percentage of sales, and the costs of poor quality as a percentage of sales. All of these examples use monetary information to measure the performance of a profit-generating organization or its segments, such as divisions, departments, product lines, sales territories, or operating activities.

Nonfinancial performance measures can include the number of times an object (product, service, activity, or person) occurs or the time taken to perform a task. Examples include number of customer complaints, number of orders shipped the same day, hours of inspection, and time to fill an order. Such performance measures are useful in reducing or eliminating waste and inefficiencies in operating activities.

Management uses performance measures in all stages of the management cycle. In the planning stage, management establishes performance measures to motivate future performance that supports the goals and objectives of the strategic plan. For example, many organizations want employees to increase quality, reduce costs, increase customer satisfaction, and increase efficiency and timeliness. As you will recall from earlier in the chapter, Abbie Awani selected the number of customer complaints as a performance measure to monitor service quality.

During the executing stage, performance measures guide and motivate the performance of employees and assist in assigning costs to products, departments, or operating activities. Abbie will record the number of customer complaints during the year. She can group the information by type of complaint or the employee involved in the service.

In the reviewing stage, management uses performance measures to improve future performance by analyzing significant differences between actual and planned performance. By comparing the actual and planned number of customer complaints, Abbie can identify problem areas and consider solutions.

In the reporting stage, performance measurement information is useful in communicating performance evaluations and developing new budgets. If Abbie needed a formal report, she could have her accountant prepare a performance evaluation analysis based on this information.

To measure increased quality, the management of a manufacturing organization needs information about and trend analysis of the number of items that require rework, the amount of scrapped materials and products, the total time devoted to inspection, and the time spent on product development, design, and testing. Improvements in production and delivery can be measured by trends in throughput time (the total production time per unit per product type), total delivery time by customer and geographic location, raw materials spoilage and scrap rates, production bottlenecks (slowdowns), and completed production. Customer satisfaction can be measured by trends in the number of product warranty claims and the number of products returned (analyzed by product line and by customer), retention of customers, product reorders by customers, and time spent on product repairs and adjustments in the field.

These analyses of nonfinancial data also measure how well management has been able to reduce operating costs. Reducing or eliminating the need to rework defective units or the incurrence of scrap also reduces the cost of a product. If throughput time is reduced, the costs connected with the time saved—such as storage costs, inspection labor time costs, and product moving costs—are also reduced. Improved product quality reduces or eliminates warranty claims and service work, thus reducing product costs.

Exhibit 1. Analysis of Nonfinancial Data—Bank

Kings Beach National Bank
Summary of Number of Customers Served
For the Quarter Ended December 31, 20xx

Part A	Number of Customers Served			
Window	October	November	December	Quarter Totals
1	5,428	5,186	5,162	15,776
2	5,280	4,820	4,960	15,060
3	4,593	4,494	4,580	13,667
Totals	15,301	14,500	14,702	44,503

Part B	Number of Customers Served per Hour			
Window	October	November	December	Quarter Averages
1	31.93	30.51	30.36	30.93
2	31.06	28.35	29.18	29.53
3	27.02	26.44	26.94	26.80
Totals	90.01	85.30	86.48	87.26
Average per hour per window	30.00	28.43	28.83	29.09

Part C: Graphic Comparison of the Number of Customers Served per Hour

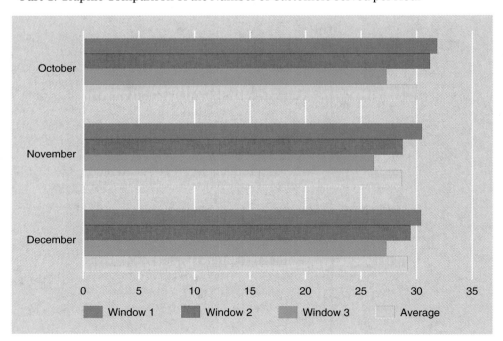

Notice that all of these performance measures are nonfinancial and are critical in today's operating environment. In addition, all are part of the decision-supporting data management needs and are expected to be supplied by the management accounting information system.

Accountants are often confronted with problems that require such nonfinancial measures as machine hours, labor hours, units of output, number of employees, and number of requests for a particular service. The following example illustrates a situation in which a manager requires nonfinancial data to make an informed decision in a service organization.

Lynda Babb supervises tellers at Kings Beach National Bank. The bank has three drive-up windows, each with a full-time teller. Historically, each teller served an average of thirty customers per hour. However, on November 1, 20xx, management implemented a new check-scanning procedure that has cut back the number of customers served per hour.

Data on the number of customers served for the three-month period ended December 31, 20xx, are shown in Part A of Exhibit 1. Each teller works an average of 170 hours per month. Window 1 is always the busiest; Windows 2 and 3 receive progressively less business. The October figure of thirty customers per hour is derived from the averages for all three windows.

Ms. Babb is preparing a report for management on the effects of the new procedure. Part B of Exhibit 1 shows her analysis of the number of customers served over the three months by each teller window. She computed the number of customers served per hour by dividing the number of customers served by the monthly average hours worked per teller (170). By averaging the customer service rates for the three tellers, she got 28.43 for November and 28.83 for December. As you can see, the service rate has decreased. But December's average is higher than November's, which means the tellers, as a whole, are becoming more accustomed to the new procedure. Part C of Exhibit 1 is a graphic comparison of the number of customers served per hour.

How to Prepare a Management Accounting Report or Analysis

OBJECTIVE 5

Identify the important questions a manager must consider before requesting or preparing a management report

As a manager, you may have to recommend the purchase of a particular machine, request money to develop a new form of packaging, or present a marketing plan for your organization's most popular product or service. Regardless of the assignment, you will have to prepare some type of report. Often the report will require relevant accounting information to support your position.

The keys to successful report preparation are the four *W*'s: Why? Who? What? and When? Keep the following points in mind as you prepare your report.

- **Why?** Know the purpose of the report. Focus on it as you write.
- **Who?** Identify the audience for your report. Communicate at a level that matches your audience's understanding of the issue and their familiarity with accounting information. A detailed, informal report may be appropriate for your manager, but a more concise summary may be necessary for other audiences, such as the president or board of directors of your organization.
- **What?** What information is needed? *Select the relevant information.* Know the sources of this information. You may draw information from specific documents or from interviews with knowledgeable managers and employees.

  What method of presentation is best? *Develop the most effective method of presentation.* The information should be relevant and easy to read and understand. You may need to include visual presentations, such as bar charts or graphs to present accounting information.

■ **When?** Know the due date for the report. Strive to prepare an accurate report on a timely basis. Remember that you may have to balance accuracy and timeliness. Some accuracy may be lost if the report is urgent.

You have an opportunity to develop your skills in reporting accounting information. At the end of each management accounting chapter, you will find Managerial Reporting and Analysis problems that ask you to formulate reports that include accounting information.

Merchandising Versus Manufacturing Organizations

OBJECTIVE 6

Compare accounting for inventories and cost of goods sold in merchandising and manufacturing organizations

Merchandising organizations and manufacturing organizations prepare income statements and balance sheets for owners, creditors, and other outside parties. Both types of organizations maintain levels of inventory and calculate gross margin using sales and cost of goods sold information. However, merchandising organizations are less complex than manufacturing organizations.

Merchandising organizations

■ purchase products that are ready for resale,
■ maintain only one inventory account on the balance sheet, and
■ include the cost of purchases in the calculation of cost of goods sold.

Manufacturing organizations

■ design and manufacture products for sale,
■ reflect three inventory accounts on the balance sheet, and
■ determine the cost of goods manufactured to include in the calculation of cost of goods sold.

Merchandising organizations, such as Wal-Mart, Toys "R" Us, and Home Depot, purchase products that are ready for resale. These organizations maintain one inventory account, called Merchandise Inventory, that reflects the costs of products held for resale. To calculate the cost of goods sold for a merchandising organization, the following equation is used:

$$\text{Cost of Goods Sold} = \begin{array}{c}\text{Beginning}\\\text{Merchandise}\\\text{Inventory}\end{array} + \begin{array}{c}\textbf{Net Cost of}\\\textbf{Purchases}\end{array} - \begin{array}{c}\text{Ending}\\\text{Merchandise}\\\text{Inventory}\end{array}$$

For example, Sweet Treasures Candy Store had a balance of $3,000 in the Merchandise Inventory account on January 1, 20xx. During the year, the company purchased candy products totaling $23,000 (adjusted for purchase discounts, purchases returns and allowances, and freight-in). At December 31, 20xx, the Merchandise Inventory balance was $4,500. The cost of goods sold is thus $21,500.

$$\text{Cost of Goods Sold} = \$3,000 + \$23,000 - \$4,500 = \$21,500$$

Manufacturing organizations, such as Motorola, Sony, and IBM, use materials, labor, and manufacturing overhead to manufacture products for sale. Materials are purchased and used in the production process. The Materials Inventory account shows the balance of the cost of unused materials. During the production process, the costs of manufacturing the product are accumulated in the Work in Process Inventory account. The balance of the Work in Process Inventory account represents the costs of unfinished product. Once the product is complete and ready for sale, the cost of the goods manufactured is reflected in the Finished Goods Inventory account. The balance in the Finished Goods Inventory account is the cost of unsold completed product. When the product is sold, the manufacturing organization calculates the cost of goods sold using the following equation:

$$\text{Cost of Goods Sold} = \begin{array}{c}\text{Beginning}\\\text{Finished Goods}\\\text{Inventory}\end{array} + \begin{array}{c}\textbf{Cost of}\\\textbf{Goods}\\\textbf{Manufactured}\end{array} - \begin{array}{c}\text{Ending}\\\text{Finished Goods}\\\text{Inventory}\end{array}$$

For example, Hatcher Candy Company, a supplier to Sweet Treasures Candy Store, had a balance of $52,000 in the Finished Goods Inventory account on January 1, 20xx. During the year, Hatcher manufactured candy products totaling $144,000. At December 31, 20xx, the Finished Goods Inventory balance was $78,000. The cost of goods sold is $118,000.

$$\text{Cost of Goods Sold} = \$52,000 + \$144,000 - \$78,000 = \$118,000$$

Both of these organizations use the following income statement format:

$$\text{Sales} - \text{Cost of Goods Sold} = \text{Gross Margin} - \text{Operating Expenses} = \text{Net Income}$$

Figure 3 compares the inventories and cost of goods sold sections for merchandising and manufacturing organizations. By combining the beginning Merchandise Inventory balance with the net cost of purchases for Sweet Treasures Candy Store, we calculate a "pie" called *cost of goods available for sale*. By counting and valuing unsold merchandise in the Merchandise Inventory account, we slice from the pie the ending Merchandise Inventory balance for the balance sheet, leaving the cost of goods sold for the income statement. Similarly, if we combine the beginning Finished Goods Inventory balance with the cost of goods manufactured for Hatcher Candy Company, we calculate a "pie" called *cost of goods available for sale*. By counting and valuing the unsold products in Finished Goods Inventory, we can slice from the pie the ending Finished Goods Inventory balance for the balance sheet, leaving the cost of goods sold for the income statement.

Cost Classifications and Their Uses

OBJECTIVE 7

Identify various approaches managers use to classify costs and show how the purpose of a manager's cost analysis can change the classification of a single cost item

Cost management is a necessary element of long-term success for an organization. Because managers are accountable to a variety of external parties, they must be aware of costs. Managers will focus on ways to operate efficiently, provide quality products or services, and satisfy customer needs. An understanding of cost classification will help managers select and use relevant information for planning, executing, reviewing, and reporting purposes.

A single cost can be classified and used in several different ways, depending on the purpose of the analysis. For example, managers may want to (1) trace costs to cost objects (cost traceability), (2) calculate the number of units that must be sold to obtain a certain level of profit (cost behavior), (3) identify costs of activities that do and do not add value to a product or service (value-adding versus nonvalue-adding costs), or (4) prepare an income statement for the owner (financial reporting).

Cost Traceability

Managers rely on management accountants to trace costs to cost objects, such as products or services, sales territories, departments, or operating activities. By tracing costs as directly as possible to cost objects, managers can thus develop a fairly

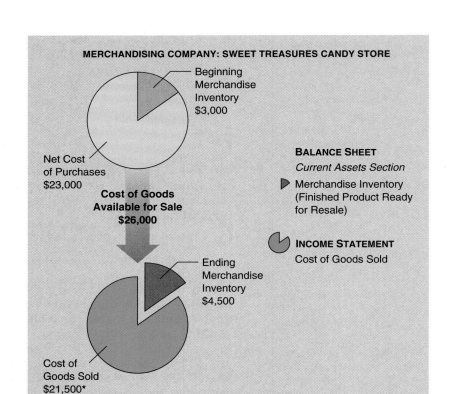

MERCHANDISING COMPANY: SWEET TREASURES CANDY STORE

Beginning Merchandise Inventory $3,000

Net Cost of Purchases $23,000

Cost of Goods Available for Sale $26,000

Ending Merchandise Inventory $4,500

Cost of Goods Sold $21,500*

BALANCE SHEET
Current Assets Section
▷ Merchandise Inventory (Finished Product Ready for Resale)

INCOME STATEMENT
Cost of Goods Sold

*Cost of goods sold = $3,000 + $23,000 − $4,500 = $21,500.

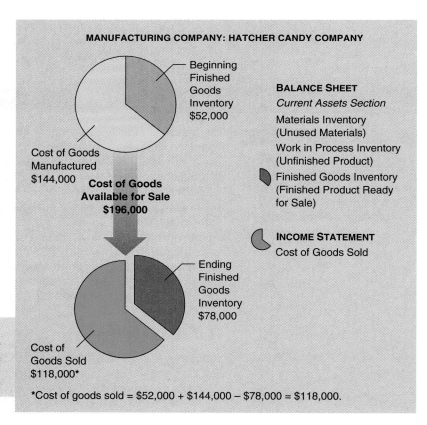

MANUFACTURING COMPANY: HATCHER CANDY COMPANY

Beginning Finished Goods Inventory $52,000

Cost of Goods Manufactured $144,000

Cost of Goods Available for Sale $196,000

Ending Finished Goods Inventory $78,000

Cost of Goods Sold $118,000*

BALANCE SHEET
Current Assets Section
Materials Inventory (Unused Materials)
Work in Process Inventory (Unfinished Product)
Finished Goods Inventory (Finished Product Ready for Sale)

INCOME STATEMENT
Cost of Goods Sold

**Figure 3
Comparison of the Inventories and Cost of Goods Sold Sections for Merchandising and Manufacturing Organizations**

*Cost of goods sold = $52,000 + $144,000 − $78,000 = $118,000.

accurate measurement of costs. Managers use these direct and indirect measures of costs to support pricing decisions or decisions to reallocate resources to other cost objects.

Direct costs are costs that can be conveniently or economically traced to a cost object. For example, the wages of production line workers can be conveniently traced to the product, because the time worked and the related hourly wages can be easily found by looking at time cards and payroll records. Similarly, the costs of an engine can be easily traced to an automobile's cost.

In some cases, however, even though a material becomes part of a finished product, the expense of actually tracing its cost is too great. Some examples include nails in furniture, bolts in automobiles, and rivets in airplanes. These costs are considered indirect costs of the product. Indirect costs are costs that cannot be conveniently or economically traced to a cost object. Even though indirect costs may be difficult to trace, they must be included in the cost of a product. Therefore, management accountants use a formula to assign indirect costs to products. For example, insurance costs for the factory cannot be conveniently traced to individual products, but, for the sake of accuracy, they must be included in each product's cost. Management accountants solve the problem by assigning a portion of the factory insurance costs to each product manufactured.

Costs are classified as direct or indirect depending on the manager's needs. Regardless of the type of organization—service, retail, or manufacturing—classifying costs is important. The following examples illustrate a cost object and its related direct and indirect costs for three kinds of organizations.

- In a service organization, such as an accounting firm, costs can be traced to a specific service, such as tax return preparation. Direct costs for tax return preparation services include the costs of tax return forms, computer usage, and labor to prepare the return. Indirect costs include the costs of office rental, utilities, secretarial labor, telephone expenses, and depreciation of office furniture.

- In a retail organization, such as a department store, costs can be traced to a department. For example, the direct costs of the shoe department include the costs of shoes and the wages of employees working in that department. Indirect costs include the costs of utilities, insurance, property taxes, storage, and handling.

- In a manufacturing organization, costs can be traced to the product. Direct costs of the product include the costs of direct materials and direct labor. Indirect costs include the costs of utilities, depreciation of equipment, insurance, property taxes, inspection, maintenance of machinery, storage, handling, and cleaning.

Cost Behavior

Managers are also interested in the way costs respond to changes in volume or activity. By analyzing these patterns of behavior, managers gain information about the impact of changes in selling prices or operating costs on the net income of the organization. Costs can be separated into variable costs or fixed costs. A variable cost is a cost that changes in direct proportion to a change in productive output (or any other measure of volume). A fixed cost is a cost that remains constant within a defined range of activity or time period.

Viewing costs as variable or fixed is important to managers of any type of organization. The following examples illustrate variable and fixed costs for service, retail, and manufacturing organizations:

- A landscaping service has variable costs that include the cost of landscaping materials and direct labor to plant the materials for each landscaping project. Fixed costs include the costs of depreciation on trucks and equipment, nursery rent, insurance, and property taxes.

- A retail used-car dealership has variable costs that include the cost of the used cars sold and sales commissions. Fixed costs include the costs of building and lot rental, depreciation on office equipment, and salaries of the receptionist and accountant.
- A lawn mower manufacturer has variable costs that include the costs of direct materials, direct labor, indirect materials (bolts, nails, lubricants), and indirect labor (inspection and maintenance labor). Fixed costs include the costs of supervisory salaries and depreciation on buildings.

Value-Adding Versus Nonvalue-Adding Costs

In the spirit of continuous improvement, managers examine operating activities and processes in their organization. Their goal is to reduce or eliminate activities that do not add value to the products or services. The organization identifies the characteristics of the product or service that customers value and would be willing to pay for. This information influences the design of future products or the delivery of future services. The organization's management also identifies the operating activities that provide the value. Activities that do not add value are reduced or eliminated. A value-adding cost is the cost of an operating activity that increases the market value of a product or service. A nonvalue-adding cost is the cost of an operating activity that adds cost to a product or service but does not increase its market value. The depreciation of a machine that shapes a part assembled into the final product is a value-adding cost; depreciation of a sales department automobile is a nonvalue-adding cost. Costs incurred to improve the quality of a product are value-adding costs if the customer is willing to pay more for the higher-quality product; if not, they are nonvalue-adding costs because they do not increase the product's market value. The costs of administrative activities such as accounting and personnel are nonvalue-adding costs; they are necessary for the operation of the business, but they do not add value to the product.

Costs for Financial Reporting

Managers must prepare financial statements for external parties using a required format based on generally accepted accounting principles. Income statements prepared for owners, creditors, and other outside parties must reflect expenditures separated into product costs and period costs. Classifying expenditures into product (cost of goods sold) and period (selling and administrative) costs is called the *absorption approach* to income statement preparation.

Table 2. Cost Classification and Cost Analyses

Cost Examples	Purpose of Cost Classification			
	Traceability to Product	Cost Behavior	Value	Financial Reporting
Sugar for candy	Direct	Variable	Value-adding	Product
Depreciation on mixing machine	Indirect	Fixed	Value-adding	Product
Sales commission	—*	Variable	Value-adding**	Period
Accountant's salary	—*	Fixed	Nonvalue-adding	Period

*Sales commission and accountant's salary are not product costs. Therefore, these costs are not directly or indirectly traceable in traditional business operations.

**Sales commission can be value-adding because customers' perceptions of the salesperson and the selling experience can strongly affect their perceptions of the product's or service's market value.

Product costs or inventoriable costs, include the three elements of manufacturing cost: direct materials, direct labor, and manufacturing overhead. The product costs for units sold in the accounting period are included in the cost of goods sold section of the income statement. The product costs of unsold units are shown in the Finished Goods Inventory balance on the balance sheet. Prime costs are the primary costs of production, which are the sum of direct materials costs and direct labor costs, while conversion costs are the costs of converting raw materials into finished product, which include direct labor and manufacturing overhead costs.

Period costs, or noninventoriable costs, are the costs of resources consumed during the current period. For example, selling and administrative expenses are period costs because those activities were performed to generate the revenues of the current period.

A single cost item can be classified in different ways depending on the purpose of the cost analysis. Table 2 provides examples.

Standards of Ethical Conduct for Practitioners of Management Accounting and Financial Management

OBJECTIVE 8

Identify the standards of ethical conduct for management accountants

Managers are responsible to external parties (for example, owners, creditors, governmental agencies, and the local community) for the proper use of organizational resources and the financial reporting of their actions. Conflicts may arise that require managers to balance the interests of all external parties. For example, the community wants a safe living environment, while owners seek to maximize profits. If management decides to purchase an expensive device to extract pollutants from the production process, it will protect the community, but profits will decline. The benefit will be greater for the community than for the owners. On the other hand, management could achieve higher profits for the owners by purchasing a less expensive, less effective pollution device that may harm the community. Such potential conflicts between external parties can create ethical dilemmas for management and for accountants.

Management accountants and financial managers have a responsibility to help management balance the needs of the various external parties. Thus the accounting profession must operate with the highest standards of performance. To provide

Exhibit 2. Standards of Ethical Conduct for Practitioners of Management Accounting and Financial Management

Practitioners of management accounting and financial management have an obligation to the public, their profession, the organization they serve, and themselves, to maintain the highest standards of ethical conduct. In recognition of this obligation, the Institute of Management Accountants has promulgated the following standards of ethical conduct for practitioners of management accounting and financial management. Adherence to these standards, both domestically and internationally, is integral to achieving the Objectives of Management Accounting. Practitioners of management accounting and financial management shall not commit acts contrary to these standards nor shall they condone the commission of such acts by others within their organizations.

Competence. Practitioners of management accounting and financial management have a responsibility to:

- Maintain an appropriate level of professional competence by ongoing development of their knowledge and skills.
- Perform their professional duties in accordance with relevant laws, regulations, and technical standards.
- Prepare complete and clear reports and recommendations after appropriate analysis of relevant and reliable information.

Confidentiality. Practitioners of management accounting and financial management have a responsibility to:

- Refrain from disclosing confidential information acquired in the course of their work except when authorized, unless legally obligated to do so.
- Inform subordinates as appropriate regarding the confidentiality of information acquired in the course of their work and monitor their activities to assure the maintenance of that confidentiality.
- Refrain from using or appearing to use confidential information acquired in the course of their work for unethical or illegal advantage either personally or through third parties.

Integrity. Practitioners of management accounting and financial management have a responsibility to:

- Avoid actual or apparent conflicts of interest and advise all appropriate parties of any potential conflict.
- Refrain from engaging in any activity that would prejudice their ability to carry out their duties ethically.
- Refuse any gift, favor, or hosptiality that would influence or would appear to influence their actions.
- Refrain from either actively or passively subverting the attainment of the organization's legitimate and ethical objectives.
- Recognize and communicate professional limitations or other constraints that would preclude responsible judgment or successful performance of an activity.

(continued)

guidance, the Institute of Management Accountants has formally adopted standards of ethical conduct for practitioners of management accounting and financial management. Those standards emphasize that management accountants have responsibilities in the areas of competence, confidentiality, integrity, and objectivity. The full statement is presented in Exhibit 2.

Chapter Review

REVIEW OF LEARNING OBJECTIVES

1. **Define *management accounting* and distinguish between management accounting and financial accounting.** Management accounting is the process of identifying, measuring, accumulating, analyzing, preparing, interpreting, and communicating information used by management to plan, evaluate, and control an organization within and to ensure that its resources are used and accounted for appropriately. Management accounting reports provide information for planning, control,

Exhibit 2. Standards of Ethical Conduct for Practitioners of Management Accounting and Financial Management (*continued*)

- Communicate unfavorable as well as favorable information and professional judgments or opinions.
- Refrain from engaging in or supporting any activity that would discredit the profession.

Objectivity. Practitioners of management accounting and financial management have a responsibility to:

- Communicate information fairly and objectively.
- Disclose fully all relevant information that could reasonably be expected to influence an intended user's understanding of the reports, comments, and recommendations presented.

Resolution of Ethical Conflict. In applying the standards of ethical conduct, practitioners of management accounting and financial management may encounter problems in identifying unethical behavior or in resolving an ethical conflict. When faced with significant ethical issues, practitioners of management accounting and financial management should follow the established policies of the organization bearing on the resolution of such conflict. If these policies do not resolve the ethical conflict, such practitioner should consider the following courses of action:

- Discuss such problems with the immediate superior except when it appears that the superior is involved, in which case the problem should be presented initially to the next higher managerial level. If a satisfactory resolution cannot be achieved when the problem is initially presented, submit the issues to the next higher managerial level.

  If the immediate superior is the chief executive officer, or equivalent, the acceptable reviewing authority may be a group such as the audit committee, executive committee, board of directors, board of trustees, or owners. Contact with levels above the immediate superior should be initiated only with the superior's knowledge, assuming the superior is not involved. Except where legally prescribed, communication of such problems to authorities or individuals not employed or engaged by the organization is not considered appropriate.
- Clarify relevant ethical issues by confidential discussion with an objective advisor (e.g., IMA Ethics Counselling Service) to obtain a better understanding of possible courses of action.
- Consult your own attorney as to legal obligations and rights concerning the ethical conflict.
- If the ethical conflict still exists after exhausting all levels of internal review, there may be no other recourse on significant matters than to resign from the organization and to submit an informative memorandum to an appropriate representative of the organization. After resignation, depending on the nature of the ethical conflict, it may also be appropriate to notify other parties.

Source: From *Standards of Ethical Conduct for Practitioners of Management Accounting and Financial Management."* Institute of Management Accountants, July 1997. Reprinted by permission.

performance measurement, and decision making to employees, managers, and suppliers when they need such information. Management accounting reports follow a flexible format and present subjective, future-oriented information expressed in dollar amounts or physical measures. In contrast, financial accounting reports provide information about the past performance of an organization to owners, lenders, customers, and government agencies on a regular basis. Financial accounting reports follow strict guidelines defined by generally accepted accounting principles and present objective information shown in historical dollars.

2. **Explain the management cycle and its connection to management accounting.** Traditionally, management operates in four stages: planning, executing, reviewing, and reporting. Strategic and operating plans prepare managers for the execution of activities that put those plans into action. A review of the actual performance in relation to planned performance helps in the evaluation of management's success in guiding and motivating personnel. Reports reflect the results of planning, executing, and reviewing operations and may be prepared externally for stockholders, creditors, or other external parties or internally for management and employees.

3. **Identify the new management philosophies for continuous improvement and discuss the role of management accounting in implementing these philosophies.** The new approaches to management include the just-in-time (JIT) operating environment, total quality management (TQM), and activity-based management

(ABM). All of these approaches are designed to achieve continuous improvement by increasing product or service quality, reducing resource waste, and reducing cost. Management accounting helps managers design better information systems that are sensitive to changes in production processes in a JIT operating environment, requests for information about quality costs (TQM), and assignment of overhead costs to products or services (ABC).

4. **Define *performance measures*, recognize the uses of these measures in the management cycle, and prepare an analysis of nonfinancial data.** Performance measures are quantitative tools that provide an indication of an organization's performance in relation to a specific goal or expected outcome. Performance measures are used in the management cycle to plan future performance, to guide and motivate current performance and assign costs during the executing stage, and to improve future performance through the analysis of significant differences between actual and planned performance. Management accountants have always been responsible for analyzing nonfinancial data. Today's globally competitive environment has created additional demand for nonfinancial analyses centered on increasing the quality of an organization's products or services, reducing production and delivery time, and satisfying customers. Among the performance measures used in these analyses are units of output, time measures, and scrap incurrence rates.

5. **Identify the important questions a manager must consider before requesting or preparing a management report.** Report preparation depends on the four *W*'s: Why? What? Who? and When? The why question is answered by stating the purpose of the report. Once that has been stated, the report maker must determine what information the report should contain to satisfy that purpose. The who question can take several forms: For whom is the report being prepared? To whom should the report be distributed? Who will read it? Finally, there is the question of when. When is the report due?

6. **Compare accounting for inventories and cost of goods sold in merchandising and manufacturing organizations.** A merchandising organization purchases a product that is ready for resale when it is received. Only one account, Merchandise Inventory, is used to record and account for items in inventory. The cost of goods sold is simply the difference between the cost of goods available for sale and the ending merchandise inventory. A manufacturing organization, because it creates a product, maintains three inventory accounts: Materials Inventory, Work in Process Inventory, and Finished Goods Inventory. Manufacturing costs flow through all three inventory accounts. During the accounting period, the cost of completed products is transferred to the Finished Goods Inventory account; the cost of units that have been sold is transferred to the Cost of Goods Sold account.

7. **Identify various approaches managers use to classify costs and show how the purpose of a manager's cost analysis can change the classification of a single cost item.** A single cost item can be classified and used by managers to (1) trace costs to cost objects (direct versus indirect costs), (2) calculate the number of units that must be sold to obtain a certain level of profit (variable versus fixed costs), (3) identify costs of activities that do and do not add value to a product or service (value-adding versus nonvalue-adding costs), or (4) prepare an income statement for outside parties (product versus period costs).

8. **Identify the standards of ethical conduct for management accountants.** Standards of ethical conduct govern management accountants' competence, confidentiality, integrity, and objectivity. These standards help management accountants recognize and avoid situations and activities that compromise their honesty, loyalty, and ability to supply management with accurate and relevant information.

REVIEW OF CONCEPTS AND TERMINOLOGY

The following concepts and terms were introduced in this chapter:

LO 3   **Activity-based costing (ABC):** A system that identifies all of an organization's major operating activities (both production and nonproduction), traces costs to those activities, and then determines which products or services use the resources and services supplied by those activities.

LO 3   **Activity-based management (ABM):** An approach to managing an organization that identifies all major operating activities, determines what resources are consumed by each activity, identifies what causes resource usage of each activity, and categorizes the activities as either adding value to a product or service or being nonvalue-adding; emphasis is on the reduction or elimination of nonvalue-adding activities.

LO 3   **Continuous improvement:** The management concept that one should never be satisfied with what is; one should always seek a better method, product, service, process, or resource.

LO 7   **Conversion costs:** The costs of converting raw materials into finished product, which are the sum of direct labor costs and manufacturing overhead costs.

LO 7   **Direct cost:** Any cost that can be conveniently or economically traced to a specific cost object; a manufacturing cost that is easily traced to a specific product.

LO 7   **Fixed cost:** A cost that remains constant within a defined range of activity or time period.

LO 7   **Indirect cost:** Any cost that cannot be conveniently or economically traced to a specific cost object.

LO 7   **Inventoriable cost:** See *product cost.*

LO 3   **Just-in-time (JIT) operating environment:** An organizational environment in which personnel are hired and raw materials and facilities are purchased and used only as needed; emphasis is on the elimination of waste.

LO 1   **Management accounting:** The process of identification, measurement, accumulation, analysis, preparation, interpretation, and communication of financial and nonfinancial information used by management to plan, evaluate, and control the organization within and to assure appropriate use and accountability for its resources.

LO 7   **Noninventoriable cost:** See *period costs.*

LO 3   **Nonvalue-adding activity:** A production- or service-related activity that adds cost to a product or service, but, from a customer's perspective, does not increase its value.

LO 7   **Nonvalue-adding cost:** The cost of an operating activity that adds cost to a product or service but does not increase its market value.

LO 4   **Performance measures:** Quantitative tools that provide an indication of an organization's performance in relation to a specific goal or expected outcome.

LO 7   **Period costs:** The costs of resources consumed during the current period; they cannot be inventoried.

LO 7   **Prime costs:** The primary costs of production, which are the sum of the direct materials costs and the direct labor costs.

LO 7   **Product cost:** Inventoriable costs that include the three elements of manufacturing cost: direct materials, direct labor, and manufacturing overhead.

LO 3   **Total quality management (TQM):** An environment in which all functions work together to build quality into the organization's product or service.

LO 3   **Value-adding activity:** A production- or service-related activity that adds cost to a product or service, but, from a customer's perspective, also increases its value.

LO 7   **Value-adding cost:** The cost of an operating activity that increases the market value of a product or service.

LO 7   **Variable cost:** A cost that changes in direct proportion to a change in productive output (or any other measure of volume).

REVIEW PROBLEM
Analysis of Nonfinancial Data

LO 4   Youngdale Painting, Inc., is a house-painting company located in Phoenix. The company employs painters specializing in interior walls or exterior trim. Recently Mr. Youngdale assigned two interior painters and three exterior trim painters to two school projects. He prepared a projection of work hours for the Yakima High School and Jerome Elementary School projects for the month of June, as shown at the top of the next page.

Projected Hours to Be Worked

	Week 1	Week 2	Week 3	Week 4	Totals
Interior	80	80	80	80	320
Exterior	120	120	120	120	480

On July 2, Mr. Youngdale assembled the actual hour data shown below:

Actual Hours Worked

	Week 1	Week 2	Week 3	Week 4	Totals
Interior	96	108	116	116	436
Exterior	104	108	116	108	436

Mr. Youngdale is concerned about the excess hours worked during June.

REQUIRED

1. For each group of painters (interior and exterior), prepare an analysis that shows the projected hours, the actual hours worked, and the number of hours over or under the projected hours for each week and in total.
2. Using the same information, prepare one line graph for the interior painters and another line graph for the exterior painters. Place the weeks on the X axis and the number of hours on the Y axis.
3. Using the information from 1 and 2, identify which group of painters worked more hours than planned and offer several reasons for the additional hours.

ANSWER TO REVIEW PROBLEM

1.

Interior Painters

Week	Projected Hours to Be Worked	Actual Hours Worked	Hours Worked Under or (Over) Projected
1	80	96	(16)
2	80	108	(28)
3	80	116	(36)
4	80	116	(36)
Total	320	436	(116)

Exterior Painters

Week	Projected Hours to Be Worked	Actual Hours Worked	Hours Worked Under or (Over) Projected
1	120	104	16
2	120	108	12
3	120	116	4
4	120	108	12
Total	480	436	44

2.

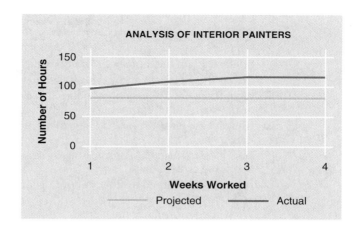

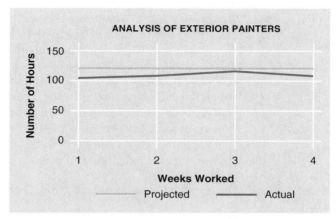

3. The interior painters took more time to complete the jobs than was anticipated by Mr. Youngdale. Possible reasons for the additional hours include:
   a. The quality of the paint or painting materials may have been poor, which would require the walls to be repainted.
   b. One of the painters may have been inexperienced or recently hired. If that person lacked training, he or she may have worked more slowly than anticipated, or the other painter may have had to take extra time to train him or her.
   c. The customer may have requested a different color or finish after the painting had started. As a result, the painters had to repaint some areas.
   d. Mr. Youngdale underestimated the amount of time required for interior painting.

Chapter Assignments

BUILDING YOUR KNOWLEDGE FOUNDATION

Questions

1. What is management accounting?
2. What effect does the size of an organization have on the amount or type of financial information needed by management?
3. How is management accounting similar to financial accounting?
4. How do management accounting and financial accounting differ in terms of report format, reasons for report preparation, and the parties to whom management is accountable?

5. How do management accounting reports and financial accounting reports differ in terms of units of measure, nature of information, and timing of preparation?
6. What are the four stages of the management cycle?
7. Briefly explain the four stages of the management cycle.
8. How is management accounting linked to the management cycle?
9. What three new management philosophies or approaches have developed in response to global competition?
10. How does each of the new management philosophies affect an organization's operating environment?
11. How have management accounting systems adapted to changes in an organization's operating environment?
12. What are the desired results of adopting any one of the three new management approaches?
13. What are performance measures?
14. Give examples of financial performance measures.
15. What are nonfinancial performance measures? Give examples.
16. How are financial and nonfinancial performance measures used?
17. What are the four *W*'s of report preparation? Explain the importance of each.
18. What is the difference between a merchandising organization and a manufacturing organization, and how does it affect accounting for inventories?
19. What is the difference between a direct cost and an indirect cost?
20. What is the difference between a value-adding cost and a nonvalue-adding cost?
21. What are product costs? period costs?
22. What are prime costs? conversion costs?
23. Why are ethical standards of competence so important to the work of management accountants?
24. Why is it so important for management accountants to maintain their integrity?

Short Exercises

SE 1.
LO 1 *Management Accounting Versus Financial Accounting*

Management accounting differs from financial accounting in a number of ways. Tell whether each of the following characteristics relates to management accounting (MA) or financial accounting (FA).

1. Focuses on various segments of the business entity
2. Demands objectivity
3. Relies on the criterion of usefulness rather than formal guidelines or restrictions for gathering information
4. Measures units in historical dollars
5. Reports information on a regular basis
6. Uses only monetary measures for reports
7. Adheres to generally accepted accounting principles
8. Prepares reports whenever needed

SE 2.
LO 2 *The Management Cycle*

Indicate whether each of the following management activities is part of the planning stage (P), the executing stage (E), the reviewing stage (REV), or the reporting stage (REP) of the management cycle.

1. Complete a balance sheet and income statement at the end of the year
2. Train a store clerk to complete a cash sale
3. Meet with department store managers to develop performance measures for sales personnel
4. Rent a local warehouse to store excess inventory of clothing
5. Evaluate the performance of the shoe department by examining the significant differences between the department's actual and planned expenses for the month
6. Prepare an annual budget of anticipated sales for each department and the entire store

SE 3.
LO 3 *JIT and Continuous Improvement*

The just-in-time operating environment focuses on reducing or eliminating the waste of resources. Resources include physical assets such as machinery and buildings, labor time, and materials and parts used in the production process. Choose one of these resources and tell how it could be wasted. How can an organization prevent the waste of that resource? How can the concept of continuous improvement be implemented to reduce the waste of that resource?

SE 4.

LO 4 *Analysis of Nonfinancial Data*

Spectrum Technologies has been having a problem with the computerized welding operation in its dialogic extractor product line. The extractors are used to sift through and separate various types of metal shavings into piles of individual metals for recycling and scrap sales. The time for each welding operation has been increasing at an erratic rate. Management has asked that the time intervals be analyzed to see if the cause of the problem can be determined. The number of parts welded per shift during the previous week is reported below. What can you deduce from the information that may help management solve the welding operation problem?

	Machine Number	Monday	Tuesday	Wednesday	Thursday	Friday
First shift:						
Kovacs	1	642	636	625	617	602
Abington	2	732	736	735	729	738
Geisler	3	745	726	717	694	686
Second shift:						
Deragon	1	426	416	410	404	398
Berwager	2	654	656	661	664	670
Grass	3	526	524	510	504	502

SE 5.

LO 5 *Managerial Report Preparation*

Melissa Mertz, president of Mertz Industries, asked controller Rick Caputo to prepare a report on the use of electricity by each of the organization's five divisions. Increases in electricity costs ranged from 20 to 35 percent in the divisions over the past year. What questions should Rick ask before he begins his analysis?

SE 6.

LO 6 *Merchandising Versus Manufacturing*

Based on the following information, decide whether the Vikram Company is a merchandising organization or a manufacturing organization. List reasons for your answer.

Beginning Work in Process Inventory	$3,800
Materials Used	2,350
Overhead Costs	4,250
Direct Labor Costs	1,500
Cost of Goods Sold	9,340
Ending Materials Inventory	2,430
Beginning Finished Goods Inventory	4,800
Ending Finished Goods Inventory	7,250

SE 7.

LO 7 *Cost Classification*

Indicate whether each of the following is a product (PR) or a period (PER) cost and a variable (V) or a fixed (F) cost. Also indicate whether each adds value (VA) or does not add value (NVA) to the product.

1. Production supervisor's salary
2. Sales commission
3. Wages of a production line worker

SE 8.

LO 8 *Ethical Conduct*

Gary Louskip, a management accountant for Pegstone Cosmetics Company, has lunch every day with his good friend Joe Blaik, a management accountant for Shepherd Cosmetics, Inc., a competitor of Pegstone. Last week, Gary couldn't decide how to treat some information in a report he was preparing, so he discussed the information with Joe. Is Gary adhering to the ethical standards of management accountants? Defend your answer.

Exercises

E 1.

LO 1 *Definitions of Management Accounting*

There are many definitions and descriptions of management accounting. The Institute of Management Accountants, in *Statement No. 1A* in its series *Statements on Management Accounting,* defined management accounting as

the process of identification, measurement, accumulation, analysis, preparation, interpretation, and communication of financial information used by management to plan, evaluate, and control within the organization and to assure appropriate use and accountability for its resources. Management accounting also comprises the preparation of financial reports for nonmanagement groups such as shareholders, creditors, regulatory agencies, and tax authorities.[5]

In *The Modern Accountant's Handbook,* management (managerial) accounting is described as follows:

> Managerial accounting, although generally anchored to the financial accounting framework, involves a broader information-processing system. It deals in many units of measure and produces a variety of reports designed for specific purposes. Its scope encompasses the past, the present, and the future. Its purposes include short- and long-range planning, cost determination, control of activities, assessment of objectives and program performance, and provision of basic information for decision making.[6]

1. Compare these two statements about management accounting.
2. Explain this statement: "It is impossible to distinguish the point at which financial accounting ends and management accounting begins."

E 2.

LO 2 *The Management Cycle*

Indicate whether each of the following management activities is part of the planning stage (P), the executing stage (E), the reviewing stage (REV), or the reporting stage (REP) of the management cycle in a local hospital.

1. Lease five Ford ambulances for the current year
2. Compare the actual number of patient days in the hospital to the planned number of patient days for the year
3. Develop a strategic plan for a new pediatric wing of the hospital
4. Prepare a report showing the past performance of the emergency room
5. Develop standards or expectations about the performance of the hospital admittance area for the next year
6. Prepare and distribute the hospital's balance sheet and income statement to the board of directors
7. Maintain an inventory of bed linens and bath towels for hospital patients
8. Formulate a corporate policy for the treatment and final disposition of hazardous waste materials in the hospital
9. Prepare a report of the types and amounts of hazardous waste materials removed from the hospital in the last three months
10. Monitor the time taken to deliver food trays to patients staying in the hospital

E 3.

LO 3 *New Management Philosophies*

Recently, you were dining with three chief financial officers who were attending a seminar on new management tools and approaches to improving operations. During dinner, they shared information about their organizations' current operating environments. Excerpts from the dinner conversation are presented below. Tell whether each excerpt describes activity-based management (ABM), just-in-time operations (JIT), or total quality management (TQM).

CFO 1: We believe that quality can be achieved through carefully designed production processes. Therefore, we have an environment in which the time to move, store, queue, and inspect materials and products is greatly reduced. We have reduced inventories by purchasing and using materials only as needed.

CFO 2: Your approach is good. However, we are more concerned with our total operating environment, so we have a strategy that asks all employees to contribute to the achievement of quality, both for our products and for our production processes. We focus on eliminating poor product quality by targeting and reducing waste and inefficiencies in our current operating methods.

CFO 3: Our organization has adopted a strategy for quality products that incorporates many of your approaches. We also want to manage our resources effectively, but we do so by monitoring operating activities. All activities are analyzed, and the ones that do not add value to products are reduced or eliminated.

E 4.

LO 4 *Nonfinancial Data Analysis*

Greenacres Landscapes, Inc., specializes in lawn installations requiring California bluegrass sod. The sod comes in 1-yard squares. The organization uses the guideline of 500 square yards per person per hour to evaluate the performance of its sod layers.

During the first week of March, the following actual data were collected.

Employee	Hours Worked	Square Yards of Sod Planted
P. Thompson	38	18,240
L. May	45	22,500
B. Pratt	40	19,800
E. Yu	42	17,640
R. Hardin	44	22,880
B. Harty	45	21,500

Evaluate the performance of the six employees.

LO 5 *Report Preparation*

E 5. Jim Herndon is the sales manager for All-Occasions Greeting Cards, Inc. At the beginning of the year, the organization introduced a new line of humorous birthday cards into the U.S. market. Now management is holding a strategic planning meeting to plan next year's operating activities. One item on the agenda is to review the success of the new birthday card line and the need to change the selling price or stimulate sales volume in the five sales territories. For the October 31 meeting, Jim was asked to prepare a report addressing these issues. His report was to include profits generated in each sales territory for the birthday card line only.

On October 31 Jim arrived late at the meeting and immediately distributed his report to the members of the strategic planning team. The report consisted of comments made by seven of Jim's leading sales representatives. The comments were broad in scope and touched only lightly on the success of the new card line. Jim was pleased that he had met the deadline to distribute the report, but the other team members were disappointed in the information he had provided.

Using the four *W*'s for report presentation, comment on Jim's effectiveness in preparing a report for the strategic planning team.

LO 6 *Merchandising Versus Manufacturing*

E 6. Indicate whether the accounting information from each of the following accounts refers to the operations of a merchandising organization (MER), a manufacturing organization (MANF), or both merchandising and manufacturing organizations (BOTH).

1. Finished Goods Inventory
2. Merchandise Inventory
3. Cost of Goods Sold
4. Net Cost of Purchases
5. Materials Inventory
6. Cost of Goods Manufactured
7. Gross Margin
8. Net Income
9. Operating Expenses

LO 7 *Cost Classifications*

E 7. Tell whether each of the following costs for a bicycle manufacturer is a product cost or a period cost, a direct cost or an indirect cost of the bicycle, and a variable cost or a fixed cost.

	Cost Classification		
	Product or Period	Direct or Indirect	Variable or Fixed
Example: Bicycle tire	Product	Direct	Variable
1. Depreciation on office computer			
2. Labor to assemble bicycle			
3. Labor to inspect bicycle			
4. President's salary			
5. Lubricant for wheels			

LO 8 *Professional Ethics*

E 8. Ron Kowalski went to work for Billings Industries five years ago. He was recently promoted to cost accounting manager and now has a new boss, Ted Young, the corporate controller. Last week, Ron and Ted went to a two-day professional development program on accounting changes in the new manufacturing environment. During the first hour of the first day's program, Ted disappeared and Ron didn't see him again until the cocktail hour. The same thing happened on the second day. During the trip home, Ron asked Ted if he enjoyed the conference. He replied:

> Ron, the golf course was excellent. You play golf. Why don't you join me during the next conference? I haven't sat in on one of those sessions in ten years. This is my

R&R time. Those sessions are for the new people. My experience is enough to keep me current. Plus, I have excellent people to help me as we adjust our accounting system to the changes being implemented on the production floor.

Does Ron have an ethical dilemma? If so, what is it? What are his options? How would you solve his problem? Be prepared to defend your answer.

Problems

P 1.

LO 4 *Using Nonfinancial Data*

Clearlake Candy Company recently developed its strategic plan based on the philosophy of total quality management. Clearlake wants to sell candies with the highest quality in color, texture, shape, and taste. To meet quality standards, management chose many quality performance measures, including the number of rejected candy canes. Working with Janeece Hammond, the process supervisor, management decided that no more than 50 candy canes should be rejected daily throughout the year.

Using the data gathered about the actual number of rejected candy canes in Week 1 of 20xx, Janeece Hammond prepared the following summary and graph.

Week 1, 20xx	Maximum Number of Rejected Allowed Candy Canes	Actual Number of Rejected Candy Canes	Variance Under (Over) Allowed Maximum
Monday	50	60	(10)
Tuesday	50	63	(13)
Wednesday	50	58	(8)
Thursday	50	59	(9)
Friday	50	62	(12)
Total for the Week	250	302	(52)
Daily Average	50	60.4	

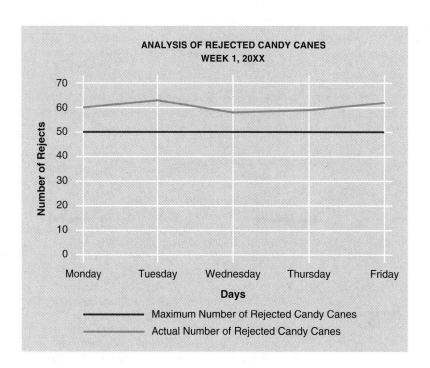

Because the variance was 20.8 percent (52 ÷ 250), Janeece decided to analyze the data further. She found that the rejected candy canes either contained too little sugar (ingredients), were not circular in shape (shaping), or were undercooked (cooking time). The number of rejects in each category follows at the top of the next page.

Week 1, 20xx	Reasons for Rejects
Ingredients	40
Shaping	195
Cooking Time	67
Total	302

Janeece worked with the cooks the following week to review the recipe, including ingredients, quantities, and cooking instructions. She trained the cooks to measure quantities more precisely, to shape the candy more carefully, and to time the cooking process more accurately. Then, in Week 3 of 20xx, she gathered the following information on the actual number of rejected candy canes and reasons for the rejects.

Week 3, 20xx	Actual Number of Rejects
Monday	20
Tuesday	21
Wednesday	22
Thursday	19
Friday	18
Total	100

Week 3, 20xx	Reasons for Rejects
Ingredients	7
Shaping	63
Cooking Time	30
Total	100

REQUIRED

1. Analyze the activity in Week 3 of 20xx by preparing a table showing each day's maximum number of rejected candy canes allowed (50 candy canes), actual number of rejected candy canes, and variance under (over) the maximum number allowed each day. In addition, prepare a graph comparing the maximum and actual numbers of rejected candy canes each day for Week 3.
2. Analyze the change in reasons for rejects between Weeks 1 and 3 by preparing a table showing the frequency of each reason for rejecting a candy cane for each week. In addition, prepare a graph comparing the reasons for each week.
3. Based on the information, how successful was Janeece in increasing the quality of the candy canes made at Clearlake? What recommendations, if any, would you make about monitoring the candy production process in the future?

P 2.

LO 4 *Nonfinancial Data Analysis: Manufacturing*

Ekin Enterprises makes shoes for every major sport. The Awesome Shoe, one of the organization's leading products, is lightweight, long wearing, and inexpensive. Production of the Awesome Shoe involves five different departments: (1) the Cutting/Lining Department, where cloth tops are cut and lined; (2) the Molding Department, where the shoe's rubber base is formed; (3) the Bonding Department, where the cloth top is bonded to the rubber base; (4) the Soling Department, where the sole is attached to the rubber base; and (5) the Finishing Department, where the shoe is trimmed, stitched, and laced.

Recently, manufacturing costs have increased for the Awesome Shoe. Controller Avery Berger has been investigating the production process to determine the problems. Everything points to the labor hours required to make the shoe. Actual labor hours worked in a recent week are as follows.

Operation	Actual Hours Worked					
	Monday	Tuesday	Wednesday	Thursday	Friday	Total
Cutting/Lining	300	310	305	300	246	1,461
Molding	144	186	183	200	246	959
Bonding	456	434	488	450	492	2,320
Soling	408	434	366	400	492	2,100
Finishing	600	620	549	625	615	3,009

The company has estimated the following labor hours for each department to complete a pair of Awesome Shoes: Cutting/Lining, .2 hour; Molding, .1 hour; Bonding, .4 hour; Soling, .3 hour; and Finishing, .5 hour. During the week under review, the number of Awesome Shoes produced was 1,200 pairs on Monday; 1,240 pairs on Tuesday; 1,220 pairs on Wednesday; 1,250 pairs on Thursday; and 1,230 pairs on Friday.

REQUIRED

1. Prepare an analysis to determine the average actual labor hours worked per day per pair of Awesome Shoes for each operation in the production process. (*Note:* Hours worked per pair of shoes = actual hours worked each day ÷ number of pairs of shoes produced each day.)
2. Prepare a graph showing the percentage of actual labor hours worked over/(under) the target level for the week.
3. By comparing the average actual labor hours worked from **1** with the expected labor hours per pair of shoes per department, prepare an analysis showing the differences in each operation for each day. Identify reasons for the differences.

P 3.

LO 5 *Approach to Report Preparation*

Lancer Industries, Inc., is deciding whether to expand its Jeans by Lorraine line of women's clothing. Sales in units of this product were 22,500, 28,900, and 36,200 in 20xx, 20x1, and 20x2, respectively. The product has been very profitable, averaging 35 percent profit (above cost) over the three-year period. Lancer has ten sales representatives covering seven states in the Northeast. Present production capacity is about 40,000 pairs of jeans per year. There is adequate plant space for additional equipment, and the labor needed can be easily hired and trained.

The organization's management is made up of four vice presidents: the vice president of marketing, the vice president of production, the vice president of finance, and the vice president of management information systems. Each vice president is directly responsible to the president, Lorraine Lancer.

REQUIRED

1. What types of information will Ms. Lancer need before she can decide whether to expand the Jeans by Lorraine product line?
2. Assume that one of the reports needed to support Ms. Lancer's decision is an analysis of sales over the past three years. This analysis should be broken down by sales representative. How would each of the four *W*'s pertain to this report?
3. Design a format for the report in **2**.

P 4.

LO 6 *Manufacturing Company Balance Sheet*

The analysis below shows the balance sheet accounts at Hooley Manufacturing Company after closing entries were made.

Ledger Accounts	Debit	Credit
Cash	$ 26,000	
Accounts Receivable	30,000	
Materials Inventory, 12/31/xx	42,000	
Work in Process Inventory, 12/31/xx	27,400	
Finished Goods Inventory, 12/31/xx	52,700	
Production Supplies and Tools	8,600	
Land	200,000	
Factory Building	400,000	
Accumulated Depreciation, Building		$ 110,000
Factory Equipment	250,000	
Accumulated Depreciation, Equipment		72,000
Sales Warehouse	148,000	
Accumulated Depreciation, Warehouse		35,000
Patents	27,300	
Accounts Payable		101,800
Mortgage Payable		400,000
Common Stock		260,000
Retained Earnings, 12/31/xx		233,200
	$1,212,000	$1,212,000

LO 6
*Manufacturing
Organization Balance
Sheet*

P 8. The analysis below shows the balance s
Company after closing entries were made.

Ledger Accounts
Cash
Accounts Receivable
Materials Inventory, 12/31/xx
Work in Process Inventory, 12/31/xx
Finished Goods Inventory, 12/31/xx
Production Supplies
Small Tools
Land
Factory Building
Accumulated Depreciation, Building
Factory Equipment
Accumulated Depreciation,
Factory Equipment
Patents
Accounts Payable
Insurance Premiums Payable
Income Taxes Payable
Mortgage Payable
Common Stock
Retained Earnings, 12/31/xx

REQUIRED

1. Manufacturing organizations use assets
   izations.
   a. List the titles of the asset accounts t
      organizations.
   b. List the titles of the asset, liability, and
      on the balance sheets of both manufa
2. Assuming that the following informatio
   calculate the (a) gross margin, (b) cost
   sale, and (d) cost of goods manufactured

   Net Income
   Operating Expenses
   Sales
   Finished Goods Inventory, 1/1/xx

REQUIRED

1. Manufacturing organizations use assets that are not needed in merchandising organizations.
   a. List the titles of the asset accounts that are specifically related to manufacturing organizations.
   b. List the titles of the asset, liability, and equity accounts that you could expect to see on the balance sheets of both manufacturing and merchandising organizations.
2. Assuming that the following information reflects the results of operations for 20xx, calculate the (a) gross margin, (b) cost of goods sold, (c) cost of goods available for sale, and (d) cost of goods manufactured.

Net Income	$133,200
Operating Expenses	48,000
Sales	450,000
Finished Goods Inventory, 1/1/xx	68,000

LO 6
*Inventories, Cost of Goods
Sold, and Net Income*

P 5. The analyses below contain incomplete data for (1) a merchandizing organization and (2) a manufacturing organization.

REQUIRED

1. Fill in the missing data for the merchandising organization.

	First Quarter	Second Quarter	Third Quarter	Fourth Quarter
Sales	$9	$ e	$15	$ k
Gross Margin	a	4	5	l
Ending Merchandise Inventory	5	f	5	m
Beginning Merchandise Inventory	4	g	h	5
Net Cost of Purchases	b	7	9	n
Net Income	3	2	i	2
Operating Expenses	c	2	2	4
Cost of Goods Sold	5	6	j	11
Cost of Goods Available for Sale	d	12	15	15

2. Fill in the missing data for the manufacturing organization.

	First Quarter	Second Quarter	Third Quarter	Fourth Quarter
Ending Finished Goods Inventory	$a	$ 3	$ h	$ 6
Cost of Goods Sold	6	3	5	l
Net Income	1	3	1	m
Cost of Goods Available for Sale	8	d	10	13
Cost of Goods Manufactured	5	e	i	8
Gross Margin	4	f	j	7
Operating Expenses	3	g	5	6
Beginning Finished Goods Inventory	b	2	3	n
Sales	c	10	k	14

Alternate Problems

LO 4
*Nonfinancial Data
Analysis: Manufacturing*

P 6. Seaflyer Surfboards, Inc., manufactures state-of-the-art surfboards and related equipment. Stacy Hopper is manager of the West Indies branch. The production process involves the following departments and tasks: (1) the Molding Department, where the board's base is molded; (2) the Sanding Department, where the base is sanded after being taken out of the mold; (3) the Fiber-Ap Department, where a fiberglass coating is applied; and (4) the Finishing Department, where a finishing coat of fiberglass is applied and the board is inspected. After the molding process, all functions are performed by hand.

Ms. Hopper is concerned about the hours being worked by her employees. The West Indies branch utilizes a two-shift labor force. The actual hours worked for the past four weeks are summarized on the next page.

Actual Ho...

Department	Week 1	Week 2
Molding	420	432
Sanding	60	81
Fiber-Ap	504	540
Finishing	768	891

Actual Hou...

Department	Week 1	Week 2
Molding	360	357
Sanding	60	84
Fiber-Ap	440	462
Finishing	670	714

Expected labor hours per product for each oper...
.5 hour; Fiber-Ap, 4.0 hours; and Finishing, 6.5...
follows:

Week	First Shift	Second Shift
1	120	100
2	135	105
3	140	115
4	130	110

REQUIRED

1. Prepare an analysis of each week to determin...
   per board for each phase of the production pr...
2. Using the information from **1** and the expecte...
   ment, prepare an analysis showing the differe...
   reasons for the differences.

P 7. Amy Green recently purchased Yardcare, Inc., a...
den-care equipment and supplies. The organ...
Maryland, has four distribution centers: Boston,...
Virginia; and Lawrenceville, New Jersey. The distr...
states. Company profits were $225,400, $337,980...
respectively.

LO 5 *Approach to Report Preparation*

Shortly after purchasing the organization, Ms...
lowing positions: vice president, marketing; vice...
troller; and vice president, research and developr...
her management group. She wishes to create a d...
would include a large, fully landscaped plant and...
center would be (1) to test equipment and supp...
distribution and (2) to showcase the effects of u...
center must also make a profit on sales.

REQUIRED

1. What types of information will Ms. Green nee...
   retail lawn and garden center?
2. One of the reports Ms. Green needs to suppor...
   ble plants and trees that could be planted a...
   locations for the new retail center. The report...
   of research and development. How would eac...
3. Design a format for the report in **2.**

EXPANDING YOUR CRITICAL THINKING, COMMUNICATION, AND INTERPERSONAL SKILLS

Skills Development

CONCEPTUAL ANALYSIS

LO 3 **LO 4** *Continuous Improvement*

SD 1. Achieving high quality requires high standards of performance. And to maintain high standards of quality, individuals and organizations must continuously improve their performance. To illustrate this, select your favorite sport or hobby.

1. Answer the following questions:
   a. What standards would you establish to assess your actual performance?
   b. What process would you design to achieve high quality in your performance?
   c. When do you know you have achieved high quality in your performance?
   d. Once you know you perform well, how easy would it be for you to maintain that level of expertise?
   e. What can you do to continuously improve your performance?
2. If you owned a business, which of the questions in **1** would be important to answer?
3. Answer the questions in **1,** assuming you own a business.

ETHICAL DILEMMA

LO 8 *Professional Ethics*

SD 2. Grace Albems is controller for the **Atlanta Corporation.** Grace has been with the company for seventeen years and is being considered for the job of chief financial officer (CFO). Her boss, the current CFO, will be Atlanta Corporation's new president. Grace has just discussed the year-end closing with her boss, who made the following statement during the conversation:

> Grace, why are you so inflexible? I'm only asking you to postpone the write-off of the $2,500,000 obsolete inventory for ten days so that it won't appear on this year's financial statements. Ten days! Do it. Your promotion is coming up, you know. Make sure you keep all the possible outcomes in mind as you complete your year-end work. Oh, and keep this conversation confidential—just between you and me. OK?

Identify the ethical issue or issues involved and state the appropriate solution to the problem. Be prepared to defend your answer.

RESEARCH ACTIVITY

LO 5 *Management Reports*

SD 3. The registrar's office is responsible for maintaining a record of each student's grades and credits for use by students, instructors, and administrators.

1. Assume that you are a manager in the registrar's office and that you recently joined a team of managers to review the grade-reporting process. State how you would prepare a grade report for students and a grade report for instructors by answering the following questions.
   a. Who will read the grade report?
   b. Why must the registrar's office prepare the grade report?
   c. What information should the grade report contain?
   d. When is the grade report due?

Communication	Critical Thinking	Group Activity	Memo	Ethics	International	Spreadsheet	Managerial Technology	Internet

2. Why do differences exist between the information in a grade report for students and the information in a grade report for instructors?
3. Visit the registrar's office of your school in person, or access it through your school's home page. Obtain a copy of your grade report and a copy of the forms the registrar's office uses to report grades to instructors at your school. Compare the information on the actual grade report forms to the information you listed in **1** above. Explain any differences.
4. What can the registrar's office do to make sure that grade reports present all necessary information in a manner that communicates effectively to users?

DECISION-MAKING PRACTICE

SD 4.

LO 4 *Nonfinancial Data Analysis*

As a subcontractor in the jet aircraft industry, **Air Gears Manufacturing Company** specializes in the production of housings for landing gears on jet airplanes. Production begins on Machine 1, which bends pieces of metal into cylinder-shaped housings and trims off the rough edges. Machine 2 welds the seam of the cylinder and pushes the entire piece into a large die to mold the housing into its final shape.

Joe Mee, the production supervisor, believes that too much scrap (wasted metal) is created in the current process. To help him, James Kincaid began preparing an analysis by comparing the amounts of actual scrap generated with the amounts of expected scrap for production in the last four weeks. His incomplete report follows.

Air Gears Manufacturing Company
Comparison of Actual Scrap and Expected Scrap
Four-Week Period

	Scrap in Pounds		Difference	
	Actual	Expected	Pounds	Percentage
Machine 1				
Week 1	36,720	36,720		
Week 2	54,288	36,288		
Week 3	71,856	35,856		
Week 4	82,440	35,640		
Machine 2				
Week 1	43,200	18,180		
Week 2	39,600	18,054		
Week 3	7,200	18,162		
Week 4	18,000	18,108		

Because of a death in his family, James is unable to complete the analysis. Joe asks you to complete the following tasks and submit a recommendation to him.

1. Present the information in two ways.
   a. Prepare a table that shows the difference between the actual and the expected scrap in pounds per machine per week. Calculate the difference in pounds and as a percentage (divide the difference in pounds by the expected pounds of scrap for each week). If the actual poundage of scrap is less than the expected poundage, record the difference as a negative. (This means there is less scrap than expected.)
   b. Prepare a line graph for each machine showing the weeks on the *X* axis and the pounds of scrap on the *Y* axis.
2. Examine the differences for the four weeks for each machine and determine which machine operation is creating excessive scrap.
3. What could cause these problems?
4. What could Joe do to identify the specific cause of such problems sooner?
5. Write a memo summarizing your findings in **1** through **4** above.

Managerial Reporting and Analysis

INTERPRETING MANAGEMENT REPORTS

MRA 1.

LO 1 *Management Information Needs*

Obtain a copy of a recent annual report for a publicly held organization in which you have a particular interest. (Copies of annual reports are available at your campus library, a local public library, on the Internet, or by direct request to an organization.) Assume that you have just been appointed to a middle-management position in a division of the organization you have chosen. You are interested in obtaining information that will help you better manage the activities of your division and have decided to thoroughly review the contents of the annual report in an attempt to learn as much as possible. You particularly want to know about:

1. Size of inventory maintained
2. Ability to earn income
3. Reliance on debt financing
4. Types, volume, and prices of products or services sold
5. Type of production process used
6. Management's long-range strategies
7. Success (profitability) of the division's various product lines
8. Efficiency of operations
9. Operating details of your division

REQUIRED

1. Write a brief description of the organization and its products, services, or activities.
2. From a review of the financial statements and the accompanying disclosure notes, prepare a written summary of the information you found that pertained to items **1** through **9** above.
3. Is any of the information you seek in other sections of the annual report? If so, which information, and where is it found?
4. The annual report also includes other types of information you may find helpful in your new position. In outline form, summarize the additional information you think will help you.

FORMULATING MANAGEMENT REPORTS

MRA 2.

LO 5 *Management Information Needs*

In **MRA 1**, you examined your new employer's annual report and noted some useful information. You still wish to find out if your new division's products are competitive, but cannot find the necessary information in the annual report.

REQUIRED

1. What kinds of information do you want to know about your competition?
2. Why is this information relevant? (Link your response to a particular decision about your organization's products or services. For example, you might seek information to help you determine a new selling price.)
3. From what sources could you obtain the information you need?
4. When would you want to obtain this information?
5. Create a report that will communicate your findings to your superior.

INTERNATIONAL COMPANY

MRA 3.

LO 4 *Management*
LO 5 *Information Needs*

McDonald's is the leading competitor in the fast-food restaurant business. More than 40 percent of McDonald's restaurants are located outside the United States. One component of McDonald's marketing strategy is to increase sales by expanding its foreign markets. The company uses financial and nonfinancial as well as quantitative and qualitative information in making decisions about new restaurant locations in foreign markets. For example, the following types of information would be important to such a decision: the cost of a new building (financial quantitative information), the estimated number of hamburgers to be sold in the first year (nonfinancial quantitative information), and site desirability (qualitative information).

REQUIRED

You are a member of a management team that must decide whether or not to open a new restaurant in England. Identify at least two examples each of the (a) financial quantitative, (b) nonfinancial quantitative, and (c) qualitative information you will need before you can make a decision.

Group Activity: Divide the class into groups and ask them to discuss this MRA. Then debrief the entire class by asking one person from each group to summarize his or her group's discussion.

EXCEL SPREADSHEET ANALYSIS

MRA 4.

LO 4 *Nonfinancial Data*

Refer to assignment **P 6** in this chapter. Ms. Hopper needs to analyze the work performed by each shift in each department during Weeks 1 through 4.

REQUIRED

1. For each department, calculate the average labor hours worked per board for each shift during Weeks 1 through 4. (*Note:* Hours worked per board = hours worked each week ÷ boards produced each week.)
2. Using the ChartWizard and the information from **1** for each department, prepare a line graph that compares the hours per board worked by the first and second shifts and the estimate for that department during Weeks 1 through 4. Below is the suggested format to use for the information table necessary to complete the line graph for the Molding Department.

Molding Department

	Week 1	Week 2	Week 3	Week 4
First shift	3.5	3.2	3.4	3.8
Second shift	3.6	3.4	3.8	4.2
Estimated	3.4	3.4	3.4	3.4

3. Examine the four graphs that you prepared in **2.** Which shift is more efficient in all four departments? List some reasons for the differences between the shifts.

ENDNOTES

1. *Source:* "Electric Car Drives Factory Innovation," *The Wall Street Journal,* February 27, 1997, p. B1.
2. Institute of Management Accountants, *Statement No. 1A* (New York, 1982). Since this definition was prepared, the importance of nonfinancial information has increased significantly. The words in brackets were added by the authors.
3. *Source:* Based on John B. MacArthur, "Cost Management at the IRS," *Management Accounting,* Institute of Management Accountants, November 1996, pp. 42–48.
4. *Source:* www.ups.com/about/inits.html
5. National Association of Accountants, "Definition of Management Accounting," from *Statements on Management Accounting,* Statement Number 1A, March 19, 1981. Copyright © 1987 by McGraw-Hill, Inc. Reprinted by permission.
6. James Don Edwards and Homer A. Black, *The Modern Accountant's Handbook* (Homewood, IL: Dow Jones-Irwin, 1976), p. 830.

CHAPTER 2

Operating Costs and Cost Allocation, Including Activity-Based Costing

LEARNING OBJECTIVES

1. State how managers use operating cost information and product costs in the management cycle.

2. Define and give examples of the three elements of product cost and compute a product's unit cost for a manufacturing organization.

3. Describe the flow of product-related activities, documents, and costs through the Materials Inventory, Work in Process Inventory, and Finished Goods Inventory accounts.

4. Prepare a statement of cost of goods manufactured and an income statement for a manufacturing organization.

5. Define *cost allocation* and explain the process of manufacturing overhead allocation using cost objects, cost pools, and cost drivers.

6. Calculate product unit cost using the traditional allocation of manufacturing overhead costs.

7. Define and explain *activity-based costing.*

8. Calculate product unit cost using activity-based costing to assign manufacturing overhead costs.

9. Apply costing concepts to a service organization.

DECISION POINT

Super Bakery supplies unique, reasonably priced, quality donuts and other baked goods to schools, hospitals, and others in the institutional baked goods market. With a staff of nine full-time employees, Super Bakery's sales reached $8.5 million in 1994. Super Bakery is a "virtual" corporation because it performs only a few strategic functions. Other functions typically performed by employees are outsourced to external companies specializing in each function. Super Bakery focuses on customer-related activities, such as taking a customer order, pricing the order, scheduling production, selecting and packing the ordered items, and billing and collecting customer accounts. A network of independent brokers sell the baked goods, and contractors produce, store, and ship them.[1]

Although Super Bakery outsources functions to outside brokers, manufacturers, and trucking companies, it must still control the quality and the

SUPER BAKERY

cost of those services to minimize the risk of losing business. Brokers must effectively sell and promote the products to customers. Quality standards must be met for the products and the production processes. Trucking companies must deliver undamaged products on time. Super Bakery also faces the challenge of pricing sales orders accurately, because the cost of serving a customer can vary depending on the size and location of the customer's organization. How can management accounting help Super Bakery?

Super Bakery uses a performance reporting and activity-based costing system. This system is a component of an organization's management accounting information system. The activity-based costing (ABC) system accumulates cost information and assigns costs to a cost object, such as products or services, and reports performance after measuring the actual performance and comparing it to the organization's plan. ABC helps determine more accurate product costs for pricing and profitability decisions and requires nonfinancial measures that are also useful for measuring and evaluating performance. To manage costs and profitability at Super Bakery, the primary focus is on the cost of a sales order, which includes the cost of the baked goods ordered and the costs of freight, storage, selling, discounts, and order-taking service associated with the order. If such cost information is estimated in advance, it will help managers make better pricing and profitability decisions about each sales order.

ABC systems include nonfinancial performance measures (called *cost drivers*) useful for both assigning costs and measuring performance. To assign indirect costs to a cost object (customer, order, common carrier), cost drivers, such as number of customer complaints, number of days from order receipt to delivery, and number of orders damaged in shipment, are selected. Cost drivers, when properly matched, can also be used to measure and evaluate employee, broker, or contractor performance. In many companies that use ABC, management will choose cost drivers that not only minimize waste or inefficiency but also persuade individuals to perform well.

Operating Costs and the Management Cycle

One of the primary goals of a company is to be profitable. Because owners expect to earn profits, managers have a responsibility to use resources wisely and generate revenues that will exceed the costs of the organization's operating, investing, and financing activities. In this chapter, we will focus on operating costs related to production activities in a manufacturing organization and to service activities in a service organization. First, let's look at operating costs and the management cycle for manufacturing, retail, and service companies.

In the management cycle, managers use operating cost information to plan, execute, review, and report the results of operating activities. Figure 1 provides an overview of operating costs and the management cycle. In the planning stage, managers of manufacturing organizations, such as John Deere, Motorola, or General Motors, use the estimated product cost portion of operating cost information to develop production, direct materials, direct labor, and manufacturing overhead budgets and to determine selling prices or sales levels required to cover all costs. In retail organizations, such as Sears, PepBoys, or Macy's, managers work with estimates of the cost of merchandise purchases to develop budgets for purchases and net income and to determine selling prices or sales levels required to cover all costs. In service organizations, like Citibank, Columbia Healthcare, or Andersen

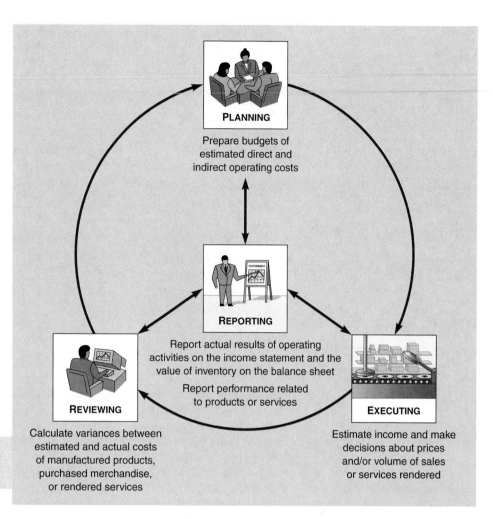

Figure 1
Operating Costs and the
Management Cycle

Consulting, managers utilize the estimated costs of rendering services to develop budgets, estimate fees, and plan human resource needs.

In the executing stage, managers of manufacturing organizations use estimated product unit costs to estimate the gross margin or operating income on products sold or to make decisions about dropping a product line, outsourcing the manufacture of a part or subassembly to another manufacturer, bidding on a special order, or negotiating a selling price. In retail organizations, managers work with the estimated cost of merchandise purchases to estimate gross margin, operating income, or value of merchandise sold or to make decisions about reducing selling prices for clearance sales, offering lower selling prices for bulk sales orders, or dropping a product line. In service organizations, managers find the estimated cost of services helpful in estimating profitability or making decisions about bidding on future service assignments or projects, lowering the fee to charge a customer, dropping a service provided, or negotiating a fee.

In the reviewing stage, managers want to know about significant differences between estimated costs and actual costs. The identification of variances between estimated and actual product costs (for manufacturing organizations), estimated and actual costs of merchandise purchased (for retail organizations), and estimated and actual costs of services rendered (for service organizations) helps managers to determine the causes of cost overruns and enables them to adjust future actions to reduce potential problems.

In the reporting stage, managers expect to see financial statements that include the actual costs associated with operating activities in the executing stage of the

Table 1. Examples of Types and Uses of Operating Cost Information for Different Types of Organizations

	Type of Organization		
	Manufacturing	Retail	Service
Operating cost information needed by management	Cost to manufacture the product	Cost to purchase the product	Cost to provide the service
Uses of cost information:			
To measure historical or future profits	Yes	Yes	Yes
To decide the selling price for regular or special sales or services provided	Yes	Yes	Yes
To value finished goods or merchandise inventories	Yes	Yes	Not applicable

management cycle and also performance evaluation reports that summarize the variance analyses calculated in the reviewing stage. This is true for manufacturing, retail, and service organizations.

Table 1 lists examples of the types and uses of operating cost information for different types of organizations. In this textbook, we will follow the traditional practices of organizations in costing products and services. For a manufacturing organization, the product costs include the costs of direct materials, direct labor, and manufacturing overhead. For a retail organization, the costs of a purchased product include adjustments for freight-in costs, purchase returns and allowances, and purchase discounts. And for a service organization, the costs to provide a service include the costs of labor and related overhead. Ultimately, a company is profitable only when revenues from sales or services rendered exceed the *full* cost of the products or services. The full cost includes the cost to manufacture or purchase a product or to render a service plus the costs of marketing, distributing, installing, repairing, and replacing a product or the costs of marketing and supporting the delivery of services.

Elements of Product Costs

OBJECTIVE 2

Define and give examples of the three elements of product cost and compute a product's unit cost for a manufacturing organization

Product costs include all costs related to the manufacturing process. The three elements of product cost are (1) direct materials costs, (2) direct labor costs, and (3) manufacturing overhead costs, which are indirect manufacturing costs.

Direct Materials Costs

All manufactured products are made from basic direct materials. Direct materials costs are the costs of materials that can be conveniently and economically traced to specific units of product. Some examples of direct materials are iron ore for steel, sheet steel for automobiles, and sugar for candy.

BUSINESS BULLETIN: TECHNOLOGY IN PRACTICE

Technology and new manufacturing processes of the 1990s have produced entirely new patterns of product costs. The three elements of product cost are still direct materials, direct labor, and manufacturing overhead. However, the percentage that each element contributes to the total cost of a product has changed. During the 1950s, 1960s, and 1970s, direct labor was the dominant cost element, making up over 40 percent of total product cost. Direct materials contributed 35 percent and manufacturing overhead around 25 percent of total cost. Seventy-five percent of total product cost was a direct cost, traceable to the product. Improved production technology caused a dramatic shift in the three product cost elements. People were replaced by machines, and direct labor was reduced significantly. Today, only 50 percent of the cost of a product is directly traceable to the product; the other 50 percent is manufacturing overhead, an indirect cost.

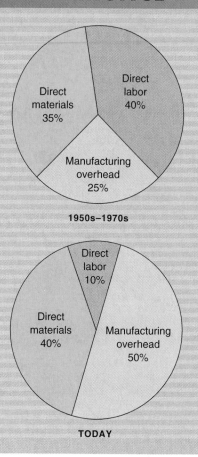

Direct Labor Costs

The manufacturing process includes all activities required to make a product, including maintenance, handling, inspecting, moving, and storing. Direct labor costs are the costs of labor to complete activities involved in the production process that can be conveniently and economically traced to specific units of product. The wages of machine operators and other workers involved in actually shaping the product are direct labor costs.

Manufacturing Overhead Costs

The third element of product cost includes all manufacturing costs that cannot be classified as direct materials or direct labor costs. Manufacturing overhead costs are production-related costs that cannot be practically or conveniently traced directly to an end product. This assortment of costs is also called *factory overhead, factory burden,* or *indirect manufacturing costs.* Two common components of manufacturing overhead costs are indirect materials costs and indirect labor costs. Indirect materials costs are the costs of materials that cannot be conveniently or economically traced to a unit of product. Labor costs for production-related activities that cannot be conveniently or economically traced to a unit of product are indirect labor costs. Examples of the major components of manufacturing overhead costs are as follows:

Indirect materials costs: costs of nails, rivets, lubricants, and small tools

Indirect labor costs: costs of labor for maintenance, inspection, engineering design, supervision, materials handling, and machine handling

Other indirect manufacturing costs: costs of building maintenance, machinery and tool maintenance, property taxes, property insurance, pension costs, depreciation on plant and equipment, rent expense, and utilities expense

As indirect costs, manufacturing overhead costs are allocated to a product's cost using traditional or activity-based costing methods, which will be explained later in this chapter.

To illustrate product costs and the manufacturing process, we will learn how Angelo Sanchez, owner of Angelo's Rolling Suitcases, Inc., operates part of his business. In 1990, Angelo Sanchez began building rolling suitcases, versions of the flight crew bag used for years by airline pilots and flight attendants. Angelo's rolling suitcases are designed to roll along easily and steadily, holding belongings for a three-day trip and providing a luggage rack with a strap to hold a briefcase and computer. The suitcases are made of ballistic nylon fabric wrapped around a rigid frame with a retractable pull handle at one end and wheels at the other end. Stair skids protect the fabric from abrasion, and carrying handles on the side and top of the bag improve handling. The direct materials costs for the rolling suitcase include the costs of the frame, ballistic nylon fabric, retractable pull handle, and wheels. Indirect materials costs include the costs of zippers, interior mesh storage pockets, garment straps, carrying handles, stair skids, and wheel lubricants. Direct labor costs include the costs of labor used to build the rolling suitcase. Indirect labor costs include the costs of labor associated with moving the materials to the production area and inspecting the rolling suitcase during its construction. In addition to the indirect materials and indirect labor costs, manufacturing overhead costs include depreciation on the building and equipment used to make the rolling suitcases and the utilities, insurance, property taxes, and insurance expenses related to the manufacturing plant.

Computing the Unit Cost of a Product for a Manufacturing Company

The product unit cost, or manufacturing cost of a single unit of product, is computed by dividing the total cost of direct materials, direct labor, and manufacturing overhead for the units produced by the total number of units produced.

$$\text{Product Unit Cost} = \frac{\text{Total Direct Materials} + \text{Direct Labor} + \text{Manufacturing Overhead for Units Produced}}{\text{Total Units Produced}}$$

Unit cost information helps managers price products and calculate gross margin and net income. Managers or accountants can calculate the product unit cost using actual costing, normal costing, or standard costing methods. Table 2 summarizes the use of actual or estimated costs for the three cost-measurement methods.

The actual costing method uses the *actual* costs of direct materials, direct labor, and manufacturing overhead to calculate the actual product unit cost at the end of the accounting period, when actual costs are known. The actual product unit cost is assigned to the finished goods inventory on the balance sheet and to the cost of goods sold on the income statement. For example, assume that Angelo's Rolling Suitcases, Inc., produced 30 rolling suitcases on December 28, 20xx, for a corporate customer in Salt Lake City. Jamie Estrada, the company's accountant, calculated

Table 2. Summary of the Use of Actual or Estimated Costs in Three Cost-Measurement Methods

Product Cost Elements	Actual Costing	Normal Costing	Standard Costing
Direct materials	Actual costs	Actual costs	Estimated costs
Direct labor	Actual costs	Actual costs	Estimated costs
Manufacturing overhead	Actual costs	Estimated costs	Estimated costs

that the actual costs for the Salt Lake City order were direct materials, $540; direct labor, $420; and manufacturing overhead, $240. The actual product unit cost for the order was $40.

Direct materials ($540 ÷ 30 rolling suitcases)	$18
Direct labor ($420 ÷ 30 rolling suitcases)	14
Manufacturing overhead ($240 ÷ 30 rolling suitcases)	8
Product cost per rolling suitcase ($1,200 ÷ 30 rolling suitcases)	$40

In this case, the product unit cost was computed when the job ended and all cost information was known. What if a company needs this information during the year, when the actual direct materials costs and direct labor costs are known but the actual manufacturing overhead costs are uncertain? Here, the product unit cost will include an estimate of the manufacturing overhead applied to the product.

The normal costing method combines the *actual* direct materials and direct labor costs with the *estimated* manufacturing overhead costs to determine a normal product unit cost. This method is simple and allows a smoother, more even assignment of manufacturing overhead costs to production during the year. It also contributes to better pricing decisions and profitability estimates. However, any difference between the estimated and the actual costs must be identified and removed so that the financial statements show only the actual product costs at the end of the year.

Assume that normal costing was used to price the Salt Lake City order, and that manufacturing overhead was applied to the product's cost using an estimated, or predetermined, overhead rate of 60 percent of direct labor costs. Based on that method, the costs for the order included the actual direct materials cost of $540.00, the actual direct labor cost of $420.00, and the *applied* manufacturing overhead cost of $252.00 ($420.00 × .6). The normalized product unit cost was $40.40.

Direct materials ($540.00 ÷ 30 rolling suitcases)	$18.00
Direct labor ($420.00 ÷ 30 rolling suitcases)	14.00
Manufacturing overhead ($252.00 ÷ 30 rolling suitcases)	8.40
Product cost per rolling suitcase ($1,212 ÷ 30 rolling suitcases)	$40.40

In this case, the product unit cost was computed using actual and estimated cost information. Later in this chapter, we will discuss various methods of assigning manufacturing overhead costs to finished products.

What if managers need product costing information before the accounting period begins, so that they can control operating activities? Or, what if an organization is pricing a proposed product for a customer? In such situations, product unit costs must be estimated, and the standard costing method can be helpful. This method allows actual costs to be compared to budgeted, or estimated, costs to identify significant variances that require management attention. The *estimated* (or standard) direct materials, direct labor, and manufacturing overhead costs determine the standard product unit cost, which is useful as a benchmark for pricing decisions during the year and for controlling product costs.

Assume Angelo's must place a bid to manufacture 20 rolling suitcases for a new Italian customer. Using standard cost information, Jamie has *estimated* the following cost information: $20 per unit for direct materials, $15 per unit for direct labor, and $9 for manufacturing overhead (assuming a standard, or predetermined, overhead rate of 60 percent of direct labor cost). The standard cost per unit would be $44.

Direct materials	$20
Direct labor	15
Manufacturing overhead ($15 × .6)	9
Product cost per rolling suitcase	$44

The $44 product unit cost is useful for estimating the gross margin for the job and deciding the price to bid for the Italian company's business. Standard costing is discussed in more detail in another chapter.

Manufacturing Inventory Accounts

OBJECTIVE 3

Describe the flow of product-related activities, documents, and costs through the Materials Inventory, Work in Process Inventory, and Finished Goods Inventory accounts

Manufacturing organizations use a number of production and production-related activities to transform materials into finished products. Materials are brought into the organization through purchasing, receiving, inspecting, moving, and storing activities. Production activities convert the materials into a finished product using labor, equipment, and other resources. Moving and storing activities transfer the completed product to the finished goods storage area. The accounting system tracks these activities as product costs flowing through the Direct Materials Inventory, Work in Process Inventory, and Finished Goods Inventory accounts. The Direct Materials Inventory account shows the balance of unused direct materials, the Work in Process Inventory account records the manufacturing costs incurred and assigned to partially completed units of product, and the Finished Goods Inventory account holds the costs assigned to all completed products that have not been sold.

Selling and administrative activities are also important in a manufacturing organization. Marketing, packaging, and shipping activities play a role in making the product available to buyers, and customer billing, collection of accounts receivable, and payment of suppliers help keep the company in sound financial shape. Such selling and administrative costs are accumulated as period costs for the purposes of financial reporting.

Document Flows and Cost Flows Through the Inventory Accounts

In many companies, accountants accumulate and report manufacturing costs based on source documents that support production and production-related activities. Looking at how the source documents for the three elements of manufacturing cost relate to the flow of costs through the three inventory accounts for a manufacturing organization provides insight into when an activity must be recorded in the accounting records. Figure 2 (on pages 50-51) summarizes the relationships among the production-related activities, the documents for each of the three cost elements, and the inventory account(s) that are affected by the activities. An organization may use paper documents or computer-transmitted information to communicate with suppliers, customers, or internal departments.

To illustrate the document flow and changes in inventory balances for production activities, we will continue with our example of Angelo's Rolling Suitcases, Inc.

Purchasing Direct Materials   When Angelo receives or expects to receive a *sales order* from a customer, the purchasing process starts with a *purchase request* for specific quantities of direct materials needed but not currently available in the materials storeroom. A qualified manager approves the request. Based on the information in the purchase request, the Purchasing Department sends *purchase orders* to its suppliers. When the direct materials arrive, an employee on the receiving dock counts and examines them and prepares a *receiving report.* Later, an accounting clerk matches the information on the receiving report with the descriptions and quantities listed on the purchase order. A material handler moves the newly arrived materials from the receiving area to the materials storeroom. Soon, Angelo receives a *vendor's invoice* requesting payment for the purchased direct materials. The cost of those materials increases the balance of Angelo's Direct Materials Inventory account.

Materials Requisition and Conversion   When the rolling suitcases are scheduled for production, the storeroom clerk receives a *materials request form.* The materials request form is essential for controlling direct materials. Besides providing the supervisor's approval signature, it describes the types and quantities of materials the storeroom clerk must pick and send to the production area, and it authorizes the release of those materials into production. If the materials request form has been approved by the appropriate manager, the storeroom clerk has the material handler move the materials to the production floor. The cost of the direct materials increases the balance of the Work in Process Inventory account and decreases the balance of the Direct Materials Inventory account.

The production employees assemble the rolling suitcases using frames, fabric, pull handles, wheels, and indirect materials. Each production employee prepares a *time card* to track the amount of time worked each day. The costs of the direct labor and manufacturing overhead used to manufacture the rolling suitcases increase the balance of the Work in Process Inventory account.

Product Completion and Sale   Employees place completed rolling suitcases in individual boxes, then move and store the boxes in the finished goods storeroom until the scheduled shipment date. The balance of the Finished Goods Inventory account increases and the balance of the Work in Process Inventory account decreases for the cost of the completed rolling suitcases.

When suitcases are sold, a clerk prepares a *sales invoice* while another clerk fills the order by removing the rolling suitcases from the storeroom, packaging them, and shipping them to the customer. A *shipping document* shows the quantity and description of the products shipped. The cost of the rolling suitcases sold increases the Cost of Goods Sold account and decreases the balance of the Finished Goods Inventory account.

The Manufacturing Cost Flow

Manufacturing cost flow is the flow of manufacturing costs (direct materials, direct labor, and manufacturing overhead) from their incurrence through the Direct Materials Inventory, Work in Process Inventory, and Finished Goods Inventory accounts into the Cost of Goods Sold account. A defined, structured manufacturing cost flow is the foundation for product costing, inventory valuation, and financial reporting. The manufacturing cost flow as it relates to the accounts in the general ledger and the production activity at Angelo's Rolling Suitcases, Inc., for the year ended December 31, 20xx, are summarized in Figure 3 on page 52. In this illus-

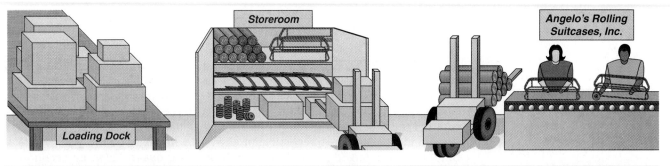

	ACTIVITY	Purchase, receive, inspect, move, and store direct materials in direct materials storeroom	Move direct materials to production area
	DOCUMENT	Purchase request Purchase order Receiving report Vendor's invoice	Materials request
INVENTORY ACCOUNT AFFECTED/ CHANGE IN BALANCE	**DIRECT MATERIALS INVENTORY**	Increases for cost of direct materials purchased	Decreases for cost of direct materials used in the production process
	WORK IN PROCESS INVENTORY		Increases for cost of direct materials used in the production process
	FINISHED GOODS INVENTORY		

Figure 2
Activities, Documents, and Cost Flows Through the Inventory Accounts of a Manufacturing Organization

tration, we will assume that the accountant has adjusted the inventory account balances to reflect only actual costs. Using the actual cost information, the accountant can prepare financial statements for the company.

The Direct Materials Inventory account shows the balance of unused direct materials. The costs of direct materials purchased increase the Direct Materials Inventory account balance, while the costs of direct materials requested and used by the Production Department decrease the balance. The following formula shows the activity in this account for Angelo's Rolling Suitcases, Inc., for the year ended December 31, 20xx:

Direct Materials Inventory, Ending Balance	=	Direct Materials Inventory, Beginning Balance	+	Cost of Direct Materials Purchased	−	Cost of Direct Materials Used
$5,000	=	$10,000	+	$20,000	−	$25,000

The Work in Process Inventory account records the balance of partially completed units of product. As direct materials and direct labor are used, their costs are added to the Work in Process Inventory account. The cost of manufacturing overhead for the current period is also added. The total costs of direct materials, direct labor, and manufacturing overhead incurred and charged to production during an accounting period are called total manufacturing costs. Total manufacturing costs increase the balance of the Work in Process Inventory account.

As goods are finished, they are moved to the finished goods storage area. The cost of all units completed and moved to the finished goods storage is the cost of goods manufactured. The cost of goods manufactured for the period decreases the balance

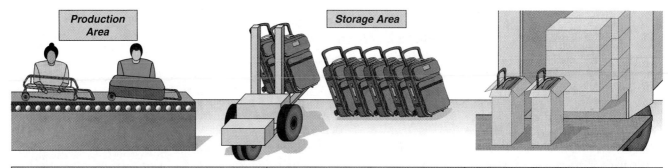

Production Area	Storage Area	
Convert direct materials into finished product using direct labor and manufacturing overhead Package some types of products	Move completed units of product of finished goods to storage area	Sell units of product to customer; pack and ship product
Time card Job card Vendors' invoices for manufacturing overhead items	Job card	Sales invoice Shipping document
Increases for costs of direct labor and manufacturing overhead	Decreases for cost of completed units of product	
	Increases for cost of completed units of product	Decreases for cost of completed units of product

of the Work in Process Inventory account. The following formulas show the activity in the Work in Process Inventory account for Angelo's Rolling Suitcases, Inc., for the year ended December 31, 20xx:

Total Manufacturing Costs	=	Cost of Direct Materials Used	+	Direct Labor Costs	+	Manufacturing Overhead Costs
$43,000	=	$25,000	+	$12,000	+	$6,000

Work in Process Inventory, Ending Balance	=	Work in Process Inventory, Beginning Balance	+	Total Manufacturing Costs	−	Cost of Goods Manufactured
$15,000	=	$2,000	+	$43,000	−	$30,000

The Finished Goods Inventory account holds the balance of costs assigned to all completed products that have not been sold by a manufacturing company. The cost of goods manufactured increases the balance, while the cost of goods sold decreases the balance. The following formula shows the activity in the Finished Goods Inventory account for Angelo's Rolling Suitcases, Inc., for the year ended December 31, 20xx:

Finished Goods Inventory, Ending Balance	=	Finished Goods Inventory, Beginning Balance	+	Cost of Goods Manufactured	−	Cost of Goods Sold
$12,000	=	$6,000	+	$30,000	−	$24,000

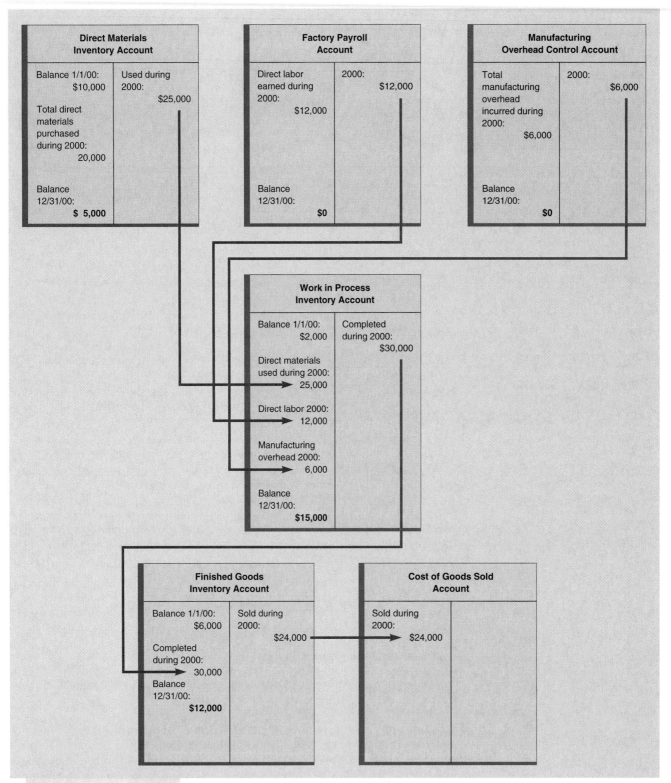

Figure 3
Manufacturing Cost Flow: An Example

Manufacturing and Reporting

The financial statements of manufacturing organizations differ very little from those of merchandising organizations. Account titles on the balance sheet of manufacturers are similar to those used by merchandisers. The primary difference between the balance sheets is the use of three inventory accounts by manufacturing organizations versus only one by merchandising organizations. Even the income statements for a merchandiser and a manufacturer are similar. However, manufacturers use the heading Cost of Goods Manufactured in place of the Purchases account. Also, the Merchandise Inventory account is replaced by the Finished Goods Inventory account.

The key to preparing an income statement for a manufacturing organization is to determine the cost of goods manufactured. This dollar amount is calculated on the statement of cost of goods manufactured. This special statement is based on an analysis of the Work in Process Inventory account.

Statement of Cost of Goods Manufactured

The flow of manufacturing costs, shown in Figure 3, provides the basis for accounting for manufacturing costs. In this process, all manufacturing costs incurred are considered product costs. They are used to compute ending inventory balances and the cost of goods sold. At the end of the period, the flow of all manufacturing costs incurred during the period is summarized in the statement of cost of goods manufactured. This statement gives the dollar amount of costs for products completed and moved to finished goods inventory during the period. The cost of goods manufactured should be the same as the amount transferred from the Work in Process Inventory account to the Finished Goods Inventory account during the period.

The statement of cost of goods manufactured for Angelo's Rolling Suitcases, Inc., is shown in Exhibit 1. The statement is complex, so we piece it together in three steps. The first step is to compute the cost of direct materials used. To do so, we add the beginning balance in the Direct Materials Inventory account to the direct materials purchased ($10,000 + $20,000). The subtotal represents the cost of direct materials available for use during the period ($30,000). Then, we subtract the ending balance of Direct Materials Inventory from the cost of direct materials available for use. The difference is the cost of direct materials used during the period ($30,000 − $5,000 = $25,000).

Calculating total manufacturing costs for the period is the second step. As shown in Figure 3, the costs of direct materials used and direct labor are added to total manufacturing overhead costs incurred during the period.

Computation of Total Manufacturing Costs

Cost of Direct Materials Used	$25,000
Add Direct Labor Costs	12,000
Add Total Manufacturing Overhead Costs	6,000
Total Manufacturing Costs	$43,000

The third step shown in Exhibit 1 is to determine the total cost of goods manufactured for the period. The beginning Work in Process Inventory balance is added to total manufacturing costs for the period to arrive at the total cost of work in process during the period. From this amount, the ending Work in Process Inventory balance is subtracted to get the cost of goods manufactured ($45,000 − $15,000 = $30,000).

The term *total manufacturing costs* should not be confused with the cost of goods manufactured. To understand the difference between these two dollar

Exhibit 1. Statement of Cost of Goods Manufactured and Income Statement for a Manufacturing Organization

Angelo's Rolling Suitcases, Inc.
Statement of Cost of Goods Manufactured
For the Year Ended December 31, 20xx

Step One	Direct Materials Used	
	Direct Materials Inventory, January 1, 20xx	$10,000
	Direct Materials Purchased	20,000
	Cost of Direct Materials Available for Use	$30,000
	Less Direct Materials Inventory, December 31, 20xx	5,000
	Cost of Direct Materials Used	$25,000
Step Two	Direct Labor	12,000
	Manufacturing Overhead	6,000
	Total Manufacturing Costs	$43,000
	Add Work in Process Inventory, January 1, 20xx	2,000
Step Three	Total Cost of Work in Process During the Year	$45,000
	Less Work in Process Inventory, December 31, 20xx	15,000
	Cost of Goods Manufactured	$30,000

Angelo's Rolling Suitcases, Inc.
Income Statement
For the Year Ended December 31, 20xx

Sales		$50,000
Cost of Goods Sold		
Finished Goods Inventory, January 1, 20xx	$ 6,000	
Cost of Goods Manufactured	30,000 ←	
Total Cost of Finished Goods Available for Sale	$36,000	
Less Finished Goods Inventory, December 31, 20xx	12,000	
Cost of Goods Sold		24,000
Gross Margin		$26,000
Selling and Administrative Expenses		16,000
Net Income		$10,000

amounts, look again at the preceding computations. Total manufacturing costs of $43,000 incurred during the period are added to the beginning balance in Work in Process Inventory. Costs of $2,000 in the beginning balance are, by definition, costs from an earlier period. The costs of two accounting periods are now being mixed to arrive at the total cost of work in process during the period ($43,000 + $2,000 = $45,000). The costs of products still in process ($15,000) are then subtracted from the total cost of work in process during the year. The remainder, $30,000, is the cost of goods manufactured (completed) during the current year. It is assumed that the items in beginning inventory were completed first. The costs attached to the ending balance of Work in Process Inventory are part of the current period's total manufacturing costs. However, they will not become part of the cost of goods manufactured until the next period, when the products are completed.

Cost of Goods Sold and the Income Statement

Exhibit 1 demonstrates the relationship between the income statement and the statement of cost of goods manufactured. The total amount of the cost of goods manufactured during the period is carried over to the income statement. There, it is used to compute the cost of goods sold. The beginning balance of Finished Goods Inventory is added to the cost of goods manufactured to get the total cost of finished goods available for sale during the period ($6,000 + $30,000 = $36,000). The cost of goods sold is then computed by subtracting the ending balance in Finished Goods Inventory (the cost of goods completed but not sold) from the total cost of finished goods available for sale ($36,000 − $12,000 = $24,000). The cost of goods sold is considered an expense in the period in which the related products are sold.

Cost Allocation

Managers need accurate and timely product costs to estimate profits and inventory values and to make pricing decisions during the year. The product cost elements of direct materials and direct labor can be easily traced to a product, but manufacturing overhead costs are indirect costs that must be collected and allocated in some manner. Cost allocation is the process of assigning collected indirect costs to specific cost objects using an allocation base that represents a major function of the business. A cost object is the destination of an assigned or allocated cost. For purposes of product costing, cost allocation is the assignment of manufacturing overhead costs to the product (cost object) during the accounting period.

To understand cost allocation, you also need to understand the terms *cost pool* and *cost driver*. For purposes of product costing, a cost pool is a collection of overhead costs related to a cost object (a production-related activity). A cost driver is an activity that causes the cost pool to increase in amount as the cost driver increases in volume. Cost allocation requires (1) the pooling of manufacturing overhead costs that are affected by a common activity and (2) the selection of a cost driver whose activity level causes a change in the cost pool.

The Manufacturing Overhead Allocation Process

The process of allocating manufacturing overhead costs is part of the management cycle presented in Figure 1. In the planning stage, manufacturing overhead costs are estimated and a rate is calculated. In the executing stage, manufacturing overhead costs are assigned to products during the production process and manufacturing overhead costs are incurred and recorded. In the reviewing stage, the difference between the actual and applied manufacturing overhead costs is calculated and analyzed. The difference is then reported in the reporting stage. In addition, the actual manufacturing overhead costs are reported in the cost of goods sold on the income statement and the ending Work in Process and Finished Goods Inventory balances on the balance sheet.

The process of manufacturing overhead allocation includes four steps. Figure 4 shows the relationship of the four steps over a time period that includes the planning process and the actual manufacturing process for one year. Figure 4 also describes each step and its timing, procedure, and journal entry, if needed. In Step 1, the planning step, the management accountant calculates a predetermined overhead rate in traditional settings or an activity pool rate in activity-based costing settings. If a rate is calculated before an accounting period begins, managers can better estimate the product costs by assigning manufacturing overhead costs more smoothly over units of production during the year. For example, using a single, plantwide overhead rate requires grouping all of the estimated manufacturing overhead costs into one cost pool with direct labor hours or machine hours as the cost driver. No journal entry is required because no business activity has occurred.

**Figure 4
The Manufacturing Overhead Allocation Process**

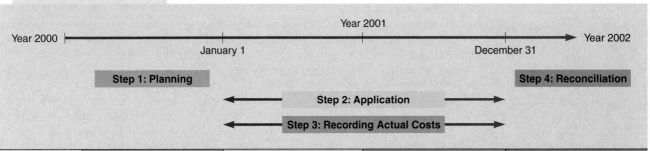

	Step 1: Planning	Step 2: Application	Step 3: Recording Actual Costs	Step 4: Reconciliation
Description	Calculate a predetermined manufacturing overhead rate	Apply manufacturing overhead costs to production	Record actual manufacturing overhead costs	Calculate the difference between applied and actual manufacturing overhead costs
When	Before accounting period	During accounting period as units are produced	During accounting period as costs are incurred	At the end of the accounting period
Procedure	Divide the cost pool of total estimated overhead costs by the total estimated cost driver level	Multiply the predetermined overhead rate for each cost pool by the actual cost driver level	Record actual manufacturing overhead costs when incurred	Calculate and record the difference between the actual and applied manufacturing overhead costs
Journal entry?	No	Yes. Increase Work in Process Inventory account. Decrease Manufacturing Overhead Control account	Yes. Increase Manufacturing Overhead Control account. Decrease asset accounts. Increase contra assets or liability accounts	Yes. If applied > actual, then Increase Manufacturing Overhead Control account. Decrease Cost of Goods Sold account. If applied < actual, then Increase Cost of Goods Sold account. Decrease Manufacturing Overhead Control account

In Step 2, the management accountant applies the estimated manufacturing overhead costs to the product's costs as units are manufactured. The actual cost driver level (for example, the actual number of direct labor hours used to complete the product) is multiplied by the predetermined manufacturing overhead rate or activity pool rate for that cost driver. The purpose of this calculation is to assign a fairly consistent manufacturing overhead cost to each unit produced during the accounting period. The accountant records the allocation, or application, of overhead to the product by increasing the Work in Process Inventory account and reducing the Manufacturing Overhead Control account.

During the accounting period the management accountant records the actual manufacturing overhead costs when incurred (Step 3). These costs will be part of the actual product cost and include the costs of indirect materials, indirect labor, depreciation, property taxes, and other accrued production costs. Recording the actual manufacturing overhead costs requires an increase in the Manufacturing Overhead Control account and a decrease in asset accounts or an increase in contra asset or liability accounts.

At the end of the accounting period, during Step 4, the reconciliation step, management accountants calculate the difference between the allocated, or applied, manufacturing overhead costs and the actual manufacturing overhead costs. If the manufacturing overhead costs applied to production during the accounting period are greater than (over) the actual manufacturing overhead costs, the difference in the amounts represents overapplied overhead costs. The accountant increases the Manufacturing Overhead Control account and decreases the Cost of Goods Sold account by this difference, assuming the difference is not material. If the difference is material, adjustments are made to the Work in Process Inventory, Finished Goods Inventory, and Cost of Goods Sold accounts. If the manufacturing overhead costs applied to production during the accounting period are less than (under) the actual manufacturing overhead costs, the difference in the amounts is underapplied overhead costs. The accountant increases the Cost of Goods Sold account and decreases the Manufacturing Overhead Control account by this difference, assuming the difference is not material. The adjustment for overapplied or underapplied overhead costs, whether it is immaterial or material, is necessary to reflect the actual manufacturing overhead costs on the income statement.

The Importance of Good Estimates

A predetermined manufacturing overhead rate has two primary uses. First, it enables managers to make more timely decisions about pricing products and controlling costs. The product cost calculated at the end of the period when all of the product costs are known is more accurate. However, when the overhead portion of product cost is estimated in advance, managers can compare actual and estimated costs throughout the year and more quickly correct the problems that caused the under- or overallocation of overhead costs. Second, an advance estimate allows the management accountant to allocate manufacturing overhead costs more equitably to each unit produced.

Actual manufacturing overhead costs fluctuate from month to month due to the timing of the costs and the variability of the amounts. For example, some manufacturing overhead costs (such as supervisors' salaries and depreciation on equipment) may be expensed monthly. Others (like payroll taxes) may be paid quarterly, and still others (like property taxes and insurance) may be paid annually. In addition, hourly indirect labor costs (such as machine maintenance and material handling) fluctuate with changes in production levels.

The successful allocation of manufacturing overhead costs depends on two factors. One is a careful estimate of the total manufacturing overhead costs. The other is a good forecast of the activity used as the cost driver.

Estimating total manufacturing overhead costs is critical. If the estimate is wrong, the manufacturing overhead rate will be wrong. This will cause an overstatement or understatement of the product unit cost. If overstated product unit cost information is relied upon, the organization may fail to bid on profitable projects because the costs appear to be too high. If understated product unit cost information is used, the organization may accept business that is not as profitable as expected. So, to provide managers with reliable product unit costs, the management accountant must be careful to include all manufacturing overhead items and to forecast the costs of those items accurately.

The budgeting process normally includes estimated manufacturing overhead costs. Managers who use production-related resources will provide cost estimates for direct and indirect production-related activities. For example, the managers for material handling and inspecting at Angelo's Rolling Suitcases, Inc., can estimate the costs related to their departments' activities. The accountant then includes their cost estimates in developing total manufacturing overhead costs. In addition, the managers need to carefully estimate the cost driver level. An understated cost driver level will cause an overstatement of the predetermined manufacturing overhead rate (the cost is spread over a lesser level), and an overstated cost driver level will cause an understatement of the predetermined manufacturing overhead rate (the cost is spread over a greater level).

In the remaining learning objectives of this chapter, we will present two approaches to manufacturing overhead allocation. We will use the first two steps of the four-step overhead allocation process to demonstrate these approaches.

Manufacturing Overhead Allocation Using the Traditional Approach

Many organizations continue to use one predetermined overhead rate to apply manufacturing overhead to a product cost. This approach is especially useful if companies manufacture only one product or a few very similar products requiring the same production processes and production-related activities, such as setup, inspection, and material handling. The total manufacturing overhead costs represent one cost pool, and a traditional activity base, such as direct labor hours, direct labor costs, machine hours, or units of production, becomes the cost driver.

Figure 5 illustrates the application of one cost pool of manufacturing overhead costs to two product lines. As we continue with our example of Angelo's Rolling Suitcases, Inc., let's assume that Angelo's will be selling two product lines in 20x1, a regular model and a deluxe model. The deluxe model has additional pockets, a wider handle that locks in a closed position, and a larger main storage area. Suppose that Jamie chooses direct labor hours as the cost driver. For the next year, Jamie estimates that manufacturing overhead costs will amount to $200,000 and that total direct labor hours worked will be 40,000 hours.

The first step using the traditional approach is to compute the predetermined overhead rate, as shown in Step 1 of Table 3:

$$\frac{\text{Predetermined}}{\text{Overhead Rate}} = \frac{\$200,000}{40,000 \text{ Direct Labor Hours}} = \$5 \text{ per Direct Labor Hour}$$

The second step is to apply manufacturing overhead to the products (see Table 3). During the year, 25,000 direct labor hours were used to produce 10,000 regular rolling suitcases and 15,000 direct labor hours were used to produce 5,000 deluxe rolling suitcases. When Jamie used the predetermined overhead rate, the portion of the manufacturing overhead cost applied to the regular rolling suitcases totaled $125,000 ($5 × 25,000 DLH), or $12.50 per unit ($125,000 ÷ 10,000 units); and the

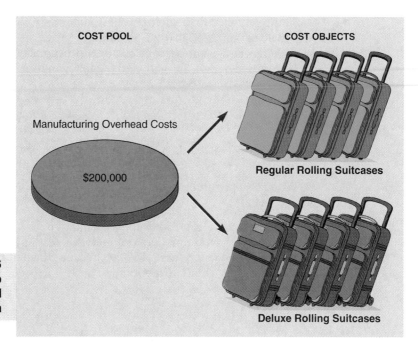

Figure 5
Using the Traditional Approach to Allocate Manufacturing Overhead Costs to Production

Table 3. Assignment of Manufacturing Overhead Costs and Calculation of Product Unit Cost: Traditional Approach

Step 1. Calculate the predetermined overhead rate.

Cost Pool Description	Estimated Cost Pool Amount	Cost Driver	Cost Driver Level	Predetermined Overhead Rate
Manufacturing overhead	$200,000	Direct labor hours (DLH)	40,000 DLH	$5 per DLH

Step 2. Apply manufacturing overhead costs to production.

	Regular		Deluxe	
	Cost Driver Level	Cost Applied	Cost Driver Level	Cost Applied
Overhead costs applied:				
Manufacturing overhead: $5 per DLH	× 25,000 DLH	$125,000	× 15,000 DLH	$75,000
Number of units		÷ 10,000		÷ 5,000
Manufacturing overhead cost per unit		$ 12.50		$ 15.00

Product Unit Cost		
	Regular Rolling Suitcase	Deluxe Rolling Suitcase
Product costs per unit:		
Direct materials	$40.00	$ 42.00
Direct labor	37.50	45.00
Manufacturing overhead	12.50	15.00
Product unit cost	$90.00	$102.00

portion applied to the deluxe rolling suitcases totaled $75,000 ($5 × 15,000 DLH), or $15.00 per unit ($75,000 ÷ 5,000 units).

Jamie also wanted to calculate the normalized product unit cost during the accounting period. She gathered the following data for the two product lines:

	Regular Rolling Suitcase	Deluxe Rolling Suitcase
Actual direct materials cost per unit	$40.00	$42.00
Actual direct labor cost per unit	37.50	45.00
Prime cost per unit	$77.50	$87.00

At the bottom of Table 3 is Jamie's calculation of the product unit cost for each product line. The deluxe model's product unit cost of $102.00 is higher than the regular model's product unit cost of $90.00 because the deluxe model required more expensive materials and more labor time.

Activity-Based Costing

OBJECTIVE 7

Define and explain activity-based costing

Suppose you and three of your friends are planning to take a skiing trip during the winter break. You call a local travel agency to obtain an estimated cost for a three-day winter skiing package. The package includes skiing, food, lodging, and entertainment. The travel agent quotes a flat fee of $400 per person, or a total of $1,600. But you and your friends prefer not to pay a flat fee. Instead, you would prefer to plan your own trip and identify the cost of each activity (skiing, eating, sleeping, entertainment).

How would you assign the $1,600 total cost of the trip to four people? The easiest way would be to follow the travel agent's approach and require each person to pay a flat fee of $400, which is one-fourth of the total cost. But what if one person does not plan to ski? Should that person pay for a portion of the skiing costs? What if another person eats much more than the other three people? Should he or she pay the same amount for food as everyone else? What if two people plan to stay only two days? Should they pay the full price?

The issue is how to assign costs fairly if each individual is involved in different activities. The people who ski should bear the skiing costs. The individual who eats more than the others should pay a larger portion of the food costs, and the ones who leave one day early should not be charged for the activities on the final day. Each individual, then, is accountable to the others for making a fair payment relative to his or her level of involvement in each activity.

The fair assignment of costs also applies to cost management. From the 1950s through the 1970s, traditional overhead allocation methods used cost drivers such as direct labor hours, direct labor costs, or machine hours to allocate a plantwide overhead cost pool to products. However, since the mid-1980s, organizations in the United States have been faced with increasing competition from foreign companies. Foreign competitors sold products of equal or better quality at lower prices than those of U.S. organizations. One weakness was that many U.S. organizations used a product costing system that did not accurately assign manufacturing overhead costs to the product lines and then used these inaccurate product unit costs when making pricing decisions. Inaccurate manufacturing overhead costs led to inaccurate product unit costs and poor pricing decisions. As a result, many organizations lost market share because they set their selling prices too high in very competitive markets. Other organizations lost profits because they set their selling prices too low in markets with little or no competition. In response, U.S. organizations began to

(1) continuously improve their product/service quality, (2) critically evaluate their operating processes, and (3) overhaul their product costing systems to more accurately identify the costs of their products or services. In the search for more accurate product costing, many organizations embraced activity-based costing (ABC). Since its introduction as a viable cost assignment technique, organizations in the United States and throughout the world have adopted ABC.

Activity-based costing (ABC) is an approach to cost assignment that calculates a more accurate product cost by categorizing all indirect costs by activity, tracing the indirect costs to those activities, and assigning activity costs to products using a cost driver that is related to the cause of the cost. A company that uses ABC to assign manufacturing overhead costs to products identifies production-related activities and the events and circumstances that cause, or drive, those activities, such as number of inspections, number of moves, or maintenance hours. As a result, many smaller cost pools are created from the single manufacturing overhead cost pool that was traditionally used. This means that the management accountant will apply manufacturing overhead costs to a product by calculating a predetermined overhead rate, or cost pool rate, for each cost pool and then using that rate and a cost driver amount to determine the portion of manufacturing overhead costs to apply. The management accountant must work with managers to select an appropriate number of cost pools for manufacturing overhead. Since each cost pool requires a cost driver, the benefit of grouping manufacturing overhead costs into several smaller pools to obtain more accurate product costs is offset by the additional costs of measuring many different cost drivers. A system must be designed to capture the actual cost driver amounts.

ABC will improve the accuracy of product costs for organizations that sell many different types of products (product diversity) or use varying, significant amounts of different production-related activities to complete the products (process complexity). To remain competitive in our current global marketplace, many organizations are selling a wider range of products or services (product or service diversity). For example, twenty years ago, Taco Bell carried only six food items. Today the menu at Taco Bell offers more than twenty-five food items. This diversity of product lines requires more careful cost allocation, especially when it comes to making decisions about pricing products, outsourcing processes to other organizations, or choosing to keep or drop a food item from the menu.

For other organizations, some products are more complicated to manufacture, store, move, package, or ship than others (process complexity). For example, an auto parts distributor receives, stores, picks, moves, consolidates, packs, and ships auto parts to auto dealers. The major operating costs of the distributor are overhead costs, which it allocates based on the cost to purchase a part for resale. Under this system, more expensive parts, such as car radios, receive a greater allocation of overhead costs than do less expensive parts, such as windshields. However, compared to a car radio, a glass windshield, because it is delicate, costs the distributor more to move, store, pack, and ship. If ABC were used, the cost of the windshield would increase to reflect a fairer allocation of the distributor's overhead costs. Thus, ABC, by fairly allocating overhead costs, would provide managers with better information for making decisions, such as pricing car radios, windshields and other auto parts; choosing to discontinue selling windshields; or reducing the amount of storage space.

Manufacturing Overhead Allocation Using ABC

OBJECTIVE 8

Calculate product unit cost using activity-based costing to assign manufacturing overhead costs

Figure 6 illustrates the use of ABC to allocate manufacturing overhead costs to two product lines. Earlier in the chapter, Jamie Estrada, accountant for Angelo's Rolling Suitcases, Inc., calculated product unit cost by computing one manufacturing overhead rate for one cost pool and applying that rate to the direct labor hours used to manufacture the regular and deluxe rolling suitcase models. As we continue with our example, we find that Angelo is concerned about the product cost for each model. Angelo believes that the difference in cost between the regular and deluxe models should be more than $12. He has asked Jamie to review her estimate. Jamie found no error when she rechecked the calculation of direct materials costs and direct labor costs. However, she believes manufacturing overhead cost allocation could be misleading, so she wants to use activity-based costing to obtain a more accurate product cost.

Jamie analyzed the production-related activities and decided that the estimated $200,000 in manufacturing overhead cost could be grouped into four cost pools. The first cost pool, setup, includes estimated total costs of $70,000 for indirect labor and indirect materials used in preparing machines and workers for each batch of production. The second cost pool, which covers inspection, includes $60,000 for salaries and other costs of indirect materials, indirect labor, and depreciation on testing equipment. Packaging, the third cost pool, includes estimated total costs of $50,000 for indirect materials, indirect labor, and equipment depreciation for each order. The last cost pool, building, includes estimated total overhead costs of $20,000 for building depreciation, maintenance, janitorial wages, property taxes, insurance, security, and all other costs not related to the first three cost pools.

After identifying the four cost pools, Jamie selected a cost driver and estimated the cost driver level for each cost pool. The following schedule shows those amounts by product line and in total.

Cost Driver	Estimated Cost Driver Level		
	Regular	**Deluxe**	**Total**
Number of setups	300	400	700
Number of inspections	150	350	500
Packaging hours	600	1,400	2,000
Machine hours	4,000	6,000	10,000

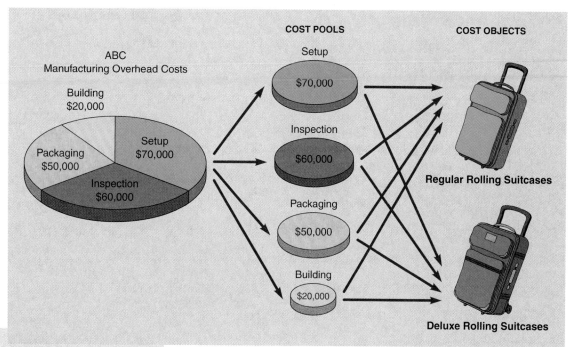

COST POOLS

COST OBJECTS

ABC
Manufacturing Overhead Costs

Setup
$70,000

Inspection
$60,000

Packaging
$50,000

Building
$20,000

Regular Rolling Suitcases

Deluxe Rolling Suitcases

Building
$20,000

Packaging
$50,000

Setup
$70,000

Inspection
$60,000

Figure 6
Using ABC to Allocate
Manufacturing Overhead Costs
to Production

After identifying cost pools, estimated cost pool amounts, cost drivers, and estimated cost driver levels, Jamie performed the first step of the overhead allocation process by calculating the cost pool rate for each cost pool. The cost pool rate is the estimated cost pool amount divided by the estimated cost driver level. Step 1 of Table 4 shows the cost pool rates to be $100 per setup, $120 per inspection, $25 per packaging hour, and $2 per machine hour.

In the second step, Jamie applied manufacturing overhead to the two product lines using the cost driver levels for each cost driver shown in the schedule above. Step 2 of Table 4 shows those calculations. For example, during the year, Jamie applied $30,000 in setup costs ($100 × 300 setups) to the regular model and $40,000 ($100 × 400 setups) to the deluxe model. After applying the overhead costs from the four cost pools to the product lines, Jamie estimated that total manufacturing overhead costs of $71,000, or $7.10 per suitcase ($71,000 ÷ 10,000 units), applied to the regular model and $129,000, or $25.80 per suitcase ($129,000 ÷ 5,000 units), applied to the deluxe model.

Jamie also wanted to calculate the normalized product unit cost for the accounting period. At the bottom of Table 4 is Jamie's calculation of the product unit cost for each product line. The product unit cost is $112.80 for the deluxe model and $84.60 for the regular model.

Jamie presented the following information to Angelo:

	Regular Rolling Suitcase	Deluxe Rolling Suitcase
Product unit cost: One manufacturing overhead cost pool	$90.00	$102.00
Product unit cost: ABC with four cost pools	84.60	112.80
Difference: decrease (increase)	$5.40	($10.80)

Table 4. Assignment of Manufacturing Overhead Costs and Calculation of Product Unit Cost: ABC Approach

Step 1. Calculate the overhead cost pool rates.

Cost Pool Description	Estimated Cost Pool Amount	Cost Driver	Cost Driver Level	Cost Pool Rates
Setup	$ 70,000	Number of setups	700 setups	$100 per setup
Inspection	60,000	Number of inspections	500 inspections	$120 per inspection
Packaging	50,000	Packaging hours	2,000 packaging hours	$ 25 per packaging hour
Building	20,000	Machine hours	10,000 machine hours	$ 2 per machine hour
	$200,000			

Step 2. Apply manufacturing overhead costs to production.

Cost Pool	Cost Pool Rate	Regular Cost Driver Level	Cost Applied	Deluxe Cost Driver Level	Cost Applied
Setup	$100 per setup	× 300 setups	$30,000	× 400 setups	$ 40,000
Inspection	$120 per inspection	× 150 inspections	18,000	× 350 inspections	42,000
Packaging	$ 25 per packaging hour	× 600 packaging hours	15,000	× 1,400 packaging hours	35,000
Building	$ 2 per machine hour	× 4,000 machine hours	8,000	× 6,000 machine hours	12,000
Total			$71,000		$129,000
Number of units			÷ 10,000		÷ 5,000
Manufacturing overhead cost per unit			$7.10		$25.80

Product Unit Cost

	Regular Rolling Suitcase	Deluxe Rolling Suitcase
Product costs per unit:		
Direct materials	$40.00	$ 42.00
Direct labor	37.50	45.00
Manufacturing overhead	7.10	25.80
Product unit cost	$84.60	$112.80

Because ABC fairly assigned more costs to the product line that used more resources, it provided a more accurate product unit cost estimate. The increased information about the production requirements for the deluxe model that went into the ABC product unit cost calculation also provided valuable insights. Angelo found that the deluxe model costs more because the product requires (1) more setups and machine hours due to changes in the handle and number of pockets, (2) more inspections to test the new handle, and (3) more hours to complete special packaging requirements that allow retailers to display the rolling suitcase in a "carry-on" package at stores in airport terminals. The product unit cost of the deluxe model is higher for two reasons. First, the product requires more production and production-related activities to be completed and ready for sale. Second, the deluxe model's manufacturing overhead cost per unit is greater, in part, because the estimated

overhead was spread over fewer units than for the regular model. Based on the results of this analysis, Angelo may want to reconsider some of his short-term decisions regarding the manufacture and sale of these two product lines.

Cost Allocation in Service Organizations

OBJECTIVE 9

Apply costing concepts to a service organization

Many organizations provide services to other organizations or to the general public. Services are labor-intensive processes supported by indirect labor and overhead costs. Managers of service organizations need to classify costs in different ways depending upon the purpose of the analysis. For example, the owner of a tax-preparation service would like to trace costs to the preparation of particular types of returns, such as personal tax returns, payroll tax reports, and estate tax returns. This allows her to see how profitable each type of service is. The manager of a nursery may classify the costs of a landscaping service into variable and fixed components to calculate the minimum number of landscaping projects needed to make a targeted profit. And the direct labor costs for tax-preparation or landscaping work will be a value-added cost to those respective services.

Processing loans, representing people in courts of law, selling insurance policies, and computing people's income taxes are typical services performed by professionals. Because no products are manufactured in the course of providing such services, service organizations have no direct materials costs. Nonetheless, specific costs arise that must be included when computing the cost of providing a service.

The most important cost in a service organization would be the professional labor involved, and the usual standard is applicable; that is, the direct labor cost must be traceable to the service rendered. In addition to the labor cost, any type of organization, whether manufacturing, retail, service, or not-for-profit—incurs overhead costs. In a service organization, the overhead costs associated with and incurred for the purpose of offering a service are classified as service overhead (like manufacturing overhead) and, along with professional labor costs, are considered service costs (like product costs) rather than period costs.

For example, assume that the Loan Department at the Seminole Bank of Commerce wants to determine the total costs incurred in processing a typical loan application. Its policy for the past five years has been to charge a $150 fee for processing a home-loan application. Barbara Hasegawa, the chief loan officer, thinks the fee is far too low. Considering the way operating costs have soared in the past five years, she proposes that the fee be doubled. You have been asked to compute the cost of processing a typical home-loan application.

The following information concerning the processing of loan applications has been given to you.

Direct professional labor:
  Loan processors' monthly salaries:

4 people at $3,000 each	$12,000

Indirect monthly Loan Department overhead costs:

Chief loan officer's salary	$ 4,500
Telephone	750
Depreciation	5,750
Legal advice	2,460
Customer relations	640
Credit check function	1,980
Internal audit function	2,400
Utilities	1,690
Clerical personnel	3,880
Miscellaneous	1,050
Total overhead costs	$25,100

In addition, you discover that all appraisals and title searches are performed by people outside the bank; their fees are treated as separate loan costs. One hundred home-loan applications are usually processed each month.

The Loan Department performs several other functions in addition to processing home-loan applications. Roughly one-half of the department is involved in loan collection. After determining how many of the processed loans were not home loans, you conclude that only 25 percent of the overhead costs of the Loan Department were applicable to the processing of home-loan applications. The cost of processing one home-loan application can be computed as follows:

Direct professional labor cost:	
$12,000 ÷ 100	$120.00
Service overhead cost:	
$25,100 × 25% ÷ 100	62.75
Total processing cost per loan	$182.75

Finally, you conclude that the chief loan officer was correct; the present fee does not cover the current costs of processing a typical home-loan application. However, doubling the loan fee seems inappropriate. To allow for a profit margin, the loan fee could be raised to $225 or $250.

Chapter Review

REVIEW OF LEARNING OBJECTIVES

1. **State how managers use operating cost information and product costs in the management cycle.** Managers use operating cost information and product costs as they plan, execute, review, and report during the management cycle. Managers in manufacturing, retail, or service organizations use operating cost and product cost information to measure historical or future profits, decide the selling price for regular or special sales or services provided, and to value finished goods or merchandise inventories.

2. **Define and give examples of the three elements of product cost and compute a product's unit cost for a manufacturing organization.** Direct materials are materials that become part of the finished product and that can be conveniently and economically traced to specific product units. The sheet metal used to manufacture cars is an example of a direct material. Direct labor costs include all labor costs for specific work that can be conveniently and economically traced to specific product units. A machine operator's wages are a direct labor cost. All other production-related costs—for utilities, depreciation on equipment, and operating supplies, for example—are classified and accounted for as manufacturing overhead costs. These costs cannot be conveniently or economically traced to end products, so they are assigned to products by a cost allocation method.

   The unit cost of a product is made up of the costs of direct materials, direct labor, and manufacturing overhead. These three cost elements are accumulated for a batch of products as they are produced. When the batch has been completed, the number of units produced is divided into the total costs incurred to determine the product unit cost. The product unit cost will include estimated costs if normal or standard costing methods are used.

3. **Describe the flow of product-related activities, documents, and costs through the Materials Inventory, Work in Process Inventory, and Finished Goods Inventory accounts.** The flow of costs through the inventory accounts begins when costs are incurred for direct materials, direct labor, and manufacturing overhead. Materials costs flow first into the Materials Inventory account, which is used to record the costs of materials when they are received and again when they are issued for use in a production process. All manufacturing-related costs—direct materials, direct labor, and manufacturing overhead—are recorded in the Work in Process Inventory account as the production process begins. When products are completed, their costs are transferred from the Work in Process Inventory account to the Finished Goods Inventory account. Costs remain in the Finished Goods Inventory account until the products are sold, at which time they are transferred to the Cost of Goods Sold account.

4. **Prepare a statement of cost of goods manufactured and an income statement for a manufacturing organization.** The cost of goods manufactured is a key component of the income statement for a manufacturing organization. Determining the cost of goods manufactured involves three steps: (1) computing the cost of materials used, (2) computing total manufacturing costs for the period, and (3) computing the cost of goods manufactured. This last figure, taken from the statement of cost of goods manufactured, is used in the income statement to compute the cost of goods sold.

5. **Define *cost allocation* and explain the process of manufacturing overhead allocation using cost objects, cost pools, and cost drivers.** Cost allocation is the process of assigning pooled indirect costs to specific cost objects using an allocation base that represents a major function of the business. The allocation of manufacturing overhead requires the pooling of manufacturing overhead costs that are affected by a common activity and the selection of a cost driver whose activity level causes a change in the cost pool. A cost pool is a pool of overhead costs related to a cost object (the destination of an assigned or allocated cost). A cost driver is an activity that causes the cost pool to increase in amount as the cost driver increases.

   The four steps of the manufacturing overhead allocation process are planning, application, recording actual costs, and reconciliation. In the planning step, the predetermined overhead rate is calculated. In the application step, manufacturing overhead costs are applied to the product costs during production. In the recording actual costs step, the actual manufacturing overhead costs are recorded in the accounting records when the costs are incurred. In the reconciliation step, the difference between the actual and applied manufacturing overhead costs is calculated and the Cost of Goods Sold account is corrected for an immaterial amount of over- or underapplied manufacturing overhead costs to the products. If the difference is material, adjustments are made to the Work in Process Inventory, Finished Goods Inventory, and Cost of Goods Sold accounts.

6. **Calculate product unit cost using the traditional allocation of manufacturing overhead costs.** The normal costing method applies manufacturing overhead costs to a product's cost by estimating a predetermined manufacturing overhead rate and multiplying that rate by the actual cost driver level. The total applied manufacturing

overhead cost is added to the actual costs of direct materials and direct labor in order to determine the total product cost. The product unit cost is the total product cost divided by the total units produced.

7. **Define and explain *activity-based costing.*** Activity-based costing (ABC) is an approach to cost assignment that calculates a more accurate product cost by (1) categorizing all indirect costs by activity and (2) tracing costs to those activities, and (3) assigning activity costs to products using a cost driver that is related to the cause of the cost. For manufacturing organizations, activity-based costing improves the accuracy of the allocation of manufacturing overhead costs to products. ABC is particularly useful for companies with product diversity or variations in the amounts of production-related activities needed to manufacture different product lines.

8. **Calculate product unit cost using activity-based costing to assign manufacturing overhead costs.** When ABC is used, manufacturing overhead costs are grouped into smaller cost pools related to specific activities. Cost drivers are identified and cost driver levels are estimated for each cost pool. Each cost pool rate is calculated by dividing the estimated cost pool amount by the cost driver level. Manufacturing overhead, which is represented in the cost pools, is applied to the product's cost by multiplying the cost pool rate by the actual cost driver amount. The total applied manufacturing overhead cost is added to the cost of direct materials and direct labor to determine the total product cost. The product unit cost is the total product cost divided by the total units produced.

9. **Apply costing concepts to a service organization.** Most types of costs incurred by a manufacturer and called product costs are also incurred by a service organization. The only important difference is that a service organization does not deal with a physical product that can be assembled, stored, and valued. Services are rendered and cannot be held in inventory. Because no products are manufactured in the course of providing services, service organizations have no materials costs. To determine the cost of performing a particular service, professional labor and service-related overhead costs are included in the analysis.

REVIEW OF CONCEPTS AND TERMINOLOGY

The following concepts and terms were introduced in this chapter.

LO 7 **Activity-based costing:** A cost assignment approach that calculates a more accurate product cost by categorizing all indirect costs by activity, tracing the indirect costs to those activities, and assigning activity costs to products using a cost driver that is related to the cause of the cost.

LO 2 **Actual costing:** A method of cost measurement using the actual costs of direct materials, direct labor, and manufacturing overhead to calculate the product unit cost.

LO 5 **Cost allocation:** The process of assigning collected indirect costs to specific cost objects using an allocation base that represents a major function of the business.

LO 5 **Cost driver:** An activity that causes the cost pool to increase in amount as the cost driver increases in volume.

LO 5 **Cost object:** The destination of an assigned, or allocated, cost.

LO 3 **Cost of goods manufactured:** The total manufacturing costs attached to units of a product completed during an accounting period and moved to finished goods storage.

LO 5 **Cost pool:** A collection of overhead costs or other indirect costs related to a cost object.

LO 2 **Direct labor costs:** Costs of labor to complete activities involved in the production process that can be conveniently and economically traced to specific units of product.

LO 2 **Direct materials costs:** Costs of materials that can be conveniently and economically traced to specific units of product.

LO 3 **Direct Materials Inventory account:** An inventory account showing the balance of the cost of unused direct materials.

LO 3 **Finished Goods Inventory account:** An inventory account that holds the costs assigned to all completed products that have not been sold by a manufacturing company.

LO 2 **Indirect labor costs:** Labor costs for production-related activities that cannot be conveniently or economically traced to a unit of product.

LO 2   **Indirect materials costs:** The costs of minor materials and other production supplies that cannot be conveniently or economically traced to a unit of product.

LO 3   **Manufacturing cost flow:** The flow of manufacturing costs (direct materials, direct labor, and manufacturing overhead) from their incurrence through the Direct Materials Inventory, Work in Process Inventory, and Finished Goods Inventory accounts to the Cost of Goods Sold account.

LO 2   **Manufacturing overhead costs:** A varied collection of production-related costs that cannot be practically or conveniently traced to an end product. Also called *factory overhead, factory burden,* or *indirect manufacturing costs.*

LO 2   **Normal costing:** A method that combines the *actual* direct materials and direct labor costs with the *estimated* manufacturing overhead costs to determine a normal product unit cost.

LO 2   **Product unit cost:** The manufacturing cost of a single unit of product; total cost of direct materials, direct labor, and manufacturing overhead for the units produced divided by the total units produced.

LO 2   **Standard costing:** A method of cost measurement using the estimated costs of direct materials, direct labor, and manufacturing overhead to calculate the product unit cost for purposes of cost control.

LO 4   **Statement of cost of goods manufactured:** A formal statement summarizing the flow of all manufacturing costs incurred during an accounting period.

LO 3   **Total manufacturing costs:** The total costs of direct materials, direct labor, and manufacturing overhead incurred and charged to production during an accounting period.

LO 3   **Work in Process Inventory account:** An inventory account used to record all manufacturing costs incurred and assigned to partially completed units of product.

REVIEW PROBLEM
Cost of Goods Manufactured—Three Fundamental Steps

LO 2
LO 3
LO 4

In addition to the year-end balance sheet and income statement, the management of Nikita Company requires the controller to prepare a statement of cost of goods manufactured. During 20xx, $361,920 of direct materials were purchased. Operating cost data and inventory account balances for 20xx follow:

Account	Balance
Direct Labor (10,430 hours at $9.50 per hour)	$ 99,085
Plant Supervision	42,500
Indirect Labor (20,280 hours at $6.25 per hour)	126,750
Factory Insurance	8,100
Utilities, Factory	29,220
Depreciation, Factory Building	46,200
Depreciation, Factory Equipment	62,800
Manufacturing Supplies	9,460
Factory Repair and Maintenance	14,980
Selling and Administrative Expenses	76,480
Direct Materials Inventory, January 1, 20xx	26,490
Work in Process Inventory, January 1, 20xx	101,640
Finished Goods Inventory, January 1, 20xx	148,290
Direct Materials Inventory, December 31, 20xx	24,910
Work in Process Inventory, December 31, 20xx	100,400
Finished Goods Inventory, December 31, 20xx	141,100

REQUIRED

1. Compute the cost of materials used during the year.
2. Given the cost of materials used, compute the total manufacturing costs for the year.
3. Given the total manufacturing costs for the year, compute the cost of goods manufactured during the year.
4. Assuming 13,397 units were manufactured during the year, what was the actual product unit cost?

ANSWER TO REVIEW PROBLEM

1. Compute the cost of materials used.

Direct Materials Inventory, January 1, 20xx	$ 26,490
Add Direct Materials Purchased (net)	361,920
Cost of Direct Materials Available for Use	$388,410
Less Direct Materials Inventory, December 31, 20xx	24,910
Cost of Direct Materials Used	$363,500

2. Compute the total manufacturing costs.

Cost of Direct Materials Used		$363,500
Add Direct Labor Costs		99,085
Add Total Manufacturing Overhead Costs		
Plant Supervision	$ 42,500	
Indirect Labor	126,750	
Factory Insurance	8,100	
Utilities, Factory	29,220	
Depreciation, Factory Building	46,200	
Depreciation, Factory Equipment	62,800	
Manufacturing Supplies	9,460	
Factory Repair and Maintenance	14,980	
Total Manufacturing Overhead Costs		340,010
Total Manufacturing Costs		$802,595

3. Compute the cost of goods manufactured.

Total Manufacturing Costs	$802,595
Add Work in Process Inventory, January 1, 20xx	101,640
Total Cost of Work in Process During the Year	$904,235
Less Work in Process Inventory, December 31, 20xx	100,400
Cost of Goods Manufactured	$803,835

4. Compute the actual product unit cost.

$$\frac{\text{Cost of Goods Manufactured}}{\text{Number of Units Manufactured}} = \frac{\$803,835}{13,397} = \$60^*$$

*Rounded.

Chapter Assignments

BUILDING YOUR KNOWLEDGE FOUNDATION

Questions

1. How do managers use operating cost information?
2. Explain the full cost of a product or service.
3. What are the three kinds of manufacturing costs included in a product's cost?
4. Define *direct materials costs.*
5. How is a direct cost different from an indirect cost?
6. What characteristics identify a cost as part of manufacturing overhead?
7. How are direct labor costs different from indirect labor costs?
8. Explain the difference between actual costing and normal costing.

9. Identify and describe the three inventory accounts used by a manufacturing company.
10. What is meant by the term *manufacturing cost flow?*
11. Describe how to compute the cost of direct materials used.
12. Describe how total manufacturing costs differ from the cost of goods manufactured.
13. How is the cost of goods manufactured used in computing the cost of goods sold?
14. What is cost allocation?
15. Explain the relationship between cost objects, cost pools, and cost drivers. Give an example of each.
16. List the four steps of the manufacturing overhead allocation process. Briefly explain each step.
17. What are two primary uses of a predetermined manufacturing overhead rate?
18. What is activity-based costing?
19. When would a company find activity-based costing to be an appropriate approach to cost assignment?
20. "The concept of product costs is not applicable to service organizations." Is this statement correct? Defend your answer.
21. Why do service organizations need unit cost information?

Short Exercises

SE 1.
LO 1 *Distinguishing the Costs of a Product*

Ray Christopher, owner of Candlelight, Inc., was given the following list of costs he incurs in his candle business. Examine the list and identify the costs that Ray should *not* include in the full cost of making and selling candles.

1. Salary of Mary, the office employee
2. Cost of delivering candles to Candles Plus, a buyer
3. Cost of wax
4. Sales commission on a sale to Candles Plus
5. Cost to custom-design Christmas candles

SE 2.
LO 2 *Elements of Manufacturing Cost*

Flora Rose, the bookkeeper at Candlelight, Inc., must group the costs to manufacture candles. Tell whether each of the following items should be classified as direct materials (DM), direct labor (DL), manufacturing overhead (MO), or none of the three (N).

1. Depreciation of the cost of vats to hold melted wax
2. Cost of wax
3. Rent on the factory where candles are made
4. Cost of George's time to dip the wicks into the wax
5. Cost of coloring for candles
6. Cost of Ray's time to design candles for Halloween
7. Sam's commission to sell candles to Candles Plus

SE 3.
LO 2 *Computing Product Unit Cost*

What is the product unit cost for Job 14, which consists of 300 units and has total manufacturing costs of direct materials, $4,500; direct labor, $7,500; and manufacturing overhead, $3,600?

SE 4.
LO 3 *Manufacturing Cost Flow*

Given the following information, compute the ending balances of the Direct Materials Inventory, Work in Process Inventory, and Finished Goods Inventory accounts.

Direct Materials Inventory, beginning balance	$ 23,000
Work in Process Inventory, beginning balance	25,750
Finished Goods Inventory, beginning balance	38,000
Direct materials purchased	85,000
Direct materials placed into production	74,000
Direct labor costs	97,000
Manufacturing overhead costs	35,000
Cost of goods completed	123,000
Cost of goods sold	93,375

SE 5.

LO 3 *Document Flows for a Manufacturing Organization*

Identify the document needed to support each of the following transactions.

1. Placing an order for direct materials with a supplier
2. Recording direct labor time at the beginning and end of each work shift
3. Receiving direct materials at the shipping dock
4. Recording the costs of a specific job requiring direct materials, direct labor, and overhead
5. Issuing direct materials into production
6. Billing the customer for a completed order
7. A request from the Production Scheduling Department for the purchase of direct materials

SE 6.

LO 4 *Income Statement for a Manufacturing Organization*

Using the following information from C.L.I.N.T. Company, prepare an income statement for 20xx.

Net Sales	$900,000
Finished Goods Inventory, January 1, 20xx	45,000
Cost of Goods Manufactured	585,000
Finished Goods Inventory, December 31, 20xx	60,000
Operating Expenses	270,000
Interest Expense	5,000
Tax Rate	34%

SE 7.

LO 5 *Calculation of Underapplied or Overapplied Overhead*

At year end, records show actual manufacturing overhead costs incurred were $25,870 and the amount of manufacturing overhead costs applied to production was $27,000. Identify the amount of under- or overapplied manufacturing overhead and indicate whether the Cost of Goods Sold account should be increased or decreased to adjust the balance to reflect actual manufacturing overhead costs.

SE 8.

LO 5
LO 6 *Computation of Predetermined Overhead Rate*

Compute the predetermined overhead rate per service request for the Maintenance Department if estimated overhead costs are $18,290 and the number of estimated service requests is 3,100.

SE 9.

LO 5
LO 6 *Application of Manufacturing Overhead to Production*

Calculate the amount of manufacturing overhead costs applied to production if the predetermined overhead rate is $4 per direct labor hour and 1,200 direct labor hours were worked.

SE 10.

LO 8 *Activity-Based Costing and Cost Drivers*

Kloezeman Clothiers Company relies on the information from its activity-based costing system when setting prices for its products. Compute ABC rates from the following budgeted data for each of the activity centers.

	Budgeted Cost	**Budgeted Cost Driver**
Cutting/Stitching	$5,220,000	145,000 machine hours
Trimming/Packing	998,400	41,600 operator hours
Designing	1,187,500	62,500 designer hours

SE 11.

LO 9 *Unit Costs in a Service Business*

Pickerson's Picking Services provides inexpensive, high-quality labor for farmers growing vegetable and fruit crops. In June, Pickerson paid laborers $4,000 to pick 500 acres of winter-grown onions. Pickerson incurred overhead costs of $2,400 for onion- and lettuce-picking services in June. This included the costs of transporting the laborers to the various fields; providing facilities, food, and beverages for the laborers; and scheduling, billing, and collecting from the farmers. Of this amount, 50 percent was related to picking onions. Compute the cost per acre to pick onions.

Exercises

E 1.

LO 1 *Distinguishing the Costs of Products*

Identify each of the following as a cost of a manufactured product (M), a cost of a purchased product (P), or both (B).

1. Warehouse costs for merchandise
2. Cost of utilities used in the factory
3. Advertising costs

4. Building rent
5. Product design costs
6. Cost of direct materials
7. Delivery costs
8. Display cases for merchandise
9. Parts in assembly operations
10. Production supervisor's salary

E 2.

LO 2 *Unit Cost Determination*

The Rose Winery is one of the finest and oldest wineries in the country. One of its most famous products is a red table wine called Olen Millot. The wine is made from Olen Millot grapes grown in Missouri's Ozark region. Recently, management has become concerned about the increasing cost of making Olen Millot and needs to find out if the current $10 per bottle selling price is adequate. The winery would like to make about a 25 percent profit on the sale of each bottle of wine. The following information is given to you for analysis.

Batch size	10,550 bottles
Costs	
Direct Materials	
Olen Millot grapes	$22,155
Chancellor grapes	9,495
Bottles	5,275
Direct Labor	
Pickers/loaders	2,110
Crusher	422
Processors	8,440
Bottler	1,688
Storage and racking	11,605
Manufacturing overhead	
Depreciation, equipment	2,743
Depreciation, building	5,275
Utilities	1,055
Indirect labor	6,330
Supervision	7,385
Supplies	3,165
Storage fixtures	2,532
Chemicals	4,220
Repairs	1,477
Miscellaneous	633
Total production costs	$96,005

1. Compute the unit cost per bottle for materials, labor, and manufacturing overhead.
2. What would you advise management regarding the price per bottle of Olen Millot wine? Defend your answer.

E 3.

LO 3 *Documentation*

Magellan Company manufactures a complete line of music boxes. Seventy percent of its products are standard items and are produced in long production runs. The remaining 30 percent of the music boxes are special orders involving specific requests for tunes. The special order boxes cost from three to six times as much as the standard product because of the use of additional materials and labor.

Howard Smith, the controller, recently received a complaint memorandum from V. Whatley, the production supervisor, because of the new network of source documents added to the existing cost accounting system. The new documents include a purchase request, a purchase order, a receiving report, and a materials request. Mr. Whatley claims that the forms represent extra busy work and interrupt the normal flow of production.

Prepare a written memorandum from Howard Smith to Mr. Whatley that fully explains the purpose of each type of document.

E 4.

LO 3 *Cost Flows and Inventory Accounts*

For each of the following activities, identify the inventory account (Direct Materials Inventory, Work in Process Inventory, Finished Goods Inventory), if any, that is affected. If an inventory account is affected, indicate whether the account balance will increase or decrease. *Example:* Moved completed units to finished goods inventory. *Answer:* Increase Finished Goods Inventory, Decrease Work in Process Inventory. If no inventory account is affected, use "None of these" as your answer.

1. Moved materials requested by production.
2. Sold units of product to customer.
3. Purchased and received direct materials for production.
4. Used direct labor and factory overhead in the production process.
5. Received payment from customer.
6. Purchased office supplies and paid cash.
7. Paid monthly office rent.

E 5.

LO 4 *Statement of Cost of Goods Manufactured*

The following information about the manufacturing costs incurred by the Earth Company for the month ended August 31, 20xx, is available.

Purchases of direct materials during August totaled $139,000.

Direct labor was 3,400 hours at $8.75 per hour.

The following manufacturing overhead costs were incurred: utilities, $5,870; supervision, $16,600; indirect supplies, $6,750; depreciation, $6,200; insurance, $1,830; and miscellaneous, $1,100.

Inventory accounts on August 1 were as follows: Direct Materials Inventory, $48,600; Work in Process Inventory, $54,250; and Finished Goods Inventory, $38,500. Inventory accounts on August 31 were as follows: Direct Materials Inventory, $50,100; Work in Process Inventory, $48,400; and Finished Goods Inventory, $37,450.

From the information given, prepare a statement of cost of goods manufactured.

E 6.

LO 5
LO 6 *Computation of Predetermined Overhead Rate*

The overhead costs used by Trinity Industries, Inc., to compute its predetermined overhead rate for 20x1 are listed below.

Indirect materials and supplies	$ 79,200
Repairs and maintenance	14,900
Outside service contracts	17,300
Indirect labor	79,100
Factory supervision	42,900
Depreciation, machinery	85,000
Factory insurance	8,200
Property taxes	6,500
Heat, light, and power	7,700
Miscellaneous manufacturing overhead	5,760
	$346,560

A total of 45,600 machine hours was used as the 20x1 allocation base. In 20x2, all overhead costs except depreciation, property taxes, and miscellaneous manufacturing overhead are expected to increase by 10 percent. Depreciation should increase by 12 percent, and a 20 percent increase in property taxes and miscellaneous manufacturing overhead is expected. Plant capacity in terms of machine hours used will increase by 4,400 hours in 20x2.

1. Compute the 20x1 predetermined overhead rate. (Carry your answer to three decimal places.)
2. Compute the predetermined overhead rate for 20x2. (Carry your answer to three decimal places.)

E 7.

LO 5
LO 6 *Computation and Application of Overhead Rate*

Bullock Compumatics specializes in the analysis and reporting of complex inventory costing projects. Materials costs are minimal, consisting entirely of operating supplies (computer diskettes, inventory sheets, and other recording tools). Labor is the highest single expense item, totaling $693,000 for 75,000 hours of work in 20xx. Manufacturing overhead costs for 20xx were $916,000 and were applied to specific jobs on the basis of labor hours worked. In 20x1 the company anticipates a 25 percent increase in manufacturing overhead costs. Labor costs will increase by $130,000, and the number of hours worked is expected to increase 20 percent.

1. Determine the total amount of manufacturing overhead anticipated by the company in 20x1.
2. Compute the predetermined manufacturing overhead rate for 20x1. (Round your answer to the nearest penny.)
3. During April 20x1, 11,980 labor hours were worked. Calculate the manufacturing overhead amount assigned to April production.

E 8.

LO 5 *Disposition of*
LO 6 *Overapplied Overhead*
(Extension of E 7)

At the end of 20x1, Bullock Compumatics had compiled a total of 89,920 labor hours worked. The actual manufacturing overhead incurred was $1,143,400.

1. Using the predetermined overhead rate computed in **E 7**, determine the total amount of manufacturing overhead applied to operations during 20x1.
2. Compute the amount of overapplied overhead for the year.
3. Will Cost of Goods Sold be increased or decreased to correct the overapplication of manufacturing overhead?

E 9.

LO 6 *Activities and Activity-*
LO 8 *Based Costing*

Yu Enterprises produces antennas for telecommunications equipment. One of the most important parts of the company's new just-in-time production process is quality control. Initially, a traditional cost accounting system was used to assign quality control costs to products. All costs of the Quality Control Department were included in the plant's overhead cost pool and allocated to products based on direct labor dollars. Recently, the firm implemented an activity-based costing system. The activities, cost drivers, and rates for the quality control function are summarized below, along with cost allocation information from the traditional system. Also shown is information related to one order of the Qian model antenna, Order HQ14. Compute the quality control cost that would be assigned to the Qian model order under both the traditional approach and the activity-based costing approach.

Traditional costing approach:
Quality control costs were assigned at a rate of 12 percent of direct labor dollars. Order HQ14 was charged with $9,350 of direct labor costs.

Activity-based costing approach:
Quality Control Function

Activities	Cost Drivers	Cost Pool Rates	Order HQ14 Activity Usage
Incoming materials inspection	Types of materials used	$17.50 per type of material	17 types of materials
In-process inspection	Number of products	$0.06 per product	2,400 products
Tool and gauge control	Number of processes per cell	$26.50 per process	11 processes
Product certification	Per order	$94.00 per order	1 order

E 10.

LO 9 *Unit Costs in a Service*
Business

Hector Franco provides custom farming services to owners of five-acre alfalfa fields. In July, he earned $2,400 by cutting, turning, and baling 3,000 bales of alfalfa. In the same month, he incurred the following costs: gas, $150; tractor maintenance, $115; and labor, $600. His annual tractor depreciation was $1,500. What was Franco's cost per bale? What was his revenue per bale? Should he increase the amount he charges the owners for his custom farming services?

Problems

P 1.

LO 2 *Computation of Unit*
Cost

Banff Industries, Inc., manufactures video discs for several of the leading recording studios in the United States and Europe. Department 85 is responsible for the electronic circuitry within each disc. Department 82 applies the plastic-like surface to the discs and packages them for shipment. A recent order for 4,000 discs from the JAZ Company was produced during July. For this job, the departments incurred the costs (at the top of the next page) to complete and ship the goods in July.

	Department	
	85	82
Direct materials used	$14,720	$1,960
Direct labor	3,400	1,280
Manufacturing overhead	3,680	2,400

REQUIRED

1. Compute the unit cost for each of the two departments.
2. Compute the total unit cost for the JAZ Company order.
3. The selling price for this order was $7 per unit. Was the selling price adequate? List the assumptions and/or computations upon which you based your answer. What suggestions would you make to Banff Industries' management concerning the pricing of future orders?

P 2.

LO 4   *Statement of Cost of Goods Manufactured*

Unger Manufacturing Company produces a line of Viking ship replicas that is sold at Scandinavian gift shops throughout the world. Inventory account balances on May 1, 20xx were Direct Materials Inventory, $190,400; Work in Process Inventory, $96,250; and Finished Goods Inventory, $52,810. April 30, 20x1 inventory account balances were Direct Materials Inventory, $186,250; Work in Process Inventory, $87,900; and Finished Goods Inventory, $56,620.

During the 20xx–20x1 fiscal year, $474,630 of direct materials were purchased, and payroll records indicated that direct labor costs totaled $215,970. Overhead costs for the period included indirect materials and supplies, $77,640; indirect labor, $192,710; depreciation, building, $19,900; depreciation, equipment, $14,240; heating, $19,810; electricity, $8,770; repairs and maintenance, $12,110; liability and fire insurance, $2,980; property taxes, building, $3,830; design and rework, $23,770; and supervision, $92,290. Other costs for the period included selling costs, $41,720, and administrative salaries, $102,750.

REQUIRED

Prepare a statement of cost of goods manufactured for the fiscal year ended April 30, 20x1.

P 3.

LO 4   *Statement of Cost of Goods Manufactured and Cost of Goods Sold*

Placita Corp. makes irrigation sprinkler systems for farmers in semi-arid and desert climates. Rajesh Balaji, the new controller for the organization, can find only partial information for the past year, which is presented below.

	Clovis Division	Lamesa Division	Childress Division	Grady Division
Direct materials used	$3	$ 7	$ g	$ 8
Total manufacturing costs	6	d	h	14
Manufacturing overhead costs	1	3	2	j
Direct labor costs	a	6	4	4
Ending Work in Process Inventory	b	3	2	5
Cost of goods manufactured	7	20	12	k
Beginning Work in Process Inventory	2	e	3	l
Ending Finished Goods Inventory	2	6	i	9
Beginning Finished Goods Inventory	3	f	5	7
Cost of goods sold	c	18	13	9

REQUIRED

Using the information given, compute the unknown values. Show your computations.

P 4.

LO 5   *Application of*
LO 6   *Manufacturing Overhead*

Classic Cosmetics Company applies manufacturing overhead costs on the basis of machine hours. The current predetermined overhead rate is computed by using data from the two prior years, in this case 20xx and 20x1, adjusted to reflect expectations for the current year, 20x2. The controller prepared the overhead rate analysis for 20x2 using the information at the top of the next page.

In 20x2, utilities are expected to increase by 40 percent over the previous year; indirect labor, employee benefits, and miscellaneous manufacturing overhead are expected to increase by 30 percent; insurance and depreciation are expected to increase by 20 percent; and supervision and janitorial services are expected to increase by 10 percent. Machine hours are expected to total 68,832.

	20xx	20x1
Machine hours	47,800	57,360
Manufacturing overhead costs:		
Indirect labor	$ 18,100	$ 23,530
Employee benefits	22,000	28,600
Manufacturing supervision	16,800	18,480
Utilities	10,350	14,490
Factory insurance	6,500	7,800
Janitorial services	11,000	12,100
Depreciation, factory and machinery	17,750	21,300
Miscellaneous manufacturing overhead	5,750	7,475
Total manufacturing overhead	$108,250	$133,775

REQUIRED

1. Compute the projected costs and the predetermined overhead rate for 20x2 using the information about expected cost increases. (Carry your answer to three decimal places.)
2. Assume that the company actually surpassed its sales and operating expectations in 20x2. Jobs completed during the year and the related machine hours used were as follows:

Job No.	Machine Hours
2214	12,300
2215	14,200
2216	9,800
2217	13,600
2218	11,300
2219	8,100

Total machine hours were 69,300. Determine the amount of manufacturing overhead to be applied to each job and to total production during 20x2. (Round answers to whole dollars.)

3. Assume that $165,845 of manufacturing overhead was incurred during the year. Was overhead underapplied or overapplied in 20x2? By how much? Should the Cost of Goods Sold account be increased or decreased to reflect actual manufacturing overhead costs?

P 5.
LO 8 *Activities and Activity-Based Costing*

Berina Computer Company, which has been in operation for ten years, produces a line of minicomputers. Holstrum, Ltd., placed an order for eighty minicomputers and the order has just been completed. Berina recently shifted to an activity-based system of cost assignment. Sandra Alvarez, the controller, is interested in finding out the impact that the ABC system had on the Holstrum order. Raw materials, purchased parts, and production labor costs for the Holstrum order are as follows:

Cost of raw materials	$36,750.00	Production direct labor hours	220
Cost of purchased parts	21,300.00	Average direct labor pay rate	$15.25

Other operating costs are as follows:

Traditional costing data using a single, plantwide overhead rate:
Manufacturing overhead costs were assigned at a rate of 270 percent of direct labor dollars.

Activity-based costing data:

Activities	Cost Drivers	Cost Pool Rates	Activity Usage for Holstrum Order
Electrical engineering design	Engineering hours	$19.50 per engineering hour	32 engineering hours
Work cell setup	Number of setups	$29.40 per setup	11 setups
Parts production work cell	Machine hours	$26.30 per machine hour	134 machine hours
Product testing cell	Cell hours	$32.80 per cell hour	52 cell hours
Packaging work cell	Cell hours	$17.50 per cell hour	22 cell hours

Building occupancy-related overhead costs are allocated at a rate of $9.80 per parts production work cell machine hour.

1. Using the traditional costing approach, compute the total cost of the Holstrum order.
2. Using the activity-based costing approach, compute the total cost of the Holstrum order.
3. What difference in the amount of cost assigned to the Holstrum order resulted from the shift to activity-based costing? Does the use of activity-based costing guarantee cost reduction for every product?

Alternate Problems

P 6.

LO 5 *Application of*
LO 6 *Manufacturing*
Overhead

Chan Products, Inc., uses a predetermined manufacturing overhead rate in its production, assembly, and testing departments. One rate is used for the entire company and is based on machine hours. The current rate was determined by analyzing data from the previous two years and projecting figures for the current year, adjusted for expected changes. Mr. Yu is about to compute the rate to be used in 20x3 using the following data.

	20x1	20x2
Machine hours	38,000	41,800
Manufacturing overhead costs:		
Indirect materials	$ 44,500	$ 57,850
Indirect labor	21,200	25,440
Supervision	37,800	41,580
Utilities	9,400	11,280
Labor-related costs	8,200	9,020
Depreciation, factory	9,800	10,780
Depreciation, machinery	22,700	27,240
Property taxes	2,400	2,880
Insurance	1,600	1,920
Miscellaneous manufacturing overhead	4,400	4,840
Total manufacturing overhead	$162,000	$192,830

In 20x3, indirect materials are expected to increase by 30 percent over the previous year. Indirect labor, utilities, machinery depreciation, property taxes, and insurance are expected to increase by 20 percent. All other expenses are expected to increase by 10 percent. Machine hours are estimated to be 45,980 for 20x3.

1. Compute the projected costs and the predetermined manufacturing overhead rate for year 20x3 using the information about expected cost increases. (Round your answer to three decimal places.)
2. During 20x3, Chan Products, Inc., produced the following jobs using the machine hours shown.

Job No.	Machine Hours	Job No.	Machine Hours
H–142	7,840	H–201	10,680
H–164	5,260	H–218	12,310
H–175	8,100	H–304	2,460

Determine the amount of manufacturing overhead applied to each job in 20x3. What was the total manufacturing overhead applied during the year? (Round answers to the nearest dollar.)
3. Actual manufacturing overhead for 20x3 was $234,485. Was overhead underapplied or overapplied in 20x3? By how much? Should the Cost of Goods Sold account be increased or decreased to reflect actual overhead costs?

P 7.

LO 8 *Activities and Activity-*
Based Costing

Maltz Products, Inc., produces a line of fax machines for wholesale distributors in the Pacific Northwest. Hines Company ordered 150 Model 14 fax machines and Maltz has just completed packaging the order. Before the Hines order is shipped, the controller has asked for a unit cost analysis comparing the amounts determined under the company's old traditional costing system with amounts computed under the new activity-based costing system. Raw materials, purchased parts, and production labor costs for the Hines order are as follows:

Cost of raw materials	$17,450.00	Production direct labor hours	140
Cost of purchased parts	$14,800.00	Average direct labor pay rate	$16.50

Other operating costs are as follows:

Traditional costing data using a single, plantwide overhead rate:
Manufacturing overhead costs were assigned at a rate of 240 percent of direct labor dollars.

Activity-based costing data:

Activities	Cost Drivers	Cost Pool Rates	Activity Usage for Hines Order
Engineering systems design	Engineering hours	$28.00 per engineering hour	18 engineering hours
Work cell setup	Number of setups	$42.00 per setup	8 setups
Parts production work cell	Machine hours	$37.50 per machine hour	84 machine hours
Product assembly cell	Cell hours	$44.00 per cell hour	36 cell hours
Packaging work cell	Cell hours	$28.50 per cell hour	28 cell hours

Building occupancy-related overhead costs are allocated at a rate of $10.40 per parts production work cell machine hour.

REQUIRED

1. Using the traditional costing approach with a single, plantwide overhead rate, compute the total cost of the Hines order.
2. Using the activity-based costing approach, compute the total cost of the Hines order.
3. What difference in the amount of cost assigned to the Hines order resulted from the shift to activity-based costing? Does the use of activity-based costing guarantee cost reduction for every product?

P 8.

LO 5
LO 6
LO 7
LO 8

Application of Manufacturing Overhead: Traditional and Activity-Based Costing Approaches

Shark Scout, Inc., manufactures underwater vehicles. Oil companies use the Rigger II to examine offshore oil rigs, and marine biology research foundations use the BioScout for research studies along coastlines. The company's San Diego factory is semiautomated and requires some direct labor. Blanca Gonzales, the controller, used normal costing to calculate the product unit cost for both product lines. Blanca calculated a traditional predetermined overhead rate of $13.75 per direct labor hour. A summary of the product unit cost and other relevant information under normal costing follow:

	Rigger II	BioScout
Product costs per unit:		
Direct materials	$ 10,000.00	$12,000.00
Direct labor	450.00	600.00
Manufacturing overhead	412.50*	550.00**
Product unit cost	$ 10,862.50	$13,150.00
Units of production	400	100
Estimated direct labor hours	12,000	4,000
Estimated manufacturing overhead costs	$220,000	

* Applied to Rigger II = $13.75 per direct labor hour × 30 direct labor hours per unit
** Applied to BioScout = $13.75 per direct labor hour × 40 direct labor hours per unit

Blanca believes that the product unit cost is too low for the BioScout line. After carefully watching the production process, she believes that the BioScout requires much more attention than the Rigger II, since suppliers perform many subassemblies for the Rigger II, and the intricate design of the BioScout requires more production-related activities to complete the production process. Blanca created four overhead activity pools, grouped the estimated manufacturing overhead costs into related cost pools, selected a cost driver for each pool, and estimated the cost driver for each product line, as shown in the following summary.

Overhead Activity Pool	Estimated Activity Cost Pool
Setup	$70,000
Inspection	20,000
Engineering	50,000
Assembly	80,000
Total	$220,000

Cost Driver	Rigger II Cost Driver Level	BioScout Cost Driver Level	Total Cost Driver Level
Number of setups	250	450	700
Number of inspections	150	350	500
Engineering hours	600	1,400	2,000
Machine hours	5,000	5,000	10,000

REQUIRED

1. Using the activity-based costing approach:
   a. Calculate the overhead cost pool rates for each cost pool.
   b. Compute the overhead costs applied to each product line by cost pool and in total.
   c. Calculate the product unit cost for each product line.
2. What differences in the costs assigned to the two product lines resulted from the shift to activity-based costing?

EXPANDING YOUR CRITICAL THINKING, COMMUNICATION, AND INTERPERSONAL SKILLS

Skills Development

CONCEPTUAL ANALYSIS

SD 1.

LO 5 *Computation of*
LO 6 *Predetermined Overhead*
LO 7 *Rates*

Both **Brown Company** and **Santo Corporation** use predetermined overhead rates for product costing, inventory valuation, and sales quotations. The two businesses are about the same size, and they compete in the corrugated box industry. Brown Company's management believes that because the predetermined overhead rate is an estimated measure, the controller's department should spend little effort in developing it. The company computes the rate once a year based on a trend analysis of the previous year's costs. No one monitors its accuracy during the year.

Santo Corporation takes a much more sophisticated approach. One person in the controller's office is responsible for developing predetermined overhead rates on a monthly basis. All cost estimates are checked carefully to make sure they are realistic. Accuracy checks are done routinely during each monthly closing analysis, and forecasts of changes in business activity are taken into account.

Assume you are a consultant who has been hired by the **Corwin Corporation,** an East Coast manufacturer of corrugated boxes. Lisa Nyman wants you to recommend the best approach for developing overhead rates. Based on your knowledge of the practices described above, write a memo to Lisa Nyman that will answer the following questions.

1. What are the advantages and disadvantages of each company's approach to developing predetermined overhead rates?
2. Which company has taken the more cost-effective approach to developing predetermined overhead rates? Defend your answer.
3. Is an accurate overhead rate most important for product costing, inventory valuation, or sales quotations? Why?
4. Would activity-based costing (ABC) be better than the two approaches discussed above? What conditions should exist before a company adopts ABC?

| Communication | Critical Thinking | Group Activity | Memo | Ethics | International | Spreadsheet | Managerial Technology | Internet |

ETHICAL DILEMMA

SD 2.

LO 9   *Preventing Pollution and the Costs of Waste Disposal*

Pleasanton Power Plant currently provides power to a metropolitan area of 4 million people. Tamika Simms, the controller for the plant, just returned from a conference about the Environmental Protection Agency's regulations concerning pollution prevention. She met with Jake Gates, the president of the company, to discuss the impact of the EPA's regulations on the plant.

"Jake, I'm really concerned. We haven't been monitoring the disposal of the radioactive material we send to the Digger Disposal Plant. If Digger is disposing of our waste material improperly, we could be sued," said Tamika. "We also haven't been recording the costs of the waste as part of our product cost. Ignoring that cost will have a negative impact on our decision about the next rate hike."

"Tamika, don't worry. I don't think we need to concern ourselves with the waste we send to Digger. We pay them to dispose of it. They take it off of our hands, and it's their responsibility to manage its disposal. As for the cost of waste disposal, I think we would have a hard time justifying a rate increase based on a requirement to record the full cost of waste as a cost of producing power. Let's just forget about waste and its disposal as a component of our power cost. We can get our rate increase without mentioning waste disposal," replied Jake.

What responsibility does Pleasanton Power Plant have to monitor the condition of the waste at the Digger Disposal Plant? Should Tamika take Jake's advice to ignore waste disposal costs in calculating the cost of power? Be prepared to discuss your response.

RESEARCH ACTIVITY

SD 3.

LO 2   *Variable and Fixed Costs*
LO 3

Make a trip to a local fast-food restaurant. Observe all aspects of the operation and take notes on the entire process. Describe the procedures used to take, process, and fill an order and get the food to the customer. Based on your observations, make a list of the costs incurred by the owner. Then identify at least three direct costs and three indirect costs of making sandwiches. Bring your notes to class and report your findings.

Group Activity: Divide the class into groups and ask them to discuss this SD. Then ask a person from each group to summarize his or her group's discussion.

DECISION-MAKING PRACTICE

SD 4.

LO 9   *Unit Costs for a Service Business*

Keaton Municipal Hospital relies heavily on cost data to keep its pricing structures in line with those of competitors. The hospital provides a wide range of services, including nursing care in intensive care units, intermediate care units, the neonatal (newborn) nursery, and nursing administration.

Ella Walton, the hospital's controller, is concerned about the profits being generated from the thirty-bed intensive care unit (ICU), so she is reviewing current billing procedures. The focus of Ella's analysis is Keaton's billing per patient day. The billing per patient day equals the cost of a patient day in the ICU plus a markup of an additional 40 percent of cost to cover other operating costs and to generate a profit.

ICU patient costs include the following:

Doctors' care	2 hours per day @ $360 per hour (actual)
Special nursing care	4 hours per day @ $85 per hour (actual)
Regular nursing care	24 hours per day @ $28 per hour (average)
Medications	$237 per day (average)
Medical supplies	$134 per day (average)
Room rental	$350 per day (average)
Food and services	$140 per day (average)

One other significant cost is equipment, which costs about $185,000 per room. Ella has determined that the cost per patient day for the equipment is $179.

Paul Sautter, the hospital director, has asked Ella to review the current billing procedure and compare it to another procedure using industry averages to determine the billing per patient day.

1. Compute the cost per patient per day.
2. Compute the billing per patient day using the hospital's existing markup rate. Round answers to whole dollars.

3. Many hospitals use separate markup rates for each cost when preparing billing statements. Industry averages revealed the following markup rates:

Equipment	30 percent	Medications	50
Doctors' care	50	Medical supplies	50
Special nursing care	40	Room rental	30
Regular nursing care	50	Food and services	25

Using these rates, recompute the billing per patient day in the ICU. Round answers to whole dollars.

4. Based on your findings in **2** and **3,** which billing procedure would you recommend to the hospital's director? Why? Be prepared to discuss your response.

Managerial Reporting and Analysis

INTERPRETING MANAGEMENT REPORTS

MRA 1.

LO 4 *Analyzing Financial Statements*

Rico Manufacturing Company makes sheet metal products for heating and air conditioning installations. For the past several years, the income of the company has been declining, and this past year, 20x1, was particularly poor. The company's statement of cost of goods manufactured and its income statement for 20xx and 20x1 are shown below and on the following page.

Rico Manufacturing Company
Statements of Cost of Goods Manufactured
For the Years Ended December 31, 20x1 and 20xx

	20x1		20xx	
Direct Materials Used				
Direct Materials Inventory, January 1	$ 91,240		$ 93,560	
Direct Materials Purchased (net)	987,640		959,940	
Cost of Direct Materials Available for Use	$1,078,880		$1,053,500	
Less Direct Materials Inventory, December 31	95,020		91,240	
Cost of Direct Materials Used		$ 983,860		$ 962,260
Direct Labor Costs		571,410		579,720
Manufacturing Overhead Costs				
Indirect Labor	$ 182,660		$ 171,980	
Power	34,990		32,550	
Insurance	22,430		18,530	
Supervision	125,330		120,050	
Depreciation	75,730		72,720	
Other Manufacturing Costs	41,740		36,280	
Total Manufacturing Overhead Costs		482,880		452,110
Total Manufacturing Costs		$2,038,150		$1,994,090
Add Work in Process Inventory, January 1		148,875		152,275
Total Cost of Work in Process During the Year		$2,187,025		$2,146,365
Less Work in Process Inventory, December 31		146,750		148,875
Cost of Goods Manufactured		$2,040,275		$1,997,490

Rico Manufacturing Company
Income Statements
For the Years Ended December 31, 20x1 and 20xx

	20x1		20xx	
Net Sales		$2,942,960		$3,096,220
Cost of Goods Sold				
Finished Goods Inventory,				
January 1	$ 142,640		$ 184,820	
Cost of Goods Manufactured	2,040,275		1,997,490	
Total Cost of Finished Goods				
Available for Sale	$2,182,915		$2,182,310	
Less Finished Goods				
Inventory, December 31	186,630		142,640	
Cost of Goods Sold		1,996,285		2,039,670
Gross Margin		$ 946,675		$1,056,550
Selling and Administrative Expenses				
Sales Salaries and				
Commission Expense	$ 394,840		$ 329,480	
Advertising Expense	116,110		194,290	
Other Selling Expenses	82,680		72,930	
Administrative Expenses	242,600		195,530	
Total Selling and Administrative Expenses		836,230		792,230
Income from Operations		$ 110,445		$ 264,320
Other Revenues and Expenses				
Interest Expense		54,160		56,815
Income Before Income Taxes		$ 56,285		$ 207,505
Less Income Taxes Expense		19,137		87,586
Net Income		$ 37,148		$ 119,919

You have been asked to comment on why the company's profitability has deteriorated.

REQUIRED

1. In preparing your comments on the decline in income, compute the following ratios for each year:
   a. Ratios of cost of direct materials used to total manufacturing costs, direct labor costs to total manufacturing costs, and total manufacturing overhead costs to total manufacturing costs. Round to one decimal place.
   b. Ratios of sales salaries and commission expense, advertising expense, other selling expenses, administrative expenses, and total selling and administrative expenses to net sales. Round to one decimal place.
   c. Ratios of gross margin to net sales, total selling and administrative expenses to net sales, and net income to net sales. Round to one decimal place.
2. From your evaluation of the ratios computed in **1,** state the probable causes of the decline in net income.
3. What other factors or ratios do you believe should be considered in determining the cause of the company's decreased income?

Formulating Management Reports

MRA 2.
LO 9 *Management Decision for a Supporting Service Function*

As the manager of grounds maintenance for **INNET**, a large insurance company in California, you are responsible for maintaining the grounds surrounding the three buildings, the six entrances to the property, and the recreational facilities, which include a golf course, a soccer field, jogging and bike paths, and tennis, basketball, and volleyball courts. Maintenance activities include gardening (watering, mowing, trimming, sweeping, and removing debris) and upkeep of land improvements (repairing concrete and gravel areas and replacing damaged or worn recreational equipment).

Early in January 20x2, you received a memo from the president requesting information about the cost of operating your department for the last twelve months. She has received a bid from Fantastic Landscapes, Inc., to perform the gardening activities you now perform. You are to prepare a cost report that will help the president in deciding whether to continue gardening activities within the company or to outsource the work to another company.

REQUIRED

1. Before preparing your report, answer the following questions.
   a. What kinds of information do you need about your department?
   b. Why is this information relevant?
   c. Where would you go to obtain this information (sources)?
   d. When would you want to obtain this information?
2. Prepare a draft of the cost report that would best communicate the costs of your department. Show only headings and line items. How would you change your report if the president asked you to reduce the costs of operating your department?
3. One of your department's costs is Maintenance Expense, Garden Equipment.
   a. Is it a direct or indirect cost for the Grounds Maintenance Department?
   b. Is it a product or a period cost?
   c. Is it a variable or a fixed cost?
   d. Does the activity add value to the provision of insurance services?
   e. Is it a budgeted or an actual cost in your report?

International Company

MRA 3.
LO 4 *Management Information Needs*

The **Muntok Pharmaceuticals Corporation** manufactures the majority of its three pharmaceutical products in Indonesia. Inventory information for April 20x1 was as follows:

Account	April 30	April 1
Direct Materials Inventory	$228,100	$258,400
Work in Process Inventory	127,200	138,800
Finished Goods Inventory	114,100	111,700

Purchases of direct materials for April were $612,600, which included natural materials, basic organic compounds, catalysts, and suspension agents. Direct labor costs were $160,000, and actual manufacturing overhead costs were $303,500. Net sales for the company's three pharmaceutical products for April were $2,188,400. General and administrative expenses were $362,000. Income is taxed at a rate of 34 percent.

REQUIRED

1. Prepare a statement of cost of goods manufactured and an income statement for the month ended April 30.
2. Explain why the total manufacturing costs do not equal the cost of goods manufactured.
3. What additional information would you need to determine the profitability of each pharmaceutical product line?
4. Tell whether each of the following is a product cost or a period cost:
   a. Import duties for suspension agent materials
   b. Shipping expenses to deliver manufactured products to the United States
   c. Rent on manufacturing facilities in Jakarta
   d. Salary of the American production line manager working at the Indonesian manufacturing facilities
   e. Training costs for an Indonesian accountant

EXCEL SPREADSHEET ANALYSIS

MRA 4.

LO 5   *Application of*
LO 6   *Manufacturing*
LO 7   *Overhead: Traditional*
LO 8   *and Activity-Based*
         Costing Approaches

REQUIRED

Refer to assignment **P 8** in this chapter. Assume that Blanca Gonzales, the controller of Shark Scout, Inc., has received some additional information from the production manager, James Koloc. Mr. Koloc reported that robotic equipment has been installed on the factory floor to increase productivity. Depreciation and other machine costs for the robots will increase total manufacturing overhead from $220,000 to $320,000 for the year, which will increase the assembly activity cost pool from $80,000 to $180,000. The cost driver level for the assembly cost pool will change from 5,000 machine hours to 2,000 machine hours for the Rigger II and from 5,000 machine hours to 8,000 machine hours for the BioScout. The cost driver levels and cost pool amounts for setup, inspection, and engineering activities will remain the same.

1. Using the traditional approach:
   a. Calculate the predetermined overhead rate.
   b. Compute the amount of the total manufacturing overhead costs applied to each product line.
   c. Calculate the product unit cost for each product line.
2. Using the activity-based costing approach:
   a. Calculate the manufacturing overhead cost pool rates for each cost pool.
   b. Compute the manufacturing overhead costs applied to each product line by cost pool and in total.
   c. Calculate the product unit cost for each product line.
3. Complete the following table and discuss the differences in the costs assigned to the two product lines resulting from the additional information in this assignment.

Product unit cost	Rigger II	BioScout
Traditional		
Activity-based costing		
Difference: decrease (increase)		

ENDNOTES

1. Tim R.V. Davis and Bruce L. Darling, "ABC in a Virtual Corporation," *Management Accounting*, Institute of Management Accountants, October 1996, pp. 18–26.

2. Neal R. Pemberton, Logan Arumugam, and Nabil Hassan, "From Obstacles to Opportunities," *Management Accounting*, Institute of Management Accountants, March 1996, pp. 20–27.

3. Kathy Williams and James Hart, "Walker: Deploying a Mainframe Solution," *Management Accounting*, Institute of Management Accountants, June 1997, pp. 49–52.

Costing Systems: Job Order Costing

1. Discuss the role costing information plays in the management cycle and explain why product unit cost is important.
2. Distinguish between the different types of product costing systems and identify the information each provides.
3. Explain the cost flow in a job order costing system for a manufacturing company.
4. Prepare a job order cost card and compute a job order's product unit cost.
5. Apply job order costing to a service organization.
6. Distinguish between job order costing and project costing.

DECISION POINT

LEVI STRAUSS & CO.

Whatever your size, Levi Strauss has the jeans that fit. Recently, Levi Strauss & Co. expanded its product strategy. In addition to producing large quantities of quality jeans in a limited variety of styles for retailers, the company began a product line of made-to-order jeans. Personal Pair jeans by Levi Strauss & Co. combine customer service with point of sale and manufacturing technology to deliver customized jeans that are guaranteed to fit.[1] The process begins when the customer's measurements are entered into the store's computer along with the customer's preference for jean length, leg opening, and color. A customer may choose from over 400 different jean prototypes. A computer link transmits the order from the store to the Levi Strauss & Co. manufacturing plant. At the factory, denim is cut to the order's specifications using state-of-the-art cutting technology. A skilled, specialized team sews the denim pieces together, and then the jeans are washed. Just before shipping, the customer's fit data are imprinted on the inside of the jeans, using a special bar code. The jeans are finally delivered either to the store or to the customer's home. The whole process takes less than three weeks to complete.

Did the methods used to make custom jeans fit Levi Strauss's existing product costing system? Why would the company consider implementing a new product costing system for Personal Pair? What performance measures would be most useful in evaluating the results of each type of business?

The type of business usually determines the product costing system that should be used. The Personal Pair approach involves producing unique, made-to-order jeans according to the specific requirements given in an individual's order. Levi Strauss & Co.'s core business is based on producing a continuous flow of certain styles of identical jeans. Because the production processes differ, each business probably will need its own costing system to determine the cost of a pair of jeans.

How the cost of a pair of jeans is computed differs because the approach to manufacturing custom orders differs from the approach to manufacturing large quantities of similar products. When products are custom-made, it is possible to collect the costs of each order. When a product is mass-produced, however, specific costs cannot be collected because there is a continuous flow of similar products. Instead, costs are collected by process, department, or activity.

Performance measures will also differ for Levi Strauss & Co.'s two types of jean businesses. For the Personal Pair business, management can measure the profitability of each order by comparing the order's cost and price. For the mass-produced jeans business, management will measure performance by comparing the budgeted and actual costs for a process or department.

Costing Information and the Management Cycle

OBJECTIVE 1

Discuss the role costing information plays in the management cycle and explain why product unit cost is important

Managers depend on relevant and reliable costing information to manage their organizations. The role of the management accountant is to develop a management information system that provides managers with the product costing information they need. Although companies vary in their approaches to gathering, analyzing, and reporting costing information, managers share the same basic concerns as they move through the management cycle. Figure 1 summarizes the management cycle and the concerns the management accountant addresses with relevant and timely costing information. Let's use the Decision Point about Levi Strauss & Co.'s Personal Pair to illustrate the use of costing information in the management cycle.

During the planning stage, knowledge of unit costs helps managers determine reasonable selling prices for products or services, and how much those products or services should cost to deliver. In addition, managers use costing information to forecast future costs and create budgets for the next operating period. Managers at Levi Strauss & Co. want to take less than three weeks to produce and deliver a pair of custom-made jeans for a reasonable selling price. Knowing the costs of making a pair of custom-made jeans helps the managers estimate the sales revenues and operating costs for that product line.

Managers often make decisions about the quality and cost of a product or service. For example, managers at Levi Strauss & Co. may decide to improve the quality of a product or to lower a product's unit cost by using cheaper direct materials. Such decisions are implemented during the executing stage of the management cycle by making changes in design, purchasing, or production.

A decision to change a product's quality or cost can have far-reaching effects. For example, a decision to improve quality may cause jeans costs to rise, and a decision to cut product costs may cause quality to decline. Managers watch for such changes during the reviewing stage of the management cycle. The information that is gathered during the reviewing stage enables managers to control operations and costs. If operating costs have risen too high, a product unit cost for a pair of jeans can be broken down into its many components to analyze where costs can be cut. If product quality is suffering, the design, purchasing, and production processes can be studied to determine the sources of the problem.

Finally, during the reporting stage of the management cycle, the management accountant prepares internal reports that compare the period's actual product costs with budgeted costs. These comparisons help managers to determine whether the

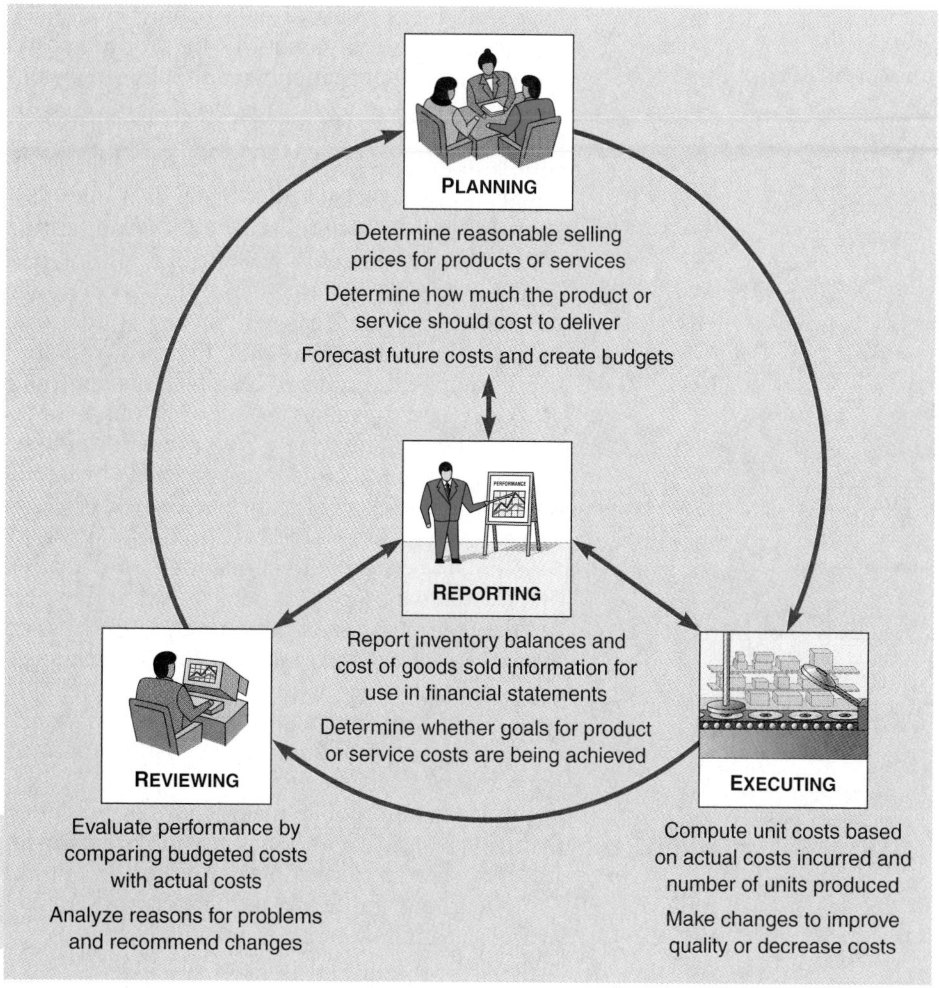

PLANNING

Determine reasonable selling prices for products or services

Determine how much the product or service should cost to deliver

Forecast future costs and create budgets

REPORTING

Report inventory balances and cost of goods sold information for use in financial statements

Determine whether goals for product or service costs are being achieved

REVIEWING

Evaluate performance by comparing budgeted costs with actual costs

Analyze reasons for problems and recommend changes

EXECUTING

Compute unit costs based on actual costs incurred and number of units produced

Make changes to improve quality or decrease costs

Figure 1
Uses of Product Costing Information in the Management Cycle

goals for product or service costs are being achieved. Managers at Levi Strauss & Co. use such reports to assess and adjust operations and plan for the future. Product unit costs are also used to determine the inventory balances on an organization's balance sheet and the cost of goods sold on its income statement.

Job Order Versus Process Costing

OBJECTIVE 2

Distinguish between the different types of product costing systems and identify the information each provides

For an organization to succeed, its managers must sell its products or services at prices that exceed the costs of creating and delivering those products or services and provide a reasonable profit. Thus, managers need extensive information about such product-related costs as setup, production, and distribution. To meet managers' needs for costing information, the management accountant must develop a highly reliable product costing system that is specifically designed to record and report the organization's operations. A product costing system is a set of procedures used to account for an organization's product costs and provide timely and accurate unit cost information for pricing, cost planning and control, inventory valuation, and financial statement preparation.

The product costing system enables managers to track costs throughout the management cycle. It provides a structure for recording the revenue earned from sales and the costs incurred for direct materials, direct labor, and manufacturing overhead. Each transaction in the product costing system is supported by source documents that are generated either internally or externally.

Two basic product costing systems have been developed: job order costing and process costing. A job order costing system is a product costing system used by companies that make large, unique, or special-order products, such as customized publications, specially-built cabinets, made-to-order draperies, or, as in our Decision Point, Levi Strauss & Co.'s Personal Pair jeans. Under such a system, the costs of direct materials, direct labor, and manufacturing overhead are traced to a specific job order or batch of products. A job order is a customer order for a specific number of specially designed, made-to-order products. Job order costing measures the cost of each complete unit. It uses a Work in Process Inventory Control account to summarize the costs of all jobs. This control account is supported by job order cost cards or a subsidiary ledger of accounts for each job.

A process costing system is a product costing system used by companies that produce large amounts of similar products or liquids, or that have a continuous production flow. Makers of paint, soft drinks, bricks, milk, or paper would use a process costing system, as would Levi Strauss & Co.'s traditional jeans business. Under such a system, the costs of direct materials, direct labor, and manufacturing overhead are first traced to a process or department and then assigned to the products manufactured by that process or department. A process costing system uses several Work in Process Inventory accounts, one for each department or process.

In reality, few actual production processes match either a job order costing system or a process costing system perfectly. Thus, the typical product costing system combines parts of both job order costing and process costing to create a hybrid system designed specifically for the organization's particular production process. For example, an automobile maker may use process costing to track the costs of manufacturing a basic car and then use job order costing to track the costs of customized features, such as convertible or hardtop, or automatic transmission or stick shift.

By learning the terms and procedures related to both the job order and the process costing systems, managers can adapt to any operating environment and help design product costing systems that fit their specific information needs.

In recent years, approaches to product costing have continued to change as a result of global competition, the limited capital available to finance organizational

growth, and the shifting mix of materials, labor, and overhead in the manufacturing process. The use of multidisciplinary teams of managers has encouraged the exploration of new management accounting practices to improve product costing. New practices emphasize the elimination of waste, the importance of quality, decreased production costs, more efficient processing, and increased customer satisfaction. Some of the new practices, including the value chain, process value analysis, activity-based management, and the just-in-time operating environment, will be discussed later.

Job Order Costing in a Manufacturing Company

OBJECTIVE 3

Explain the cost flow in a job order costing system for a manufacturing company

Remember that a job order costing system is designed to gather costs for a specific order or batch of products to help determine product unit costs. Price setting, production scheduling, and other management tasks related to job orders depend on information from the management accounting system. This is why it is necessary to maintain a system that gives timely, correct data about product costs. In this section, we see how the three main cost elements—materials, labor, and manufacturing overhead—are accounted for in a job order costing system. Notice that all inventory balances in a job order costing system are kept on a perpetual basis and that all production costs are included in the analysis.

Incurring Materials, Labor, and Manufacturing Overhead Costs

A basic part of a job order costing system is the set of procedures and accounts used when the company incurs materials, labor, and manufacturing overhead costs. To help control such costs, businesses use various documents to support each transaction. The effective use of procedures and documents generates timely, accurate information for managers and facilitates the smooth and continuous flow of information through the accounting records.

Materials   Careful use of materials improves a company's overall efficiency and profitability by conserving productive resources and saving their related costs. At the same time, good records ensure accountability. So, controlling the physical materials used in production and keeping good records increase the opportunity to earn a profit.

To help record and control materials costs, accountants rely on a series of documents, including purchase requisitions, purchase orders, receiving reports, inventory records, and materials requisitions. Through these documents, materials are ordered, received, stored, and issued into production. Information from purchase requisitions enables the tracing of direct materials costs to specific jobs or batches of product, and identifies the amount of indirect materials to be charged to manufacturing overhead.

Labor   Labor is one production resource that cannot be stored and used later, so it must be accounted for carefully. Time cards and job cards are used to record labor costs as they are incurred. Time cards keep track of the total amount of time each employee works per day, and job cards track the amount of time each employee works on a particular job or other labor classification. Direct labor costs that can be traced directly to a job or batch of products are charged to the Work in Process Inventory Control account, and all indirect labor costs flow through the Manufacturing Overhead Control account.

Manufacturing Overhead   All indirect manufacturing costs are classified as manufacturing overhead. Like direct materials and direct labor costs, manufacturing overhead costs require documents to support their recording and payment. As described above, materials requisitions support the use of indirect materials and supplies, and job cards track indirect labor; vendors' invoices support most of the other indirect costs. In a job order costing system, all manufacturing overhead costs are charged to the Manufacturing Overhead Control account, and separate subsidiary accounts are maintained to keep track of the individual kinds of overhead costs. Using a predetermined overhead rate, manufacturing overhead costs are assigned to individual jobs by decreasing the Manufacturing Overhead Control account and increasing the Work in Process Inventory Control account.

Exhibit 1. The Job Order Costing System—Wasa Boat Company

Materials Inventory Control

Beg. Bal.	123,000	Requisitions:		
(1) Purchases	91,200	Direct Materials	188,000	(3)
(2) Purchases	8,200	Supplies	9,600	(3)
End. Bal.	24,800			

Work in Process Inventory Control

Beg. Bal.	40,080			
(3) Direct Materials Used	188,000	Completed	388,080	(9)
(5) Direct Labor	164,000			
(8) Overhead	139,400			
End. Bal.	143,400			

Factory Labor

(4) Wages Earned	240,000	Direct Labor	164,000	(5)
		Indirect Labor	76,000	(5)

Manufacturing Overhead Control

(3) Supplies Used	9,600	Applied	139,400 (8)
(5) Indirect Labor	76,000		
(6) Other	29,500		
(7) Adjustment	24,000		
	139,100		139,400
(11) To close	300		
	—		

SUBSIDIARY LEDGERS

MATERIALS LEDGER

Material 5X

Beg. Bal.	83,000	Used	124,000	(3)
(1) Purchases	57,200			
End. Bal.	16,200			

Material 14Q

Beg. Bal.	37,000	Used	64,000	(3)
(1) Purchases	34,000			
End. Bal.	7,000			

Operating Supplies Inventory

Beg. Bal.	3,000	Used	9,600	(3)
(2) Purchases	8,200			
End. Bal.	1,600			

JOB ORDER COST CARDS

Job 16F

Costs from the previous period	40,080
Direct Materials	103,800
Direct Labor	132,000
Manufacturing Overhead	112,200
Completed Cost	388,080

Job 23H

Direct Materials	84,200
Direct Labor	32,000
Manufacturing Overhead	27,200
Ending Balance	143,400

Cost Flow in a Job Order Costing System

Because a job order costing system emphasizes cost flow, it is important to understand how the various costs are incurred, recorded, and transferred within the system. This cost flow, along with the job order cost cards and the subsidiary ledgers for materials and finished goods inventories, forms the core of the job order costing system. Understanding the cost flow enables you to fully understand how the system works. The job order cost flow at Wasa Boat Company is diagrammed in Exhibit 1. Referring to Exhibit 1 will help you picture the flow of each cost in the following discussion.

Exhibit 1. The Job Order Costing System—Wasa Boat Company (continued)

Finished Goods Inventory Control

Beg. Bal.	—	Sold	352,800 (10)
(9) Completed During Period	388,080		
End. Bal.	35,280		

Cost of Goods Sold

(10) Sold During Period	352,800	Adjustment	300 (11)
End. Bal.	352,500		

FINISHED GOODS LEDGER

Product 16F

Beg. Bal.	—	Sold	352,800 (10)
(9) Completed	388,080		
End. Bal.	35,280		

Product 23H

Beg. Bal.	—

Beginning Inventory Balances   In Exhibit 1, the word *control* is found in all three inventory account titles, which means that each inventory account has a subsidiary ledger backing up its totals. The beginning balance of the Materials Inventory Control account is $123,000. This includes $83,000 of Material 5X, $37,000 of Material 14Q, and $3,000 of operating supplies. Those amounts correspond to the beginning balances in the materials subsidiary ledger, shown in the lower part of Exhibit 1. The Work in Process Inventory Control account's beginning balance of $40,080 is related entirely to Job 16F, as shown on the subsidiary ledger's job order cost card. There is no beginning balance in Finished Goods Inventory Control, which means that all previously completed orders have been shipped.

Purchase of Direct Materials and Supplies   During the period, the Wasa Boat Company bought direct materials and supplies totaling $99,400. Two transactions supported those purchases. Transaction 1 totaled $91,200 and involved the purchase of $57,200 of Material 5X and $34,000 of Material 14Q. Transaction 2 was the purchase of $8,200 of operating supplies.

Requisition of Direct Materials and Supplies into Production   Transaction 3 shows the requisition of direct materials and supplies into production. A total of $188,000 of direct materials costs are transferred from the Materials Inventory Control account to the Work in Process Inventory Control account. From the materials subsidiary ledger, you can see that the $188,000 is made up of $124,000 of Material 5X and $64,000 of Material 14Q. In addition, $9,600 of operating supplies were used. Since supplies are an indirect material, their cost was transferred to the Manufacturing Overhead Control account.

Labor Costs for the Period   The total cost of factory labor for the period was $240,000. As shown by Transaction 4, this amount was entered in the Factory Labor account. Factory Labor is a clearing account, which means that it holds costs for only a short time, until they are distributed to the various production accounts. This distribution is shown in Transaction 5. Of the total, $164,000 is for direct labor and is transferred directly to the Work in Process Inventory Control account. The remaining $76,000 is for indirect labor and is transferred to the Manufacturing Overhead Control account.

Accounting for Other Manufacturing Overhead Costs   Thus far, indirect materials and indirect labor have been the only costs charged to the Manufacturing Overhead Control account. Transaction 6 shows that other cash payments totaling $29,500 have also been made during the period. Those cash payments were for electricity, $6,300; maintenance and repairs, $16,900; factory liability and fire insurance, $2,800; and property taxes, $3,500. The noncash expense of depreciation must also be accounted for in Manufacturing Overhead. Transaction 7 records an adjustment of $24,000 for the depreciation of plant, machinery, and equipment.

Applying Manufacturing Overhead Costs to Production   For manufacturing overhead costs to be included in the production costs of the period, they must be applied using a predetermined overhead rate. The Wasa Boat Company's current overhead rate is 85 percent of direct labor dollars. In Transaction 8, manufacturing overhead costs are applied to production by transferring $139,400 (85% of $164,000) from the Manufacturing Overhead Control account to the Work in Process Inventory Control account.

Tracing Costs to Specific Jobs   At this point, all of the period's production costs have been transferred to the Work in Process Inventory Control account. Now it is necessary to relate the costs to specific jobs. This is done by tracing each cost in the

Work in Process Inventory Control account to the job order cost cards in the subsidiary ledgers. (A job order cost card is a document on which all costs incurred in the production of a particular job order are recorded.) The Work in Process Inventory Control account at the top of Exhibit 1 shows that the total cost of direct materials used was $188,000. By looking at the job order cost cards at the bottom of Exhibit 1, you can see that $103,800 of the total cost of direct materials was used for Job 16F and $84,200 was used for Job 23H. In the same way, the total direct labor costs of $164,000 can be traced to $132,000 for Job 16F and $32,000 for Job 23H. And the total manufacturing overhead cost of $139,400 can be traced to $112,200 for Job 16F and $27,200 for Job 23H.

At the end of the period, Job 16F has a total cost of $388,080 and Job 23H has a total cost of $143,400. At this point, Job 16F has been completed, and so its total cost is transferred to the Finished Goods Inventory Control account, as shown by Transaction 9. The ending balance in the Work in Process Inventory Control account is $143,400. That amount corresponds to the ending balance shown on the job order cost card for Job 23H because Job 23H is still in process at the end of the period.

Accounting for Completed Units   The costs of completed units are placed in the Finished Goods Inventory Control account until the units are shipped to customers. At the Wasa Boat Company, units costing $388,080 (Job 16F) were completed and transferred to the Finished Goods Inventory Control account during the period. Units from Job 16F with costs totaling $352,800 were then sold to customers, as shown by Transaction 10. Their sale left an ending balance of $35,280 in the Finished Goods Inventory Control account. That balance corresponds to the ending balance for Product 16F in the finished goods subsidiary ledger.

Accounting for Units Sold   The costs of all units sold during the period are transferred from the Finished Goods Inventory Control account to the Cost of Goods Sold account. Transaction 10 shows this transfer of costs at the Wasa Boat Company.

Disposing of Underapplied or Overapplied Overhead   For the final step, we return to the Manufacturing Overhead Control account. During the period, a total of $139,100 was charged to this account and $139,400 of manufacturing overhead was applied to production activities. As a result, manufacturing overhead was overapplied by $300. Rather than trying to trace such a small amount to all of the units worked on during the period, the company prefers to close the overapplied balance to the Cost of Goods Sold account. Since production was overcharged by the amount of overapplied overhead, Transaction 11 closes out the balance in the Manufacturing Overhead Control account and reduces the total charges in the Cost of Goods Sold account by the $300.

The Job Order Cost Card

OBJECTIVE 4

Prepare a job order cost card and compute a job order's product unit cost

As shown in the discussion of Exhibit 1, job order cost cards play a key role in the job order costing system. Because all manufacturing costs are accumulated in the Work in Process Inventory Control account, a separate accounting procedure is needed to relate those costs to specific jobs. The solution is a subsidiary ledger made up of job order cost cards. Each job being worked on has a job order cost card. As costs are incurred, they are classified by job and recorded on the appropriate job order cost card.

A typical job order cost card is shown in Figure 2. Each card has space for direct materials, direct labor, and manufacturing overhead costs. It also includes the job order number, product specifications, the name of the customer, the date of the order, the projected completion date, and a cost summary. As each department incurs direct materials and direct labor costs, the individual job order cost cards are

JOB ORDER COST CARD
Wasa Boat Company
New Port Richey, Florida

Job Order No. **16F**

Product Specs: **Model GB30-Mark I: 30 foot fiberglass sailing sloop with full galley**

Customer: **Hinds Yachts, Inc.**

Date of Order: **February 10, 20xx**

Date of Completion: **October 28, 20xx**

Cost Summary:
Direct Materials **$120,200**
Direct Labor **144,800**
Manufacturing Overhead **123,080**
Total **$388,080**
Units Completed **11 (eleven)**
Product Unit Cost **$35,280**

Direct Materials:
Dept. 1 **$96,500**
Dept. 2 **23,700**
Dept. 3 **–0–**
Total **$120,200**

Direct Labor:
Dept. 1 **$43,440**
Dept. 2 **60,960**
Dept. 3 **40,400**
Total **$144,800**

Applied Manufacturing Overhead:
Dept. 1 **$36,924**
Dept. 2 **51,816**
Dept. 3 **34,340**
Total **$123,080**

Figure 2
Job Order Cost Card–
Manufacturing Company

updated. Manufacturing overhead, as applied, is also posted to the job order cost cards. Job order cost cards for incomplete jobs make up the subsidiary ledger for the Work in Process Inventory Control account. To ensure correctness, the ending balance in the Work in Process Inventory Control account is compared with the total of the costs shown on the job order cost cards.

Computing Product Unit Costs

Product unit costs are fairly simple to calculate in a job order costing system. All costs of direct materials, direct labor, and manufacturing overhead are recorded on a job order cost card as a job progresses toward completion. When a job is finished, the costs on its job order cost card are totaled. The product unit cost is computed by dividing the total costs for the job by the number of good units produced.

The cost data for completed Job 16F are shown on the job order cost card in Figure 2. Eleven sailing sloops were produced at a total cost of $388,080. This worked out to a cost of $35,280 per sloop before adjustments. As shown in Exhibit 1, however, only ten of the sloops were actually shipped during the year. Because the amount of overapplied overhead was small, the entire $300 was used to reduce the cost of the ten sloops sold. The cost of one sloop still remains in the Finished Goods Inventory Control account at the unadjusted amount.

BUSINESS BULLETIN: BUSINESS PRACTICE

Some companies, such as R. R. Donnelley and Sons Company, AMOCO, and Hexacomb Corporation, have adopted open-book management practices to encourage employee accountability and responsibility for results. Companies that practice open-book management make the organization's financial records available to all interested parties. Employees are taught the basics of budgeting, product costing, and key performance measures. By attending regular meetings, or huddles, where the organization's or their department's scoreboard is discussed, employees learn how their job actions affect the organization's performance. The scoreboard contains information about the company's income statement, balance sheet, and other key performance measures. Since employee compensation is tied to scoreboard results, employees can see that by improving the company's financial performance , they will undoubtedly increase their own financial success.[3]

Job Order Costing in a Service Organization

OBJECTIVE 5

Apply job order costing to a service organization

Many service organizations use job order costing to compute the cost of providing their services. The only significant difference between service and manufacturing organizations is that in service organizations, costs are not associated with a physical product that can be assembled, stored, and valued. Services are rendered and cannot be held in inventory. Examples of services include auto repair, swimming pool maintenance, income tax return preparation, Red Cross disaster relief, and medical care. Because service organizations do not manufacture products, they have little or no cost for materials. The most important cost in a service organization is labor, which is carefully accounted for through the use of time cards.

The cost flow for services is similar to the cost flow for manufactured products. Job order cost cards are used to keep track of the costs incurred for each job. Job costs include labor, materials and supplies, and service overhead. For many service organizations, each job is based on a contract that requires the customer to pay for all costs incurred plus a predetermined amount of profit. Such contracts are called cost-plus contracts, and the "plus" provides a profit based on the amount of costs incurred. When the job is complete, the costs on the completed job order cost card become the cost of services. The cost of services is adjusted at the end of the accounting period for the difference between the applied service overhead costs and the actual service overhead costs.

For example, Gartner Landscaping Services employs fifteen people and serves the San Francisco Bay area. The company earns its revenue from designing and installing landscapes for homes and offices. The job order cost card for the Rico Corporation's landscaping job is shown in Figure 3. Costs have been categorized into three separate activities: Landscape Design, Landscape Installation, and Job-Site Cleanup. Costs have been tracked to the Rico Corporation job for its duration, and now that the job is finished, it is time to complete the job order cost card. The service overhead charge for Landscape Design is 40 percent of design labor cost, and the service overhead cost for Landscape Installation is 50 percent of installation labor cost. Total costs incurred for this job were $5,400. The cost-plus contract has a 15 percent profit guarantee; therefore, $810 of profit margin is added to the total cost to arrive at the total contract revenue of $6,210, which is the amount billed to Rico.

JOB ORDER COST CARD
Gartner Landscaping Services

Customer: Rico Corporation
Job Order Number: _____
Contract Type: Cost-Plus
Type of Service: Landscape Corporate Headquarters
Date Completed: May 31, 20xx

Costs Charged to Job	Previous Months	Current Month	Total Cost
Landscape Design			
Supplies	$ 100	$ –	$ 100
Design Labor	850	–	850
Service Overhead (40% of design labor)	340	–	340
Totals	$1,290	$ –	$1,290
Landscape Installation			
Planting Materials	$ 970	$1,200	$2,170
Installation Labor	400	620	1,020
Service Overhead (50% of installation labor)	200	310	510
Totals	$1,570	$2,130	$3,700
Job-Site Cleanup			
Janitorial Service Cost	$ 90	$ 320	$ 410
Totals	$2,950	$2,450	$5,400

Cost Summary to Date	Total Cost
Landscape Design	$ 1,290
Landscape Installation	3,700
Job-Site Cleanup	410
Totals	$ 5,400
Profit Margin (15%)	810
Contract Revenue	$ 6,210

Figure 3
Job Order Cost Card–
Service Organization

Job Order Costing Versus Project Costing

OBJECTIVE 6

Distinguish between job order costing and project costing

While the concept of a job order costing system that collects the costs of direct materials, direct labor, and manufacturing overhead by specific job order to make unique items or special-order products remains valid, new approaches to costing for more complex products and services are being developed. In today's business environment, many jobs have become extremely complex, take a long time to complete, and require the talents of many departments, consultants, and subcontractors. They have evolved into projects, which are broad, complex, multidisciplinary

BUSINESS BULLETIN: ETHICS IN PRACTICE

A tip from the Department of Defense's fraud hotline triggered another audit of The Boeing Co. by the Inspector General, the watchdog agency for the Pentagon. The audit found several examples of overcharging for parts, including charging $1.24 for each of 31,108 springs previously priced at five cents and $403 each for 246 actuator sleeves priced earlier at $24.72.

Boeing spokesperson Dick Dalton said, "This is a story that looks a whole lot worse than it is." According to Boeing, the audit quoted prices that dated back fifteen to twenty years when the Pentagon bought and stored large quantities of products. Today, the Pentagon receives small deliveries of parts on short notice, as needed. The new system saves the Pentagon huge inventory storage costs, but the price per part is higher because of the higher cost of frequent deliveries and on-demand ordering.

The Inspector General, Eleanor Hill, told a Senate Armed Services subcommittee, "We found considerable evidence that the Department of Defense had not yet learned how to be an astute buyer in the commercial marketplace."[4]

approaches to the production of goods or services. Examples of projects include the construction of a building or the development of a computer software program. Effective project management requires a product costing system that accommodates today's environment of multidisciplinary work groups, neighborhoods of shared computer files, and multitasking computers. In the past, managers tended to focus on products or customer requests one at a time. Today, however, managers must develop the ability to coordinate many jobs or tasks being performed at many different times in many different places. Therefore, project costing links many different job orders and processes by transferring costs from one job or process to another, collecting and summarizing costs in a variety of ways, and providing appropriate internal controls to manage these complicated projects. The detailed processes involved in project costing and project management are covered in more advanced accounting courses.

Chapter Review

REVIEW OF LEARNING OBJECTIVES

1. Discuss the role costing information plays in the management cycle and explain why product unit cost is important. During the planning stage, costing information helps managers to determine reasonable selling prices for products or services, to determine how much those products or services should cost to deliver, and to forecast future costs and create budgets for the next operating period. During the executing stage, managers compute unit costs based on actual costs incurred and make changes to improve quality or decrease costs. During the reviewing stage, managers evaluate performance by comparing budgeted costs with actual costs, analyze reasons for problems, and recommend changes. During the reporting stage, reports comparing actual product costs with budgeted costs help managers to determine whether goals for product or service costs are being achieved. Product unit costs are used to determine the inventory balances reported on the balance sheet and the cost of goods sold reported on the income statement, so they also assist in financial reporting.

2. **Distinguish between the different types of product costing systems and identify the information each provides.** The job order costing system is a product costing system used by companies that make large, unique, or special-order products. Under such a system, the costs of direct materials, direct labor, and manufacturing overhead are traced to a specific job order or batch of products. Job order costing measures the cost of each complete unit and summarizes the cost of all jobs in a Work in Process Control account that is supported by job cost cards or a subsidiary ledger of accounts for each job.

   A process costing system is a product costing system used by companies that produce large amounts of similar products or liquids, or that have a continuous production flow. Under such a system, the costs of direct materials, direct labor, and manufacturing overhead are first traced to a process or department and then assigned to the products manufactured by that process or department. Process costing uses several Work in Process Inventory accounts, one for each department or process.

3. **Explain the cost flow in a job order costing system for a manufacturing company.** A job order costing system uses a perpetual inventory approach. The costs of direct materials and supplies are first charged to the Materials Inventory Control account and to the respective materials accounts in the subsidiary ledger. Labor costs are first accumulated in the Factory Labor account. The various manufacturing overhead costs are charged to the Manufacturing Overhead Control account. As products are manufactured, the costs of direct materials and direct labor are transferred to the Work in Process Inventory Control account. Manufacturing overhead costs are applied and charged to the Work in Process Inventory Control account using a predetermined overhead rate. Those charges are used to reduce the balance in the Manufacturing Overhead Control account. When products and jobs are complete, the costs assigned to them are transferred to the Finished Goods Inventory Control account. Then, when the products are sold and shipped, their costs are transferred to the Cost of Goods Sold account.

4. **Prepare a job order cost card and compute a job order's product unit cost.** All costs of direct materials, direct labor, and manufacturing overhead for a particular job are accumulated on a job order cost card. When the job has been completed, those costs are totaled. The total is then divided by the number of good units produced to find the product unit cost for that order. The product unit cost is entered on the job order cost card and used to value items in inventory.

5. **Apply job order costing to a service organization.** Service organizations can use job order costing to track the costs of labor, materials and supplies, and service overhead to specific customer jobs. For many service organizations, each job is based on a cost-plus contract that requires the customer to pay for all costs incurred plus a predetermined amount of profit. Labor is an important cost for service organizations, whereas there are usually few or no materials costs.

6. **Distinguish between job order costing and project costing.** A project is larger, more complex, and more time-consuming to complete than a job order. Projects require the talents of many departments, consultants, and subcontractors. They take a multidisciplinary approach to the production of products or services.

REVIEW OF CONCEPTS AND TERMINOLOGY

The following concepts and terms were introduced in this chapter:

LO 5 **Cost-plus contract:** A form of contract that requires the customer to pay for all costs incurred plus a predetermined amount of profit.

LO 2 **Job order:** A customer order for a specific number of specially designed, made-to-order products.

LO 3 **Job order cost card:** A document on which all costs incurred in the production of a particular job order are recorded; part of the subsidiary ledger for the Work in Process Inventory Control account.

LO 2 **Job order costing system:** A product costing system used by companies that make large, unique, or special-order products; the costs of direct materials, direct labor, and manufacturing overhead are traced to specific job orders for products.

LO 2 **Process costing system:** A product costing system used by companies that produce large amounts of similar products or liquids, or that have a continuous production flow; the costs of direct materials, direct labor, and manufacturing overhead are first traced to a process or department and then assigned to the products manufactured by that process or department.

LO 2 **Product costing system:** A set of procedures that accounts for an organization's product costs and provides timely and accurate unit cost information for pricing, planning and control, inventory valuation, and financial statement preparation.

LO 6 **Project:** A broad, complex, multidisciplinary approach to the production of a good or service.

REVIEW PROBLEM
Job Order Costing in a Service Organization

Sanibel Plumbing Company employs thirty people and serves the metropolitan Jacksonville area. The company earns roughly half of its revenue from plumbing installations in new homes and half from plumbing repairs and remodeling of existing homes. Job order cost cards are used to keep track of the costs incurred on each plumbing job. Job costs are categorized as direct materials, direct labor, or service overhead. Costs have been categorized into three activities: Plumbing System Design, System Installation, and Job-Site Cleanup. Costs have been tracked for the duration of the Clary job, and now that all work has been finished, it is time to complete the job order cost card. The service overhead charge for Plumbing System Design is 30 percent of engineering labor costs, and the service overhead charge for System Installation is 50 percent of direct labor cost. The cost-plus contract has a 25 percent profit guarantee. The costs for the Clary job are shown below.

Beginning balances	
Plumbing System Design	$ 2,635
System Installation	14,250
Job-Site Cleanup	75
Costs during October	
Plumbing System Design	
Supplies	0
Engineering labor	$ 250
System Installation	
Materials and supplies	$ 2,150
Direct labor	6,400
Job-Site Cleanup	
Janitorial service cost	$ 525

REQUIRED

1. Create the job order cost card for the Clary job.
2. What amount will Sanibel Plumbing Company bill for the Clary job?
3. Using a T account for the Clary job, reconstruct the beginning balance for the current month and the current month's transactions.

ANSWER TO REVIEW PROBLEM

1. Create the job order cost card for the Clary job.

JOB ORDER COST CARD
Sanibel Plumbing Company

Customer: Clary
Job Order No.:
Contract Type: Cost-Plus
Type of Service: New Home Plumbing   **Date of Completion:** October 31, 20xx

Costs Charged to Job	Previous Months	Current Month	Total
Plumbing System Design			
Beginning balance	$ 2,635		
Current month's costs			
Supplies		$ 0	
Engineering labor		250	
Service overhead (30% of engineering labor)		75	
Totals	$ 2,635	$ 325	$ 2,960
System Installation			
Beginning balance	$14,250		
Current month's costs			
Materials and supplies		$ 2,150	
Direct labor		6,400	
Service overhead (50% of direct labor)		3,200	
Totals	$14,250	$11,750	$26,000
Job-Site Cleanup			
Beginning balance	$ 75		
Current month's costs		$ 525	
Totals	$ 75	$ 525	$ 600

Cost Summary to Date	Total Cost
Plumbing System Design	$ 2,960
System Installation	26,000
Job-Site Cleanup	600
Total	$29,560
Profit margin (25% of total cost)	7,390
Contract revenue	$36,950

---

2. Sanibel Plumbing will bill Clary $36,950 for this job.

3. Using a T account, reconstruct the transactions for the Clary job for the current month.

Clary Job

Beg. Bal.	16,960	29,560
	250	
	75	
	2,150	
	6,400	
	3,200	
	525	
End. Bal.	0	

Chapter Assignments

BUILDING YOUR KNOWLEDGE FOUNDATION

Questions

1. How is costing information used in the planning stage of the management cycle?
2. How is costing information used in the executing stage of the management cycle?
3. How is costing information used in the reviewing stage of the management cycle?
4. How is costing information used in the reporting stage of the management cycle?
5. What is a product costing system?
6. What is a job order costing system? What types of companies use this kind of system?
7. What is a job order?
8. What are the main similarities and differences between a job order costing system and a process costing system? (Focus on the characteristics of each system.)
9. How does materials usage influence a company's efficiency and profitability?
10. "Purchased labor services cannot be stored and used later." Discuss this statement.
11. What is the nature of the Manufacturing Overhead Control account?
12. What is the purpose of the job order cost card? Identify the types of information recorded on this document.
13. Explain the process of computing product unit cost in a job order costing system. How are the necessary data accumulated?
14. What is the main difference between a service organization and a manufacturing organization? How does that affect the costing system of a service organization?
15. How does a project differ from a job order?

Short Exercises

SE 1.
LO 1 *Uses of Product Costing Information*

Kerri's Kennel provides boarding for dogs and cats. Kerri must make several decisions soon. Write *yes* or *no* to indicate whether knowing the cost to board one animal per day (i.e., the product unit cost) can help Kerri answer the following questions.

1. Is the boarding fee high enough to cover my costs?
2. How much profit will I make if I board an average of ten dogs per day for fifty weeks?
3. What costs can I reduce so that I can compete with the boarding fee charged by my competitor?

SE 2.
LO 2 *Industries Using a Job Order Costing System*

Write *yes* or *no* to indicate whether each of the following industries would normally use a job order costing system for product costing.

1. Soft drink producer
2. Jeans manufacturer
3. Submarine contractor
4. Office building contractor
5. Stuffed toy maker

SE 3.

LO 2 *Job Order Versus Process Costing Systems*

State whether a job order costing system or a process costing system would typically be used to account for the costs of producing the following:

1. Dog collars
2. Custom-designed fencing for outdoor breeding kennels
3. Pet grooming
4. Aquariums
5. Dog food
6. Veterinary services

SE 4.

LO 3 *Manufacturing Transactions in a Job Order Costing System*

For each of the following transactions, tell which account(s) would be affected in a job order costing system.

1. Purchased materials, $12,890.
2. Charged direct labor to production, $3,790.
3. Requisitioned direct materials into production, $6,800.
4. Applied manufacturing overhead to jobs in process, $3,570.

SE 5.

LO 3 *Transactions in a Job Order Costing System*

Enter the following transactions into T accounts.

1. Incurred $34,000 of direct labor, $18,000 of indirect labor, and $7,000 of marketing labor.
2. Applied service overhead based on 12,680 labor hours @ $6.50 per labor hour.

SE 6.

LO 4 *Concept of Product Costing*

Write *yes* or *no* to indicate whether each of the following costs is included in a product unit cost. Then explain your answers.

1. Direct materials costs
2. Fixed manufacturing overhead costs
3. Variable selling costs
4. Fixed administrative costs
5. Direct labor costs
6. Variable manufacturing overhead costs

SE 7.

LO 4 *Computation of Product Unit Cost for a Project*

Complete the following job order cost card for six custom-built computer systems.

Job Order No. 168		Gatekeeper 3000 Apache City, North Dakota	
Customer: Robert Arthur		Direct Materials:	
		Dept. 1	$ 3,540
		Dept. 2	2,820
Date of Order: April 4, 20xx		Total	$
Date of Completion: June 18, 20xx		Direct Labor:	
		Dept. 1	$ 2,340
		Dept. 2	1,620
Cost Summary:		Total	$
Direct Materials	$		
Direct Labor		Applied Manufacturing Overhead:	
Manufacturing Overhead		Dept. 1	$ 2,880
Total	$	Dept. 2	2,550
Units Completed		Total	$
Cost per Unit	$		

SE 8.

LO 5 *Job Order Costing in a Service Organization*

For each of the following transactions, tell which account(s) would be affected in a job order costing system for a desert landscaping business.

1. Charged customer for landscape design.
2. Purchased cactus plants and gravel on credit for one job.
3. Paid three employees to prepare soil for gravel.
4. Paid for rental equipment to move gravel to job site.

Exercises

E 1.

LO 2 *Product Costing*

Pandora's Printing Company specializes in wedding invitations. Pandora needs information to budget next year's activities. Write *yes* or *no* to indicate whether each piece of information listed below is likely to be available in the company's product costing system.

1. Cost of paper and envelopes
2. Printing machine setup costs
3. Depreciation of printing machinery
4. Advertising costs
5. Repair costs for printing machinery
6. Costs to deliver stationery to customers
7. Office supplies costs
8. Costs to design a wedding invitation
9. Cost of ink
10. Sales commissions

E 2.

LO 2 *Costing Systems: Industry Linkage*

Which of the following products would normally be accounted for using a job order costing system? Which would be accounted for using a process costing system? (a) paint, (b) automobiles, (c) jet aircraft, (d) bricks, (e) large milling machines, (f) liquid detergent, (g) aluminum compressed-gas cylinders of standard size and capacity, (h) aluminum compressed-gas cylinders with a special fiberglass overwrap for a Mount Everest expedition, (i) standard nails produced from wire, (j) television sets, (k) printed wedding invitations, (l) a limited edition of lithographs, (m) flea collars for pets, (n) high-speed lathes with special-order thread drills, (o) breakfast cereal, and (p) an original evening gown.

E 3.

LO 3 *Job Order Cost Flow*

The three manufacturing cost elements—direct materials, direct labor, and manufacturing overhead—flow through a job order costing system in a structured, orderly fashion. Specific general ledger accounts, subsidiary ledgers, and source documents are used to verify and record cost information. In both paragraph and diagram form, describe the cost flow in a job order costing system.

E 4.

LO 3 *Work in Process Inventory Control Account: T Account Analysis*

On July 1, Schneider Specialty Company's Work in Process Inventory Control account showed a beginning balance of $29,400. Production activity for July was as follows: (a) Direct materials costing $238,820, along with $28,400 of operating supplies, were requisitioned into production. (b) Schneider Specialty Company's total manufacturing payroll for July was $140,690, of which $52,490 was used to pay for indirect labor. (c) Manufacturing overhead was applied at a rate of 150 percent of direct labor costs.

1. Record the materials, labor, and manufacturing overhead costs for July in T accounts.
2. Compute the ending balance in the Work in Process Inventory Control account. Assume a transfer of $461,400 to the Finished Goods Inventory Control account during the period.

E 5.

LO 4 *Job Order Costs and Computation of Product Unit Cost*

During the month of January, the Kasik Cabinet Company worked on six different job orders for specialty kitchen cabinets. Job A-62, manufactured for T. J. Products, Inc., was begun and completed during the month. Partial data from Job A-62's job order cost card are summarized on the next page.

	Costs	Machine Hours Used
Direct materials:		
Cedar	$7,900	
Pine	6,320	
Hardware	2,930	
Assembly supplies	988	
Direct labor:		
Sawing Department	$2,840	120
Shaping Department	2,200	220
Finishing Department	2,250	180
Assembly Department	2,890	50

A total of 34 cabinets were produced for Job A-62. The current predetermined manufacturing overhead rate is $21.60 per machine hour. From the information given, prepare a job order cost card and compute the job order's product unit cost. The cedar and pine are placed into production in the Sawing Department. The hardware and supplies are placed into production in the Assembly Department. (Round to whole dollars.)

E 6.
LO 4 *Computation of Product Unit Cost*

Using job order costing, determine the product unit cost from the following costs incurred during March: liability insurance, manufacturing, $2,500; rent, sales office, $2,900; depreciation, manufacturing equipment, $6,100; materials used, $32,650; indirect labor, manufacturing, $3,480; manufacturing supplies, $1,080; heat, light, and power, manufacturing, $1,910; fire insurance, manufacturing, $2,600; depreciation, sales equipment, $4,250; rent, manufacturing, $3,850; direct labor, $18,420; manager's salary, manufacturing, $3,100; president's salary, $5,800; sales commissions, $8,250; and advertising expenses, $2,975. The Inspection Department reported that 48,800 good units were produced during March. Carry your answer to three decimal places.

E 7.
LO 4 *Computation of Product Unit Cost*

Wild Iris Corporation manufactures specialty lines of women's apparel. During February, Wild Iris Corporation worked on three special orders: A-25, A-27, and B-14. Cost and production data for each order are shown in the following table.

	Job A-25	Job A-27	Job B-14
Direct materials:			
Fabric Q	$10,840	$12,980	$17,660
Fabric Z	11,400	12,200	13,440
Fabric YB	5,260	6,920	10,900
Direct labor:			
Garmentmaker	8,900	10,400	16,200
Layout	6,450	7,425	9,210
Packaging	3,950	4,875	6,090
Manufacturing overhead:			
120% of direct labor dollars	?	?	?
Number of units produced	700	775	1,482

1. Compute the total cost associated with each job. Show the subtotals for each cost category.
2. Compute the product unit cost for each job. (Round your computations to the nearest penny.)

E 8.
LO 5 *Job Costing in a Service Organization*

A job order cost card for Clovis Computer Services appears at the top of the next page. Complete the missing information. The organization's profit factor is 30 percent of total cost.

JOB ORDER COST CARD
Clovis Computer Services

Customer:	Ray Dove
Job Order No.:	
Contract Type:	Cost-Plus
Type of Service:	Software Installation and Internet Interfacing
Date of Completion:	October 6, 20xx

Costs Charged to Job	Total
Software Installation Services	
Installation labor	$ 300
Service overhead (? % of installation labor costs)	?
Totals	$ 450
Internet Services	
Internet labor	$ 200
Service overhead (20% of Internet labor costs)	40
Total	$?

Cost Summary to Date:	Total Cost
Software Installation Services	$?
Internet Services	?
Total	$?
Profit margin	?
Contract revenue	$?

Problems

LO 3 *Job Order Costing: Unknown Quantity Analysis*

P 1. Partial operating data for the Privata Picture Company are presented below. Management has decided that the predetermined overhead rate for the current year is 120 percent of direct labor costs.

Account/Transaction	June	July
Beginning Materials Inventory Control	$ a	$ e
Beginning Work in Process Inventory Control	89,605	f
Beginning Finished Goods Inventory Control	79,764	67,660
Direct Materials Requisitioned	59,025	g
Materials Purchased	57,100	60,216
Direct Labor Costs	48,760	54,540
Manufacturing Overhead Applied	b	h
Cost of Units Completed	c	231,861
Cost of Goods Sold	166,805	i
Ending Materials Inventory Control	32,014	27,628
Ending Work in Process Inventory Control	d	j
Ending Finished Goods Inventory Control	67,660	30,515

REQUIRED Using the data provided, compute the unknown values. Show all your computations.

P 2.

Lektro-Cart Manufacturing, Inc., produces electric golf carts. The carts are special-order items, so the company uses a job order costing system. Manufacturing overhead is applied at the rate of 90 percent of direct labor cost. Following is a list of events and transactions for January.

Jan. 1 Direct materials costing $215,400 were purchased on account.
  2 Operating supplies were purchased on account, $49,500.
  4 Production personnel requisitioned direct materials costing $193,200 (all used on Job X) and operating supplies costing $38,100 into production.
  10 The following manufacturing overhead costs were paid: utilities, $4,400; manufacturing rent, $3,800; and maintenance charges, $3,900.
  15 Payroll was recorded for employees. Gross wages and salaries were as follows: direct labor, $120,000 (all for Job X); indirect labor, $60,620; sales commissions, $32,400; and administrative salaries, $38,000.
  15 Manufacturing overhead was applied to production.
  19 Operating supplies costing $27,550 and direct materials listed at $190,450 were purchased on account.
  21 Direct materials costing $214,750 (Job X, $178,170; Job Y, $18,170; Job Z, $18,410) and operating supplies costing $31,400 were requisitioned into production.
  31 The following gross wages and salaries were recorded: direct labor, $132,000 (Job X, $118,500; Job Y, $7,000; Job Z, $6,500); indirect labor, $62,240; sales commissions, $31,200; and administrative salaries, $38,000.
  31 Manufacturing overhead was applied to production.
  31 Jobs X and Y were completed and transferred to Finished Goods Inventory; total cost was $855,990.
  31 Job X was shipped to the customer; the total production cost was $824,520 and the sales price was $996,800.
  31 The following manufacturing overhead costs (adjusting entries) were recorded: prepaid insurance expired, $3,700; property taxes (payable at year end), $3,400; and depreciation, machinery, $15,500.

REQUIRED

1. Record the entries for all transactions and events in January in T accounts. Determine the partial account balances. Include T accounts for Jobs X, Y, and Z. Assume no beginning inventory balances. Also assume that when the payroll was recorded, entries were made to the Factory Labor account.
2. Compute the amount of underapplied or overapplied overhead as of January 31 and transfer it to the Cost of Goods Sold account.

P 3.

The three September 1 inventory balances of Tannehill House, a manufacturer of high-quality children's clothing, were as follows:

Account	Balance
Materials Inventory Control	$21,360
Work in Process Inventory Control	15,112
Finished Goods Inventory Control	17,120

Job order cost cards for jobs in process as of September 30, 20xx, had the following totals:

Job No.	Direct Materials	Direct Labor	Manufacturing Overhead
24-A	$1,596	$1,290	$1,677
24-B	1,492	1,380	1,794
24-C	1,984	1,760	2,288
24-D	1,608	1,540	2,002

Materials purchased and received in September:
September 4	$33,120
September 16	28,600
September 22	31,920

Direct labor costs for September:
September 15 payroll	$23,680
September 29 payroll	25,960

Predetermined overhead rate:
   130 percent of direct labor cost

Direct materials requisitioned into production
   during September:

September 6	$37,240
September 23	38,960

Finished goods with a 75 percent markup over cost were sold during September for $320,000.

REQUIRED

1. Using T accounts, reconstruct the transactions for September.
2. Compute the cost of units completed during the month.
3. What was the total cost of units sold during September?
4. Determine the ending inventory balances.
5. Jobs 24-A and 24-C were completed during the first week of October. No additional materials costs were incurred, but Job 24-A required $960 more direct labor, and Job 24-C needed additional direct labor of $1,610. Job 24-A was composed of 1,200 pairs of trousers; Job 24-C, of 950 shirts. Compute the product unit cost for each job. (Round your answers to three decimal places.)

P 4.

LO 5 *Job Order Costing: Service Company*

Nedeau Engineering Co. specializes in designing automated characters and displays for theme parks. Cost-plus profit contracts are used, and the company's profit factor is 30 percent of total cost. A job order costing system is used to track the costs associated with the development of each job. Costs are accumulated for three primary activities: Bid and Proposal, Design, and Prototype Development. Current service overhead rates based on engineering hours are as follows: Bid and Proposal, $18 per hour; Design, $22 per hour; and Prototype Development, $20 per hour. Supplies are treated as direct materials, traceable to each job. Three jobs, P-12, P-15, and P-19, were worked on during January. The following table contains the costs for these jobs.

	P-12	P-15	P-19
Beginning balances:			
Bid and Proposal	$2,460	$2,290	$ 940
Design	1,910	460	0
Prototype Development	2,410	1,680	0
Costs during January:			
Bid and Proposal			
Supplies	0	$ 280	$2,300
Labor: hours	12	20	68
dollars	$ 192	$ 320	$1,088
Design			
Supplies	$ 400	$ 460	$ 290
Labor: hours	64	42	26
dollars	$1,280	$ 840	$ 520
Prototype Development			
Special materials	$6,744	$7,216	$2,400
Labor: hours	120	130	25
dollars	$2,880	$3,120	$ 600

REQUIRED

1. Using the format shown in the chapter's review problem, create the job order cost cards for each of the three jobs.
2. Jobs P-12 and P-15 were completed and the customers approved of the prototype products. Customer A plans to produce 12 special characters using the design and specifications created by Job P-12. Customer B plans to make 18 displays from the design developed by Job P-15. What dollar amount will each customer use as the cost of design for each of these products (i.e., what is the product unit cost for Jobs P-12 and P-15)? Round to the nearest dollar.
3. What is Nedeau Engineering Co.'s January ending Contract in Process balance for the three jobs?

LO 4   *Job Order Costing:*
LO 5   *Service Company*

P 5.   Savannah House, a restored Victorian mansion located in Florala, Tennessee, caters and services special events for businesses and social occasions. The company earns 60 percent of its revenue from weekly luncheon meetings of local clubs such as Rotary International and Kiwanis. The remainder of its business comes from bookings for weddings and receptions. Job order cost cards are used to keep track of the costs incurred. Job costs are categorized into three types: Food and Beverages, Labor, and Facility Overhead. The facility overhead cost for weekly events is 10 percent of food and beverage costs, the facility overhead cost for sit-down receptions is 40 percent of food and beverage costs, and the facility overhead cost for standup receptions is 20 percent of food and beverage costs. Accumulated costs for three different Savannah House clients in the current quarter are as follows:

	Food and Beverage	**Labor**	**Facility Overhead**
Monday Club meetings	Last month: $2,000 This month: $2,500	Last month: $200 This month: $250	Last month: ? This month: ?
Huang-Smith engagement and wedding parties	Last month: $3,000 This month: $8,000 Both sit-down affairs	Last month: $1,000 This month: $2,000	Last month: ? This month: ?
Reception for the new president	This month: $5,000 A standup affair	This month: $1,000	This month: ?

The number of attendees served at Monday Club meetings is generally 200 per month. The Huang-Smith parties paid for 500 guests. The organizers of the reception for the new president provided for 1,000 invitees.

1. Using the format shown in the chapter's review problem, create a job card for each of the three clients.
2. Calculate the total cost of each of the three jobs on their job cost card.
3. Calculate the cost per attendee for each job.
4. Rank the jobs in order of most to least costly based upon the job's total cost and by the cost per attendee. Based upon these rankings of cost, what observations can be made?
5. Speculate on what price should be charged by Savannah House for these types of jobs.

Alternate Problems

LO 3   *Job Order Costing:*
          T Account Analysis

P 6.   Buxton Industries, Inc., the finest name in parking attendant apparel, has been in business for over thirty years. Its colorful and stylish uniforms are special-ordered by exclusive hotels and country clubs all over the world. During April, Buxton completed the following transactions.

Apr. 1   Materials costing $59,400 were purchased on account.
      3   Materials costing $26,850 were requisitioned into production (all were used on Job A).
      4   Operating supplies were purchased for cash, $22,830.
      8   The company issued checks for the following manufacturing overhead costs: utilities, $4,310; manufacturing insurance, $1,925; and repairs, $4,640.
     10   The Cutting Department manager requisitioned $29,510 of materials (all used on Job A) and $6,480 of operating supplies into production.
     15   Payroll was recorded for the employees. Gross wages and salaries were as follows: direct labor, $62,900 (all for Job A); indirect labor, $31,610; manufacturing supervision, $26,900; and sales commissions, $32,980.
     15   Overhead was applied to production.
     22   Manufacturing overhead costs were paid: utilities, $4,270; maintenance, $3,380; and rent, $3,250.
     23   The Receiving Department recorded the purchase on account and receipt of $31,940 of materials and $9,260 of operating supplies.
     27   Production requisitioned $28,870 of materials (Job A, $2,660; Job B, $8,400; Job C, $17,810) and $7,640 of operating supplies.

Apr. 30   The following gross wages and salaries were recorded for employees: direct labor, $64,220 (Job A, $44,000; Job B, $9,000; Job C, $11,220); indirect labor, $30,290; manufacturing supervision, $28,520; and sales commissions, $36,200.

    30   Manufacturing overhead was applied to production.

    30   Jobs A and B were completed and transferred to Finished Goods Inventory; the total cost was $322,400.

    30   Job A was shipped to the customer; the total production cost was $294,200, and the sales price was $418,240.

    30   Adjusting entries for the following were recorded: $2,680 for depreciation, manufacturing equipment; $1,230 for property taxes, manufacturing, payable at month end.

Manufacturing overhead was applied at a rate of 120 percent of direct labor cost.

REQUIRED

1. Record the entries for all transactions and events in April in T accounts. Determine the partial account balances. Include T accounts for Jobs A, B, and C. Assume no beginning inventory balances. Assume that when payroll was recorded, entries were made to the Factory Labor account. (Round your answers to the nearest whole dollar.)
2. Compute the amount of underapplied or overapplied overhead for April and transfer it to the Cost of Goods Sold account.

P 7.

LO 3
LO 4

Job Order Cost Flow

Vandana Jain is the chief financial officer for Quick Industries, a company that makes special-order printers for personal computers. Her records for February revealed the following information.

Beginning inventory balances:

Materials Inventory Control	$27,450
Work in Process Inventory Control	22,900
Finished Goods Inventory Control	19,200

Direct materials purchased and received:

February 6	$ 7,200
February 12	8,110
February 24	5,890

Direct labor costs:

February 14	$13,750
February 28	13,230

Direct materials requisitioned into production:

February 4	$ 9,080
February 13	5,940
February 25	7,600

Job order cost cards for jobs in process on February 28 had the following totals.

Job No.	Direct Materials	Direct Labor	Manufacturing Overhead
AJ-10	$3,220	$1,810	$2,534
AJ-14	3,880	2,110	2,954
AJ-30	2,980	1,640	2,296
AJ-16	4,690	2,370	3,318

The predetermined manufacturing overhead rate for the month was 140 percent of direct labor costs. Sales for February totaled $152,400, which represented a 70 percent markup over the cost of production.

REQUIRED

1. Using T accounts, reconstruct the transactions for February.
2. Compute the cost of units completed during the month.
3. What was the total cost of units sold during February?
4. Determine the ending balances in the inventory accounts.
5. During the first week of March, Jobs AJ-10 and AJ-14 were completed. No additional direct materials costs were incurred, but Job AJ-10 needed $720 more direct labor, and Job AJ-14 required additional direct labor of $1,140. Job AJ-10 was 40 units; Job AJ-14, 55 units. Compute the product unit cost for each completed job (round to three decimal places).

LO 5

Job Order Costing: Service Company

P 8. Napier & Associates is a CPA firm located in Homewood, Illinois. The firm deals primarily in tax and audit work. For billing of major audit engagements, the firm uses cost-plus profit agreements, and the profit factor used is 25 percent of total job cost. Costs are accumulated for three primary activities: Preliminary Analysis, Field Work, and Report Development. Current service overhead rates based on billable hours are: Preliminary Analysis, $12 per hour; Field Work, $20 per hour; and Report Development, $16 per hour. Supplies are treated as direct materials, traceable to each engagement. Audits for three clients, Adams, Inc., Brodahl Bakeries, and Hill House Restaurants, are currently in process. During March, costs related to these projects were:

	Adams, Inc.	Brodahl Bakeries	Hill House Restaurants
Beginning balances:			
Preliminary Analysis	$1,160	$2,670	$2,150
Field Work	710	1,980	3,460
Report Development	0	1,020	420
Costs during March:			
Preliminary Analysis			
Supplies	$ 710	$ 430	$ 200
Labor: hours	60	10	12
dollars	$1,200	$ 200	$ 240
Field Work			
Supplies	$ 450	$1,120	$ 890
Labor: hours	120	240	230
dollars	$4,800	$9,600	$9,200
Report Development			
Supplies	$ 150	$ 430	$ 390
Labor: hours	30	160	140
dollars	$ 900	$4,800	$4,200

REQUIRED

1. Using the format shown in the chapter's review problem, create the job order cost cards for each of the three audit engagements.
2. The Brodahl Bakeries and Hill House Restaurants audits were completed by the end of March. What will be the billing amount for each of those audit engagements?
3. What is Napier & Associates' March ending Audit in Process account balance for the three jobs?

Skills Development

CONCEPTUAL ANALYSIS

LO 1   *Business Plans*
LO 3

SD 1. In the past twenty years, *Fortune* 500 companies have eliminated over five million jobs, yet the overall U.S. economy has grown by almost thirty million jobs. Most of the new jobs have been created by new businesses. A key step in starting a new company is a realistic analysis of the people, opportunity, context, risks, and rewards of the venture and the formulation of a business plan. Notice the similarities between the questions accountants answer in the management cycle and the nine questions every great business plan should answer:[5]

- Who is the new venture's customer?
- How does the customer make decisions about buying this product or service?
- To what degree is the product or service a compelling purchase for the customer?
- How will the product or service be priced?
- How will the venture reach all the identified customer segments?
- How much does it cost (in time and resources) to acquire a customer?
- How much does it cost to produce and deliver the product or service?
- How much does it cost to support a customer?
- How easy is it to retain a customer?

Assume you are a consultant who has been hired for your knowledge of the management cycle. Write a memo that discusses how the nine questions fit into the management cycle.

ETHICAL DILEMMA

LO 3   *Ethical Job Order Costs*

SD 2. Kevin Rogers, the production manager for **Stitts Metal Products Company,** entered the office of controller Ed Harris and asked, "Ed, what gives here? I was charged for 330 direct labor hours on Job AD22 and my records show that we only spent 290 hours on that job. That 40-hour difference caused the total cost of direct labor and manufacturing overhead for the job to increase by over $5,500. Are my records wrong, or was there an error in the direct labor assigned to the job?" Ed responded, "Don't worry about it, Kevin. This job won't be used in your quarterly performance evaluation. Job AD22 was a federal government job, a cost-plus-fixed-fee contract, so the more costs we assign to it, the more profit we make. We decided to add a few hours to the job in case there is some follow-up work to do. You know how fussy the feds are with their close tolerances."

What should Kevin Rogers do? Discuss Ed Harris's costing procedure.

    Communication   **Critical Thinking**   **Group Activity**   **Memo**   **Ethics**   **International**   **Spreadsheet**   **Managerial Technology**   **Internet**

SD 3.

LO 3 *Job Order Costing*

Many businesses accumulate costs for each job performed. Examples of businesses that use a job order costing system include print shops, car repair shops, health clinics, and kennels. Visit a local business that uses job order costing, and interview the owner, manager, or accountant about the process and the documents the business uses to accumulate product costs. Write a paper that summarizes the information you obtained. Include the following items in your written summary:

1. The name of the business and the type of operations performed
2. The name and position of the individual you interviewed
3. A description of the process of starting and completing a job
4. A description of the accounting process and the documents used to track a job
5. Your response to the following questions:
   a. Did the person you interviewed know the *actual* amount of materials, labor, and overhead charged to a particular job? If the job includes some estimated costs, how are the estimates calculated? Is the determination of the selling price of the product or service affected by the product costs?
   b. Compare the documents discussed in the chapter to the documents used in the company that you visited. How are they similar, and how are they different?
   c. In your opinion, does the business record and accumulate its product costs effectively? Explain.

Group Activity: Group students according to type of business selected and ask them to concentrate on Part 5.

DECISION-MAKING PRACTICE

SD 4.

LO 3 *Analysis of Job*
LO 4 *Order Costing Systems*

Zavala Manufacturing Company is a small family-owned business that makes specialty plastic products. Since it was started three years ago, the company has grown quickly and now employs ten production people. Because of the nature of its products, the company uses a job order costing system. The company's manual accounting system is falling behind in processing transactions.

Two months ago, in May, the company's accountant quit. You have been called in to help management. The following information has been given to you.

Beginning inventory balances (January):	
Materials	$50,420
Work in Process (Job K-2)	59,100
Finished Goods (Job K-1)	76,480

Direct materials requisitioned into production during the year:	
Job K-2	$33,850
Job K-4	53,380
Job K-6	82,400

Direct labor for the year:	
Job K-2	$25,300
Job K-4	33,480
Job K-6	45,600

The company purchased materials only once (in February), for $126,500. All jobs use the same materials. For the current year, the company has been using an overhead application rate of 150 percent of direct labor costs. So far, two jobs, K-2 and K-4, have been completed, and Jobs K-1 and K-2 have been shipped to customers. Job K-1 contained 3,200 units; Job K-2, 5,500 units; and Job K-4, 4,600 units.

1. Calculate the product unit costs for jobs K-1, K-2, and K-4, and the costs so far for job K-6.
2. From the information given, prepare a T account analysis, and compute the current balances in the Materials Inventory Control, Work in Process Inventory Control, Finished Goods Inventory Control, and Cost of Goods Sold accounts. Also show T accounts for each job.

3. The president has asked you to analyze the current job order costing system. Do you think the system should be changed? How? Why? Prepare an outline of your response to the president.

Managerial Reporting and Analysis

INTERPRETING MANAGEMENT REPORTS

MRA 1.

LO 1   *Interpreting Nonfinancial Data*

Eagle Manufacturing supplies engine parts to ***Cherokee Cycle Company,*** a major U.S. manufacturer of motorcycles. Eagle, like all parts suppliers for Cherokee, has always added a healthy profit margin to its cost when calculating its selling price to Cherokee. Recently, however, several new suppliers have offered to provide parts to Cherokee for lower prices than Eagle has been charging.

Because Eagle wants to keep Cherokee's business, a team of managers analyzed the company's product costs and decided to make minor changes in the company's manufacturing process. No new equipment was purchased, and no additional labor was required. Instead, the machines were rearranged and some of the work was reassigned.

To monitor the effectiveness of the changes, Eagle introduced three new performance measures to its information system: inventory levels, lead time (total time required for a part to move through the production process), and productivity (number of parts manufactured per person per day). Eagle's goal was to reduce the quantities of the first two performance measures and to increase the quantity of the third.

A section of a recent management report, shown below, summarizes the quantities for each performance measure before and after the changes in the manufacturing process were made.

Measure	Before	After	Improvement
Inventory in dollars	$21,444	$10,772	50%
Lead time in minutes	17	11	35%
Productivity			
(parts per person per day)	515	1,152	124%

REQUIRED

1. Do you believe Eagle improved the quality of its manufacturing process and the quality of its engine parts? Explain your answer.
2. Can Eagle lower its selling price to Cherokee? Explain your answer.
3. Was the design of the product costing system affected by the introduction of the new measures? Explain your answer.
4. Do you believe that the new measures caused a change in Eagle's cost per engine part? In what way?

FORMULATING MANAGEMENT REPORTS

MRA 2.

LO 1   *Product Costing Systems*
LO 2   *and Nonfinancial Data*

Refer to the information in MRA 1. Jordan Smith, who is the president of ***Eagle Manufacturing,*** wants to improve the quality of the company's operations and products. She believes waste exists in the design and manufacture of standard engine parts. To begin the improvement process, she has asked you to (1) identify sources of waste, (2) develop performance measures to account for the waste, and (3) estimate the current costs associated with such waste. She has asked you to write a memo presenting your findings within two weeks so that she can begin strategic planning to revise the selling price for engine parts to Cherokee.

You have identified two sources of costly waste. The Production Department is redoing work that was not done correctly the first time, and the Engineering Design Department is redesigning products that were not designed according to customer specifications the first time. Having improper designs has caused the company to buy parts that are not used in production. You have also obtained the following information from the product costing system:

Direct labor costs	$673,402
Engineering design costs	124,709
Indirect labor costs	67,200
Depreciation on production equipment	84,300
Supervisors' salaries	98,340
Direct materials costs	432,223
Indirect materials costs	44,332

REQUIRED

1. In preparation for writing your memo, answer the following questions.
   a. For whom are you preparing the memo? What is the appropriate length of the memo?
   b. Why are you preparing the memo?
   c. What information is needed for the memo? Where can you get such information? What performance measure would you suggest for each activity? Is the accounting information sufficient for your memo?
   d. When is the memo due? What can be done to provide accurate and timely information?
2. Prepare an outline of the sections you would want in your memo.

INTERNATIONAL COMPANY

MRA 3.
LO 1   *Design of a Product*
LO 2   *Costing System*

The **Al Khali Corporation**'s copper mines hold 63 percent of the 23.2 million tons of copper in Saudi Arabia. The owners of the mining operation are willing to invest millions of dollars in the latest pyrometallurgical copper extraction processes. The production managers are currently examining both batch and continuous methods of the new copper extraction process. The method they choose will replace the hydrometallurgical process now in use.

What impact will the method selected by the production managers have on the design of the product costing system? What impact would changing from hydrometallurgical to pyrometallurgical processing have on the design of the product costing system if both processes use continuous methods of extraction?

EXCEL SPREADSHEET ANALYSIS

MRA 4.
LO 5   *Job Order Costing:*
      Service Organization

Refer to assignment P 4 in this chapter. Nedeau Engineering Co. needs to analyze its jobs in process during the month of January.

REQUIRED

1. Using the Chart Wizard and the job order cost cards for Jobs P-12, P-15, and P-19, prepare a bar chart that compares the Bid and Proposal costs, Design costs, and Prototype Development costs of the jobs. Below is the suggested format to use for the information table necessary to complete the bar chart.

	P-12	P-15	P-19
Bid and Proposal			
Design			
Prototype Development			
Total Job Cost			

2. Examine the chart you prepared in **1.** List some reasons for the differences between the costs of the various jobs.

ENDNOTES

1. Personal Pair is a registered trademark from Levi Strauss & Co.
2. Jack Stack, *The Great Game of Business* (New York: Currency Doubleday, 1992).
3. John Case, "Opening the Books," *Harvard Business Review,* March–April 1997, pp. 118–127.
4. Associated Press, "$75 Screws? The Pentagon Pays It," *The Gainesville Sun,* March 19, 1998, p. 1.
5. William A. Sahlman, "How to Write a Great Business Plan," *Harvard Business Review,* July–August 1997, pp. 98–108.

CHAPTER 4

Costing Systems: Process Costing

LEARNING OBJECTIVES

1. Describe the process costing system, discuss its role in the management cycle, and identify the reasons for its use.
2. Relate the patterns of product flows in a process costing environment to the process cost flow approaches.
3. Explain the role of the Work in Process Inventory account(s) in a process costing system.
4. Prepare a process cost report: (a) Use a schedule of equivalent production to compute equivalent units of production, (b) use a unit cost analysis schedule to compute product unit cost for a specific time period, and (c) complete a cost summary schedule that assigns costs to units completed and transferred out during the period, and compute the ending balance in the Work in Process Inventory account.
5. Apply activity-based costing to a process costing system.
6. Evaluate operating performance using product costing information.

SUPPLEMENTAL OBJECTIVE

7. Compute equivalent units, product unit cost, and the ending Work in Process Inventory balance in a process costing system that uses the average costing approach.

DECISION POINT

KUNDE ESTATE WINERY

Kunde Estate Winery is located in California's Sonoma Valley. Kunde is considered an estate winery because it grows or controls the growth of at least 95 percent of the grapes it uses in its wines. The winemaking process differs for white and red wines, but both must be aged from eight to eighteen months in stainless steel tanks or oak barrels before being bottled and released for distribution.

Because of this aging process, determining the product unit cost of a bottle of wine creates special problems and requires the blending of the job order and process costing approaches into a hybrid system. The process of taking the picked grapes and turning them into a fermented solution requires a process costing approach. But once the winemaker begins to work with the fermented solutions, blending other types of grapes with varietals such as Cabernet sauvignon or Chardonnay, the uniqueness of the resulting wines suggests the need for a job order system. Tracing production and aging costs to specific lots of wine involves many allocations, but tracking the cost of blending and refining the wine requires a different kind of attention.[1] What types of problems do wineries encounter in this critical costing area? How could Kunde Estate Winery overcome this problem?

Blending takes place during the aging process and usually begins about three months after the initial solution of crushed, destemmed grapes was produced. The winemaker experiments with different combinations of grapes at different stages in the eight- to eighteen-month aging process. Some white varietals can be easily developed, whereas some red varietals are very complex and take months to develop. The controller at Kunde Estate Winery created a tracking system that records the activities of the winemaker. The time spent on each batch of each varietal wine is recorded. Then, all costs connected with the winemaker's activities are assigned to a batch or lot of wine based on the amount of time the winemaker took to produce it. The new approach is a version of activity-based costing applied to a hybrid product costing system.

The Process Costing System

A product costing system is expected to provide unit cost information, supply cost data to support management decisions, and furnish ending values for the Materials, Work in Process, and Finished Goods Inventory accounts. The job order costing system is one approach to satisfying those objectives. The process costing system is a second approach. A process costing system is a product costing system used by companies that produce large amounts of similar products or liquids, or that have a continuous production flow. In a process costing system, the costs of materials, labor, and manufacturing overhead are traced to processes or work cells and then assigned to the products produced by those processes or work cells.

Since process costing is another product costing system, its role in the management cycle is similar to the role described for job order costing in the previous chapter. Figure 1 reviews that role. In the planning stage of the management cycle, past and projected product costing information and customer preferences can help managers decide what a product should cost and if that amount is reasonable. After management has determined a target number of units to be sold, all product-related costs for that targeted amount can be computed and used in the budget. In the executing stage of the cycle, actual costs are incurred and units are produced, so actual unit costs can be computed. In the reviewing stage, managers evaluate performance by comparing what was planned with what was actually produced. Reasons for not achieving targeted costs or for overproducing are analyzed, and changes are recommended. In the reporting stage, actual units produced and costs incurred are used to value inventory on the balance sheet and cost of goods sold on the income statement. Managers are also interested in whether goals for product costs are being achieved.

Continuous flow of a production process signals the need for a process costing system. In a continuous flow environment, liquid products or large numbers of similar products are produced. Tracking individual costs to individual products is too difficult and too expensive and does not result in significantly different product costs. One gallon of green paint is identical to the next gallon. One brick looks just like the next brick. Each product is similar to the next and should cost the same amount to produce. A process costing system accumulates the costs of materials, labor, and manufacturing overhead for each process or work cell and assigns those costs equally to the products produced during a particular time period. Industries that produce paint, beverages, bricks, canned foods, milk, and paper are typical users of the process costing system. Companies that adopt the just-in-time operating philosophy also usually employ process costing procedures, because a continuous flow work cell or process is central to a JIT operation.

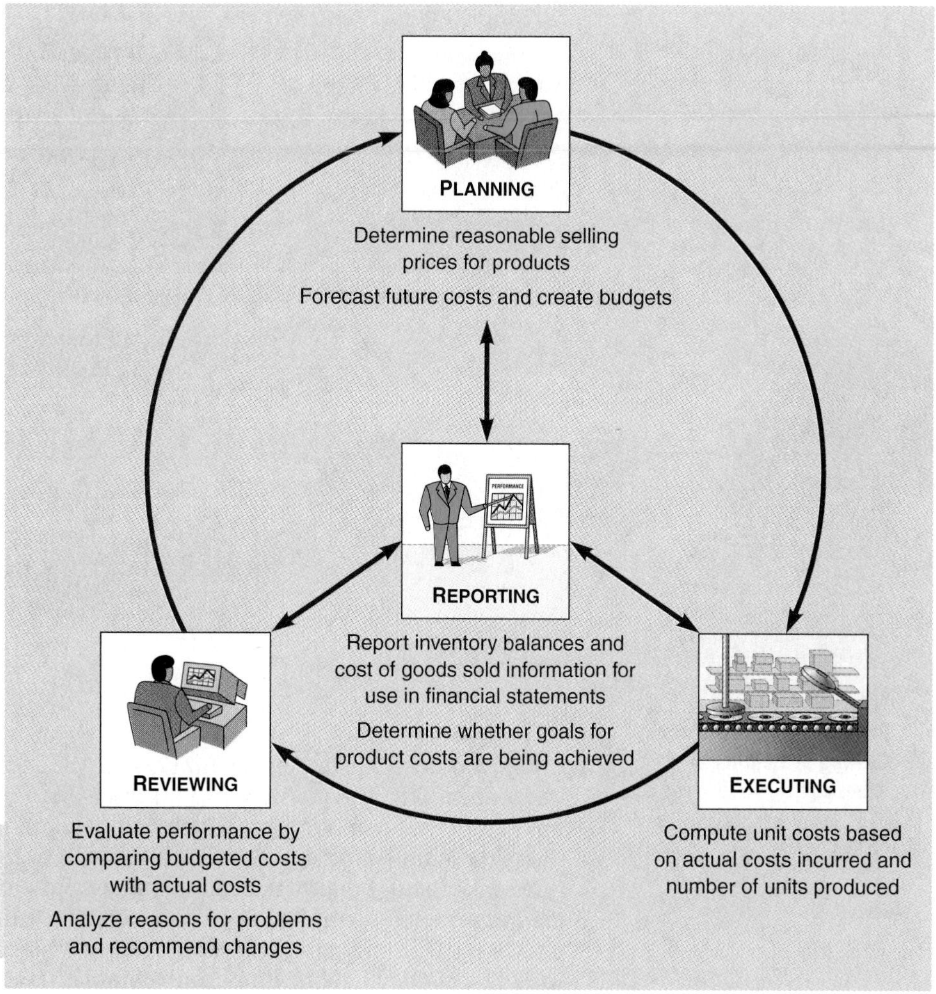

Figure 1
Uses of Product Costing Information in the Management Cycle

PLANNING
Determine reasonable selling prices for products
Forecast future costs and create budgets

REPORTING
Report inventory balances and cost of goods sold information for use in financial statements
Determine whether goals for product costs are being achieved

REVIEWING
Evaluate performance by comparing budgeted costs with actual costs
Analyze reasons for problems and recommend changes

EXECUTING
Compute unit costs based on actual costs incurred and number of units produced

Patterns of Product Flows

OBJECTIVE 2

Relate the patterns of product flows in a process costing environment to the process cost flow approaches

During production in a process costing environment, products flow through several departments or processes and may undergo many different combinations of operations. The simplest product flow follows a linear pattern, like the product flow in winemaking, illustrated in Figure 2.

- In Department A (Crushing), the grapes, which are the direct materials, are crushed to extract the liquid that will become wine. Direct labor is provided by workers who feed the grapes into the crusher and route the resulting liquid to the next department. Overhead includes the costs of the equipment and the resources necessary to operate and maintain the equipment.

- In Department B (Aging), the wine is placed in metal or wooden casks and aged in a climate-controlled cellar. Some direct labor costs are incurred during aging, but most of the costs are overhead costs related to storing and caring for the wine in ways that will ensure a quality finished product.

- In Department C (Bottling), the wine is bottled, labeled, and boxed before being transferred to finished goods inventory in the warehouse. Here, more direct materials are needed in the form of bottles, labels, and boxes. Although this operation is usually highly automated, direct labor is still needed to run the equipment and move the finished product to the warehouse.

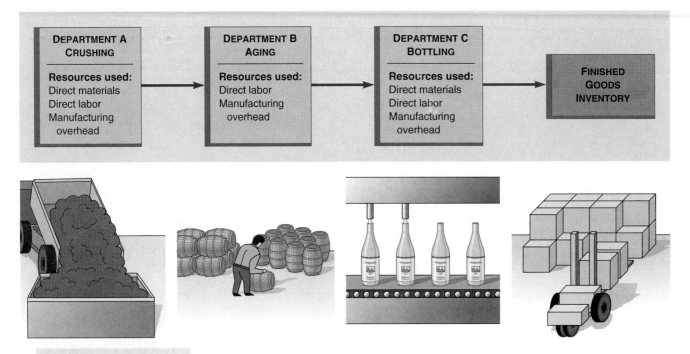

DEPARTMENT A CRUSHING	DEPARTMENT B AGING	DEPARTMENT C BOTTLING	FINISHED GOODS INVENTORY
Resources used: Direct materials Direct labor Manufacturing overhead	**Resources used:** Direct labor Manufacturing overhead	**Resources used:** Direct materials Direct labor Manufacturing overhead	

**Figure 2
Product Flows in a Process Costing System for Winemaking**

Many process costing environments are much more complex than the winemaking process. A company may use a number of separate processes to manufacture many different components, which will become the direct materials that are ultimately assembled into a finished product. For example, when making sofas, a furniture maker would manufacture the frames and cushions separately, then upholster the frames and assemble frames and cushions into finished products. In this chapter, we present only the linear approach because it illustrates all the concepts that would be applied in both simple and complex environments.

Cost Flow Approaches

In process costing, costs are accumulated by department and are passed to each subsequent department as the product is made. The accumulated costs may be assigned to products using either the FIFO costing approach or the average costing approach. The FIFO costing approach is a costing method in which the cost flow follows the logical product flow. The costs assigned to the first products made are the first costs transferred from one department to the next department. This corresponds to the order in which products normally flow in and out of production

BUSINESS BULLETIN: BUSINESS PRACTICE

How important are the concepts and techniques presented in this chapter? How much are they used in practice? A study conducted by the Institute of Management Accountants determined that 52 percent of the 112 companies surveyed used process costing procedures. Of the companies using the process costing approach, 58 percent were using the FIFO costing approach, 21 percent used a variant of the FIFO approach, and 21 percent used the average costing approach.[2]

departments. The product flow illustrated in Figure 2 is based on a FIFO pattern. The average costing approach assigns an average cost to all products made during an accounting period; cost assignment is not linked to the physical product flow. We have chosen to use the FIFO costing approach in our discussion of the process costing system for two reasons. First, since products flow through the manufacturing process in a FIFO pattern, it is easier to learn how to account for their costs if those costs also follow a FIFO pattern. Second, most companies in industries that employ process costing systems use the FIFO approach. We describe the average costing method in the Supplemental Objective at the end of this chapter.

Cost Flows Through the Work in Process Inventory Accounts

OBJECTIVE 3

Explain the role of the Work in Process Inventory account(s) in a process costing system

Accounting for the costs of direct materials, direct labor, and manufacturing overhead is similar for job order costing and process costing. Under both systems, costs must be recorded and eventually charged to production. Direct materials and supplies must be purchased and requisitioned into production. Wages for direct labor must be paid to employees and charged to production accounts. Finally, manufacturing overhead costs must be assigned to production. Therefore, the flow of costs *into* the Work in Process Inventory account is very similar to the two product costing systems.

The main difference between job order costing and process costing is the way in which costs are assigned to products. In a job order costing system, costs are traced to specific jobs and products. In a process costing system, an averaging technique is used. All products worked on during a specific time period (a week or a month) are used for computing unit cost. Total costs of direct materials, direct labor, and manufacturing overhead accumulated in the Work in Process Inventory account (or accounts) are divided by the equivalent units for products worked on during the period.

Work in Process Inventory, Finished Goods Inventory, and Product Unit Cost

The Work in Process Inventory accounts are the focal point of process costing. There is one Work in Process Inventory account for each process or department in the production process. Figure 3 shows how costs flow through the Work in Process Inventory accounts during the winemaking process. As direct materials, direct labor, and manufacturing overhead are used, their costs flow to the Work in Process

BUSINESS BULLETIN: ETHICS IN PRACTICE

Downsizing is one tactic American management is using to regain competitiveness in today's global marketplace. Other terms for this action are *rightsizing* and *reengineering*. When a company downsizes, it is often attempting to reduce product and other operating costs by replacing a significant portion of its work force with automated manufacturing and other operating systems. Such wholesale layoffs have caused employees to question their loyalty to their employers, a loyalty that has always been crucial to American success in world markets. Does a business owe loyalty to its employees, and do employees owe loyalty to their employers? These are important questions. Perhaps American businesses need to try other approaches to enhancing competitiveness, such as retraining employees in new skills. Certainly college students should recognize the importance of continuing to upgrade their skills throughout their careers so that they always have value in the marketplace.

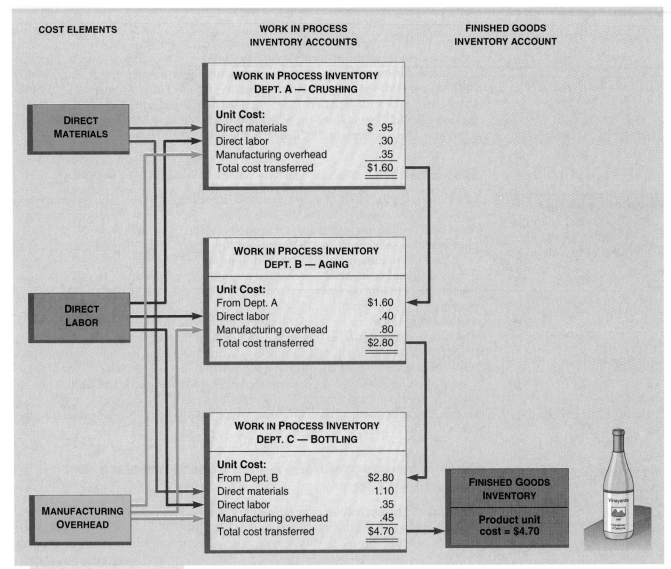

COST ELEMENTS

WORK IN PROCESS
INVENTORY ACCOUNTS

FINISHED GOODS
INVENTORY ACCOUNT

DIRECT MATERIALS

**WORK IN PROCESS INVENTORY
DEPT. A — CRUSHING**

Unit Cost:	
Direct materials	$ .95
Direct labor	.30
Manufacturing overhead	.35
Total cost transferred	$1.60

**WORK IN PROCESS INVENTORY
DEPT. B — AGING**

Unit Cost:	
From Dept. A	$1.60
Direct labor	.40
Manufacturing overhead	.80
Total cost transferred	$2.80

DIRECT LABOR

**WORK IN PROCESS INVENTORY
DEPT. C — BOTTLING**

Unit Cost:	
From Dept. B	$2.80
Direct materials	1.10
Direct labor	.35
Manufacturing overhead	.45
Total cost transferred	$4.70

MANUFACTURING OVERHEAD

FINISHED GOODS INVENTORY

Product unit
cost = $4.70

**Figure 3
Cost Flows and Product
Unit Cost in a Process
Costing System for
Winemaking**

Inventory account of the department that uses them. Department A (Crushing) and Department C (Bottling) use direct materials, and all three processes use direct labor and manufacturing overhead. Once the wine bottles are filled, labled, and packaged, they are ready for sale and are transferred to finished goods inventory. The unit costs for each bottle of wine are calculated for each department in the production process and are transferred to the next department. The product unit cost of $4.70 includes all costs from all departments. This amount is made up of $2.05 ($.95 + $1.10) in direct materials, $1.05 ($.30 + $.40 + $.35) in direct labor, and $1.60 ($.35 + $.80 + $.45) in manufacturing overhead.

The Process Cost Report

A process cost report helps managers track and analyze costs in a process costing system. The process cost report consists of three schedules: the schedule of equivalent production, the unit cost analysis schedule, and the cost summary schedule.

The Schedule of Equivalent Production

A key feature of a process costing system is the computation of equivalent units of production for each department or process for each accounting period. This computation is needed before unit costs can be computed. In process costing, an averaging approach is used. No attempt is made to associate costs with particular job orders. Instead, all manufacturing costs incurred in a department or process are divided by the units produced during the period. There are, however, several important questions to answer about the number of units produced. Exactly how many units were produced? Do we count only those units completed during the period? What about partly completed units in the beginning work in process inventory? Do we count them even if only part of the work needed to complete them was done during the period? And what about products in the ending work in process inventory? Is it proper to focus on only those units started and completed during the period?

The answers to all these questions relate to the concept of equivalent production. Equivalent production (also called *equivalent units*) is a measure of the number of equivalent whole units produced in a period of time. This measure restates partly completed units in terms of equivalent whole units. The number of equivalent units produced is equal to the sum of (1) total units started and completed during the period and (2) an amount representing the work done on partially completed products in both the beginning and the ending work in process inventories. A percentage of completion factor is applied to partially completed units to calculate the number of equivalent whole units.

Figure 4 illustrates the computation of equivalent units. One computer was in process at the beginning of Week 2, three were started and completed during Week 2, and one was still in process at period end. Actually, one-half (.5) of Computer A and three-quarters (.75) of Computer E were completed during Week 2. The total equivalent units for the week are found by adding together the units started and

**Figure 4
Computation of Equivalent
Units**

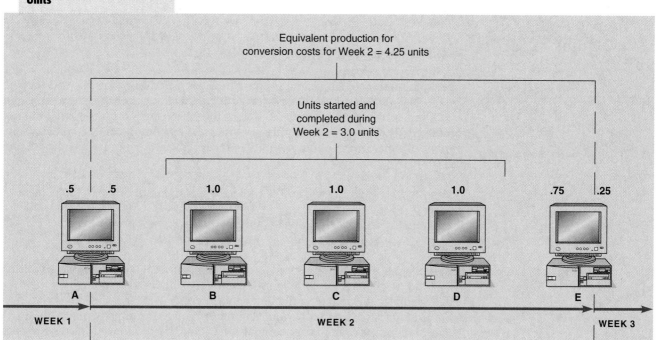

Conversion costs (the cost of direct labor and manufacturing overhead) are incurred uniformly as each computer moves through production. Equivalent production for Week 2 is 4.25 units for conversion costs. But materials costs are all added to production at the beginning of the process. Since four computers entered production in Week 2 (computers B, C, D, and E), equivalent production for the week is 4.0 units for materials costs.

completed (3.0) and the units partly completed (.5 and .75). Therefore, equivalent production for Week 2 is 4.25 units.

The foregoing method is used to determine equivalent production for conversion costs, which are the combined total of direct labor and manufacturing overhead costs incurred by a production department. Because direct labor and manufacturing overhead are often incurred uniformly throughout the production process, it is convenient to combine them when determining unit cost.

Direct materials are usually added at the beginning of a process, however, so equivalent units for *materials* costs are computed separately. As shown in Figure 4, materials for Computer A were added in Week 1 and therefore do not influence equivalent units for materials in Week 2. However, materials for Computer E were *all* added to production in Week 2. So, 3.0 (units started and completed—Computers B, C, and D) is added to 1.0 (unit started but not completed—Computer E) to get the equivalent units for materials for Week 2, 4.0 units.

Once you know the number of equivalent units produced, you can compute unit costs for materials and conversion costs for each department or work cell in the production process. The equations for computing the unit cost amounts are as follows (note the role of equivalent units):

$$\text{Unit Cost for Materials} = \frac{\text{Total Materials Costs}}{\text{Equivalent Units for Materials Costs}}$$

$$\text{Unit Cost for Conversion Costs} = \frac{\text{Total Labor and Manufacturing Overhead Costs}}{\text{Equivalent Units for Conversion Costs}}$$

Earlier we noted that direct labor and manufacturing overhead costs are usually combined and called conversion costs when computing unit cost because both types of costs are usually incurred uniformly throughout the production process. Materials costs are generally not used uniformly within the process. Such costs are usually incurred either at the beginning of the process (raw materials input) or at the end of the process (packing materials). Because of this difference, the number of equivalent units for raw materials will differ from the number for conversion costs. Separate computations of equivalent units for materials and conversion costs are necessary.

Computing Equivalent Production: No Beginning Work in Process Inventory

We will now take a closer look at the computation of equivalent production. First, we will assume that there are no units in beginning work in process inventory. In such a case, we need to consider only (1) units started and completed during the period and (2) units started but not completed. By definition, the number of units started but not completed equals the number of units in the ending work in process inventory. Equivalent production consists of two amounts:

Amount 1: Units Started and Completed = (Number of Units) × 100 percent

Amount 2: Equivalent Units in Ending Work in Process Inventory = (Number of Units) × (Average Percentage of Completion)

The *sum* of these two amounts equals the equivalent whole units completed during the period. Percentage of completion factors are obtained from engineering estimates or supervisors in the production departments.

For example, assume that Kernan Computer Products Company makes products for sale to computer mail-order companies. One of the products it makes is cables for connecting computers to monitors, modems, and other peripherals. Each cable is considered a unit in the manufacturing process. Company records for January 20xx contain the following information: (1) 47,500 units were started during

Exhibit 1. Step 1: Schedule of Equivalent Production: No Beginning Inventory

Kernan Computer Products Company
Schedule of Equivalent Production—Cables
For the Month Ended January 31, 20xx

Units—Stage of Completion	Units to Be Accounted For	Direct Materials Costs	Conversion Costs
Beginning inventory—units started last period but completed in this period	—	—	—
Units started and completed in this period	41,300	41,300	41,300
Ending inventory—units started but not completed in this period	6,200		
Direct materials costs—100% complete		6,200	
Conversion costs—60% complete			3,720
Totals	47,500	47,500	45,020

January; (2) 6,200 units were partially complete at the end of January; (3) the units in the ending work in process inventory were 60 percent completed; (4) direct materials (the parts for making the cables) were added at the beginning of the process; and (5) no units were lost or spoiled during the month.

The schedule of equivalent production, in which the period's equivalent units are computed for both direct materials costs and conversion costs, is shown in Exhibit 1. Because there were no partially complete cables in beginning work in process inventory, dashes are entered in the appropriate columns. All 41,300 units started and completed during the period (47,500 units started − 6,200 units not completed) have received 100 percent of the direct materials, direct labor, and manufacturing overhead needed to complete them. Therefore, 41,300 equivalent units are recorded in both the Direct Materials Costs and the Conversion Costs columns.

The next step is to account for the equivalent units in ending inventory. The 6,200 units have received all direct materials because the materials were added to each product as it entered the production process. Therefore, 6,200 equivalent units are entered in the Direct Materials Costs column. However, conversion costs (direct labor and manufacturing overhead) are added uniformly as the products move through the process. The 6,200 units in ending inventory are only 60 percent complete. Equivalent whole units are determined by multiplying the number of units by the percentage completed:

6,200 Units × 60% Completion = 3,720 Equivalent Units

When the columns are totaled, we find that for January, there were 47,500 equivalent units for direct materials costs and 45,020 equivalent units for conversion costs. From the standpoint of direct materials, the company has made 47,500 cables, but from the standpoint of conversion costs, the equivalent of only 45,020 cables were completed.

Computing Equivalent Production: With Beginning Work in Process Inventory
In reality, it is rare to find a manufacturer that has no beginning work in process inventory. By definition, process costing techniques are used in industries where production flows continuously or where there are long runs of identical products. Because there is usually something in process at month end, there are always units in beginning work in process inventory in the following period. Thus, we turn our analysis to such a situation, expanding the previous example.

For February 20xx, the records for Kernan Computer Products Company showed that (1) the 6,200 units in beginning work in process inventory (60 percent complete at the beginning of February) were finished during the month and (2) 57,500 units were started during the period, of which 5,000 units were partially complete (45 percent) at period end and constituted the ending work in process inventory.

In February, Kernan Computer Products Company had both beginning and ending balances for cables in work in process inventory. To compute equivalent units, we must be careful to account for only the work done in February. The computation of equivalent units is illustrated in Exhibit 2. Units in beginning inventory were 60 percent complete for conversion costs before the period began, and 100 percent complete for materials costs. All materials were added during the preceding period. Therefore, for those units, no equivalent units of materials costs were applicable to February, and only 40 percent of the conversion costs were needed to complete the units. As shown in Exhibit 2, equivalent units of conversion costs are 2,480 (6,200 units × 40 percent, the remaining percentage of completion). Computations for units started and completed and for ending inventory are similar to those for January.

Exhibit 2. Step 1: Schedule of Equivalent Production: With Beginning Inventory

Kernan Computer Products Company
Schedule of Equivalent Production—Cables
For the Month Ended February 28, 20xx

Units—Stage of Completion	Units to Be Accounted For	Equivalent Units	
		Direct Materials Costs	Conversion Costs
Beginning inventory—units started last period but completed in this period	6,200		
Direct materials costs—100% complete		—	
Conversion costs—60% complete			2,480
Units started and completed in this period	52,500	52,500	52,500
Ending inventory—units started but not completed in this period	5,000		
Direct materials costs—100% complete		5,000	
Conversion costs—45% complete			2,250
Totals	63,700	57,500	57,230

Note that our examples cover only two of the hundreds of possible process costing situations. Nevertheless, they establish the procedures necessary to solve all process costing problems using FIFO product and cost flows.

The Unit Cost Analysis Schedule

Thus far we have focused on accounting for *units* of productive output—in our example, computer cables. In the schedule of equivalent production, we computed the units to be accounted for and equivalent units for direct materials costs and conversion costs. Once we have determined this unit information, we can turn to dollar information.

The unit cost analysis schedule is used to accumulate all costs charged to the Work in Process Inventory account of each department or production process and to compute the cost per equivalent unit for direct materials costs and conversion costs. As shown in Exhibit 3, a unit cost analysis schedule has two parts: the total cost analysis and the computation of equivalent units.

The following additional information about the manufacture of computer cables is available for February 20xx:

Costs from beginning inventory
Direct materials costs	$ 20,150
Conversion costs	21,390

Current period costs
Direct materials costs	189,750
Conversion costs	320,488

This information enables us to complete the unit cost analysis schedule. As shown in Exhibit 3, all costs for the period are accumulated in the part of the schedule called "Total Cost Analysis." Included are the direct materials costs and conversion costs from beginning inventory and the direct materials costs and conversion costs incurred during the current period. All direct materials costs and conversion costs

Exhibit 3. Step 2: Unit Cost Determination

Kernan Computer Products Company
Unit Cost Analysis Schedule—Cables
For the Month Ended February 28, 20xx

Total Cost Analysis	Costs from Beginning Inventory	Current Period Costs	Total Costs to Be Accounted For
Direct materials costs	$20,150	$189,750	$209,900
Conversion costs	21,390	320,488	341,878
Totals	$41,540	$510,238	$551,778

Computation of Equivalent Unit Costs	Current Period Costs	÷ Equivalent Units*	= Cost per Equivalent Unit
Direct materials costs	$189,750	57,500	$3.30
Conversion costs	320,488	57,230	5.60
Totals	$510,238		$8.90

*From Exhibit 2.

for the period are summed in the Total Costs to Be Accounted For column. Total costs for cables to be accounted for equal $551,778, which is the sum of $209,900 in direct materials costs and $341,878 in conversion costs.

In the second part of the unit cost analysis, the part called "Computation of Equivalent Unit Costs," the costs of making the products during the current period are computed. Thus, *only current period costs* are used. The direct materials costs and conversion costs for the period are divided by their respective units of equivalent production for the period to arrive at the cost per equivalent unit. The second part of Exhibit 3 shows that the total cost of $8.90 per equivalent unit consists of $3.30 per equivalent unit for direct materials costs ($189,750 ÷ 57,500 equivalent units) plus $5.60 per equivalent unit for conversion costs ($320,488 ÷ 57,230 equivalent units). Note that the equivalent units were taken from the schedule of equivalent production in Exhibit 2.

Costs attached to units in beginning inventory are *not* included in the computation of equivalent unit costs. Under the FIFO cost flow assumption, separate costing analyses are used for each accounting period. Therefore, costs attached to beginning inventory are treated separately, in the cost summary schedule.

The Cost Summary Schedule

The final phase of the process costing analysis is to prepare the cost summary schedule, shown in Exhibit 4. This schedule helps to determine the costs to be transferred to the Finished Goods Inventory account of a department or production process and the ending balance in the Work in Process Inventory account. The information in this schedule comes from the schedule of equivalent production and the unit cost analysis schedule.

Continuing the example of computer cables, Exhibit 4 shows that the costs transferred to the Finished Goods Inventory account included $41,540 attached to the 6,200 units in beginning inventory, the costs of completing the units in beginning inventory, and the costs of producing the 52,500 units started and completed during February. Exhibit 2 shows that 2,480 equivalent units of conversion costs were required to complete the 6,200 units in the beginning work in process inventory. Because the equivalent unit conversion cost for February is $5.60, the cost to complete the units carried over from January was $13,888 (2,480 units × $5.60). The 52,500 units started and completed in February each cost $8.90 to produce. Their combined cost of $467,250 is added to the $55,428 required to produce the 6,200 units from beginning inventory to arrive at the total of $522,678 transferred to the Finished Goods Inventory account.

All costs remaining in the Work in Process Inventory account for cables after the costs of completed units have been transferred out represent the cost of the cables still in the process of being made at the end of February. As shown in the second column of Exhibit 4, the ending Work in Process Inventory balance of $29,100 is made up of $16,500 of direct materials costs (5,000 units × $3.30 per unit) and $12,600 of conversion costs (5,000 units × 45 percent × $5.60 per unit). Note that the unit figures come from the schedule of equivalent production (Exhibit 2).

When the cost summary schedule is completed, a computational check is performed, as shown in the far right column of Exhibit 4. The total cost of completed units transferred to the Finished Goods Inventory account is added to the costs of unfinished units in the Work in Process Inventory account to arrive at the total costs to be accounted for. This figure is compared with the total costs to be accounted for as calculated in the unit cost analysis schedule (Exhibit 3). The two totals should be equal, except possibly for a minor difference due to rounding. In Exhibit 4, the two figures are the same, so we know that all costs of the computer cables have been accounted for and that no calculation errors were made in the February cost analysis.

Exhibit 4. Step 3: Cost Summary Schedule

Kernan Computer Products Company
Cost Summary Schedule—Cables
For the Month Ended February 28, 20xx

	Cost of Goods Transferred to Finished Goods Inventory		Cost of Ending Work in Process Inventory		Total Costs to Be Accounted For
Beginning inventory*					
Costs from preceding period	$ 41,540				
Costs to complete this period					
Direct materials costs: none	—				
Conversion costs: 2,480					
units × $5.60	13,888				
Subtotal	$ 55,428				
Units started and completed*					
52,500 units × $8.90	467,250				
Ending inventory*					
Direct materials costs: 5,000 units × $3.30			$16,500		
Conversion costs: 2,250 units × $5.60			12,600		
Totals	$522,678	+	$29,100	=	$551,778†

*Unit figures come from the schedule of equivalent production for February (Exhibit 2).
†See the unit cost analysis schedule (Exhibit 3).

Process Costing and Activity-Based Costing

OBJECTIVE 5

Apply activity-based costing to a process costing system

In the traditional approach to process costing, two kinds of costs are accumulated in the Work in Process Inventory account: costs that can be traced directly to the process (direct materials costs and direct labor costs) and indirect production costs, which are assigned using a predetermined overhead rate, usually based on direct labor hours, labor dollars, or machine hours. This traditional approach was used in the Kernan Computer Products Company case in Learning Objective 4.

Activity-based costing (ABC) may also be used to assign costs in a process costing system. You will recall that in an activity-based costing system, all costs are first divided into two groups—those that are directly traceable to a product, process, or department (including directly traceable overhead costs such as electricity and operating supplies) and those that are not directly traceable to a cost objective. The nontraceable costs are then categorized by activity (such as setup costs, engineering costs, and materials purchasing costs), and a cost driver is identified for each activity. Companywide costs that cannot be linked to an operating activity, such as

Figure 5
Cost Flows in an Activity-Based Costing System

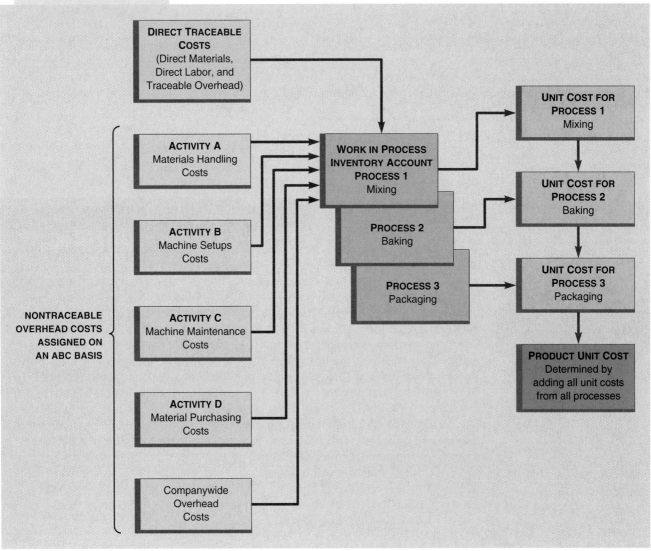

Exhibit 5. Computation and Assignment of Activity-Based Costs

Step 1. Compute assignment rates for May.

Activity	Cost Driver	Cost Driver Level	Total Cost	Assignment Rate
Materials handling	Number of moves	230	$57,500	$250 per move
Machine setups	Number of setups	90	18,000	200 per setup
Machine maintenance	Maintenance hours	450	6,750	15 per hour
Materials purchasing	Number of purchases	150	7,500	50 per purchase
Companywide overhead	Number of square feet	20,000	66,000	3.30 per square foot

Step 2. Assign ABC overhead to Mixing Department for May.

Activity	Cost Driver Level	Assignment Rate	Cost Assigned
Materials handling	70 moves	$250	$17,500
Machine setups	60 setups	200	12,000
Machine maintenance	200 hours	15	3,000
Materials purchasing	30 purchases	50	1,500
Companywide overhead	3,000 square feet	3.30	9,900
Total overhead costs assigned			$43,900

Step 3. Prepare process cost report.

Compute equivalent units, unit costs, and cost summary of cost of goods transferred and cost of ending work in process inventory in the usual way. Include ABC-assigned costs as a conversion cost in the computation of unit cost.

plant insurance and building and grounds maintenance, are grouped together and assigned using a base such as square footage.

In a traditional process costing system, only direct materials and conversion costs are assigned to the Work in Process Inventory account. However, in an ABC system, more detailed information is gathered about costs and activities. As a result, more overhead costs may be assigned to a process because costs related to activities or cost drivers can be directly traced to the incurrence of the costs. To illustrate cost assignment using activity-based costing, assume that Dolcini Products Company manufactures several different kinds of Italian-style breads. The company has three processes—mixing, baking, and packaging—and employs an activity-based costing system.

Figure 5 illustrates the cost flow in Dolcini's activity-based costing system. The Work in Process Inventory account for each process receives costs that can be identified as directly traceable—direct materials costs, direct labor costs, and traceable overhead costs—and nontraceable overhead costs assigned on the basis of specifically identified activities, such as materials handling, machine setups, machine maintenance, and materials purchasing. Nontraceable companywide overhead costs are assigned on a predetermined basis, such as square feet occupied by the department. Each process's contribution to the bread's cost is then determined, and these figures are summed to determine the product unit cost.

Exhibit 5 illustrates the application of ABC costing to Dolcini's Mixing Department for the month of May. The first step is the calculation of the assignment rate for each cost driver for the overall company. Each assignment rate is calculated by dividing the total cost of the activity by the cost driver level. For instance, the cost of materials handling is to be assigned at a rate of $250 per move required by the department. For companywide overhead, number of square feet is used.

The second step is to assign the costs applicable to the Mixing Department. This is done by multiplying the cost driver level used by each activity in the Mixing Department by the assignment rate. For materials handling, a total of $17,500 is assigned (70 moves during the month at the rate of $250 per move). The portion of the company's nontraceable overhead assigned to the Mixing Department for the month of May was $43,900.

The next step is to prepare a process cost report for the Mixing Department similar to the one prepared for Kernan Computer Products Company earlier in this chapter. The process cost report differs in only one way when ABC is used. In the unit cost analysis, the calculation of conversion costs is expanded to include one amount for directly traceable labor and a separate amount for ABC-assigned overhead. A unit cost analysis schedule using ABC is illustrated in this chapter's Review Problem.

Using Product Costing Information to Evaluate Performance

OBJECTIVE 6

Evaluate operating performance using product costing information

The job order and process costing systems provide valuable information to managers. Both approaches provide unit costs that can be used in determining a product's price. In addition, the information supplied by the two systems is used to compute the balances in the Materials Inventory, Work in Process Inventory, and Finished Goods Inventory accounts on the balance sheet and the cost of goods sold on the income statement.

Both the job order and process costing systems also supply managers with much more information that is useful in tracking and evaluating operating performance. The following measurements help managers analyze operating efficiency:

Cost trends of a product or product line

Units produced per time period

Materials usage per unit produced

Labor cost per unit produced

Special order needs of customers

Comparisons of the cost-effectiveness of changing to a more advanced production process

Cost trends can be developed from product cost data over several time periods. Such trends can help managers identify areas of rising costs or areas in which cost-effectiveness has improved. Tracking units produced per time period, a figure easily pulled from a product costing analysis, can help managers evaluate operating efficiency.

Direct materials and labor costs represent a significant part of a product's cost and should be monitored constantly. Trends in direct materials usage and labor costs per unit produced can help managers determine optimal resource usage.

Anticipating customers' needs is very important to managers. Job order cost cards summarize the size, costs, and type of product a specific customer has ordered. By tracking such information, managers can see which customers are increasing their orders and which are reducing them and take action to improve customer relations.

Finally, decisions to purchase new, automated machinery and equipment are often based on the savings that the change is expected to produce. Managers can estimate product unit costs for the new equipment and compare them with cost trends for the existing equipment to decide whether or not to make a purchase.

Honda Motor Corp. has been highly successful because of management's ability to simultaneously cut product costs and refine the company's automated assembly line. The company has found that by cutting the time it takes to make an automobile, it also cuts the costs of making the product. With a standardized, continuous flow production process, would Honda Motor Corp. use a process costing system? The answer is that the company would probably use a system designed around the process costing approach, but some aspects of job order costing would also be incorporated. Why? Because even though a continuous assembly line is in operation, all custom-ordered variants of a particular model are manufactured at the same time as non-custom-ordered cars. This product costing system is called *operation costing*.[3]

The Average Costing Approach to Process Costing

SUPPLEMENTAL OBJECTIVE 7

Compute equivalent units, product unit cost, and the ending Work in Process Inventory balance in a process costing system that uses the average costing approach

Figure 2 shows how products flow through a manufacturing process in a first-in, first-out (FIFO) order. In the FIFO approach to process costing, the assignment of costs follows the same order as the product flow. Another approach to process costing, the average costing approach, assigns costs in a different way. The average costing approach assumes that the items in beginning work in process inventory were started and completed during the current period. The process cost report under the average costing approach uses the same three schedules as that under the FIFO approach, but the procedures for completing the schedules differ.

The Schedule of Equivalent Production

No Beginning Work in Process Inventory   When there is no beginning work in process inventory, the computation of equivalent units is exactly the same under the average costing approach as it is under the FIFO method. The two approaches generate different amounts of equivalent units only in cases in which there is beginning inventory.

With Beginning Work in Process Inventory   The first difference between the FIFO costing and average costing methods is found in the computation of equivalent units when there is beginning work in process inventory. Remember that under the average costing approach, all units in beginning inventory are treated as if they were started and completed in the current period. However, equivalent units can still be calculated in three parts:

Part 1:   Units in Beginning Inventory = Number of Units × 100 percent

Part 2:   Units Started and Completed = Number of Units × 100 percent

Part 3:   Equivalent units in ending work in process inventory:

Materials Costs = Number of Units × Percentage of Completion

Conversion Costs = Number of Units × Percentage of Completion

Notice that the computation of parts 2 and 3 is the same under both costing approaches.

Part **A** of Exhibit 6 shows the use of the average costing approach to compute equivalent units for Jansson Manufacturing Company, a company that makes paint. For April 20xx, there were 1,450 units in beginning Work in Process Inventory, 100 percent complete for direct materials costs and 40 percent complete for conversion

Exhibit 6. Process Cost Report: Average Costing Approach

Jansson Manufacturing Company
Mixing Department—Process Cost Report Using Average Costing
For the Month Ended April 30, 20xx

A. Schedule of Equivalent Production

		Equivalent Units	
Units—Stage of Completion	Units to Be Accounted For	Direct Materials Costs	Conversion Costs
Beginning inventory	1,450	1,450	1,450
Units started and completed in this period	53,350	53,350	53,350
Ending inventory—units started but not completed in this period	2,250		
Direct materials costs—100% complete		2,250	
Conversion costs—70% complete			1,575 (70% of 2,250)
Totals	57,050	57,050	56,375

B. Unit Cost Analysis Schedule

	Total Costs			Equivalent Unit Costs	
	(1) Costs from Beginning Inventory	(2) Current Period Costs	(3) Total Costs to Be Accounted For	(4) Equivalent Units	(3 ÷ 4) Cost per Equivalent Unit
Direct materials costs	$12,760	$489,280	$502,040	57,050	$ 8.80
Conversion costs	1,760	278,975	280,735	56,375	4.98
Totals	$14,520	$768,255	$782,775		$13.78

C. Cost Summary Schedule

	Cost of Goods Transferred to Cooling Department	Cost of Ending Work in Process Inventory	Total Costs to Be Accounted For
Beginning inventory: 1,450 units × $13.78 per unit	$ 19,981		
Units started and completed: 53,350 units × $13.78 per unit	735,163		
Ending inventory			
Direct materials costs: 2,250 units × $8.80		$19,800**	
Conversion costs: 1,575 units × $4.98		7,844	
Totals	$755,144	$27,644	$782,788*

*Difference of $13 due to rounding.
**Rounded.

costs. In addition, 53,350 units were started and completed during the month. Ending Work in Process Inventory contained 2,250 units, 100 percent complete for direct materials costs and 70 percent complete for conversion costs. As shown in Exhibit 6, the full amount of the 1,450 units in beginning inventory is entered in both the Direct Materials Costs and the Conversion Costs columns. The full amount of the 53,350 units started and completed during April is also entered in the Direct Materials Costs and Conversion Costs columns. Ending inventory is 100 percent complete for direct materials, so 2,250 equivalent units are entered in the Direct

Materials Costs column. Since these units are only 70 percent complete, 1,575 equivalent units (2,250 × 70 percent) are entered in the Conversion Costs column. The end result is a monthly total of 57,050 equivalent units for direct materials costs and 56,375 equivalent units for conversion costs for the Mixing Department at Jansson Manufacturing Company.

The Unit Cost Analysis Schedule

There is one significant difference between the unit cost analysis schedule computed under the average costing method and the one prepared using the FIFO method. Under the FIFO approach, to compute the cost per equivalent unit, we divide the amount in the Current Period Costs column by the respective amount in the Equivalent Units column. Under the average costing approach, we divide the amount in the Total Costs to Be Accounted For column by the respective amount in the Equivalent Units column. The costs in beginning inventory and the costs of the current period are added together and treated as current costs (averaged), just as beginning inventory units are treated as if they were started and completed during the period.

As shown in part **B** of Exhibit 6, Jansson's total cost per equivalent unit computed under the average costing approach is $13.78. Materials costs per unit are $8.80 (found by dividing the total materials costs to be accounted for, $502,040, by 57,050 equivalent units). To compute the conversion costs per unit, the total conversion costs to be accounted for—$280,735—are divided by 56,375 equivalent units to arrive at $4.98 per unit.

The Cost Summary Schedule

The cost summary schedule identifies the cost of goods completed and transferred to the next department, process, or finished goods inventory. Under the average costing method, because beginning work in process inventory is treated as if it were started and completed during the current period, the units in beginning inventory and the units actually started and completed in this period are treated alike. Both are costed out at the total unit cost computed in the unit cost analysis schedule. Costs of units in ending work in process inventory are computed in exactly the same way as they were under the FIFO costing approach. The units in ending inventory are multiplied by the respective percentages of completion and cost per equivalent unit for materials costs and conversion costs to compute the ending balance of the Work in Process Inventory account.

Part **C** of Exhibit 6 shows the completed cost summary schedule for the Jansson Manufacturing Company. To compute the cost of goods completed and transferred to the Cooling Department during April, both the units in beginning work in process inventory (1,450) and the units started and completed in April (53,350) are multiplied by the $13.78 cost per equivalent unit. The 1,450 units in beginning inventory are valued at $19,981 (1,450 × $13.78), and the 53,350 units started and completed are valued at $735,163 (53,350 × $13.78). The total costs transferred out in April are $755,144.

The final step needed to complete the cost summary schedule is to compute the dollar value of the units in ending work in process inventory. Since all materials are added at the beginning of the process, the 2,250 units are multiplied by a 100 percent completion factor and by $8.80 to arrive at the $19,800 for total materials costs. Conversion costs of $7,844 are computed by multiplying 2,250 units times the 70 percent completion factor (equals 1,575 equivalent units) times $4.98 per unit. The total cost of the units in ending work in process inventory of $27,644 is found by adding $19,800 and $7,844.

Chapter Review

REVIEW OF LEARNING OBJECTIVES

1. **Describe the process costing system, discuss its role in the management cycle, and identify the reasons for its use.** A process costing system is a product costing system used by companies that produce large amounts of similar products or liquids, or that have a continuous production flow. In a process costing system, the costs of materials, labor, and manufacturing overhead are traced to processes or work cells and then assigned to the products manufactured by those processes or work cells during a particular time period. Industries that produce paint, beverages, bricks, canned foods, milk, and paper are typical users of the process costing system.

   The product costs provided by the process costing system play a key role in the management cycle. During the planning stage of the management cycle, past and projected product costing information can help managers set selling prices and prepare budgets. During the executing stage of the cycle, actual costs are incurred as units are produced. During the reviewing stage, performance is evaluated by comparing budgeted costs with actual costs. In the reporting stage, actual units produced and costs incurred are used to value inventory on the balance sheet and cost of goods sold on the income statement.

2. **Relate the patterns of product flows in a process costing environment to the process cost flow approaches.** Process costing is used to account for the production of large amounts of similar products or liquids or for long, continuous production runs of identical products. Thus, products flow in a FIFO fashion (first in, first out). Once a product is started into production, it flows on to completion. In a process costing system, manufacturing costs are handled differently from the way they are in a job order cost system. Following a FIFO costing approach, unit costs are computed using only current period cost and unit data. Costs attached to units in the beginning work in process inventory are treated separately. The unit costs are assigned to completed units and to units in the ending work in process inventory.

3. **Explain the role of the Work in Process Inventory account(s) in a process costing system.** The Work in Process Inventory account is the heart of the process costing system. Each production department or operating unit has its own Work in Process Inventory account. All costs charged to that department flow into this inventory account. A process cost report is completed at period end to determine the costs flowing out of the Work in Process Inventory account.

4. **Prepare a process cost report: (a) Use a schedule of equivalent production to compute the equivalent units of production, (b) use a unit cost analysis schedule to compute product unit cost for a specific time period, and (c) complete a cost summary schedule that assigns costs to units completed and transferred out during the period, and compute the ending balance in the Work in Process Inventory account.** Equivalent units are computed from unit information, including (1) units in the beginning work in process inventory and their percentage of completion, (2) units started and completed during the period, and (3) units in the ending work in process inventory and their percentage of completion. If materials are added at the beginning of the manufacturing process, no materials are added to the units in beginning inventory during the current period, so no materials costs are included in the computation of equivalent units. All units started during the period receive the full amount of materials. Equivalent units for costs added uniformly throughout the process are computed by multiplying the percentage completed in the current period by the total units in the respective categories mentioned above. Unit costs are found by using a unit cost analysis schedule. Materials costs for units in beginning inventory and materials costs for the current period are added. The same procedure is followed for conversion costs. Total costs to be accounted for are found by adding the total materials costs and conversion costs. Following FIFO costing procedures, the unit cost for materials is found by dividing the materials costs for the current period by the equivalent unit amount for materials. The same procedure is followed for conversion costs. Then the unit costs for materials and conversion costs are added to yield the total unit cost for the period. The first part of the cost summary schedule is used to compute the costs assigned to units completed and transferred out during the period.

The cost of producing the units in the beginning inventory is determined by adding the costs transferred in from the preceding period and the conversion costs needed to complete the units during the current period. That amount is added to the total cost of producing all units started and completed during the period. The result is the total cost to be transferred to the Finished Goods Inventory account. The second part of the cost summary schedule assigns costs to units still in process at period end. Unit costs for materials and conversion costs are multiplied by their respective equivalent units. The total equals the balance in the Work in Process Inventory account at the end of the period.

5. Apply activity-based costing to a process costing system. In an activity-based costing system, more costs are directly traceable to a product, process, or department than in a traditional system. As a result, when ABC is used in a process costing system, there are three categories of costs. The category for materials costs stays the same as in a traditional process costing system, but there are two categories of conversion costs: (1) traceable conversion costs, which include traceable labor costs and traceable overhead costs, and (2) nontraceable conversion costs, which are companywide overhead costs that cannot be traced to an activity. The costs of activities are assigned to the Work in Process Inventory accounts using predetermined cost drivers as bases. The companywide costs that cannot be traced to activities are accumulated in a companywide overhead pool and assigned using a predetermined base, such as square footage. Product unit cost is determined by adding all unit costs for all processes.

6. Evaluate operating performance using product costing information. Both the job order and the process costing systems supply information that managers can use to track and evaluate the operating performance of an organization. The following measurements can help managers analyze operating efficiency: cost trends of a product or product line; units produced per time period; materials usage per unit produced; labor cost per unit produced; special order needs of customers; and comparisons of the cost-effectiveness of changing to a more advanced production process.

Supplemental Objective

7. Compute equivalent units, product unit cost, and the ending Work in Process Inventory balance in a process costing system that uses the average costing approach. The average costing approach to process costing is an alternative method of accounting for production costs in a continuous flow manufacturing environment. The same three schedules that were completed under the FIFO method—the schedule of equivalent production, the unit cost analysis schedule, and the cost summary schedule—must be completed for each process. The only difference between the FIFO and average costing approaches is that the latter assumes that the items in beginning work in process inventory were started and completed during the current period. Costs in beginning inventory are averaged with current period costs to compute the product unit costs used to value the ending balance in Work in Process Inventory and goods completed and transferred out of the process or work cell.

REVIEW OF CONCEPTS AND TERMINOLOGY

The following concepts and terms were introduced in this chapter:

LO 2 **Average costing approach:** A process costing method that assigns an average cost to all products made during an accounting period; cost assignment is not linked to the physical product flow.

LO 4 **Conversion costs:** The combined total of direct labor and manufacturing overhead costs incurred by a production department.

LO 4 **Cost summary schedule:** A process costing schedule that is used to determine the costs to be transferred to the Finished Goods Inventory account of a department or production process and the ending balance of the Work in Process Inventory account.

LO 4 **Equivalent production:** A measure of the number of equivalent whole units produced in a period of time. Also called *equivalent units*.

LO 2 **FIFO costing approach:** A process costing method in which the cost flow follows the logical product flow; the costs assigned to the first products made are the first costs transferred from the department to the next department.

LO 1   **Process costing system:** A product costing system used by companies that produce large amounts of similar products or liquids, or that have a continuous production flow; the costs of materials, labor, and manufacturing overhead are traced to processes or work cells and then assigned to the products produced by those processes or work cells.

LO 4   **Process cost report:** A set of three schedules that help managers track and analyze costs in a process costing system; it consists of the schedule of equivalent production, the unit cost analysis schedule, and the cost summary schedule.

LO 4   **Schedule of equivalent production:** A process costing schedule in which a period's equivalent units are computed for both materials costs and conversion costs.

LO 4   **Unit cost analysis schedule:** A process costing statement used to accumulate all costs charged to the Work in Process Inventory account of each department or production process and to compute cost per equivalent unit for direct materials costs and conversion costs.

REVIEW PROBLEM
Activity-Based Costing in a Process Costing System

LO 4
LO 5
Newell Company of Scottsdale, Arizona, produces a line of sunscreen products, all of which must go through the same blending process. The company employs an activity-based costing system and assigns many overhead costs to the various parts of the operating process using ABC assignment rates. However, some overhead costs, such as supplies and electric power, are traced directly to the production processes. At September 1, 20xx, there were 1,400 units in process in the Blending Department, 100 percent complete for materials costs and 40 percent complete for conversion costs. During September, 52,600 units were started into production. At the close of operations on September 30, 1,300 units remained in process, with all materials and 20 percent of the conversion costs added. Activity-based costing information for September was as follows:

			Cost Driver Amounts	
Activity	Total Costs	Cost Driver	Total Company	Blending Department
Materials handling	$22,496	Number of moves	152 moves	55 moves
Machine setups	65,120	Number of setups	296 setups	63 setups
Machine maintenance	19,200	Maintenance hours	480 hours	56 hours
Materials purchasing	17,920	Number of purchases	64 purchases	16 purchases
Companywide overhead	26,000	Number of square feet	10,000 square feet	1,650 square feet

Other cost information for September for the Blending Department is summarized below:

Beginning work in process inventory	
Direct materials costs	$ 3,575
Conversion costs:	
Directly traceable labor and overhead	718
ABC-assigned overhead	336
Costs for September	
Direct materials costs	131,500
Conversion costs:	
Directly traceable labor and overhead	66,550
ABC-assigned overhead	?

Output of the Blending Department is transferred to the Bottling Department, where, prior to bottling, special ingredients are added to the blended solution to form the company's various sunscreen products.

REQUIRED

1. Compute the activity-based costing assignment rates for September.
2. Compute the amount of ABC-assigned overhead that was charged to the Blending Department in September.
3. Using the FIFO process costing approach, prepare a process cost report for the Blending Department for September. Include (a) a schedule of equivalent production, (b) a unit cost analysis schedule, and (c) a cost summary schedule.
4. From the information in the cost summary schedule, identify the amount that should be transferred out of the Work in Process Inventory account, and state where those dollars should be transferred.

ANSWER TO REVIEW PROBLEM

1. Activity-based cost assignment rates for September:

Activity	Cost Driver	Cost Driver Level	Total Cost	Assignment Rate
Materials handling	Number of moves	152	$22,496	$148.00 per move
Machine setups	Number of setups	296	65,120	220.00 per setup
Machine maintenance	Maintenance hours	480	19,200	40.00 per hour
Materials purchasing	Number of purchases	64	17,920	280.00 per purchase
Companywide overhead	Number of square feet	10,000	26,000	2.60 per square foot

2. ABC-assigned overhead charged to the Blending Department in September:

Activity	Cost Driver Level	Assignment Rate	Cost Assigned
Materials handling	55 moves	$148.00	$ 8,140
Machine setups	63 setups	220.00	13,860
Machine maintenance	56 hours	40.00	2,240
Materials purchasing	16 purchases	280.00	4,480
Companywide overhead	1,650 square feet	2.60	4,290
Total overhead costs assigned			$33,010

3. Preparation of process cost report:

Newell Company
Blending Department
Process Cost Report
For the Month Ended September 30, 20xx

A. Schedule of Equivalent Production

| Units—Stage of Completion | Units to Be Accounted For | Equivalent Units | |
		Direct Materials Costs	Conversion Costs
Beginning inventory—units started last period but completed in this period	1,400		
Direct materials costs—100% complete		0	
Conversion costs—40% complete			840 (60% of 1,400)
Units started and completed in this period (52,600 − 1,300)	51,300	51,300	51,300
Ending inventory—units started but not completed in this period	1,300		
Direct materials costs—100% complete		1,300	
Conversion costs—20% complete			260 (20% of 1,300)
Totals	54,000	52,600	52,400

B. Unit Cost Analysis Schedule

	Costs from Beginning Inventory	Current Period Costs	Total Costs to Be Accounted For
Direct materials costs	$3,575	$131,500	$135,075
Conversion costs:			
Directly traceable labor and overhead	718	66,550	67,268
ABC-assigned overhead	336	33,010	33,346
Total conversion costs	$1,054	$ 99,560	$100,614
Totals	$4,629	$231,060	$235,689

Computation of Equivalent Unit Costs	Current Period Costs	÷	Equivalent Units	=	Cost per Equivalent Unit
Direct materials costs	$131,500		52,600		$2.50
Conversion costs	99,560		52,400		1.90
Totals	$231,060				$4.40

C. Cost Summary Schedule

	Cost of Goods Transferred to Bottling Department	Cost of Ending Work in Process Inventory	Total Costs to Be Accounted For
Beginning inventory			
Beginning balance	$ 4,629		
Cost to complete:			
1,400 units × 60% × $1.90 per unit	1,596		
Total beginning inventory	$ 6,225		
Units started and completed			
51,300 units × $4.40 per unit	225,720		
Ending inventory			
Direct materials costs:			
1,300 units × $2.50 per unit		$3,250	
Conversion costs:			
260 units × $1.90 per unit		494	
Totals	$231,945	$3,744	$235,689

4. Units costing $231,945 were completed during September and should be transferred to the Work in Process Inventory account of the Bottling Department.

Chapter Assignments

BUILDING YOUR KNOWLEDGE FOUNDATION

Questions

1. What is a process costing system?
2. What types of companies are likely to employ a process costing system?
3. What two methods may be used to assign costs to products in a process costing system?
4. Explain the FIFO costing approach to assigning costs to products in a process costing system.
5. Explain the similarity between job order and process costing systems in accounting for the costs of materials, labor, and overhead.
6. Explain the difference between job order and process costing systems in accounting for the costs of materials, labor, and overhead.
7. "In job order costing, one Work in Process Inventory account is used for all jobs. In process costing, several Work in Process Inventory accounts are used." Explain these statements.
8. What three schedules are used in a process cost report?
9. Define the term *equivalent production* (or *equivalent units*).
10. Why must actual unit data be changed to equivalent unit data to cost products in a process costing system?
11. Define the term *conversion costs*. Why are conversion costs used in process costing computations?
12. Why is it easier to compute equivalent units without units in beginning inventory than with units in beginning inventory?
13. What are the purposes of the unit cost analysis schedule?

14. What two important dollar amounts come from the cost summary schedule? How do they relate to the year-end financial statements?

15. Describe how to check the accuracy of the results in the cost summary schedule.

16. Which of the three schedules in a process cost report is affected by a switch to activity-based costing? Describe the changes.

17. What type of operating performance can be evaluated by (a) units produced per time period, (b) labor cost per unit produced, and (c) special order needs of customers?

18. Explain the average costing approach to assigning costs to products in a process costing system.

19. Briefly describe the similarities and differences in the uses of the process cost report in the FIFO and average costing approaches to process costing.

Short Exercises

SE 1.
LO 1 *Process Versus Job Order Costing*

Indicate whether the manufacturer of each of the following products should use a job order costing system or a process costing system to accumulate product costs.

1. Plastics
2. Ocean cruise ships
3. Cereal
4. Medical drugs for veterinary practices

SE 2.
LO.1 *Process Versus Job Order Costing*

Indicate whether each of the following is a characteristic of job order costing or of process costing.

1. Several Work in Process Inventory accounts are used, one for each department or part in the process.
2. Costs are grouped by department, process, or work cell.
3. Costs are measured for each completed job.
4. Only one Work in Process Inventory account is used.
5. Costs are measured in terms of units completed in specific time periods.
6. Costs are assigned to specific jobs or batches of product.

SE 3.
LO 3 *Process Costing and the Work in Process Inventory Account*

BioCo Chemical uses an automated mixing machine to combine three raw materials into a product called Triogo. On the average, each unit of Triogo contains $3 of Material X, $6 of Material Y, $9 of Material Z, $2 of direct labor, and $12 of manufacturing overhead. Total costs charged to the Work in Process Inventory account during the month were $208,000. There were no units in beginning or ending work in process inventory. How many units were completed and transferred to finished goods inventory during the month?

SE 4.
LO 4 *Equivalent Production: No Beginning Inventory*

Given the following information from Blue Blaze's records for July 20xx, compute the equivalent units of production.

Beginning inventory	—
Units started during the period	17,000
Units partially completed	2,500
Percentage of completion of ending work in process inventory	70%

Direct materials are added at the beginning of the process, and conversion costs are added uniformly throughout the process.

SE 5.
LO 4 *Equivalent Production: Beginning Inventory*

Assume the same information as in **SE 4**, except that there were 3,000 units in beginning work in process inventory, 100 percent complete for direct materials and 40 percent complete for conversion costs. Compute the equivalent units of production for the month.

LO 4 *Unit Cost Determination*

SE 6. Using the information from **SE 4** and the following information, compute the total cost per equivalent unit.

Costs for the period
Direct materials costs	$20,400
Conversion costs	32,500

LO 4 *Cost Summary Schedule*

SE 7. Using the information from **SE 4** and **SE 6** and the FIFO method, prepare a cost summary schedule.

LO 5 *ABC and Process Costing*

SE 8. From the following data, assemble a detailed analysis of the conversion costs that should be charged to the process for the period:

Direct materials costs, $12,675

Labor costs, $2,790

Directly traceable overhead costs, $8,910

12 machine setups at $40 per setup

9 purchases at $60 per purchase order

Plant building maintenance: 200 square feet at $18 per square foot

LO 6 *Measuring Performance with Product Costing Data*

SE 9. The following are weekly average direct materials costs per unit for two products. What use could a manager of the department that is producing these products make of this information?

Week	Product A	Product B
1	$45.20	$23.90
2	46.10	23.80
3	48.30	23.80
4	49.60	23.60

SO 7 *Average Costing Method*

SE 10. The cost summary schedule below is based on the average costing method. It was prepared for the Peretti Pasta Company for the year ended July 31, 20xx.

Peretti Pasta Company
Cost Summary Schedule
For the Year Ended July 31, 20xx

	Cost of Goods Transferred to Finished Goods Inventory	Cost of Ending Work in Process Inventory
Beginning inventory		
3,140 units at $4.60	$ 14,444	
Units started and completed		
94,960 units at $4.60	436,816	
Ending inventory		
Direct materials costs:		
4,200 units at $3.20		$13,440
Conversion costs:		
2,100 units at $1.40		2,940
Totals	$451,260	$16,380

Prepare the company's schedule of equivalent production. Assume that direct materials are added at the beginning of the process.

Exercises

LO 1 *Process Versus Job Order Costing*

E 1. Indicate whether the manufacturer of each of the following products should use a job order costing system or a process costing system to accumulate product costs.

1. Paint
2. Fruit juices
3. Tailor-made suits
4. Milk
5. Coffee cups printed with your school insignia
6. Paper
7. Roller coaster for a theme park
8. Posters for a fund-raising event

LO 2 *Use of Process Costing Information*

E 2. Bernard's Bakery makes a variety of cakes, cookies, and pies for distribution to five major grocery store chains in the Tri-City area. A standard process is used to manufacture all items except the special-order birthday cakes. Bernard wants to know if the process costing system currently used in the company can help him find some crucial information. Which of the following questions can be answered using information from a process costing system? Which of the following questions can be best answered using a job order costing system? Explain.

1. How much does it cost to make one chocolate cheesecake?
2. Did the cost of making special-order birthday cakes exceed the cost budgeted for this month?
3. What is the value of the pie inventory at the end of June?
4. What were the costs of the cookies sold during June?
5. At what price should we sell our famous brownies to the grocery store chains?
6. Did we exceed our planned production costs of $3,000 for making pies in June?

LO 3 *Work in Process Inventory Accounts in Process Costing Systems*

E 3. Grant, Inc., makes a chemical used as a food preservative through a manufacturing process involving Departments A and B. The company had the following total costs and unit costs for completed production last month, when 10,000 pounds of chemicals were manufactured.

	Total Cost	Unit Cost
Department A		
Direct materials	$10,000	$1.00
Direct labor	2,600	.26
Manufacturing overhead	1,300	.13
Totals, Dept. A	$13,900	$1.39
Department B		
Direct materials	$ 3,000	$ .30
Direct labor	700	.07
Manufacturing overhead	1,000	.10
Totals, Dept. B	$ 4,700	$ .47
Totals	$18,600	$1.86

1. How many Work in Process Inventory accounts would Grant use?
2. What dollar amount of the chemical's production cost was transferred from Department A to Department B last month?
3. What dollar amount was transferred from Department B to the Finished Goods Inventory account?
4. What dollar amount is useful in order to estimate a selling price for one pound of the chemical?

LO 4 *Equivalent Units: No Beginning Inventories*

E 4. Salazar Stone Company produces slumpstone bricks. Though it has been in operation for only twelve months, the company already enjoys a good reputation. During its first year, direct materials for 600,000 bricks were put into production; 586,000 were completed and transferred to finished goods inventory. The remaining bricks were still in process at year end, 60 percent complete. In the company's process costing system, all direct materials are added at the beginning of the process. Conversion costs are incurred uniformly throughout the production process.

From this information, prepare a schedule of equivalent production for the year ending December 31, 20xx. Use the FIFO costing approach.

LO 4 *Equivalent Units: Beginning Inventories—FIFO Method*

E 5. Zwick Enterprises makes Dewberry Shampoo for professional hair stylists. On January 1, 20xx, 5,200 liters of shampoo were in process, 80 percent complete as to conversion costs and 100 percent complete as to direct materials costs. During the month, 212,500 liters of direct materials were put into production. Data for work in process inventory on January 31, 20xx, were as follows: shampoo, 4,500 liters; stage of completion, 60 percent of conversion costs and 100 percent of direct materials content.

From this information, prepare a schedule of equivalent production for the month. Use the FIFO costing approach.

LO 4 *Work in Process Inventory Accounts: Total Unit Cost*

E 6. Scientists at Toguri Laboratories, Inc., have just perfected a liquid substance called D. K. Rid that dissolves tooth decay. The substance, which is generated by a complex process involving five departments, is very expensive. Cost and equivalent unit data for the latest week are as follows (units are in ounces).

	Direct Materials Costs		**Conversion Costs**	
		Equivalent		**Equivalent**
Dept.	**Dollars**	**Units**	**Dollars**	**Units**
A	$12,000	1,000	$33,825	2,050
B	21,835	1,985	13,065	1,005
C	23,896	1,030	20,972	2,140
D	—	—	22,086	2,045
E	—	—	15,171	1,945

From these data, compute the unit cost for each department and the total unit cost of producing one ounce of D. K. Rid.

LO 4 *Unit Cost Determination*

E 7. Neff Kitchenwares, Inc., manufactures sets of heavy-duty cookware. Production has just been completed for July 20xx. At the beginning of July, the Work in Process Inventory account showed direct materials costs of $31,700 and conversion costs of $29,400. The cost of direct materials used in July was $275,373; conversion costs were $175,068. During the month, 15,190 sets were started and completed. A schedule of equivalent production for July has already been prepared. It shows a total of 16,450 equivalent sets for direct materials costs and 16,210 equivalent sets for conversion costs.

With this information, prepare a unit cost analysis schedule for July. Use the FIFO costing approach.

LO 4 *Cost Summary Schedule*

E 8. The Kristoff Bakery produces Kringle coffee bread. It uses a process costing system for internal recordkeeping. In August 20xx, beginning inventory was 450 units, 100 percent complete for direct materials costs and 10 percent for conversion costs, and had a value of $655. Units started and completed during the month totaled 14,200. Ending inventory was 410 units, 100 percent complete for direct materials costs and 70 percent for conversion costs. Unit costs per equivalent unit for August were direct materials costs, $1.40, and conversion costs, $.80.

Using the information given, compute the cost of goods transferred to the Finished Goods Inventory account, the cost remaining in the Work in Process Inventory account, and the total costs to be accounted for. Use the FIFO costing approach.

LO 5 *ABC and Product Unit Cost*

E 9. Golden Enterprises produces copies of famous lithographs for artists around the world. The lithograph duplicating process is done on a series of copying machines arranged into a work cell for continuous production. At the end of August 20xx, the following data were made available for the work cell:

Beginning work in process inventory
  1,400 lithographs
  Direct materials costs, $4,060
  Conversion costs
    Directly traceable labor and overhead costs, $3,660
    ABC-assigned overhead costs, $820

August data:
  Equivalent units: Direct materials costs, 25,200 units; conversion costs, 25,430 units
    Direct materials costs incurred, $73,080
    Directly traceable labor and overhead costs, $63,766
    Activity-based cost drivers and assignment rates:

Activity	Cost Driver Level	Assignment Rate
Engineering design	25 engineering hours	$68.00 per engineering hour
Design layouts	80 design hours	$120.00 per design hour
Layout setups	6 setups	$210.00 per setup
Materials purchasing	9 purchases	$330.00 per purchase
Companywide overhead	650 square feet	$3.20 per square foot

From this information, prepare a unit cost analysis schedule for August, using the format appropriate for a process costing system using the ABC approach.

LO 6 *Measuring Performance with Nonfinancial Product Data*

E 10. During the month of December, Lazar Products Company conducted a study of the productivity of its three-machine metal-trimming center. The data were condensed into product units per hour so that managers could analyze the productivity of individual machine operators. The target output established for the year was 125 units per hour. From the data presented below, analyze the productivity of the three machine operators.

Week	Operator 1	Operator 2	Operator 3
1	119 per hour	129 per hour	124 per hour
2	120 per hour	127 per hour	124 per hour
3	122 per hour	125 per hour	123 per hour
4	124 per hour	122 per hour	124 per hour

SO 7 *Average Costing Method*

E 11. Uncle Fun Corporation produces children's toys using a liquid plastic formula and a continuous production process. In the Toy Truck Work Cell, the plastic is heated and fed into a molding machine. The molded toy trucks are then cooled and trimmed and sent to the Packaging Work Cell. All direct materials are added at the beginning of the process. In July, the beginning work in process inventory was 420 units, 40 percent complete; the ending balance was 400 units, 70 percent complete.

During the month, 15,000 units were started into production. The Work in Process Inventory account had a beginning balance of $937 for direct materials costs and $370 for conversion costs. During July, $35,300 of direct materials were added to the process and $31,760 of conversion costs were assigned to the work cell. Using the average costing method, prepare a process cost report that computes the equivalent units for July, the product unit cost for the toy trucks, and the ending balance in the Work in Process Inventory account.

Problems

P 1.

LO 4 *Process Costing: No Beginning Inventories*

LO 4 *Process Costing: No Beginning Inventories*

The Cee Gee Chewing Gum Company, which produces several flavors of bubble gum, began production of a new kumquat-flavored gum on June 1, 20xx. Two basic direct materials, gum base and kumquat-flavored sweetener, are blended at the beginning of the process. Direct labor and manufacturing overhead costs are incurred uniformly throughout the blending process. During June, 135,000 kilograms of gum base and 270,000 kilograms of kumquat additive were used at costs of $122,500 and $80,000, respectively. Direct labor charges were $299,200, and manufacturing overhead costs applied during June were $284,000. The ending work in process inventory was 21,600 kilograms. All direct materials have been added to those units, and 25 percent of the conversion costs have been assigned. Output from the Blending Department is transferred to the Packing Department.

REQUIRED

1. Prepare a process cost report with (a) a schedule of equivalent production, (b) a unit cost analysis schedule, and (c) a cost summary schedule for the Blending Department for June.
2. From the information in the cost summary schedule, identify the amount that should be transferred out of the Work in Process Inventory account, and state where those dollars should be transferred.

P 2.

LO 4 *Process Costing: With Beginning Inventories—FIFO Method*

Waukesha Bottling Company manufactures and sells several different kinds of soft drinks. Direct materials (sugar syrup and artificial flavor) are added at the beginning of production in the Mixing Department. Direct labor and manufacturing overhead costs are applied to products throughout the process. During August 20xx, beginning inventory for the citrus flavor was 1,200 gallons, 80 percent complete. Ending inventory was 1,800 gallons, 50 percent complete. Production data showed 120,000 gallons started during August. A total of 119,400 gallons was completed and transferred to the Bottling Department. Beginning inventory costs were $610 for direct materials and $676 for conversion costs. Current period costs were $60,000 for direct materials and $83,538 for conversion costs.

REQUIRED

1. Using the FIFO costing approach, prepare a process cost report for the Mixing Department for August with (a) a schedule of equivalent production, (b) a unit cost analysis schedule, and (c) a cost summary schedule.
2. From the information in the cost summary schedule, identify the amount that should be transferred out of the Work in Process Inventory account, and state where those dollars should be transferred.

P 3.

LO 4 *Process Costing: One Process/Two Time Periods—FIFO Method*

The Verdant Valley Company produces organic honey for sale to health food stores and restaurants. The company owns thousands of beehives. No direct materials other than the honey are used. The production operation is a simple one in which the impure honey is added at the beginning of the process. The honey flows through a series of filterings, leading to a pure finished product. Costs of labor and manufacturing overhead are incurred uniformly throughout the filtering process. Production data for April and May 20xx are shown below:

	April	May
Beginning Work in Process Inventory		
Units (liters)	7,100	?
Direct materials costs	$ 2,480	?
Conversion costs	$ 5,110	?
Production during the period		
Units started (liters)	286,000	312,000
Direct materials costs	$100,100	$124,800
Conversion costs	$251,190	$278,901
Ending Work in Process Inventory		
Units (liters)	10,400	14,900

The April beginning inventory was 80 percent complete for conversion costs, and ending inventory was 20 percent complete. The ending inventory for May was 30 percent complete for conversion costs. Assume that there was no loss from spoilage or evaporation.

REQUIRED

1. Using the FIFO approach, prepare a process cost report for April with (a) a schedule of equivalent production, (b) a unit cost analysis schedule, and (c) a cost summary schedule.
2. From the information in the cost summary schedule, identify the amount that should be transferred out of the Work in Process Inventory account, and state where those dollars should be transferred.
3. Repeat parts **1** and **2** for May.

P 4.

LO 4 *Process Costing*
LO 5 *System and ABC*

Huizinga Company of Azusa, California, manufactures a line of plastic products. Each type of product must go through a special bonding process before being sent to the Packaging Work Cell. The company employs an activity-based costing system and assigns many overhead costs to the various parts of the operating process using ABC assignment rates. Some overhead costs, such as supplies and electric power, are traced directly to the production processes. At July 1, 20xx, there were 800 units in process in the Bonding Work Cell, 100 percent complete for direct materials and 60 percent complete for conversion costs. During July, 32,800 units were started into production. At the close of operations on July 31, 600 units remained in process, with all direct materials and 80 percent of the conversion costs added. The following activity-based costing information was available for July:

| | | | Cost Driver Amounts | |
| | Total | Cost | Total | Bonding |
Activity	Costs	Driver	Company	Work Cell
Materials purchasing	$18,430	Number of purchase orders	97 purchase orders	36 purchase orders
Machine repairs	29,440	Repair hours	640 hours	88 hours
Machine setups	96,750	Number of setups	430 setups	108 setups
Materials moving	35,640	Number of moves	220 moves	38 moves
Companywide overhead	31,500	Number of square feet	15,000 square feet	2,260 square feet

Other cost information for July for the Bonding Work Cell is summarized below:

Beginning work in process inventory:	
Direct materials	$ 4,975
Conversion costs:	
Directly traceable labor and overhead	1,295
ABC-assigned overhead	860
Costs added to production in July:	
Direct materials	203,360
Conversion costs:	
Directly traceable labor and overhead	102,410
ABC-assigned overhead	?

Output of the Bonding Work Cell is transferred to the Packaging Work Cell, where the products are packaged in an assortment of unique containers, based on precise customer specifications.

REQUIRED

1. Compute the activity-based costing assignment rates for July.
2. Compute the amount of ABC-assigned overhead that was charged to the Bonding Work Cell in July.
3. Using the FIFO process costing approach, prepare a process cost report for the Bonding Work Cell for July 20xx. Include (a) a schedule of equivalent production, (b) a unit cost analysis schedule, and (c) a cost summary schedule.
4. From the information in the cost summary schedule, identify the amount that should be transferred out of the Work in Process Inventory account, and state where those dollars should be transferred.

P 5.

LO 4 *Process Costing:*
With Beginning
Inventories/Two
Departments—FIFO
Method

Canned fruits and vegetables are the main products made by Freeland Foods, Inc. All direct materials are added at the beginning of the Mixing Department's process. When the ingredients have been mixed, they go to the Cooking Department. There the mixture is heated to 100° Celsius and simmered for twenty minutes. When cooled, the mixture goes to the Canning Department for final processing. Throughout the operations, direct labor and manufacturing overhead costs are incurred uniformly. No direct materials are added in the Cooking Department.

Cost data and other information for January 20xx were as follows:

Production Cost Data	Direct Materials Costs	Conversion Costs
Mixing Department		
Beginning inventory	$ 28,560	$ 5,230
Current period costs	$450,000	$181,200

	Transferred-In Costs	Conversion Costs
Cooking Department		
Beginning inventory	$ 62,380	$ 12,320
Current period costs	?	$671,148
Work in Process Inventories		
Beginning inventories		
Mixing Department (40% complete)	5,000 liters	
Cooking Department (20% complete)	8,000 liters	
Ending inventories		
Mixing Department (60% complete)	6,000 liters	
Cooking Department (70% complete)	9,000 liters	

Unit Production Data	Mixing Department	Cooking Department
Units started during January	90,000 liters	89,000 liters
Units transferred out during January	89,000 liters	88,000 liters

Assume that no spoilage or evaporation loss took place during January.

REQUIRED

1. Using the FIFO costing approach, prepare a process cost report for the Mixing Department for January with (a) a schedule of equivalent production, (b) a unit cost analysis schedule, and (c) a cost summary schedule.
2. Prepare the same schedules as in **1,** this time for the Cooking Department. (Round unit costs to three decimal places.)

Alternate Problems

P 6.

LO 4 *Process Costing:*
With Beginning
Inventories—FIFO
Method

Lacho Liquid Extracts Company produces a line of fruit extracts for use in making home-made products such as wines, jams and jellies, pies, and meat sauces. Fruits are introduced into the production process in pounds; the product emerges in quarts (one pound of input equals one quart of output). On June 1, 20xx, 4,250 units were in process. All direct materials had been added, and the units were 70 percent complete as to conversion costs. Direct materials costs of $5,070 and conversion costs of $2,910 were attached to the units in beginning work in process inventory. During June, 61,300 pounds of fruit were added: apples, 23,500 pounds costing $21,600; grapes, 22,600 pounds costing $29,920; and bananas, 15,200 pounds costing $22,040. Direct labor for the month totaled $24,630, and overhead costs applied were $31,375. On June 30, 20xx, 3,400 units remained in process. All direct materials had been added, and 50 percent of conversion costs had been incurred.

REQUIRED

1. Using the FIFO costing approach, prepare a product cost report for June with (a) a schedule of equivalent production, (b) a unit cost analysis schedule, and (c) a cost summary schedule.

2. From the information in the cost summary schedule, identify the amount that should be transferred out of the Work in Process Inventory account, and state where those dollars should be transferred.

P 7.

LO 4 *Process Costing: One Process/Two Time Periods—FIFO Method*

Coconino Laboratories produces liquid detergents that leave no soap film. All elements are biodegradable. The production process has been automated, so that the product can now be produced in one operation instead of a series of heating, mixing, and cooling operations. All direct materials are added at the beginning of the process, and conversion costs are incurred uniformly throughout the process. Operating data for July and August 20xx are as follows:

	July	August
Beginning work in process inventory		
Units (pounds)	2,400	?
Direct materials costs	$ 4,700	?
Conversion costs	$ 1,220	?
Production during the period		
Units started (pounds)	31,000	32,800
Direct materials costs	$65,100	$67,240
Conversion costs	$53,448	$56,420
Ending work in process inventory		
Units (pounds)	3,100	3,600

The beginning work in process inventory was 30 percent complete as to conversion costs. The points of completion for ending work in process inventories were July, 60 percent, and August, 50 percent. Assume that the loss from spoilage and evaporation was negligible.

REQUIRED

1. Using the FIFO costing approach, prepare a process cost report for July with (a) a schedule of equivalent production, (b) a unit cost analysis schedule, and (c) a cost summary schedule.
2. From the information in the cost summary schedule, identify the amount that should be transferred out of the Work in Process Inventory account, and state where those dollars should be transferred.
3. Repeat parts **1** and **2** for August.

P 8.

SO 7 *Process Costing: With Beginning Inventories— Average Costing Method*

Hi-E Food Products, Inc., makes high-vitamin, calorie-packed wafers used by professional sports teams to supply quick energy to players. The thin white wafers are produced in a continuous flow. The company, which uses a process costing system based on the average costing approach, recently purchased several automated machines so that the wafers can be produced in a single department. Direct materials are all added at the beginning of the process. The costs for the machine operators' labor and production-related overhead are incurred uniformly throughout the process.

In February 20xx, a total of 232,000 liters of direct materials was put into production at a cost of $271,400. Two liters of direct materials were used to produce one unit of output (one unit = 144 wafers). Direct labor costs for February were $60,530. Manufacturing overhead was $144,820. The beginning work in process inventory on February 1 was 12,000 units, 100 percent complete for direct materials and 20 percent complete for conversion costs. The total cost of those units was $55,000, with $48,600 assigned to the cost of direct materials. The ending work in process inventory of 10,000 units was fully complete for direct materials, but only 30 percent complete for conversion costs.

REQUIRED

1. Assuming an average costing approach and no loss due to spoilage, prepare a process cost report with (a) a schedule of equivalent production, (b) a unit cost analysis schedule, and (c) a cost summary schedule.
2. From the information in the cost summary schedule, identify the amount that should be transferred out of the Work in Process Inventory account, and state where those dollars should be transferred.

EXPANDING YOUR CRITICAL THINKING, COMMUNICATION, AND INTERPERSONAL SKILLS

Skills Development

CONCEPTUAL ANALYSIS

LO 2 *Changing the*
LO 3 *Accounting System*

SD 1. **Transnational Cablecom** produces several types of communications cable for a worldwide market. Since the manufacturing process is continuous, a process costing system is used to develop product costs. Until recently, costs were accumulated monthly, and revised product costs were made available to management by the tenth of the following month. With the installation of a computer-integrated manufacturing system, cost information is now available as soon as each production run is finished. The production superintendent has asked the controller to change the accounting system so that product unit costs are available the day following production.

Prepare a memorandum to the corporate vice president justifying the proposed change in the accounting system. Identify reasons that the controller can use to support the production superintendent's request. What benefits would be obtained from the proposed modification? Be prepared to share your ideas with your classmates.

ETHICAL DILEMMA

LO 1 *Continuing*
LO 2 *Professional*
Education

SD 2. Paula Sciarretta is the head of the Information Systems Department at **Moreno Manufacturing Company.** Harold Randolph, the company's controller, is meeting with Paula to discuss changes in data gathering connected with the company's new automated flexible manufacturing system. Paula opened the conversation by saying, "Harold, the old job order costing methods just will not work for the new flexible manufacturing system. The new system is based on continuous product flow, not batch processing. We need to change to a process costing system for both data gathering and product costing. Otherwise, our product costs will be way off, and it will affect our pricing decisions. I found out about the need for this change at a professional seminar I attended last month. You should have been there with me." Harold responded, "Paula, who is the accounting expert here? I know what product costing approach is best for this situation. Job order costing has provided accurate information for this product line for more than fifteen years. Why should we change just because we've purchased a new machine? We've purchased several machines for this line over the years. And as for your seminar, I don't need to learn about costing methods. I was exposed to them all when I studied management accounting back in the late 1970s."

Is Harold's behavior ethical? If not, what has he done wrong? What can Paula do if Harold continues to refuse to update the product costing system?

Group Activity: Divide the class into groups and direct the groups to develop a strategy for Paula. Debrief the groups in class.

RESEARCH ACTIVITY

LO 1 *Process Costing*
LO 5 *Systems*

SD 3. Locate an article about a company that you believe would use a process costing system. Make a special effort to see if it also uses activity-based costing. Conduct your search using the business section of your local newspaper, *The Wall Street Journal,* company annual reports, or the Needles Accounting Resource Center Web site at http://www.hmco.com/college/needles/home.html.

| Communication | Critical Thinking | Group Activity | Memo | Ethics | International | Spreadsheet | Managerial Technology | Internet |

Prepare a short report that includes the company's name, its product(s), and a description of its production process. Bring this information to class to share with your classmates. Be sure to identify the article's title, author(s), and publication date.

DECISION-MAKING PRACTICE

SD 4.

LO 4 *Setting a Selling Price*

For the past four years, three companies have dominated the soft drink industry, holding a combined 85 percent of market share. **Wonder Cola, Inc.,** ranks second nationally in soft drink sales; the company had gross revenues of $27,450,000 last year. Management is thinking about introducing a new low-calorie drink called Slimit Cola.

Wonder soft drinks are processed in a single department. All direct materials (ingredients) are added at the beginning of the process. The beverages are bottled at the end of the process in bottles costing one cent each. Direct labor and manufacturing overhead costs are applied uniformly throughout the process.

Corporate controller Sam Blimley believes that costs for the new cola will be very much like those for the company's Cola Plus drink. Last year, he collected the following data about Cola Plus.

	Units	Costs
Work in Process Inventory		
January 1, 20x0[*]	2,200	
Direct materials costs		$ 2,080
Conversion costs		620
December 31, 20x0[†]	2,000	
Direct materials costs		1,880
Conversion costs		600
Units started during the year	458,500	
Costs for 20x0		
Liquid materials added		430,990
Direct labor and manufacturing overhead		229,400
Bottles		110,068

[*]50% complete.   [†]60% complete.   *Note:* Each unit is a twenty-four-bottle case.

The company's variable general administrative and selling costs are $1.10 per unit. Fixed administrative and selling costs are assigned to products at the rate of $.50 per unit. Wonder's two main competitors have already introduced a diet cola in the marketplace. Company A's product sells for $4.10 per unit, Company B's for $4.05. All costs are expected to increase by 10 percent from 20x0 to 20x1. The company tries to earn a profit of at least 15 percent on the total unit cost.

1. What factors should the company consider in setting a selling price for Slimit Cola?
2. Using the FIFO costing approach, compute (a) equivalent units for direct materials, bottle, and conversion costs; (b) the total production cost per unit; and (c) the total cost per unit of Cola Plus for 20x0.
3. What is the expected unit cost of Slimit Cola for 20x1?
4. Recommend a unit selling price range for Slimit Cola for 20x1 and give the reason(s) for your choice.

Managerial Reporting and Analysis

INTERPRETING MANAGEMENT REPORTS

MRA 1.

LO 4   *Analysis of Product Cost*

Sturdy Tire Corporation makes several lines of automobile and truck tires. The company operates in a competitive marketplace, so it relies heavily on cost data from its FIFO process costing system. It uses that information to set prices for its most competitive tires. The company's Blue Radial line has lost some of its market share during each of the past four years. Management believes that price breaks allowed by the three competitors are the main reason for the decline in sales.

The company controller, Becky Birdsong, has been asked to review the product costing information that supports price decisions on the Blue Radial line. In preparing her report, she collected the following data related to 20x2, the last full year of operations.

		Units	Dollars
Equivalent units:	Direct materials costs	84,200	
	Conversion costs	82,800	
Manufacturing costs:	Direct materials		$1,978,700
	Direct labor		800,400
	Manufacturing overhead applied		1,600,800
Unit cost data:	Direct materials costs		23.50
	Conversion costs		29.00
Work in process inventory:	Beginning (70% complete)	4,200	
	Ending (30% complete)	3,800	

Units started and completed during 20x2 totaled 80,400. Attached to the beginning Work in Process Inventory account were direct materials costs of $123,660 and conversion costs of $57,010. Birdsong found that little spoilage had occurred. The proper cost allowance for spoilage was included in the predetermined overhead rate of $2.00 per direct labor dollar. The review of direct labor cost revealed, however, that $90,500 was charged twice to the production account, the second time in error. This resulted in too much labor and overhead costs being charged to the above accounts.

So far in 20x3, the Blue Radial has been selling for $92 per tire. This price was based on the 20x2 unit data plus a 75 percent markup to cover operating costs and profit. During 20x3, the three competitors' prices for comparable tires have been about $87 per tire. In the company's process costing system, all direct materials are added at the beginning of the process, and conversion costs are incurred uniformly throughout.

REQUIRED

1. Explain how the cost-charging error is affecting the company.
2. Prepare a revised unit cost schedule for 20x2.
3. What should have been the minimum selling price per tire in 20x3?
4. Suggest ways of preventing such errors in the future.

FORMULATING MANAGEMENT REPORTS

MRA 2.

LO 2   *Using the Process*
LO 4   *Costing System*

You are the production manager for **Sargent Mills Corp.,** a manufacturer of four cereal products. The company's leading product in the market is Smackaroos, a sugar-coated puffed rice cereal. Yesterday, Walter Bonarski, the controller, reported that the production cost for each box of Smackaroos has increased approximately 22 percent in the last four months. Since the company is unable to increase the selling price for a box of Smackaroos, the increased production costs will reduce profits significantly.

Today you received a memo from Hilda Wilfong, the company president, asking you to review your production process to identify inefficiencies or waste that can be eliminated. Once you have completed your analysis, you are to write a memo presenting your findings and suggesting ways to reduce or eliminate the problems. The president will use your information during a meeting with the top management team in ten days.

You are aware of previous problems in the Baking Department and the Packaging Department. Upon your request, Walter has provided you with schedules of equivalent production, unit cost analysis schedules, and cost summary schedules for the two departments. He has also given you the following detailed summary of the cost per equivalent unit for a box of cereal.

	April	May	June	July
Baking Department				
Direct materials	$1.25	$1.26	$1.24	$1.25
Direct labor	.50	.61	.85	.90
Manufacturing overhead	.25	.31	.34	.40
Department totals	$2.00	$2.18	$2.43	$2.55
Packaging Department				
Direct materials	$ .35	$ .34	$ .33	$ .33
Direct labor	.05	.05	.04	.06
Manufacturing overhead	.10	.16	.15	.12
Department totals	$ .50	$ .55	$ .52	$ .51
Total cost per equivalent unit	$2.50	$2.73	$2.95	$3.06

REQUIRED

1. In preparation for writing your memo, answer the following questions.
   a. For whom are you preparing the memo? Does this affect the length of the memo? Explain.
   b. Why are you preparing the memo?
   c. What actions should you take to gather information for the memo? What information is needed? Is the information provided by Walter sufficient for analysis and reporting?
   d. When is the memo due? What can be done to provide accurate and timely information?
2. Based on your analysis of the information provided by Walter, where is the main problem in the production process?
3. Prepare an outline of the sections you would want in your memo.

INTERNATIONAL COMPANY

MRA 3.

LO 1 *Process Costing and*
LO 3 *the Work-in-Process Inventory Account*

SvenskStål, AB is an iron and steel producing company located in Solentuna, Sweden. Ingrid Bjornsson, the company controller, has recently redesigned the management accounting system to accommodate changes in the company's steel processing systems. Prior to the beginning of this year, the company produced only specialty iron and steel products that were made-to-order for their customers. A job order product costing system is used for the made-to-order products. With the purchase of three continuous processing work cells, the company created a new division that produces three types of sheet steel in continuous rolls. Process costing is used in this new division for product costing purposes.

At a recent meeting of the Executive Committee, Ingrid outlined the changes in the product costing system caused by the new work cells. As part of her explanation, she stated that three new Work in Process (WIP) Inventory accounts would be used, one for each of the three work cells. Lars Karlsson, the Production Superintendent, questioned the need to change product costing approaches and did not understand why so many new WIP Inventory accounts were necessary.

Why did Ingrid install a process costing system in the new division? Was a new division necessary or could the three new work cells have been merged with the specialty steel production facilities? Why were three new WIP Inventory accounts installed? Could the work of the three new work cells have been incorporated into the single WIP Inventory account used for the specialty steel orders?

EXCEL SPREADSHEET ANALYSIS

MRA 4.

LO 4 *FIFO Process Costing: One Process—Two Time Periods*

Seader Corporation produces a line of home products in its Fargo, North Dakota, plant. The Shaping Department has been making two-gallon chili pots for the past three months. The production process has been automated, so the product can now be produced in one operation rather than in the three operations that were needed before the automated machinery was purchased. All direct materials are added at the beginning of the process, and conversion costs are incurred uniformly throughout the process. Operating data for May and June 20xx were as follows:

	May	June
Beginning Work in Process Inventory		
Units (May: 40% complete)	220	?
Direct materials costs	$ 400	$ 360
Conversion costs	$ 125	$ 134
Production during the month		
Units started	24,000	31,000
Direct materials costs	$35,000	$74,400
Conversion costs	$26,000	$29,695
Ending Work in Process Inventory		
Units (May: 70% complete; June: 60% complete)	200	320
Unit costs		
Direct materials costs	$1.800	$?
Conversion costs	.958	?
Product unit cost	$2.758	$?

REQUIRED

1. Using the appropriate template on your Computer-Aided Learning diskette, prepare a complete process costing analysis for June 20xx, including (a) a schedule of equivalent units, (b) a unit cost analysis schedule, and (c) a cost summary schedule. (Round unit costs to three decimal places; round all other dollar amounts to the nearest dollar.)

2. From the information in the cost summary schedule, identify the amount that should be transferred out of the Work in Process Inventory account, and state where those dollars should be transferred.

3. Analyze the product costing results of the Shaping Department for the current month versus those for the previous month. What is the most significant change? What are some possible causes of this change?

ENDNOTES

1. John Y. Lee and Brian G. Jacobs, "Kunde Estate Winery: A Case Study in Cost Accounting," *CMA Magazine*, The Society of Management Accountants (Canada), April 1993, pp. 15–19.

2. Rex C. Hunter, Frank R. Urbancic, and Donald E. Edwards, "Process Costing: Is It Relevant?" *Management Accounting*, Institute of Management Accountants, December 1989, p. 53.

3. "Honda Sees Performance and Profits from New Accord," *The Wall Street Journal*, August 27, 1997, p. B4.

CHAPTER 5

Activity-Based Systems: Activity-Based Management and Just-in-Time

1. **Explain the role of activity-based systems in the management cycle.**
2. **Define *activity-based management (ABM)* and discuss its relationship with the supply chain and the value chain.**
3. **Distinguish between value-adding and nonvalue-adding activities, and describe process value analysis.**
4. **Define a *cost hierarchy,* describe its elements, and explain how a cost hierarchy and a bill of activities are used in activity-based costing.**
5. **Define the *just-in-time (JIT) operating philosophy* and identify the elements of a JIT operating environment.**
6. **Identify the changes in product costing that result when a firm adopts a JIT operating environment.**
7. **Define and apply *backflush costing,* and compare the cost flows in traditional and backflush costing.**
8. **Compare ABM and JIT as activity-based systems.**

DECISION POINT

TEVA PHARMACEUTICAL INDUSTRIES, LTD.

Teva Pharmaceutical Industries, Ltd., is an Israel-based company that manufactures and markets prescription drugs internationally. Its Operations Division includes four manufacturing plants in Israel that produce goods to fill orders placed by the company's three marketing divisions. The U.S. marketing division (Teva's Lemmon subsidiary) markets about 30 products, each sold in large quantities. Most of these products are generic drugs, which are drugs without a brand name. The Israeli marketing division handles 1,200 products in different packages and dosage forms, sold in small quantities. The third marketing division handles special-order sales to customers in other countries. Teva wants to expand its manufacturing of both generic and specialized pharmaceutical products. Its marketing strategy includes both high-volume sales of a few product lines and low-volume sales of many different product lines.[1] How can activity-based systems help Teva's managers compete globally in the generic drug market, particularly in the United States?

Teva can use activity-based systems to better determine the costs of its products and to identify and reduce or eliminate business activities that do not add value to the product. Activity-based systems are information systems that provide quantitative information about activities in an organization. When companies compete globally, their managers can use activity-based systems to determine the costs of a product or service. Activity-based management (ABM) and just-in-time (JIT) operating environments rely on the examination of activities to minimize waste, reduce costs, and improve the allocation of resources. Teva can use ABM and its tool, activity-based costing (ABC), to improve product costing and to help managers make better decisions about pricing products, adding or dropping product lines, changing production processes, and contracting with other companies to provide products or services. JIT can help Teva improve its production processes and manage inventory levels and timely production.

Activity-Based Systems and Management

OBJECTIVE 1

Explain the role of activity-based systems in the management cycle

Many companies operate in volatile business environments that are strongly influenced by customer demands. Company managers know that customers buy value, usually in the form of quality products or services that are delivered on a timely basis for a reasonable price. Companies generate revenue when customers see value and buy their product or service. Thus, companies measure value as the revenue generated by the company (customer value = revenue generated).

Value exists when some characteristic of a product or service satisfies customers' wants or needs. For example, Dell Computer Corporation knows that one market segment is customers who appreciate convenience. In response to their needs, Dell creates value and increases revenue by selling computer systems, called Dell Dimension Systems, that include the latest microprocessor, monitor, video card, CD-ROM drive, sound card, modem, speakers, and preinstalled Microsoft software products. Microsoft creates value and increases revenue by offering its customers "free" upgrades of selected software on the Internet.

To create value and to satisfy customer needs for quality, reasonable price, and timely delivery, managers must

- Work with suppliers and customers
- View the organization as a collection of value-adding activities
- Use resources for value-adding activities
- Reduce or eliminate nonvalue-adding activities
- Know the total cost of creating value for a customer

If an organization's strategic plan focuses on providing products or services that customers esteem, then managers will work with suppliers and customers to find ways to collectively improve quality, reduce costs, and improve delivery time. Managers will also focus their attention internally to find the best ways of using resources to create or maintain value in their products or services. This requires matching the resources to operating activities that add value to a product or service. Managers will examine all business activities, including research and development, purchasing, production, storing, selling, shipping, and customer service, so that they can successfully allocate resources. In addition, managers need to know the full product cost, which includes not only the costs of direct materials and direct labor, but also the costs of all production and nonproduction activities required to satisfy the customer. For example, the full product cost of a Dell Dimension System includes not only the cost of the computer components and software, but also the costs of taking the sales order, processing the order, packaging and shipping the system, and providing subsequent customer service for warranty work and software upgrades. If the activities are executed well and in agreement with the strategic plan and if costs are assigned fairly, the company can improve product pricing and product quality, increase productivity, and generate revenues (value) and profits.

Activity-Based Systems

Organizations that focus on customers redesign their accounting information systems to provide customer-related, activity-based information. Activity-based systems, which are information systems that provide quantitative information about the activities in an organization, create opportunities to improve the costing information supplied to managers. Activity-based systems help managers view their organization as a collection of activities. The activity-based costing information helps managers improve operating processes and make better pricing decisions.

In this chapter, we will look at two types of activity-based systems—activity-based management (ABM) and just-in-time (JIT)—and consider the changes made to product costing systems when either of these systems is used. Both systems help organizations manage activities, not costs. By managing activities, organizations can reduce or eliminate many nonvalue-adding activities, which leads to reduced costs and increased income.

Using Activity-Based Systems in the Management Cycle

When organizations operate in more volatile business environments, their managers must plan, execute, evaluate, and report differently. In this chapter, we expand our view of the management cycle to consider an organization as a collection of activities. As mentioned earlier, managers depend on relevant and reliable financial and nonfinancial information to manage the organization. One role of the management accountant is to develop an accounting information system that supplies easy-to-understand product costing information to answer the basic questions that arise at each stage in the management cycle.

Figure 1 summarizes how managers use activity-based costing information during the management cycle. Let's use Teva Pharmaceutical Industries, Ltd. (Teva) as an example. In the planning stage, managers want answers to questions like "Which activities add value to a product or service?" "What resources are needed to perform those activities?" and "How much should the product or service cost?" We know that Teva wants to increase its sales in the generic drug market. By examining Teva's value-adding activities and their related costs, management can ensure that the company is manufacturing quality products at the lowest cost. If budgeted cost information is prepared for each activity, management can better allocate resources to cost objects (for example, product lines, customer groups, or sales territories) and measure operating performance. If managers assume that resource-consuming activities cause costs and that products incur costs by the activities they require, the estimated product unit cost will be more accurate.

In the executing stage, managers want an answer to the question "What is the actual cost of making our product or providing our service?" They want to know what activities are being performed, how well the activities are being performed, and what resources are actually being consumed. The managers at Teva will focus on activities that add the most value to the products that customers buy. However, they will also monitor some nonvalue-adding activities that have been reduced but not completely eliminated. The accounting information system measures actual

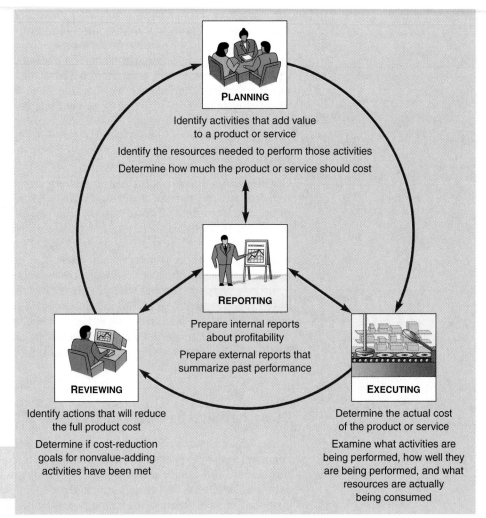

Figure 1
Activity-Based Systems and the
Management Cycle

quantities of activity (a nonfinancial quantitative measure) and accumulates related activity costs (a financial quantitative measure). Gathering quantitative information at the activity level allows Teva's managers the flexibility to create cost pools for different types of cost objects. For example, the costs of the selling activity can be assigned to a customer (Wal-Mart), to a sales territory (Israel), or to a product line (cough syrup).

In the reviewing stage, managers want answers to the questions "What actions will reduce the full product cost?" and "Did we meet our cost-reduction goals for nonvalue-adding activities?" Managers can measure an activity's performance by reviewing the difference between its actual and budgeted costs. With this information, they can analyze the variances in activity levels, identify waste and inefficiencies, and take action to improve processes and activities. They can also continue to monitor the costs of nonvalue-adding activities to see if the company met its goals to reduce or eliminate those costs. Careful review and analysis will lead to increased customer value by improving quality and reducing costs and cycle time.

Finally, in the reporting stage of the management cycle, managers communicate with internal and external users about the company. Internally, Teva's managers will want to see reports that show the application of the costs of activities to cost objects

in order to better measure profitability, as will be shown with bills of activities later in this chapter. External financial reports summarize past performance and answer such questions as "How much does inventory cost?" and "Did the company earn a profit?"

Activity-Based Management and Activity-Based Costing

OBJECTIVE 2

Define activity-based management (ABM) *and discuss its relationship with the supply chain and the value chain*

As defined in an earlier chapter, activity-based management (ABM) is an approach to managing an organization that includes identifying all major operating activities, determining what resources are consumed by each activity, identifying how resources are consumed by each activity, and categorizing the activities as either adding value to a product or service or not adding value. ABM is beneficial for both strategic planning and operational decision making because it provides financial and operational performance information at the activity level that is useful for making decisions about business segments, such as product lines, market segments, and customer groups. It also helps managers eliminate waste and inefficiencies and redirect resources to activities that add value to the product or service. Activity-based costing (ABC) is the tool used in an ABM environment to assist in assigning activity costs to cost objects for product costing and decision making. ABC helps managers make better pricing decisions, inventory valuations, and profitability decisions.

Supply Chains and Value Chains

Two tools of ABM, supply chains and value chains, help managers better understand their organization's external and internal operations. A supply chain is an interdependent collection of organizations that supply materials, products, or services to a customer. When managers understand their product's or service's supply chain, they can better understand their organization's role in the total process of creating their product or service and delivering it to customers. Every organization can create a variety of supply chains because of its variety of suppliers and customers. As shown in Figure 2, a supply chain includes suppliers and suppliers' suppliers as well as customers and customers' customers, and moves from materials through production, distribution, and retailing to the final customer. For example,

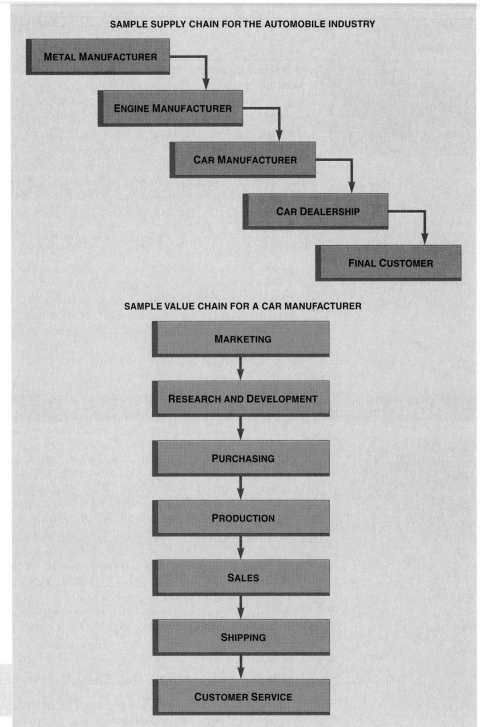

SAMPLE SUPPLY CHAIN FOR THE AUTOMOBILE INDUSTRY

METAL MANUFACTURER → ENGINE MANUFACTURER → CAR MANUFACTURER → CAR DEALERSHIP → FINAL CUSTOMER

SAMPLE VALUE CHAIN FOR A CAR MANUFACTURER

MARKETING → RESEARCH AND DEVELOPMENT → PURCHASING → PRODUCTION → SALES → SHIPPING → CUSTOMER SERVICE

**Figure 2
Supply Chain and Value Chain for
a Manufacturing Company**

in the automobile industry, a metal manufacturer supplies metal to an engine manufacturer, who supplies engines to the car manufacturer. The car manufacturer supplies cars to car dealerships, who supply cars to the final customers. Except for the metal manufacturer, each organization in the supply chain is a customer of a supplier earlier in the chain. Each organization in the supply chain has its own value-creating activities.

A value chain is a related sequence of value-creating activities within an organization. It helps managers better understand the interdependencies of those activities. The sequence of value-creating activities varies from company to company depending on a number of factors, including the size of the company and the types of products or services sold. For example, Figure 2 shows the value chain of activities for a car manufacturer. Such a value chain is commonly found within manufacturing companies. The value chain includes activities for marketing, research and development, purchasing, production, sales, shipping, and customer service (installation, maintenance, replacement, handling complaints, billing, and collection). A company's value chain is part of its supply chain. That supply chain also includes the value chains of its suppliers and customers.

A company can enhance its profitability by understanding not only its own value chain, but also how its value-adding activities fit into its suppliers' and customers' value chains. Working with suppliers and customers across the entire supply chain provides opportunities to reduce the total cost of making a product, even though costs for one activity may be increased. For example, assume that Ford Motor Co. decided to place order entry computers in its car dealerships. The new computers would streamline the entry and processing of orders and make the orders more accurate. In this case, even though Ford would incur the cost of the computers, the total cost of making and delivering a car would decrease because the cost of placing and processing an order would decrease. When organizations work cooperatively with others in their supply chain, new processes can be introduced that will reduce the total costs of products or services.

ABM in a Service Organization

Let's look at how ABM can be implemented in a service organization. Western Data Services, Inc. (WDSI) offers strategic database marketing to help organizations increase sales. WDSI's basic package of services includes the design of a mail piece (either a Classic Letter with or without inserts or a Self-Mailer), creation and maintenance of marketing databases containing information about the client's target group, and a production process that prints a promotional piece and prepares it for mailing. WDSI's primary customers tend to be financial institutions throughout the western states, but the company also serves small businesses and nonprofit organizations.

Carl Marcus, the owner and manager of WDSI, reviewed his company's supply chain as part of his strategic plan. As shown in Figure 3, WDSI's supply chain includes one supplier, WDSI as a service provider, one customer group (financial institutions), and the customer group's customers. In reality, WDSI has a number of suppliers, including office supply companies, printers, and computer stores. However, Carl chose to include only WDSI's most significant supplier, Pitney Bowes, the manufacturer of the Series Nine Model Inserter, because of the major expense involved in using Pitney Bowes's equipment to fold, insert, address, seal, and meter mail pieces. Carl chose financial institutions as the primary customer group in the supply chain because they represented 75 percent of his revenues. The customers of the financial institutions are included in the supply chain because those individuals and businesses receive the mail pieces prepared by WDSI. Based on his understanding of the supply chain, Carl has changed WDSI's strategy to work with Pitney Bowes and the financial institutions to improve WDSI's services.

Another part of Carl's strategy is to manage processes and activities using ABM and ABC. Carl developed a value chain of activities for the company so that he could identify all major operating activities, the resources each activity consumes, and the cause for the resource usage. As shown in Figure 3, WDSI's value chain includes marketing, preparing marketing databases, purchasing supplies, processing orders, mailing promotional pieces, and customer relations.

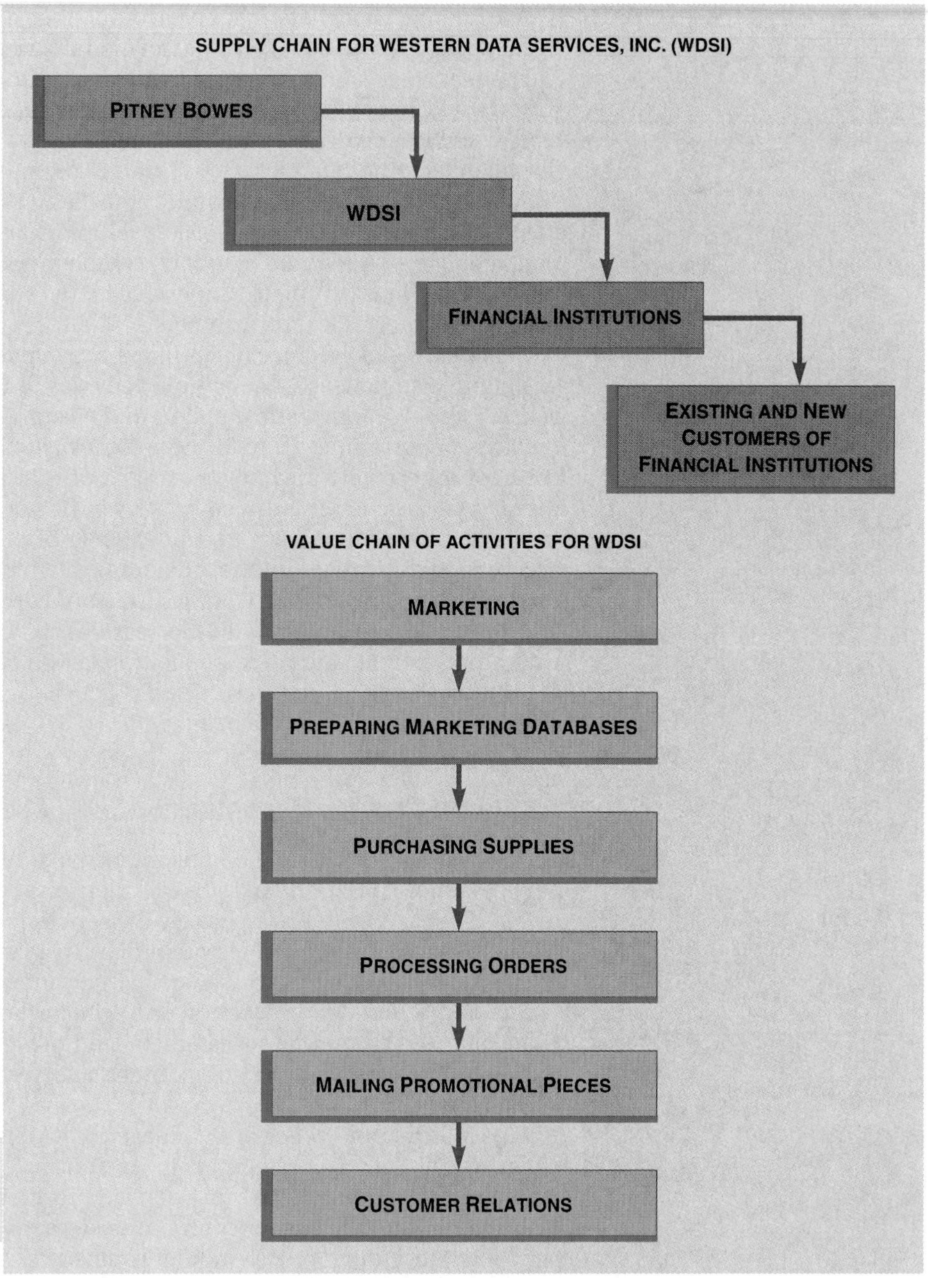

SUPPLY CHAIN FOR WESTERN DATA SERVICES, INC. (WDSI)

PITNEY BOWES → WDSI → FINANCIAL INSTITUTIONS → EXISTING AND NEW CUSTOMERS OF FINANCIAL INSTITUTIONS

VALUE CHAIN OF ACTIVITIES FOR WDSI

MARKETING → PREPARING MARKETING DATABASES → PURCHASING SUPPLIES → PROCESSING ORDERS → MAILING PROMOTIONAL PIECES → CUSTOMER RELATIONS

Figure 3
Supply Chain and Value Chain for a Service Organization

Value-Adding and Nonvalue-Adding Activities and Process Value Analysis

OBJECTIVE 3

Distinguish between value-adding and nonvalue-adding activities, and describe process value analysis

An important element of activity-based management is the identification of value-adding and nonvalue-adding activities. A value-adding activity is an activity that adds value to a product or service as perceived by the customer. Examples include preparing the engineering design of a new car, assembling the car, painting the car, and installing seats and airbags. A nonvalue-adding activity is an activity that adds cost to a product or service but does not increase its market value. Examples include the repair of machines, shop floor clean-up, moving materials, and building mainte-nance. All of these activities require time and use resources but add no value for the customer. The costs of both types of activities are accumulated to measure performance and to determine if the goal of reducing nonvalue-adding activities has been achieved.

Process value analysis (PVA) is an analytical method of identifying all activities and relating them to the events that cause or drive the need for the activities and the resources consumed. This is helpful for companies using ABM to manage activities. PVA forces managers to look critically at all existing phases of their operations. When nonvalue-adding activities and costs are reduced or eliminated and cost traceability is improved, product costs become significantly more accurate. This in turn improves management decisions and increases profitability.

Customers value a quality product delivered on a timely basis for a reasonable price. To keep costs down, company managers continuously seek to improve processes and activities. To manage the cost of an activity, a manager can reduce the activity's frequency or eliminate it. For example, inspection costs can be reduced if an inspector samples one of every three engines received from a supplier rather than inspecting every engine. If the supplier is a reliable source of high-quality engines, such a reduction in inspection activity is appropriate.

Other activities can be eliminated completely if business processes are changed or if outside suppliers can do the work at lower costs. For example, some accounting recordkeeping activities can be eliminated when a company purchases materials just in time for production and makes the product just in time for customer delivery. This change to a just-in-time operating environment eliminates the need to accumulate costs as the product is made. Another way to eliminate an activity is to contract to have it performed by an external party, also called *outsourcing*. Companies are outsourcing purchasing, accounting, and information systems maintenance to companies that either have more expertise or can perform the work at a lower cost.

By identifying nonvalue-adding activities, companies can reduce costs and redirect resources to value-adding activities. For example, PVA has enabled companies such as Westinghouse Electric, Pepsi-Cola North America, and Land 'O Lakes, Inc., to significantly reduce the costs of managing small-dollar purchases. Managers reviewed and analyzed the activities of purchasing supplies, recording and paying small bills, setting up accounts, and establishing credit with seldom-used suppliers. Once managers identified the nonvalue-adding activities, they were able to determine their costs. Management's response was to stop performing those activities internally. Instead, they chose the less expensive alternative of using a special credit card known as a procurement card (or purchasing card) with Visa, MasterCard, or American Express to handle large volumes of small-dollar purchases.

Value-Adding and Nonvalue-Adding Activities in a Service Organization

Let's look at the value-adding and nonvalue-adding activities in a service organization by continuing with our illustration. Carl Marcus, owner and manager of WDSI, a strategic database marketing company, has examined the activities related to the design, processing, and mailing of Classic Letters. Table 1 shows the value-adding activities for Classic Letters and how those activities add value. When Carl's customers ask for database marketing services, these are the activities they pay for. Carl also identified a number of nonvalue-adding activities, which include the following:

- Prepare a job order form and schedule the job
- Order, receive, inspect, and store paper, envelopes, and supplies
- Set up machines to process a specific letter size
- Log the total number of items processed in a batch
- Bill the client and record and deposit payments from the client

Table 1. Value-Adding Activities for a Service Organization

Western Data Services, Inc.
Value-Adding Activities for the Classic Letter

Value-Adding Activities	How the Activity Adds Value
Design the letter	Enhances the effectiveness of the communication
Create a database of customer names and addresses sorted in ZIP code order	Increases the probability that the client will efficiently and effectively reach the targeted customer group
Verify the conformity of mailing information with USPS requirements	Ensures that the client's mailing will receive the best postal rate
Process the job: A computer prints a personalized letter. A machine folds the letter, inserts it and other information into an envelope, prints the address on the envelope, and seals and meters the envelope.	Creates the client mailing
Deliver the letters to the post office	Begins the delivery process

After reviewing the list of nonvalue-adding activities, Carl arranged with his suppliers to have paper, envelopes, and other supplies delivered the day a job was performed. This helped reduce WDSI's storage costs. Carl was also able to reduce the cost of verifying the conformity of mailing information with United States Postal Service (USPS) requirements by purchasing computer software that verifies addresses and helps WDSI's employees select a sorting scheme that eliminates sorting by hand. Now Carl is ready to determine the unit costs for the Classic Letter service and the Self-Mailer service.

BUSINESS BULLETIN: BUSINESS PRACTICE

Federal Express, a major shipping company, changed its pricing structure after analyzing its shipping activities and costs. For many years, FedEx based its shipping costs on weight and delivery priority (overnight or two-day). However, as its business expanded throughout the United States and the world, FedEx realized that the number of miles a shipment traveled was a better indicator of costs for long-distance deliveries. Thus, FedEx decided to assign costs to a shipment based on weight, delivery priority, and distance traveled. More accurate costing led FedEx to increase its prices for longer-distance deliveries (for example, from New York City to San Francisco) and to reduce its prices for local deliveries (for example, from Boston to Philadelphia). Although shipping to local destinations will be more cost-efficient for FedEx customers, FedEx risks losing long-distance, coast-to-coast business to its competitors—unless those companies also reexamine their activities and make similar adjustments.[3]

Implementing Activity-Based Costing

OBJECTIVE 4

Define a cost hierarchy, describe its elements, and explain how a cost hierarchy and a bill of activities are used in activity-based costing

Activity-based costing is important to activity-based management because it improves the assignment of activity-driven costs to cost objects. To implement activity-based product costing, the management accountant works with a team to

1. Identify and classify each activity
2. Estimate the cost of resources for each activity
3. Identify a cost driver for each activity and estimate the quantity of each cost driver
4. Calculate a cost pool rate
5. Assign costs to cost objects based on the level of activity required to make the product or provide the service

Two tools help in the implementation of ABC—a cost hierarchy and a bill of activities.

The Cost Hierarchy   A cost hierarchy is a framework for classifying activities according to the level at which their costs are incurred. Many companies use this framework to manage the assignment of activity-based costs to products or services. In a manufacturing company, the cost hierarchy typically has four levels: the unit level, the batch level, the product level, and the facility level. Unit-level activities are performed each time a unit is produced. For example, in the engine-installation process for a car manufacturer, unit-level activities include assembling engine subassemblies and connecting engines to car frames. These activities vary with the number of cars produced. Batch-level activities are performed each time a batch of goods is produced. These activities vary with the number of batches prepared. Examples of batch-level activities in an engine-installation process include setup, inspection, scheduling, and materials handling. Product-level activities are performed to support the diversity of products in a manufacturing plant. Examples of product-level activities include implementing engineering change notices and redesigning the installation process. Facility-level activities are performed to support a facility's general manufacturing process. Examples for a car manufacturer include managing, maintaining, lighting, securing, and insuring the manufacturing plant. Note that the frequency of activities varies across levels and that both value-adding and nonvalue-adding activities are included in the cost hierarchy. Service organizations can also use a cost hierarchy to group activities. The four levels typically are the unit level, the batch level, the service level, and the operations level. Table 2 lists

Table 2. Sample Activities in Cost Hierarchies

Activity Level	Car Manufacturer: Engine Installation	Direct Mail Service: Preparing a Mailing to Bank Customers
Unit level	Install engine Test engine	Print and fold letter Insert letter and other information into envelope Seal and meter envelope
Batch level	Set up installation process Move engines Inspect engines	Retool machines Verify correct postage Bill client
Product or service level	Redesign installation process	Train employees Develop and maintain computer systems and databases
Facility or operations level	Provide facility management, maintenance, lighting, security, and space	Provide facility management, maintenance, lighting, security, and space

Exhibit 1. Bill of Activities for a Service Organization

Western Data Services, Inc.
Bill of Activities for Classic Letter and Self-Mailer
For the Month Ended May 31, 20x1

Activity/ Cost Pool	Cost Pool Rate	Classic Letter (110,000 letters)		Self-Mailer (48,000 self-mailers)	
		Cost Driver Level	Activity Cost	Cost Driver Level	Activity Cost
Unit level					
Process letters	$20 per machine hour	300 machine hours	$ 6,000	120 machine hours	$ 2,400
Batch level					
Prepare databases	$85 per 1,000 names	50,000 names	4,250	20,000 names	1,700
Retool machines	$10 per direct labor hour	220 direct labor hours	2,200	100 direct labor hours	1,000
Inspect for USPS compliance	$12 per inspection hour	100 inspection hours	1,200	80 inspection hours	960
Service level					
Develop databases	$25 per design hour	118 design hours	2,950	81 design hours	2,025
Solicit new customers	$3 per solicitation	300 solicitations	900	95 solicitations	285
Operations level					
Provide utilities and space	$15 per machine hour	300 machine hours	4,500	50 machine hours	750
Total activity costs assigned to services			$ 22,000		$ 9,120
Total volume			110,000		48,000
Activity costs per unit (total activity costs ÷ total volume)			$ 0.20		$ 0.19
Cost summary					
Activity costs (includes labor and overhead)			$ 22,000		$ 9,120
Direct materials cost			7,700		5,280
Postage costs			17,600		7,680
Total costs for month			$ 47,300		$22,080
Unit cost			$ .43		$ .46

examples of activities in the cost hierarchies for a manufacturing company and a service organization.

The Bill of Activities   Once the cost hierarchy is created, the management accountant groups the activities into the specified levels and prepares a summary of the activity costs assigned to the selected cost objects. A bill of activities is a list of activities and related costs that is used to compute the costs assigned to activities and the product unit cost. More complex bills of activities include cost pool rates and cost driver levels used to assign costs to cost objects. A bill of activities may be used as the primary document or a supporting schedule to calculate the product unit cost in job order or process costing. It may also be used in a service organization.

Exhibit 1 illustrates a bill of activities for WDSI. In this example, Carl Marcus uses the bill of activities to see how activity costs contributed to unit costs. WDSI provides two types of services. The Classic Letter service involves the printing, folding, collating, and inserting of letters and other materials into a printed, addressed envelope that is then metered and sealed. The cost of the Classic Letter service includes the cost of direct materials (envelopes, letters, other materials), postage, and service overhead. The Self-Mailer is a one-page solicitation that can be refolded and returned to the client's address. The cost of the Self-Mailer service includes the costs of direct materials (a single page of paper for each mailer), postage, and service overhead. During the month, the volume of mailings for a customer could vary from 150 to 20,000 addresses in a single mailing. The sizes of the databases that were prepared and the number of machine setups and inspection hours varied from job to job. The service overhead costs for the activities and related cost pools identified in the cost hierarchy are assigned to the two services using ABC. The activity costs are calculated for the service overhead related to each service and then added to the costs of direct materials and postage to calculate a unit cost.

Carl chose to group activities by unit level, batch level, service level, and operations level. At the unit level, he included the costs of all activities required for processing each Classic Letter and Self-Mailer and used machine hours as the cost driver. At the batch level, for each job, he included the costs of all activities required to prepare the database of names and addresses for mailing, to set up the machines, and to inspect the letters for compliance with the regulations of the United States Postal Service. Carl selected the number of names in the database, direct labor hours, and inspection hours, respectively, as the cost drivers. At the service level, Carl included the costs of all activities required to develop databases for new clients and to solicit new business for WDSI, and he used design hours and number of solicitations as the cost drivers. Finally, at the operations level, he included the costs of all activities related to providing utilities and space and used machine hours as the cost driver.

Carl prepared a bill of activities for one month ending May 31, 20x1. He grouped cost pools related to each activity level and supported the activity's cost with cost information about the cost pool rate and cost pool driver level. He calculated the total activity costs and activity cost per unit assigned to each type of service. At the bottom of the bill of activities for the month, he prepared a summary of the total costs of the services and calculated the unit cost for each service (the total costs divided by the number of units mailed).

The cost information gathered in the bill of activities helped Carl Marcus estimate the company's profits by allowing him to compare his costs with his revenues. To be competitive, he is currently offering the Classic Letter services for $.50 per letter and the Self-Mailer services for $.45 per mailer. The Classic Letter services are generating a positive gross margin of $.07 ($.50 − $.43) per letter, but the Self-Mailer service shows a negative gross margin of $.01 ($.45 − $.46) per mailer. Carl must find ways to increase fee revenue, reduce costs, or increase service volume for the Self-Mailer service. ABC can help him reduce costs, because the activity costs, including labor and overhead, are categorized by activities and grouped into activity levels. Carl can examine those activities to identify and reduce or eliminate some of the company's nonvalue-adding activities.

Activity-Based Costing for Selling and Administrative Activities

Customer groups and sales territories differ in their complexity and diversity. Customers who buy the most products or services often place larger or more frequent orders. Thus, a larger portion of the costs of selling and administrative activities can be traced to those customers than to customers who buy smaller amounts or order less frequently. Sales territories can differ in size and number of customers served. As a result, some sales territories may require more support services than other sales territories.

ABC can be applied to other operating activities besides production. ABC can be used to group selling and administrative activities and assign the costs of those activities to cost objects, such as customer groups and sales territories. For many companies, similar customers, such as distributors or retailers, are often treated as a single group because it is difficult to assign costs to individual customers. The resources associated with selling and administrative activities include salaries, benefits, depreciation on buildings and equipment, sales commissions, and utilities. The costs of those resources are grouped into cost pools and assigned to cost objects, such as customer groups or sales territories, using cost drivers, such as the number of sales calls, sales orders, invoices, or billings.

Exhibit 2 presents an income statement for one of WDSI's customers. A similar format can be used to create income statements for any cost object. Service organizations typically group clients according to significant characteristics, such as length of time required to perform the service or frequency of service. In our example, Carl Marcus can use the ABC information to review the profitability of each customer or customer group. He can also use the information to compare selling and administrative costs across customer groups or to plan profits based on changes in those activities.

The New Manufacturing Environment and JIT Operations

OBJECTIVE 5

Define the just-in-time (JIT) operating philosophy *and identify the elements of a JIT operating environment*

Organizations face more challenges today than ever before. Once, organizations in the United States were almost automatically assured of a reasonable share of the world market. But over the last twenty years, changes in technology and communications and the growing expertise of foreign enterprises have forced U.S. companies to reorganize to compete successfully. Foreign firms, most notably those from Asia and Europe, have issued a challenge by producing high-quality products at prices often below those charged by many U.S. businesses. To gain a foothold in world markets, foreign companies had to look for ways to streamline their operating processes and improve productivity. Their strategies included the following:

1. Eliminate the waste of materials, labor, space, and production time.
2. Reduce inventories, which tie up working capital.
3. Simplify approaches to measuring productivity and keeping records.

The same strategies have now been adopted by forward-thinking U.S. companies. Those companies have had to update their operating processes and rethink their basic operating methods. Many companies that formerly relied on traditional production processes are changing to new operating and managing approaches, particularly the just-in-time (JIT) operating environment. Companies that adopt the JIT approach must redesign their manufacturing facilities and the events that trigger the production process. The just-in-time (JIT) operating philosophy requires

Exhibit 2. Income Statement for a Cost Object

Western Data Services, Inc.
Customer-Related Income Statement
Gila State Bank
For the Month Ended May 31, 20x1

Fee revenue ($.50 × 12,000 Classic Letters)			$6,000
Cost of processing order ($.43 × 12,000 Classic Letters)			5,160
Gross margin			$ 840
Less: Selling and administrative activity costs			

Activity/ Cost Pool	Cost Pool Rate	Cost Driver Level	Activity Cost
Make sales calls	$12 per sales call	10 sales calls	$120
Prepare sales orders	$6 per sales order	25 sales orders	150
Handle inquiries	$.50 per minute	120 minutes	60
Process credits	$20 per notice	1 notice	20
Process invoices	$10 per invoice	12 invoices	120
Follow-ups	$8 per follow-up	20 follow-ups	160
Process billings and collections	$4 per billing	24 billings	96
Total selling and administrative activity costs			726
Net income contributed by Gila State Bank			$ 114

that all resources, including materials, personnel, and facilities, be used only as needed. Its objectives are to improve productivity and eliminate waste.

The first step in achieving JIT operating efficiencies is to redesign the plant layout, moving machines and processes closer together to cut production time. But the Japanese took the redesign one step further by automating the new processes. Automated JIT operations brought Japanese industry to world prominence. Japanese manufacturers were able to improve product quality while decreasing waste. The result was significant cost savings, which were reflected in lower prices. The Japanese also increased the productivity of their factories as they approached total capacity. Their success has prompted manufacturers in other countries to change from traditional production methods to the new automated JIT environments. And the movement toward automated JIT operations will continue as more and more companies enter world markets.

Organizations that want to adopt a JIT operating environment must reevaluate their current operations and implement new ways of producing goods or services. Underlying the new methods are several basic concepts.

Simple is better.

The quality of the product or service is critical.

The work environment must emphasize continuous improvement.

Maintaining inventories wastes resources and may hide poor work.

Any activity or function that does not add value to the product should be eliminated or reduced.

Goods should be produced only when needed.

Workers must be multiskilled and must participate in improving efficiency and product quality.

In a traditional operating environment, a company usually

1. Maintains large amounts of inventory
2. Uses push-through production methods
3. Purchases materials in larger lot sizes with fewer deliveries
4. Performs infrequent setups
5. Manufactures products in batches
6. Uses a work force skilled in only one area

Whereas, to implement a JIT operating environment, a company must be prepared to

1. Maintain minimum inventory levels.
2. Develop pull-through production planning and scheduling.
3. Purchase materials and produce products as needed, in smaller lot sizes.
4. Perform quick, inexpensive machine setups.
5. Create flexible manufacturing work cells.
6. Develop a multiskilled work force.
7. Maintain high levels of product quality.
8. Enforce a system of effective preventive maintenance.
9. Encourage continuous improvement of the work environment.

This section describes each element and its impact on costs, product quality, and productivity.

Maintain Minimum Inventory Levels

One objective of a JIT operating environment is to maintain minimum inventory levels. In contrast to the traditional environment, in which parts, materials, and supplies are purchased far in advance and stored until the production department needs them, in a JIT environment, materials and parts are purchased and received only when needed. The system lowers costs by reducing (1) the space needed for inventory storage, (2) the amount of materials handling, and (3) the amount of inventory obsolescence. There is less need for inventory control facilities, personnel, and recordkeeping. The amount of work in process inventory waiting to be processed and the amount of working capital tied up in all inventories decrease significantly.

Develop Pull-Through Production Planning and Scheduling

Pull-through production is a system in which a customer's order triggers the purchase of materials and the scheduling of production for the required products. In contrast, traditional manufacturing operations use the push-through method, whereby products are manufactured in long production runs and stored in anticipation of customers' orders.

Purchase Materials and Produce Products as Needed, in Smaller Lot Sizes

With pull-through production, the size of customers' orders determines the size of production runs, and the company purchases materials and parts as needed. Low inventory levels are maintained, but machines have to be set up more frequently, resulting in more work stoppages.

Perform Quick, Inexpensive Machine Setups

In the past, managers felt that it was more cost-effective to produce large inventories because producing small batches increases the number of machine setups. The success of JIT over the last ten years has disproved this. By placing machines in more efficient locations and scheduling similar products on common machine groupings, setup time can be minimized. In addition, workers become more experienced and more efficient when they perform frequent setups.

Create Flexible Manufacturing Work Cells

In a traditional factory layout, all similar machines are grouped together, forming functional departments. Products are routed through each department in sequence, so that all necessary operations are completed in order. This process can take several days or weeks, depending on the size and complexity of the job.

By changing the factory layout, the JIT operating environment may cut the manufacturing time of a product from days to hours, or from weeks to days. In many cases, time can be reduced more than 80 percent by ensuring that all the machines needed for sequential processing are placed together. The new cluster of machinery forms a flexible work cell, an autonomous production line that can perform all required operations efficiently and continuously. The flexible work cell handles products of similar shape or size—what is called a family of products. Product families require minimum setup changes as workers move from one job to the next. The more flexible the work cell, the greater the potential to minimize total production time.

Develop a Multiskilled Work Force

In the flexible work cells of a JIT environment, workers may be required to operate several types of machines simultaneously. Therefore, they must learn new operating skills. Many work cells are run by only one operator, who, for example, may have to set up and retool machines and even perform routine maintenance on them. In short, a JIT operating environment requires a multiskilled work force.

Multiskilled workers have been very effective in contributing to the high levels of productivity achieved by Japanese companies. In the United States, union contracts often restrict workers to a single skill. Thus, some companies may encounter difficulties in training workers to run work cells.

Maintain High Levels of Product Quality

JIT operations result in high-quality products because high-quality direct materials are used and because inspections are routinely made throughout the production process. According to the JIT philosophy, inspection as a separate step does not add value to the product, so the JIT environment incorporates inspection into ongoing operations. JIT machine operators inspect the products as they pass through the manufacturing process. Once an operator detects a flaw, he or she shuts down the work cell and determines its cause. The operator either fixes the problem or helps the engineer or quality control person find a way to correct the problem to prevent the production of similarly flawed products. This integrated inspection procedure, combined with quality raw materials, produces high-quality finished goods.

Enforce a System of Effective Preventive Maintenance

When a company rearranges its machinery into flexible manufacturing cells, each machine becomes an integral part of its cell. If one machine breaks down, the entire cell stops functioning. Because the product cannot be easily routed to another machine while the malfunctioning machine is being repaired, continuous JIT operations require an effective system of preventive maintenance. Preventing machine breakdowns is considered more important and more cost-effective than keeping machines running continuously. Machine operators are trained to perform minor repairs as they detect problems. Machines are serviced regularly—much like an automobile—to help guarantee continued operation. The machine operator conducts routine maintenance during periods of downtime between orders. (Remember that in a JIT setting, the work cell does not operate unless there is a customer order for the product. Machine operators take advantage of such downtime to perform maintenance.)

Encourage Continuous Improvement of the Work Environment

The JIT environment fosters loyalty among workers, who are likely to see themselves as part of a team because they are so deeply involved in the production process. Machine operators must have the skills to run several types of machines, be able to detect defective products, suggest measures to correct problems, and maintain the machinery within their work cell. In addition, each worker is encouraged to make suggestions for improving the production process. Japanese companies receive thousands of employee suggestions and implement a high percentage of them. And workers are rewarded for suggestions that improve the process. Such an environment supports workers' initiative and benefits the company.

Accounting for Product Costs in the New Manufacturing Environment

OBJECTIVE 6

Identify the changes in product costing that result when a firm adopts a JIT operating environment

When a firm shifts from a traditional to the new manufacturing environment, the management accounting system must take a new approach to evaluating costs and controlling operations. The changes in the manufacturing operations will affect how costs are determined and what measures are used to monitor performance.

Many traditional management accounting procedures depend on measures of direct labor. For example, accountants use measures of direct labor to find standard cost variances and to estimate the costs of potential projects. Most important, they rely on measures of direct labor to compute product unit costs. However, because direct labor hours and dollars are significantly reduced in the JIT environment, many believe that costs should be assigned differently. They argue that traditional product costing techniques have become obsolete, and they cite three reasons: (1) JIT operations have changed many of the relationships and cost patterns associated with traditional manufacturing; (2) automation has replaced direct labor hours with machine hours; and (3) computerized processes and systems have increased the accountant's ability to trace costs to the specific activities that generate them.[4]

This section examines how product costing procedures can be changed to determine accurate costs for products manufactured in the new manufacturing environment. After looking at changes in how costs are categorized and assigned, the backflush costing method will be used to compute product costs.

Classifying Costs

The JIT work cell and the goal of reducing or eliminating nonvalue-adding activities change the way costs are classified and assigned in a JIT operating environment. The traditional production process can be divided into five parts, or time frames:

Processing time   The actual amount of time spent working on a product

Inspection time	The time spent either looking for product flaws or reworking defective units
Moving time	The time spent moving a product from one operation or department to another
Queue time	The time a product spends waiting to be worked on once it arrives at the next operation or department
Storage time	The time a product spends in materials storage, work in process inventory, or finished goods inventory

In product costing under JIT, costs associated with processing time are grouped as either materials costs or conversion costs. Conversion costs include the total of direct labor costs and manufacturing overhead costs incurred by a production department, JIT work cell, or other work center.

Assigning Costs

In the JIT operating environment, indirect costs have little correlation with direct labor hours. The key measure is throughput time, the time it takes to move a product through the entire production process. So machine hours become more important than labor hours. Measures of product movement are used to apply conversion costs to products.

Sophisticated computer monitoring of the work cells allows many costs to be traced directly to the cells where products are manufactured. As Table 3 shows, several costs that used to be treated as indirect costs and applied to products using a labor base are treated as direct costs of a work cell. They are directly traceable to the JIT production cell. If standard costs are used, products are costed using predetermined rates for materials and conversion costs. Because each cell manufactures similar products to minimize setup time, materials and conversion costs should be nearly uniform per product per cell. The costs of materials handling, utilities, operating supplies, and supervision can be traced directly to work cells as they are incurred. Depreciation charges are based on units of output, not on time, so depreciation can also be charged directly to work cells based on the number of units produced. Building occupancy costs, property and casualty insurance premiums, and property taxes remain indirect costs and must be assigned to the production cells for inclusion in the conversion cost.

Table 3. Changes Caused by JIT: Direct Versus Indirect Costs

Traditional Environment		JIT Environment
Direct	Materials and parts	Direct
Direct	Direct labor	Direct
Indirect	Repairs and maintenance	Direct to work cell
Indirect	Materials handling	Direct to work cell
Indirect	Operating supplies	Direct to work cell
Indirect	Utility costs	Direct to work cell
Indirect	Supervision	Direct to work cell
Indirect	Depreciation	Direct to work cell
Indirect	Supporting service functions	Mostly direct to work cell
Indirect	Building occupancy	Indirect
Indirect	Insurance and taxes	Indirect

Backflush Costing

OBJECTIVE 7

Define and apply backflush costing, and compare the cost flows in traditional and backflush costing

In a just-in-time environment, managers continuously seek ways to reduce wasted resources and time. Thus far, we have focused on how waste can be trimmed from production operations, but waste can also be reduced in other areas. For example, it is possible to decrease the amount of time it takes to record and account for the costs of the production process. This is accomplished by simplifying the cost flow through the accounting records. First, since labor costs are reduced in a JIT environment, the accounting system combines direct labor costs and manufacturing costs into a single category, conversion costs. Second, since materials arrive just in time to be used in the production process, there is little reason to maintain a separate Materials Inventory account. Instead, the Materials Inventory account and the Work in Process Inventory account are often combined into a single account called Raw in Process Inventory.

A JIT organization may also streamline its accounting process by using backflush costing. When backflush costing is used, all product costs are first accumulated in the Cost of Goods Sold account. Then, at period end, the costs are "flushed back," or worked backward, into the appropriate inventory accounts. Some organizations prefer to record costs first in the Finished Goods Inventory account instead of in the Cost of Goods Sold account, but the objective is the same: to save recording time by having all product costs flow straight to a final destination and then, at period end, working backward to determine the proper balances for the inventory accounts. This approach avoids the recording of several transactions, as illustrated below.

Comparison of Cost Flows in Traditional and Backflush Costing

The cost flows in a traditional costing system are illustrated at the top of Figure 4. When direct materials arrive at the factory, their costs flow into the Materials Inventory account. Then, when the materials are requisitioned into production, their costs flow into the Work in Process Inventory account. When direct labor is used, its costs are added to the Work in Process Inventory account. Manufacturing overhead is applied to production using a base such as direct labor hours, machine hours, or number of units produced. The amount of applied overhead is added to the other costs in the Work in Process Inventory account. At the end of the manufacturing process, the costs of the finished units are transferred to the Finished Goods Inventory account, and when the units are sold, their costs are transferred to the Cost of Goods Sold account.

In a JIT setting, materials arrive just in time to be placed into production. When backflush costing is used, the direct materials costs and the conversion costs (direct labor and manufacturing overhead) are immediately charged to the Cost of Goods Sold account. At the end of the period, the costs of goods in raw in process invento-

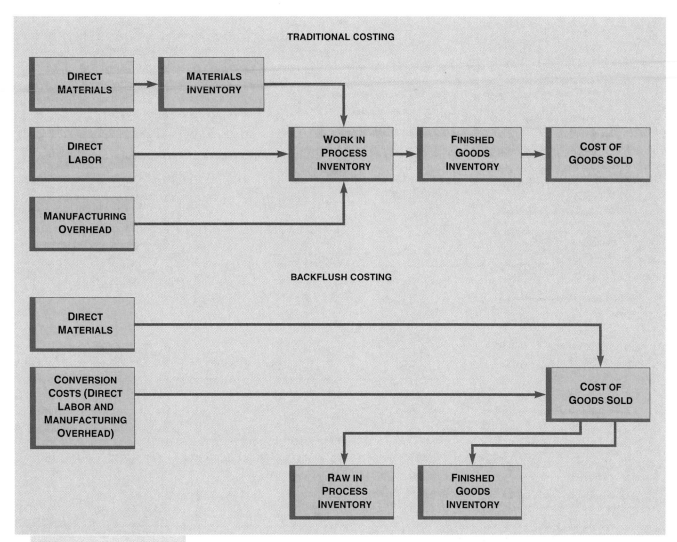

Figure 4
Comparison of Cost Flows in Traditional and Backflush Costing

ry and in finished goods inventory are determined, and those costs are flushed back to the Raw in Process Inventory account and the Finished Goods Inventory account. Once those costs have been flushed back, the Cost of Goods Sold account contains only the costs of units completed and sold during the period. The cost flows in a backflush costing system are shown in the bottom diagram in Figure 4.

To illustrate, assume that the following transactions occurred at Allegro Company last month:

1. Purchased $20,000 of direct materials on account.
2. Used all of the materials in production during the month.
3. Incurred direct labor costs of $8,000.
4. Applied $24,000 of manufacturing overhead to production.
5. Completed units costing $51,600 during the month.
6. Sold units costing $51,500 during the month.

The top diagram in Figure 5 shows how those transactions would be entered in T accounts when traditional product costing is used. You can trace the flow of each cost by following its transaction number.

The bottom diagram in Figure 5 shows how the same transactions would be treated in a JIT environment using backflush costing. The cost of direct materials (Transaction 1) is charged directly to the Cost of Goods Sold account. Transaction 2 is not included because there is no Materials Inventory account when backflush

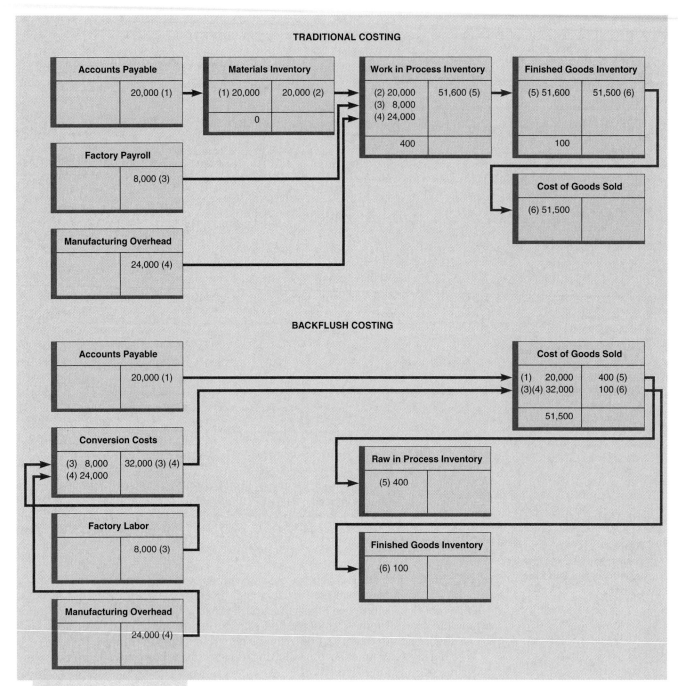

Figure 5
Cost Flows Through T Accounts in Traditional and Backflush Costing

costing is used. The costs of direct labor (Transaction 3) and manufacturing overhead (Transaction 4) are combined in the Conversion Costs account and transferred to the Cost of Goods Sold account. The total in the Cost of Goods Sold account is then $52,000 ($20,000 for direct materials and $32,000 for conversion costs). Once all product costs for the month have been entered in the Cost of Goods Sold account, the amounts to be transferred to the inventory accounts are calculated. The amount to be transferred to the Raw in Process Inventory account is determined by subtracting the cost of completed units (Transaction 5) from the total costs charged to the Cost of Goods Sold Account ($52,000 − $51,600 = $400). The amount to be transferred to the Finished Goods Inventory account is calculated by subtracting the cost of units sold (Transaction 6) from the cost of completed units

($51,600 − $51,500 = $100). The ending balance in the Cost of Goods Sold account is $51,500, which is the same as the ending balance when traditional costing is used. The difference is that backflush costing enabled us to use fewer accounts and to avoid recording several transactions.

Comparison of ABM and JIT

OBJECTIVE 8

Compare ABM and JIT as activity-based systems

ABM and JIT are similar in that both, as activity-based systems, analyze processes and identify value-adding and nonvalue-adding activities. Both seek to eliminate or reduce nonvalue-adding activities and to improve the allocation of resources. In addition, by providing more accurate product costing information, both help managers make decisions about bidding, pricing, product lines, and outsourcing.

However, the two systems differ in their primary goals. One goal of ABM is to calculate the most accurate product cost possible by using cost drivers to fairly assign indirect costs of production-related activities to cost objects. ABM accomplishes this through the use of activity-based costing (ABC), which is often a fairly complex accounting information system used with job order or process costing systems. Job order and process costing systems track the direct materials, direct labor, and manufacturing overhead costs throughout the production process. ABC helps assign only the manufacturing overhead costs to the product cost. Note that ABC can also be used to examine nonproduction-related activities, such as marketing and shipping.

The primary goal of JIT is to simplify and standardize production and purchasing activities. JIT minimizes complexity in the production process by using work cells, standardizing parts, and reducing or eliminating inventories. JIT reorganizes many service activities so that they are performed within the work cells. The cost of those activities become direct costs to the work cell and to the products made by the work cell. The total production costs within the work cell can then be assigned using simple cost drivers such as process hours or direct materials cost. Companies that have implemented JIT in their operating environment may use backflush costing rather than job order costing or process costing. This approach focuses on the output at the end of the production process and simplifies the accounting system. The characteristics of ABM and JIT are summarized in Table 4.

Table 4. Comparison of ABM and JIT Approaches to Activity-Based Systems

	ABM	JIT
Purpose	Reduce or eliminate nonvalue-adding activities	Reduce complexity by using work cells, standardizing parts, and reducing or eliminating inventories and nonvalue-adding production activities
Cost assignment	Use ABC to assign manufacturing overhead costs to the product cost by using appropriate cost drivers	Reorganize service activities so that they are performed within work cells and manufacturing overhead costs incurred in the work cell become direct costs of the products made in the work cell
Costing method	Integrate ABC with either job order or process costing to calculate product costs	May use backflush costing to calculate product costs when the products are completed

Teva Pharmaceutical Industries, Ltd., which was presented in the Decision Point at the beginning of the chapter, can use both JIT and ABM/ABC. Teva can use either JIT or ABM/ABC in the operations divisions that manufacture relatively similar products or product lines, such as the generic pharmaceutical products marketed to the United States. On the other hand, ABM/ABC would be more appropriate in the operations divisions that manufacture a variety of product lines to satisfy the Israeli and other markets. Companies that want to remain competitive in a global marketplace will want to use activity-based systems, and each company will choose the activity-based system that best fits the needs of its long-range strategic plan.

Chapter Review

REVIEW OF LEARNING OBJECTIVES

1. **Explain the role of activity-based systems in the management cycle.** Activity-based systems are information systems that provide quantitative information about activities in an organization. Because activity-based systems help managers view the organization as a collection of related activities, they enable managers to improve operating processes and make better pricing decisions. During the planning phase of the management cycle, activity-based systems help managers identify value-adding activities, determine the resources needed for those activities, and estimate product costs. In the executing and reviewing stages, these systems help managers to determine the full product cost, identify actions that will reduce the full product cost, and determine if cost-reduction goals for nonvalue-adding activities were reached. Activity-based systems also help managers report the cost of inventory and determine the degree to which product goals were achieved.

2. **Define *activity-based management (ABM)* and discuss its relationship with the supply chain and the value chain.** Activity-based management (ABM) is an approach to managing an organization that involves identifying all major operating activities, determining what resources are consumed by each activity, identifying how resources are consumed by each activity, and categorizing the activities as either adding value to a product or service or not adding value. ABM enables managers to see their organization as a collection of value-creating activities (a value chain) operating as part of a larger system that includes suppliers' and customers' value chains (a supply chain). This perspective helps managers work cooperatively both within and outside their organization to reduce costs by eliminating waste and inefficiencies and by redirecting resources toward value-adding activities.

3. **Distinguish between value-adding and nonvalue-adding activities, and describe process value analysis.** A value-adding activity is an activity that adds value to a product or service as perceived by the customer. Examples include preparing the engineering design of a new car, assembling the car, painting the car, and installing seats and airbags. A nonvalue-adding activity is an activity that adds cost to a product or service but does not increase its market value. Examples include the repair of machines, shop floor clean-up activities, moving materials, and building maintenance. Process value analysis (PVA) is an analytical method of identifying all activities and relating them to events that cause or drive the need for the activities and the resources consumed.

4. **Define a *cost hierarchy,* describe its elements, and explain how a cost hierarchy and a bill of activities are used in activity-based costing.** To create a cost hierarchy, production activities are identified and classified into four levels. Unit-level activities are activities performed each time a unit is produced. Batch-level activities are activities performed each time a batch of goods is produced. Product-level activities are activities performed to support the diversity of products in a manufacturing plant. Facility-level activities are activities performed to support a facility's general manufacturing process. For ABC product costing, the management accountant works with a team to (1) identify each activity and classify it into one of the four categories, (2) esti-

mate the cost of resources for each activity, (3) identify all cost drivers and estimate the quantity of each cost driver, (4) calculate a cost pool rate, and (5) assign all costs to cost objects based on the level of activity required to make the product or provide the service.

5. **Define the *just-in-time (JIT) operating philosophy* and identify the elements of a JIT operating environment.** Just-in-time (JIT) is an overall operating philosophy in which all resources, including materials, personnel, and facilities, are used only as needed. The objectives are to improve productivity and reduce waste. The elements of a JIT operating environment are (1) maintain minimum inventory levels; (2) develop pull-through production planning and scheduling; (3) purchase materials and produce parts as needed, in smaller lot sizes; (4) perform quick, inexpensive machine setups; (5) create flexible manufacturing work cells; (6) develop a multiskilled work force; (7) maintain high levels of product quality; (8) enforce a system of effective preventive maintenance; and (9) encourage continuous improvement of the work environment.

6. **Identify the changes in product costing that result when a firm adopts a JIT operating environment.** In the JIT operating environment, as a firm increases its reliance on automation, machine hours replace direct labor hours as the dominant source of costs. This means that measures of direct labor are no longer a reliable means of determining product costs. In product costing under JIT, processing costs are grouped as either materials costs or conversion costs. The costs associated with inspection time, moving time, queue time, and storage time are reduced or eliminated. The shift to automation also affects the assignment of manufacturing overhead costs. Other measures of production replace the job order cost card, and direct labor and manufacturing overhead costs are combined into conversion costs. Computerized facilities improve cost tracking, so that many costs that are considered indirect costs in traditional manufacturing settings, such as electricity and factory supplies, can be traced directly to work cells. Only costs associated with building occupancy, insurance, and property taxes remain indirect costs and must be assigned to work cells.

7. **Define and apply *backflush costing,* and compare the cost flows in traditional and backflush costing.** Backflush costing is commonly used to account for product costs in a JIT operating environment. When backflush costing is used, all product costs are first accumulated in the Cost of Goods Sold account. Then, at period end, the costs are "flushed back," or worked backward, into the appropriate inventory accounts. This differs from the traditional approach, in which the Materials Inventory account is used to record the costs of materials purchased and used and the Work in Process Inventory account is used to record the costs of direct materials, direct labor, and manufacturing overhead during the production process. The objective of backflush costing is to save recording time, which cuts costs.

8. **Compare ABM and JIT as activity-based systems.** ABM and JIT are similar in that both, as activity-based systems, analyze processes and identify value-adding and nonvalue-adding activities so that managers can eliminate or reduce nonvalue-adding activities and improve resource allocation. The primary difference between the two systems is that ABM focuses on using activity-based costing to more fairly assign costs to cost objects, whereas JIT focuses on simplifying and standardizing production and purchasing activities.

REVIEW OF CONCEPTS AND TERMINOLOGY

The following concepts and terms were introduced in this chapter:

LO 2 **Activity-based management (ABM):** An approach to managing an organization that involves identifying all major operating activities, determining what resources are consumed by each activity, identifying how resources are consumed by each activity, and categorizing the activities as either adding value to a product or service or not adding value; emphasis is on the reduction or elimination of nonvalue-adding activities.

LO 1 **Activity-based system:** An information system that provides quantitative information about activities in an organization.

LO 7   **Backflush costing:** A product costing approach, used in a JIT operating environment, in which all product costs are first accumulated in the Cost of Goods Sold account and then, at period end, flushed back into the appropriate inventory accounts.

LO 4   **Batch-level activities:** Activities performed each time a batch of goods is produced; such activities vary with the number of batches prepared.

LO 4   **Bill of activities:** A list of activities and related costs that is used to compute the costs assigned to activities and the product unit cost.

LO 6   **Conversion costs:** The total of direct labor costs and manufacturing overhead costs incurred by a production department, JIT work cell, or other work center.

LO 4   **Cost hierarchy:** A framework for classifying production-related activities according to the level at which their costs are incurred.

LO 4   **Facility-level activities:** Activities performed to support a facility's general manufacturing process.

LO 1   **Full product cost:** A cost that includes not only the costs of direct materials and direct labor, but also the costs of all production and nonproduction activities required to satisfy the customer.

LO 6   **Inspection time:** The time spent either looking for product flaws or reworking defective units.

LO 5   **Just-in-time (JIT) operating philosophy:** An operating philosophy that requires that all resources, including materials, personnel, and facilities, be used only as needed; its objectives are to improve productivity and eliminate waste.

LO 6   **Moving time:** The time spent moving a product from one operation or department to another.

LO 3   **Nonvalue-adding activity:** An activity that adds cost to a product or service but does not increase its market value.

LO 6   **Processing time:** The actual amount of time spent working on a product.

LO 3   **Process value analysis (PVA):** An analytical method of identifying all activities and relating them to the events that cause or drive the need for the activities and the resources consumed.

LO 4   **Product-level activities:** Activities performed to support the diversity of products in a manufacturing plant.

LO 5   **Pull-through production:** A production system in which a customer's order triggers the purchase of materials and the scheduling of production for the required products.

LO 5   **Push-through method:** A production system in which products are manufactured in long production runs and stored in anticipation of customers' orders.

LO 6   **Queue time:** The time a product spends waiting to be worked on once it arrives at the next operation or department.

LO 7   **Raw in Process Inventory account:** An inventory account in the just-in-time operating environment that combines the Materials Inventory and the Work in Process Inventory accounts.

LO 6   **Storage time:** The time a product spends in materials storage, work in process inventory, or finished goods inventory.

LO 2   **Supply chain:** An interdependent collection of organizations that supply materials, products, or services to a customer.

LO 6   **Throughput time:** The time it takes to move a product through the entire production process.

LO 4   **Unit-level activities:** Activities performed each time a unit is produced; such activities vary with the number of units produced.

LO 3   **Value-adding activity:** An activity that adds value to a product or service as perceived by the customer.

LO 2   **Value chain:** A related sequence of value-creating activities within an organization.

LO 5   **Work cell:** An autonomous production line that can perform all required operations efficiently and continuously.

REVIEW PROBLEM
Activity-Based Costing

LO 4 Alvelo Corporation produces more than a dozen types of boat motors. The 240-horsepower motor is the most expensive and most difficult to produce. The 60-horsepower model is the easiest to produce and is the leading seller for the company. The other models range from 70 horsepower to 220 horsepower and get more complex as the horsepower increases. Rodak Company recently ordered 175 of the 80-horsepower model. Song Shin, the controller of Alvelo Corporation, is interested in testing the activity-based approach to product costing on this order because the company is considering a shift to that method. Costs directly traceable to the Rodak order are as follows:

Cost of direct materials	$57,290
Cost of purchased parts	$76,410
Direct labor hours	1,320
Average direct labor pay rate per hour	$14.00

Other operating costs are as follows:

Traditional costing approach:
Manufacturing overhead costs were assigned at a rate of 320 percent of direct labor dollars.

Activity-based costing approach:

Activities	Cost Drivers	Cost Assignment Rates	Activity Usage for Rodak Order
Product design	Engineering hours	$62 per engineering hour	76 engineering hours
Work cell setup	Number of setups	$90 per setup	16 setups
Parts production	Machine hours	$38 per machine hour	380 machine hours
Assembly	Direct labor hours	$19 per direct labor hour	84 direct labor hours
Product simulation	Testing hours	$90 per testing hour	28 testing hours
Packaging and shipping	Product units	$26 per unit	175 units
Building occupancy	Direct labor cost	125% of direct labor cost	$18,480 direct labor cost

REQUIRED

1. Use the traditional costing approach to compute the total cost and the product unit cost of the Rodak order.
2. Using the cost hierarchy, identify each activity as occurring at the unit level, batch level, product level, or facility level.
3. Prepare a bill of activities for the operating costs.
4. Using the activity-based costing approach, compute the total cost and the product unit cost of the Rodak order.
5. What difference in the product unit cost of the Rodak order resulted from the shift to activity-based costing? Does the use of activity-based costing guarantee cost reduction for every order?

ANSWER TO REVIEW PROBLEM

1. Apply the traditional costing approach to the Rodak order.

Direct materials cost	$ 57,290
Cost of purchased parts	76,410
Direct labor cost	18,480
Manufacturing overhead (320% of direct labor dollars)	59,136
Total cost of order	$ 211,316
Product unit cost (total cost ÷ 175 units)	$1,207.52

2. Assign activities to the categories of the cost hierarchy

Unit level:	Parts production
	Assembly
	Packaging and shipping
Batch level:	Work cell setup
Product level:	Product design
	Product simulation
Facility level:	Building occupancy

3 and 4. Create a bill of activities and apply activity-based costing to the Rodak order.

Alvelo Corporation
Bill of Activities
Rodak Order

Activity/Cost Pool	Cost Pool Rate	Cost Driver Level	Activity Cost
Unit level			
Parts production	$38 per machine hour	380 machine hours	$ 14,440
Assembly	$19 per direct labor hour	84 labor hours	1,596
Packaging and shipping	$26 per unit	175 units	4,550
Batch level			
Work cell setup	$90 per setup	16 setups	1,440
Product level			
Product design	$62 per engineering hour	76 engineering hours	4,712
Product simulation	$90 per testing hour	28 testing hours	2,520
Facility level			
Building occupancy	125% of direct labor cost	$18,480 direct labor cost	23,100
Total activity costs assigned to job			$ 52,358
Total units of job			175
Activity costs per unit (total activity costs ÷ total units)			$ 299.19
Cost summary			
Direct materials			$ 57,290
Costs of purchased parts			76,410
Direct labor cost			18,480
Activity costs			52,358
Total cost of order			$ 204,538
Product unit cost (total cost ÷ 175 units)			$1,168.79

5. Compare traditional costing and ABC costing.

Product unit cost—traditional costing approach	$1,207.52
Product unit cost—activity-based costing approach	1,168.79
Difference	$ 38.73

In this case, the ABC product unit cost is lower than the product unit cost computed using the traditional costing approach. Activity-based costing does not guarantee cost reduction for every product, however. It does improve cost traceability, which often identifies products that have been undercosted or overcosted by a traditional product costing system.

Chapter Assignments

BUILDING YOUR KNOWLEDGE FOUNDATION

Questions

1. How do companies measure customer value? What can managers do to create value and satisfy customers' needs?
2. Define an activity-based system. Identify two activity-based systems. What are some benefits of using activity-based systems?
3. How is costing information from activity-based systems used in each of the four stages of the management cycle?
4. What assumption should managers make about resource-consuming activities when they estimate a product unit cost?
5. What is the value of gathering quantitative information at the activity level?
6. What is activity-based management (ABM)? How does ABM benefit both strategic planning and operational decision making?
7. How does a supply chain differ from a value chain?
8. What is the difference between a value-adding activity and a nonvalue-adding activity? Give an example of each.
9. Define process value analysis.
10. List the five steps of activity-based product costing.
11. List and define the four categories in the cost hierarchy for a manufacturing company.
12. What is a bill of activities?
13. What is pull-through production? In what ways does it differ from push-through production?
14. What changes occur in the responsibilities of a machine operator in the JIT operating environment?
15. How does the inspection function change in a JIT environment?
16. Why is preventive maintenance of machinery critical to the operation of a JIT work cell?
17. How has the movement to JIT operations and automated manufacturing facilities affected the role of direct labor in management accounting practices?
18. When is backflush costing used? How does it reduce the time spent on record-keeping?
19. How do ABM and JIT differ in their approaches to product costing?

Short Exercises

SE 1.
LO 1 *Activity-Based Systems*

Laveta Hicks started a retail clothing business two years ago. Laveta's first year was very successful, but sales dropped 50 percent in the second year. Laveta's husband, a business consultant, analyzed her business and came up with two basic reasons for the decline in sales: (1) Laveta has been placing orders late in each season, and (2) shipments of clothing have been arriving late and in poor condition. What measures can Laveta take to improve her business and persuade customers to return?

SE 2.
LO 2 *Identifying a Product's Value Chain*

Which of the following activities would be part of the value chain of a manufacturing company?

Product inspection	Plating/packing
Machine drilling	Cost accounting
Materials storage	Moving work in process
Product engineering	Inventory control

SE 3.

LO 2 *Supply Chain*

Horace Blake is developing plans to open Ribs 'n Chicken restaurant. He has located a building and will lease all the furniture and equipment he needs to place his restaurant in operation. Food Servers, Inc., will supply all of the restaurant's personnel. Identify the components of Ribs 'n Chicken's supply chain.

SE 4.

LO 3 *Value-Adding Versus Nonvalue-Adding Activities*

Identify which of the following activities related to a local submarine sandwich shop are value-adding (V) and which are nonvalue-adding (NV).

Purchasing sandwich ingredients	Cleaning up the shop
Storing condiments	Making home deliveries
Making sandwiches	Accounting for store sales and costs

SE 5.

LO 4 *ABC Cost Hierarchy*

Engineering design is vital to the success of any motor vehicle manufacturing company. Based on the four categories of the cost hierarchy in an activity-based costing system, how would the engineering design activity be classified for:

1. The maker of unique, single editions of Rolls Royces
2. The maker of built-to-order city and county emergency vehicles (orders are usually placed for 10 to 12 identical vehicles)
3. The maker of a line of automobiles sold throughout the world

SE 6.

LO 5 *Elements of a JIT Operating Environment*

Maintaining minimum inventory levels, developing pull-through production planning and scheduling, and purchasing materials as needed in smaller lot sizes are three elements of a just-in-time operating environment. How do pull-through production and producing as needed help to accomplish the objective of minimizing inventories?

SE 7.

LO 6 *Product Costing Changes in a JIT Environment*

Zygmont Tool Products Company is in the process of adopting the just-in-time operating philosophy for its tool-making operations. Identify which of the following manufacturing overhead costs are nonvalue-adding costs (NVA) and which can be traced directly to the new tool-making work cell (D).

Storage barrels for work in process inventory
Inspection labor
Machine electricity
Machine repairs
Depreciation of the storage barrel movers
Machine setup labor

SE 8.

LO 7 *Backflush Costing*

During August, Hagen Printing Company incurred direct materials costs of $123,450 and conversion costs of $265,200. The company employs a just-in-time operating philosophy and a backflush costing system. At the end of August, it was determined that the Raw in Process Inventory account had been assigned $980 of costs and the ending balance of the Finished Goods Inventory account was $1,290. There were no beginning inventory balances. How much was charged to the Cost of Goods Sold account during August? What was the ending balance of Cost of Goods Sold?

SE 9.

LO 8 *ABM and JIT Compared*

Dextra Corp. recently completed the installation of three just-in-time work cells in its Screen-Making Division. The work cells will make large quantities of products for major window- and door-producing companies. Should Dextra use backflush costing or ABM/ABC to account for product costs? Defend your choice of activity-based system.

Exercises

E 1.

LO 2 *Supply Chains and Value Chains*

Identify which of the following people, events, and activities associated with a lawn and garden nursery are part of the supply chain (S) and which are part of the value chain (V).

Plant and tree vendor
Purchasing potted trees
Computer and software salesperson
Creating marketing plans
Advertising company manager
Scheduling delivery trucks
Customer service

LO 3   *Process Value Analysis*

E 2.   Arakawa Enterprises has been in business for 30 years. Last year, the company purchased Chemcraft Laboratory and entered the chemical processing business. Arakawa's controller prepared a process value analysis of the new operation and identified the following activities:

New product research	Product sales	Product bottling process
Solicitation of vendor bids	Packaging process	Product warranty work
Materials storage	Materials inspection	Product engineering
Product curing process	New product marketing	Purchasing of materials
Product scheduling	Product inspection	Finished goods storage
Product spoilage	Product delivery	Processing areas clean-up
Customer follow-up	Materials delivery	Product mixing process

From the list above, identify the value-adding activities and classify them into the activity areas of the value chain illustrated in Figure 2. Prepare a separate list of the nonvalue-adding activities.

LO 4   *ABC Cost Hierarchy*

E 3.   Orval Electronics makes sound speakers and speaker systems. Its customers range from new hotels and restaurants that need specially designed sound systems to nationwide retail outlets that order large quantities of similar products. The following activities are part of the company's operating process:

New product design	Direct materials costs	Assembly labor costs
Product line marketing	Repairing the building	Assembly line setup
Unique system design	Sales commissions	Securing the building
Unique system packaging	Bulk packing of orders	Product line supervision

Classify each activity as either unit level (UL), batch level (BL), product level (PL), or facility level (FL).

LO 5   *Elements of JIT*

E 4.   The following basic concepts underlie activity-based systems such as ABM and JIT. Match each numbered concept to the related lettered element(s) of the JIT operating environment.

Basic Concepts

1. Simple is better.
2. Product quality is critical.
3. The work environment must emphasize continuous improvement.
4. Maintaining inventories wastes resources and may hide bad work.
5. Any activity or function that does not add value to the product should be reduced or eliminated.
6. Goods should be produced only when needed.
7. Workers must be multiskilled and must participate in the improvement of efficiency and product quality.

Related Elements of the JIT Operating Environment

a. Maintain minimum inventory levels.
b. Develop pull-through production planning and scheduling.
c. Purchase materials and produce products as needed, in smaller lot sizes.
d. Perform quick, inexpensive machine setups.
e. Create flexible manufacturing work cells.
f. Develop a multiskilled work force.
g. Maintain high levels of product quality.
h. Enforce a system of effective preventive maintenance.
i. Encourage continuous improvement in the work environment.

LO 6   *Direct Versus Indirect Costs*

E 5.   The cost categories in the following list are common in a manufacturing and assembly operation.

Direct materials	Operating supplies
Sheet steel	Small tools
Iron castings	Depreciation, plant

Assembly parts	Depreciation, machinery
Part 24RE6	Supervisory salaries
Part 15RF8	Electrical power
Direct labor	Insurance and taxes, plant
Engineering labor	President's salary
Indirect labor	Employee benefits

Identify each cost as either direct or indirect, assuming it was incurred in (1) a traditional manufacturing setting and (2) a JIT environment. State the reasons for any changes in classification.

E 6.

LO 7 *Raw in Process Inventory*

Martinez Products Co. installed a JIT work environment in its Shovel Division, and the system has been operating at near capacity for eight months. The division's accounting system was changed to combine the Raw Materials Inventory and Work in Process Inventory accounts into a single Raw in Process Inventory account and to combine direct labor and manufacturing overhead into a Conversion Costs account. The following transactions took place last week.

May 28 Ordered and received handles and sheet metal costing $11,340.
    29 Direct labor costs incurred, $5,400.
    29 Manufacturing overhead costs incurred, $8,100.
    30 Completed shovels costing $24,800.
    31 Sold shovels costing $24,000.

Using backflush costing, calculate the ending balances in the Raw in Process Inventory and the Finished Goods Inventory accounts.

E 7.

LO 7 *Backflush Costing*

Tarkoff Enterprises produces several varieties of digital alarm clocks. The company recently installed a just-in-time assembly process and uses backflush costing to record production costs. Manufacturing overhead is applied using a rate of $17 per assembly labor hour. There were no beginning inventories in March. During the month, the following operating data were generated:

Cost of direct materials and parts purchased and used	$53,200
Direct labor costs incurred	$27,300
Manufacturing overhead costs applied	?
Assembly hours worked	3,840 hours
Ending raw in process inventory	$1,050
Ending finished goods inventory	$960

Using T accounts show the flow of costs through the backflush costing system. What was the total cost of goods sold for March?

E 8.

LO 8 *ABM Versus JIT*

Identify each of the following as a characteristic of ABM or JIT.

1. Uses backflush costing
2. Uses ABC to assign manufacturing overhead costs to the product cost
3. Integrates ABC with either job order or process costing systems
4. Reduces complexity by using work cells, standardizing parts, and reducing or eliminating inventories and nonvalue-adding production activities
5. Reorganizes service activities so that they are performed within work cells

Problems

P 1.

LO 2 *Value Chain and Process*
LO 3 *Value Analysis*

Valporo Industries, Inc., produces a line of yard maintenance equipment for major retail store chains. Among the company's products are chain saws, lawn weed eaters, trimmers, and lawn mowers. These products are made to order in large quantities for each customer. The company has adopted an activity-based management philosophy, and the controller is in the process of developing an activity-based costing system. He has identified the following primary activities of the company.

Production scheduling	Materials moving
Product delivery	Production—assembly
Customer follow-up	Engineering design
Materials and parts purchasing	Product inspection

Materials storage	Processing areas clean-up
Materials inspection	Product marketing
Production—drilling	Building maintenance
Product packaging	Product sales
New product testing	Product rework
Finished goods storage	Production—grinding
Production—machine setup	Personnel services

REQUIRED

1. Identify the activities that are nonvalue-adding.
2. Assist the controller's process value analysis by grouping the value-adding activities into the activity areas of the value chain illustrated in Figure 2.
3. State whether each nonvalue-adding activity is necessary or unnecessary. Suggest how the controller could reduce or eliminate each unnecessary activity.

P 2.

LO 4   *ABM and Activity-Based Costing*

Kalina Products, Inc., produces a line of printers for wholesale distributors in the South. Life Spring Company ordered 150 Model G printers, and Kalina has just completed packaging the order. Before shipping the Life Spring order, the controller has asked for a unit cost analysis comparing costs determined by the traditional costing system with costs computed under the new activity-based costing system.

Direct materials, purchased parts, and production labor costs for the Life Spring order are as follows:

Cost of direct materials	$17,552
Cost of purchased parts	$14,856
Direct labor hours	140
Average direct labor pay rate per hour	$17

Other operating costs are as follows:

Traditional costing data:

Manufacturing overhead costs were assigned at a rate of 240 percent of direct labor cost.

Activity-based costing data:

Activities	Cost Drivers	Cost Assignment Rates	Activity Usage for Life Spring Order
Engineering systems design	Engineering hours	$28 per engineering hour	18 engineering hours
Setup	Number of setups	$36 per setup	12 setups
Parts production	Machine hours	$37 per machine hour	82 machine hours
Product assembly	Labor hours	$42 per labor hour	36 labor hours
Packaging	Number of packages	$28 per package	30 packages

Building occupancy-related costs are assigned at a rate of $10 per machine hour.

REQUIRED

1. Use the traditional costing approach to compute the total cost and the product unit cost of the Life Spring order.
2. Using the cost hierarchy, identify each activity as unit level, batch level, product level, or facility level.
3. Prepare a bill of activities for the operating costs.
4. Use activity-based costing to compute the total cost and the product unit cost of the Life Spring order.
5. What difference in the product unit cost of the Life Spring order resulted from the shift to activity-based costing? Does the use of activity-based costing guarantee cost reduction for every order?

P 3.

LO 6   *Product Costing in a JIT Work Cell*

Allen Company produces a complete line of bicycle seats in its Flagstaff plant. The four versions of Model J17-21 are made in JIT work cell 2. The four seats have different shapes but identical processing operations and production costs. During July, the following costs were incurred and traced to JIT 2.

Materials	
Leather	$25,430
Metal frame	39,180
Bolts	3,010

Materials handling	
Labor	$8,232
Equipment depreciation	4,410
Electrical power	2,460
Maintenance	5,184
Direct labor	
Machinists	13,230
Engineering design	
Labor	4,116
Electrical power	1,176
Engineering overhead	7,644
JIT overhead	
Equipment depreciation	7,056
Indirect labor	30,870
Supervision	17,640
Operating supplies	4,410
Electrical power	10,584
Repairs and maintenance	21,168
Building occupancy overhead	52,920

July's output totaled 29,400 units. Each unit requires three machine hours of effort. Materials handling costs are allocated to the products based on unit materials cost; engineering design costs are allocated based on units produced; and JIT overhead is allocated based on machine hours.

REQUIRED

1. Compute the following:
   a. The materials handling cost allocation rate
   b. The engineering design cost allocation rate
   c. JIT overhead allocation rate
2. Compute the product unit cost of one bicycle seat. Show your computation.

P 4.

LO 7   *Backflush Costing*

Killough Corp. produces metal fasteners using six work cells, one for each of the company's product lines. Just-in-time operations and costing methods were implemented two years ago. Manufacturing overhead is applied using a rate of $14 per machine hour for the Machine Screw Work Cell. There were no beginning inventories on April 1. Operating details for April for the Machine Screw Work Cell are shown below.

Cost of direct materials purchased on account and used	$104,500
Cost of parts purchased on account and used	$78,900
Direct labor costs incurred	$39,000
Costs of goods completed during April	$392,540
Manufacturing overhead costs applied	?
Machine hours used	12,220 machine hours
Ending raw in process inventory	$940
Ending finished goods inventory	$1,020

REQUIRED

1. Using T accounts, show the flow of costs through a backflush costing system.
2. Using T accounts, show the flow of costs through a traditional costing system.
3. What was the total cost of goods sold for the month?

Alternate Problems

P 5.

LO 4   *Activities and Activity-Based Costing*

Crampton Cellular Company, which has been in operation for six years, produces a line of cellular telephones. Johanna Realtors, Ltd., placed an order for eighty cellular phones, and the order has just been completed. Crampton recently shifted its cost assignment approach to an activity-based system. Himzo Seta, the controller, is interested in finding out what impact the ABC system had on the Johanna order. Direct materials, purchased parts, and production labor costs for the Johanna order are as follows:

| Cost of direct materials | $36,950 | Direct labor hours | 220 |
| Cost of purchased parts | 21,100 | Average direct labor pay rate per hour | $15 |

Other operating costs are as follows:

Traditional costing data:

Manufacturing overhead costs were assigned at a rate of 270 percent of direct labor cost.

Activity-based costing data:

Activities	Cost Drivers	Cost Assignment Rates	Activity Usage for Johanna Order
Electrical engineering design	Engineering hours	$19 per engineering hour	32 engineering hours
Setups	Number of setups	$29 per setup	11 setups
Parts production	Machine hours	$26 per machine hour	134 machine hours
Product testing	Number of tests	$32 per test	52 tests
Packaging	Number of packages	$17 per package	22 packages

Building occupancy-related costs are assigned at a rate of $9.80 per machine hour.

REQUIRED

1. Use the traditional costing approach to compute the total cost and the product unit cost of the Johanna order.
2. Using the cost hierarchy, identify each activity as unit level, batch level, product level, or facility level.
3. Prepare a bill of activities for the operating costs.
4. Use activity-based costing to compute the total cost and the product unit cost of the Johanna order.
5. What difference in the product unit cost of the Johanna order resulted from the shift to activity-based costing? Does the use of activity-based costing guarantee cost reduction for every order?

P 6.

LO 7 *Backflush Costing*

B&K Automotive Parts Co. produces twelve automotive body parts that are purchased by three automobile assembly companies in the United States. The Fender Work Cell is operated by four employees and involves a flexible manufacturing system with fourteen work stations. The work cell produces automotive fenders that are completely detailed and ready to install when received by the customer. Just-in-time operating and costing procedures have been implemented since the work cell became operational three years ago. Manufacturing overhead is applied using a rate of $26 per work cell hour used. All materials and parts are used as they are received. Operating details for February for the Fender Work Cell are shown below.

Beginning raw in process inventory	—
Beginning finished goods inventory	$420
Cost of direct materials purchased on account and used	$213,400
Cost of parts purchased on account and used	$111,250
Direct labor costs incurred	$26,450
Costs of goods completed during February	$564,650
Manufacturing overhead costs applied	?
Work cell hours used	8,260 work cell hours
Ending raw in process inventory	$1,210
Ending finished goods inventory	$670

REQUIRED

1. Using T accounts, show the flow of costs through a backflush costing system. (*Note:* In backflush costing, costs in beginning inventories remain in the accounts until the end of the period, when the accounts are adjusted to their ending balances.)
2. Using T accounts, show the flow of costs through a traditional costing system.
3. What was the total cost of goods sold for the month?

EXPANDING YOUR CRITICAL THINKING, COMMUNICATION, AND INTERPERSONAL SKILLS

Skills Development

CONCEPTUAL ANALYSIS

SD 1.

LO 5 *JIT in a Service Business*

The initiation banquet for new members of your business club is being held at an excellent restaurant. You are sitting next to two marketing majors. In discussing the accounting course they are taking, they mention that they are having difficulty understanding the just-in-time (JIT) concept. They have read that a company's JIT operating system contains elements that support the concepts of simplicity, continuous improvement, waste reduction, timeliness, and efficiency. They realize that in order to understand JIT in a complex manufacturing environment, they must first understand JIT in a simpler context. They ask you to explain the term and provide an example.

Briefly explain the just-in-time philosophy. Apply the elements of a JIT operating system presented in this chapter to the restaurant where your banquet is being held. Do you believe the JIT philosophy applies in all restaurant operations? Explain.

ETHICAL DILEMMA

SD 2.

LO 5 *Ethics and JIT Implementation*

For almost a year, **Traki Company** has been changing its manufacturing process from a traditional to a JIT approach. Management has asked for employee assistance in the transition and has offered bonuses for suggestions that cut time from the production operation. Deb Hinds and Jack Snow each identified a time-saving opportunity and, independently, turned in their suggestions to their manager, Randall Soder.

When Soder sent the suggestions to the vice president of production, they were inadvertently identified as being Soder's own. After careful analysis, the company's Production Review Committee decided that the two suggestions were worthy of reward and voted a large bonus to Soder. When notified by the vice president, Soder could not bring himself to identify the true authors of the suggestions.

When Hinds and Snow heard about Soder's ill-gained bonus, they were very upset and confronted him with their grievance. He told them that he needed the recognition to be eligible for an upcoming promotion and promised that if they kept quiet about the matter, he would make sure that they both received significant raises. Prepare written responses so that you can discuss the following questions in class.

1. Should Hinds and Snow keep quiet? What other options are open to them?
2. Given that Soder committed a fraudulent act, how should he have dealt with the complaint of Hinds and Snow?

RESEARCH ACTIVITY

SD 3.

LO 6 *Just-in-Time Production*

Many large, multinational companies, as well as many smaller companies, have recently installed automated just-in-time production processes to compete for new domestic and foreign business. Locate an article about a company that has recently installed a JIT system. Conduct your search using the company annual reports in your campus library, the business section of your local newspaper, *The Wall Street Journal*, or the Needles Accounting Resource Center Web site at http//www.hmco.com/college/needles/home.html.

Choose a source that describes the changes the company made within its plant to increase product quality and to compete as a world-class manufacturer. Prepare a one-page description of those changes. Include in your report the name of the company, its geographic location, the name of the chief executive officer and/or president, and the

 Communication

 Critical Thinking

 Group Activity

 Memo

 Ethics

 International

 Spreadsheet

 Managerial Technology

 Internet

dollar amount of the company's total sales for the most recent year, if stated. Be prepared to present your findings to your classmates.

DECISION-MAKING PRACTICE

SD 4.
LO 3   *Activities, Cost Drivers,*
LO 5   *and JIT*
LO 6

Atlanta, Georgia, is home of the **Sable Corporation.** Fifteen years ago Bruce Sable teamed up with ten financial supporters and created a roller skate manufacturing company. Company design people soon turned the roller skate idea into a riding skateboard. Twelve years and more than 4 million skateboards later, Sable Corporation finds itself an industry leader in both volume and quality. To retain market share, Sable Corporation has decided to automate its manufacturing process. Flexible manufacturing systems have been ordered for the wheel assembly and the board shaping lines. Manual operations will be retained for the board decorating line because some hand painting is involved. All operations will be converted to a just-in-time environment.

You have been called in as a consultant to Sable, who wants some idea of the impact of the new JIT approach on the company's product costing practices.

1. Summarize the elements of a JIT environment.
2. What product costing changes should be anticipated when the new automated systems are installed?
3. What are some cost drivers that the company should employ? In what situations?

Managerial Reporting and Analysis

INTERPRETING MANAGEMENT REPORTS

MRA 1.
LO 3   *ABC and Selling and*
LO 4   *Administrative Expenses*

Sally Star, the owner of Star Bakery, wants to know the profitability of each of the bakery's customer groups. She is especially interested in the State Prisons customer group, which is one of Star Bakery's largest customer groups. Currently, the bakery is selling doughnuts and snack foods to ten state prisons in three states. The controller has prepared the income statement shown below for the State Prisons customer group. The controller also provided information about selling and administrative activities for customer groups

Star Bakery
Income Statement for State Prisons Customer Group
For the Year Ending December 31, 20x1

Sales ($5 per case × 50,000 cases)	$250,000
Cost of goods sold ($3.50 per case × 50,000 cases)	175,000
Gross margin	$ 75,000
Less: Selling and administrative activities costs	

Activity/ Cost Pool	Cost Pool Rate	Cost Driver Level	Activity Cost
Make sales calls	$60 per sales call	60 sales calls	$3,600
Prepare sales orders	$10 per sales order	900 sales orders	9,000
Handle inquiries	$5 per minute	1,000 minutes	5,000
Ship products	$1 per case sold	50,000 cases	50,000
Process invoices	$2 per invoice	950 invoices	19,000
Process credit	$20 per notice	40 notices	800
Process billings and collections	$7 per billing	1,050 billings	7,350

Total selling and administrative activity costs	94,750
Net income (loss) contributed by state prisons	$ (19,750)

with similar characteristics. For 20x1, the planned cost pool rates and annual cost driver levels for each selling and administrative activity included:

Activity/ Cost Pool	Planned Cost Pool Rate	Planned Annual Cost Driver Level
Make sales calls	$60 per sales call	59 sales calls
Prepare sales orders	$10 per sales order	850 sales orders
Handle inquiries	$5.10 per minute	1,000 minutes
Ship products	$.60 per case sold	50,000 cases
Process invoices	$1 per invoice	500 invoices
Process credit	$10 per notice	5 notices
Process billings and collections	$4 per billing	600 billings

You have been called in as a consultant on the State Prisons customer group.

REQUIRED

1. Calculate the planned activity cost for each activity/cost pool item.
2. Calculate the differences between the planned activity costs and the State Prisons customer group's activity costs for 20x1.
3. From your evaluation of the differences calculated in **2** and your review of the income statement, identify the nonvalue-adding activities and state which selling and administrative activities should be examined.
4. What actions might the company take to reduce the costs of nonvalue-adding selling and administrative activities?

Group Activity: Provide data for Parts 1 and 2 to groups and ask them to discuss and answer Parts 3 and 4.

FORMULATING MANAGEMENT REPORTS

MRA 2.

LO 5 *Manufacturing Processes and Management Reporting Systems*

Classic Clubs, Inc., manufactures professional golf clubs. Demand is so great that the company built a special plant that makes only custom-crafted clubs. The clubs are shaped by machines but vary according to the customer's sex, height, weight, and arm length. Ten basic sets of clubs are produced, five for females and five for males. Slight variations in machine setup provide the differences in the club weights and lengths. In the past six months, several problems have developed. Even though one computer numerically controlled machine is used in the manufacturing process, the company's backlog is growing rapidly. Customers are complaining that delivery is too slow. Quality is declining because clubs are pushed through production without proper inspection. Working capital is tied up in excessive amounts of inventory and storage space. Workers are complaining about the pressure to produce the backlogged orders. Machine breakdowns are increasing. Production control reports are not useful because they are not timely and contain irrelevant information. The company's profitability and cash flow are suffering.

Classic Clubs, Inc., has hired you as a consultant to define the problem and suggest a possible solution to the current dilemma. Denise Rodemeyer, the president, asks that you complete your work within a month so that she can prepare an action plan to present to the board of directors at the mid-year board meeting.

REQUIRED

1. In memo form, prepare a response to Rodemeyer. Recommend specific changes in the manufacturing process and the management accounting system. Defend each change that you suggest.
2. To help you prepare this report, answer the following questions.
   a. What kinds of information do you need to prepare this report?
   b. Why is this information relevant?
   c. Where would you go to obtain this information (sources)?
   d. When would you want to obtain this information?

INTERNATIONAL COMPANY

MRA 3.

LO 4 *ABM and ABC in a Service Business*

Kendle and Watson, a CPA firm, has provided audit, tax, and management advisory services to businesses in the London area for over fifty years. Recently, the firm decided to use ABM and activity-based costing to assign its overhead costs to those service functions. Bellamy Kendle is interested in seeing the difference in the average cost per audit job between the traditional and the activity-based costing approaches. The following information has been provided to assist in the comparison.

Total direct labor costs	£400,000
Other direct costs	120,000
Total direct costs	£520,000

Overhead costs are as follows:

Traditional costing data:

Overhead costs were assigned at a rate of 120 percent of direct labor costs.

Activity-based costing data:

Activities	Cost Drivers	Cost Assignment Rates	Activity Usage for Audit Function
Professional development	Number of employees	£2,000 per employee	50 employees
Administration	Number of jobs	£1,000 per job	50 jobs
Client development	Number of new clients	£5,000 per new client	29 new clients

REQUIRED

1. Using direct labor cost as the cost driver, calculate the total costs for the audit function. What is the average cost per job?
2. Using activity-based costing to assign overhead, calculate the total costs for the audit function. What is the average cost per job?
3. Calculate the difference in total costs between both approaches. Why would activity-based costing be the better approach to assigning overhead to the audit function?

EXCEL SPREADSHEET ANALYSIS

MRA 4.

LO 3 *ABC in Planning and*
LO 4 *Control*

Refer to the income statement for the State Prisons customer group for the year ending December 31, 20x1, in **MRA 1.** Sally Star, the owner of Star Bakery, is in the process of budgeting net income for 20x2. She has asked the controller to prepare a budgeted income statement for the State Prisons customer group. Sally estimates that the selling price per case, the number of cases sold, the cost of goods sold per case, and the activity costs for making sales calls, preparing sales orders, and handling inquiries will remain the same for 20x2. She has contracted with a new freight company to ship the 50,000 cases at $.60 per case sold. She has also analyzed the processes for invoicing, reviewing credit, billing, and collecting and has decided it would be less expensive for a customer service agency to do the work. The agency will charge the bakery 1.5 percent of the total sales revenue.

REQUIRED

Using an Excel spreadsheet:

1. Prepare a budgeted income statement for the State Prisons customer group for the year ending December 31, 20x2.
2. Refer to the information in MRA 1. Assuming the planned cost pool rate and planned annual cost driver level for each selling and administrative activity remain the same in 20x2, calculate the planned activity cost for each activity/cost pool item.
3. Calculate the differences between the planned activity costs and the State Prisons customer group's activity costs for 20x2.
4. Evaluate the results of changing freight companies and outsourcing the customer service activities.

ENDNOTES

1. Robert S. Kaplan, Dan Weiss, and Eyal Desheh, "Transfer Pricing with ABC," *Management Accounting*, Institute of Management Accountants, May 1997, pp. 20–29.
2. Alexander Kogan, Ephraim F. Sudit, and Miklos A. Visarhelyi, "Management Accounting in the Era of Electronic Commerce," *Management Accounting*, Institute of Management Accountants, September 1997, pp. 26–30.
3. Richard Ashton, "Federal Excess?" *Home Office Computing*, October 1997, p. 28.
4. Several of the ideas in this section are from Robert D. McIlhattan, "How Cost Management Systems Can Support the JIT Philosophy," *Management Accounting*, Institute of Management Accountants, September 1987, pp. 20–26.
5. Alexander Kogan, Ephraim F. Sudit, and Miklos A. Visarhelyi, "Management Accounting in the Era of Electronic Commerce," *Management Accounting*, Institute of Management Accountants, September 1997, pp. 26–30.

CHAPTER 6

Cost-Volume-Profit Analysis and Variable Costing

1. Define *cost behavior* and explain how managers make use of this concept in the management cycle.
2. Identify specific types of variable and fixed cost behavior, and define and discuss the relationships of operating capacity and relevant range to cost behavior.
3. Define *mixed cost,* and use the high-low method to separate the variable and fixed components of a mixed cost.
4. Define *cost-volume-profit analysis* and discuss how managers use this analysis.
5. Compute a breakeven point in units of output and in sales dollars, and prepare a breakeven graph.
6. Define *contribution margin* and use the concept to determine a company's breakeven point for a single product and for multiple products.
7. Apply cost-volume-profit analysis to estimated levels of future sales and to changes in costs and selling prices.
8. Apply cost-volume-profit analysis to a service business.

DECISION POINT

Cummins Engine Company, Inc., is a manufacturing company whose main office is located in Columbus, Indiana.[1] Cummins facilities in the United States, Mexico, and China manufacture diesel engines and other parts for large trucks. The costs of manufacturing equipment used to produce engines (which include the B and C Series) are considered fixed because the equipment can be used over a long period of time.

But equipment does not last forever. Equipment deteriorates, and some pieces become outdated when new, more productive models are introduced. The depreciable costs of the equipment are assigned to engines using a modified units-of-production method. This method considers both the life of the equipment (maximum economic life) and its usage (total productive capacity).

Management must decide when to replace equipment as well as when to purchase additional equipment so that the business can change its manufacturing processes to produce a new series of engines that will meet the latest emissions requirements. How does the relationship of fixed costs to

CUMMINS ENGINE COMPANY, INC.

the company's production volume and its profit play a role in the decision process?

To generate income, the revenue generated from the sale of B and C Series engines must exceed the costs of using the equipment to produce the engines (depreciation expense) and other costs related to designing, manufacturing, selling, and shipping the engines. Management decides the best method of assigning equipment costs to the units produced. When making plans to purchase additional equipment, management must first estimate the projected volume of engine production, the costs involved, and the projected net income. With those projections in mind, management can decide how much new equipment it needs to meet the company's goal.

Cost Behavior Patterns

OBJECTIVE 1

Define cost behavior *and explain how managers make use of this concept in the management cycle*

The expectation that an organization's management will generate income for its owners and maintain liquidity for its creditors requires managers to find ways to make good decisions. One common way to make good decisions is to use cost behavior to analyze alternative courses of action. Cost behavior is the way costs respond to changes in volume or activity. Some costs vary with volume or operating activity; others remain fixed as volume changes. Between these two extremes are costs that exhibit characteristics of both. An understanding of cost behavior is most helpful as managers move through the planning, executing, and reporting stages of the management cycle, as shown in Figure 1.

In the planning stage, managers want to know how many units must be sold to cover all costs or to generate a targeted amount of income. Managers want to know how changes in planned operating, investing, or financing activities will affect income. As German sports shoe manufacturer Adidas completed the acquisition of Salomon SA, a French ski and sporting goods maker, its management began to estimate income from future operations. They used cost behavior to estimate how the addition of new lines of sporting equipment, such as Salomon skis and snowboards, Taylor Made golf clubs, and Mavic cycling equipment, would contribute to the organization's income.

Car manufacturers, such as Chrysler, also use cost behavior in the planning stage to decide how to change the output of trucks and cars to meet changing sales demand. If increased demand for trucks suggests the need to increase truck production and decrease car production, management can use cost behavior analysis to estimate the changes in income for those product lines. Since the truck segment is more profitable for Chrysler, the company's net income should increase if truck production is increased.

Managers use information about cost behavior in almost every decision they make. For example, the management at Cummins Engine must understand the changes in income that can be caused by a decision to buy new, more productive manufacturing equipment or to launch an advertising campaign to promote a new series of engines. Throughout the executing stage of the management cycle, management must understand cost behavior to determine the impact of its decisions on income.

Managers at Adidas, Chrysler, and Cummins Engine will also need to understand cost behavior during the reporting stage of the management cycle. Variable costing income statements, which are discussed later in this chapter, are commonly used to analyze the impact of changes in cost and sales on the profitability of product lines, sales territories, customers, departments, or other segments. Other reports based on cost behavior are used in decisions about eliminating a product line, accepting

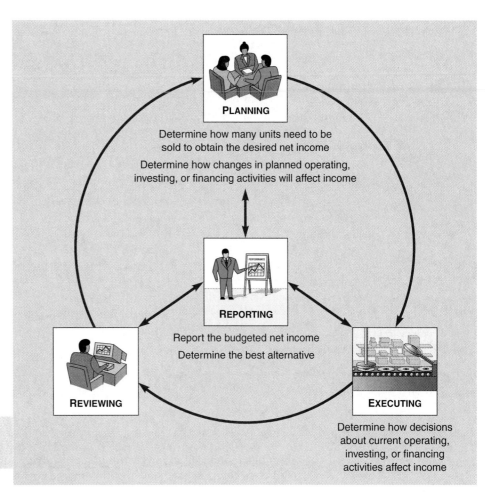

**Figure 1
The Use of Cost Behavior in
the Management Cycle**

special orders, and contracting with other companies to provide services previously performed internally.

Our discussion in this chapter will focus primarily on cost behavior as it relates to production activity. But cost behavior can be observed in other activities. For example, increases in the number of shipments affect shipping costs; the number of units sold or total sales revenue affects the cost of sales commissions; and the number of customers billed or the number of hours to bill affects total billing costs. Costs behave in much the same way in service organizations as they do in manufacturing organizations. We look specifically at the costs of service organizations later in the chapter.

The Behavior of Variable Costs

Total costs that change in direct proportion to changes in productive output (or any other measure of volume) are called variable costs. To explore how variable costs work, consider tire costs for Land Rover, a maker of off-road vehicles. Each new vehicle has four tires, and each tire costs $48. The total cost of tires, then, is $192 for one car, $384 for two, $576 for three, $768 for four, $960 for five, $1,920 for ten, and $19,200 for one hundred. In the production of off-road vehicles, the total cost of tires is a variable cost. On a per unit basis, however, a variable cost remains constant. In this case, the cost of tires per vehicle is $192 whether the auto maker produces one car or one hundred cars. True, the cost of tires varies depending on the

Table 1. Examples of Variable, Fixed, and Mixed Costs

Costs	Manufacturing Company—Desk Manufacturer	Service Company—Bank	Merchandising Company—Department Store
Variable	Direct materials Direct labor (hourly) Indirect labor (hourly) Operating supplies Small tools	Computer equipment leasing (based on usage) Computer operators (hourly) Operating supplies Data storage disks	Merchandise to sell Sales commissions Shelf stockers (hourly)

Fixed	Depreciation, machinery and building
	Insurance premiums
	Labor (salaried)
	Supervisory salaries
	Property taxes
		Depreciation, furniture and fixtures
		Insurance premiums
		Salaries:
		  Programmers
		  Systems designers
		  Bank administrators
		Rent, buildings
			Depreciation, building
			Insurance premiums
			Buyers (salaried)
			Supervisory salaries
			Property taxes (on equipment and building)

Mixed	Electrical power Telephone Heat	Electrical power Telephone Heat	Electrical power Telephone Heat

number purchased, and discounts are available for purchases of large quantities. But once the purchase has been made, the cost per tire is established. Table 1 lists other examples of variable costs. All of those costs—whether incurred by a manufacturer, a service business, or a merchandiser—are variable based on either productive output or total sales.

Operating Capacity   Because variable costs increase or decrease in direct proportion to volume or output, it is important to know an organization's operating capacity. Operating capacity is the upper limit of an organization's productive output capability, given its existing resources. It describes just what an organization can accomplish in a given time period. Operating capacity, or volume, can be expressed in several ways, including total labor hours, total machine hours, and total units of output. Any increase in volume or activity over operating capacity requires additional expenditures for building, machinery, personnel, and operations. In our discussion of cost behavior patterns, we assume that operating capacity is constant and that all activity occurs within the limits of current operating capacity. Cost behavior patterns can change when additional operating capacity is added.

There are three common measures, or types, of operating capacity: theoretical, or ideal, capacity; practical capacity; and normal capacity. Theoretical (ideal) capacity is the maximum productive output for a given period, assuming that all machinery and equipment are operating at optimum speed, without interruption. Theoretical capacity is useful in estimating maximum production levels, but an organization never operates at ideal capacity. In fact, the concept had little relationship to actual operations until the advent of the just-in-time operating environment. The concept that drives the just-in-time environment is the continuous improvement of operations, with the long-term goal of approaching ideal capacity.

Practical capacity is theoretical capacity reduced by normal and expected work stoppages. Production is interrupted by machine breakdowns and downtime for retooling, repairs and maintenance, and employees' work breaks. Such normal interruptions and the resulting reductions in output are considered when measuring practical capacity.

Most organizations do not operate at either theoretical or practical capacity. Both measures include excess capacity, extra machinery and equipment kept on standby. This extra equipment is used when regular equipment is being repaired. Also, during a slow season, a company may use only part of its equipment, or it may work just one or two shifts instead of around the clock. Because it is necessary to consider so many different circumstances, managers often use a measure called normal capacity, rather than practical capacity, when planning operations. Normal capacity is the average annual level of operating capacity needed to meet expected sales demand. The sales demand figure is adjusted for seasonal changes and business and economic cycles. Therefore, normal capacity is a realistic measure of what an organization is likely to produce, not what it can produce.

Each variable cost should be related to an appropriate measure of capacity, but, in many cases, more than one measure of capacity applies. Operating costs can be related to machine hours used or total units produced. Sales commissions, on the other hand, usually vary in direct proportion to total sales dollars.

There are two reasons for carefully selecting the basis for measuring the activity of variable costs. First, an appropriate activity base simplifies cost planning and control. Second, the management accountant must combine (aggregate) many variable costs with the same activity base so that the costs can be analyzed in a reasonable way. Such aggregation also provides information that allows management to predict future costs.

The general guide for selecting an activity base is to relate costs to their most logical or causal factor. For example, machinery setup costs should be considered variable in relation to the number of setup operations needed for a particular job or function. This approach allows machinery setup costs to be budgeted and controlled more effectively.

Linear Relationships and the Relevant Range   The traditional definition of a variable cost assumes that there is a linear relationship between cost and volume, that costs go up or down as volume increases or decreases. You saw that relationship in our tire example earlier. Figure 2 shows another linear relationship. Here, each unit of output requires $2.50 of labor cost. Total labor costs grow in direct proportion to the increase in units of output: For two units, total labor costs are $5.00; for six units, the organization incurs $15.00 in labor costs.

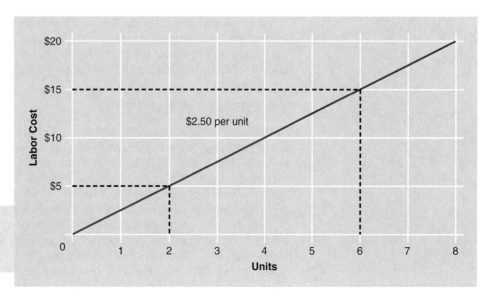

Figure 2
A Common Variable-Cost Behavior Pattern: A Linear Relationship

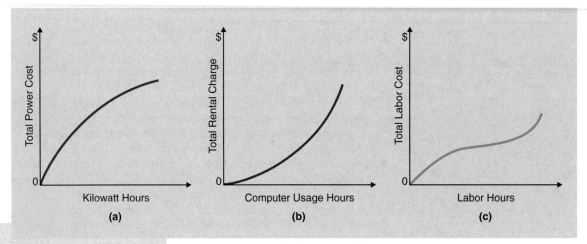

Figure 3
Other Variable-Cost Behavior Patterns: Nonlinear Relationships

Many costs, however, vary with operating activity in a nonlinear fashion. In Figure 3, graph (a) shows the behavior of power costs as usage increases and the unit cost of power consumption falls. Graph (b) shows the behavior of rental costs when each additional hour of computer usage costs more than the previous hour. And graph (c) shows how labor costs vary as efficiency increases and decreases. These three nonlinear cost patterns are variable in nature, but they differ from the straight-line variable-cost pattern shown in Figure 2.

Variable costs with linear relationships to a volume measure are easy to analyze and project for cost planning and control. Nonlinear variable costs are not easy to use. But all costs must be included in an analysis if the results are to be useful to management. To simplify cost analysis procedures and make variable costs easier to use, accountants have developed a method of converting nonlinear variable costs into linear variable costs. This method is called *linear approximation* and relies upon the concept of relevant range. Relevant range is the span of activity in which a company expects to operate. Within that range, many nonlinear costs can be estimated using the straight-line linear approximation approach illustrated in Figure 4. Those estimated costs can then be treated as part of the other variable costs.

A linear approximation of a nonlinear variable cost is not a precise measure, but it allows the inclusion of nonlinear variable costs in cost behavior analysis, and the loss of accuracy is usually not significant. The goal is to help management estimate costs and prepare budgets, and linear approximation helps accomplish that goal.

The Behavior of Fixed Costs

Fixed costs behave much differently from variable costs. Fixed costs are total costs that remain constant within a relevant range of volume or activity. Remember that a relevant range of activity is the range in which actual operations are likely to occur.

Look back at Table 1 for examples of fixed costs. The desk manufacturer, the bank, and the department store all incur depreciation costs and fixed annual insurance premiums. In addition, all salaried personnel have fixed earnings for a particular period. The desk manufacturer and the department store own their buildings and must pay annual property taxes. The bank, on the other hand, pays an annual fixed rental charge for the use of its building.

As the examples in Table 1 suggest, a particular time period is identified when discussing fixed costs because, according to economic theory, all costs tend to be

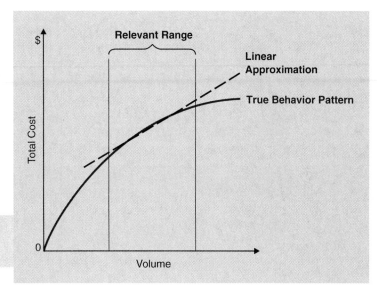

Figure 4
The Relevant Range and
Linear Approximation

variable in the long run. A change in plant capacity, machinery, labor requirements, or other production factors causes fixed costs to increase or decrease. Thus, a cost is fixed only within a limited time period. For planning purposes, management usually considers a one-year time period: Fixed costs are expected to be constant within that period.

Of course, fixed costs change when activity exceeds the relevant range. For example, assume that a local manufacturing organization needs one supervisor for an eight-hour work shift. Production can range from zero to 500,000 units per month per shift; the relevant range, then, is from zero to 500,000 units. The supervisor's salary is $4,000 per month. The cost behavior analysis is as follows:

Units of Output per Month	Total Supervisory Salaries per Month
0–500,000	$4,000
Over 500,000	**$8,000**

If a maximum of 500,000 units can be produced per month per shift, any output above 500,000 units would require another work shift and another supervisor. Like all fixed costs, the new fixed cost remains constant in total within the new relevant range.

What about unit costs? Fixed costs per unit change as volume increases or decreases. *Unit fixed costs vary inversely with activity or volume.* On a per unit basis, fixed costs go down as volume goes up. That pattern holds true as long as the firm is operating within the relevant range of activity. Look at how supervisory costs per unit fall as the volume of activity increases within the relevant range.

Volume of Activity	Cost per Unit
100,000 units	$4,000 ÷ 100,000 = $.0400
300,000 units	$4,000 ÷ 300,000 = $.0133
500,000 units	$4,000 ÷ 500,000 = $.0080
600,000 units	**$8,000** ÷ 600,000 = $.0133

The per unit cost increases to $.0133 at the 600,000-unit level because that activity level is above the relevant range, which means another shift must be added and another supervisor must be hired.

Figure 5 shows this behavior pattern. The fixed supervisory costs for the first 500,000 units of production are $4,000. Those costs hold steady at $4,000 for any

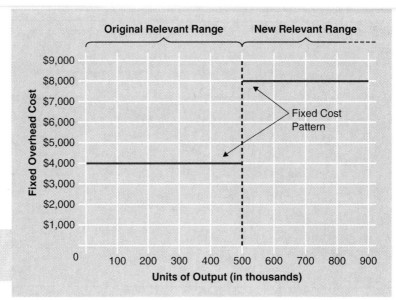

Figure 5
A Common Fixed-Cost
Behavior Pattern

level of output within the relevant range. But if output goes above 500,000 units, another supervisor must be hired, pushing fixed supervisory costs to $8,000.

Mixed Costs

OBJECTIVE 3

Define mixed cost, *and use the high-low method to separate the variable and fixed components of a mixed cost*

Some costs cannot be classified as either variable or fixed. A mixed cost has both variable and fixed cost components. Part of the cost changes with volume or usage, and part of the cost is fixed over the period. Telephone cost is an example. Monthly telephone cost includes charges for long-distance calls plus a service charge and charges for extra telephones. The long-distance charges are variable because they depend on the amount of use; the service charge and the cost of the additional telephones are fixed costs.

Examples of Mixed Costs   Many costs have both variable and fixed components. Utilities costs often fall into this category. Like telephone costs, electricity and gas heat costs normally consist of a fixed base amount and additional charges related to usage. Figure 6 shows just two of the many behavior patterns of mixed costs. Graph (a) depicts the total telephone cost for an organization. The monthly bill begins with a fixed charge for the service and increases as long-distance calls are made. Graph (b)

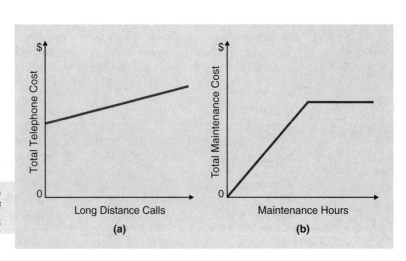

Figure 6
Behavior Patterns of
Mixed Costs

depicts a special contractual arrangement: The annual cost of equipment mainte-nance provided by an outside company increases for each maintenance hour worked, up to a maximum per period. After the maximum is reached, additional maintenance is done at no cost.

High-Low Method of Separating Costs   For cost planning and control, mixed costs must be divided into their respective variable and fixed components. The sep-arate components can then be grouped with other variable and fixed costs for analysis. When there is doubt about the behavior pattern of a particular cost, espe-cially a mixed cost, it helps to plot past costs and related measures of volume in a scatter diagram. A scatter diagram is a chart of plotted points that helps determine if there is a linear relationship between a cost item and its related activity measure. It is a form of linear approximation. If the diagram suggests that a linear relationship exists, a cost line can be imposed on the data by either visual means or statistical analysis.

For example, last year, the Evelio Corporation's Winter Park Division incurred the following machine hours and electricity costs.

Month	Machine Hours	Electricity Costs
January	6,250	$ 24,000
February	6,300	24,200
March	6,350	24,350
April	6,400	24,600
May	6,300	24,400
June	6,200	24,300
July	6,100	23,900
August	6,050	23,600
September	6,150	23,950
October	6,250	24,100
November	6,350	24,400
December	6,450	24,700
Totals	75,150	$290,500

Figure 7 shows a scatter diagram of these data. The diagram suggests that there is a linear relationship between machine hours and the cost of electricity. To determine

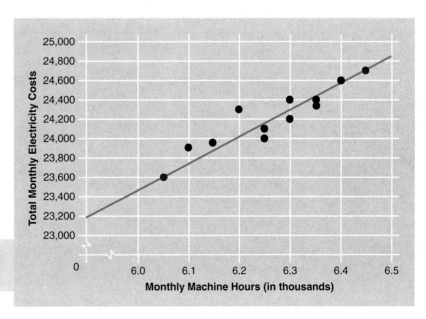

Figure 7
Scatter Diagram of Machine Hours and Electricity Costs

the variable and fixed components of this mixed cost, we apply the high-low method, a common, three-step approach to separating variable and fixed costs.

Step 1: Calculate the variable cost per activity base.

Select the periods of highest and lowest activity within the accounting period. In our example, the Winter Park Division experienced its highest machine-hour activity in December and its lowest machine-hour activity in August. Find the difference between the highest and lowest amounts for both the machine hours and their related electricity costs.

Volume	Month	Activity Level	Cost
Highest	December	6,450 machine hours	$24,700
Lowest	August	6,050 machine hours	23,600
Difference		400 machine hours	$ 1,100

To determine the variable cost per machine hour, divide the difference in cost by the difference in machine hours.

$$\text{Variable Cost per Machine Hour} = \$1,100 \div 400 \text{ Machine Hours}$$
$$= \$2.75 \text{ per Machine Hour}$$

Step 2: Calculate the total fixed costs.

Compute total fixed costs for a month by selecting the information from the month with either the highest or the lowest volume. Let's select the month with the highest volume.

$$\text{Total Fixed Costs} = \text{Total Costs} - \text{Total Variable Costs}$$
$$\text{Total Fixed Costs for December} = \$24,700.00 - (6,450 \times \$2.75) = \$6,962.50$$

You can check your answer by recalculating total fixed costs using the month with the lowest activity. Total fixed costs will be the same.

$$\text{Total Fixed Costs for August} = \$23,600.00 - (6,050 \times \$2.75) = \$6,962.50$$

BUSINESS BULLETIN: BUSINESS PRACTICE

Socially conscious investors are seeking more environmental information from companies. Companies must disclose in the notes to the financial statements any information about contingencies or liabilities from environmental contamination. Companies may also voluntarily include environmental information in their annual reports. Because environmental information affects investors' decisions, managers must consider the financial consequences of business decisions that affect the environment. Information that must be considered in profit planning and cost-volume-profit analysis includes:

- An estimate of the costs (or range of costs) necessary to meet environmental obligations
- An indication of when, if, and how those costs have been recorded in the accounting records
- The possible effects of those environmental obligations on the future financial well-being of the company[2]

Step 3: Calculate the formula to estimate the total costs within the relevant range.

$$\text{Total Cost per Month} = \$6,962.50 + \$2.75 \text{ per Machine Hour}$$

Remember that the cost formula will work only within the relevant range. In this example, the formula would work for amounts between 6,050 machine hours and 6,450 machine hours. To estimate the electricity costs for machine hours outside the relevant range (in this case, below 6,050 machine hours or above 6,450 machine hours), a new cost formula must be calculated.

Cost-Volume-Profit Analysis

OBJECTIVE 4

Define cost-volume-profit analysis *and discuss how managers use this analysis*

Suppose Ford Motor Co. wants to plan operations for the upcoming model year. How do managers know the correct amounts of materials and parts to purchase? Will additional workers need to be hired? Will there be enough space on existing assembly lines or must new facilities be constructed? What should the selling price of the cars be to meet the company's target net income for the year? These questions cannot be answered until the anticipated volume for the year is estimated. Once a target volume has been developed, the costs of production for the period and product pricing can be computed using cost-volume-profit analysis.

Cost-volume-profit (C-V-P) analysis is an examination of the cost behavior patterns that underlie the relationships among cost, volume of output, and profit, which we will refer to as net income. C-V-P analysis is a tool for both planning and control. The process involves a number of techniques and problem-solving procedures based on the cost behavior patterns in an organization. The techniques express relationships among revenue, sales mix, cost, volume, and net income. These relationships provide a general model of financial activity that management can use for short-range planning, evaluating performance, and analyzing alternatives.

For planning, managers can use C-V-P analysis to calculate net income when sales volume is known. Or, through C-V-P analysis, management can decide the level of sales needed to reach a target amount of net income. C-V-P analysis is also used extensively in budgeting.

The C-V-P relationship is expressed in a simple equation.

$$\text{Sales Revenue} = \text{Variable Costs} + \text{Fixed Costs} + \text{Net Income}$$

Or,

$$S = VC + FC + NI$$

Cost-volume-profit analysis is a way of measuring how well the departments in an organization are doing. At the end of a period, sales volume and related actual costs are analyzed to find actual net income. A department's performance is measured by comparing actual costs with expected costs, costs that have been computed by applying C-V-P analysis to actual sales volume. The result is a performance report on which management can base the control of operations.

Basic C-V-P analysis can also be applied to measure the effects of alternative choices: changes in variable and fixed costs, expansion or contraction of sales volume, increases or decreases in selling prices, or other changes in operating methods or policies. Cost-volume-profit analysis is useful for making decisions about product pricing, product mix analysis (when an organization produces more than one product or offers more than one service), adding or deleting a product line, and accepting special orders. There are many applications of C-V-P analysis, and all are used by managers to plan and control operations effectively.

Breakeven Analysis

OBJECTIVE 5

Compute a breakeven point in units of output and in sales dollars, and prepare a breakeven graph

Breakeven analysis uses the basic elements of cost-volume-profit relationships. The breakeven point is the point at which total revenues equal total costs. Breakeven, then, is the point at which an organization begins to earn net income. When a new venture or product line is being planned, the likelihood of success can be quickly measured by finding the project's breakeven point. If, for instance, breakeven is 50,000 units and the total market is only 25,000 units, the idea should be abandoned promptly.

Sales (S), variable costs (VC), and fixed costs (FC) are used to compute the breakeven point, which can be stated in terms of sales units or sales dollars. The general equation for finding the breakeven point is:

$$S = VC + FC$$

For example, Dakota Products, Inc., makes special wooden stands for portable compact disk players that include a protective storage compartment for the disks. Variable costs are $50 per unit, and fixed costs average $20,000 per year. Each wooden stand sells for $90. Given this information, we can compute the breakeven point for this product in sales units (x equals sales units):

$$
\begin{aligned}
S &= VC + FC \\
\$90x &= \$50x + \$20,000 \\
\$40x &= \$20,000 \\
x &= 500 \text{ Units}
\end{aligned}
$$

and in sales dollars:

$$\$90 \times 500 \text{ Units} = \$45,000$$

We can also make a rough estimate of the breakeven point using a graph. This method is less exact, but it does yield meaningful data. Figure 8 shows a breakeven graph for Dakota Products, Inc. This graph has five parts.

1. A horizontal axis in volume or units of output
2. A vertical axis in dollars of revenue
3. A line running horizontally from the vertical axis at the level of fixed costs
4. A total cost line that begins at the point where the fixed cost line crosses the vertical axis and slopes upward to the right (The slope of the line depends on the variable cost per unit.)
5. A total revenue line that begins at the origin of the vertical and horizontal axes and slopes upward to the right (The slope depends on the selling price per unit.)

At the point where the total revenue line crosses the total cost line, revenues equal total costs. The breakeven point, stated in either units or dollars of sales, is

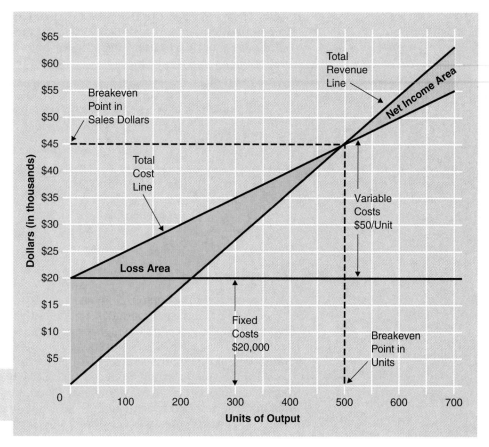

Figure 8
Graphic Breakeven Analysis:
Dakota Products, Inc.

found by extending broken lines from this point to the axes. As Figure 8 shows, Dakota Products, Inc., will break even when 500 wooden stands have been made and sold for $45,000.

Contribution Margin

A simpler method of determining the breakeven point uses contribution margin. Contribution margin is what remains after total variable costs are subtracted from sales. A product line's contribution margin represents its net contribution to paying off fixed costs and earning net income.

$$S - VC = CM$$

And net income is what remains after fixed costs are paid and subtracted from the contribution margin.

$$CM - FC = NI$$

The following example uses contribution margin to determine the profitability of Dakota Products, Inc.

		Units Produced and Sold		
Symbols		250	500	750
S	Sales revenue ($90 per unit)	$22,500	$45,000	$67,500
VC	Less variable costs ($50 per unit)	12,500	25,000	37,500
CM	Contribution margin ($40 per unit)	$10,000	$20,000	$30,000
FC	Less fixed costs	20,000	20,000	20,000
NI	Net income (net loss)	($10,000)	—	$10,000

The breakeven point (BE) can be expressed as the point at which contribution margin minus total fixed costs equals zero (or the point at which contribution margin equals total fixed costs). In terms of units of product, the equation for the breakeven point looks like this:

$$(\text{CM per Unit} \times \text{BE Units}) - \text{FC} = 0$$

The formula that also generates the breakeven point in units is

$$\text{BE Units} = \frac{\text{FC}}{\text{CM per Unit}}$$

To show how the formula works, we use the data for Dakota Products, Inc.

$$\text{BE Units} = \frac{\text{FC}}{\text{CM per Unit}} = \frac{\$20,000}{\$90 - \$50} = \frac{\$20,000}{\$40} = 500 \text{ Units}$$

Multiple Products

Many manufacturing organizations sell a variety of products to satisfy different customer needs. Often each product has different variable and fixed costs or different selling prices. To calculate the breakeven point for each product, the unit contribution margin for each product must be weighted by the sales mix. The sales mix is the proportion of each product's unit sales relative to the organization's total unit sales. Let's assume that Dakota Products, Inc., sells two types of wooden stands for portable compact disk players: the Floor Stand model, which is placed on the floor and has high storage capacity, and the Tabletop model, which is smaller and can be placed in entertainment units. If Dakota sells 500 units, of which 300 units are Floor Stands and 200 units are Tabletops, the sales mix would be 3:2. For every 3 Floor Stand models sold, 2 Tabletop models are sold. The sales mix can also be stated in percentages. Of the 500 units sold, 60 percent (300 ÷ 500) are Floor Stand sales and 40 percent (200 ÷ 500) are Tabletop sales (see Figure 9).

The breakeven point for multiple products can be completed in three steps. We will illustrate using Dakota Products, Inc.'s 60/40 percent sales mix, total fixed costs of $32,000, and the selling price, variable cost per unit, and contribution margin per unit for each product line presented in Step 1 below.

Step 1: Compute the weighted-average contribution margin.
Calculate the weighted-average contribution margin by multiplying the contribution margin for each product by its percentage of the sales mix.

	Sales		Variable Costs		Contribution Margin (CM)		Percentage of Sales Mix		Weighted-Average CM
Floor Stand	$90	−	$50	=	$40	×	.60	=	$24
Tabletop	$40	−	$20	=	$20	×	.40	=	$ 8
Weighted-average contribution margin									$32

Step 2: Calculate the weighted-average breakeven point.
Compute the weighted-average breakeven point by dividing total fixed costs by the weighted-average contribution margin.

Weighted-Average Breakeven Point = Total Fixed Costs ÷ Weighted-Average Contribution Margin

$$1,000 \text{ Units} = \$32,000 \div \$32$$

Step 3: Calculate the breakeven point for each product.
Multiply the weighted-average breakeven point by each product's percentage of the sales mix.

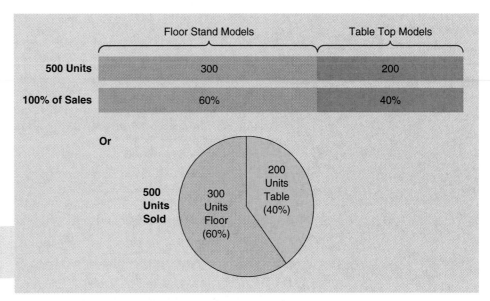

Figure 9
Sales Mix for Dakota Products, Inc.

	Weighted-Average Breakeven Point		Sales Mix		Breakeven Point
Floor Stand	=	1,000 units	×	.60	= 600 units
Tabletop	=	1,000 units	×	.40	= 400 units

To verify, determine the contribution margin of each product and subtract the total fixed costs.

Contribution margin
Floor Stand = 600 × $40 =	$24,000	
Tabletop = 400 × $20 =	8,000	
Total contribution margin	$32,000	
Less fixed costs	32,000	
Net income	—	

Planning Future Sales

OBJECTIVE 7

Apply cost-volume-profit analysis to estimated levels of future sales and to changes in costs and selling prices.

The primary goal of a business venture is not to break even; it is to generate net income. C-V-P analysis adjusted for targeted net income can be used to estimate the profitability of a venture. In fact, the approach is excellent for "what if" analysis, in which the accountant selects several scenarios and computes the anticipated net income for each. For instance, what if sales increase by 17,000 units? What effect will the increase have on anticipated net income? What if sales increase by only 6,000 units? What if fixed costs are reduced by $14,500? What if the variable unit cost increases by $1.40? Each of these scenarios generates a different amount of net income or loss.

To illustrate how C-V-P analysis can be applied, assume that the president of Dakota Products, Inc., Les Tibbs, has set $4,000 in net income as the goal for the year. If all the data in our earlier example stay as they were, how many compact disk stands must Dakota Products, Inc., make and sell to reach the target net income? Again, x equals the number of units.

$$S = VC + FC + NI$$
$$\$90x = \$50x + \$20,000 + \$4,000$$
$$\$40x = \$24,000$$
$$x = 600 \text{ Units}$$

The answer is 600 units. To check the accuracy of the answer, insert all known data into the equation.

$$S - VC - FC = NI$$
$$(600 \text{ Units} \times \$90) - (600 \times \$50) - \$20,000 = \$4,000$$
$$\$54,000 - \$30,000 - \$20,000 = \$4,000$$

The contribution margin approach can also be used for profit planning. To do so, we simply add the target net income to the numerator of the contribution margin breakeven equation:

$$\text{Target Sales Units} = \frac{FC + NI}{CM \text{ per Unit}}$$

Using the data from the Dakota Products, Inc., example, the number of sales units needed to generate $4,000 in net income is computed this way:

$$\text{Target Sales Units} = \frac{FC + NI}{CM \text{ per Unit}} = \frac{\$20,000 + \$4,000}{\$40} = \frac{\$24,000}{\$40} = 600 \text{ Units}$$

Let's continue to look at the planning activities of Dakota Products, Inc. The contribution income statement below focuses on cost behavior, not cost function. All variable costs related to production, selling, and administration are subtracted from sales to determine the total contribution margin. All fixed costs related to production, selling, and administration are subtracted from the total contribution margin to determine net income. This format is used internally by managers to help make decisions about the company's operations.

	Dakota Products, Inc. **Contribution Income Statement** **For the Year Ended December 31, 20xx**	
	Per Unit	**Total for 600 Units**
Sales revenue	$90	$54,000
Less variable costs	50	30,000
Contribution margin	$40	$24,000
Less fixed costs		20,000
Net income		$ 4,000

Mr. Tibbs wants the members of the planning team to consider three alternatives to the original plan shown in the contribution income statement. In the following sections, we examine each alternative and its impact on net income. In the summary, we will review our work and analyze the different breakeven points.

Alternative 1: Decrease Variable Costs, Increase Sales Volume   The planning team worked with production, purchasing, and sales employees to determine the net income if the company purchased and used pine rather than oak to make the wooden compact disk stands. If pine is used, the direct materials cost per unit will decrease by $3. The company plans to stain the pine to meet the needs of a new customer group, which will increase the sales volume by 10 percent. What will be the estimated net income for this alternative? What will be the impact of this alternative on net income?

SOLUTION

	Per Unit	Total for 660 units
Sales revenue	$90	$59,400
Less variable costs	47	31,020
Contribution margin	$43	$28,380
Less fixed costs		20,000
Net income		$ 8,380
Increase in net income ($8,380 − $4,000)		$ 4,380

A different way to determine the impact of changes in selling price, cost, or sales volume on net income is to analyze only the information that changes between the original plan and the proposed alternative. In Alternative 1, variable costs will decrease by $3 (from $50 to $47), which will increase the contribution margin per unit by $3 (from $40 to $43) for the 600 wooden stands planned to be sold. This will increase the total contribution margin and net income by $1,800 ($3 × 600).

In addition, a sales increase of 60 units (.10 × 600) will increase the total contribution margin and net income by $2,580 ($43 × 60). The total increase in net income due to the decrease in variable costs and the increase in sales volume will be $4,380.

SOLUTION

Analysis of Changes Only

Increase in contribution margin from	
Planned sales [($43 − $40) × 600 units]	$1,800
Additional sales ($43 × 60 units)	2,580
Increase in net income	$4,380

Alternative 2: Increase Fixed Costs, Increase Sales Volume   Rather than change the direct materials, the marketing department suggested that a $500 increase in advertising costs would increase sales volume by 5 percent. What will be the estimated net income for this alternative? What will be the impact of this alternative on net income?

SOLUTION

	Per Unit	Total for 630 units
Sales revenue	$90	$56,700
Less variable costs	50	31,500
Contribution margin	$40	$25,200
Less fixed costs		20,500
Net income		$ 4,700
Increase in net income ($4,700 − $4,000)		$ 700

Additional advertising costs will affect both sales volume and fixed costs. The sales volume will increase by 30 stands from 600 units to 630 units (600 × 1.05), which increases the total contribution margin and net income by $1,200 (from $24,000 to $25,200). Fixed costs will increase from $20,000 to $20,500, which decreases net income by $500. The increase in net income will be $700 ($1,200 − $500).

SOLUTION

Analysis of Changes Only

Increase in contribution margin from additional units sold [$40 × (600 × .05)]	$1,200
Less increase in fixed costs	500
Increase in net income	$700

Alternative 3: Increase Selling Price, Decrease Sales Volume   Mr. Tibbs asked the planning team to evaluate the impact of a $10 increase in selling price on the company's net income. The planning team believes that their competitors are selling the same product at a lower price. By increasing the selling price, the team estimates that the sales volume will decrease by 15 percent. What will be the estimated net income for this alternative? What will be the impact of this alternative on net income?

SOLUTION

	Per Unit	Total for 510 Units
Sales revenue	$100	$51,000
Less variable costs	50	25,500
Contribution margin	$ 50	$25,500
Less fixed costs		20,000
Net income		$ 5,500
Increase in net income ($5,500 − $4,000)		$ 1,500

The $3,000 decrease in sales revenue is more than offset by the $4,500 decrease in variable costs, resulting in an increase in the contribution margin and net income of $1,500.

SOLUTION

Analysis of Changes Only

Increase in contribution margin from increasing selling price ($10 increase in selling price × 510 units sold)	$5,100
Decrease in contribution margin from decrease in sales volume ($40 contribution margin per unit × 90 sales units lost)	(3,600)
Increase in net income	$1,500

Comparative Summary   In preparation for a meeting with Mr. Tibbs, the planning team at Dakota Products, Inc., compiled the summary presented in Exhibit 1. It compares the three alternatives to the original plan and shows how changes in variable and fixed costs, selling price, and sales volume will affect the breakeven point.

Note that the decrease in variable costs (direct materials) proposed in Alternative 1 increases the contribution margin per unit (from $40 to $43), which reduces the breakeven point. Since fewer sales dollars are required to cover variable costs, the breakeven point is reached sooner, at a sales volume of 465 units, which is lower than the breakeven point of 500 units in the original plan. In Alternative 2 the increase in fixed costs has no effect on the contribution margin per unit, but it does require the total contribution margin to cover more fixed costs before reaching the breakeven point. Thus, the breakeven point of 513 units is higher than the breakeven point of 500 units in the original plan. The increase in selling price in Alternative 3 increases the contribution margin per unit, which reduces the

Exhibit 1. Comparative Summary of Alternatives at Dakota Products, Inc.

	Original Plan Totals for 600 Units	Alternative 1 Decrease Direct Materials Cost for 660 Units	Alternative 2 Increase Advertising for 630 Units	Alternative 3 Increase Selling Price for 510 Units
Sales revenue	$54,000	$59,400	$56,700	$51,000
Less variable costs	30,000	31,020	31,500	25,500
Contribution margin	$24,000	$28,380	$25,200	$25,500
Less fixed costs	20,000	20,000	20,500	20,000
Net income	$ 4,000	$ 8,380	$ 4,700	$ 5,500
Breakeven point in whole units				
$20,000 FC ÷ $40 CM	500			
$20,000 FC ÷ $43 CM		465		
$20,500 FC ÷ $40 CM			513	
$20,000 FC ÷ $50 CM				400

breakeven point. Since more sales dollars are available to cover fixed costs, the breakeven point of 400 units is lower than the breakeven point for the original plan.

Which plan should Mr. Tibbs choose? If he selects the alternative with the highest net income shown in Exhibit 1, he would choose Alternative 1. However, if he focuses on the breakeven point, he may prefer to choose Alternative 3. Since the breakeven point for that alternative is 400 units, Dakota Products, Inc., can begin generating net income more quickly.

Remember that the breakeven point provides a "ballpark" estimate of the number of units that must be sold to cover the total costs. Additional qualitative information may help Mr. Tibbs make a better decision. Will customers perceive that the quality of the compact disk stands is lower if the company uses pine rather than oak as proposed in Alternative 1? Has the company chosen the best form of advertising to yield a 5 percent increase in sales volume for Alternative 2? Will the increase in selling price suggested in Proposal 3 create more than a 15 percent decline in unit sales? Management accountants provide the quantitative information for planning, but managers must also be sensitive to qualitative factors, such as product quality, reliability and quality of suppliers, and availability of human and technical resources.

Assumptions Underlying C-V-P Analysis

Cost-volume-profit analysis is useful only under certain conditions and only when certain assumptions hold true. These assumptions and conditions are as follows:

1. The behavior of variable and fixed costs can be measured accurately.
2. Costs and revenues have a close linear approximation. For example, if costs rise, revenues rise proportionately.
3. Efficiency and productivity hold steady within the relevant range of activity.
4. Cost and price variables also hold steady during the period being planned.
5. The sales mix does not change during the period being planned.
6. Production and sales volume are roughly equal.

If one or more of these conditions and assumptions are absent, the C-V-P analysis may be misleading.

Applying Cost-Volume-Profit Analysis to a Service Business

Now we will see how C-V-P analysis can be applied to a service business by studying four decisions that were made by a mortgage company. Assume that Lynn Chumbley, the manager of the Appraisal Department at Portland Mortgage Company, wants to plan the home appraisal activities that are required for each mortgage loan application. The following information has been estimated for the next year.

Service fee revenue: $400 per appraisal

Variable costs: Direct professional labor, $160 per appraisal
County survey map fee, $99 per appraisal

Mixed costs: Monthly service overhead:

Volume	Month	Activity Level	Cost
Highest	March	106 appraisals	$20,346
Lowest	February	98 appraisals	20,018

Estimated average home appraisals per month next year: 100

Decision 1: Estimating Service Overhead Costs   Lynn would like to estimate the total service overhead cost of appraisals for next year. Use the high-low method to calculate the cost formulas that will estimate service overhead costs for next year.

Step 1: Calculate the variable service overhead cost per appraisal.

$$\text{Variable Service Overhead Cost per Appraisal} = \text{(Highest Cost} - \text{Lowest Cost)} \div$$
$$\text{(Highest Volume} - \text{Lowest Volume)}$$
$$= (\$20{,}346 - \$20{,}018) \div (106 - 98)$$
$$= \$328 \div 8 \text{ Appraisals} = \$41$$

Step 2: Calculate the total fixed service overhead costs.

$$\text{Total Fixed Service Overhead Costs} = \text{Total Service Overhead Costs} -$$
$$\text{Total Variable Service Overhead Costs}$$
$$\text{Total Fixed Service Overhead Costs for March} = \$20{,}346 - (\$41 \times 106) = \$16{,}000$$

Step 3: State the formula for total service overhead costs for one month.

$$\text{Total Service Overhead Costs} = \text{Total Fixed Service Overhead Costs} + \text{(Variable Rate} \times$$
$$\text{Estimated Number of Appraisals)}$$
$$= \$16{,}000 + (\$41 \text{ per Appraisal} \times \text{Number of Appraisals)}$$

Step 4: Calculate the total service overhead costs for one month, assuming that 100 appraisals will be made.

$$\text{Total Overhead Service Costs} = \$16{,}000 + (\$41 \times 100) = \$20{,}100$$

Decision 2: Determining the Breakeven Point   Lynn would also like to know how many appraisals must be performed each month to cover the fixed and variable appraisal costs. Calculate the breakeven point.

$$\text{Let } x = \text{Number of Appraisals per Month at Breakeven Point}$$
$$S = VC + FC$$
$$\$400x = \$300x + \$16{,}000$$
$$\$100x = \$16{,}000$$
$$x = 160 \text{ Appraisals per Month}$$

The variable rate of $300 per appraisal includes the variable service overhead rate, the direct professional labor, and the county survey map fee ($41 + $160 + $99).

Decision 3: Determining the Effect of a Change in Operating Costs Lynn is worried because an average of only 100 appraisals can be performed each month and the estimated breakeven point is 160 appraisals per month. Due to strong competition in the community, the mortgage company cannot increase its fee. Lynn has been asked to reduce costs so that the mortgage company can profit from home appraisal activities. Lynn reviewed the appraisal activity and determined that improved scheduling of appraisals would reduce travel time. The current professional labor cost of $160 per appraisal covers the fee of one appraiser working four hours at $40 per hour. By scheduling the jobs based on location, Lynn can reduce the appraisers' travel time by 50 percent. As a result, the professional labor cost will decrease to $80 [(.50 × 4 hours) × $40 per hour] for one appraiser working two hours at $40 per hour. The new scheduling process will increase fixed costs by $200 per month. What would be the new breakeven point?

$$\text{Let } x = \text{Number of Appraisals per Month at Breakeven Point}$$
$$S = VC + FC$$
$$\$400x = \$220x + \$16{,}200$$
$$\$180x = \$16{,}200$$
$$x = 90 \text{ Appraisals per Month}$$

Variable costs become $220 ($300 − $80) per appraisal due to the reduced labor costs. This change increases the contribution margin by $80 per appraisal. Fixed costs increase from $16,000 to $16,200. The increase in the contribution margin is greater than the increase in the fixed costs, so the breakeven point decreases from 160 appraisals per month to 90 appraisals per month.

Decision 4: Estimating Net Income What would be the net income if the new scheduling process is implemented and 100 appraisals are performed each month?

$$\text{Let NI} = \text{Net Income When 100 Appraisals Are Performed}$$
$$NI = S - VC - FC$$
$$NI = \$400(100) - \$220(100) - \$16{,}200$$
$$NI = \$40{,}000 - \$22{,}000 - \$16{,}200 = \$1{,}800$$

Chapter Review

REVIEW OF LEARNING OBJECTIVES

1. **Define** *cost behavior* **and explain how managers make use of this concept in the management cycle.** Cost behavior is the way costs respond to changes in volume or activity. Some costs vary in relation to volume or operating activity; other costs remain fixed as volume changes. Cost behavior depends on whether the focus is total costs or cost per unit. Variable costs vary in total as volume changes but are fixed per unit; fixed costs are fixed in total as volume changes but vary per unit. Managers use information about cost behavior in almost every decision they make. Whenever managers are asked to make a decision, they must always deal with cost ramifications, and they must understand and anticipate cost behavior patterns if they are to decide correctly.

2. **Identify specific types of variable and fixed cost behavior, and define and discuss the relationships of operating capacity and relevant range to cost behavior.** Total costs that change in direct proportion to changes in productive output (or any other volume measure) are called variable costs. Hourly wages, the cost of operating supplies, direct materials costs, and the cost of merchandise are all variable costs. Total fixed costs remain constant within a relevant range of volume or activity. They change only when activity exceeds the anticipated relevant range because, for example, new equipment or new buildings must be purchased, higher insurance premiums and property taxes must be paid, or additional supervisory personnel must be hired to accommodate the increased activity.

3. **Define** *mixed cost,* **and use the high-low method to separate the variable and fixed components of a mixed cost.** A mixed cost, such as the cost of electricity, has both variable and fixed cost components. The high-low method, which identifies a linear relationship between activity level and cost, is the easiest way to separate variable costs from fixed costs in a mixed cost.

4. **Define** *cost-volume-profit analysis* **and discuss how managers use this analysis.** Cost-volume-profit analysis is an examination of the cost behavior patterns that underlie the relationships among cost, volume of output, and net income. C-V-P analysis is a tool for both planning and control. The process involves a number of techniques and problem-solving procedures based on the cost behavior patterns in an organization. This form of analysis provides a general model of financial activity that management can use for short-range planning, evaluating performance, and analyzing alternatives.

5. **Compute a breakeven point in units of output and in sales dollars, and prepare a breakeven graph.** The breakeven point is the point at which total revenues equal total costs, the point at which net sales equal variable costs plus fixed costs. Once the number of units needed to break even is known, the number can be multiplied by the product's selling price to determine the breakeven point in sales dollars.

   A breakeven graph is made up of a horizontal axis (units) and a vertical axis (dollars). Three lines are plotted: The fixed cost line runs horizontally from the point on the vertical axis representing total fixed cost. The total cost line begins at the intersection of the fixed cost line and the vertical axis and runs upward to the right. The total revenue line runs from the intersection of the two axes upward to the right. The slope of the total cost line is determined by the variable cost per unit; the slope of the total revenue line is determined by the selling price per unit. The point at which the total cost and the total revenue lines cross determines the breakeven point in units or in dollars.

6. **Define** *contribution margin* **and use the concept to determine a company's breakeven point for a single product and for multiple products.** Contribution margin is the excess of revenues over all variable costs related to a particular sales volume. A product's contribution margin represents its net contribution to paying off fixed costs and earning net income. The breakeven point in units can be computed by dividing total fixed costs by the contribution margin per unit. A sales mix is used to calculate the breakeven point for each product when a company sells more than one product.

7. Apply cost-volume-profit analysis to estimated levels of future sales and to changes in costs and selling prices. The addition of targeted net income to the breakeven equation makes it possible to plan levels of operation that yield targeted net income. The formula in terms of contribution margin is

$$\text{Target Sales Units} = \frac{\text{FC} + \text{NI}}{\text{CM per Unit}}$$

8. Apply cost-volume-profit analysis to a service business. A service business can use cost-volume-profit analysis to separate mixed costs into their variable and fixed portions, calculate a breakeven point, and plan net income when changes in cost, volume, or price occur.

REVIEW OF CONCEPTS AND TERMINOLOGY

The following concepts and terms were introduced in this chapter.

LO 5 **Breakeven point:** The point at which total revenues equal total costs.

LO 6 **Contribution margin:** The remainder after total variable costs are subtracted from sales.

LO 1 **Cost behavior:** The way costs respond to changes in volume or activity.

LO 4 **Cost-volume-profit (C-V-P) analysis:** An examination of the cost behavior patterns that underlie the relationships among cost, volume of output, and net income.

LO 2 **Excess capacity:** Machinery and equipment kept on standby.

LO 2 **Fixed costs:** Total costs that remain constant within a relevant range of volume or activity.

LO 3 **High-low method:** A three-step approach to separating a mixed cost into its variable and fixed components.

LO 3 **Mixed costs:** Costs that have both variable and fixed components; part of the cost changes with volume or usage, and part of the cost is fixed over the period.

LO 2 **Normal capacity:** The average annual level of operating capacity needed to meet expected sales demand.

LO 2 **Operating capacity:** The upper limit of an organization's productive output capability, given its existing resources.

LO 2 **Practical capacity:** Theoretical capacity reduced by normal and expected work stoppages.

LO 2 **Relevant range:** The span of activity in which a company expects to operate.

LO 6 **Sales mix:** The proportion of each product's unit sales relative to the organization's total unit sales.

LO 3 **Scatter diagram:** A chart of plotted points that helps determine if there is a linear relationship between a cost item and its related activity measure.

LO 2 **Theoretical capacity:** The maximum productive output for a given period, assuming that all machinery and equipment are operating at optimum speed, without interruption. Also called *ideal capacity*.

LO 2 **Variable costs:** Total costs that change in direct proportion to changes in productive output or any other measure of volume.

REVIEW PROBLEM
Breakeven/Profit Planning Analysis

LO 5 Instrument City, Inc., is a major producer of pipe organs. Its Model D14 is a double-man-
LO 6 ual organ with a large potential market. On the next page is a summary of data from 20x1
LO 7 operations for Model D14.

Variable costs per unit	
Direct materials	$ 2,300
Direct labor	800
Manufacturing overhead	600
Selling expense	500
Total fixed costs	
Manufacturing overhead	195,000
Advertising	55,000
Administrative expense	68,000
Selling price per unit	9,500

REQUIRED

1. Compute the 20x1 breakeven point in units.
2. Instrument City sold sixty-five D14 models in 20x1. How much net income did the firm realize?
3. Management is considering alternative courses of action for 20x2. (Use the figures from **2** and treat each alternative independently.)
   a. Calculate the number of units that must be sold to generate a net income of $95,400. Assume that costs and selling price remain constant.
   b. Calculate the net income if the company increases the number of units sold by 20 percent and cuts the selling price by $500 per unit.
   c. Determine the number of units that must be sold to break even if advertising is increased by $47,700.
   d. If variable costs are cut by 10 percent, find the number of units that must be sold to generate net income of $125,000.

ANSWER TO REVIEW PROBLEM

1. Compute the breakeven point in units for 20x1.

$$\text{Breakeven Units} = \frac{\text{FC}}{\text{CM per Unit}} = \frac{\$318,000}{\$9,500 - \$4,200} = \frac{\$318,000}{\$5,300} = 60 \text{ Units}$$

2. Calculate net income from sales of sixty-five units.

Units sold	65
Units required to break even	60
Units over breakeven	5

20x1 net income = $5,300 per unit × 5 = $26,500

Contribution margin equals sales minus all variable costs. Contribution margin per unit equals the amount of sales dollars remaining, after variable costs have been subtracted, to cover fixed costs and earn net income. If all fixed costs have been absorbed by the time breakeven is reached, the entire contribution margin of each unit sold in excess of breakeven represents net income.

3. a. Calculate the number of units that must be sold to generate net income of $95,400.

$$\text{Target Sales Units} = \frac{\text{FC} + \text{NI}}{\text{CM per Unit}}$$

$$= \frac{\$318,000 + \$95,400}{\$5,300} = \frac{\$413,400}{\$5,300} = 78 \text{ Units}$$

b. Calculate net income if unit sales increase 20 percent and unit selling price decreases by $500.

Sales revenue [78(65 × 1.20) units at $9,000 per unit]	$702,000
Less variable costs (78 units × $4,200)	327,600
Contribution margin	$374,400
Less fixed costs	318,000
Net income	$ 56,400

c. Determine the number of units needed to break even if advertising costs (fixed cost) increase by $47,700.

$$\text{BE Units} = \frac{FC}{\text{CM per Unit}}$$

$$= \frac{\$318,000 + \$47,700}{\$5,300} = \frac{\$365,700}{\$5,300} = 69 \text{ Units}$$

d. Calculate the number of units that must be sold to generate a net income of $125,000 if variable costs decrease by 10 percent.

$$\text{CM per Unit} = \$9,500 - (\$4,200 \times .9) = \$9,500 - \$3,780 = \$5,720$$

$$\text{Target Sales Units} = \frac{FC + NI}{\text{CM per Unit}}$$

$$= \frac{\$318,000 + \$125,000}{\$5,720} = \frac{\$443,000}{\$5,720} = 77.45 \text{ or } 78 \text{ Units}$$

Chapter Assignments

BUILDING YOUR KNOWLEDGE FOUNDATION

Questions

1. Define *cost behavior.*
2. Why is an understanding of cost behavior useful to managers?
3. What is the difference between theoretical capacity and practical capacity?
4. Why does a company never operate at theoretical capacity?
5. Define *excess capacity.*
6. What is normal capacity? Why is normal capacity considered more relevant and useful than either theoretical or practical capacity?
7. What does *relevant range of activity* mean?
8. What makes variable costs different from fixed costs?
9. "Fixed costs remain constant in total but decrease per unit as productive output increases." Explain this statement.
10. What is a mixed cost? Give an example.
11. What is a scatter diagram?
12. Describe the high-low method of separating mixed costs.
13. Define *cost-volume-profit analysis.*
14. Identify two uses of C-V-P analysis and explain their significance to management.
15. Define *breakeven point.* Why is information about the breakeven point important to managers?
16. Define *contribution margin* and describe its use in breakeven analysis.
17. State the equation that determines target sales units using the elements of fixed costs, target net income, and contribution margin per unit.
18. What conditions must be met for C-V-P computations to be accurate?
19. Give examples of ways in which C-V-P analysis can be used in a service organization.
20. Compare and contrast breakeven analysis for manufacturing organizations to breakeven analysis for service organizations.

Short Exercises

SE 1.

LO 1   *Concept of Cost Behavior*

Patrick's Hat Makers is in the business of designing specialty hats. The material that goes into producing a derby costs $4.50 per unit, and Patrick's pays each of its two full-time hat makers $250 per week. If hat maker A makes 15 derbies in one week, what is the variable cost per derby, and what is this worker's fixed cost per derby? If hat maker B makes only 12 derbies in one week, what are this worker's variable and fixed costs per derby? (Round to two decimal places where necessary.)

SE 2.
LO 2 *Identification of Variable,*
LO 3 *Fixed, and Mixed Costs*

Identify the following as either fixed costs, variable costs, or mixed costs.

1. Direct materials
2. Telephone expense
3. Operating supplies
4. Personnel manager's salary
5. Factory building rent payment

SE 3.
LO 3 *Mixed Costs: High-Low*
Method

Using the high-low method and the following information, compute the monthly variable costs per telephone hour and fixed costs for Sadiko Corporation.

Month	Business Telephone Hours	Telephone Expenses
April	96	$4,350
May	93	4,230
June	105	4,710

SE 4.
LO 4 *Cost-Volume-Profit*
Analysis

Delacruz, Inc., wishes to make a net income of $20,000. The company has variable costs of $80 per unit and fixed costs of $12,000. How much must Delacruz charge per unit if 4,000 units are sold?

SE 5.
LO 5 *Computing the*
Breakeven Point

How many units must Marsik Company sell to break even if the selling price per unit is $8.50, variable costs are $4.30 per unit, and fixed costs are $3,780?

SE 6.
LO 6 *Contribution Margin*

Using the contribution margin approach, find the breakeven point in units for Dubois Consumer Products if the selling price per unit is $11, the variable cost per unit is $6, and the fixed costs are $5,500.

SE 7.
LO 6 *Cost-Volume-Profit*
Analysis for Multiple
Products

Using the contribution margin approach, find the breakeven point in units for Lacy Products' two products. Product A's selling price per unit is $10 and its variable cost per unit is $4. Product B's selling price per unit is $8 and its variable cost per unit is $5. Fixed costs are $15,000 and the sales mix of Product A to Product B is 2:1.

SE 8.
LO 7 *Contribution Margin*
and Projected Profit

If Sandoval Watches sells 300 watches at $48 per watch and has variable costs of $18 per watch and fixed costs of $4,000, what is the projected net income?

SE 9.
LO 8 *Cost Behavior in a*
Service Business

Eye Spy, a private investigation firm, has the following costs for December.

Direct labor: $190 per case
Service overhead, December

Salary for director of investigations	$ 4,800
Telephone	930
Depreciation	8,300
Legal advice	2,300
Supplies	590
Advertising	360
Utilities	1,560
Wages for clerical personnel	2,000
Total service overhead	$20,840

Service overhead for October: $21,150
Service overhead for November: $21,350

The number of cases investigated during October, November, and December was 93, 97, and 91, respectively.

Compute the variable and fixed cost components of service overhead. Then determine the variable and fixed costs per case for December. (Round to nearest dollar where necessary.)

Exercises

E 1.

LO 2 *Identification of Variable and Fixed Costs*

Indicate whether each of the following costs of productive output is usually considered variable or fixed: (1) packing materials for stereo components, (2) real estate taxes, (3) gasoline for a delivery truck, (4) property insurance, (5) depreciation expense of buildings (straight-line method), (6) supplies, (7) indirect materials, (8) bottles used to package liquids, (9) license fees for company cars, (10) wiring used in radios, (11) machine helper's wages, (12) wood used in bookcases, (13) city operating license, (14) machine depreciation based on machine hours of usage, (15) machine operator's hourly wages, and (16) cost of required outside inspection of each unit produced.

E 2.

LO 2 *Variable Cost Analysis*

Speedy Oil Change has been in business for six months. Each oil change requires an average of four quarts of oil. The cost of oil to Speedy Oil Change is $.50 per quart. The estimated number of cars that will be serviced in the next three months is 240, 288, and 360.

1. Compute the cost of oil for each of the three months and the total cost for all three months. Fill in the blanks in the following table.

Month	Cars to Be Serviced	Required Quarts/Car	Cost/Quart	Total Cost/Month
1	240	4	$.50	____
2	288	4	.50	____
3	360	4	.50	____
Three-month total	888			====

2. Complete the following sentences by choosing the words that best describe the cost behavior at Speedy Oil Change.

Cost per unit (increased, decreased, remained constant).

Total variable cost per month (increased, decreased) as the quantity of oil used (increased, decreased).

E 3.

LO 3 *Mixed Costs: High-Low Method*

Elder Electronics Company manufactures major appliances. The company just had its most successful year because of increased interest in its refrigerators. While preparing the budget for next year, Arnelle Autrey, the company's controller, compiled the following data.

Month	Volume in Machine Hours	Electricity Costs
July	6,000	$60,000
August	5,000	53,000
September	4,500	49,500
October	4,000	46,000
November	3,500	42,500
December	3,000	39,000

Using the high-low method, determine (1) the variable electricity cost per machine hour, (2) the monthly fixed electricity cost, and (3) the total variable electricity costs and fixed electricity costs for the six-month period.

E 4.

LO 5 *Graphical Analysis*

Identify the letter of the point, line segment, or area of the breakeven graph on the next page that correctly completes each of the following statements.

1. The maximum possible operating loss is
   a. *A.*   c. *B.*
   b. *D.*   d. *F.*

2. The breakeven point in sales dollars is
   a. *C.*   c. *A.*
   b. *D.*   d. *G.*

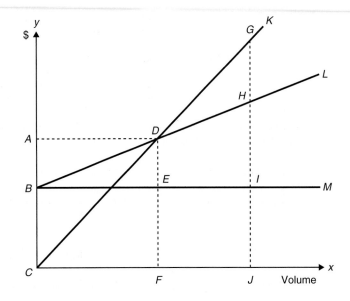

3. At volume *F*, total contribution margin is
   a. *C.*   c. *E.*
   b. *D.*   d. *G.*

4. Net income is represented by area
   a. *KDL.*   c. *BDC.*
   b. *KCJ.*   d. *GCJ.*

5. At volume *J*, total fixed costs are represented by
   a. *H.*   c. *I.*
   b. *G.*   d. *J.*

6. If volume increases from *F* to *J*, the change in total costs is
   a. *HI* minus *DE.*   c. *BC* minus *DF.*
   b. *DF* minus *HJ.*   d. *AB* minus *DE.*

E 5.

LO 5 *Breakeven Analysis*
LO 6

Gleason Manufacturing Company produces head covers for golf clubs. The company expects to generate net income next year. It anticipates fixed manufacturing costs of $126,500 and fixed general and administrative expenses of $82,030 for the year. Variable manufacturing and selling costs per set of head covers will be $4.65 and $2.75, respectively. Each set will sell for $13.40.

1. Compute the breakeven point in sales units.
2. Compute the breakeven point in sales dollars.
3. If the selling price is increased to $14 per unit and fixed general and administrative expenses are cut by $33,465, what would the new breakeven point be in units?
4. Prepare a graph to illustrate the breakeven point found in **2.**

E 6.

LO 6 *Calculate Breakeven Point for Multiple Products*

Marine Aquarium, Inc., manufactures and sells aquariums, water pumps, and air filters using a sales mix of 1:2:2. Using the contribution margin approach, find the breakeven point in units for each product. The company's fixed costs are $26,000. Other information is as follows:

	Selling Price per Unit	**Variable Cost per Unit**
Aquariums	$60	$25
Water pumps	20	12
Air filters	10	3

E 7.

LO 6 *Contribution*
LO 7 *Margin/Profit Planning*

ICT Systems, Ltd., makes undersea missiles for nuclear submarines. Management has just been offered a government contract that may generate a net income for the company. The contract purchase price is $130,000 per unit, but the number of units to be purchased has not yet been decided. The company's fixed costs are budgeted at $3,973,500, and the variable costs are $68,500 per unit.

1. Compute the number of units the company should agree to make at the stated contract price to earn a target net income of $1,500,000.
2. Using a lighter material, the variable unit cost can be reduced by $1,730, but total fixed overhead will increase by $27,500. How many units must be produced to make $1,500,000 in net income?
3. Using the figures in **2**, how many additional units must be produced to increase net income by $1,264,600?

E 8.

LO 7 *Planning Future Sales*
LO 8

Short-term automobile rentals are the specialty of Frugal Auto Rentals, Inc. Average variable operating costs have been $12.50 per day per automobile. The company owns sixty cars. Fixed operating costs for the next year are expected to be $145,500. Average daily rental revenue per automobile is expected to be $34.50. Management would like to earn a net income of $47,000 during the year.

1. Calculate the total number of daily rentals the company must have during the year to earn the target net income.
2. On the basis of your answer to **1**, determine the number of days on the average that each automobile must be rented.
3. Find the total revenue for the year needed to earn net income of $47,000.
4. What would the total rental revenue be if fixed operating costs could be lowered by $5,180 and target net income increased to $70,000?

E 9.

LO 8 *Cost Behavior in a Service Business*

Leo Zapata, CPA, provides tax services in Rio Bravo. To prepare standard short-form tax returns, he incurred the following costs for the previous three months.

Direct professional labor: $50 per tax return

Service overhead (included telephone, depreciation on equipment and building, tax forms, office supplies, wages of clerical personnel, and utilities): January, $18,500; February, $20,000; March, $17,000.

Number of tax returns prepared: January, 850; February, 1,000; March, 700.

1. Determine the variable and fixed cost components of the Service Overhead account.
2. What would be the estimated total cost per tax return if Leo's CPA firm prepares 825 standard short-form tax returns in April?

Problems

P 1.

LO 2 *Cost Behavior and*
LO 3 *Projection*
LO 8

Bright Auto, Inc., which opened for business on March 1, 20x1, specializes in revitalizing automobile exteriors. *Detailing* is the term used to describe the process. The objective is to detail an automobile until it looks like it just rolled off the showroom floor. Area market research indicates that a full exterior detail should cost about $100. The company has just completed its first year of business and has asked its accountants to analyze the operating results. Management wants costs divided into variable, fixed, and mixed components and would like them projected for the coming year. Anticipated volume for next year is 1,100 jobs.

The process used to detail a car's exterior is as follows:

1. One $20-per-hour employee spends twenty minutes cleaning the car's exterior.
2. One can per car of Tars-Off, a cleaning compound, is used on the trouble spots.
3. A chemical compound called Buff Glow 7 is used to remove oxidants from the paint surface and restore the natural oils to the paint.
4. Poly Wax is applied by hand, allowed to sit for ten minutes, and then buffed off.
5. The final step is an inspection to see that all wax and debris have been removed.

On average, two hours are spent on each car, including the cleaning time and wait time for the wax. The following first-year operating information for Bright Auto is provided to the accountant.

Number of automobiles detailed	840
Labor per auto	2 hours at $20.00 per hour
Containers of Tars-Off consumed	840 at $3.50 per can
Pounds of Buff Glow 7 consumed	105 pounds at $32.00 per pound
Pounds of Poly Wax consumed	210 pounds at $8.00 per pound
Rent	$1,400.00 per month

During the year, utilities costs ranged from $800 for 40 jobs in March to $1,801 for 110 jobs in August.

REQUIRED

1. Classify the costs as variable, fixed, or mixed.
2. Using the high-low method, separate the mixed costs into their variable and fixed components. Use number of jobs as the basis.
3. Project the same costs for next year, assuming that the anticipated increase in activity will occur and that fixed costs will remain constant.
4. Compute the unit cost per job for next year.
5. Based on your answer to **4,** should the price remain at $100 per job?

P 2.

LO 5
LO 6
LO 7 *Breakeven Analysis*

Billings & Brown, a law firm in downtown San Diego, is considering the development of a legal clinic for middle- and low-income clients. Paraprofessional help would be employed, and a billing rate of $18 per hour would be used. The paraprofessionals would be law students who would work for only $9 per hour. Other variable costs are anticipated to be $5.40 per hour, and annual fixed costs are expected to total $27,000.

REQUIRED

1. Compute the breakeven point in billable hours.
2. Compute the breakeven point in total billings.
3. Find the new breakeven point in total billings if fixed costs should go up by $2,340.
4. Using the original figures, compute the breakeven point in total billings if the billing rate is decreased by $1 per hour, variable costs are decreased by $.40 per hour, and fixed costs go down by $3,600.

P 3.

LO 7 *Planning Future Sales*

Lesko Financial Corporation is a subsidiary of Polansky Enterprises. Processing loan applications is the main task of the corporation. Last year, Polly Bar, the manager of the Loan Department, established a policy of charging a $250 fee for every loan application processed. Next year's variable costs have been projected as follows: loan consultant's wages, $15.50 per hour (a loan application takes five hours to process); supplies, $2.40 per application; and other variable costs, $5.60 per application. Annual fixed costs include depreciation of equipment, $8,500; building rental, $14,000; promotional costs, $12,500; and other fixed costs, $8,099.

REQUIRED

1. Using the contribution margin approach, compute the number of loan applications the company must process to (a) break even and (b) earn a net income of $14,476.
2. Continuing the same approach, compute the number of applications the company must process to earn a target net income of $20,000 if promotional costs increase by $5,662.
3. Assuming the original information and the processing of 500 applications, compute the loan application fee the company must charge if the target net income is $41,651.
4. Bar believes that 750 loan applications is the maximum number her staff can handle. How much more can be spent on promotional costs if the highest fee tolerable to the customer is $280, if variable costs cannot be reduced, and if the target net income for such an application loan is $50,000?

P 4.

LO 6
LO 7 *Planning Future Sales*

Vitale Company has a maximum capacity of 200,000 units per year. Variable manufacturing costs are $12 per unit. Fixed manufacturing overhead is $600,000 per year. Variable selling and administrative costs are $5 per unit, and fixed selling and administrative costs are $300,000 per year. The current sales price is $23 per unit.

REQUIRED

1. What is the breakeven point in (a) sales units and (b) sales dollars?
2. How many units must be sold to earn a target net income of $240,000 per year?
3. A strike at a major supplier has caused a material shortage, so the current year's production and sales are limited to 160,000 units. Top management is planning to reduce fixed costs to $841,000 to partially offset the effect on net income of the reduced sales. Variable cost per unit is the same as last year. The company already has sold 30,000 units at the regular selling price of $23 per unit.
   a. How much of the fixed costs was covered by the total contribution margin of the first 30,000 units sold?
   b. What contribution margin per unit will be needed on the remaining 130,000 units to cover the remaining fixed costs and to earn $210,000 in net income this year?

Alternate Problems

P 5.

LO 5 *Breakeven Analysis*
LO 6

At the beginning of each year, the accounting department at Zia Lighting, Ltd., must find the point at which projected sales revenue will equal total budgeted variable and fixed costs. The company makes custom-made, low-voltage outdoor lighting systems. Each system sells for an average of $435. Variable costs per unit are $210. Total fixed costs for the year are estimated to be $166,500.

REQUIRED

1. Compute the breakeven point in sales units.
2. Compute the breakeven point in sales dollars.
3. Find the new breakeven point in sales units if the fixed costs should go up by $10,125.
4. Using the original figures, compute the breakeven point in sales units if the selling price decreases to $425 per unit, fixed costs go up by $15,200, and variable costs decrease by $15 per unit.

P 6.

LO 7 *Planning Future Sales:*
         Contribution Margin
         Approach

Yoli Bingaman is president of the ASU Plastics Division of Land Industries. Management is considering a new product featuring a dashing medieval knight posed on a beautiful horse. Called Chargin' Knight, this product is expected to have global market appeal and become the mascot for many high school and university athletic teams. Expected variable unit costs are as follows: direct materials, $18.50; direct labor, $4.25; production supplies, $1.10; selling costs, $2.80; and other, $1.95. The following are annual fixed costs: depreciation, building and equipment, $36,000.00; advertising, $45,000.00; and other, $11,400.00. Land Industries plans to sell the product for $55.00.

REQUIRED

1. Using the contribution margin approach, compute the number of products the company must sell to (a) break even and (b) earn a net income of $70,224.
2. Using the same data, compute the number of products that must be sold to earn a target net income of $139,520 if advertising costs rise by $40,000.
3. Assuming the original information and sales of 10,000 units, compute the new selling price the company must use to make a net income of $131,600.
4. According to the vice president of marketing, Pete Rice, the most optimistic annual sales estimate for the product would be 15,000 units, and the highest competitive selling price the company can charge is $52.00 per unit. How much more can be spent on fixed advertising costs if the selling price is $52.00, if the variable costs cannot be reduced, and if the target net income for 15,000 unit sales is $251,000?

Skills Development

CONCEPTUAL ANALYSIS

SD 1.

LO 1
LO 2
Concept of Cost Behavior

Pacific Coast Shrimp Company is a very small company. It owns an ice house and shrimp preparation building, a refrigerated van, and three shrimp boats. Steven Black inherited the company from his father three months ago. The company employs three boat crews of four people each and five processing workers. Willman and Yang, a local accounting firm, has kept the company's financial records for many years.

In her last analysis of operations, Su Yang stated that the company's fixed-cost base of $100,000 is satisfactory for this type and size of business. However, variable costs have averaged 70 percent of sales over the last two years, a percentage that is too high for the volume of business. For example, last year only 30 percent of the company's sales revenue of $300,000 contributed toward covering the fixed costs. As a result, the company reported a $10,000 operating loss.

Black wants to improve the company's net income, but he is confused by Yang's explanation of the fixed and variable costs. Prepare a response to Black from Yang in which you explain the concept of cost behavior as it relates to Pacific Coast's operations. Include ideas for improving the company's net income based on changes in fixed and variable costs.

ETHICAL DILEMMA

SD 2.

LO 5
Breaking Even and Ethics

Cindy Ginsberg is the supervisor of the new product division of **Fricker Corp.,** located in Jackson, Wyoming. Ginsberg's annual bonus is based on the success of new products and is computed on the amount of sales over and above each product's projected breakeven point. In reviewing the computations supporting her most recent bonus, she found that a large order for 7,500 units of product WR4, which had been refused by a customer and returned to the company, had been included in the calculations. She later found out that the company's accountant had labeled the return as an overhead expense and had charged the entire cost of the returned order to the plantwide manufacturing overhead account. The result was that product WR4 exceeded breakeven by more than 5,000 units and Cindy's bonus from that product amounted to over $800. What actions should Ginsberg take? Be prepared to discuss your response.

RESEARCH ACTIVITY

SD 3.

LO 6
LO 7
Projecting Revenues and Costs

Select a company on the Internet or refer to the Needles Accounting Resource Center Web site at http://www.hmco.com/college/needles/home.html for links to selected companies. Study the Letter to the Stockholders in the most recent annual report for the company you have chosen. Many initiatives or actions discussed in this section were part of the company's strategic plan and were included in planning activities for the year. Identify at least three initiatives or actions that you believe were part of the company's planning activities for the year that affected sales or costs. Also identify one initiative or action that the company is planning for the coming year that you would expect to affect revenue or expenses for next year.

Group Activity: Divide the class into groups and ask them to discuss this SD. Then debrief the entire class by asking one person from each group to summarize his or her group's findings.

Communication	Critical Thinking	Group Activity	Memo	Ethics	International	Spreadsheet	Managerial Technology	Internet

DECISION-MAKING PRACTICE

SD 4.

LO 2 *Mixed Costs*
LO 3

Officials of the ***Minnetonka Golf and Tennis Club*** are putting together a budget for the year ending December 31, 20xx. A problem has caused the budget to be delayed by more than four weeks. Ray Lobo, the club treasurer, indicated that two expense items were creating the problem. The items were difficult to account for because they were called "mixed costs," and he did not know how to break them down into their variable and fixed components. An accountant friend and golfing partner told him to use the high-low method to divide the costs into their variable and fixed parts.

The two cost categories are Electricity Expense and Repairs and Maintenance Expense. Information pertaining to last year's spending patterns and the measurement activity connected with each cost are as shown below.

| Month | Electricity Expense | | Repairs and Maintenance | |
	Amount	Kilowatt Hours	Amount	Labor Hours
January	$ 7,500	210,000	$ 7,578	220
February	8,255	240,200	7,852	230
March	8,165	236,600	7,304	210
April	8,960	268,400	7,030	200
May	7,520	210,800	7,852	230
June	7,025	191,000	8,126	240
July	6,970	188,800	8,400	250
August	6,990	189,600	8,674	260
September	7,055	192,200	8,948	270
October	7,135	195,400	8,674	260
November	8,560	252,400	8,126	240
December	8,415	246,600	7,852	230
Totals	$92,550	2,622,000	$96,416	2,840

1. Using the high-low method, compute the variable cost rates used last year for each expense. What was the monthly fixed cost for electricity and for repairs and maintenance?
2. Compute the total variable cost and total fixed cost for each expense category for last year.
3. Lobo believes that for the coming year the electricity rate will increase by $.005 and the repairs rate will rise by $1.20. Usage of all items and their fixed cost amounts will remain constant. Compute the projected total cost for each category. How will these increases in costs affect the club's profits and cash flow?

Managerial Reporting and Analysis

INTERPRETING MANAGEMENT REPORTS

MRA 1.

LO 4 *Cost-Volume-Profit*
LO 5 *Analysis*
LO 6

Nambe-Casa, Ltd., is an international importer-exporter of fine china. The company was formed in 1963 in Albuquerque, New Mexico. The company has distribution centers in the United States, Europe, and Australia. Although very successful in its early years, the company's profitability has steadily declined. As a member of a management team selected to gather information for the next strategic planning meeting, you are asked to review the most recent income statement for the company. The income statement is on the next page. Sales in 20x1 were 15,000 sets of fine china.

Nambe-Casa, Ltd.
Contribution Income Statement
For the Year Ended December 31, 20x1

Sales		$13,500,000
Less Variable Costs		
Purchases	$6,000,000	
Distribution	2,115,000	
Sales Commissions	1,410,000	
Total Variable Costs		9,525,000
Contribution Margin		$ 3,975,000
Less Fixed Costs		
Distribution	$ 985,000	
Selling	1,184,000	
General and Administrative	871,875	
Total Fixed Costs		3,040,875
Net Income		$ 934,125

REQUIRED

1. For each set of fine china, calculate the (a) selling price, (b) variable purchases cost, (c) variable distribution cost, (d) variable sales commission; and (e) contribution margin.
2. Calculate the breakeven point in units and in sales dollars.
3. Historically, variable costs should be about 60 percent of sales. What was the ratio of variable costs to sales for 20x1? List three actions Nambe-Casa could take to correct the difference.
4. What would have been the impact on fixed costs if Nambe-Casa had sold only 14,000 sets of fine china?

FORMULATING MANAGEMENT REPORTS

MRA 2.

LO 7 *Cost-Volume-Profit Analysis*

Refer to the information in **MRA 1**. In January 20x2, Laura Casa, the president and chief executive officer of Nambe-Casa, Ltd., conducted a strategic planning meeting with her officers. Below is a summary of the information provided by two of the officers.

Rita O'Toole, vice president of sales: A review of the competitors indicates that the selling price of a set of china should be lowered to $890. We plan to sell 15,000 sets of fine china again in 20x2. To encourage increased sales, we should raise sales commissions to 12 percent of the selling price.

Maurice Moonitz, vice president of distribution: We have signed a contract with a new shipping line for foreign shipments. We will be able to reduce the fixed distribution costs by 10 percent and reduce variable distribution costs by 4 percent.

Laura needs your help. She is concerned that the changes may not improve net income sufficiently in 20x2. If net income does not increase by at least 10 percent, she will want to find other ways to reduce the company's costs. Since the new year has already started and changes need to be made quickly, she requests your report within five days.

REQUIRED

1. Prepare an estimated contribution income statement for 20x2. Your report should show the budgeted (estimated) net income based on the information provided above and in **MRA 1**. Will the changes improve net income sufficiently? Explain.
2. In preparation for writing your report, answer the following questions:
   a. Who needs the report?
   b. Why are you preparing the report?
   c. What were the sources of information for your report?
   d. When is the report due?

INTERNATIONAL COMPANY

MRA 3.

LO 4   *C-V-P Analysis and
Decision Making*

The ***Goslar Corporation*** cuts stones used in the construction and restoration of cathedrals throughout Europe. Granite, marble, and sandstone are cut into a variety of dimensions for walls, ceilings, and floors. The German-based company has operations in Italy and Switzerland. Otto Schrock, the controller, recently determined that the breakeven point was $325,000 in sales. In preparation for a quarterly planning meeting, Otto must provide information for the following six proposals, which will be discussed individually by the planning team.

a. Increase the selling price of marble slabs by 10 percent.
b. Change the sales mix to respond to the increased sales demand for marble slabs. As a result, the company would increase production of marble slabs and decrease the production and sales of sandstone, the least profitable product.
c. Increase fixed production costs by $40,000 annually for the depreciation of new stone-cutting equipment.
d. Increase the variable costs by 1 percent for increased export duties on foreign sales.
e. Decrease the sales volume of the sandstone slabs because of political upheavals in eastern Europe.
f. Decrease the number of days that a customer can wait before paying without being charged interest.

REQUIRED

1. For each proposal, determine if cost-volume-profit (C-V-P) analysis would provide useful financial information.
2. Indicate whether each proposal that lends itself to C-V-P analysis would show an increase, decrease, or no impact on net income. Consider each decision separately.

EXCEL SPREADSHEET ANALYSIS

MRA 4.

LO 7   *Planning Future Sales*

Refer to the information in **MRA 2**. In January 20x2, Laura Casa gathered information about a decrease in the selling price of a set of china to $890, an increase in sales commissions to 12 percent of the selling price, a decrease in fixed distribution costs of 10 percent, a decrease in variable distribution costs of 4 percent, and planned sales of 15,000 sets. Based on an analysis of this information she found that Nambe-Casa would not increase its 20x2 net income by at least 10 percent over the previous year's income.

Rita O'Toole reported that a new salesperson had just obtained a sales contract with an Australian distributor for 4,500 sets of china. The selling price, variable purchases cost per unit, 12 percent sales commission, and total fixed costs will be the same, but the variable distribution costs will be $160 per unit.

REQUIRED

Using Excel spreadsheet, complete the following:

1. Calculate the desired net income for 20x2.
2. Prepare a contribution margin income statement for 20x2 based on the information presented in **MRA 1** and the adjustments presented in **MRA 2**. Do you agree with Ms. Casa that Nambe-Casa's projected net income for 20x2 will be less than the net income for 20x1? Explain.
3. Calculate the total contribution margin from the Australian sales.
4. Prepare a revised contribution margin income statement for 20x2 by combining the information from **2** and **3** above.
5. Does Nambe-Casa need the Australian sales to satisfy the desired net income requirement for 20x2?

ENDNOTES

1. Linda Hall and Jane Lambert, "Cummins Engine Changes Its Depreciation," *Management Accounting*, Institute of Management Accountants, July 1996, pp. 30–36.
2. Jerry G. Kreuze, Gale E. Newell, and Stephen J. Newell, "What Companies Are Reporting," *Management Accounting*, Institute of Management Accountants, July 1996, p. 42.
3. Paul Hooper and John Page, "Relational Databases: An Accountant's Primer," *Management Accounting*, Institute of Management Accountants, October 1996, pp. 48–53.

CHAPTER 7

The Budgeting Process

1. Define *budgeting* and explain its role in the management cycle.
2. Explain the basic principles of budgeting.
3. Describe the master budget process for different types of organizations, and list the guidelines for preparing budgets.
4. Prepare a budgeted income statement and supporting operating budgets.
5. Prepare a cash budget.
6. Prepare a budgeted balance sheet.
7. Define *responsibility accounting* and discuss its relation to responsibility centers.

DECISION POINT

THE HON COMPANY

The HON Company, the largest manufacturer of mid-priced office furniture in the United States and Canada, wants to improve productivity and customer service while developing new products and services. However, balancing incremental improvements with innovation is difficult. The HON Company, one of nine subsidiaries of HON Industries, operates as a profit center. The managers of HON Company are responsible for generating profits and managing resources in accordance with its parent company's strategic plan. The company feels tremendous pressure to compete in an industry that has a few major customers who want good quality, low prices, and on-time delivery. To manage costs and make full use of production capacity, managers at the HON Company use a process called continuous quarterly budgeting to implement their budgets. At the beginning of each quarter, teams work to create a four-quarter budget. Through this budgeting process, top management expects to motivate others to continuously improve productivity and reduce delivery time while planning the introduction of new products and variations of existing products.[1]

How does the quarterly budget process work? First, a team from sales and marketing develops a sales budget by product, geographic territory, and distribution channel. The president and senior staff review the sales budget to see that it meets the goals of the strategic plan. Second, the scheduling team prepares a production and shipping schedule to coordinate those activities at the different manufacturing plants. Third, managers responsible for one of the five functional areas (research and development; production; distribution; customer service; and selling, general, and administrative) prepare cost/expense budgets. Fourth, the company accounting group reviews the budgets and analyzes the contents to see that the budgets reflect the strategic plan. Fifth, the HON Company controller prepares a complete set of budgeted financial statements and additional information, including

VIDEOCASE

ENTERPRISE RENT-A-CAR

OBJECTIVES

- To become familiar with the budgeting process and budgets
- To understand the relationship between strategic plans and operating budgets
- To describe the role of budgeting in the management cycle

BACKGROUND FOR THE CASE

Enterprise Rent-A-Car does not have the high profile most of its competitors enjoy because it does not rent vehicles at airport locations; however, with over $3.5 billion in annual revenues (revenue growth of more than 25 percent per year for the last eleven years) and more than 3,300 locations, it is the largest car rental company in the United States and one of the top fifty privately owned companies. The forty-year old company focuses on the home-city market, which is divided into two segments. The first segment serves people who need replacement vehicles when their own cars are not available—for instance, when they are scheduled for lengthy repair work. The second segment serves people with discretionary needs for another or different type of car for a short period, such as for a weekend trip or vacations. Enterprise prides itself on providing excellent customer service, including free delivery and pickup of all rentals. The company accomplishes its goals by providing incentives to motivate employees, coupled with a decentralized organization that allows great latitude in decision making. Enterprise's managers prepare budgets to integrate, coordinate, and communicate the operating plans necessary to achieve these strategic objectives. The budgeting system must allow measurement of performance for each location and each employee. Good systems and budgeting also facilitate the company's objective of expanding into global markets in Canada, the United Kingdom, and Germany.

 For more information about Enterprise Rent-A-Car, visit the company's Web site through the Needles Accounting Resource Center at
http://www.hmco.com/college/needles/home.html

REQUIRED

 View the video on Enterprise Rent-A-Car that accompanies this book. As you are watching the video, take notes related to the following questions:

1. As part of the planning process, many large, successful companies prepare budgets. In your words, explain what a budget is and list all of the reasons you believe a company like Enterprise would prepare a set of budgets.
2. Companies that prepare strategic plans also prepare budgets. What is the relationship between Enterprise's strategic plans and its operating budgets?
3. What is the role of budgeting in the management cycle?

productivity measures, budgeted sales attributable to new product introductions, and major equipment expenditures.

The value of this approach for HON Company results from the preparation of the budgets on a quarterly basis. This continuous process informs employees about new products and procedures and permits improvements to occur more quickly. Continuous quarterly budgeting successfully connects strategic planning to operations by helping the workers see the corporate vision, target their actions to support the vision, and monitor the results of their actions. Continuous quarterly budgeting helps the managers and employees of the HON Company to continuously improve productivity and customer service while integrating innovation through the development of new products.

The Budgeting Process

OBJECTIVE 1

Define budgeting *and explain its role in the management cycle*

Planning is an important ongoing process for organizations. A review of the current use of available resources for financing, investing, and operating activities is necessary to plan for the efficient use of future resources. Budgeting is the process of identifying, gathering, summarizing, and communicating financial and nonfinancial information about an organization's future activities. The budgeting process provides managers with the opportunity to carefully match the goals of the organization with the resources necessary to accomplish those goals.

Budgets are synonymous with managing an organization. The term *organization* is important because budgets are used in government and not-for-profit organizations (such as hospitals, universities, professional organizations, and charities) as well as in profit-oriented businesses. All types of organizations rely on plans to help them accomplish their objectives. All types of organizations have managers whose responsibilities are determined by top management or a board of directors; budgets are used to plan for and assess those areas of responsibility and to measure managers' performance. All organizations need cash to purchase resources to accomplish their goals. Whenever cash needs to be managed and accounted for, budgets are used. Budgets establish (1) minimum desired or target levels of cash receipts and (2) limits on the spending of cash for particular purposes. The primary difference between not-for-profit and profit-oriented organizations is that a profit-oriented organization sells a product or service for the purpose of making a profit. Profit-oriented organizations often call their budgeting function a profit-planning activity.

A budget is a plan of action that forecasts future transactions, activities, and events in financial or nonfinancial terms. Used as planning documents, budgets can communicate information, coordinate activities and resource usage, motivate employees, and evaluate performance. Budgets come in many forms. Some budgets present financial information based on the availability of resources. Those budgets should reflect a fair assignment of resources to various organizational activities over a future period. For example, a cash budget shows the planned use of cash resources for operating, investing, and financing activities. Other budgets show planned activities to meet certain requirements or standards established in the planning stage. For example, a production budget shows planned production in units. Exhibit 1 contains two simple budgets prepared for diverse purposes. These budgets are illustrations rather than official guidelines for budget preparation.

The budgeting process is as important in today's globally competitive operating environment as it is in more traditional settings. In fact, budgeting becomes even

Exhibit 1. Examples of Budgets

Example A

State University Knights
Alumni Club
Revenues and Expenditures Budget
Homecoming Activities—20x1

Budgeted Revenues		
Football Concession Sales	$32,500	
Homecoming Dance Tickets		
(1,200 at $20)	24,000	
Parking Fees	1,425	
Total Budgeted Revenues		$57,925
Budgeted Expenditures		
Dance Music Group	$ 7,500	
Hall Rental	2,000	
Refreshments	2,600	
Printing Costs	1,450	
Concession Purchases	12,200	
Clean-up Costs	4,720	
Miscellaneous	800	
Total Budgeted Expenditures		31,270
Excess of Revenues Over Expenditures*		$26,655

*To be contributed to State University's Scholarship Fund.

Example B

Scottsdale Resort
Room Occupancy Budget
For the Year Ended December 31, 20x2

	Projected Occupancy							
	Singles (50)		Doubles (80)		Mini Suites (10)		Luxury Suites (6)	
Month	Rooms	%	Rooms	%	Rooms	%	Rooms	%
January	20	40.0	30	37.5	2	20.0	1	16.7
February	24	48.0	36	45.0	3	30.0	1	16.7
March	28	56.0	42	52.5	4	40.0	2	33.3
April	32	64.0	50	62.5	5	50.0	2	33.3
May	44	88.0	60	75.0	6	60.0	2	33.3
June	46	92.0	74	92.5	7	70.0	3	50.0
July	50	100.0	78	97.5	9	90.0	4	66.7
August	50	100.0	80	100.0	10	100.0	5	83.3
September	48	96.0	78	97.5	10	100.0	6	100.0
October	34	68.0	60	75.0	8	80.0	5	83.3
November	30	60.0	46	57.5	2	20.0	3	50.0
December	34	68.0	50	62.5	4	40.0	4	66.7

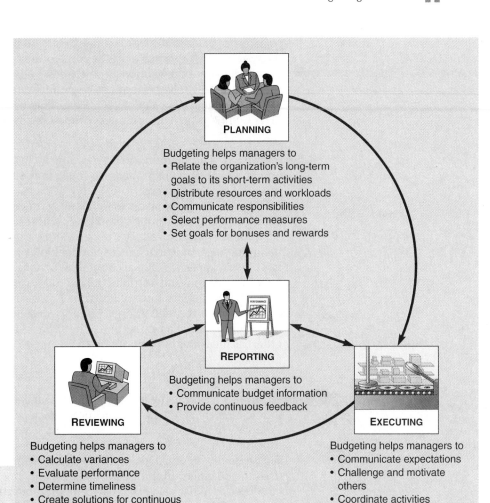

more important when just-in-time (JIT) or total quality management (TQM) concepts are applied and when computers and other electronic operating and data accumulation devices are used. In these new environments, actual operating data are made available quickly, and budgets are updated continuously to accommodate management's need for performance evaluation. The principles of budgeting do not change in the new operating environments, but the speed and timing with which they are applied does.

Budgeting and the Management Cycle

Managers in profit-oriented organizations work to generate profits and pay debts as they become due because investors and creditors expect them to do so. To achieve the goals of profitability and liquidity, managers of many organizations use the budgeting process throughout the management cycle to help plan, execute, review, and report the organization's financing, investing, and operating activities. Figure 1 illustrates the relationships between budgeting and the management cycle. Budgets originate in the planning stage, which is the stage that we emphasize in this chapter. It is important to develop relevant, timely budgets during the planning stage because managers will rely on the resulting budget information when making decisions during the executing and reviewing stages. Budget information is quantifiable information about an organization's future activities and the revenues or expenses associated with those activities. Reports formally communicate budget information. We will illustrate the relationship between budgeting and the management cycle in the context of Hi-Flyer Company, a manufacturer of flying disks used for recreation and tournament play. The owner, Skye King, believes that the future growth of Hi-Flyer Company depends on a good budgeting process.

Planning   The planning process often includes the development of long-range and short-range plans to achieve important success factors, such as high-quality products, reasonable cost, and timely delivery. Mr. King believes that budgets help his organization's managers match long-term goals with short-term business activities by carefully distributing workloads and resources throughout the organization, such as to specific products, departments, sales territories, and activities. In the planning stage, budget teams use budget information to communicate responsibilities to individuals who are accountable for a particular segment of the organization. Careful selection and introduction of performance measures can challenge and influence the performance of individuals or teams to achieve goals and earn bonuses and rewards for their efforts. Senior management recently selected profits, number of units sold, and cycle time (the time to take, manufacture, and ship a sales order) as measures of performance for bonuses to individuals and teams at Hi-Flyer Company.

Executing   During the executing stage, managers use budget information for communication, benchmarking, and problem recognition. The managers of Hi-Flyer Company use budget information daily, weekly, and monthly to communicate expectations about the performance of activities and the availability of resources for segments of the organization. For example, Abe Dillon, the production manager, uses the planned units of production as an operating target for the production employees. He has also established the number of reworks as a performance measure to motivate workers to manufacture quality products. In addition, Mr. King uses standard product costs, generated during the budget process, to submit bids for sales orders, estimate profits, and calculate the expected profitability of a product during the operating period.

Reviewing   In the reviewing stage, managers calculate variances, evaluate performance, review the timeliness of activities performed, and create solutions for continuous improvement. As mentioned earlier, Hi-Flyer's managers use the performance measures developed during the planning stage as targets for actual performance during the executing stage. By comparing the budget and actual information, they can identify variances between planned and actual activity. They review the variances to identify waste and inefficiencies in production, sales, purchasing, packing, shipping, accounting, and other business activities. If problems are identified, they can work together to find solutions that will enable the organization to continuously improve its products and processes. Hi-Flyer's managers perform budget analyses on a regular basis because it helps chart the course of future operations and provides a means of evaluating past performance. If Hi-Flyer Company establishes realistic goals, then comparing the actual results with budgeted targets can help management assess how well the organization performed.

Reporting   The reporting stage occurs throughout the year because managers need to continuously report on budget information and provide feedback about the organization's operating, investing, and financing activities. Budgets are reports showing plans for future actions. As such, they serve as a reference point for many other reports. For example, performance reports based on budget information sup-

BUSINESS BULLETIN: TECHNOLOGY IN PRACTICE

When an organization decides to market its products or services on the Internet's World Wide Web, it must create a Web site and build the site's costs into its budget. Developing a Web site includes making decisions about access to the Internet, content on the site (online brochures or product news), graphic design, and functionality. In addition to basic development costs, the organization will incur costs for faster connections, database applications that update information easily, and animations and three-dimensional logos. After the Web site has been developed, additional costs include monthly site maintenance fees, database development, and network integration. In addition, those who choose to use a custom domain server pay a yearly licensing fee to Internic, a government agency that oversees Internet activity.

port bonuses and promotions. Other budget-based reports support operating decisions. In this chapter, we will focus on how budgets are prepared during the planning stage. In the next chapter, we will discuss the use of budget information in the reviewing stage of the management cycle.

Basic Principles of Budgeting

OBJECTIVE 2
Explain the basic principles of budgeting

Budget preparation contributes to an organization's success in three ways. First, preparing a budget forces management to look ahead and plan both long- and short-range goals and events. Second, the entire management team must work together to make and carry out the plans. Third, by comparing the budget with actual results, it is possible to review performance at all levels of management.

Long-Range Goals   Annual operating plans cannot be made unless the people preparing the budget know the direction that top management expects for the organization. Long-range goals, which are projections covering a five- to ten-year period, must be set by top management. Those goals should take into consideration economic and industry forecasts, employee-management relationships, and the structure and role of management in leading the organization. And they should include statements about the expected quality of products or services, growth rates, and desired market share.

Vague aims are not sufficient. The long-term goals should set specific targets and expected timetables and name the people responsible for achieving the goals. For example, assume that one of O'Toole Corporation's long-term goals is to control 15 percent of its product's market. At present the company holds only 4 percent of the market. The company's long-term goals may state that the vice president of marketing is to develop plans and strategies to ensure that the company controls 10 percent of the market in five years and increases its share to 15 percent by the end of ten years.

Once all goals have been developed, they should be compiled into a total long-range plan. This plan should include a spectrum of targets and goals and give direction to the company's efforts to achieve those goals. It should include future profit projections and spell out in general terms new products and services.

Short-Range Goals and Strategies   The long-range goals must be carefully developed because they are used to prepare yearly operating plans and targets. The short-range plan involves every part of the enterprise and is much more detailed than the long-range goals.

To arrive at the short-range plan, the long-range goals must be restated in terms of what should be accomplished during the next year. Decisions must be made about sales and profit targets by product or service, human resource needs and expected changes, and plans for introducing new products or services. The resulting short-range targets and goals form the basis for the organization's operating budget for the year.

Once management has set the short-range goals, the controller or budget director takes charge of preparing the budget. This person designs a complete set of budget-development plans and a timetable with deadlines for all levels and parts of the year's operating plan. Specific people must be named to carry out each part of the budget's development, and their responsibilities, targets, and deadlines must be clearly described.

The Master Budget

OBJECTIVE 3

Describe the master budget process for different types of organizations, and list the guidelines for preparing budgets

Suppose you want to start a new business, but you must obtain a bank loan to supply some of the cash you need to begin operations. Before the bank will agree to loan you money, you must demonstrate that you can repay the principal and interest with cash generated by profitable operations. To do so, you will prepare a set of budgeted, or pro forma, financial statements for the bank to review. Now assume that you receive the bank loan and that, over ten years, your company becomes quite successful. Every year you would continue to prepare a set of budgeted financial statements so that you could match long-term goals to short-term activities and plan for the resources necessary to operate, finance, and invest in your business.

A master budget is a set of budgets that consolidate an organization's financial information into budgeted financial statements for a future period of time. A master budget includes a set of operating budgets that support a budgeted income statement. In addition, a master budget presents a set of financial budgets that include a budgeted balance sheet, a cash budget, and a capital expenditures budget. Regardless of the type of organization, the master budget provides helpful information for planning, executing, reviewing, and reporting organizational activities. Figures 2, 3, and 4 display the preparation of a master budget for a manufacturing organization, a retail organization, and a service organization, respectively.

The master budget process has some similarities in all three types of organizations. All three types of organizations need a set of operating budgets to support the budgeted income statement. The budget information from the operating budgets and the capital expenditures budget affects the cash budget and the budgeted balance sheet. The cash budget also provides information for the budgeted balance sheet.

The main difference in the master budget process for the three types of organizations involves the preparation of operating budgets for the budgeted income statement. The operating budgets for a manufacturing organization like Intel or John Deere include budgets for sales, production, direct materials purchases, direct labor, manufacturing overhead, cost of goods manufactured, and selling and administrative expenses. The preparation of those budgets for a manufacturing organization will be explained under the next learning objective.

A retail organization like J.C. Penney or Home Depot must know what products to sell, the estimated quantities to be sold, and the selling price for each. This helps the organization plan the amount of resources needed to sell the merchandise. A retail organization must purchase merchandise for resale and incur expenses for employee payroll, utilities, taxes, insurance, rent, advertising, sales commissions, accounting, and other expenses. Managers may need to purchase long-term assets, such as buildings, equipment, and display cases to store, display, and sell merchan-

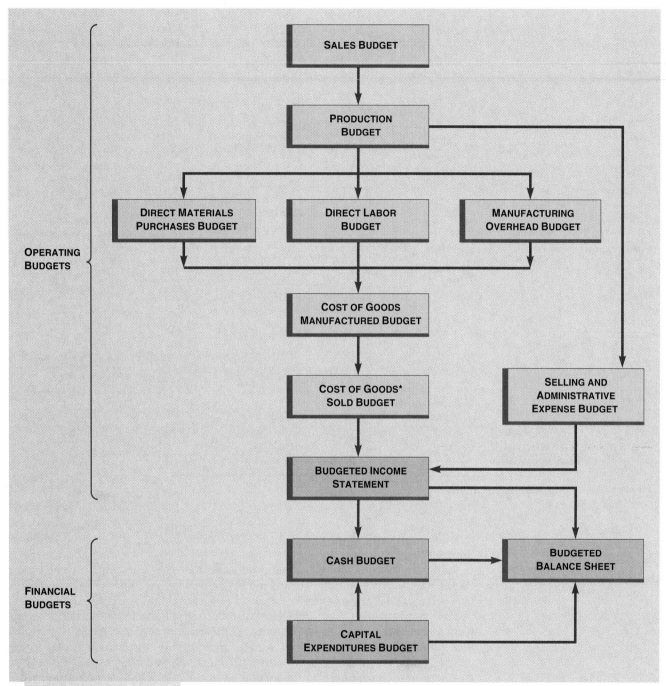

Figure 2
Preparation of a Master
Budget for a Manufacturing
Organization

*Some organizations choose to include the cost of goods sold budget in the budgeted income statement.

dise. To manage the use of these resources, retail managers and accountants prepare operating budgets to support a budgeted income statement. The operating budgets for a retail organization include a sales budget, a purchases budget, a cost of goods sold budget, and a selling and administrative expense budget. The sales budget is prepared first because it is used to estimate sales volume and revenues. Once managers know how many sales dollars to expect, and the quantity to be sold, they can develop other budgets that will enable them to manage the organization's resources to generate profits on those sales. The purchases budget determines the

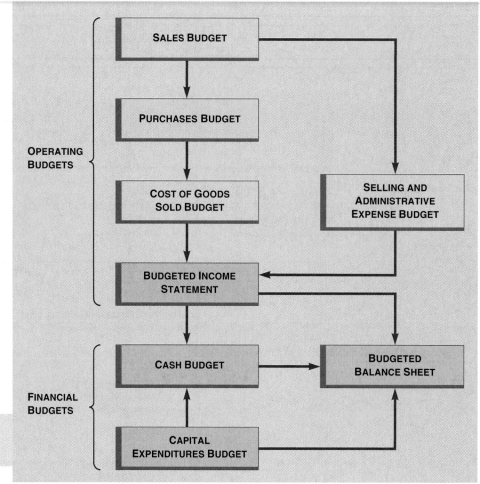

Figure 3
Preparation of a Master Budget
for a Retail Organization

quantity of merchandise needed to meet the sales demand and maintain a minimum level of inventory.

Rather than manufacture and sell products, service organizations such as Union Pacific Railroad or Columbia Healthcare invest money in human resources to provide services. Managers of service organizations must know the types and amounts of services to perform. Managers must also know the labor hours needed to complete those services, the level of expertise of their employees, and the labor rates for the planned services. In addition, service organizations must incur expenses for utilities, taxes, insurance, rent, advertising, accounting, and other expenses.

A service organization also prepares a set of operating budgets to support the budgeted income statement. The operating budgets include budgets for service revenue, labor, services overhead, and selling and administrative expenses. The labor budget reflects the estimated labor hours and labor rates to provide the services. The managers use this information to estimate the amount of human and technical resources needed for the accounting period and to set prices for services.

Guidelines for Budget Preparation

Attention to the suggestions presented in Table 1 will help managers improve the quality of the budgets they prepare. Managers need to know why the budget is being prepared, who will read and use it, how the information will be presented, and where the information can be found. Meaningful, accurate information is gathered from

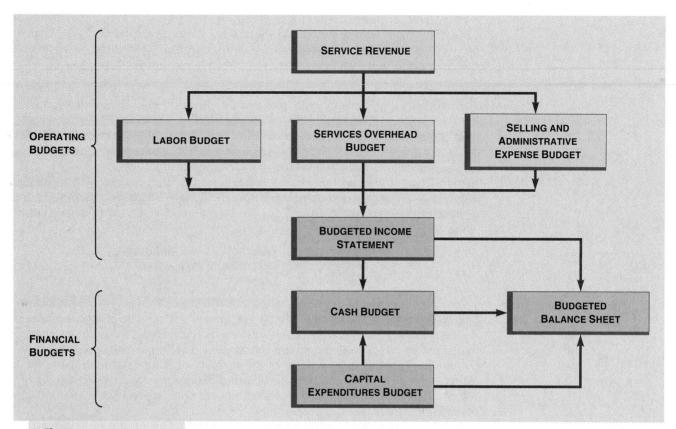

Figure 4
Preparation of a Master Budget for a Service Organization

appropriate documents or interviews with the employees, suppliers, or managers who are responsible for the related areas. The title or heading includes the organization's name, the type of budget, and the accounting period under consideration. Several revisions may be required before the final version is ready to distribute.

The Operating Budgets

OBJECTIVE 4

Prepare a budgeted income statement and supporting operating budgets

Procedures for preparing a master budget vary from one organization to another. Since it is impossible to cover all procedures found in actual practice, the following discussion will illustrate one approach to preparing a budgeted income statement and supporting operating budgets for a manufacturing organization. Remember that by applying the tools of cost behavior and cost-volume-profit analysis and by

Table 1. Guidelines for Budget Preparation

- Know the purpose of the budget.
- Identify the user group and their information needs.
- Begin the budget with a clearly stated title or heading.
- Identify the format for the budget, and use appropriate formulas and calculations to derive the quantitative information.
- Label the budget's components, and list the unit and financial data in an orderly manner.
- Know the sources of budget information.
- Revise the budget until all planning decisions are included.

working with a particular product costing method, you can prepare any kind of budget. We have already stated that there is no standard format to use for budget preparation; the only universal requirements are that the budget be clear and understandable and that it communicate the intended information to the reader.

Sales Budget   The beginning point for the preparation of the master budget is the sales budget. The sales budget is a detailed plan, expressed in both units and dollars, that identifies expected product (or service) sales for a future period. Sales managers use this information to plan sales- and marketing-related activities as well as human, physical, and technical resource needs. Accountants use the information to determine estimated cash receipts for the cash budget. To prepare the sales budget, management must know the estimated selling price per unit and the estimated sales demand in units. The sales budget reflects the total budgeted sales using the following equation:

$$\begin{array}{ccc} \text{Total} & & \text{Estimated} & & \text{Estimated} \\ \text{Budgeted} & = & \text{Selling Price} & \times & \text{Sales in} \\ \text{Sales} & & \text{per Unit} & & \text{Units} \end{array}$$

Although the calculation is easy, selecting the best estimates for the selling price and the sales volume can be difficult. The estimated selling price may be the current selling price, or it may change in response to such factors as competition. An estimated selling price below the current selling price may be needed if competitors are currently selling the same product at lower prices or if the organization wants to increase its share of the market. On the other hand, the organization may plan to sell at a higher price because the product's quality has increased due to improved materials or production processes.

In addition, the estimated sales volume is very important because it will affect the level of operating activities and the amount of resources necessary to operate. Production, packing, shipping, accounting, purchasing, selling, and administrative activities require resources that will increase in varying degrees with increases in the estimated sales volume. A sales forecast can help to determine an estimated sales volume. A sales forecast is a projection of sales demand (the estimated sales in units) based on an analysis of external and internal factors. External factors influencing a sales forecast include:

1. The state of the local and the national economies
2. The state of the industry's economy
3. The nature of the competition, their sales volume, and selling price

Internal factors influencing a sales forecast include:

1. The number of units sold in prior periods
2. The organization's credit policies
3. The organization's collection policies
4. The organization's pricing policies
5. Any new products the organization plans to introduce into the market
6. The capacity of the organization's manufacturing facilities

Exhibit 2 illustrates the sales budget for Hi-Flyer Company. The sales budget states sales information for the Hi-Flyer products in both units and dollar revenue amounts for each quarter and for the entire year. The estimated selling price is $5 per unit in response to the highly competitive marketplace. The sales forecast shows highly seasonable sales activity that causes the estimated sales volume to fluctuate between 10,000 and 40,000 Hi-Flyers per quarter in 20x1. If Hi-Flyer Company sold more than one product, separate schedules or a comprehensive sales budget could be prepared to show the total budgeted sales by product.

Exhibit 2. Sales Budget

Hi-Flyer Company
Sales Budget
For the Year Ended December 31, 20x1

	Quarter				
	1	2	3	4	Year
Sales in Units	10,000	30,000	10,000	40,000	90,000
× Selling Price per Unit	$ 5	$ 5	$ 5	$ 5	$ 5
Total Sales	$50,000	$150,000	$50,000	$200,000	$450,000

Production Budget   The production budget is a detailed schedule that identifies the products or services that must be produced or provided to meet sales and inventory needs. Production managers use this information to plan for the technical and human resources needed to complete production-related activities. To prepare this budget, management must know the sales target in units (see the sales budget in Exhibit 2) and the desired level of ending finished goods inventory for each period. The desired level of ending finished goods inventory is often stated as a percentage of the next period's budgeted unit sales. For example, Hi-Flyer Company's desired level of ending finished goods inventory is 10 percent of the next quarter's unit sales of Hi-Flyers.

The following formula identifies the production needs for each accounting period.

$$\begin{array}{ccccc} \text{Total} & & \text{Budgeted} & \text{Desired Units} & \text{Desired Units of} \\ \text{Production} & = & \text{Sales in} & + \text{ of Ending} & - \text{ Beginning} \\ \text{Units} & & \text{Units} & \text{Finished} & \text{Finished} \\ & & & \text{Goods} & \text{Goods} \\ & & & \text{Inventory} & \text{Inventory} \end{array}$$

BUSINESS BULLETIN: INTERNATIONAL PRACTICE

An organization selling in foreign markets must consider each market's special characteristics when developing a sales budget. The differences among regions and countries require the preparation of a separate sales budget for each market. Here are some examples of factors a company must consider when marketing abroad.[2]

Region/Country	Dominant and Distinctive Market Characteristic
Canada	North American Free Trade Agreement
Eastern Europe	Recent democratization and uncertain trade regulations
France	Price controls
Japan	Complex distribution system
Pacific Rim	New area with many developing countries offering a growing consumer base

Exhibit 3. Production Budget

Hi-Flyer Company
Production Budget
For the Year Ended December 31, 20x1

	Quarter				
	1	2	3	4	Year
Sales in Units (Exhibit 2)	10,000	30,000	10,000	40,000	90,000
Add Desired Units of Ending Finished Goods Inventory	3,000	1,000	4,000	1,500	1,500
Desired Total Units	13,000	31,000	14,000	41,500	91,500
Less Desired Units of Beginning Finished Goods Inventory	1,000	3,000	1,000	4,000	1,000
Total Production Units	12,000	28,000	13,000	37,500	90,500

Note 1: Desired units of ending finished goods inventory = 10% of *next* quarter's budgeted sales.
Note 2: Desired units of beginning finished goods inventory = 10% of *current* quarter's budgeted sales.
Note 3: Assume that budgeted sales for the first quarter of 20x2 = 15,000 units.

Exhibit 3 illustrates the production budget for Hi-Flyer Company. Notice that each quarter's desired total units of ending finished goods inventory become the next quarter's desired total units of beginning finished goods inventory. If we assume that the budgeted units for the first quarter of 20x2 are 15,000 units, then the ending finished goods inventory for the fourth quarter of 20x1 will be 1,500 units (.10 × 15,000 units). This amount also represents the desired total units of ending finished goods inventory for 20x1. The 1,000 units in the beginning finished goods inventory for the first quarter are also the desired total units of beginning finished goods inventory for the year 20x1. A production budget for a service organization will show the required labor hours to generate the planned revenues for each period. Organizations that manufacture a variety of products or provide many different types of services may prepare either separate schedules for each product or service or one comprehensive production budget. This information helps managers to schedule production and service activities.

Direct Materials Purchases Budget   The direct materials purchases budget is a detailed schedule that identifies the purchases required for budgeted production and inventory needs and the costs associated with those needs. The purchasing function uses this information to plan purchases of direct materials, while the accountant uses the same information to estimate cash payments to suppliers. Thus, this budget reflects both the quantity and the cost of direct materials purchases.

To prepare this budget, management must know the production needs (see the production budget in Exhibit 3), the desired level of the direct materials inventory for each period, and the estimated per unit cost of direct materials. The desired level of ending direct materials inventory is usually stated as a percentage of the next period's production needs. In our example, Hi-Flyer Company's desired level of ending direct materials inventory is 20 percent of the next quarter's production needs.

The first step is to calculate the total production needs in ounces because the Hi-Flyer flying disk requires 10 ounces of plastic per disk. The total production needs in ounces for the quarter is the number of Hi-Flyer disks budgeted for production in the quarter multiplied by 10 ounces of plastic per disk. In the second step, the fol-

Exhibit 4. Direct Materials Purchases Budget

Hi-Flyer Company
Direct Materials Purchases Budget
For the Year Ended December 31, 20x1

	Quarter				
	1	2	3	4	Year
Total Production Units (Exhibit 3)	12,000	28,000	13,000	37,500	90,500
× 10 Ounces per Unit	10	10	10	10	10
Total Production Needs in Ounces	120,000	280,000	130,000	375,000	905,000
Add Desired Ounces of Ending Direct Materials Inventory	56,000	26,000	75,000	30,000	30,000
	176,000	306,000	205,000	405,000	935,000
Less Desired Ounces of Beginning Direct Materials Inventory	24,000	56,000	26,000	75,000	24,000
Total Ounces of Direct Materials to Be Purchased	152,000	250,000	179,000	330,000	911,000
× Cost per Ounce	$ .05	$ .05	$ .05	$ .05	$ .05
Total Cost of Direct Materials Purchases	$ 7,600	$ 12,500	$ 8,950	$ 16,500	$ 45,550

Note 1: Desired ounces of ending direct materials inventory = 20% of *next* quarter's budgeted production needs in ounces.
Note 2: Desired ounces of beginning direct materials inventory = 20% of *current* quarter's budgeted production needs in ounces.
Note 3: Assume that budgeted production needs in ounces for the first quarter of 20x2 = 150,000 ounces.
Note 4: The desired direct materials inventory balance at January 1, 20x1 = 24,000 ounces × $.05 per ounce = $1,200 and at December 31, 20x1 = 30,000 ounces × $.05 per ounce = $1,500.

lowing formula creates the direct materials purchases in units for each accounting period in the budget.

Total Units of Direct Materials To Be Purchased	=	Total Production Needs in Units of Direct Materials	+	Desired Units of Ending Direct Materials Inventory	−	Desired Units of Beginning Direct Materials Inventory

The third step is to calculate the cost of the direct materials purchases by multiplying the total unit purchases of direct materials by the direct materials cost of $.05 per ounce (the cost that was estimated by the Purchasing Department). Exhibit 4 illustrates the direct materials purchases budget for Hi-Flyer Company. Notice that each quarter's desired units of ending direct materials inventory becomes the next quarter's desired units of beginning direct materials inventory. If we assume that the budgeted ounces for the first quarter of 20x2 are 150,000 ounces, then the ending direct materials inventory for the fourth quarter of 20x1 will be 30,000 ounces (.20 × 150,000 ounces). This amount also represents the desired units of ending direct materials inventory for the year 20x1. The 24,000 ounces of the first quarter's beginning direct materials inventory is also the desired units of beginning direct materials inventory for the year 20x1. In this example, Hi-Flyer Company uses only one direct material. Organizations that purchase a large variety of materials or parts for production may prepare either separate schedules for each material required or one comprehensive direct materials purchases budget.

Exhibit 5. Direct Labor Budget

Hi-Flyer Company
Direct Labor Budget
For the Year Ended December 31, 20x1

	Quarter				
	1	2	3	4	Year
Total Production Units (Exhibit 3)	12,000	28,000	13,000	37,500	90,500
× Direct Labor Hours per Unit	.1	.1	.1	.1	.1
Total Direct Labor Hours	1,200	2,800	1,300	3,750	9,050
× Direct Labor Cost per Hour	$ 6	$ 6	$ 6	$ 6	$ 6
Total Direct Labor Cost	$ 7,200	$16,800	$ 7,800	$22,500	$54,300

Direct Labor Budget   The direct labor budget is a detailed schedule that identifies the direct labor needs for a future period and the labor costs associated with those needs. The Production Department uses direct labor hours to schedule the number of employees and the hours that each will work, while the accountant uses direct labor costs to estimate the cash payments to direct labor workers. The information in the direct labor budget also helps the Human Resources Department plan for hiring new employees, training current and new employees, or reducing the number of employees.

The first step in preparing a direct labor budget is to estimate the total direct labor hours by multiplying the estimated direct labor hours per unit by the anticipated units of production (see Exhibit 3). The second step is to calculate the total budgeted direct labor cost by multiplying the estimated total direct labor hours by the estimated direct labor cost per hour. The Human Resources Department provides an estimate of the hourly labor wages for these workers.

$$\begin{array}{ccc} \text{Total Budgeted} & & \text{Estimated} & & \text{Estimated} \\ \text{Direct Labor} & = & \text{Total Direct} & \times & \text{Direct Labor} \\ \text{Cost} & & \text{Labor Hours} & & \text{Cost per Hour} \end{array}$$

Exhibit 5 illustrates the direct labor budget for Hi-Flyer Company using these formulas to estimate the total budgeted direct labor cost. The Production Department needs an estimated .10 direct labor hours to complete one Hi-Flyer. The Human Resources Department estimates a direct labor cost of $6 per direct labor hour. In this example, Hi-Flyer Company needs only one production department. Organizations that require varying production processes and varying levels of expertise may prepare either separate schedules for each type of labor or one comprehensive direct labor budget.

Manufacturing Overhead Budget   The manufacturing overhead budget is a detailed schedule of anticipated manufacturing costs, other than direct materials and direct labor costs, that must be incurred to meet the production expectations of a future period. The manufacturing overhead budget has two purposes: (1) to integrate the overhead cost budgets developed by the managers of production and production-related service departments and (2) to group information for the calculation of manufacturing overhead rates for the forthcoming accounting period.

The presentation of manufacturing overhead budget information is flexible. Grouping information by activities is useful for organizations using activity-based

Exhibit 6. Manufacturing Overhead Budget

Hi-Flyer Company
Manufacturing Overhead Budget
For the Year Ended December 31, 20x1

	Quarter				Year
	1	2	3	4	
Variable Overhead Costs					
Indirect Materials	$ 2,160	$ 5,040	$ 2,340	$ 6,750	$ 16,290
Employee Benefits	2,880	6,720	3,120	9,000	21,720
Inspection	1,080	2,520	1,170	3,375	8,145
Maintenance and Repair	1,920	4,480	2,080	6,000	14,480
Utilities	3,600	8,400	3,900	11,250	27,150
Total Variable Overhead	$11,640	$27,160	$12,610	$36,375	$ 87,785
Fixed Overhead Costs					
Depreciation, Machinery	$ 2,810	$ 2,810	$ 2,810	$ 2,810	$ 11,240
Depreciation, Building	3,225	3,225	3,225	3,225	12,900
Supervision	9,000	9,000	9,000	9,000	36,000
Maintenance and Repair	2,150	2,150	2,150	2,150	8,600
Other Overhead Expenses	3,175	3,175	3,175	3,175	12,700
Total Fixed Overhead	$20,360	$20,360	$20,360	$20,360	$ 81,440
Total Manufacturing Overhead Costs	$32,000	$47,520	$32,970	$56,735	$169,225

costing. This approach helps the accountant to more easily determine the application rates for each cost pool. The Hi-Flyer Company prefers to group information into variable and fixed costs for cost-volume-profit analysis during the executing stage of the management cycle (see Exhibit 6). The manufacturing overhead rate for Hi-Flyer Company is the estimated total manufacturing costs divided by the estimated total direct labor hours. The predetermined manufacturing overhead rate for 20x1 is $18.70 per direct labor hour ($169,225 ÷ 9,050 direct labor hours), or $1.87 per unit ($18.70 per direct labor hour ÷ .10 direct labor hours per unit). The variable portion of the manufacturing overhead rate is $9.70 per direct labor hour, which includes indirect materials, $1.80; employee benefits, $2.40; inspection, $.90; maintenance and repair, $1.60; and utilities, $3.00.

Selling and Administrative Expense Budget   A selling and administrative expense budget is a detailed plan of operating expenses, other than those of the production function, needed to support the sales and overall operations of the organization for a future period. The accountant uses the estimated selling and administrative expense budget to estimate cash payments for products or services used in nonproduction-related activities. Exhibit 7 illustrates the selling and administrative expense budget for Hi-Flyer Company, which groups expenses into variable and fixed components for purposes of cost-volume-profit analysis and profit planning.

Cost of Goods Manufactured Budget   The cost of goods manufactured budget is a detailed schedule that summarizes the costs of production for a future period. The sources of budget information for the total manufacturing costs are the budgets for direct materials, direct labor, and manufacturing overhead (Exhibits 4, 5, and 6).

Exhibit 7. Selling and Administrative Expense Budget

Hi-Flyer Company
Selling and Administrative Expense Budget
For the Year Ended December 31, 20x1

	Quarter				
	1	2	3	4	Year
Variable Selling and Administrative Expenses					
Delivery Expenses	$ 800	$ 2,400	$ 800	$ 3,200	$ 7,200
Sales Commissions	1,000	3,000	1,000	4,000	9,000
Accounting	700	2,100	700	2,800	6,300
Other Administrative Expenses	400	1,200	400	1,600	3,600
Total Variable Selling and Administrative Expenses	$ 2,900	$ 8,700	$ 2,900	$11,600	$ 26,100
Fixed Selling and Administrative Expenses					
Sales Salaries	$ 4,500	$ 4,500	$ 4,500	$ 4,500	$ 18,000
Executive Salaries	12,750	12,750	12,750	12,750	51,000
Depreciation, Office Equipment	925	925	925	925	3,700
Taxes and Insurance	1,700	1,700	1,700	1,700	6,800
Total Fixed Selling and Administrative Expenses	$19,875	$19,875	$19,875	$19,875	$ 79,500
Total Selling and Administrative Expenses	$22,775	$28,575	$22,775	$31,475	$105,600

Exhibit 8. Cost of Goods Manufactured Budget

Hi-Flyer Company
Cost of Goods Manufactured Budget
For the Year Ended December 31, 20x1

			Sources of Data
Direct Materials Used			
Direct Materials Inventory, January 1, 20x1	$ 1,200		Exhibit 4, Note 4
Purchases for 20x1	45,550		Exhibit 4
Cost of Direct Materials Available for Use	$46,750		
Less Direct Materials Inventory, December 31, 20x1	1,500		Exhibit 4, Note 4
Cost of Direct Materials Used		$ 45,250	
Direct Labor Costs		54,300	Exhibit 5
Manufacturing Overhead Costs		169,225	Exhibit 6
Total Manufacturing Costs		$268,775	
Work-in-Process Inventory, January 1, 20x1*		—	
Less Work-in-Process Inventory, December 31, 20x1*		—	
Cost of Goods Manufactured		$268,775	

*It is a company policy to have no units in process at the beginning or end of the year.

Most manufacturing organizations anticipate some work in process at the beginning or end of the future period, although we assume that the Hi-Flyer Company has a policy of no work in process on January 1 or December 31 of any year. Exhibit 8 summarizes the costs of production for Hi-Flyer Company. The budgeted, or standard, product unit cost for one Hi-Flyer is rounded to $2.97 ($268,775 ÷ 90,500 units).

Budgeted Income Statement

Once the operating budgets have been prepared, the budget director or the controller can prepare the budgeted income statement for the period. A budgeted income statement projects an organization's net income based on the estimated revenues and expenses for a future period. Information about projected sales and costs comes from several operating budgets. Hi-Flyer Company's budgeted income statement for 20x1 is shown in Exhibit 9. Note that the right side of the exhibit identifies the sources of key elements so you can trace the statement's development. At this point, you can review the overall preparation of the operating budgets by comparing the preparation flow in Figure 2 to the schedules in Exhibits 2 through 9. You will notice that the budgeted cost of goods sold was included in the budgeted income statement instead of being shown as a separate schedule.

Exhibit 9. Budgeted Income Statement

Hi-Flyer Company
Budgeted Income Statement
For the Year Ended December 31, 20x1

			Sources of Data
Sales		$450,000	Exhibit 2
Cost of Goods Sold			
Finished Goods Inventory, January 1, 20x1*	$ 2,970		
Cost of Goods Manufactured	268,775		Exhibit 8
Total Cost of Goods Available for Sale	$271,745		
Less Finished Goods Inventory, December 31, 20x1*	4,455		
Cost of Goods Sold		267,290	
Gross Margin		$182,710	
Less Selling and Administrative Expenses		105,600	Exhibit 7
Income from Operations		$ 77,110	
Less Interest Expense (8% × $70,000)		5,600	
Income Before Income Taxes		$ 71,510	
Less Income Taxes Expense (30%)		21,453	
Net Income		$ 50,057	

*Finished goods inventory balances assume that product unit costs were the same in 20x0 and 20x1.

January 1	December 31	
1,000 units	1,500 units	(Exhibit 3)
× $2.97	× $2.97	(Exhibit 8)
$2,970	$4,455	

Capital Expenditures Budget

A capital expenditures budget is a detailed plan outlining the amount and timing of anticipated capital expenditures for a future period. Buying equipment, building a new store outlet, purchasing and installing a materials handling system, or acquiring another business are examples of capital expenditure decisions that require a capital expenditures budget. Budgeting for capital expenditures decisions is discussed in another chapter. In our illustration, Hi-Flyer Company plans to purchase a new extrusion machine for $30,000. The company will pay $15,000 in the first quarter of 20x1, when the order is placed, and $15,000 in the second quarter of 20x1, when the equipment is received.

Cash Budgeting

OBJECTIVE 5

Prepare a cash budget

A cash budget is a projection of the cash receipts and cash payments for a future period. It summarizes the cash flow forecasts of planned transactions in all phases of a master budget. This information helps managers plan for short-term loans when the cash balance is low and for short-term investments when the cash balance is high. The elements of a cash budget can relate to operating, investing, or financing activities, as shown by the examples in Table 2.

The cash budget excludes some planned noncash transactions, such as depreciation expense, amortization expense, issuance and receipt of stock dividends, uncollectible accounts expense, and gains and losses on sales of assets. Some organizations also exclude deferred taxes and accrued interest.

Information about cash receipts comes from several sources, including the sales budget, cash collection records and trends, the budgeted income statement, the cash budgets from previous periods, and financial records of notes, stocks, and bonds. Information about cash payments comes from operating budgets, capital expenditures budgets, the previous year's financial statements, loan records, and the budgeted income statement. The accountant will convert credit sales to cash inflows and materials purchases to cash outflows and disclose those conversions on supporting schedules for the cash budget.

Table 2. Elements of a Cash Budget

Activities	Cash Receipts From	Cash Payments For
Operating	Cash sales Cash collections on credit sales	Purchases of direct materials Purchases of operating supplies Direct labor Manufacturing overhead expenses Selling expenses Administrative expenses
Investing	Sale of investments Sale of long-term assets Interest income from investments Cash dividends from investments	Purchase of investments Purchase of long-term assets
Financing	Loan proceeds Proceeds from sale of stock Proceeds from sale of bonds	Loan repayment Interest expense Cash dividends to stockholders

Exhibit 10. Schedule of Expected Cash Collections from Customers

Hi-Flyer Company
Schedule of Expected Cash Collections from Customers
For the Year Ended December 31, 20x1

	Quarter				
	1	2	3	4	Year
Accounts Receivable, Dec. 31, 20x0	$38,000	$ 10,000	—	—	$ 48,000
Cash Sales	10,000	30,000	$10,000	$ 40,000	90,000
Collections of Credit Sales					
First Quarter ($40,000)	24,000	12,000	4,000		40,000
Second Quarter ($120,000)		72,000	36,000	12,000	120,000
Third Quarter ($40,000)			24,000	12,000	36,000
Fourth Quarter ($160,000)				96,000	96,000
Total Cash to Be Collected from Customers	$72,000	$124,000	$74,000	$160,000	$430,000

Note 1: 20% of sales are cash sales, 80% are credit sales. Credit sales are collected as follows: 60% of all credit sales collected in quarter of sale, 30% collected in quarter following sale, 10% collected in second quarter following sale.

Note 2: The Accounts Receivable balance at December 31, 20x0, is $48,000, which is $8,000 from 20x0 third quarter sales [($100,000 × .80) × .10] and $40,000 from 20x0 fourth quarter sales [($125,000 × .80) × .40].

Note 3: The Accounts Receivable balance at December 31, 20x1, is $68,000, which is $4,000 from the third quarter's sales [($50,000 × .80) × .10] and $64,000 from the fourth quarter's sales [($200,000 × .80) × .40].

Preparing a Cash Budget In our illustration, the cash budget summarizes cash inflows and cash outflows for the four quarters of 20x1 and for the entire year. A useful format for the preparation of a cash budget is:

$$\begin{array}{ccccc} \text{Estimated} & & \text{Total} & \text{Total} & \text{Estimated} \\ \text{Ending} & = & \text{Estimated} & - \text{Estimated} & + \text{Beginning} \\ \text{Cash Balance} & & \text{Cash Receipts} & \text{Cash Payments} & \text{Cash Balance} \end{array}$$

Many organizations also need to prepare supporting schedules for cash inflows or cash outflows that fluctuate over time. For example, the Hi-Flyer Company expects to receive cash from cash sales and credit sales in 20x1. The projected collection of that cash is shown in Exhibit 10, the schedule of expected cash collections from customers. Cash sales will represent 20 percent of the current quarter's sales, and the remaining 80 percent of sales will be credit sales. Experience has shown that 60 percent of all credit sales are collected in the quarter of sale, 30 percent are collected in the quarter following sale, and 10 percent are collected in the second quarter following sale.

Exhibit 10 shows that in the first quarter of 20x1, Hi-Flyer Company will collect $38,000 of the $48,000 balance of accounts receivable at December 31, 20x0. The company will collect the remaining portion of the $48,000 balance ($10,000) in the second quarter of 20x1. The estimated ending balance of Accounts Receivable at December 31, 20x1, is $68,000, which is $4,000 from the third quarter's credit sales [($50,000 × .80) × .10] plus $64,000 from the fourth quarter's sales [($200,000 × .80) × .40]. The expected cash collections from this exhibit flow to the total cash receipts section of the cash budget.

Our illustration continues with the preparation of a schedule of expected cash payments for direct materials. To simplify the illustration, Hi-Flyer Company will

Exhibit 11. Schedule of Expected Cash Payments for Direct Materials

Hi-Flyer Company
Schedule of Expected Cash Payments for Direct Materials
For the Year Ended December 31, 20x1

	Quarter				
	1	2	3	4	Year
Accounts Payable, Dec. 31, 20x0	$4,200	—	—	—	$ 4,200
First Quarter ($7,600)	3,800	$ 3,800			7,600
Second Quarter ($12,500)		6,250	$ 6,250		12,500
Third Quarter ($8,950)			4,475	$ 4,475	8,950
Fourth Quarter ($16,500)				8,250	8,250
Total Cash Payments for Direct Materials	$8,000	$10,050	$10,725	$12,725	$41,500

Note 1: 50% of the direct materials purchases are paid in the quarter of purchase and 50% are paid in the following quarter.
Note 2: The Accounts Payable balance at December 31, 20x0, is $4,200, or 50% of the 20x0 fourth-quarter direct materials purchases of $8,400.
Note 3: The Accounts Payable balance at December 31, 20x1 is $8,250, or 50% of the fourth-quarter direct materials purchases of $16,500.

pay 50 percent of the invoices it receives in the quarter of purchase and the remaining 50 percent in the following quarter. The estimated ending balance of Accounts Payable at December 31, 20x1, is $8,250 (50 percent of the fourth-quarter direct materials purchases of $16,500). Exhibit 11 shows the schedule for 20x1, which supports the first line of the cash payments section of the cash budget.

The cash budget in Exhibit 12 lists the cash receipts and cash payments, as well as the cash increase or decrease for the period. The cash increase or decrease plus the period's beginning cash balance equals the ending cash balance for the period. In the example in Exhibit 12, you can see that the beginning cash balance for the first quarter was $20,000. This amount also represents the beginning cash balance for the year 20x1. In addition, notice that each quarter's budgeted ending cash balance becomes the next quarter's beginning cash balance. To assist you in following the development of this budget, the sources for all information are listed on the right side of the exhibit.

Many organizations maintain a minimum cash balance to cover unusual expenditures. If the ending cash balance on the cash budget falls below the minimum required cash level, short-term borrowing may be necessary during the year to cover planned cash payments. If the ending cash balance is significantly larger than the organization needs, the excess cash may be invested in short-term securities to generate additional income.

Let's examine the 20x1 cash budget for the Hi-Flyer Company presented in Exhibit 12. If we assume that management wants a minimum of $10,000 cash available at the end of each quarter, the balance at the end of the first quarter indicates a problem. Hi-Flyer's management has several options in managing the low cash balance for the first quarter. The organization can borrow cash to cover the first quarter's cash needs, delay purchase of the equipment until the second quarter, or reduce some of the operating expenses. On the other hand, the balance at the end of the fourth quarter may be excessively high, thus leading management to invest a portion of the idle cash in short-term securities.

Exhibit 12. Cash Budget

Hi-Flyer Company
Cash Budget
For the Year Ended December 31, 20x1

	Quarter 1	Quarter 2	Quarter 3	Quarter 4	Year	Sources of Data
Cash Receipts						
Expected Cash Collections from Customers	$ 72,000	$124,000	$74,000	$160,000	$430,000	Exhibit 10
Total Cash Receipts	$ 72,000	$124,000	$74,000	$160,000	$430,000	
Cash Payments						
Direct Materials	$ 8,000	$ 10,050	$10,725	$ 12,725	$ 41,500	Exhibit 11
Direct Labor	7,200	16,800	7,800	22,500	54,300	Exhibit 5
Indirect Materials	2,160	5,040	2,340	6,750	16,290	
Employee Benefits	2,880	6,720	3,120	9,000	21,720	
Inspection	1,080	2,520	1,170	3,375	8,145	
Maintenance and Repair	1,920	4,480	2,080	6,000	14,480	Exhibit 6
Utilities	3,600	8,400	3,900	11,250	27,150	
Supervision	9,000	9,000	9,000	9,000	36,000	
Maintenance and Repair	2,150	2,150	2,150	2,150	8,600	
Other Overhead Expenses	3,175	3,175	3,175	3,175	12,700	
Delivery Expenses	800	2,400	800	3,200	7,200	
Sales Commissions	1,000	3,000	1,000	4,000	9,000	
Accounting	700	2,100	700	2,800	6,300	
Other Administrative Expenses	400	1,200	400	1,600	3,600	Exhibit 7
Sales Salaries	4,500	4,500	4,500	4,500	18,000	
Executive Salaries	12,750	12,750	12,750	12,750	51,000	
Taxes and Insurance	1,700	1,700	1,700	1,700	6,800	
Capital Expenditures	15,000	15,000	—	—	30,000	Note 1
Interest Expense	1,400	1,400	1,400	1,400	5,600	Exhibit 9
Income Taxes	5,363	5,363	5,363	5,364	21,453	
Total Cash Payments	$ 84,778	$117,748	$74,073	$123,239	$399,838	
Cash Increase (Decrease)	$(12,778)	$ 6,252	$ (73)	$ 36,761	$ 30,162	
Beginning Cash Balance	20,000	7,222	13,474	13,401	20,000	
Ending Cash Balance	$ 7,222	$ 13,474	$13,401	$ 50,162	$ 50,162	

Note: A new extrusion machine costing $30,000 will be paid in two quarterly installments of $15,000 each in the first and second quarter of 20x1.

Budgeted Balance Sheet

OBJECTIVE 6
Prepare a budgeted balance sheet

The final step in developing the master budget is to prepare a budgeted balance sheet. A budgeted balance sheet projects the financial position of an organization for a future period. As shown in Figure 2, all budgeted information is used in this process. The budgeted balance sheet at December 31, 20x1, for the Hi-Flyer

Company is illustrated in Exhibit 13. To assist you in following the development of this statement, the sources of all information are listed on the right side of the exhibit and notes are included at the bottom.

Budget Implementation

When the master budget is completed, management must decide whether to accept the proposed master budget and the planned operating results it presents, or change the plans and revise the budget. Once the master budget has been accepted, it must be implemented.

Budget implementation is the responsibility of the budget director. Two elements discussed earlier—communication and support—determine the success of this process. Proper communication of expectations and targets to all key people in the organization is essential. All involved employees must know what is expected of them and must receive directions on how to achieve their goals. Equally important, top management must support the budgeting process and encourage implementation of the budget. The process will succeed only if middle- and lower-level managers can see that top management is truly interested in the outcome and willing to reward people for meeting the budget goals.

Responsibility Accounting

OBJECTIVE 7

Define responsibility accounting *and discuss its relation to responsibility centers*

Many organizations develop strategic plans that include the allocation of resources to areas of responsibility. For example, Chrysler Corp. allocates resources to its Eagle, Jeep, and Plymouth automotive divisions. The managers of those divisions will be responsible for revenue generation and cost management. In addition, those managers may also be given resources to invest in assets that will support the growth of the automotive division. Within each division, other managers are responsible for manufacturing subassemblies or assembling automobiles. The performance of all the managers is evaluated in terms of their ability to manage their areas of responsibility.

To assist in the strategic planning process, many organizations have established responsibility accounting systems. Responsibility accounting is an information system that (1) classifies financial data according to areas of responsibility in an organization and (2) reports each area's activities by including only the revenue and

BUSINESS BULLETIN: BUSINESS IN PRACTICE

Hexacomb Corporation and other companies use budgets in their "open-book management" system to motivate employees to achieve company goals. Hexacomb's "beat the budget" bonus system helps employees earn bonuses based on their plant's performance. Management consults with employees at each of the company's seven plants to develop an annual budget. Scorecards, which include an income statement, a balance sheet, and relevant nonfinancial measures, are distributed throughout the plants to track performance against budget. Managers and employees review the financial information each month and adjust operating activities, if necessary. If profits exceed the budgeted amount for the seven plants, half of the excess profits are placed into a bonus pool. Employees collect the bonus if their plant beats its budget.[3]

Exhibit 13. Budgeted Balance Sheet

Hi-Flyer Company
Budgeted Balance Sheet
For the Year Ended December 31, 20x1

Sources
of Data

Assets

Current Assets

Cash		$ 50,162	Exhibit 12
Accounts Receivable		68,000	Exhibit 10
Direct Materials Inventory		1,500	Exhibit 8
Work in Process Inventory		—	Exhibit 8, Note
Finished Goods Inventory		4,455	Exhibit 9, Note
Total Current Assets		$124,117	

Property, Plant, and Equipment

Land		$ 50,000	
Plant and Equipment	$200,000		Note 1
Less Accumulated Depreciation	45,000	155,000	Note 2
Total Property, Plant, and Equipment		205,000	
Total Assets		$329,117	

Liabilities

Current Liabilities

Accounts Payable		$ 8,250	Exhibit 11, Note 3
Total Current Liabilities		$ 8,250	

Long-Term Liabilities

Notes Payable		70,000	Note 3
Total Liabilities		$ 78,250	

Stockholders' Equity

Contributed Capital

Common Stock	$150,000		Note 4
Retained Earnings	100,867		Note 5
Total Stockholders' Equity		250,867	
Total Liabilities and Stockholders' Equity		$329,117	

Note 1: The Plant and Equipment balance includes the $30,000 equipment purchase.
Note 2: The Accumulated Depreciation balance includes the 20x1 depreciation expense totaling $27,840 for Machinery, Building, and Equipment ($11,240, $12,900, and $3,700, respectively).
Note 3: Management plans no change in the Notes Payable balance.
Note 4: Management plans no change in the Common Stock balance.
Note 5: The Retained Earnings balance at December 31 equals the beginning Retained Earnings balance plus the 20x1 projected net income ($50,810 and $50,057, respectively).

cost categories that the assigned manager can control. A responsibility center is an organizational unit whose manager has been assigned the responsibility of managing a portion of the organization's resources. The activity of a responsibility center dictates the extent of the manager's responsibility. If a responsibility center involves only costs, it is called a cost center. On the other hand, if a manager is responsible for both revenues and costs, and for the resulting profits, the department is called a profit center. Finally, an investment center is a responsibility center whose manager is responsible for profit generation and can, in addition, make significant decisions about the assets the center uses. In the case of Chrysler Corp., the Eagle, Jeep, and Plymouth divisions may be investment centers or profit centers, whereas a single assembly plant may be a cost center.

Organizational Structure and Reporting

A responsibility accounting system establishes a communications network within the organization that is ideal for gathering information about operations in the planning, executing, and reviewing stages of the management cycle. The system is used to prepare budgets by areas of responsibility and to report the actual results of each responsibility center. The report for a responsibility center includes only those cost and revenue items the manager of that center can control. This approach ensures that managers will not be held responsible for items they cannot control.

By examining a corporate organization chart and a series of related managerial reports, you can see how a responsibility accounting system works. Figure 5 shows a typical management hierarchy, with the three vice presidents reporting to the corporate president. In the figure, the sales and finance areas are condensed to emphasize the manufacturing area. The production managers of Divisions A and B report to the vice president of manufacturing. In Division B, the managers of the Stamping Department, Painting Department, and Assembly Department report to the division's production manager.

In a responsibility accounting system, operating reports for each level of management are tailored to individual needs. Because a responsibility accounting system provides a report for every manager and because lower-level managers report

BUSINESS BULLETIN: ETHICS IN PRACTICE

Managers need to develop a strong ethical culture within their organizations so that they can minimize unethical or illegal activities. Unethical behavior in organizations hurts business. As employee productivity and loyalty decrease, employee turnover and absenteeism increase. As a result the organization may project a poor image to customers, suppliers, and the community. A loss of faith and confidence in the organization becomes expensive. Organizations can spend as much as $5,000 per employee on efforts to control unethical behavior. So, how can managers influence the ethical culture of their organizations? They can:

- Develop a code of ethics that communicates the organization's ethical values.
- Increase employee awareness through training programs.
- Provide a process to guide employees when they are facing an ethical dilemma.
- Develop a process to promote, watch, and positively influence the ethical behavior of the organization's employees.
- Demonstrate ethical behavior personally.[4]

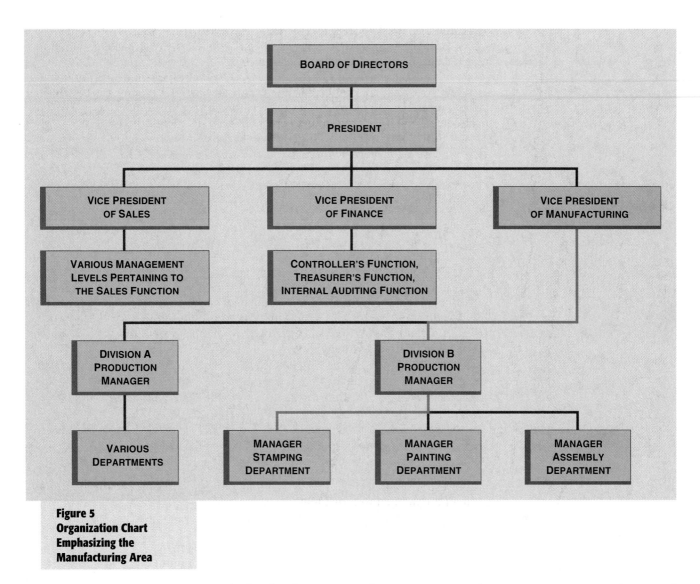

Figure 5
Organization Chart Emphasizing the Manufacturing Area

to higher-level managers, the same costs and revenues may appear in several reports. When lower-level operating data are included in higher-level reports, the data are summarized.

Based on the managerial hierarchy presented in Figure 5, Exhibit 14 illustrates how the responsibility reporting network is tied together. At the department level, the report lists cost items under the manager's control and compares expected (or budgeted) costs with actual costs. This comparison is a measure of operating performance. The manager who receives the report on the Stamping Department should be particularly concerned with direct materials costs and maintenance salaries, for they are significantly over budget. Also, the underutilization of small tools may signal problems with productivity in that department.

The production manager of Division B is responsible for the three operating departments plus controllable divisionwide costs. The production manager's report includes a summary of results from the Stamping Department as well as from the other areas of responsibility. At the division level, the report does not present detailed data for each department; only department totals appear. As shown in Exhibit 14, the data are even more condensed in the vice president's report. Only corporate and summarized divisional data about costs controllable by the vice president are included.

Exhibit 14. Reporting Within a Responsibility Accounting System

Manufacturing: Vice President   Monthly Report: November

Amount Budgeted	Controllable Cost	Actual Amount	Over (Under) Budget
$ 281,400	Central production scheduling	$ 298,100	$16,700
179,600	Office expenses	192,800	13,200
19,800	Operating expenses	26,200	6,400
339,500	Division A	348,900	9,400
→ 426,200	Division B	399,400	(26,800)
$1,246,500	Totals	$1,265,400	$18,900

Division B: Production Manager   Monthly Report: November

Amount Budgeted	Controllable Cost	Actual Amount	Over (Under) Budget
	Division expenses		
$101,800	Salaries	$ 96,600	($ 5,200)
39,600	Utilities	39,900	300
25,600	Insurance	21,650	(3,950)
	Departments		
→ 46,600	Stamping	48,450	1,850
69,900	Painting	64,700	(5,200)
142,700	Assembly	128,100	(14,600)
$426,200	Totals	$399,400	($26,800)

Stamping Department: Manager   Monthly Report: November

Amount Budgeted	Controllable Cost	Actual Amount	Over (Under) Budget
$22,500	Direct materials	$23,900	$1,400
14,900	Factory labor	15,200	300
2,600	Small tools	1,400	(1,200)
5,100	Maintenance salaries	6,000	900
1,000	Supplies	1,200	200
500	Other costs	750	250
$46,600	Totals	$48,450	$1,850

Chapter Review

REVIEW OF LEARNING OBJECTIVES

1. **Define *budgeting* and explain its role in the management cycle.** Budgeting is the process of identifying, gathering, summarizing, and communicating financial and nonfinancial information about future activities in an organization. Budgeting helps managers (1) relate the organization's long-term goals to short-term activities and distribute resources during the planning stage; (2) communicate expectations, motivate others, and coordinate activities during the executing stage; (3) evaluate performance and solve problems during the reviewing stage; and (4) communicate budget information, report the organization's financing, investing, and operating activities, and provide continuous feedback during the reporting stage of the management cycle.

2. **Explain the basic principles of budgeting.** Budgeting principles relate to (1) long-range goals and (2) short-range goals and strategies. Every organization needs to set long-range goals and convert them into plans for product or service offerings. The long-range goals must be restated in terms of short-range goals and strategies, which provide plans for the annual product or service offerings and associated profit plans. The budget development plans and timetable must also be set up.

3. **Describe the master budget process for different types of organizations, and list the guidelines for preparing budgets.** A master budget is a set of budgets that consolidate an organization's financial information into budgeted financial statements for a future period of time. A master budget includes a budgeted income statement supported by a set of operating budgets, a budgeted balance sheet, and a cash budget. The operating budgets (1) for a manufacturing organization include budgets for sales, production, direct materials purchases, direct labor, manufacturing overhead, and selling and administrative expenses; (2) for a retail organization include budgets for sales, merchandise purchases, and selling and administrative expenses; and (3) for a service organization include budgets for service revenue, labor, services overhead, and selling and administrative expenses. Preliminary planning involves knowing the purpose of the budget, the user group and their information needs, the sources of budget information, and the budget components.

4. **Prepare a budgeted income statement and supporting operating budgets.** The initial step in preparing a budgeted income statement is to prepare a sales budget. After preparing the sales budget, managers or accountants at a manufacturing organization prepare a production budget followed by budgets for direct materials purchases, direct labor, manufacturing overhead, selling and administrative expenses, cost of goods manufactured, and cost of goods sold. The information from these operating budgets supports the information on the budgeted income statement.

5. **Prepare a cash budget.** A cash budget is a projection of the cash receipts and cash payments for a future period. A cash budget summarizes the cash flow results of planned transactions for a future period. A cash budget discloses the organization's projected ending cash balance and shows a manager when short-term borrowing or investing may be appropriate.

   The preparation of a cash budget begins with the projection of all expected sources of cash. Next, all expected cash payments are found by analyzing all other operating budgets and the capital expenditures budget within the master budget. The difference between these two totals is the cash increase or decrease anticipated for the period. This total, combined with the period's beginning cash balance, yields the ending cash balance.

6. **Prepare a budgeted balance sheet.** The final step in the master budget process is to prepare a budgeted balance sheet for the company. All budgeted data are used in this process.

7. **Define *responsibility accounting* and discuss its relation to responsibility centers.** Responsibility accounting is an information reporting system that (1) classifies financial data according to areas of responsibility in an organization and (2) reports each area's activities by including only revenue and cost categories that the assigned manager can control. A responsibility accounting system personalizes accounting

reports. It is composed of a series of reports, one for each person with responsibility for cost control. Within a responsibility accounting system, a responsibility center is an organizational unit for which reports are prepared.

REVIEW OF CONCEPTS AND TERMINOLOGY

The following concepts and terms were introduced in this chapter:

LO 1 **Budget:** A plan of action that forecasts future transactions, activities, and events in financial or nonfinancial terms.

LO 6 **Budgeted balance sheet:** A statement that projects the financial position of an organization for a future period.

LO 4 **Budgeted income statement:** A statement that projects an organization's net income based on estimated revenues and expenses for a future period.

LO 1 **Budget information:** Quantifiable information about an organization's future activities and the revenues or expenses associated with those activities.

LO 1 **Budgeting:** The process of identifying, gathering, summarizing, and communicating financial and nonfinancial information about an organization's future activities.

LO 4 **Capital expenditures budget:** A detailed plan outlining the amount and timing of anticipated capital expenditures for a future period.

LO 5 **Cash budget:** A projection of the cash receipts and cash payments for a future period.

LO 7 **Cost center:** A responsibility center, such as a department or division, whose manager is responsible only for the costs incurred by that center.

LO 4 **Cost of goods manufactured budget:** A detailed schedule that summarizes the costs of production for a future period.

LO 4 **Direct labor budget:** A detailed schedule that identifies the direct labor needs for a future period and the labor costs associated with those needs.

LO 4 **Direct materials purchases budget:** A detailed schedule that identifies the purchases required for budgeted production and inventory needs and the costs associated with those needs.

LO 7 **Investment center:** A responsibility center whose manager is responsible for profit generation and can make significant decisions about the assets the center uses.

LO 4 **Manufacturing overhead budget:** A detailed schedule of anticipated manufacturing costs, other than direct materials and direct labor costs, that must be incurred to meet the production expectations of a future period.

LO 3 **Master budget:** A set of budgets that consolidate an organization's financial information into budgeted financial statements for a future period of time.

LO 4 **Production budget:** A detailed schedule that identifies the products or services that must be produced or provided to meet budgeted sales and inventory needs.

LO 7 **Profit center:** A responsibility center whose manager is responsible for revenues and costs and the resulting profits.

LO 7 **Responsibility accounting:** An information reporting system that (1) classifies financial data according to areas of responsibility in an organization and (2) reports each area's activities by including only the revenue and cost categories that the assigned manager can control.

LO 7 **Responsibility center:** An organizational unit whose manager has been assigned the responsibility of managing a portion of the organization's resources. This includes, but is not limited to, cost centers, profit centers, and investment centers.

LO 4 **Sales budget:** A detailed plan, expressed in both units and dollars, that identifies expected product (or service) sales for a future period.

LO 4 **Sales forecast:** A projection of sales demand based on an analysis of external and internal factors.

LO 4 **Selling and administrative expense budget:** A detailed plan of operating expenses, other than those of the production function, needed to support the sales and overall operations of the organization for a future period.

REVIEW PROBLEM

Cash Budget Preparation

LO 5   Pearce Information Processing Company provides word processing services for its clients. Pearce uses state-of-the-art equipment and employs five data entry personnel, who each average 160 hours of work a month. The following table sets out information developed by the budget officer.

| | Actual—20x0 | | Forecast—20x1 | | |
	November	December	January	February	March
Client billings (sales)	$25,000	$35,000	$25,000	$20,000	$40,000
Selling and administrative expenses	12,000	13,000	12,000	11,000	12,500
Operating supplies purchased	2,500	3,500	2,500	2,500	4,000
Processing overhead	3,200	3,500	3,000	2,500	3,500

The company has a bank loan of $12,000 at a 12 percent annual interest rate. Interest is paid monthly, and $2,000 of the principal of the loan is due on February 28, 20x1. No capital expenditures are anticipated for the first quarter of the coming year. Income taxes of $4,550 for calendar year 20x0 are due and payable on March 15, 20x1. The company's five employees earn $8.50 an hour, and all payroll-related labor benefit costs are included in processing overhead. For the items included in the table, assume the following conditions.

Client billings	60% are cash sales collected during the month of sale
	30% are collected in the first month following the sale
	10% are collected in the second month following the sale
Operating supplies	Paid for in the month purchased
Selling and administrative expenses and processing overhead	Paid in the month following the cost's incurrence

The beginning cash balance on January 1, 20x1, is expected to be $13,840.

REQUIRED   Prepare a monthly cash budget for Pearce Information Processing Company for the three-month period ending March 31, 20x1.

ANSWER TO REVIEW PROBLEM

Here is the three-month cash budget for Pearce Information Processing Company.

Pearce Information Processing Company
Monthly Cash Budget
For the Three-Month Period Ended March 31, 20x1

	January	February	March	Totals
Cash Receipts				
Client billings	$28,000	$23,000	$32,500	$83,500
Cash Payments				
Operating supplies	$ 2,500	$ 2,500	$ 4,000	$ 9,000
Direct labor	6,800	6,800	6,800	20,400
Selling and administrative expenses	13,000	12,000	11,000	36,000
Processing overhead	3,500	3,000	2,500	9,000
Interest expense	120	120	100	340
Loan payment	—	2,000	—	2,000
Income tax payment	—	—	4,550	4,550
Total cash payments	$25,920	$26,420	$28,950	$81,290
Cash Increase (Decrease)	$ 2,080	($ 3,420)	$ 3,550	$ 2,210
Beginning Cash Balance	13,840	15,920	12,500	13,840
Ending Cash Balance	$15,920	$12,500	$16,050	$16,050

Details supporting the individual computations within the cash budget are as follows:

	January	February	March
November	$ 2,500	—	—
December	10,500	$ 3,500	—
January	15,000	7,500	$ 2,500
February	—	12,000	6,000
March	—	—	24,000
	$28,000	$23,000	$32,500
Operating supplies			
All paid in the month purchased	$ 2,500	$ 2,500	$ 4,000
Direct labor			
5 employees × 160 hours a month × $8.50 an hour	6,800	6,800	6,800
Selling and administrative expenses			
Paid in the month following incurrence	13,000	12,000	11,000
Processing overhead			
Paid in the month following incurrence	3,500	3,000	2,500
Interest expense			
January and February = 1% of $12,000	120	120	
March = 1% of $10,000			100
Loan payment	—	2,000	—
Income tax payment	—	—	4,550

The ending cash balances of $15,920, $12,500, and $16,050 for January, February, and March 20x1, respectively, appear to be comfortable but not too large for the company.

Chapter Assignments

BUILDING YOUR KNOWLEDGE FOUNDATION

Questions

1. Define *budgeting*.
2. What is a budget? What type of information can be included in a budget?
3. Give examples of ways that budgeting can help managers during the planning stage of the management cycle.
4. Give examples of ways that budgeting can help managers during the executing stage of the management cycle.
5. Give examples of ways that budgeting can help managers during the reviewing stage of the management cycle.
6. Give examples of ways that budgeting can help managers during the reporting stage of the management cycle.
7. List three ways in which budget preparation contributes to an organization's success.
8. Distinguish between long-range plans and yearly operating plans.
9. What factors should influence the development of long-range goals?
10. What is the purpose of the following budgeting principle? "Restate the long-range plans in terms of short-range plans for products or services and a detailed profit plan."
11. Explain how budgets are developed once management has set short-range goals.
12. What is a master budget? What is its purpose?
13. In what ways are master budgets similar for manufacturing, retail, and service organizations?
14. Explain the differences between the master budget for a retail organization and the master budget for a service organization.
15. List the guidelines for the preparation of a budget.
16. What is a sales forecast? What are some factors that influence the estimation of future unit sales?
17. What are the three steps in preparing a direct materials purchases budget?
18. What are the two steps in preparing a direct labor budget?
19. List four items not found on a cash budget.
20. Define *responsibility accounting*.
21. Describe a responsibility accounting system.
22. How does a company's organizational structure affect its responsibility accounting system?
23. Compare and contrast a cost or expense center, a profit center, and an investment center.

Short Exercises

LO 1 *Budgeting and the Management Cycle*

SE 1. State whether each of the following management activities requiring the use of budget information is part of the planning stage (P), the executing stage (E), the reviewing stage (REV), or the reporting stage (REP) of the management cycle.

1. Coordinate the purchasing, production, selling, and shipping activities.
2. Select performance measures to monitor the timeliness of the shipping activities.
3. Calculate variances between the planned direct materials and the actual direct materials used in production last month.
4. Develop a budget to distribute the organization's resources to the various operating segments.
5. Prepare a report showing the performance of the production department for the last three months.

SE 2.
LO 1 *Manager's Budget Uses*

Jim Gray is the manager of a shoe department in a local discount department store. His supervisor has indicated that Jim's goal is to increase the number of pairs of shoes sold by 20 percent. The department sold 8,000 pairs of shoes last year. Two shoe salespersons currently work for Jim. What type of budgets should Jim use to help achieve his sales goal? What kinds of information should these budgets provide?

SE 3.
LO 1 *Budgetary Control*

Andrea Kral likes to analyze the results of her tree nursery operations by comparing the actual operating results with budgeted figures from the beginning of the year. If the business generates large profits, she often overlooks the differences between actual and budgeted data. But if profits are low, she spends many hours analyzing those differences. If you were Andrea, would you approach budgetary control in a similar manner? If not, what changes would you make to her approach?

SE 4.
LO 2 *Budgeting Principles*

The basic principles of budgeting have just been discussed with the dashboard assembly team at the Rockford Automobile Company. The team is participating in the company's budgeting process for the first time. One team member asked the controller to explain how the long-range goals principles relate to the short-range goals and strategies principles. How should the controller respond?

SE 5.
LO 3 *Master Budget Components*

The master budget is a compilation of many departmental or functional forecasts for the coming year or operating cycle. What is the most important forecast made in relation to the master budget? List the reasons for your answer. Which budgets must be prepared before you can develop a direct materials purchases budget?

SE 6.
LO 4 *Operating Budget Preparation*

Lockwood Company expects to sell 50,000 units of its product in the coming year. Each unit sells for $45. Sales brochures and supplies are expected to cost $7,000 for the year. Three sales representatives cover the southeast region. Their individual base salary is $20,000, and they earn a sales commission of 5 percent of the selling price of the units they sell. The sales representatives supply their own transportation, and they are reimbursed for travel at a rate of $.40 per mile. Based on the current year's mileage, the sales representatives are expected to drive a total of 75,000 miles next year. From the information provided, calculate the budgeted selling expenses for the coming year.

SE 7.
LO 5 *Operating Budget Preparation*

BK Insurance Co. specializes in term life insurance contracts. Cash collection experience shows that 20 percent of billed premiums are collected in the month prior to being due, 60 percent are paid in the month they are due, and 16 percent are paid in the month following their due date. Four percent of the billed premiums are paid late (in the second month following their due date) and include a 10 percent penalty payment. Total billing notices were: January, $58,000; February, $62,000; March, $66,000; April, $65,000; May, $60,000; and June, $62,000. How much cash does the company expect to collect in May?

SE 8.
LO 4 *Budgeted Gross Margin*

Operating budgets for the Constantine Company revealed the following information: net sales, $450,000; beginning direct materials inventory, $23,000; materials purchased, $185,000; beginning work in process inventory, $64,700; beginning finished goods inventory, $21,600; direct labor costs, $34,000; manufacturing overhead applied, $67,000; ending work in process inventory, $61,200; ending direct materials inventory, $18,700; and ending finished goods inventory, $16,300. Compute the company's budgeted gross margin.

SE 9.
LO 5 *Cash Budget*

The following direct materials purchase projections are for the Martinson Corp. Experience has shown that the company pays 60 percent of the purchases on account in the month of purchase and 40 percent in the month following the purchase. Prepare a schedule of expected cash payments for direct materials for the first quarter of 20x1.

	Purchases on Account	Cash Purchases
December 20x0	$40,000	$20,000
January 20x1	60,000	30,000
February 20x1	50,000	25,000
March 20x1	70,000	35,000

SE 10.
LO 6 *Budgeted Balance Sheet*

Shadow Corporation's budgeted data showed total projected assets for the coming year of $4,650,000. Total liabilities were expected to be $1,900,000. Common stock and retained earnings make up the entire stockholders' equity section of the balance sheet.

Common stock remains at its beginning balance of $1,500,000. The projected net income for the year is $349,600. What was the balance of retained earnings at the beginning of the budget period?

LO 7 *Identification of Controllable Costs*

SE 11. Bill Faries is the manager of the Paper Cutting Department in Division A of Warren Paper Products. From the following list, identify the costs that are controllable by Bill.

1. Salaries of cutting machine workers
2. Cost of cutting machine parts
3. Cost of electricity for Division A
4. Lumber Department hauling costs
5. Vice president's salary

LO 7 *Cost Centers, Profit Centers, and Investment Centers*

SE 12. Identify the following as a cost center, a profit center, or an investment center.

1. In business unit A, the manager is responsible for generating cash inflows and incurring costs with the goal of making the most money for the company. The manager has no responsibility for assets.
2. Business unit B produces a component that is not sold to an external party.

Exercises

LO 1 *Budgeting and the Management Cycle*

E 1. Joe Mee manages a golf and tennis resort. Indicate whether each of the following management activities requiring the use of budget information is part of the planning stage (P), the executing stage (E), the reviewing stage (REV), or the reporting stage (REP) of the management cycle.

1. Joe develops a budget to distribute limited resources to the Pro Shop, facilities maintenance, golf and tennis operations, hotel operations, and restaurant operations.
2. Joe challenges the employees to increase the volume of customers eating in the restaurant by 10 percent as set forth in the restaurant's budget.
3. Joe selects the number of golf lessons given each month as a measure of performance for the golf course operations.
4. After three months of operations, the resort's accountant prepares a performance report for the restaurant.
5. Joe analyzes the restaurant's performance report and finds that sales volume is 25 percent lower than planned.
6. Joe meets with restaurant managers and employees to discuss operations and surveys resort guests for one month. Based on his findings, Joe expands the number of food items offered on the menu, increases advertising for the restaurant, and replaces the cook.
7. Rita Baines, the manager of golf operations, uses the budgeted number of golf lessons to motivate the golf pros to provide more lessons. However, Rita notices that the quality of the golf lessons does not improve.
8. At the end of the month, Rita calculates the variance between the actual number of golf lessons given and the budgeted number of golf lessons. She finds that fewer lessons were given than originally planned.
9. Rita prepares a variance report and gives it to the golf pros for review.
10. Rita selects the number of hours of golf instruction as a new performance measure for the remainder of the year.

LO 1 *Budget Objectives*

E 2. You recently attended a workshop on budgeting and overheard the following comments as you moved to the refreshment table.

1. "Budgets look the same regardless of the size of an organization and the role of the budget process in management."
2. "Budgets can include financial or nonfinancial data. In our organization, we plan the number of hours to be worked and the number of customer contacts we want our salespeople to make."
3. "All budgets are complicated. You have to be an expert to prepare one."
4. "Budgets do not need to be highly accurate or very meaningful. No one stays within a budget in our organization."

Do you agree or disagree with each comment? Explain.

E 3.

LO 2 *Budgeting Principles*

The managers of Colorado Calendars, Inc., recently held a planning meeting to develop goals for the company. The company's success has been influenced by the managers' willingness to effectively follow budgeting principles. These principles include long-range goals and short-range goals and strategies. Identify the group of budgeting principles related to the following actions taken by the management team.

(long-range goals)
1. The management team considered economic and industry forecasts, employee-management relationships, and the structure and role of management in forecasting the next ten-year period.

(short-range goals)
2. Decisions were made about next year's sales and profit targets by calendar line and sales territory based on the forecast for the next ten years.

E 4.

LO 2 *Budgeting Principles*

Assume that you work in the accounting department of a small wholesale warehousing business. Inspired by a seminar on budgeting that she recently attended, the president wants to develop a budgeting system and has asked you to direct it.

State the points that you should communicate to the president about the initial steps in the budgeting process. Concentrate on principles related to long-range goals and short-range goals and strategies.

E 5.

LO 3 *Components of a Master Budget*

Identify the order in which the following budgets are prepared within the master budget process. Use the letters *a* through *g*, with the first budget to be prepared as *a*.

b 1. Production budget
d 2. Direct labor budget
c 3. Direct materials purchases budget
a 4. Sales budget
g 5. Budgeted balance sheet
f 6. Cash budget
e 7. Budgeted income statement

E 6.

LO 4 *Sales Budget Preparation*

Quarterly and annual sales for 20x1 for the Crosson Manufacturing Company are shown below.

Crosson Manufacturing Company
Actual Sales Revenue
For the Year Ended December 31, 20x1

Product Class	January–March	April–June	July–September	October–December	Annual Totals	Estimated 20x2 Percent Increases by Product Class
Marine Products	$ 44,500	$ 45,500	$ 48,200	$ 47,900	$ 186,100	10%
Mountain Products	36,900	32,600	34,100	37,200	140,800	5%
River Products	29,800	29,700	29,100	27,500	116,100	30%
Hiking Products	38,800	37,600	36,900	39,700	153,000	15%
Running Products	47,700	48,200	49,400	49,900	195,200	25%
Biking Products	65,400	65,900	66,600	67,300	265,200	20%
Totals	$263,100	$259,500	$264,300	$269,500	$1,056,400	

Prepare the 20x2 sales budget for the company. Show both quarterly and annual totals for each product class.

E 7.

LO 4 *Production Budget Preparation*

Ed Julius, the controller for the All-in-One Door Company, is preparing a production budget for 20xx. The company's policy is to maintain a finished goods inventory equal to one-half of the following month's sales. Complete the following production budget for the first quarter using the information provided. Budgeted sales for April are 7,000 doors.

	January	February	March
Desired sales in units	5,000	4,000	6,000
Desired ending finished goods inventory	2,000	?	?
Desired total units	7,000		
Less desired beginning finished goods inventory	2,500	?	?
Production needs	4,500	?	?

LO 4   *Direct Materials Purchases Budget*

E 8. The All-in-One Door Company manufactures garage door units. These units include hinges, door panels, and other hardware. Prepare a direct materials purchases budget for the first quarter of 20xx based on budgeted production of 16,000 garage door units. Ed Julius, the controller, has provided the following information.

Hinges	4 sets per door	$11.00 a set
Door panels	4 panels per door	$27.00 a panel
Other hardware	1 lock per door	$31.00 a lock
	1 handle per door	$22.50 a handle
	2 roller tracks per door	$16.00 for a set of 2 roller tracks
	8 rollers per door	$4.00 a roller

Assume no beginning or ending quantities of direct materials inventory.

LO 4   *Direct Labor Budget Preparation*

E 9. Whitmore Metals Company manufactures three products in a single plant with two departments: Cutting and Grinding. The company has estimated costs for products T, M, and B and is currently analyzing direct labor hour requirements for the budget year 20x1. The department data follow:

	Cutting	Grinding
Estimated Hours per Unit		
Product T	1.1	.5
Product M	.6	2.9
Product B	3.2	1.0
Hourly Labor Rate	$9	$7

Budgeted unit production in 20x1 is 21,000 of Product T, 36,000 of Product M, and 30,000 of Product B. Prepare a direct labor budget for 20x1 that shows the budgeted direct labor costs for each department and for the company as a whole.

LO 4   *Manufacturing Overhead Budget*

E 10. Denise Talley is chief financial officer of the London division of Talley Corporation, a multinational company operating with three divisions. As part of the budgeting process, Talley's staff is developing the manufacturing overhead budget for 20x1. The division estimates that 50,000 units will be manufactured during the year. The budgeted cost information follows:

	Variable Rate per Unit	Total Fixed Costs
Indirect Materials	$1.00	
Indirect Labor	4.00	
Supplies	.40	
Repairs and Maintenance	3.00	$ 40,000
Electricity	.10	20,000
Factory Supervision		180,000
Insurance		25,000
Property Taxes		35,000
Depreciation, Machinery		82,000
Depreciation, Building		72,000

From the data given, prepare the 20x1 manufacturing overhead budget for the division.

E 11.

LO 5 *Cash Budget Preparation—Revenues*

E 11. Magrone Car Care, Inc., is an automobile maintenance and repair organization with outlets throughout the midwestern United States. Judy McCullough, the budget director for the home office, is beginning to assemble next quarter's cash budget. Sales are projected as follows:

	On Account	Cash
October 20x1	$452,000	$196,800
November 20x1	590,000	214,000
December 20x1	720,500	218,400

McCullough's past collection results for sales on account indicate the following pattern.

Month of sale	40%
1st month following sale	30%
2nd month following sale	28%
Uncollectible	2%

Sales on account during the months of August and September were $346,000 and $395,000, respectively.

What are the purposes of preparing a cash budget? Compute the amount of cash to be collected from customers during each month of the last quarter.

LO 7 *Identification of Controllable Costs*

E 12. Contro Corporation produces computer equipment. Production has a three-tier management structure, as follows:

Vice president, production

Plant superintendent

Production supervisors

Identify each cost item below as variable (V), fixed (F), or mixed (M). Then identify the manager responsible for that cost.

1. Repair and maintenance costs
2. Materials handling costs
3. Direct labor
4. Supervisors' salaries
5. Maintenance of plant grounds
6. Depreciation, equipment
7. Plant superintendent's salary
8. Materials usage costs
9. Storage, finished goods inventory
10. Property taxes, plant
11. Depreciation, plant

Problems

LO 4 *Budget Preparation*

P 1. The main product of Cho Sun Enterprises, Inc., is a multipurpose hammer that carries a lifetime guarantee. The steps in the manufacturing process have been combined by using modern, automated equipment. A list of cost and production information for the Cho Sun hammer follows.

Direct materials
   Anodized steel: 2 kilograms per hammer at $1.60 per kilogram
   Leather strapping for the handle: .5 square meter per hammer at $4.40 per square meter
   (Packing materials are returned to the manufacturer and thus are not included as part of cost of goods sold.)
Direct labor
   Forging operation: $12.50 per labor hour; 6 minutes per hammer
   Leather-wrapping operation: $12.00 per direct labor hour; 12 minutes per hammer
Manufacturing overhead
   Forging operation: rate equals 70 percent of department's direct labor dollars
   Leather-wrapping operation: rate equals 50 percent of department's direct labor dollars

For the three months ending December 31, 20x1, Cho Sun's management expects to produce 54,000 hammers in October, 52,000 hammers in November, and 50,000 hammers in December.

Assume no beginning or ending balances of direct materials inventory or work in process inventory for the year.

1. For the three-month period ending December 31, 20x1, prepare monthly production cost information for the manufacture of the Cho Sun hammer. Classify the costs as direct materials, direct labor, or manufacturing overhead and show the computation methods used.
2. Prepare a cost of goods manufactured budget for the hammer. Show monthly cost data and combined totals for the quarter for each cost category.

P 2.
LO 4 *Comprehensive Budgeted Income Statement*

Bobby Blue began manufacturing operations for Blue's Bath Oils in 20x2. His biggest customer is a national retail store chain that sells hair and bath products. Mr. Blue would like an estimate of the company's income from operations for 20x2.

Calculate the company's income from operations by completing the following operating budgets and budgeted income statement for Blue's Bath Oils.

1. Sales Budget

Blue's Bath Oils
Sales Budget
For the Year Ended December 31, 20x2

	Quarter				
	1	2	3	4	Year
Sales in Units	4,000	3,000	5,000	5,000	17,000
× Selling Price per Unit	$ 5	?	?	?	?
Total Sales	$20,000	?	?	?	?

2. Production Budget

Blue's Bath Oils
Production Budget
For the Year Ended December 31, 20x2

	Quarter				
	1	2	3	4	Year
Sales in Units (Budget 1)	4,000	?	?	?	?
Add Desired Units of Ending Finished Goods Inventory	300	?	?	600	600
Desired Total Units	4,300				
Less Desired Units of Beginning Finished Goods Inventory	400	?	?	?	400
Total Production Units	3,900	?	?	?	?

Note 1: Desired units of ending finished goods inventory = 10% of *next* quarter's budgeted sales.
Note 2: Desired units of beginning finished goods inventory = 10% of *current* quarter's budgeted sales.

3. Direct Materials Purchases Budget

Blue's Bath Oils
Direct Materials Purchases Budget
For the Year Ended December 31, 20x2

	Quarter				
	1	2	3	4	Year
Total Production Units (Budget 2)	3,900	3,200	5,000	5,100	17,200
× 3 Ounces per Unit	3	?	?	?	?
Total Production Needs in Ounces	11,700	?	?	?	?
Add Desired Ounces of Ending Direct Materials Inventory	1,920	?	?	**3,600**	**3,600**
	13,620				
Less Desired Ounces of Beginning Direct Materials Inventory	**2,340**	?	?	?	**2,340**
Total Ounces of Direct Materials to be Purchased	11,280	?	?	?	
× Cost per Ounce	$ .10	?	?	?	?
Total Cost of Direct Materials Purchases	$ 1,128	?	?	?	?

Note 1: Desired ounces of ending direct materials inventory = 20% of *next* quarter's budgeted production needs in ounces.

Note 2: Desired ounces of beginning direct materials inventory = 20% of *current* quarter's budgeted production needs in ounces.

Note 3: Assume that budgeted production needs in ounces for the first quarter of 20x3 = 18,000 ounces.

4. Direct Labor Budget

Blue's Bath Oils
Direct Labor Budget
For the Year Ending December 31, 20x2

	Quarter				
	1	2	3	4	Year
Total Production Units (Budget 2)	3,900	?	?	?	?
× Direct Labor Hours per Unit	.1	?	?	?	?
Total Direct Labor Hours	390	?	?	?	?
× Direct Labor Cost per Hour	$ 7	?	?	?	?
Total Direct Labor Cost	$2,730	?	?	?	?

5. Manufacturing Overhead Budget

Blue's Bath Oils
Manufacturing Overhead Budget
For the Year Ended December 31, 20x2

| | Quarter | | | | |
	1	2	3	4	Year
Variable Overhead Costs					
Indirect Materials ($.05)	$ 195	?	?	?	?
Employee Benefits ($.25)	975	?	?	?	?
Inspection ($.10)	390	?	?	?	?
Maintenance and Repair ($.15)	585	?	?	?	?
Utilities ($.05)	195	?	?	?	?
Total Variable Overhead	$2,340	?	?	?	?
Fixed Overhead Costs					
Depreciation, Machinery	$ 500	?	?	?	?
Depreciation, Building	700	?	?	?	?
Supervision	1,800	?	?	?	?
Maintenance and Repair	400	?	?	?	?
Other Overhead Expenses	600	?	?	?	?
Total Fixed Overhead	$4,000	?	?	?	?
Total Manufacturing Overhead Costs	$6,340	?	?	?	?

6. Selling and Administrative Expense Budget

Blue's Bath Oils
Selling and Administrative Expense Budget
For the Year Ended December 31, 20x2

| | Quarter | | | | |
	1	2	3	4	Year
Variable Selling and Administrative Expenses					
Delivery Expenses ($.10)	$ 400	?	?	?	?
Sales Commissions ($.15)	600	?	?	?	?
Accounting ($.05)	200	?	?	?	?
Other Administrative Expenses ($.20)	800	?	?	?	?
Total Variable Selling and Administrative Expenses	$2,000	?	?	?	?
Fixed Selling and Administrative Expenses					
Sales Salaries	$5,000	?	?	?	?
Depreciation, Office Equipment	900	?	?	?	?
Taxes and Insurance	1,700	?	?	?	?
Total Fixed Selling and Administrative Expenses	$7,600	?	?	?	?
Total Selling and Administrative Expenses	$9,600	?	?	?	?

7. Cost of Goods Manufactured Budget

Blue's Bath Oils
Cost of Goods Manufactured Budget
For the Year Ended December 31, 20x2

Direct Materials Used		
Direct Materials Inventory, January 1, 20x2		
Purchases for 20x2	?	(Budget 3)
Cost of Materials Available for Use		
Less Direct Materials Inventory, December 31, 20x2	?	
Cost of Direct Materials Used		
Direct Labor Costs		(Budget 4)
Manufacturing Overhead Costs	?	(Budget 5)
Total Manufacturing Costs		
Work-in-Process Inventory, January 1, 20x2*		
Less Work-in-Process Inventory, December 31, 20x2*	?	
Cost of Goods Manufactured	?	

*It is a company policy to have no units in process at year end.

8. Budgeted Income Statement

Blue's Bath Oils
Budgeted Income Statement
For the Year Ended December 31, 20x2

Sales		
Cost of Goods Sold		
Finished Goods Inventory, January 1, 20x2		
Cost of Goods Manufactured	?	(Budget 7)
Cost of Goods Available for Sale		
Less Finished Goods Inventory, December 31, 20x2	?	
Cost of Goods Sold		?
Gross Margin		
Less Selling and Administrative Expenses		?	(Budget 6)
Income from Operations		?

LO 5   *Basic Cash Budget*

P 3. Produce Mart, Inc., is the creation of Leo Lynz. Lynz's dream was to develop the biggest produce store with the widest selection of fresh fruits and vegetables in the northern Illinois area. In three years, he accomplished his objective. Eighty percent of his business is conducted on credit with area retail enterprises, and 20 percent of the produce sold is to walk-in customers at his retail outlet on a cash only basis.

   Collection experience has shown that 50 percent of all credit sales are collected during the month of sale, 30 percent are received in the month following the sale, and 20 percent are collected in the second month after the sale. Lynz has asked you to prepare a cash budget for the quarter ending September 30, 20x3.

Operating data for the period are as follows: Total sales in May were $132,000, and in June, $135,000. Anticipated sales include July, $139,000; August, $152,500; and September, $168,500. Purchases for the quarter are expected to be $87,400 in July; $97,850 in August; and $111,450 in September. All purchases are for cash.

Other projected costs for the quarter include salaries and wages of $36,740 in July, $38,400 in August, and $40,600 in September; and monthly costs of $2,080 for heat, light, and power; $750 for bank collection fees; $3,850 for rent; $2,240 for supplies; $3,410 for depreciation of equipment; $2,570 for equipment repairs; and $950 for miscellaneous expenses. The corporation's cash balance at June 30, 20x3, was $5,490.

REQUIRED

1. Prepare a cash budget by month for the quarter ending September 30, 20x3.
2. Should Produce Mart, Inc., anticipate taking out a loan during the quarter? How much should be borrowed? When? (**Note:** Management has a $3,000 minimum monthly cash balance policy.)

P 4.

LO 4 *Budgeted Financial*
LO 6 *Statements*

The Bank of the West has asked the president of Montoya Products, Inc., for a budgeted income statement and budgeted balance sheet for the quarter ending June 30, 20x1. These documents will be used to support the company's request for a loan. A quarterly master budget is routinely prepared by the company, so the president indicated that the requested documents would be forwarded to the bank.

To date (April 2), the following operating budgets have been developed. Sales: April, $220,400, May, $164,220, and June, $165,980; direct materials purchases for the period, $96,840; direct materials usage, $102,710; direct labor expenses, $71,460; manufacturing overhead, $79,940; selling and administrative expenses, $143,740; capital expenditures, $125,000 (to be spent on June 29); cost of goods manufactured, $252,880; and cost of goods sold, $251,700.

Balance sheet account balances at March 31, 20x1 were: Cash, $28,770; Accounts Receivable, $26,500; Direct Materials Inventory, $23,910; Work in Process Inventory, $31,620; Finished Goods Inventory, $36,220; Prepaid Expenses, $7,200; Plant, Furniture, and Fixtures, $498,600; Accumulated Depreciation, Plant, Furniture, and Fixtures, $141,162; Patents, $90,600; Accounts Payable, $39,600; Notes Payable, $105,500; Common Stock, $250,000; and Retained Earnings, $207,158.

Monthly cash balances for the quarter are projected to be: April 30, $20,490; May 31, $35,610; and June 30, $45,400. During the quarter, accounts receivable are supposed to increase by 30 percent, patents will go up by $6,500, prepaid expenses will remain constant, accounts payable will go down by 10 percent, and the company will make a $5,000 payment on the note payable ($4,100 is principal reduction). The federal income tax rate is 34 percent and the second quarter's tax is paid in July. Depreciation for the quarter will be $6,420, which was already included in the manufacturing overhead budget. No dividends were paid.

REQUIRED

1. Prepare a budgeted income statement for the quarter ending June 30, 20x1. Round answers to the nearest dollar.
2. Prepare a budgeted balance sheet as of June 30, 20x1.

P 5.

LO 5 *Cash Budget*
Preparation:
Comprehensive

Black Hills Ski Resort, Inc., has been in business for twenty-two years. Although the skiing season is difficult to predict, the company operates under the assumption that all of its revenues will be generated during the first three months of the calendar year. Routine maintenance and repair work are done during the remaining nine-month period. The following projections for 20x2 were developed by Sandy Potts, the company budget director.

Cash Receipts

Lift tickets: January, 16,800 people @ $22; February, 17,400 people @ $23; and March, 17,800 people @ $24
Food sales: January, $62,000; February, $56,000; and March, $62,000
Skiing lessons: January, $158,000; February, $134,000; and March, $158,000
Equipment sales and rental: January, $592,000; February, $496,000; and March, $592,000
Liquor sales: January, $124,000; February, $92,000; and March, $104,000

Cash Payments

Salaries:
  Ski area:
    Lift operators: 12 people @ $2,500 per month for January, February, and March (first quarter)
    Instruction and equipment rental: 24 people @ $2,700 per month for first quarter
    Maintenance: $35,000 per month for first quarter, and a total of $96,000 for the rest of the year
  Customer service: Shuttle bus drivers, 10 people @ $1,400 per month for first quarter
  Medical: 8 people @ $6,400 per month for first quarter
  Food service: 24 people @ $1,800 per month for first quarter
Purchases:
  Food: $30,000 per month for the first quarter
  Ski equipment: Purchases of $340,000 in both January and February plus a $700,000 purchase anticipated in December 20x2
  Liquor: $50,000 in each month of the first quarter
  Tickets and supplies: $50,000 in January, $40,000 in February, and $80,000 in December 20x2
Advertising: $40,000 in January, $30,000 in February, and a total of $90,000 from April through the end of the year
Fire and liability insurance: January and June premium payments of $8,000
Medical facility costs: $15,000 per month during first quarter
Utilities: $5,000 per month for the first quarter and $1,000 per month for the rest of the year
Lift maintenance: $25,000 per month for the first quarter and $10,000 per month for the rest of the year
Property taxes: $180,000 due in June
Federal income taxes: 20x1 taxes of $364,000 due in March

The beginning cash balance for 20x2 is anticipated to be $10,000.

REQUIRED

Prepare a cash budget for Black Hills Ski Resort, Inc., for 20x2, using the following column headings.

Item	January	February	March	April–December	Year

Alternate Problems

LO 4
Budgeted Income Statement

P 6. Catie Burns is the budget director for Overland Spectaculars, Inc., a multinational company based in Maryland. Overland Spectaculars, Inc., organizes and coordinates art shows and auctions throughout the world. Budgeted and actual costs and expenses for 20x4 are compared in the following schedule.

Expense Item	20x4 Amounts Budget	Actual
Salaries expense, staging	$ 240,000	$ 256,400
Salaries expense, executive	190,000	223,600
Travel costs	320,000	326,010
Auctioneer services	270,000	224,910
Space rental costs	125,500	123,290
Printing costs	96,000	91,250
Advertising expense	84,500	91,640
Insurance, merchandise	42,400	38,650
Insurance, liability	32,000	33,550
Home office costs	104,600	109,940
Shipping costs	52,500	56,280
Miscellaneous	12,500	12,914
Total expenses	$1,570,000	$1,588,434
Net receipts	$3,100,000	$3,184,600

For 20x5, the following fixed costs have been budgeted: executive salaries, $220,000; advertising expense, $95,000; merchandise insurance, $40,000; and liability insurance, $34,000. Additional information follows.

a. Net receipts are expected to be $3,200,000 in 20x5.
b. Staging salaries will increase 20 percent over 20x4 actual figures.
c. Travel costs are expected to be 11 percent of net receipts.
d. Auctioneer services will be billed at 9.5 percent of net receipts.
e. Space rental costs will go up 20 percent from 20x4 budgeted amounts.
f. Printing costs are expected to be $95,000 in 20x5.
g. Home office costs are budgeted for $115,000 in 20x5.
h. Shipping costs are expected to rise 20 percent over 20x4 budgeted amounts.
i. Miscellaneous expenses for 20x5 will be budgeted at $14,000.

REQUIRED

1. Prepare the company's budgeted income statement for 20x5. Assume that only services are being sold and that there is no cost of sales. (Net receipts equal gross margin.) Use a 34 percent federal income tax rate.
2. Should the budget director be worried about the trend in the company's operations? Be specific.

P 7.

LO 5 *Basic Cash Budget*

Lisa Santelli is president of Tri-State Nurseries, Inc. This corporation has four locations and has been in business for six years. Each retail outlet offers over 300 varieties of plants and trees. James Ash, the controller, has been asked to prepare a cash budget for the Southern Division for the first quarter of 20x2.

Projected data supporting the budget are summarized as follows. Collection history for the accounts receivable has shown that 30 percent of all credit sales are collected in the month of sale, 60 percent in the month following the sale, and 8 percent in the second month following the sale. Two percent of the credit sales are uncollectible. Purchases are all paid for in the month following the purchase. As of December 31, 20x1 the Southern Division had a cash balance of $4,800.

Sales (60 percent on credit)		Purchases	
November 20x1	$ 80,000	December 20x1	$43,400
December 20x1	100,000	January 20x2	62,350
January 20x2	60,000	February 20x2	49,720
February 20x2	80,000	March 20x2	52,400
March 20x2	70,000		

Salaries and wages are projected to be $12,600 in January; $16,600 in February; and $10,600 in March. Monthly costs are estimated to be: utilities, $2,110; collection fees, $850; rent, $2,650; equipment depreciation, $2,720; supplies, $1,240; small tools, $1,570; and miscellaneous, $950.

REQUIRED

1. Prepare a cash budget by month for the Southern Division for first quarter 20x2.
2. Should Tri-State Nurseries, Inc., anticipate taking out a loan for the Southern Division during the quarter? How much should be borrowed? When? (**Note:** Management maintains a $3,000 minimum cash balance at each location.)

P 8.

LO 4 *Budgeted Financial*
LO 6 *Statements*

Voyager Video Company, Inc., produces and markets two popular video games, "Fifth Galaxy" and "Young Pathfinder." The company's closing balance sheet account balances for 20x0 are as follows: Cash, $18,735; Accounts Receivable, $19,900; Direct Materials Inventory, $18,510; Work in Process Inventory, $24,680; Finished Goods Inventory, $21,940; Prepaid Expenses, $3,420; Plant and Equipment, $262,800; Accumulated Depreciation, Plant and Equipment, $55,845; Other Assets, $9,480; Accounts Payable, $52,640; Mortgage Payable, $70,000; Common Stock, $90,000; and Retained Earnings, $110,980.

Operating budgets for the first quarter of 20x1 revealed the following: direct materials purchases, $58,100; direct materials usage, $62,400; direct labor expense, $42,880; manufacturing overhead, $51,910; selling expenses, $35,820; general and administrative expenses, $60,240; capital expenditures, $0; ending cash balances by month: January, $34,610; February, $60,190; March, $54,802; cost of goods manufactured, $163,990; and cost of goods sold, $165,440.

Sales per month are projected to be $125,200 for January, $105,100 for February, and $112,600 for March. Accounts receivable will double during the quarter, and accounts payable will decrease by 20 percent. Mortgage payments for the quarter will total $6,000, of which $2,000 is interest expense. Prepaid expenses are expected to go up by $20,000, and other assets are projected to increase 50 percent over the budget period. Depreciation for plant and equipment (already included in the manufacturing overhead budget) averages 5 percent of total Plant and Equipment per year. Federal income taxes (34 percent of profits) are payable in April. No dividends were paid.

REQUIRED

1. Prepare a budgeted income statement for the quarter ending March 31, 20x1.
2. Prepare a budgeted balance sheet as of March 31, 20x1.

EXPANDING YOUR CRITICAL THINKING, COMMUNICATION, AND INTERPERSONAL SKILLS

Skills Development

CONCEPTUAL ANALYSIS

SD 1.

LO 1 *The Budgeting Process*
LO 2
LO 3

Many organizations believe the budgeting process is wasteful and ineffective. Managers and employees can spend too much time focusing on budgeting mechanics rather than on strategic issues. They can also forget to review nonvalue-adding activities that waste resources. Finally, they may select budget information and use budget formats that fail to communicate the short-term business activities needed to achieve long-term goals. Place yourself in the role of a budget director for a company. Prepare a memorandum to the company's owner justifying the need for budgeting. Also suggest ways to make the budgeting process, the budget information, and the budgets themselves efficient, effective, and meaningful. (**Note:** For help in completing this assignment, look for the article written by Jeffrey A. Schmidt, "Is It Time to Replace Traditional Budgeting?" *Journal of Accountancy,* October 1992, pp. 103–107, located on the Needles Accounting Resource Center Web site at http://www.hmco.com/college/needles/home.html.)

Group Activity: Ask students to complete the assignment individually. Then have students work in groups to prepare (1) an argument justifying the use of budgeting and (2) a list of ways to make the budgeting process, the budget information, and the budgets efficient, effective, and meaningful. Select one person from each group to report the group's findings to the class.

ETHICAL DILEMMA

SD 2.

LO 2 *Ethical Considerations in*
LO 3 *the Budgeting Process*
LO 4

Gus Kamp is manager of the Repairs and Maintenance (R&M) Department, a cost center at *Phoenix Industries.* Mr. Kamp is responsible for preparing the annual budget for his department. For 20x2, he turned in the following budgeted information to the company's budget director. The 20x2 figures are 20 percent above the 20x1 budget figures. Most managers in the company inflate their budget numbers by at least 10 percent because their bonuses depend upon how much below budget they operate.

Cost Category	Budget 20x1	Actual 20x1	Budget 20x2
Supplies	$ 20,000	$ 16,000	$ 24,000
Labor	80,000	82,000	96,000
Utilities	8,500	8,000	10,200
Tools	12,500	9,000	15,000
Hand-carried equipment	25,000	16,400	30,000
Cleaning materials	4,600	4,200	5,520
Miscellaneous	2,000	2,100	2,400
Totals	$152,600	$137,700	$183,120

The director has questioned some of the numbers. Mr. Kamp defended them by saying that he expects a significant increase in repairs and maintenance activity in 20x2.

What are the real reasons for the increased budgeted data? What are the ethical considerations of this situation?

Communication	Critical Thinking	Group Activity	Memo	Ethics	International	Spreadsheet	Managerial Technology	Internet

RESEARCH ACTIVITY

LO 1
LO 2
SD 3.
The Budgeting Process

Managers of the HON Company and HON Industries use relevant operational information to prepare quarterly budgets for the next year. HON's Web site presents the actual results of some of the long-range and short-range plans that were originally included in company budgets. Prepare a short, typewritten report that includes a list of the historical or planned events, activities, or factors that would influence the information in the next period's budget for HON Industries. Conduct your research by reviewing the Decision Point in this chapter, the *Management Accounting* article on which the Decision Point is based, and/or the most recent Operations Review in the Investor Relations section of the HON Industries Web site (see the Needles Accounting Resource Center Web site at http://www.hmco.com/college/needles/home.html for access to these materials.)

DECISION-MAKING PRACTICE

LO 2
LO 3
LO 4
SD 4.
Effective Budgeting Procedures

During the past ten years, **Squizzero Enterprises** has practiced participative budgeting all the way from the maintenance personnel to the president's staff. Gradually, however, the objectives of honesty and decisions made in the best interest of the company as a whole have given way to division-benefiting decisions. Ralph Banerjee, the corporate controller, has asked Maggie Neff, the budget director, to carefully analyze this year's divisional budgets before incorporating them into the company's master budget.

The Motor Division was the first of six divisions to submit its 20x5 budget request to the corporate office. Its summary income statement and notes appear on the next page.

1. Recast the Motor Division's budgeted income statement into the following format (round percentages to two places):

	Budget–12/31/x4		Budget–12/31/x5	
Account	Amount	Percent of Sales	Amount	Percent of Sales

2. Actual results for 20x4 revealed the following information about revenues and cost of goods sold.

	Amount	Percent of Sales
Net Sales		
Radios	$ 780,000	43.94%
Appliances	640,000	36.06%
Telephones	280,000	15.77%
Miscellaneous	75,000	4.23%
Net Sales	$1,775,000	100.00%
Less Cost of Goods Sold	763,425	43.01%
Gross Margin	$1,011,575	56.99%

On the basis of this information and your analysis in **1,** what should the budget director say to the managers of the Motor Division? Mention specific areas of the budget that need to be revised.

Squizzero Enterprises
Motor Division
Budgeted Income Statement
For the Years Ended December 31, 20x4 and 20x5

	Budget 12/31/x4	Budget 12/31/x5	Increase (Decrease)
Net Sales			
Radios	$ 850,000	$ 910,000	$ 60,000
Appliances	680,000	740,000	60,000
Telephones	270,000	305,000	35,000
Miscellaneous	84,400	90,000	5,600
Net Sales	$1,884,400	$2,045,000	$160,600
Less Cost of Goods Sold	750,960	717,500[1]	(33,460)
Gross Margin	$1,133,440	$1,327,500	$194,060
Operating Expenses			
Wages			
Warehouse	$ 94,500	$ 102,250	$ 7,750
Purchasing	77,800	84,000	6,200
Delivery/Shipping	69,400	74,780	5,380
Maintenance	42,650	45,670	3,020
Salaries			
Supervisory	60,000	92,250	32,250
Executive	130,000	164,000	34,000
Purchases, Supplies	17,400	20,500	3,100
Merchandise Moving Equipment			
Maintenance	72,400	82,000	9,600
Depreciation	62,000	74,750[2]	12,750
Building Rent	96,000	102,500	6,500
Sales Commissions	188,440	204,500	16,060
Insurance			
Fire	12,670	20,500	7,830
Liability	18,200	20,500	2,300
Utilities	14,100	15,375	1,275
Taxes			
Property	16,600	18,450	1,850
Payroll	26,520	41,000	14,480
Miscellaneous	4,610	10,250	5,640
Total Operating Expenses	$1,003,290	$1,173,275	$169,985
Income from Operations	$ 130,150	$ 154,225	$ 24,075

1. Less expensive merchandise will be purchased in 20x5 to boost profits.
2. Depreciation is increased because of a need to buy additional equipment to handle increased sales.

Managerial Reporting and Analysis

INTERPRETING MANAGEMENT REPORTS

MRA 1.

LO 2 *Interpreting Budget Formulation Policies*

Husin Corporation is a manufacturing company with annual sales of $25,000,000. The controller, Victor Subroto, appointed Yolanda Alvillar as budget director. She created the following budget formulation policy based on a calendar-year accounting period.

May 20x2 Meeting of corporate officers and budget director to discuss corporate plans for 20x3.

June 20x2 Meeting(s) of division managers, department heads, and budget director to communicate 20x3 corporate objectives. At this time, relevant background data are distributed to all managers and a time schedule is established for development of 20x3 budget data.

July 20x2 Managers and department heads continue to develop budget data. Complete 20x3 monthly sales forecasts by product line and receive final sales estimates from sales vice president.

Aug. 20x2 Complete 20x3 monthly production activity and anticipated inventory level plans. Division managers and department heads should communicate preliminary budget figures to budget director for coordination and distribution to other operating areas.

Sept. 20x2 Development of preliminary 20x3 master budget. Revised budget data from all functional areas to be received. Budget director will coordinate staff activities, integrating labor requirements, direct materials and supplies requirements, unit cost estimates, cash requirements, and profit estimates, and prepare preliminary 20x3 master budget.

Oct. 20x2 Meeting with corporate officers to discuss preliminary 20x3 master budget; any corrections, additions, or deletions to be communicated to budget director by corporate officers; all authorized changes to be incorporated into the 20x3 master budget.

Nov. 20x2 Submit final draft of 20x3 master budget to corporate officers for approval. Publish approved budget and distribute to all corporate officers, division managers, and department heads.

REQUIRED

1. Comment on the proposed budget formulation policy.
2. What changes in the policy would you recommend?

FORMULATING MANAGEMENT REPORTS

MRA 2.

LO 2 *Budgeted Financial*
LO 3 *Statement Preparation*
LO 4

Assume that you have just signed a partnership agreement with your cousin Eddie to open a bookstore near the college campus. You believe that you will be able to provide excellent services at prices lower than your local competition. In order to begin operations, Eddie and you have decided to apply for a small business loan from the Small Business Administration (SBA). Part of the application requires that you submit financial statements that will forecast the bookstore's first two years of operating activity and its financial position at the end of the second year. The application is due within six weeks. Because of your expertise in accounting and business, Eddie has asked you to develop the budgeted financial statements.

REQUIRED

1. List the budgeted financial statements and supporting schedules you believe you must prepare. *2yr. cash budget, budgeted Inc. statement, budg. bal. sheet.*
2. Who needs the budgeted financial statements? *SBA*
3. Why are you preparing budgeted financial statements? *To get a loan.*
4. What information do you need to develop on the budgeted financial statements? How will you obtain the information?
5. When must you have the budgeted financial statements prepared? *6 weeks*
6. In what ways can Eddie and you use the budgeted financial statements that you have prepared?
   - planning & controlling activities
   - measuring management performance.

INTERNATIONAL COMPANY

MRA 3.
LO 5 *Goals and the Budgeting Process*

3M manufactures a variety of products ranging from office supplies to household sponges and laser imagers for CAT scanners to reflective materials for roads. Because of the company's aggressive research and development activities, many of these products have been redesigned to satisfy the needs of Asian customers. Business has been so successful that sales in the Asia-Pacific division of 3M have doubled in the past five years. Facilities are in Malaysia, South Korea, India, Thailand, and Taiwan.[5]

Based on 3M's strategic plan for next year, two goals for the Asia-Pacific division have been developed. These goals include a 25 percent growth in sales volume and construction of a $14 million manufacturing plant in Shanghai that will begin operations in the third quarter of the year.

REQUIRED

The manager for the Asia-Pacific division is preparing the cash budget for next year's operations. How would the budgeted cash receipts and cash payments on the cash budget be affected by these two goals?

EXCEL SPREADSHEET ANALYSIS

MRA 4.
LO 3
LO 4 *The Budgeting Process*

Refer to the Hi-Flyer Company's master budget presented in this chapter for the year ending December 31, 20x1. Skye King has decided to increase the budgeted sales in the first quarter by 5,000 units to reflect sales to a new customer in Canada. The expenses for this sale will include direct materials, direct labor, variable manufacturing overhead, and variable selling and administrative expenses. The delivery expense for the Canadian customer will be $.18 per unit rather than the regular $.08 per unit. The desired units of beginning finished goods inventory will remain at 1,000 units.

REQUIRED

Use the Excel spreadsheet of the exhibits found in the chapter and the changes stated above to complete the following:

1. Prepare a revised budgeted income statement and supporting operating budgets.
2. What was the change in income from operations? Would you recommend accepting the order? Why?

ENDNOTES

1. Ralph Drtina, Steve Hoeger, and John Schaub, "Continuous Budgeting at the HON Company," *Management Accounting,* Institute of Management Accountants, January 1996, pp. 20–24.
2. From, "Budgeting for an International Business," Paul V. Mannino and Ken Milani. *Management Accounting,* February, 1992, p. 39. Reprinted courtesy of the Institute of Management Accountants.
3. John Case, "Opening the Books," *Harvard Business Review,* March–April 1997, pp. 118–126.
4. Adapted from Larry Ponemon, "Building an Effective Business Ethics Process," *Management Accounting,* Institute of Management Accountants, June 1996, p. 16.
5. "3M: Business Booms in Asia," *Asian Business,* Vol. 29, No. 22, February 1993, pp. 9–10.

CHAPTER 8

Cost Control Using Standard Costing and Variance Analysis

1. Define *standard costs* and describe how managers use standard costs in the management cycle.
2. State the purposes for using standard costs.
3. Identify the six elements of, and compute, a standard unit cost.
4. Describe how to control costs through variance analysis.
5. Compute and analyze direct materials variances.
6. Compute and analyze direct labor variances.
7. Define and prepare a flexible budget.
8. Compute and analyze manufacturing overhead variances.
9. Explain how variances are used to evaluate managers' performance.

DECISION POINT

THE RUBICON GROUP

The Rubicon Group, of Oak Brook, Illinois, is an employee-owned consulting company that specializes in identifying computer hardware, software, and process-support solutions to business problems. It designs and installs comprehensive distribution, financial, and manufacturing software systems. One of the company's specialties is cost control. As part of its service in this area, Rubicon provides clients with current and standard cost updates, a comprehensive cost worksheet package, a variance report tracking standard and actual costs, and a gross profit and price evaluation. For manufacturers, the cost control analysis looks at current and standard costs for machine setup, materials, labor, and variable and fixed manufacturing overhead. Rubicon's cost control system can track variances for making an individual part, specific routed parts, or all parts manufactured by a client company. The company's operating manual states that its cost control system "offers users both the tools and the flexibility to establish, analyze, and report the following financial management functions: standard cost generation, cost inquiries, and evaluation of cost changes."[1] How can these three functions aid management in controlling operating costs?

Creating a set of standard costs provides management with benchmarks to use in evaluating actual operating costs. They are targets for analyzing actual spending trends. Cost inquiries are used to continuously monitor market price and operating cost changes. If these changes are permanent, the changes are used to update standard costs. The evaluation of changes in costs provides management with information about the causes of variances. Once the cause of a variance is known, management can make decisions to correct any related operating problem.

Standard Costs in Today's Business Environment

OBJECTIVE 1

Define standard costs *and describe how managers use standard costs in the management cycle*

Standard costing is a budgetary control technique. In a standard costing system, standard costs for direct materials, direct labor, and manufacturing overhead flow through the inventory accounts and eventually into the Cost of Goods Sold account. Instead of using actual costs for product costing purposes, standard costs are used. Standard costs are realistically predetermined costs that are developed from analyses of both past operating costs, quantities, and times and future costs and operating conditions.

Once standard costs have been developed, managers use them as tools for cost planning and control. Figure 1 shows how standard costs are used during the management cycle. During the planning stage, after projected sales and production targets for the upcoming year are established, standard costs can be used to estimate costs for direct materials, direct labor, and variable manufacturing overhead. The estimated costs serve as goals for product costing. They can also be used in product distribution and pricing. Standard costs not only aid in the development of budgets, but they also serve as yardsticks for evaluating capital expenditures. If the price a vendor charges differs from the anticipated standard price, the manager should question the difference.

During the executing stage, dollar, time, and quantity standards are applied to the work being done. The reviewing stage occurs at the end of the accounting period—whether it be a week, a month, or a quarter. At that time, the actual costs incurred are compared with standard costs, and the difference is computed. The difference between a standard cost and an actual cost is called a variance. Variances provide measures of performance that can be used to control costs. The amount of a variance provides one measure of the significance of the variance. But managers should look beyond the amount of a variance and try to determine its cause or causes. By analyzing the causes of variances, managers can identify inefficient functions within departments or work cells and take action to improve them. Variances from standard costs can also be used to evaluate an individual manager's performance.

During the reporting stage, standard costs are used to report on operations and managerial performance. When a variance report is tailored to a manager's specific responsibilities, it will provide much useful information about how well operations are proceeding and how well the manager is controlling them.

Standard costing has traditionally been used to measure and evaluate operating performance in manufacturing settings. Today, standard costing can be applied by managers in service organizations such as Barnett Bank and Liberty Mutual Insurance Company. The only difference between using standard costs in a manufacturing company and in a service organization is that there are no direct materials costs in a service environment. But labor and overhead costs are very much a part of providing services and must be planned and controlled. Therefore, managers in service organizations can also use standard costs and measure performance through variance analysis.

In today's globally competitive manufacturing environment, managers use new approaches to performance evaluation. Instead of concentrating exclusively on production efficiency and cost control, they are also concerned with reducing processing time and improving quality, customer satisfaction, and the number of on-time

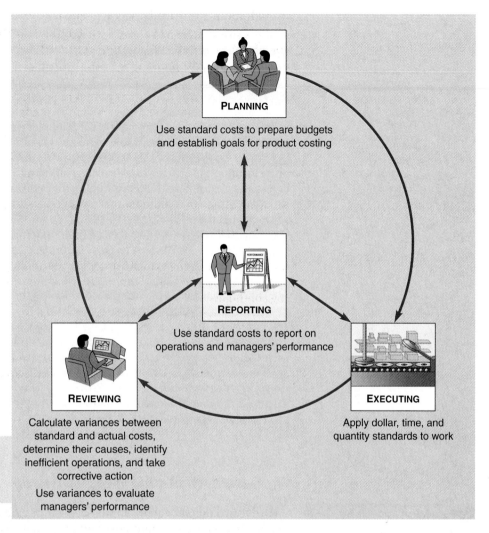

Figure 1
Standard Costing, Variance Analysis, and the Management Cycle

PLANNING

Use standard costs to prepare budgets and establish goals for product costing

REPORTING

Use standard costs to report on operations and managers' performance

EXECUTING

Apply dollar, time, and quantity standards to work

REVIEWING

Calculate variances between standard and actual costs, determine their causes, identify inefficient operations, and take corrective action

Use variances to evaluate managers' performance

deliveries. This approach requires new measures of performance that track processing time, quality, customer responses, and delivery results. The importance of labor-related standard costs and variances has been reduced because direct labor costs have dropped significantly. However, standard costs and variance analysis are still very much in use for direct materials and manufacturing overhead.

The Nature and Purpose of Standard Costing

OBJECTIVE 2

State the purposes for using standard costs

Accountants do not build a full cost accounting system from standard costs alone. Standard costs are used with existing job order or process costing systems. When a company uses standard costs, all costs affecting the inventory accounts and the Cost of Goods Sold account are recorded using standard, or predetermined, costs rather than actual costs incurred. In this section, we examine the nature and purpose of standard costs—their components, their development, and their use in product costing. Later in the chapter we concentrate on their use in cost control and evaluating managers' performance.

Standard costs are predetermined costs for direct materials, direct labor, and manufacturing overhead. They are usually expressed as the cost per unit of finished product or process. Standard costs share two very important characteristics with predetermined overhead costs: both forecast the dollar amounts to be used in product costing, and both depend on projected costs for budgeted items. But that is where the similarity ends.

Standard costing focuses on *total* unit cost, which includes all three elements of manufacturing cost. The computation of standard costs is more detailed than that of predetermined overhead costs. Whereas predetermined overhead rates are usually based on past costs, standard costs are based on engineering estimates, forecasted demand, worker input, time and motion studies, and type and quality of direct materials. One drawback to standard costing is that it is expensive to use. Since a predetermined overhead rate provides some of the same data as a standard overhead rate, a company that cannot afford to add standard costing to its cost system should continue to use predetermined overhead rates.

Standard costing is a total cost concept. In a fully integrated standard costing system, standard costs replace all actual manufacturing costs. Accounts such as Direct Materials Inventory, Work in Process Inventory, Finished Goods Inventory, and Cost of Goods Sold are maintained and reported in terms of standard costs. All inventory balances are computed using standard unit costs. The management accountant keeps separate records of actual costs to compare what should have been spent (the standard costs) with the actual costs incurred.

There are, then, several reasons for introducing standard costs into a cost accounting system. They are useful in preparing operating budgets. They make it easier to pinpoint production costs that must be controlled and to evaluate the performance of managers and workers. They help in setting realistic prices, and they simplify procedures for valuing inventories and product costing. Although expensive to set up and maintain, a standard costing system can save a company money by helping to reduce waste and inefficiency.

The Development of Standard Costs

OBJECTIVE 3

Identify the six elements of, and compute, a standard unit cost

A standard unit cost for a manufactured product has six parts: (1) the direct materials price standard, (2) the direct materials quantity standard, (3) the direct labor time standard, (4) the direct labor rate standard, (5) the standard variable manufacturing overhead rate, and (6) the standard fixed manufacturing overhead rate. To develop a standard unit cost, we must identify and analyze each of these elements. For service organizations, only the last four apply because those organizations do not use raw materials or parts in their operations.

Standard Direct Materials Cost The standard direct materials cost is found by multiplying the standard price for direct materials by the standard quantity for direct materials. If the standard price for a certain item is $2.75 and a specific job calls for a standard quantity of 8 of the items, the standard direct materials cost for that job is $22.00 (8 × $2.75).

The direct materials price standard is a careful estimate of the cost of a specific direct material in the next accounting period. The purchasing agent is responsible for developing price standards for all direct materials. When estimating a direct materials price standard, the purchasing agent must take into account all possible price increases, changes in available quantities, and new sources of supply. The purchasing agent also makes the actual purchases.

The direct materials quantity standard is an estimate of the amount of direct materials to be used. It is influenced by product engineering specifications, the quality of direct materials, the age and productivity of machinery, and the quality and experience of the work force. Some scrap and waste may be unavoidable, so they are included in the estimate. Production managers or cost accountants usually establish and monitor direct materials quantity standards, although engineers, purchasing agents, and machine operators may contribute to the development of these standards.

Standard Direct Labor Cost   The standard direct labor cost for a product, task, or job order is calculated by multiplying the standard hours of direct labor by the standard wage for direct labor. If a product takes 1.5 standard direct labor hours to produce and the standard direct labor rate is $8.40 per hour, then the product's standard direct labor cost is $12.60 ($8.40 × 1.5).

The direct labor time standard is the expected time required for each department, machine, or process to complete the production of one unit or one batch of output. Current time and motion studies of workers and machines as well as past employee and machine performance are the basic input for the development of this standard. In many cases, standard time per unit is a small fraction of an hour. The direct labor time standard should be revised whenever a machine is replaced or the quality of the labor force changes. Meeting time standards is the responsibility of the department manager or supervisor.

Standard labor rates are fairly easy to develop because labor rates are either set by a labor contract or defined by the company. Direct labor rate standards are the hourly direct labor costs that are expected to prevail during the next accounting period for each function or job classification. Although rate ranges are established for each type of worker and rates vary within these ranges based on experience and length of service, an average standard rate is developed for each task. Even if the person actually making the product is paid more or less than the standard rate, the standard rate is used to calculate the standard direct labor cost.

Standard Manufacturing Overhead Cost   The standard manufacturing overhead cost is the sum of the estimates for variable and fixed manufacturing overhead costs in the next accounting period. It is based on standard rates computed in much the same way as the predetermined manufacturing overhead rate discussed earlier. One important difference, however, is that the standard manufacturing overhead rate is made up of two parts, one for variable costs and one for fixed costs. The reason for computing the standard variable and fixed manufacturing overhead rates separately is that different application bases are generally required. The standard variable manufacturing overhead rate is total budgeted variable manufacturing overhead costs divided by an expression of capacity, such as the expected number of standard machine hours or direct labor hours. (Other bases may be used if machine hours or direct labor hours are not good predictors (or drivers) of variable manufacturing overhead costs.) Using standard machine hours as the basis, the formula is:

$$\text{Standard Variable Manufacturing Overhead Rate} = \frac{\text{Total Budgeted Variable Manufacturing Overhead Costs}}{\text{Expected Number of Standard Machine Hours}}$$

The standard fixed manufacturing overhead rate is total budgeted fixed manufacturing overhead costs divided by an expression of capacity, usually normal capacity in terms of standard hours or units. The denominator is expressed in the same terms (direct labor hours, machine hours, and so forth) used to compute the variable manufacturing overhead rate. The formula is:

$$\text{Standard Fixed Manufacturing Overhead Rate} = \frac{\text{Total Budgeted Fixed Manufacturing Overhead Costs}}{\text{Normal Capacity in Terms of Standard Machine Hours}}$$

Using normal capacity as the application basis ensures that all fixed manufacturing overhead costs have been applied to units produced by the time normal capacity is reached.

Using Standards for Product Costing

Using standard costs eliminates the need to calculate unit costs from actual cost data every week or month or for each batch produced. Once standard costs are developed for direct materials, direct labor, and manufacturing overhead, a total standard unit cost can be computed at any time.

With standard cost elements, the following amounts are determined: (1) cost of purchased direct materials entered into Direct Materials Inventory, (2) cost of goods requisitioned out of Direct Materials Inventory and into Work in Process Inventory, (3) cost of direct labor charged to Work in Process Inventory, (4) cost of manufacturing overhead applied to Work in Process Inventory, (5) cost of goods completed and transferred to Finished Goods Inventory, and (6) cost of units sold and charged to Cost of Goods Sold. In other words, all transactions affecting the three inventory accounts and the Cost of Goods Sold account are expressed in terms of standard costs, no matter what the amount of actual costs incurred.

For example, Bokinski Industries, Inc., uses a standard costing system. Recently, the company updated the standards for its line of automatic pencils. New standards include the following: Direct materials price standards are $9.20 per square foot for casing materials and $2.25 for each movement mechanism. Direct materials quantity standards are .025 square foot of casing materials per pencil and one movement mechanism per pencil. Direct labor time standards are .01 hour per pencil for the Stamping Department and .05 hour per pencil for the Assembly Department. Direct labor rate standards are $8.00 per hour for the Stamping Department and $10.20 per hour for the Assembly Department. Standard manufacturing overhead rates are $12.00 per direct labor hour for the standard variable manufacturing overhead rate and $9.00 per direct labor hour for the standard fixed manufacturing overhead rate. The standard cost of making one automatic pencil would be computed as follows.

Direct materials costs	
Casing ($9.20 per sq. ft. $\times$ .025 sq. ft.)	$ .23
One movement mechanism	2.25
Direct labor costs	
Stamping Department (.01 hour per pencil $\times$ $8.00 per hour)	.08
Assembly Department (.05 hour per pencil $\times$ $10.20 per hour)	.51
Manufacturing overhead	
Variable manufacturing overhead (.06 hour per pencil $\times$ $12.00 per hour)	.72
Fixed manufacturing overhead (.06 hour per pencil $\times$ $9.00 per hour)	.54
Total standard cost of one automatic pencil	$4.33

Using Variance Analysis to Control Operations

OBJECTIVE 4

Describe how to control costs through variance analysis

Although a standard costing system can be useful in both cost planning and cost control, it has traditionally been associated primarily with cost control and the evaluation of operating performance. Managers of manufacturing operations, as well as those responsible for selling and service functions, constantly compare the costs of what was expected to happen with the costs of what did happen. By examining the differences—or variances—between standard and actual costs, managers can learn much valuable information.

Variance analysis is the process of computing the differences between standard (or budgeted) costs and actual costs and identifying the causes of those differences.

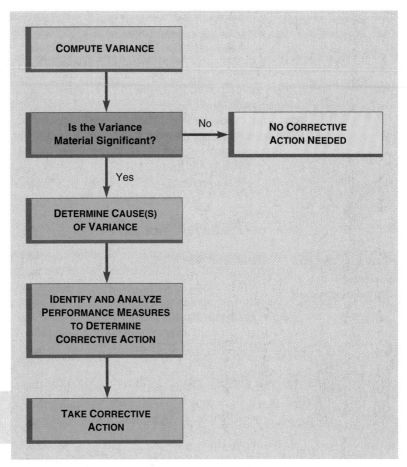

Figure 2
Using Variance Analysis to Control Costs

But just identifying the cause(s) of a variance does not necessarily solve the problem. Therefore we will also discuss some financial and nonfinancial performance measures that can be used to track the cause of a problem and suggest possible ways to correct it.

Several steps are needed to get to the root of a problem and to correct it. As shown in Figure 2, first you must compute the variance. If the variance is insignificant, actual operating results are close to anticipated operating conditions and no corrective action is needed. If the variance is significant, the management accountant analyzes it to identify its cause. Knowing the cause of a variance usually helps the accountant pinpoint the areas or activities that need to be monitored. The accountant then chooses the best performance measures to track those activities, analyzes the results, and determines the action needed to correct the problem. The final step is to take the required corrective action.

As we focus on the variances related to direct materials, direct labor, and manufacturing overhead, we will follow the process outlined in Figure 2. Computing the amount of the variance is important. But it is also important to remember that identifying the amount of a variance does nothing to prevent it from occurring again in the future. Managers need to know the cause of a variance. We will identify many examples of operating problems that might cause each of the variances to occur. Once the cause is known, specific performance measures can be identified and analyzed to help the manager determine the best solution to the problem so corrective action can be taken.

Computing and Analyzing Variances

Management accountants compute variances for whole cost categories, such as total direct materials costs, and for elements of that category, like the price of each direct material and the quantity of each direct material used. The more detailed an analysis is, the more effective it is in controlling costs. We will limit our analysis to six variances, two for each of the main cost elements of direct materials, direct labor, and manufacturing overhead. In practice, companies can use dozens of variances in many different types of activities to assist them in controlling and improving operating conditions.

Direct Materials Variances

OBJECTIVE 5

Compute and analyze direct materials variances

The total direct materials cost variance is the difference between the standard cost of direct materials and the actual cost incurred for those items. Let us assume, for example, that Ramos Company makes leather chairs. Each chair should use 4 yards of leather (standard quantity), and the standard price of leather is $6.00 per yard. During August, Ramos Company purchased 760 yards of leather costing $5.90 per yard and used the leather to produce 180 chairs. The total direct materials cost variance is calculated as follows:

Standard cost

Standard quantity × standard price	=
(180 chairs × 4 yards per chair) × $6.00 per yard	=
720 yards × $6.00 per yard	= $4,320

Less actual cost

Actual quantity × actual price	=
760 yards × $5.90 per yard	= 4,484
Total direct materials cost variance	$ 164 (U)

Here actual cost exceeds standard cost. The situation is unfavorable, as indicated by the *U* placed in parentheses after the dollar amount. An *F* designates a favorable situation.

To find the area or people responsible for the variance, the total direct materials cost variance must be broken down into two parts: the direct materials price variance and the direct materials quantity variance. The direct materials price variance is the difference between the standard price and the actual price, multiplied by the actual quantity purchased. For Ramos Company, the direct materials price variance is computed as follows:

Standard price	$6.00
Less actual price	5.90
Difference	$ .10 (F)

Direct Materials Price Variance = (Standard Price − Actual Price) × Actual Quantity
= $ .10 (F) × 760 yards
= $76 (F)

Because the direct materials purchased cost less than the standard cost, the variance is favorable.

The direct materials quantity variance is the difference between the standard quantity and the actual quantity used, multiplied by the standard price.

BUSINESS BULLETIN: **BUSINESS PRACTICE**

The globally competitive business environment has caused managers in many companies to revise their costing systems, in particular their standard costing systems. In traditional systems, variance analysis focused on the efficient use of direct materials and direct labor. Defects and product rework were expected, and their anticipated amounts were incorporated into the standards. Excess production that built inventories was not penalized. Today, tracking product quality and avoiding inventory buildups are major concerns. Consequently, revised standard costing systems track product quality and rates of production as well as the efficient use of resources. Quality variances are computed to indicate the production costs wasted on defective units. One approach to calculating a quality variance is as follows:

(Total Units Produced − Good Units Produced) × Standard Cost per Unit

Overproduction is also frowned on in the new global operating environment. To help track overproduction, a production variance can be computed as follows:

(Good Units Produced − Scheduled Units) × Standard Cost per Unit

The two new variances can be incorporated into an existing standard costing system to monitor product defects and prevent overproduction. Direct materials price and quantity variances and direct labor rate and efficiency variances are still necessary to help measure the efficiency of resource usage.[2]

Standard quantity (180 × 4 yards per chair)	720 yards
Less actual quantity	760 yards
Difference	40 yards (U)

$$
\begin{aligned}
\text{Direct Materials Quantity Variance} &= (\text{Standard Quantity} - \text{Actual Quantity}) \times \\
&\quad \text{Standard Price} \\
&= 40 \text{ yards (U)} \times \$6 \text{ per yard} \\
&= \$240 \text{ (U)}
\end{aligned}
$$

Because more direct material was used than prescribed, the direct materials quantity variance is unfavorable.

If the calculations are correct, the sum of the direct materials price variance and the direct materials quantity variance should equal the total direct materials cost variance.

Direct materials price variance	$ 76 (F)
Direct materials quantity variance	240 (U)
Total direct materials cost variance	$164 (U)

Sometimes cost relationships are easier to interpret in diagram form. Figure 3 illustrates the analysis just described. Notice that direct materials are purchased at actual cost but entered into the Direct Materials Inventory account at standard price; therefore, the direct materials price variance of $76 (F) is known when costs are entered into Direct Materials Inventory. As shown in Figure 3, the standard quantity times the standard price is the amount entered into the Work in Process Inventory account.

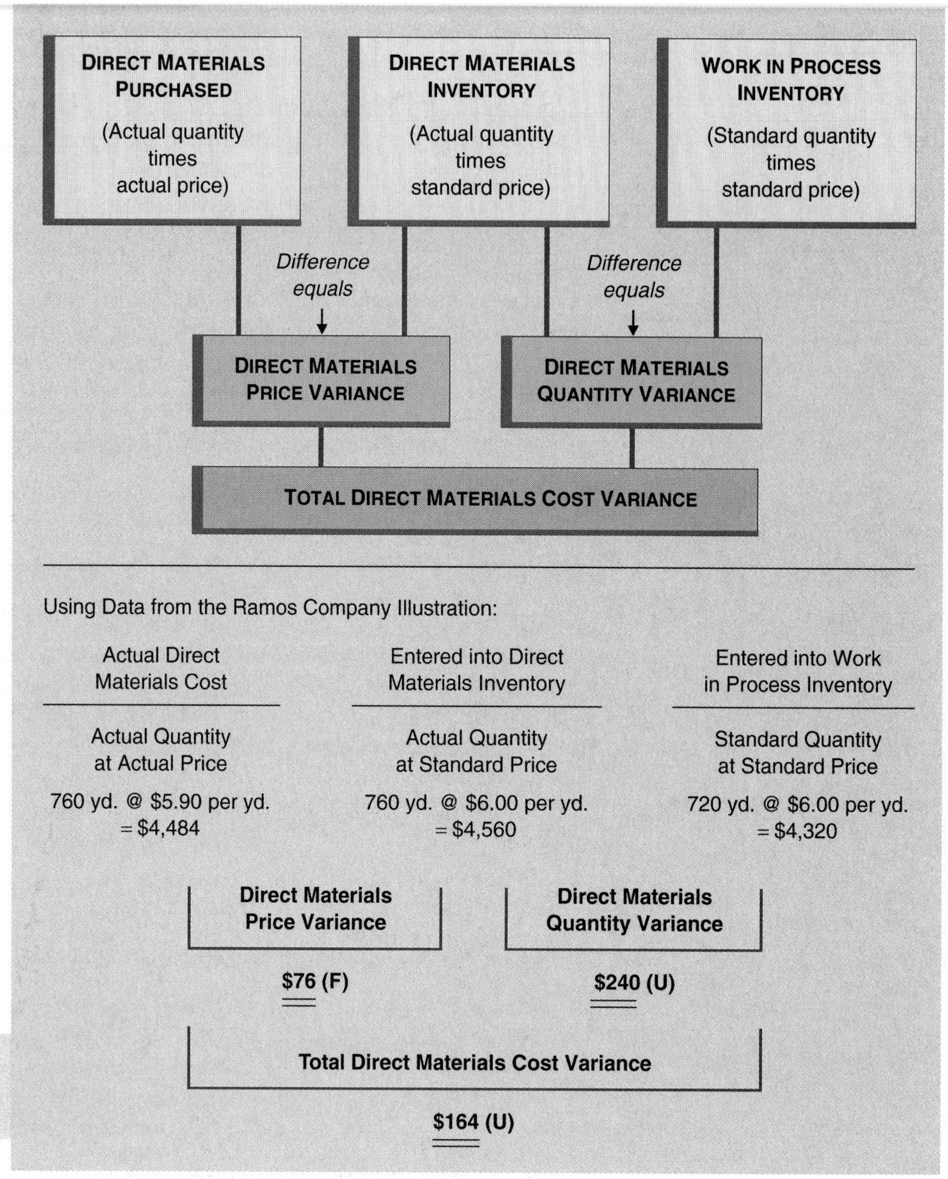

DIRECT MATERIALS PURCHASED	DIRECT MATERIALS INVENTORY	WORK IN PROCESS INVENTORY
(Actual quantity times actual price)	(Actual quantity times standard price)	(Standard quantity times standard price)

Difference equals → DIRECT MATERIALS PRICE VARIANCE

Difference equals → DIRECT MATERIALS QUANTITY VARIANCE

TOTAL DIRECT MATERIALS COST VARIANCE

Using Data from the Ramos Company Illustration:

Actual Direct Materials Cost	Entered into Direct Materials Inventory	Entered into Work in Process Inventory
Actual Quantity at Actual Price	Actual Quantity at Standard Price	Standard Quantity at Standard Price
760 yd. @ $5.90 per yd. = $4,484	760 yd. @ $6.00 per yd. = $4,560	720 yd. @ $6.00 per yd. = $4,320

Direct Materials Price Variance	Direct Materials Quantity Variance
$76 (F)	$240 (U)

Total Direct Materials Cost Variance

$164 (U)

Figure 3
Direct Materials
Variance Analysis

Taking Corrective Action—Ramos Company   Managers of the Ramos Company were concerned because the direct materials price variances and quantity variances had been occurring in the production of leather chairs for some time and because, as in our analysis, the price variances were always favorable and the quantity variances were always unfavorable. The purchasing manager had contacted vendors about possible price changes, but no changes had occurred. By tracking the purchasing activity for three months, the management accountant discovered that a lower grade of leather had been purchased at a reduced price. No authorization had been given to the purchasing agent for such a substitution. After a careful analysis, the manager of engineering determined that the substitute leather was not appropriate and that the company should return to purchasing the originally specified leather. Further analysis revealed that the unfavorable quantity variance was also caused by using the substitute leather. By tracking the purchasing activity, the managers at Ramos Company were able to solve the variance problem in the direct materials costs of producing leather chairs.

Direct Labor Variances

OBJECTIVE 6

Compute and analyze direct labor variances

The procedure for finding cost variances in direct labor parallels the procedure for finding variances in direct materials. The total direct labor cost variance is the difference between the standard direct labor cost for the good units produced and the actual direct labor costs incurred. (Good units are the total units produced less the units that are scrapped or need to be reworked.) At the Ramos Company, each chair requires 2.4 standard direct labor hours, and the standard direct labor rate is $8.50 per hour. During August, 450 direct labor hours were used to make 180 chairs at an average pay rate of $9.20 per hour. The total direct labor cost variance is computed below.

Standard cost
$$\text{Standard hours allowed} \times \text{standard rate} =$$
$$(180 \text{ chairs} \times 2.4 \text{ hours per chair}) \times \$8.50 \text{ per hour} =$$
$$432 \text{ hours} \times \$8.50 \text{ per hour} = \$3,672$$

Less actual cost
$$\text{Actual hours} \times \text{actual rate} = 450 \text{ hours} \times \$9.20 = \underline{4,140}$$

Total direct labor cost variance $\underline{\underline{\$\ 468}}$ (U)

Both the actual direct labor hours per chair and the actual direct labor rate varied from the standard. For effective performance evaluation, management must know how much of the total cost arose from differing direct labor rates and how much from varying direct labor hours. This information is found by computing the direct labor rate variance and the direct labor efficiency variance.

The direct labor rate variance is the difference between the standard direct labor rate and the actual direct labor rate, multiplied by the actual direct labor hours worked.

Standard rate	$8.50
Less actual rate	9.20
Difference	$ .70 (U)

$$\text{Direct Labor Rate Variance} = (\text{Standard Rate} - \text{Actual Rate}) \times \text{Actual Hours}$$
$$= \$.70 \text{ (U)} \times 450 \text{ hours}$$
$$= \underline{\underline{\$315}} \text{ (U)}$$

The direct labor efficiency variance is the difference between standard direct labor hours allowed for the good units produced and the actual direct labor hours worked, multiplied by the standard direct labor rate.

Standard hours allowed (180 chairs × 2.4 hours per chair)	432 hours
Less actual hours worked	450 hours
Difference	18 hours (U)

$$\text{Direct Labor Efficiency Variance} = (\text{Standard Hours Allowed} - \text{Actual Hours Worked})$$
$$\times \text{ Standard Rate}$$
$$= 18 \text{ hours (U)} \times \$8.50 \text{ per hour}$$
$$= \underline{\underline{\$153}} \text{ (U)}$$

The following check shows that the direct labor rate and efficiency variances have been computed correctly:

Direct labor rate variance	$315 (U)
Direct labor efficiency variance	153 (U)
Total direct labor cost variance	$468 (U)

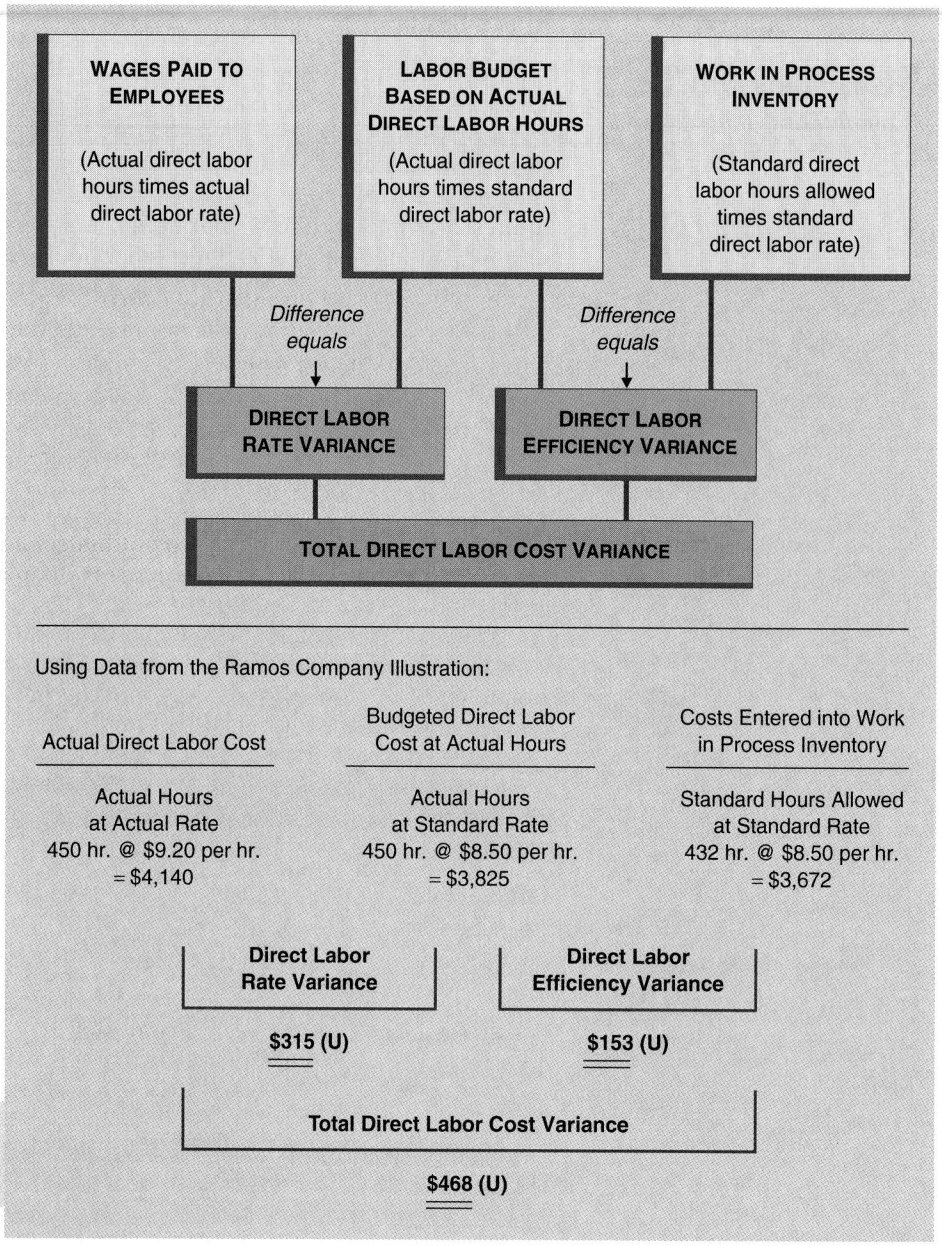

WAGES PAID TO EMPLOYEES (Actual direct labor hours times actual direct labor rate)	LABOR BUDGET BASED ON ACTUAL DIRECT LABOR HOURS (Actual direct labor hours times standard direct labor rate)	WORK IN PROCESS INVENTORY (Standard direct labor hours allowed times standard direct labor rate)

Difference equals ↓ **DIRECT LABOR RATE VARIANCE**

Difference equals ↓ **DIRECT LABOR EFFICIENCY VARIANCE**

TOTAL DIRECT LABOR COST VARIANCE

Using Data from the Ramos Company Illustration:

Actual Direct Labor Cost	Budgeted Direct Labor Cost at Actual Hours	Costs Entered into Work in Process Inventory
Actual Hours at Actual Rate 450 hr. @ $9.20 per hr. = $4,140	Actual Hours at Standard Rate 450 hr. @ $8.50 per hr. = $3,825	Standard Hours Allowed at Standard Rate 432 hr. @ $8.50 per hr. = $3,672

Direct Labor Rate Variance
$315 (U)

Direct Labor Efficiency Variance
$153 (U)

Total Direct Labor Cost Variance
$468 (U)

Figure 4
Direct Labor
Variance Analysis

Figure 4 summarizes the direct labor variance analysis. Unlike direct materials variances, the direct labor rate and efficiency variances are usually computed and recorded at the same time, because direct labor is not stored in an inventory account before use. Data from Ramos Company in the lower portion of Figure 4 illustrate this approach to direct labor variance analysis.

Taking Corrective Action—Ramos Company   Because both the direct labor rate variance and the direct labor efficiency variance were unfavorable, the management of the Ramos Company wanted to find out their causes. By analyzing employee time cards, it was discovered that a machine operator from another department had taken the place of a chair assembly worker who was ill. The machine operator made $9.20 per hour while the assembly worker earned the standard $8.50 per hour rate. When questioned about the unfavorable efficiency variance, the assembly supervisor identified two causes. First, the machine operator had to learn assembly skills on the job, so his assembly time was longer than the standard time per chair. Second, the materials handling people were partially to blame because they delivered parts late on five different occasions. Management decided to keep a close eye on the materials handling function by tracking delivery times and number of delays for the next three months. Once the new data are collected and analyzed, corrective action can be taken.

Manufacturing Overhead Variances

Controlling manufacturing overhead costs is more difficult than controlling direct materials and direct labor costs because the responsibility for manufacturing overhead costs is hard to assign. In addition, many types of both variable and fixed manufacturing overhead costs may contribute to variances from standard costs. Most fixed manufacturing overhead costs are not controlled by specific department managers, but if variable manufacturing overhead costs can be related to departments or activities, some control is possible.

Using a Flexible Budget   The type of budget a company uses strongly affects the accuracy of its manufacturing overhead variance analysis. The budgets discussed earlier were *static*, or fixed, budgets. They forecast revenues and expenses for one level of sales and production. The entire master budget is usually prepared for a single level of output, but many things can happen over a year's time that will cause actual output to differ from the estimated output. If a company produces more products than predicted, total production costs should also rise. In such a situation, comparing actual production costs with static budgeted amounts will automatically show large variances.

OBJECTIVE 7

Define and prepare a flexible budget

Exhibit 1 presents data for Bradford Industries, Inc. As you can see, actual costs exceed budgeted costs by $14,300, or 7.2 percent. Most managers would consider

Exhibit 1. Performance Analysis: Comparison of Actual and Budgeted Data

Bradford Industries, Inc.
Performance Report—Berwyn Division
For the Year Ended December 31, 20xx

Cost Category	Budget*	Actual†	Difference Under (Over) Budget
Direct materials	$ 42,000	$ 46,000	($ 4,000)
Direct labor	68,250	75,000	(6,750)
Manufacturing overhead			
Variable			
Indirect materials	10,500	11,500	(1,000)
Indirect labor	14,000	15,250	(1,250)
Utilities	7,000	7,600	(600)
Other	8,750	9,750	(1,000)
Fixed			
Supervisory salaries	19,000	18,500	500
Depreciation	15,000	15,000	—
Utilities	4,500	4,500	—
Other	10,900	11,100	(200)
Totals	$199,900	$214,200	($14,300)

*Budget based on expected productive output of 17,500 units.
†Actual cost of producing 19,100 units.

CHAPTER 8

Exhibit 2. Flexible Budget: Total Performance

Bradford Industries, Inc.
Flexible Budget—Berwyn Division
For the Year Ended December 31, 20xx

Cost Category	Units Produced 15,000	17,500	20,000	Variable Cost per Unit*
Direct materials	$ 36,000	$ 42,000	$ 48,000	$2.40
Direct labor	58,500	68,250	78,000	3.90
Variable manufacturing overhead				
Indirect materials	9,000	10,500	12,000	.60
Indirect labor	12,000	14,000	16,000	.80
Utilities	6,000	7,000	8,000	.40
Other	7,500	8,750	10,000	.50
Total variable costs	$129,000	$150,500	$172,000	$8.60
Fixed manufacturing overhead				
Supervisory salaries	$ 19,000	$ 19,000	$ 19,000	
Depreciation	15,000	15,000	15,000	
Utilities	4,500	4,500	4,500	
Other	10,900	10,900	10,900	
Total fixed manufacturing overhead costs	$ 49,400	$ 49,400	$ 49,400	
Total costs	$178,400	$199,900	$221,400	

Flexible budget formula:
Total budgeted costs = (variable cost per unit × number of units produced) +
   budgeted fixed costs = ($8.60 × units produced) + $49,400

Note: Activity expressed in units was used as the basis for this analysis. When units are used, direct material and direct labor costs are included in the analysis. Flexible budgets are commonly restricted to overhead costs. In such cases, machine hours or direct labor hours are used in place of units produced.
*Computed by dividing the dollar amount in any column by the respective level of activity.

such an overrun to be significant. But was there really a cost overrun? The budgeted amounts are based on an expected output of 17,500 units, but actual output was 19,100 units. Thus, the static budget for 17,500 units is inadequate for judging performance. Before analyzing the performance of the Berwyn Division, we must change the budgeted data to reflect an output of 19,100 units.

This can be accomplished by using a flexible budget. A flexible budget is a summary of expected costs for a *range* of activity levels, geared to changes in the level of productive output. Unlike a static budget, a flexible budget provides forecasted data that can be adjusted automatically for changes in the level of output. The flexible budget (also called a *variable budget*) is primarily a cost control tool used in evaluating performance.

Exhibit 2 presents a flexible budget for Bradford Industries, Inc., with budgeted data for 15,000, 17,500, and 20,000 units of output. The total cost of a variable cost item is found by multiplying the number of units produced by the variable cost for one unit of that item. For example, in the Berwyn Division, direct materials will cost $36,000 if 15,000 units are produced (15,000 units × $2.40). The important part of

Exhibit 3. Performance Report Using Flexible Budget Data

Bradford Industries, Inc.
Performance Report—Berwyn Division
For the Year Ended December 31, 20xx

Cost Category (Variable Unit Cost)	Budget Based on 19,100 Units Produced	Actual Costs of 19,100 Units	Difference Under (Over) Budget
Direct materials ($2.40)	$ 45,840	$ 46,000	($160)
Direct labor ($3.90)	74,490	75,000	(510)
Manufacturing overhead			
Variable			
Indirect materials ($.60)	11,460	11,500	(40)
Indirect labor ($.80)	15,280	15,250	30
Utilities ($.40)	7,640	7,600	40
Other ($.50)	9,550	9,750	(200)
Fixed			
Supervisory salaries	19,000	18,500	500
Depreciation	15,000	15,000	—
Utilities	4,500	4,500	—
Other	10,900	11,100	(200)
Totals	$213,660	$214,200	($540)

this illustration is the flexible budget formula shown at the bottom. The flexible budget formula is an equation that determines the correct budgeted cost for any level of productive activity. It consists of a per unit amount for variable costs and a total amount for fixed costs. In Exhibit 2, the $8.60 variable cost per unit is computed in the far right column, and the $49,400 is found in the fixed cost section of the analysis. Using this formula, you can draw up a budget for the Berwyn Division at any level of output.

Exhibit 3 shows a performance report prepared using the flexible budget data in Exhibit 2. Variable unit costs have been multiplied by 19,100 units to arrive at the total budgeted figures. Fixed overhead information has been carried over from the flexible budget developed in Exhibit 2. As the new performance report shows, costs exceeded budgeted amounts during the year by only $540, or less than three-tenths of one percent. In other words, when we use a flexible budget, we find that the performance of the Berwyn Division is almost on target.

At the Bradford Company, a flexible budget is used to analyze overall performance. At the Ramos Company, a flexible budget is used only to analyze manufacturing overhead costs. Exhibit 4 shows the Ramos Company's flexible budget for manufacturing overhead costs for the Chair Assembly Department. Whereas the Bradford Industries' flexible budget was based on units of output, the Ramos Company's budget uses direct labor hours as the expression of activity. Thus, in the Ramos budget, variable costs vary with the number of direct labor hours worked. Total fixed manufacturing overhead costs remain constant. The flexible budget formula in such cases is (variable costs per direct labor hour × number of direct labor hours) + budgeted fixed manufacturing overhead costs. As shown at the bottom of Exhibit 4, the specific flexible budget formula for the Ramos Company is ($5.75 × number of DLH) + $1,300.

Exhibit 4. Flexible Budget: Manufacturing Overhead Costs

Ramos Company
Flexible Budget—Manufacturing Overhead
Chair Assembly Department
For an Average One-Month Period

Cost Category	Direct Labor Hours (DLH)			Variable Cost per DLH
	300	400	500	
Budgeted variable manufacturing overhead				
Indirect materials	$ 450	$ 600	$ 750	$1.50
Indirect labor	600	800	1,000	2.00
Supplies	225	300	375	.75
Utilities	300	400	500	1.00
Other	150	200	250	.50
Total budgeted variable manufacturing overhead costs	$1,725	$2,300	$2,875	$5.75
Budgeted fixed manufacturing overhead				
Supervisory salaries	$ 600	$ 600	$ 600	
Depreciation	400	400	400	
Other	300	300	300	
Total budgeted fixed manufacturing overhead costs	$1,300	$1,300	$1,300	
Total budgeted manufacturing overhead costs	$3,025	$3,600	$4,175	

Flexible budget formula:

Total budgeted manufacturing overhead costs = (variable costs per direct labor hour × number of DLH) + budgeted fixed manufacturing overhead costs = ($5.75 × number of DLH) + $1,300

The flexible budget in Exhibit 4 shows overhead costs for 300, 400, and 500 direct labor hours. However, this month Ramos Company did not operate at exactly one of those activity levels. Instead, it operated at 432 direct labor hours. To find the total budgeted manufacturing overhead costs for the month, simply insert 432 direct labor hours in the flexible budget formula: ($5.75 × 432 DLH) + $1,300 = $3,784.

Analyzing Manufacturing Overhead Variances   Analyses of manufacturing overhead variances differ in degree of detail. The basic approach is to compute the total manufacturing overhead variance, which is the difference between the actual manufacturing overhead costs incurred and the standard manufacturing overhead costs applied to production using the standard variable and fixed manufacturing overhead rates. The total manufacturing overhead variance is then divided into two parts: the controllable manufacturing overhead variance and the manufacturing overhead volume variance.

OBJECTIVE 8

Compute and analyze manufacturing overhead variances

In our example, Ramos Company budgeted standard variable manufacturing overhead costs of $5.75 per direct labor hour plus $1,300 of fixed manufacturing overhead costs for the month of August (see the flexible budget formula). Normal capacity was set at 400 direct labor hours per month. The company incurred $4,100 of actual manufacturing overhead costs in August.

Before finding the manufacturing overhead variances, the total standard manufacturing overhead rate must be calculated. The total standard manufacturing overhead rate has two parts. One is the variable rate of $5.75 per direct labor hour. The other is the standard fixed manufacturing overhead rate, which is found by dividing budgeted fixed manufacturing overhead ($1,300) by normal capacity. The result is $3.25 per direct labor hour ($1,300 ÷ 400 hours). So, the total standard manufacturing overhead rate is $9.00 per direct labor hour ($5.75 + $3.25). The total budgeted fixed manufacturing overhead costs divided by normal capacity provides a rate that assigns fixed manufacturing overhead costs to products in a way that is consistent with expected output. The total manufacturing overhead variance is computed as follows:

Standard manufacturing overhead costs applied to good units produced		
$9.00 per direct labor hour × (180 chairs × 2.4 hr. per chair)		$3,888
Less actual manufacturing overhead costs incurred		4,100
Total manufacturing overhead variance		$ 212 (U)

This amount can be divided into two parts: the controllable manufacturing overhead variance and the manufacturing overhead volume variance. The controllable manufacturing overhead variance is the difference between the actual manufacturing overhead costs incurred and the manufacturing overhead costs budgeted for the level of production reached. Thus, the controllable manufacturing overhead variance for Ramos Company for August is as follows:

Budgeted manufacturing overhead (flexible budget) for 180 chairs:		
Variable manufacturing overhead cost for 432 direct labor hours (180 chairs × 2.4 hr. per chair) × $5.75 per direct labor hour	$2,484	
Budgeted fixed manufacturing overhead cost	1,300	
Total budgeted manufacturing overhead		$3,784
Less actual manufacturing overhead costs incurred		4,100
Controllable manufacturing overhead variance		$ 316 (U)

In this example, the controllable manufacturing overhead variance is unfavorable; the company spent more than had been budgeted.

The manufacturing overhead volume variance is the difference between the manufacturing overhead costs budgeted for the level of production achieved and the manufacturing overhead costs applied to production using the standard variable and fixed manufacturing overhead rates. Continuing with the Ramos Company example, we have the following:

Standard manufacturing overhead costs applied for 432 direct labor hours (180 chairs × 2.4 hr. per chair) × $9.00 per direct labor hour	$3,888
Less budgeted manufacturing overhead (see above)	3,784
Manufacturing overhead volume variance	$ 104 (F)

Checking the computations, we find that the two variances do equal the total manufacturing overhead variance.

Controllable manufacturing overhead variance	$316 (U)
Manufacturing overhead volume variance	104 (F)
Total manufacturing overhead variance	$212 (U)

Because the manufacturing overhead volume variance gauges the use of existing facilities and capacity, a volume variance will occur if more or less capacity than normal is used. In this example, 400 direct labor hours is considered normal use of facilities. Fixed manufacturing overhead costs are applied on the basis of standard hours allowed. So in the example, manufacturing overhead was applied on the basis of 432 hours, even though the fixed manufacturing overhead rate was computed using 400 hours (normal capacity). Thus, more fixed costs would be applied to products than were budgeted. Because the products can absorb no more than actual costs incurred, this level of production would tend to lower unit cost. Thus, when capacity exceeds the expected amount, the result is a favorable manufacturing overhead volume variance. When capacity does not meet the normal level, not all of the fixed manufacturing overhead costs will be applied to units produced. It is then necessary to add the amount of underapplied fixed manufacturing overhead to the cost of the good units produced, thereby increasing their unit cost. This condition is unfavorable.

Figure 5 summarizes the analysis of manufacturing overhead variance. As explained earlier, to determine the controllable manufacturing overhead variance, the management accountant subtracts the budgeted manufacturing overhead amount (using a flexible budget for the level of output achieved) from the actual manufacturing overhead costs incurred. A positive result means an unfavorable variance because actual costs were greater than budgeted costs. The controllable manufacturing overhead variance is favorable if the difference is negative. Subtracting total manufacturing overhead applied from budgeted manufacturing overhead at the level of output achieved yields the manufacturing overhead volume variance. Again, a positive result means an unfavorable variance; a negative result, a favorable variance. The data from the Ramos Company example are shown in the lower part of Figure 5. Carefully check the solution in the figure with that computed on the previous page.

Taking Corrective Action—Ramos Company   The manager of Ramos Company's Chair Assembly Department found that the unfavorable controllable variance of $316 was caused by higher than anticipated usage of indirect materials and the inefficient assembly skills of the borrowed machine operator. To obtain more specific information, the manager asked the management accountant to study the use of indirect materials over a period of three months.

The borrowed machine operator took 450 hours to do 432 standard hours of work, but the 432 standard hours were well above normal capacity of 400 direct labor hours. The overutilization of capacity resulted in a favorable volume variance of $104. The cause was traced to high seasonal demand for the product that pressed the company to use almost all of its capacity. Management decided not to do anything about the volume variance because it fell within a range that had been anticipated.

Manufacturing Overhead Variance Analysis in an Activity-Based Costing System

When organizations such as Ingersoll Milling Machine Co. and Saturn Automobile Co. adopt an activity-based costing system, costs are traced to activities within departments rather than accumulated for whole departments, as in a traditional costing system. Thus, if Department A has three activities, costs are accumulated separately for each of the three activities rather than for the department as a whole. The approach to variance analysis then changes to focus on the activities, not the department. Direct materials costs and direct labor costs are traced directly to an activity, just as if each activity were a department. From that point on, variance analyses of direct materials and direct labor costs for an activity are the same as they were in our previous discussion based on departments.

Activity-based costing changes the analysis of overhead variance in one very significant way: Each activity has a different cost driver, so the basis of the variance analysis changes from one activity to another. We no longer analyze overhead using a single measure, such as direct labor hours or machine hours, as an expression of capacity.

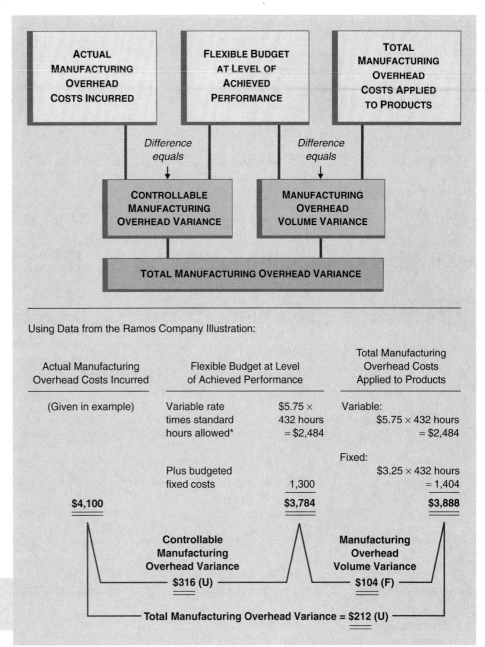

**Figure 5
Manufacturing Overhead
Variance Analysis**

* Standard hours allowed (achieved performance level) is computed by multiplying good units produced times required standard direct labor time per unit. The computation is as follows:

180 chairs produced x 2.4 hours per chair = 432 standard hours allowed

Figure 6 illustrates how overhead variance analysis changes when an organization uses an activity-based system. We still want to compute a controllable overhead variance and an overhead volume variance, but we now must compute those variances for each activity. Assume, as shown in Figure 6, that an organization has three activities: Setup Activity, Work Cell Activity, and Repairs and Maintenance Activity. The overhead variance analysis for the Setup Activity shown in Figure 6 is structured in the same way as the analysis shown in Figure 5, and it is very similar to that used to analyze the overhead variances of a department. The primary difference is the cost driver used in the analysis. Here the cost driver is the number of setup hours.

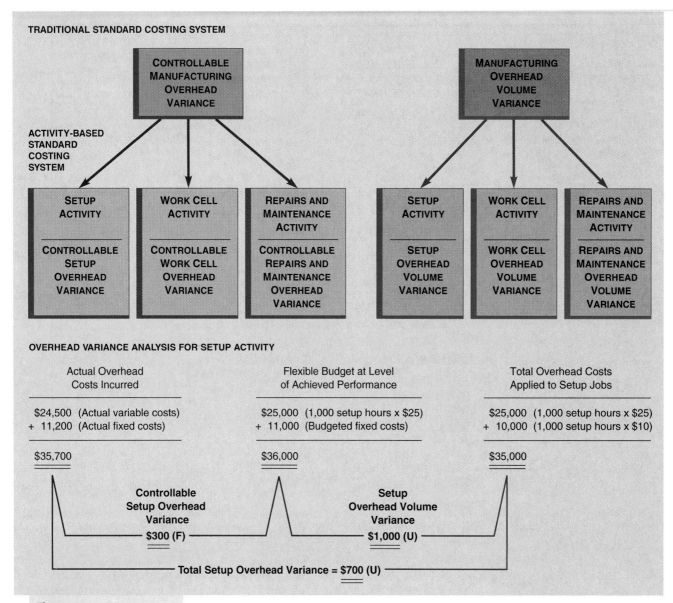

TRADITIONAL STANDARD COSTING SYSTEM

ACTIVITY-BASED STANDARD COSTING SYSTEM

OVERHEAD VARIANCE ANALYSIS FOR SETUP ACTIVITY

Actual Overhead Costs Incurred	Flexible Budget at Level of Achieved Performance	Total Overhead Costs Applied to Setup Jobs
$24,500 (Actual variable costs) + 11,200 (Actual fixed costs)	$25,000 (1,000 setup hours x $25) + 11,000 (Budgeted fixed costs)	$25,000 (1,000 setup hours x $25) + 10,000 (1,000 setup hours x $10)
$35,700	$36,000	$35,000

Controllable Setup Overhead Variance
$300 (F)

Setup Overhead Volume Variance
$1,000 (U)

Total Setup Overhead Variance = $700 (U)

Figure 6
Manufacturing Overhead Variance Analysis: Traditional Versus Activity-Based Standard Costing Systems

To analyze the controllable overhead variance and the overhead volume variance of the Setup Activity, you need to know the following information:

Actual variable overhead costs of the Setup Activity	$24,500
Actual fixed overhead costs of the Setup Activity	$11,200
Setup hours worked	1,000 hours
Total capacity of the Setup Activity in hours	1,100 hours
Budgeted fixed overhead costs	$11,000
Variable overhead rate for the Setup Activity	$25 per setup hour
Fixed overhead rate for the Setup Activity	$10 per setup hour

Using the same approach to overhead variance analysis discussed earlier, we determine that the controllable overhead variance for the Setup Activity is $300 (F), which is computed by subtracting $35,700 of actual overhead costs from the budgeted total of $36,000. It is favorable because the activity spent less than anticipated.

The overhead volume variance of $1,000 (U) occurred because the activity did not operate at full capacity. They failed to use 100 hours of setup labor, which resulted in $1,000 of underapplied fixed overhead (100 hours × $10 fixed overhead rate). A similar approach would be used to analyze overhead variances for the Work Cell Activity and the Repairs and Maintenance Activity. As mentioned earlier, a different cost driver would be used for each of those activities.

Using Variances in Performance Evaluation

OBJECTIVE 9

Explain how variances are used to evaluate managers' performance

The effective evaluation of managers' performance depends on both human factors and company policies. Using variances from standard costs in a manager's performance report adds accuracy to the evaluation process.

The human factor is the key to meeting corporate goals. People do the planning, people perform the operating processes, and people evaluate and are evaluated. To ensure effectiveness and fairness when setting up a performance evaluation process, management should develop appropriate policies and get direct input from managers and employees. More specifically, a company's management should establish policies and procedures for (1) preparing operational plans, (2) assigning responsibility for performance, (3) communicating operational plans to key personnel, (4) evaluating each area of responsibility, (5) identifying the causes of significant variances, and (6) taking corrective action to eliminate problems.

Variance analysis tends to pinpoint efficient and inefficient operating areas better than do basic comparisons of actual and budgeted data. Breaking down cost differences into more detailed variances helps to identify the causes for the differences. The key to preparing a performance report based on standard costs and related variances is to follow company policy by (1) identifying the personnel responsible for each significant variance, (2) determining the causes for each variance, and (3) developing a reporting format suited to the task. Performance reports should be tailored to each manager's responsibilities. They should be clear and accurate and should explain in detail why the department or activity met or did not meet operating expectations. Managers should be held accountable for only those cost areas under their control.

Exhibit 5 shows a performance report for the manager of Ramos Company's Chair Assembly Department. The report summarizes all of the cost data and variances for direct materials, direct labor, and manufacturing overhead. In addition, it identifies the causes of all of the variances and the corrective actions taken. This

Exhibit 5. Managerial Performance Report Using Variance Analysis

Ramos Company
Managerial Performance Report
Chair Assembly Department
For the Month Ended August 31, 20xx

Productivity Summary

Normal capacity (direct labor hours, or DLH)	400 DLH
Capacity performance level achieved (standard hours allowed)	432 DLH
Good units produced	180 chairs

Cost and Variance Analysis

	Standard Cost	Actual Cost Incurred	Total Variance	Variance Breakdown Amount	Type
Direct materials	$ 4,320	$ 4,484	$164 (U)	$ 76 (F)	Direct materials price variance
				240 (U)	Direct materials quantity variance
Direct labor	3,672	4,140	468 (U)	315 (U)	Direct labor rate variance
				153 (U)	Direct labor efficiency variance
Manufacturing overhead	3,888	4,100	212 (U)	316 (U)	Controllable manufacturing overhead variance
				104 (F)	Manufacturing overhead volume variance
Totals	$11,880	$12,724	$844 (U)	$844 (U)	

Causes of Variances

Direct materials price variance:
Substitute direct material purchased at reduced price

Direct materials quantity variance:
Poor quality of substitute direct material

Direct labor rate variance:
Machine operator replaced assembly worker

Direct labor efficiency variance:
Machine operator replaced assembly worker
Late delivery of parts to assembly floor

Controllable manufacturing overhead variance:
Indirect materials usage too high—caused by replacement worker's lack of skill

Manufacturing overhead volume variance:
High number of product orders caused by seasonal demand

Actions Taken

Substitute direct material not appropriate—returned to original direct material

Substitute direct material not appropriate—returned to original direct material

Temporary replacement—assembly worker ill

Temporary replacement—assembly worker ill
Material delivery times and number of delays being tracked

Study of indirect materials usage being conducted

No action necessary

report enables the plant superintendent to review the manager's actions and evaluate his or her performance. A point to remember is that the mere occurrence of a variance does not indicate poor performance. However, if a variance consistently occurs, if no cause is identified, and if no corrective action is taken, the manager may be suspected of poor performance. The report in Exhibit 5 suggests that the manager of the Chair Assembly Department has the operation under control because the causes of the variances have been identified and corrective actions have been taken.

Chapter Review

REVIEW OF LEARNING OBJECTIVES

1. **Define *standard costs* and describe how managers use standard costs in the management cycle.** Standard costs are realistically predetermined costs that are developed from analyses of both past costs, quantities, and times and future costs and operating conditions. In a standard costing system, standard costs for direct materials, direct labor, and manufacturing overhead flow through the inventory accounts and eventually into the Cost of Goods Sold account. Instead of using actual costs for product costing purposes, standard costs are used.

   Once standard costs have been developed, managers use them as tools for planning and budgeting. Once the projected sales and production unit targets for the upcoming year are established, planned costs for direct materials, direct labor, and variable manufacturing overhead can be computed using standard costs. The resulting costs serve as targets or goals for product costing. They can also be used in product distribution and pricing. At the end of an accounting period, actual costs incurred are compared with standard costs and the differences are computed. These differences, called variances, provide measures of performance that can be used to control costs.

2. **State the purposes for using standard costs.** Standard costs are predetermined costs for direct materials, direct labor, and manufacturing overhead that are usually expressed as a cost per unit of finished product. Standard costs are useful for preparing operating budgets and evaluating performance. They help in identifying production costs that require control, in establishing realistic prices, and in simplifying procedures for valuing inventories and product costing.

3. **Identify the six elements of, and compute, a standard unit cost.** The six elements of a standard unit cost are (1) the direct materials price standard, (2) the direct materials quantity standard, (3) the direct labor time standard, (4) the direct labor rate standard, (5) the standard variable manufacturing overhead rate, and (6) the standard fixed manufacturing overhead rate. The direct materials price standard is found by carefully considering expected price increases, changes in available quantities, and possible new sources of supply. The direct materials quantity standard expresses the expected quantity to be used. It is affected by product engineering specifications, the quality of direct materials, the age and productivity of the machines, and the quality and experience of the work force. The direct labor time standard is based on current time and motion studies of workers and machines and by past employee and machine performance. Labor union contracts and company personnel policies influence direct labor rate standards. Standard variable and fixed manufacturing overhead rates are found by dividing total budgeted variable and fixed manufacturing overhead costs by an appropriate application base.

   A product's total standard unit cost is computed by adding the following costs: (1) direct materials cost (equals direct materials price standard times direct materials quantity standard), (2) direct labor cost (equals direct labor time standard times direct labor rate standard), and (3) manufacturing overhead cost (equals standard variable and standard fixed manufacturing overhead rate times standard direct labor hours allowed per unit).

4. **Describe how to control costs through variance analysis.** A standard costing system has traditionally been associated with cost control activities and the evaluation of operating performance. Managers of manufacturing operations, as well as those responsible for selling and service functions, constantly compare the costs of what was expected to happen with the costs of what did happen. By examining the differences—or variances—between standard and actual costs, managers can learn much valuable information. Variance analysis is a four-step approach. The first step is to compute the variance. If the variance is insignificant, actual operating results are close to or equal to anticipated operating conditions and no corrective action is needed. If the variance is significant, the management accountant analyzes it to identify its cause (step 2). Knowing the cause of a problem or variance usually helps the accountant pinpoint the areas or activities that need to be monitored. Step 3 involves identifying the performance measures that track those activities. The final step is to take the approaches needed to correct the problem.

5. **Compute and analyze direct materials variances.** An analysis of the direct materials price and quantity variances helps to explain causes of differences between standard and actual direct materials costs. The direct materials price variance is computed by finding the difference between the standard price and the actual price per unit and multiplying it by the actual quantity purchased. The direct materials quantity variance is the difference between the standard quantity that should have been used and the actual quantity used, multiplied by the standard price.

6. **Compute and analyze direct labor variances.** Causes for the difference between standard direct labor costs and actual direct labor costs are identified by analyzing the direct labor rate and direct labor efficiency variances. The direct labor rate variance is computed by determining the difference between the standard labor rate and the actual labor rate and multiplying it by the actual labor hours worked. The direct labor efficiency variance is equal to the difference between the standard hours allowed for the number of good units produced and the actual hours worked, multiplied by the standard direct labor rate for the operation being analyzed.

7. **Define and prepare a flexible budget.** A flexible budget is a summary of anticipated costs for a range of activity levels, geared to changes in productive output. Variable, fixed, and total costs are given for several levels of capacity or output. From those data the management accountant derives the flexible budget formula. This formula, which can be applied to any level of productive output, allows management to evaluate the performance of individuals, departments, or processes.

8. **Compute and analyze manufacturing overhead variances.** The total manufacturing overhead variance is equal to the amount of under- or overapplied manufacturing overhead costs for the period. An analysis of the controllable manufacturing overhead variance and the manufacturing overhead volume variance will help to explain why the amount of manufacturing overhead applied to units produced differed from the manufacturing overhead costs incurred. The controllable manufacturing overhead variance is the difference between the actual manufacturing overhead costs incurred and the manufacturing overhead costs budgeted for the level of production achieved (based on the flexible budget). The manufacturing overhead volume variance is the difference between the manufacturing overhead budgeted for the level of production achieved and the total manufacturing overhead costs applied to production using the standard variable and fixed manufacturing overhead rates. When an organization adopts an activity-based costing system, costs are traced to activities within departments rather than accumulated for whole departments. If a department has three activities, costs are accumulated separately for each of the three activities rather than for the department as a whole. Direct materials costs and direct labor costs are traced to an activity, just as if the activity were a department. From that point on, variance analyses for those two costs follow the same approach as variance analyses for a department. Activity-based costing changes the analysis of overhead costs in one very significant way: Each activity has a different cost driver, so the basis of the variance analysis changes from one activity to another.

9. **Explain how variances are used to evaluate managers' performance.** The effective evaluation of managers' performance depends on both human factors and company policies. Using variances from standard costs in a manager's performance report adds accuracy to the evaluation process. To ensure effectiveness and fairness when

setting up a performance evaluation process, management should develop appropriate policies and get direct input from managers and employees. More specifically, a company's management should establish policies and procedures for (1) preparing operational plans, (2) assigning responsibility for performance, (3) communicating operational plans to key personnel, (4) evaluating each area of responsibility, (5) identifying the causes of significant variances, and (6) taking corrective action to eliminate problems.

The key to preparing a performance report based on standard costs and related variances is to follow company policy by (1) identifying the personnel responsible for each variance, (2) determining the causes for each variance, and (3) developing a reporting format suited to the task. Performance reports should be tailored to each manager's responsibilities.

REVIEW OF CONCEPTS AND TERMINOLOGY

The following concepts and terms were introduced in this chapter.

LO 8   **Controllable manufacturing overhead variance:** The difference between actual manufacturing overhead costs incurred and the manufacturing overhead costs budgeted for the level of production reached.

LO 6   **Direct labor efficiency variance:** The difference between standard direct labor hours allowed for the good units produced and actual direct labor hours worked, multiplied by the standard direct labor rate.

LO 3   **Direct labor rate standards:** The hourly direct labor costs that are expected to prevail during the next accounting period for each function or job classification.

LO 6   **Direct labor rate variance:** The difference between the standard direct labor rate and the actual direct labor rate, multiplied by the actual direct labor hours worked.

LO 3   **Direct labor time standard:** The expected time required for each department, machine, or process to complete production of one unit or one batch of output.

LO 3   **Direct materials price standard:** A careful estimate of the cost of a specific direct material in the next accounting period.

LO 5   **Direct materials price variance:** The difference between the standard price and the actual price, multiplied by the actual quantity purchased.

LO 3   **Direct materials quantity standard:** An estimate of the amount of direct materials to be used, influenced by product engineering specifications, quality of direct materials, age and productivity of machinery, and quality and experience of the work force.

LO 5   **Direct materials quantity variance:** The difference between the standard quantity and the actual quantity used, multiplied by the standard price.

LO 7   **Flexible budget:** A summary of expected costs for a range of activity levels, geared to changes in the level of productive output; also called *variable budget*.

LO 7   **Flexible budget formula:** An equation that determines the correct budgeted cost for any level of productive output.

LO 8   **Manufacturing overhead volume variance:** The difference between the manufacturing overhead costs budgeted for the level of production achieved and the manufacturing overhead costs applied to production using the standard variable and fixed manufacturing overhead rates.

LO 1   **Standard costs:** Realistically predetermined costs that are developed from analyses of both past operating costs, quantities, and times and future costs and operating conditions.

LO 3   **Standard direct labor cost:** The standard hours of direct labor multiplied by the standard wage for direct labor.

LO 3   **Standard direct materials cost:** The standard price for direct materials multiplied by the standard quantity for direct materials.

LO 3   **Standard fixed manufacturing overhead rate:** Total budgeted fixed manufacturing overhead costs divided by an expression of capacity, usually normal capacity in terms of standard hours or units.

LO 3 **Standard manufacturing overhead cost:** The sum of the estimates for variable and fixed manufacturing overhead costs in the next accounting period.

LO 3 **Standard variable manufacturing overhead rate:** Total budgeted variable manufacturing overhead costs divided by an expression of capacity, such as the expected number of standard machine hours or standard direct labor hours.

LO 6 **Total direct labor cost variance:** The difference between standard direct labor cost for the good units produced and the actual direct labor costs incurred.

LO 5 **Total direct materials cost variance:** The difference between the standard cost for direct materials and the actual cost incurred for those items.

LO 8 **Total manufacturing overhead variance:** The difference between the actual manufacturing overhead costs incurred and the standard manufacturing overhead costs applied to production using the standard variable and fixed manufacturing overhead rates.

LO 1 **Variance:** The difference between a standard cost and an actual cost.

LO 4 **Variance analysis:** The process of computing the differences between standard (or budgeted) costs and actual costs and identifying the causes of those differences.

REVIEW PROBLEM
Variance Analysis

LO 3
LO 5
LO 6
LO 7
LO 8

Sosnow Manufacturing Company has a standard costing system and keeps all cost standards up to date. The company's main product is copper water pipe, which is made in a single department. The standard variable costs for one unit of finished pipe are:

Direct materials (3 sq meters @ $12.50 per sq. meter)	$37.50
Direct labor (1.2 hours @ $9.00 per hour)	10.80
Variable manufacturing overhead (1.2 hr. @ $5.00 per direct labor hour)	6.00
Standard variable cost per unit	$54.30

Normal capacity is 15,000 direct labor hours, and budgeted fixed manufacturing overhead costs for the year were $54,000. During the year, the company produced and sold 12,200 units. Related transactions and actual cost data for the year were as follows: Direct materials consisted of 37,500 square meters purchased and used; unit purchase cost was $12.40 per square meter. Direct labor consisted of 15,250 direct labor hours worked at an average labor rate of $9.20 per hour. Actual manufacturing overhead costs incurred for the period consisted of variable manufacturing overhead costs of $73,200 and fixed manufacturing overhead costs of $55,000.

REQUIRED

Using the data given, compute the following:

1. Standard hours allowed
2. Standard fixed manufacturing overhead rate
3. Direct materials price variance
4. Direct materials quantity variance
5. Direct labor rate variance
6. Direct labor efficiency variance
7. Controllable manufacturing overhead variance
8. Manufacturing overhead volume variance

ANSWER TO REVIEW PROBLEM

1. Standard Hours Allowed = Good Units Produced × Standard Direct Labor Hours
   per Unit

   = 12,200 units × 1.2 direct labor hours per unit = 14,640 hours

2. Standard Fixed Manufacturing Overhead Rate $= \dfrac{\text{Budgeted Fixed Manufacturing Overhead Cost}}{\text{Normal Capacity}}$

$= \dfrac{\$54,000}{15,000 \text{ direct labor hours}}$

$= \underline{\$3.60}$ per direct labor hour

3. Direct materials price variance:

Price difference:		
	Standard price	$12.50 per sq. meter
	Less actual price paid	12.40 per sq. meter
	Difference	$ .10 (F)

Direct Materials Price Variance = (Standard Price − Actual Price) × Actual Quantity
= $.10 (F) × 37,500 sq. meters
= $3,750 (F)

4. Direct materials quantity variance:

Quantity difference:		
	Standard quantity	
	(12,200 units × 3 sq. meters)	36,600 sq. meters
	Less actual quantity used	37,500 sq. meters
	Difference	900 (U)

Direct Materials Quantity Variance = (Standard Quantity − Actual Quantity) × Standard Price
= 900 sq. meters (U) × $12.50 per sq. meter
= $11,250 (U)

5. Direct labor rate variance:

Rate difference:		
	Standard labor rate	$9.00 per hour
	Less actual labor rate	9.20 per hour
	Difference	$ .20 (U)

Direct Labor Rate Variance = (Standard Rate − Actual Rate) × Actual Hours
= $.20 (U) × 15,250 hours
= $3,050 (U)

6. Direct labor efficiency variance:

Difference in hours:		
	Standard hours allowed	14,640 hours*
	Less actual hours worked	15,250 hours
	Difference	610 (U)

Direct Labor Efficiency Variance = (Standard Hours Allowed − Actual Hours Worked) × Standard Rate
= 610 hours (U) × $9.00 per hour
= $5,490 (U)

*12,200 units produced × 1.2 hours per unit = 14,640 hours.

7. Controllable manufacturing overhead variance

Budgeted manufacturing overhead for 14,640 hours		
Variable manufacturing overhead cost		
(14,640 labor hours × $5.00 per hour)	$73,200	
Budgeted fixed manufacturing overhead	54,000	
Total budgeted manufacturing overhead		$127,200
Less actual manufacturing overhead incurred		$128,200
Controllable manufacturing overhead variance		$ 1,000 (U)

8. Manufacturing overhead volume variance

Total budgeted manufacturing overhead (see computation in 7)		$127,200
Less manufacturing overhead applied		
Variable: 14,640 labor hours × $5.00 per hour	$73,200	
Fixed: 14,640 labor hours × $3.60 per hour	52,704	
Total manufacturing overhead applied		125,904
Manufacturing overhead volume variance		$ 1,296 (U)

Chapter Assignments

BUILDING YOUR KNOWLEDGE FOUNDATION

Questions

1. What are standard costs?
2. Can standard costing be used by a service organization? Explain your answer.
3. What do predetermined overhead costing and standard costing have in common? How are they different?
4. "Standard costing is a total cost concept in that standard unit costs are determined for direct materials, direct labor, and manufacturing overhead." Explain this statement.
5. Name the six elements used to compute a standard unit cost.
6. Identify three factors that could affect a direct materials price standard.
7. What general ledger accounts are affected by a standard costing system?
8. "Performance is evaluated by comparing what did happen with what should have happened." What is meant by this statement? Relate your comments to the budgetary control process.
9. What is a variance?
10. What is variance analysis?
11. How can variances help management control operations?
12. What is the formula for computing a direct materials price variance?
13. How would you interpret an unfavorable direct materials price variance?
14. Identify two possible causes of a direct labor rate variance and describe the measures used to track performance in those areas. Then do the same for a direct labor efficiency variance.
15. Can an unfavorable direct materials quantity variance be caused, at least in part, by a favorable direct materials price variance? Explain.
16. What is a flexible budget? What is its purpose?
17. What are the two parts of the flexible budget formula? How are they related to each other?
18. Distinguish between the controllable manufacturing overhead variance and the manufacturing overhead volume variance.
19. If standard hours allowed exceed normal hours, will the period's manufacturing overhead volume variance be favorable or unfavorable? Explain your answer.
20. What is the key to preparing a performance report based on standard costs and related variances?

Short Exercises

SE 1.

LO 1 *Uses of Standard Costs*

Jensen Corporation is considering the installation of a standard costing system. Dan Barkus, the manager of the Missouri Division, attended the corporate meeting where Leah Eisen, the controller, discussed the proposal. Dan asked, "Leah, how will this new system benefit me? How will I use the new system?" Prepare Leah's response to Dan.

SE 2.

LO 2 *Purposes of Standard Costs*

You are a consultant and a client asks you why companies augment their cost accounting systems with standard costs. Prepare your response, listing several purposes for introducing standard costs into a cost accounting system.

SE 3.

LO 3 *Standard Unit Cost Computation*

Given the following information, compute the standard unit cost of Product JLT.

Direct materials quantity standard:	5 pounds per unit
Direct materials price standard:	$10.20 per pound
Direct labor time standard:	.4 hours per unit
Direct labor rate standard:	$10.75 per hour
Variable manufacturing overhead rate standard:	$7.00 per machine hour
Fixed manufacturing overhead rate standard:	$11.00 per machine hour
Machine hour standard:	2 hours per unit

SE 4.

LO 4 *Cost Variance Analysis*

Des Jardins Metal Works produces lawn sculptures. The company follows a practice of analyzing only variances that differ by more than 5 percent from the standard cost. The controller computed the following direct labor efficiency variances for March.

	Direct Labor Efficiency Variance	Standard Direct Labor Cost
Product 4	$1,240 (U)	$26,200
Product 6	3,290 (F)	41,700
Product 7	2,030 (U)	34,300
Product 9	1,620 (F)	32,560
Product 12	2,810 (U)	59,740

Identify the variances that should be analyzed for cause. Round to two decimal places. Also identify possible causes of the variances.

SE 5.

LO 5 *Direct Materials Variances*

Given the standard costs in **SE 3** and the following actual cost and usage data, compute the direct materials price and direct materials quantity variances.

Direct materials purchased and used	55,000 pounds
Price paid for direct materials	$10.00 per pound
Number of good units produced	11,000 units

SE 6.

LO 6 *Direct Labor Variances*

Given the standard costs in **SE 3** and the following actual cost and usage data, compute the direct labor rate and direct labor efficiency variances.

Direct labor hours used	4,950 hours
Total cost of direct labor	$53,460
Number of good units produced	11,000 units

SE 7.

LO 7 *Flexible Budget Preparation*

Prepare a flexible budget for 10,000, 12,000, and 14,000 units of output, given the following information.

Variable costs	
Direct materials	$8.00 per unit
Direct labor	$2.50 per unit
Variable manufacturing overhead	$6.00 per unit
Total budgeted fixed manufacturing overhead	$81,200

<table>
<tr><td>

LO 8 *Manufacturing Overhead Variances*

</td><td>

SE 8. Ron-Mar Products uses a standard costing system. The following information about manufacturing overhead was generated during August:

</td></tr>
</table>

Standard variable manufacturing overhead rate	$2 per machine hour
Standard fixed manufacturing overhead rate	$3 per machine hour
Actual variable manufacturing overhead costs	$443,200
Actual fixed manufacturing overhead costs	$698,800
Budgeted fixed manufacturing overhead costs	$700,000
Standard machine hours per unit	12
Good units produced	18,940
Actual machine hours	228,400

Compute the controllable manufacturing overhead variance and the manufacturing overhead volume variance.

LO 9 *Evaluating Managerial Performance*

SE 9. Derrick Shirley, the production manager at AWA Industries, received a report containing the following information from Gina Masamoto, the company controller.

	Actual	Standard	Variance
Direct Materials	$38,200	$36,600	$1,600 (U)
Direct Labor	19,450	19,000	450 (U)
Manufacturing overhead	62,890	60,000	2,890 (U)

Gina asked for a response. If you were Derrick, what would you do? What additional information does Derrick need to prepare his response?

Exercises

LO 1 *Uses of Standard Costs*

E 1. Deb Nicodemus has just assumed the duties of controller for Hinkley Market Research Company. She is concerned that the methods used for cost planning and control do not accurately track the operations of the business. She plans to suggest to the company's president, Jefferson Hinkley, that a standard costing system be created for budgeting and cost control. The new system could be incorporated into the existing accounting system. The anticipated cost of installing the new costing system and training managers is around $7,500. Prepare a memo from Deb to Jefferson Hinkley that defines a standard costing system and outlines its uses and benefits.

LO 3 *Development of Standard Costs*

E 2. McCain Corp. maintains a complete standard costing system and is in the process of updating its direct materials and direct labor standards for Product 20B. The following data have been accumulated.

Direct Materials
   In the previous period, 20,500 units were produced and 32,800 square yards of direct materials were used to produce them.
   Three suppliers of direct materials will be used in the coming period: Supplier A will provide 20 percent of the materials at a cost of $3.60 per square yard, Supplier B will be responsible for 50 percent at a cost of $3.80 per square yard, and Supplier C will ship 30 percent at a cost of $3.70 per square yard.

Direct Labor
   During the previous period, 57,400 direct labor hours were worked, 34,850 hours on machine H and 22,550 hours on machine K.
   Machine H operators earned $9.40 per hour and machine K operators earned $9.20 per hour last period. The new labor contract calls for a 10 percent increase in labor rates for the coming period.

From the information above, compute the direct materials quantity and price standards and the direct labor time and rate standards for each machine listed for the coming accounting period.

LO 3 *Standard Unit Cost Computation*

E 3. Tara Aerodynamics, Inc., makes electronically equipped weather-detecting balloons for university meteorology departments. Recent nationwide inflation has caused the company management to order that standard costs be recomputed. New direct materials price standards are $600.00 per set for electronic components and $13.50 per square meter for heavy-duty canvas. Direct materials quantity standards include one set of electronic components and 100 square meters of heavy-duty canvas per balloon. Direct labor time standards are 26 hours per balloon for the Electronics Department and 19 hours per balloon for the Assembly Department. Direct labor rate standards are $11.00 per hour for the Electronics Department and $10.00 per hour for the Assembly Department. Standard manufacturing overhead rates are $16.00 per direct labor hour for the standard variable manufacturing overhead rate and $12.00 per direct labor hour for the standard fixed manufacturing overhead rate.

Using the production standards provided, compute the standard unit cost of one weather balloon.

E 4.
LO 5 *Direct Materials Price and Quantity Variances*

The Febor Elevator Company manufactures small hydroelectric elevators with a maximum capacity of ten passengers. One of the direct materials used by the Production Department is heavy-duty carpeting for the floor of the elevator. The direct materials quantity standard used for the month ended April 30, 20xx was 8 square yards per elevator. During April, the purchasing agent purchased this carpeting at $11 per square yard; the standard price for the period was $12. Ninety elevators were completed and sold during April; the Production Department used an average of 8.5 square yards of carpet per elevator.

Calculate Febor Elevator Company's direct materials price and quantity variances for carpet for April 20xx.

E 5.
LO 6 *Direct Labor Rate and Efficiency Variances*

Goetz Foundry, Inc., manufactures castings used by other companies in the production of machinery. For the past two years, the largest selling product has been a casting for an eight-cylinder engine block. Standard direct labor hours per engine block are 1.8 hours. The labor contract requires that $14 per hour be paid to all direct labor employees. During June, 16,500 engine blocks were produced. Actual direct labor hours and costs for June were 29,900 hours and $433,550, respectively.

1. Compute the direct labor rate variance for eight-cylinder engine blocks during June.
2. Using the same data, compute the direct labor efficiency variance for eight-cylinder engine blocks during June. Check your answer, assuming that the total direct labor variance is $17,750 (U).

E 6.
LO 7 *Flexible Budget Preparation*

Fixed manufacturing overhead costs for the Bernard Company for 20xx are expected to be as follows: depreciation, $72,000; supervisory salaries, $92,000; property taxes and insurance, $26,000; and other fixed manufacturing overhead, $14,500. Total fixed manufacturing overhead is thus expected to be $204,500. Variable costs per unit are expected to be as follows: direct materials, $16.50; direct labor, $8.50; operating supplies, $2.60; indirect labor, $4.10; and other variable manufacturing overhead costs, $3.20.

Prepare a flexible budget for the following levels of production: 18,000 units, 20,000 units, and 22,000 units. What is the flexible budget formula for 20xx?

E 7.
LO 8 *Manufacturing Overhead Variances*

Theodore Company produces handmade clamming buckets that are sold to distributors along the Atlantic coast of North Carolina. The company incurred $12,400 of actual manufacturing overhead costs in May. Budgeted standard manufacturing overhead costs for May were $4 of variable manufacturing overhead costs per direct labor hour plus $1,500 in fixed manufacturing overhead costs. Normal capacity was set at 2,000 direct labor hours per month. In May, the company was able to produce 10,100 clamming buckets. The time standard is .2 direct labor hours per clamming bucket.

Compute the total manufacturing overhead variance, the controllable manufacturing overhead variance, and the manufacturing overhead volume variance for May.

E 8.
LO 8 *Manufacturing Overhead Variances*

Ridgeway Industries uses a standard costing system that includes flexible budgeting for cost planning and control. The 20xx monthly flexible budget for manufacturing overhead costs is $200,000 of fixed costs plus $5.20 per machine hour. Monthly normal capacity of 100,000 machine hours is used to compute the standard fixed manufacturing overhead rate. During December 20xx, plant workers recorded 105,000 actual machine hours. The standard machine hours allowed for good production during December was only 98,500. Actual manufacturing overhead costs incurred during December totaled $441,000 of variable costs and $204,500 of fixed costs.

Compute (1) the under- or overapplied manufacturing overhead during December and (2) the controllable manufacturing overhead variance and the manufacturing overhead volume variance.

LO 8 *Overhead Variance Analysis in an ABC System*

E 9. Lewis Paper Company produces rolled paper products that are used by various book publishing and newspaper companies. The company adopted an activity-based costing system and now analyzes variances for over thirty activities within the Production Division. The Machine Setup Activity is used by seven different work cells and is involved in each product line's size or type of paper change. Information about the Machine Setup Activity for June follows.

Actual variable overhead costs of the activity	$95,900
Actual fixed overhead costs of the activity	$38,000
Setup hours worked	3,400 hours
Total capacity of the activity in hours	3,200 hours
Budgeted fixed overhead costs	$38,400
Variable overhead rate for the activity	$28 per setup hour
Fixed overhead rate for the activity	$12 per setup hour

Compute (1) the under- or overapplied overhead for the Machine Setup Activity during June and (2) the activity's controllable overhead variance and the overhead volume variance for the month.

E 10. Scott Loman is a project manager for Beam Construction Company. Recently the company's controller sent him a performance report for the Aims Apartment Complex project. Included in the report was an unfavorable direct labor efficiency variance of $1,900 for roof structure. What types of information does Scott need to analyze before he can respond to the unfavorable direct labor efficiency variance that is his responsibility?

LO 9 *Evaluating Managerial Performance*

Problems

P 1. Prefabricated houses are the specialty of Kentish Homes, Inc., of Dallas, Texas. Although Kentish Homes produces many models, and customers can even special order a home, 60 percent of the company's business comes from the sale of the Citadel, a three-bedroom, 1,400-square-foot home with an impressive front entrance. The six basic direct materials used to manufacture the entrance with their standard costs for 20x1 are as follows: wood framing materials, $2,140; deluxe front door, $480; door hardware, $260; exterior siding, $710; electrical materials, $580; and interior finishing materials, $1,520.

LO 3 *Developing and Using Standard Costs*

Three types of direct labor are used to build this section: carpenter, 30 hours at $12 per hour; door specialist, 4 hours at $14 per hour; and electrician, 8 hours at $16 per hour. In 20x1, the company used a manufacturing overhead rate of 40 percent of total direct materials cost.

During 20x2, the cost of wood framing materials is expected to increase by 20 percent. The deluxe front door will need two suppliers: Supplier A will produce 40 percent of the company's needs at $490 per door; Supplier B, 60 percent at $500 per door. The cost of the door hardware will increase by 10 percent, and the cost of electrical materials will increase by 20 percent. Exterior siding cost should decrease by $16 per unit. The cost of interior finishing materials is expected to remain the same. The carpenter's wages will increase by $1 per hour, while the door specialist's wages should remain the same. The electrician's wages will increase by $.50 per hour. Finally, the manufacturing overhead rate will decrease to 25 percent of total direct materials cost. All other costs will remain the same.

REQUIRED

1. Compute the total standard cost of direct materials per front entrance for 20x1.
2. Using your answer to **1,** compute the total standard unit cost for the Citadel's entrance in 20x1.
3. Compute the new standard unit cost per front entrance for the year 20x2.

LO 5 *Direct Materials and*
LO 6 *Direct Labor Variances*

P 2. Neff Trophy Company produces a variety of athletic awards, most in the form of trophies or mounted replicas of athletes in action. Lisa Neff, the president of the company, is in the process of developing a standard costing system. The company produces six standard sizes. The deluxe trophy stands three feet tall above the base. Direct materials standards include one pound of metal supported by an 8-ounce wooden base. Standard prices for 20xx were $3.30 per pound of metal and $.45 per ounce of wood.

Alternate Problems

P 6.

LO 3 *Development of Standards: Direct Materials*

Clockworks, Ltd., assembles clock movements for grandfather clocks. Each movement has four components to assemble: the clock facing, the clock hands, the time movement, and the spring assembly. For the current year, 20x1, the company used the following standard costs: clock facing, $15.90; clock hands, $12.70; time movement, $66.10; and spring assembly, $52.50.

Prices and sources of materials are expected to change in 20x2. Sixty percent of the facings will be supplied by Company A at $19.50 each, and the remaining 40 percent will be purchased from Company B at $18.80 each. The hands are produced for Clockworks, Ltd., by Olesha Hardware, Inc., and will cost $16.40 per set in 20x2. Time movements will be purchased from three Swiss sources: Company Q, 30 percent of total need at $70.50 per movement; Company R, 20 percent at $69.50; and Company S, 50 percent at $71.90. Spring assemblies will be purchased from a French company and are expected to increase in cost by 20 percent.

REQUIRED

1. Determine the total standard direct materials cost per unit for 20x2.
2. If the company could guarantee the purchase of 2,500 sets of hands from Olesha Hardware, Inc., the unit cost would be reduced by 20 percent. Find the resulting standard direct materials unit cost.
3. Substandard spring assemblies can be purchased at $50.00, but 20 percent of them will be unusable and cannot be returned. Compute the standard direct materials unit cost if the company follows this procedure, assuming the original facts of the case for the remaining data. The cost of the defective materials will be spread over good units produced.

P 7.

LO 5 *Direct Materials and*
LO 6 *Direct Labor Variances*

The Kawalski Packaging Company makes plastic baskets for food wholesalers. Each Type R basket is made of .8 grams of liquid plastic and .6 grams of an additive that includes color and hardening agents. The standard prices are $.15 per gram of liquid plastic and $.09 per gram of additive.

Two kinds of direct labor are required: molding and trimming/packing. The direct labor time and rate standards per 100-basket batch are as follows: molding, 1.0 hours per batch at an hourly rate of $12; trimming/packing, 1.2 hours per batch at $10 per hour.

During 20xx, the company produced 48,000 Type R baskets. Actual materials used were 38,600 grams of liquid plastic at a total cost of $5,404 and 28,950 grams of additive at a cost of $2,895. Actual direct labor included 480 hours for molding at a total cost of $5,664, and 560 hours for trimming/packing at $5,656.

REQUIRED

1. Compute the direct materials price and quantity variances for both the liquid plastic and the additive.
2. Compute the direct labor rate and efficiency variances for the molding and trimming/packing processes.

P 8.

LO 5 *Direct Materials, Direct*
LO 6 *Labor, and*
LO 8 *Manufacturing Overhead Variances*

The Doormat Division of Robertson Rug Company produces a line of all-vinyl mats. Each doormat calls for .4 meters of vinyl material that costs $3.10 per meter. Standard direct labor hours and cost per doormat are .2 hour and $1.84 (.2 hour × $9.20 per hour), respectively. The division's current standard variable overhead rate is $1.50 per direct labor hour, and the standard fixed manufacturing overhead rate is $.80 per direct labor hour.

In August the division manufactured and sold 60,000 doormats. During the month, 25,200 meters of vinyl material were used at a total cost of $73,080. The total actual manufacturing overhead costs for August were $28,200, of which $18,200 were variable. The total number of direct labor hours worked was 10,800, and the factory payroll for direct labor for August was $95,040. Normal monthly capacity for the year has been set at 58,000 doormats. Budgeted fixed manufacturing overhead for the period was $9,280.

REQUIRED

Compute (1) the direct materials price variance, (2) the direct materials quantity variance, (3) the direct labor rate variance, (4) the direct labor efficiency variance, (5) the controllable manufacturing overhead variance, and (6) the manufacturing overhead volume variance.

Skills Development

CONCEPTUAL ANALYSIS

SD 1.

LO 4 *Cost Control Using Variance Analysis*

Holding down operating costs is an ongoing challenge for managers. The lower the costs incurred, the higher the profit. But two factors make a target profit difficult to achieve. First, dozens of possible operating inefficiencies may occur, ranging from human error to unexpected machine breakdowns. Each occurrence causes costs to escalate. On the other hand, if costs are so strictly controlled that cheaper resources are used, the quality of the product or service may suffer and total sales may decline. To control costs and still produce high-quality goods or services, managers must continually assess operating activities by analyzing both financial and nonfinancial data.

Write a short paper discussing how variance analysis helps managers to accomplish cost control objectives. Focus on both the financial and the nonfinancial data used in a standard costing system.

ETHICAL DILEMMA

SD 2.

LO 2 *An Ethical Question*
LO 4 *Involving Standard Costs*

Jason Bramwell is the manager of standard costing systems at **Ragnar Industries, Inc.** Standard costs are developed for all product-related direct materials, direct labor, and manufacturing overhead costs and are used for pricing products, for costing all inventories, and for performance evaluation of all purchasing and production line managers. The company updates standard costs whenever costs, prices, or rates change by 3 percent or more; in addition, all standard costs are reviewed and updated annually in December. This practice provided currently attainable standards that were appropriate for use in valuing year-end inventories on Ragnar Industries' financial statements.

On November 30, 20x2, Jason received a memo from the company's chief financial officer. The memo said that the company was considering the purchase of another company and that Jason and his staff were to concentrate their full effort on analyzing the proposed transaction and ignore adjusting the standards until February or March. In late November, prices on over twenty raw materials were reduced by 10 percent or more and a new labor contract reduced several categories of labor rates. Lower standard costs would result in lower inventories, higher cost of goods sold due to inventory write-downs, and lower net income for the year. Jason believed that the company was facing an operating loss and that the assignment to evaluate the proposed major purchase was designed primarily to keep his staff from revising and lowering the standards. Jason questioned the CFO about the assignment and reiterated the need for updating the standard costs, but he was again told to ignore the update procedure and concentrate on the company purchase. The proposed purchase never materialized, and Jason and his staff were removed from the assignment in early February.

Assess Jason's actions in this situation. Did he follow all ethical paths to solve the problem? What are the consequences of not adjusting the standard costs?

Communication	Critical Thinking	Group Activity	Memo	Ethics	International	Spreadsheet	Managerial Technology	Internet

RESEARCH ACTIVITY

SD 3.

LO 1   *The Relevance of*
LO 2   *Standard Costing*

Standard costs and the variances for direct materials, direct labor, and manufacturing overhead generated by a standard costing system have been used to control costs and evaluate performance for many years. Standard costs are also used in the pricing of new products. In recent years, the standard costing approach has been called irrelevant to the measurement of operations. Locate an article written about this topic within the last five years in the periodical *Management Accounting,* published monthly by the Institute of Management Accountants or on the Needles Accounting Resource Center Web site at http://www.hmco.com/college/needles/home.html. Identify the issues addressed by the author(s). Is the article positive or negative toward standard costs? What role does the globally competitive environment play in the points being made by the author(s)? Prepare a formal two-page summary of the article. Also prepare an outline that you would use if called upon to report your findings to your classmates.

Group Activity: Have students work in groups to complete **SD 3**. Select one person from each group to report the group's findings to the class.

DECISION-MAKING PRACTICE

SD 4.

LO 6   *Annuity Life Insurance*
LO 8   *Company—Standard*
       Costing in a Service
       Industry

The ***Annuity Life Insurance Company*** (ALIC) markets several types of life insurance policies, but its permanent, twenty-year life annuity policy (P20A) is its most popular product. The P20A policy sells in $10,000 increments and features variable percentages of whole life insurance and single-payment annuity, depending on the potential policyholder's needs and age. An entire department is devoted to developing and marketing the P20A policy. ALIC has determined that both the policy developer and the policy salesperson contribute to the creation of each policy, so ALIC categorizes these people as direct labor for variance analysis, cost control, and performance evaluation. For unit costing, each $10,000 increment is considered 1 unit. Thus, a $90,000 policy is counted as 9 units.

    Standard unit cost information for the period is as follows:

Direct labor	
Policy developer	
3 hours at $12.00 per hour	$ 36.00
Policy salesperson	
8.5 hours at $14.20 per hour	120.70
Operating overhead	
Variable operating overhead	
11.5 hours at $26.00 per hour	299.00
Fixed operating overhead	
11.5 hours at $18.00 per hour	207.00
Standard unit cost	$662.70

Actual costs incurred during January for the 265 units sold were as follows:

Direct labor	
Policy developers	
848 hours at $12.50 per hour	$10,600.00
Policy salespeople	
2,252.5 hours at $14.00 per hour	31,535.00
Operating overhead	
Variable operating overhead	78,440.00
Fixed operating overhead	53,400.00

Normal monthly capacity was 260 units, and the budgeted fixed operating overhead for the month was $53,820.

1. Compute the standard hours allowed in January for policy developers and policy salespeople.
2. What should have been the total standard costs for January? What were the total actual costs incurred for January? Compute the total cost variance for the period.
3. Compute the direct labor rate and efficiency variances for policy developers and policy salespeople.
4. Compute the operating overhead variances for January.
5. Identify possible causes for each variance and suggest possible solutions.

Managerial Reporting and Analysis

INTERPRETING MANAGEMENT REPORTS

MRA 1.
LO 7 *Flexible Budgets and*
LO 9 *Performance Evaluation*

Boris Realtors, Inc., specializes in home resales. Revenue is earned from selling fees. Commissions for salespersons, listing agents, and listing companies are the main costs for the company. Business has improved steadily over the last ten years. As usual, Bonnie Boris, the managing partner of Boris Realtors, Inc., received a report summarizing the performance for the most recent year.

Boris Realtors, Inc.
Performance Report
For the Year Ended December 31, 20xx

	Budget*	Actual**	Difference Under (Over) Budget
Total Selling Fees	$2,052,000	$2,242,200	($190,200)
Less Variable Costs			
Sales Commissions	$1,102,950	$1,205,183	($102,233)
Automobile	36,000	39,560	(3,560)
Advertising	93,600	103,450	(9,850)
Home Repairs	77,400	89,240	(11,840)
General Overhead	656,100	716,970	(60,870)
	$1,966,050	$2,154,403	($188,353)
Less Fixed Costs			
General Overhead	60,000	62,300	(2,300)
Total Costs	$2,026,050	$2,216,703	($190,653)
Net Income	$ 25,950	$ 25,497	$ 453

*Budgeted data based on 180 home resales.
**Actual selling fees and operating costs of 200 home resales.

1. Analyze the performance report. What does it say about the performance of the company? Is the performance report reliable? Explain.
2. Calculate the budgeted selling fee and budgeted variable costs per home resale.
3. Prepare a performance report using a flexible budget based on the actual number of home resales.
4. Analyze the report you prepared in **3.** What does it say about the performance of the company? Is the performance report reliable? Explain.
5. What recommendations would you make to improve next year's performance?

FORMULATING MANAGEMENT REPORTS

MRA 2.

LO 4   *Preparing Performance*
LO 6   *Reports*
LO 8
LO 9

Troy Corrente, the president of **Forest Valley Spa,** is concerned about the spa's operating performance in March 20xx. He carefully budgeted his costs so that he could reduce the 20xx membership fees. Now he needs to monitor those costs to make sure that the spa's profits are at the level he expected.

He has asked you, as the controller for the spa, to prepare a performance report for the operating labor and overhead costs. He also wants you to analyze the report and suggest possible causes for any problems you find. He needs your work immediately so that any problems can be quickly solved.

The following information is available:

	Standard	Actual
Variable costs		
Operating labor	$10,880	$12,150
Utilities	2,880	3,360
Repairs and maintenance	5,760	7,140
Fixed costs		
Depreciation, equipment	2,600	2,680
Rent	3,280	3,280
Other	1,704	1,860
Totals	$27,104	$30,470

Normal operating hours call for eight operators to work 160 hours each per month. During March, nine operators worked an average of 150 hours each.

1. Answer the following questions about preparing performance reports.
   a. Who needs the performance report?
   b. Why are you preparing the performance report?
   c. What information do you need to develop the performance report? How will you obtain that information?
   d. When must you have the performance report and analysis prepared?
2. With this limited information, compute the operating labor rate variance, the operating labor efficiency variance, and the operating controllable overhead variance.
3. Prepare a performance report for the month. Analyze the report and suggest possible causes for any problems that you find.

INTERNATIONAL COMPANY

MRA 3.

LO 5   *Variance Analysis*
LO 6

Ming Nu recently became the controller of a joint venture in Hong Kong. Ming created a standard costing system to help plan for and control the company's activities. After completing the first quarter of operations using standard costing, Ming met with the budget team, which included managers from purchasing, engineering, production, and personnel. He asked them to share any problems that occurred during the quarter. He planned to use the information to analyze the variances that his staff would calculate.

For each of the following situations, identify the direct materials and/or direct labor variance(s) that could be affected and indicate the direction (favorable or unfavorable) of those variances.

a. The production department used highly skilled, higher-paid workers.
b. Machines were improperly adjusted.
c. Direct labor personnel worked more carefully to manufacture the product.
d. The product design engineer substituted a direct material that was less expensive and of lower quality.
e. The Purchasing Department bought higher-quality materials at a higher price.
f. A major supplier used a less-expensive mode of transportation to deliver the raw materials.
g. Work was halted for two hours because of a power disruption.

EXCEL SPREADSHEET ANALYSIS

MRA 4.

LO 7 *Flexible Budget*
LO 8 *Development and Manufacturing Overhead Variance Analysis*

Ella Mae Collins is the controller for *FH Industries.* She has asked you, her new assistant, to prepare an analysis from the following data related to projected and actual manufacturing overhead costs for October 20xx:

	Standard Variable Costs per Machine Hour (MH)	Actual Variable Costs Incurred in October
Indirect materials and supplies	$1.10	$ 2,380
Indirect machine setup labor	2.50	5,090
Materials handling	1.40	3,950
Maintenance and repair	1.50	2,980
Utilities	.80	1,490
Miscellaneous	.10	200
Totals	$7.40	$16,090

	Budgeted Fixed Manufacturing Overhead	Actual Fixed Manufacturing Overhead in October
Supervisory salaries	$ 3,630	$ 3,630
Machine depreciation	8,360	8,580
Other	1,210	1,220
Totals	$13,200	$13,430

During October, the number of good units produced was used to compute the 2,100 standard machine hours allowed. Your analysis of this data should include the steps outlined below.

REQUIRED

1. Prepare a monthly flexible budget for the company for operating activity at 2,000 machine hours, 2,200 machine hours, and 2,500 machine hours.
2. Formulate a flexible budget formula for the company.
3. The company's normal operating capacity is 2,200 machine hours per month. Compute the fixed manufacturing overhead rate at this level of activity. Then break the rate down into individual rates for each element of fixed manufacturing overhead.
4. Prepare a detailed comparative cost analysis for October. All variable and fixed manufacturing overhead costs should be included. Your report form should include the following five columns: (a) cost category, (b) cost per machine hour, (c) costs applied, (d) actual costs incurred, and (e) variance.
5. Develop a manufacturing overhead variance analysis for October that identifies the controllable manufacturing overhead variance and the manufacturing overhead volume variance.
6. Prepare an analysis of the variances. Are some of the fixed costs controllable by the manager? Defend your answer.

ENDNOTES

1. http://www.rubgrp.com/main.html. Other sources include brochures and practice manual pages received from The Rubicon Group and a personal telephone interview with Dennis Evans, of the Rubicon Group, January 30, 1998.

2. Carole Cheatham, "Updating Standard Cost Systems," *Journal of Accountancy*, The American Institute of Certified Public Accountants, December 1990, pp. 57–60.

3. http://www.euro.net/innovation/Management_Base_/Man_Guide_Rel_1.081/controlandmonitoring.html, July 14, 1997.

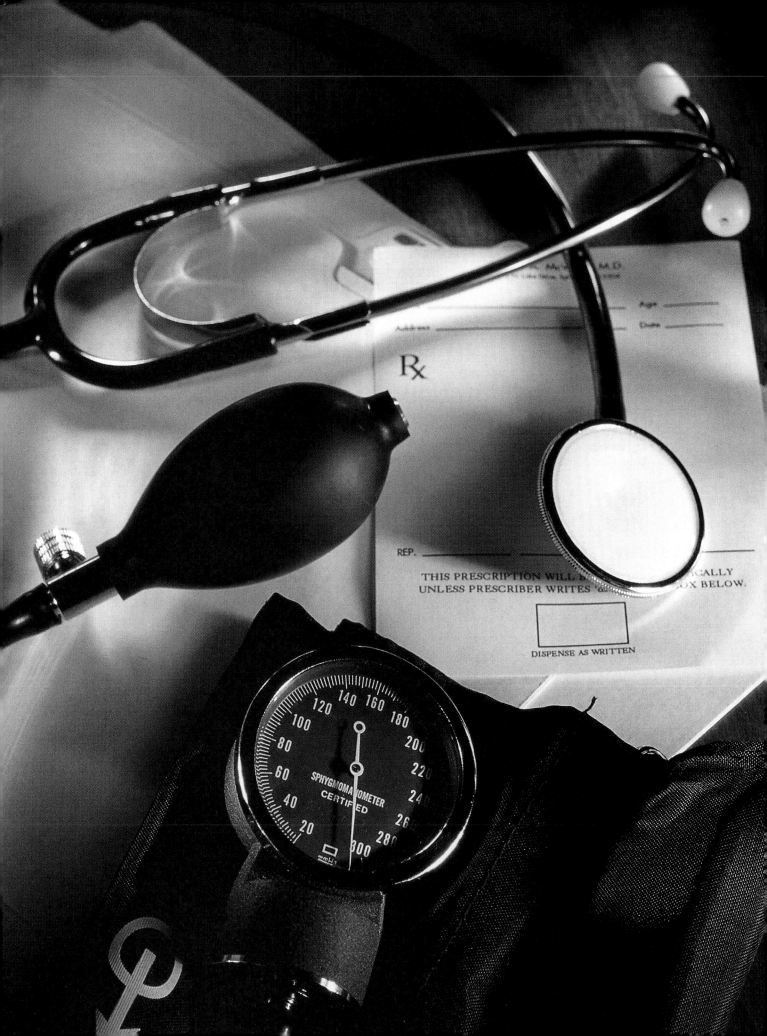

CHAPTER 9

Short-Run Decision Analysis

LEARNING OBJECTIVES

1. Discuss the role of cost information in short-run decision analysis and the management cycle.
2. Identify the steps in the management decision cycle and discuss the role of relevant decision information and incremental analysis in short-run decision analysis.
3. Prepare decision analyses in a manufacturing organization for (a) outsourcing decisions, (b) special order decisions, (c) segment profitability decisions, (d) product mix decisions involving constrained resources, and (e) sell or process-further decisions.
4. Apply short-run decision analysis to nonmanufacturing organizations.

DECISION POINT

OMNI HEALTHCARE

Omni Healthcare is a health maintenance organization (HMO) that serves approximately twenty-six counties in northern California and has more than 130,000 members. Omni wants to compete successfully in the health care market by operating efficiently and finding new members. Omni Healthcare's goal is to provide affordable health care services that preserve members' freedom to choose their own physician and member hospital. Omni wants its front-line managers to make better, more informed decisions using timely, relevant information. For example, Omni's actuarial staff, who review the cost of medical supplies, services, and pharmaceuticals, want to ask questions such as, "What are the expenses of the most requested medical procedures in San Francisco County?" They need information in order to negotiate the best contracts. Omni's marketing managers want to know, "What is the membership growth in Marin County compared to Santa Clara County?" They need information in order to identify successful marketing methods and new markets. The provider group staff, who are responsible for obtaining new providers, want to know, "Do we have enough providers in Santa Clara County to support our membership base?" They need information about provider group expenses in order to sign profitable contracts with provider groups.[1]

How can a management accountant help Omni? The management accountant can use an information system, or data warehouse, to improve decision making by providing timely reports designed to summarize relevant information in a useful manner. The senior management of companies like Omni work to develop strategic plans that include the development and use of data warehouses. Such warehouses enable organizations to simultaneously pursue a wide variety of complex goals because they are designed to provide the specific, high-quality information managers need to make decisions and monitor progress.

Cost Information for Short-Run Decisions

In financial reporting, we are interested in *what happened.* The historical information disclosed in financial reports helps to answer that question. For planning and control purposes, managers want to know *why it happened.* Historical financial and nonfinancial quantitative information is used to analyze the results of business actions. In this chapter, we focus on *what will happen.* Managers make many decisions that will affect their organization's activities in the short run. They need historical and estimated quantitative information that is both financial *and* nonfinancial in nature. Such information should be relevant, timely, and presented in a format that is easy to use in decision making. The information will help them to consider the question, "What will happen if we choose one alternative over another?"

As illustrated in Figure 1, short-run decision analysis is an important component of the management cycle. In the planning stage of the management cycle, managers estimate cost and revenue information that can be used to make short-run decisions during the coming year. In this chapter, we focus on the executing stage of the management cycle, which is the stage in which managers must adapt to changing environments and take advantage of opportunities that will improve the organization's profitability and liquidity in the short run. During the year, managers may have an opportunity to sell a special order, examine the profitability of a segment, select the appropriate product mix given a resource constraint, contract with outside suppliers of goods and services, or sell a product as is or process it further. All of those decisions affect operations in the current operating period. In the reviewing stage of the management cycle, each decision is evaluated to determine if the forecasted results were obtained. If the results are not as predicted, corrective action must be identified and taken. Finally, the reporting stage takes place continuously during the management cycle. Budgets will include relevant estimated cost and revenue information for some decisions. Short-run decision reports will show the analysis that supports a decision. Other reports will provide information to review the results of a decision.

As a general rule, the managers of companies like Omni Healthcare will make decisions that support the company's strategic plan. For example, Omni management may have to make a decision about keeping or eliminating one of its prestigious medical procedures, performing heart transplants. Both quantitative and qualitative factors will influence the decision. The quantitative information includes the costs of performing a heart transplant and the fee revenues that the procedure generates. Management may also want to know the number of heart transplants performed each year, the average time taken to complete the operation, and the average number of patient days in the hospital. Examples of qualitative factors that would influence the decision include the qualifications of the medical team, the efficiency and effectiveness of the equipment, health insurers' restrictions on the procedure, and the community's needs. Some of this information is generated in the planning stage of the management cycle.

In the executing stage, Omni management might choose to eliminate the procedure if its costs exceed the revenues generated. However, they may choose to keep the procedure because the community expects the organization to provide this service. Other qualitative factors that can be weighed in the decision include:

- Competition (Do our competitors perform this operation?)
- Economic conditions (Do insurance companies cover such operations?)
- Social issues (Are people willing to have the operation because they want to live longer?)
- Product or service quality (Can we attract more business by providing the best service?)
- Timeliness (Can we promote a quick and healthy recovery?)

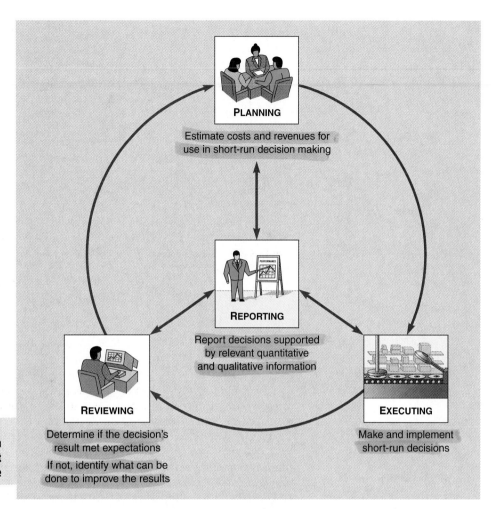

Figure 1
Cost Information for Short-Run Decisions in the Management Cycle

Managers must identify and assess the importance of all such factors when making short-run decisions. They must also make sure that the decision is compatible with their organization's strategic plan. During the reviewing stage, the managers will measure the impact of their decision on the net income of the organization. Omni managers will prepare reports to support the information selected, the decision made, and the impact of that decision on the organization.

The Decision-Making Process

OBJECTIVE 2

Identify the steps in the management decision cycle and discuss the role of relevant decision information and incremental analysis in short-run decision analysis

The Management Decision Cycle

Although many decisions are unique and are not made according to strict rules, certain events occur frequently in the analysis of business problems. These events form a pattern called the management decision cycle. The five steps managers take in making decisions and following up on them are shown in Figure 2.

The first step in the cycle is the discovery of a problem or need. Then in step **2,** the accountant works with the managers involved in the decision to identify all reasonable courses of action that will solve the problem or meet the need. In step **3,** the accountant prepares a thorough analysis of each possible solution, identifying its total cost, savings, and other financial effects. Each alternative may require

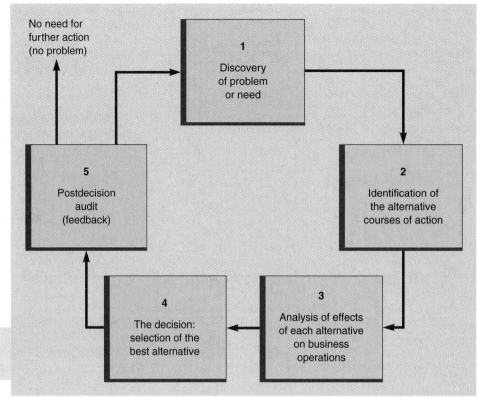

Figure 2
The Management Decision
Cycle

different cost information. In **step 4,** after studying the information the accountant has gathered and organized in a meaningful way, the managers select the best course of action. In step **5,** after the decision has been carried out, the accountant studies its effects on the operation. The resulting postdecision audit gives management feedback about the results of the decision. If the solution is not completely satisfactory or if problems remain, the decision cycle begins again. If the solution settled the problem, then the decision process is complete.

Relevant Information for Management

Once managers determine that a problem or need is worthy of consideration, they must evaluate how each possible solution will affect the organization's operations. The management accountant is responsible for providing managers with relevant information for each alternative.

How does the management accountant decide what is relevant and what is not? Facts that are the same for each alternative are not relevant. If total sales are unchanged in a proposal to reduce labor costs by installing an automated machine, then that information should not appear in the evaluation of the machines being considered. Similarly, although the accountant may use past data to prepare cost estimates of alternatives, historical data are not relevant to projections of future operations and do not guide managers in choosing among alternatives. The accountant should include only those cost projections or estimates that are relevant to the decision. Relevant decision information is the data about future costs, revenues, and resource usage that differ among the alternatives being evaluated. The analyses and reports accountants use to present decision data to management should include only relevant information and omit past data and data that are common to each alternative under study. Relevant costs are costs that differ among alternatives. Such costs are also called *avoidable costs*. Irrelevant costs may be either sunk costs or costs that do not differ among alternatives. Sunk costs are costs incurred because of a previous decision that cannot be recovered through the current decision. For example, the cost of delivery vans acquired last year is not relevant when deciding whether to purchase a new van. Sunk costs are omitted from decision analyses. Opportunity costs are the revenues forfeited or lost when one alternative is chosen over another. For example, a full-time teller at a bank would lose his salary if he returned to college full-time to complete his degree in finance. The lost salary is an opportunity cost and is relevant to his decision about whether to return to college or to continue to work as a teller. If managers want their short-run decision analyses to be efficient and effective, they must recognize the differences between relevant and irrelevant decision information and use only relevant information.

Incremental Analysis

Incremental analysis helps managers to compare alternative projects by focusing on the differences in their projected revenues and costs. The accountant organizes relevant information to determine which alternative contributes the most to profits or incurs the lowest costs. Only data that are different for the different alternatives appear in the report.

For example, assume that a management accountant is preparing a report to help the management of the Lennox Company decide which of two mill blade grinders—C or W—to buy. The accountant has collected the following annual sales and operating cost estimates for the two machines.

	Grinder C	Grinder W
Increase in revenue	$16,200	$19,800
Increase in annual operating costs		
Direct materials	4,800	4,800
Direct labor	2,200	4,100
Variable manufacturing overhead	2,100	3,050
Fixed manufacturing overhead (depreciation included)	5,000	5,000

An incremental analysis shows increases or decreases in revenues and costs that arise from each alternative. Since direct materials and fixed manufacturing overhead costs are the same for each alternative, they are not included in the analysis.

If you assume that the purchase price and the useful life of the two grinders are the same, the incremental analysis in Exhibit 1 shows that Grinder W generates $750 more in income than Grinder C. Thus, the decision based on this report is to purchase Grinder W.

Since the incremental analysis focuses on the differences between alternatives, it identifies both the benefits and the drawbacks of each. An incremental analysis simplifies the evaluation for the decision maker and reduces the time needed to choose the best course of action.

Contribution Margin and Short-Run Decisions

The contribution margin format of income reporting, as discussed in the chapter on cost-volume-profit analysis and variable costing, is often used in decision analysis. Contribution margin is most commonly used to examine the profitability of a segment. It is also used to make decisions about selling special orders and to select the appropriate product mix when a resource is constrained.

Exhibit 1. Incremental Analysis

	Lennox Company Incremental Analysis		
	Grinder C	Grinder W	Difference in Favor of Grinder W
Increase in revenues	$16,200	$19,800	$3,600
Increased operating costs that differ between alternatives			
Direct labor	2,200	4,100	(1,900)
Variable manufacturing overhead	2,100	3,050	(950)
Total relevant operating costs	$ 4,300	$ 7,150	($2,850)
Resulting change in net income	$11,900	$12,650	$ 750

Decision: Purchase Grinder W.

Special Decision Reports

Income statements in the contribution margin format and incremental analyses work best when quantitative information is being compared. In some cases, however, managers may be considering many alternatives, each of which would be best in certain circumstances. One alternative may generate more profits, whereas another diversifies the company's product line. A third alternative may prevent a huge layoff, bolstering the company's goodwill. Even though several alternatives may be equally good, management must choose only one. In such cases, qualitative information must support or replace the quantitative analyses, and the accountant must use imagination to prepare the special decision report that demonstrates which alternative is best under the circumstances.

For most special decision reports, there is no one correct, set structure. Experienced accountants prepare such reports to fit individual situations. In this course, you can solve most of the problems by following the examples in the text. But remember that in practice, management accountants must create formats appropriate to existing circumstances. Such challenges contribute to the dynamic role of the management accountant.

Operating Decisions

Many business decisions can be made using incremental analysis. In this section, we use various forms of incremental analysis to select the best alternative when managers face (1) outsourcing decisions, (2) special order decisions, (3) segment profitability decisions, (4) product mix decisions involving constrained resources, or (5) sell or process-further decisions.

OBJECTIVE 3a

Prepare decision analyses in a manufacturing organization for outsourcing decisions

Outsourcing Decisions

Outsourcing is the use of suppliers outside the organization to perform services or produce goods that could be performed or produced internally. Outsourcing includes make-or-buy decisions, which are decisions about whether to make a part internally or buy it from an external supplier. But outsourcing also includes using external companies to perform traditional operating activities.

To compete effectively in global markets, many companies are identifying their core competencies, or the activities they perform best, so that they can improve their profits by focusing on those activities. One way to obtain the financial, physical, human, and technological resources needed to perform those competencies is to outsource expensive, nonvalue-adding activities. Strong candidates for outsourcing include payroll processing, training, managing fleets of vehicles, sales and marketing, custodial services, and information management. Many such areas involve either relatively low employee skill levels (such as payroll processing or custodial services) or highly specialized knowledge (such as information management) that could be better acquired from experts outside the company.

Many companies benefit from outsourcing. Outsourcing production or operating activities can reduce a company's investment in physical assets and human resources, which can improve cash flow. Outsourcing can also help a company reduce operating costs and improve profits. For example, Amazon.com, a bookseller on the Internet, made the decision to outsource the distribution of 80 percent of its books to Ingram Books. By using Internet commerce and outsourcing the distribution function, Amazon.com has been able to reduce its storage and distribution costs enough to be able to provide discounts of up to 40 percent off the list price on selected bestsellers. Outsourcing also enables Amazon.com to provide additional value-adding services such as on-line reviews of books by their authors, reviews by others, and discussions and interviews about current books. Other companies use outsourcing to benefit from specialized supplier knowledge. For example, Sun Life Assurance Group, a Canadian life insurance company, provides better services to its customers by relying on the expertise of companies like Dodge Group's Financial Data Warehouse, an information systems service provider, to manage large volumes of data.

Although outsourcing provides many benefits, organizations may still consider making the product or providing the service internally. Some of the problems associated with outsourcing include loss of control, loss of expertise within the organization, the organization's growing dependence on the supplier, the supplier's growing dependence on the organization, and potential loss of critical information to competitors. In addition, as detailed in Table 1, there are hidden costs associated with maintaining a long-term relationship with a supplier. Because such costs are often

---

Table 1. Hidden Costs of Outsourcing the Production of Parts for Assembly Operations

When manufacturers purchase parts from suppliers, they expect quality parts to be delivered quickly for a reasonable price. The hidden costs of maintaining an outsourcing relationship with a supplier can include the following:

Costs of Quality for Parts Purchased from Suppliers

- Cost of inspecting parts delivered to the company
- Cost of labor and shipping to return defective parts to suppliers
- Cost of training suppliers to follow quality methods
- Cost of reworking products due to poor-quality parts

Costs of Late Deliveries from Suppliers

- Cost of lost customer sales due to late parts deliveries from suppliers
- Cost of carrying extra direct materials and finished goods inventory to compensate for late parts deliveries from suppliers
- Cost of back orders due to partial shipments

overlooked when outsourcing decisions are made, management accounting systems must be specifically designed to evaluate them. To help manage the hidden costs of outsourcing, many companies also add clauses to their contracts with suppliers that specify penalties for poor quality and late deliveries. To ensure a successful outsourcing experience, companies must develop and implement quality controls, carefully analyze outsourcing opportunities to make sure the benefits exceed the costs, monitor and measure the supplier relationship, select the right partner, and connect the outsourcing decision with corporate strategy.

A common problem facing managers of manufacturing companies is whether to make or to outsource some or all of the parts used in product assembly. The goal is to help management select the more profitable choice by identifying the costs of each alternative and their effects on revenues and existing costs. The following factors are needed for this analysis.

To Make	**To Outsource**
Need for additional machinery	Purchase price of item
Variable costs of making the item	Rent or net cash flow to be generated
Incremental fixed costs	from vacated space in factory
	Salvage value of unused machinery

The case of the Kriegel Electronics Company illustrates an outsourcing decision. For the past five years, the firm has purchased a small transistor casing from an outside supplier at a cost of $1.25 per casing. The supplier has just informed Kriegel Electronics that it is raising the price 20 percent, effective immediately. Kriegel has idle machinery that could be adjusted to produce the casings. Kriegel estimates the cost of direct materials at $84 per 100 casings, the amount of direct labor at three minutes of labor per casing at a rate of $8 per direct labor hour, and the cost of variable manufacturing overhead at $4 per direct labor hour. Fixed manufacturing overhead includes $4,000 of depreciation per year and $6,000 of other fixed costs. Annual production and usage would be 20,000 casings. The company has space and machinery to produce the casing; these are currently idle and would continue to be idle if the part is purchased. Should Kriegel Electronics Company continue to outsource the casings?

Incremental analysis enables the accountant to organize the relevant data in an outsourcing decision. Management can then use the accountant's report to quickly analyze all relevant costs or revenues and use that information to select the best alternative.

Exhibit 2 presents an incremental analysis of the two alternatives. All relevant costs are listed. Because the machinery has already been purchased and neither the machinery nor the required factory space has any other use, the depreciation costs and other fixed manufacturing overhead costs are the same for both alternatives; therefore, they are not relevant to the decision. The cost of making the needed cas-

Exhibit 2. Incremental Analysis: Outsourcing Decision

Kriegel Electronics Company
Outsourcing Decision
Incremental Analysis

	Make	Outsource	Difference in Favor of Make
Direct materials (20,000 ÷ 100 × $84)	$16,800	—	($16,800)
Direct labor (20,000 ÷ 20 × $8)*	8,000	—	(8,000)
Variable manufacturing overhead (20,000 ÷ 20 × $4)*	4,000	—	(4,000)
To purchase completed casings (20,000 × $1.50)	—	$30,000	30,000
Totals	$28,800	$30,000	$ 1,200

Decision: Make the transistor casing.

*Rate of pieces per hour.

ings is $28,800. The cost of buying 20,000 casings will be $30,000 at the increased purchase price. The company would save $1,200 by making the casings, and indeed it should do so.

Special Order Decisions

OBJECTIVE 3b

Prepare decision analyses in a manufacturing organization for special order decisions

Management is often faced with special order decisions, which are decisions about whether to accept or reject special product orders at prices below the normal market prices. Special orders usually involve large numbers of similar products that are sold in bulk (packaged in large containers). Because management does not expect such orders, they are not included in annual cost or sales estimates. And, because such orders are one-time events, they should not be included in revenue or cost estimates for subsequent years. Before a firm accepts a special order, it must be sure that the products involved are sufficiently different from its regular product line to avoid violating federal price discrimination laws.

The objective of a special order decision is to determine whether a special order should be accepted. A special order should be accepted only if it maximizes net income, based on the organization's strategic plan and objectives, the relevant costs of the special order, and qualitative factors. One approach to such a decision is to compare the special order price to the relevant costs to produce, package, and ship the order. The relevant costs include the variable manufacturing costs, variable selling costs, if any, and other costs directly associated with the special order (freight, insurance, packaging, and/or labeling the product). Another approach is to prepare a special order bid price by calculating a minimum selling price for the special order. The bid price equals the relevant costs plus an estimated profit.

In many situations, sales commission expenses are excluded from a special order decision analysis because the manufacturing company was approached directly by the special order customer. In addition, the fixed costs of existing facilities usually would not change if a special order were accepted, and therefore are usually irrelevant to the decision. If additional fixed costs would have to be incurred to facilitate the transaction, they would be relevant to the decision. Examples of relevant fixed costs include the purchase of additional machinery, an increase in supervisory help, or an increase in insurance premiums required by a specific order.

Jens Sporting Goods, Inc., manufactures a complete line of sporting equipment. Leiden Enterprises operates a large chain of discount stores. Leiden has approached Jens with a special order for 30,000 deluxe baseballs to be bulk packed in boxes containing 500 baseballs each. Leiden is willing to pay $2.45 per baseball. The Jens Accounting Department knows that annual expected production is 400,000 baseballs. It also knows that the current year's production is 410,000 baseballs and the the maximum production capacity is 450,000 baseballs. The following additional information is available:

Standard unit cost data	
Direct materials	$ .90
Direct labor	.60
Manufacturing overhead	
Variable	.50
Fixed ($100,000 ÷ 400,000)	.25
Packaging per unit	.30
Advertising ($60,000 ÷ 400,000)	.15
Other fixed selling and administrative	
expenses ($120,000 ÷ 400,000)	.30
Product unit cost	$ 3.00
Unit selling price	$ 4.00
Total estimated bulk packaging costs	
(30,000 baseballs: 500 per box)	$2,500

Should Jens Sporting Goods, Inc., accept Leiden's offer?

An incremental analysis in the contribution margin reporting format appears in Exhibit 3. The report shows contribution margin for the Baseball Division's operations both with and without the Leiden order. Fixed costs are not included because

Exhibit 3. Incremental Analysis: Special Order Decision

Jens Sporting Goods, Inc.
Special Order Decision
Incremental Analysis

	Without Leiden Order (410,000 products)	With Leiden Order (440,000 products)	Difference in Favor of Accepting Leiden Order
Sales	$1,640,000	$1,713,500	$73,500
Less: Variable costs			
Direct materials	$ 369,000	$ 396,000	($27,000)
Direct labor	246,000	264,000	(18,000)
Variable manufacturing			
overhead	205,000	220,000	(15,000)
Packaging costs	123,000	125,500	(2,500)
Total variable costs	$ 943,000	$1,005,500	($62,500)
Contribution margin	$ 697,000	$ 708,000	$11,000

Decision: Accept the order.

the only costs affected by the order are direct materials, direct labor, variable manufacturing overhead, and packaging. Packaging costs will increase, but only by the amount of the added bulk packaging. All other costs will remain the same. The net result of accepting the special order is an $11,000 increase in contribution margin (and net income). This amount is verified by the following computation.

$$
\begin{aligned}
\text{Net Gain} \ &= \ [(\text{Unit Selling Price} \ - \ \text{Unit Variable Mfg. Costs}) \ \times \ \text{Units}] \\
&\quad - \ \text{Bulk Packaging Costs} \\
&= \ [(\$2.45 \ - \ \$2.00) \ \times \ 30{,}000] \ - \ \$2{,}500 \\
&= \ \$13{,}500 \ - \ \$2{,}500 \\
&= \ \$11{,}000
\end{aligned}
$$

Thus, the analysis reveals that Jens should accept the special order from Leiden Enterprises.

Now let us assume that Leiden is asking Jens to give a special price on the order. What would be the minimum special order price? If the total costs for the special order are $62,500, the cost per baseball is $2.083 ($62,500 divided by 30,000). The special order price should cover this cost and generate a profit. If Jens would like to earn $3,000 from the special order, the special order price should be $2.19 ($2.083 cost per ball, rounded to $2.09, plus $.10 profit per ball [$3,000 divided by 30,000 balls]).

Of course, the decision made by Jens's management must be consistent with the company's strategic plan. Qualitative factors that might influence the decision are (1) the special order's impact on sales to regular customers, (2) the potential of the special order to lead into new sales areas, and (3) the customer's ability to maintain an ongoing relationship that includes good ordering and paying practices. Notice that the sales of $1,640,000 in baseballs before the special order absorbed all the fixed costs of manufacturing overhead, advertising, and selling and administration.

Segment Profitability Decisions

OBJECTIVE 3c

Prepare decision analyses in a manufacturing organization for segment profitability decisions

Another type of operating decision managers must face is whether to keep or drop unprofitable segments, such as product lines, services, sales territories, divisions, or departments. The manager must select the alternative that maximizes net income, based on the organization's strategic plan and objectives, the relevant revenues and costs, and qualitative factors. The objective of this analysis is to identify the segments that have a negative segment margin.

A segment margin is a segment's sales revenue minus its direct costs (direct variable costs and direct fixed costs traceable to the segment). Such costs are assumed to be avoidable. If the segment were dropped, those costs would not be incurred. If a segment has a positive segment margin (that is, if the segment's revenue is greater than its direct costs), the segment is kept. The segment is able to cover its own direct costs and contribute a portion of its revenue to cover common costs and add to net income. If a segment has a negative segment margin (if the segment's revenue is less than its direct costs), the segment is dropped. Recognize that certain common costs will be incurred regardless of the decision. Those are unavoidable costs, and the remaining segments must have sufficient contribution margin to cover their own direct costs and the common costs for the company.

An analysis of segment profitability includes the preparation of a segmented income statement using variable costing to identify variable and fixed costs. The fixed costs that are traceable to the segments are called *direct fixed costs*. The remaining fixed costs are common costs and are not assigned to segments.

Assume that management at Lebo Corporation wants to determine if Division Y should be eliminated. A segmented income statement is prepared, separating variable and fixed costs to calculate the contribution margin. The total fixed costs of $84,000 are separated further by directly tracing $55,500 to Division X and $16,500 to Division Y. The remaining $12,000 is common fixed costs. The following segmented income statement shows the segment margins for Divisions X and Y and the net income for the total company:

Lebo Corporation			
Segmented Income Statement			
For the Year Ended December 31, 20xx			
	Division X	**Division Y**	**Total Company**
Sales	$135,000	$15,000	$150,000
Less variable costs	52,500	7,500	60,000
Contribution margin	$ 82,500	$ 7,500	$ 90,000
Less direct fixed costs	55,500	16,500	72,000
Segment margin	$ 27,000	($ 9,000)	$ 18,000
Less common fixed costs			12,000
Net income			$ 6,000

The analysis of Situation 1 in Exhibit 4 shows that dropping Division Y will increase net income by $9,000. Unless the company is able to increase Division Y's segment margin by increasing sales revenue or reducing direct costs, the segment should be dropped. The incremental approach to analyzing this decision isolates the segment and focuses on its segment margin, as shown in the last column of the exhibit.

The decision to drop a segment also requires a careful review of the other segments to see if they will be affected. Let's extend the illustration by assuming that Division X's sales volume and variable costs will decrease 20 percent if Division Y is eliminated. The reduction in sales volume stems from the loss of customers who purchase products from both divisions. The analysis of Situation 2 in Exhibit 4 shows that dropping Division Y would reduce the segment margin and also net income for the company by $7,500. In this situation, Lebo Corporation would want to keep Division Y.

Product Mix Decisions

OBJECTIVE 3d

Prepare decision analyses in a manufacturing organization for product mix decisions involving constrained resources

A company may be unable to provide the full variety of products that customers demand in a given time period. Limits to resources such as machine time or available labor may restrict the types or quantities of products manufactured. Resource constraints can also be associated with other production activities, such as inspection and equipment setup. The question is, Which product or products contribute the most to company profitability in relation to the amount of capital assets or other constrained resources needed to produce those items? To satisfy customers' demands and maximize net income, managers will choose to manufacture the most profitable product lines first. To identify such product lines, the contribution margin per constrained resource (such as labor hours or machine hours) for each product is calculated.

The objective of a product mix decision is to select the alternative that maximizes the contribution margin per constrained resource based on the organization's strategic plan and objectives, the relevant revenues and costs, and qualitative factors. The decision analysis, which uses incremental analysis to identify the relevant costs and revenues, is completed in two steps. First, calculate the contribution margin per unit for each product line affected by the constrained resource. The contri-

Question: Keep or drop Division Y with no change in activity of Division X

Exhibit 4. Incremental Analysis: Segment Profitability Decision

Lebo Corporation
Segment Profitability Decision
Incremental Analysis—Situation 1

	Keep Division Y	Drop Division Y	Difference in Favor of Dropping Division Y
Sales	$150,000	$135,000	($15,000)
Less variable costs	60,000	52,500	7,500
Contribution margin	$ 90,000	$ 82,500	($ 7,500)
Less direct fixed costs	72,000	55,500	16,500
Segment margin	$ 18,000	$ 27,000	$ 9,000
Less common fixed costs	12,000	12,000	-0-
Net income	$ 6,000	$ 15,000	$ 9,000

Decision: Drop Division Y.

Question: Keep or drop Division Y with a 20 percent decrease in sales volume for Division X

Lebo Corporation
Segment Profitability Decision
Incremental Analysis—Situation 2

	Keep Division Y	Drop Division Y	Difference in Opposition to Dropping Division Y
Sales	$150,000	$108,000	($42,000)
Less variable costs	60,000	42,000	18,000
Contribution margin	$ 90,000	$ 66,000	($24,000)
Less direct fixed costs	72,000	55,500	16,500
Segment margin	$ 18,000	$ 10,500	($ 7,500)
Less common fixed costs	12,000	12,000	-0-
Net income	$ 6,000	($ 1,500)	($ 7,500)

Decision: Keep Division Y.

bution margin per unit equals the selling price per unit less the variable costs per unit. Next, calculate the contribution margin per unit of the constrained resource. The contribution margin per unit of the constrained resource equals the contribution margin per unit divided by the quantity of the constrained resource required per unit.

Assume that Grady Enterprises manufactures three computer games—Rising Star, Ghost Master, and Road Warrior. The product line data are as follows:

	Rising Star	Ghost Master	Road Warrior
Current unit sales demand	20,000	30,000	18,000
Machine hours per unit	2	1	2.5
Selling price per unit	$24.00	$18.00	$32.00
Unit variable manufacturing costs	$12.50	$10.00	$18.75
Unit variable selling costs	$6.50	$5.00	$6.25

The current production capacity is 100,000 machine hours.

Question 1: *Which computer game should be manufactured first? Second? Last?*

The product mix analysis is shown in Exhibit 5. It indicates that the Ghost Master computer game should be manufactured first because it provides the highest contribution margin per machine hour. Road Warrior would be manufactured next, and Rising Star would be manufactured last.

Question 2: *How many of each type of computer game should be produced and sold to maximize the company's contribution margin based on the current production activity of 100,000 machine hours? What is the total contribution margin for that combination?*

Question: Determine the order in which the products should be manufactured.

Decision: Manufacture games in the following order: Ghost Master, Road Warrior, and Rising Star.

Question: Determine the quantity of each product that will be produced if sales demand exceeds the machine hours available.

Decision: Manufacture 30,000 units of Ghost Master, 18,000 units of Road Warrior, and 12,500 units of Rising Star.

Exhibit 5. Incremental Analysis: Product Mix Decision Involving Constrained Resources

Grady Enterprises
Product Mix Decision: Ranking the Order of Production
Incremental Analysis

	Rising Star	Ghost Master	Road Warrior
Selling price per unit	$24.00	$18.00	$32.00
Less variable costs			
Manufacturing	$12.50	$10.00	$18.75
Selling	6.50	5.00	6.25
Total unit variable costs	$19.00	$15.00	$25.00
Contribution margin per unit (A)	$ 5.00	$ 3.00	$ 7.00
Machine hours per unit (B)	2	1	2.5
Contribution margin per machine hour (A ÷ B)	$ 2.50	$ 3.00	$ 2.80

Grady Enterprises
Product Mix Decision: Number of Units to Make
Incremental Analysis

	Machine Hours
Total machine hours available	100,000
Less machine hours to produce Ghost Master (30,000 units × 1 machine hour per unit)	30,000
Balance of machine hours available	70,000
Less machine hours to produce Road Warrior (18,000 units × 2.5 machine hours per unit)	45,000
Balance of machine hours available	25,000
Less machine hours to produce Rising Star (12,500 units × 2 machine hours per unit)	25,000
Balance of machine hours available	0

To begin the analysis, compare the current production activity to the required production activity to meet the current unit sales demand. The company needs 115,000 machine hours to meet the current unit sales demand: 40,000 machine hours for Rising Star (20,000 units × 2 machine hours per unit), 30,000 machine hours for Ghost Master (30,000 units × 1 machine hour per unit), and 45,000 machine hours for Road Warrior (18,000 units × 2.5 machine hours per unit). Since that amount exceeds the current capacity of 100,000 machine hours, management must determine the product mix that maximizes the company's contribution margin, which will also maximize its net income. The calculations in the second part of Exhibit 5 show that Grady Enterprises should manufacture 30,000 units of Ghost Master, 18,000 units of Road Warrior, and 12,500 units of Rising Star. The total contribution margin is:

	Contribution Margin
Ghost Master (30,000 units × $3.00 per unit)	$ 90,000
Road Warrior (18,000 units × $7.00 per unit)	126,000
Rising Star (12,500 units × $5 per unit)	62,500
Total contribution margin	$278,500

Sell or Process-Further Decisions

OBJECTIVE 3e

Prepare decision analyses in a manufacturing organization for sell or process-further decisions

Some manufacturing companies make products that can either be sold in a basic condition or be processed further and sold as a more refined product to a different market. For example, a meatpacking company processes cattle into meat and meat-related products, such as bones and hides. The company may choose to sell sides of beef and pounds of bones and hides to other companies for further processing. Alternatively, it could choose to cut and package the meat for immediate sale in grocery stores, process bone into fertilizer for gardeners, or tan hides into refined leather for purses.

A sell or process-further decision is a decision about whether to sell a joint product at the split-off point or sell it after further processing. Joint products are two or more products, made from a common material or process, that cannot be identified as separate products during some or all of the production process. Only at a specific point, called the split-off point, do joint products become separate and identifiable. At that point, a company may choose to sell the product as is or to process it into another form for sale to a different market.

The objective of a sell or process-further decision is to select the alternative that maximizes net income, based on the organization's strategic plan and objectives, the relevant revenues and costs, and qualitative factors. To complete the analysis, calculate the incremental revenue, which is the difference between the total revenue if the product is sold at the split-off point and the total revenue if the product is sold after further processing. Compare the incremental revenue to the incremental costs of processing further. Choose to process a product further if the incremental revenue is greater than the incremental costs of processing further. If the incremental costs are greater than the incremental revenue, choose to sell the product at the split-off point. Be sure to ignore joint costs (or common costs) in your analysis, since they are incurred *before* the split-off point and do not change if further processing occurs. Although accountants assign joint costs to products when valuing inventories and calculating cost of goods sold, joint costs are not relevant to a sell or process-further decision and are omitted from the decision analysis.

For example, H & L Beef Products, Inc., processes cattle. It can sell the meat as sides of beef or process it further into final cuts (steaks, roasts, and hamburger). As part of the company's strategic plan, management is looking for new markets for meat or meat byproducts. Part of the production process separates hides and bones for sale to other manufacturers. However, management is considering whether it

BUSINESS BULLETIN: BUSINESS PRACTICE

Review the following quantitative and qualitative factors before deciding whether to keep your information system operations in-house or outsource the work to others.

1. The vendor's fee for each year of the contract period. Fees in subsequent years may be higher than expected or may be adjusted according to the cost-of-living index.
2. Costs of administering the outsourcing contract.
3. Contracting and legal costs, including the monetary and opportunity costs involved in contracting, renegotiating, or settling vendor disputes.
4. Costs associated with transfer of software licenses.
5. Information system salaries and severance payments. Consider salaries of staff who are to be retained and payments required for employees who are to be terminated.[3]

would be profitable to process the hides into leather and the bones into fertilizer. The costs of the cattle and of transporting, hanging, storing, and cutting sides of beef were $125,000. The company's accountant provided the following information.

Product	Sales Revenue if Sold at Split-off	Sales Revenue if Sold After Further Processing	Additional Processing Costs
Meat	$100,000	$200,000	$80,000
Bones	20,000	40,000	15,000
Hides	50,000	55,000	10,000

The decision analysis in Exhibit 6 indicates that meat and bones can be profitably processed further, but the hides should be sold at the split-off point. Notice that the $125,000 joint costs were ignored because they are sunk costs that will not influence the decision.

As mentioned earlier, the final decision is based on the company's strategic plan and objectives, the relevant revenues and costs, and qualitative factors. A decision to process further must agree with the company's strategic plan to expand into new markets. In addition, the company's ability to obtain the resources to manufacture a quality product must be considered.

Decision: Sell hides at the split-off point and further process meat and bones into final cuts of meat and fertilizer.

Exhibit 6. Incremental Analysis: Sell or Process-Further Decision

H & L Beef Products, Inc.
Sell or Process-Further Decision
Incremental Analysis

	Meat	Bones	Hides
Incremental revenue if processed further:			
Process further	$200,000	$40,000	$55,000
Split-off	100,000	20,000	50,000
Incremental revenue	$100,000	$20,000	$ 5,000
Less incremental costs	80,000	15,000	10,000
Net income (loss) from processing further	$ 20,000	$ 5,000	($ 5,000)

Short-Run Decisions in a Nonmanufacturing Organization

OBJECTIVE 4

Apply short-run decision analysis to nonmanufacturing organizations

Managers of nonmanufacturing organizations must also make short-run decisions. Typical short-run decisions in service organizations include whether to outsource a service, accept or bid for a special order, drop an unprofitable service, and provide one service before another because of limited labor hours. Managers of retail operations must also make decisions about whether to add or drop a product line and what products to display for sale when shelf and floor space are limited.

To see how short-run decision analysis applies to a nonmanufacturing organization, let's consider CyberWeb Services, a small company owned by Simon Orozco. Simon provides Web page services to small businesses. His services include the preparation of Basic Web Pages and Custom Web Pages. A Basic Web Page includes designing a home page with three links to supporting pages, installing the pages on the Web, and maintaining the Web pages for one year. The design is limited to one of three basic color schemes, icons for three connecting sites, and no pictures or graphics.

A Custom Web Page includes designing a home page with multiple links to supporting pages, installing the pages on the Web, and redesigning the format and refreshing the content of the pages for six months. The design reflects the client's preferences in color scheme, icons, pictures, and graphics.

The following summary of information will be used to make several short-run decisions for CyberWeb Services.

	Basic Web Page	Custom Web Page
Service revenue per page	$200	$750
Variable costs per page	77	600
Contribution margin per page	$123	$150

Total fixed costs for 20xx are $78,000.

Service Mix Decisions   One of CyberWeb Service's two graphic designers, Taylor Campbell, was planning to take maternity leave in July and August 20xx. As a result, there would be only one designer available to perform the work, and design labor hours would be a resource constraint. Simon planned to help the other designer complete the 160 orders for Basic Web Pages and 30 orders for Custom Web Pages for those two months. However, he wanted to know which pages should be completed first. Although Custom Web Pages had a higher contribution margin per service, each Custom Web Page required 12.5 design hours, whereas Basic Web Pages required only 1 design hour per page.

Exhibit 7 shows the analysis that the accountant prepared. The contribution margin per design labor hour was calculated for Basic Web Pages and Custom Web Pages. The analysis indicates that Basic Web Pages had a lower contribution margin per service ($123) than Custom Web Pages ($150) but a higher contribution margin per design hour ($123) than Custom Web Pages ($12). Based on this analysis, Simon decided that he would help the other graphic designer complete Basic Web Pages first.

Outsourcing Decisions   In mid-August, Taylor Campbell notified Simon that she was moving to another state and would no longer be able to work at CyberWeb Services. She suggested that Simon contract the work out to Ky To, a freelance graphic designer who works at home. Simon had to decide whether to hire a new employee or to outsource some of the Web design work to someone outside of his company, like Ky To. If he hired a new employee, he would pay $32 per design hour for the employee to work 600 hours and incur service overhead costs of $2 per design hour. If he outsourced the work to Ky To, he would pay $36 per design hour to

Exhibit 7. Incremental Analysis: Service Mix Decision Involving Constrained Resources

CyberWeb Services
Service Mix Decision: Ranking the Order in Which the Services Are Provided

	Basic Web Pages	Custom Web Pages
Service revenue per page	$200	$750
Less variable costs per page	77	600
Contribution margin per page (A)	$123	$150
Design hours per page (B)	1	12.5
Contribution margin per design hour (A ÷ B)	$123	$ 12

Decision: Prepare the Basic Web Pages first.

work 600 hours. He would also be able to redirect the use of a computer and server to generate $4,000 in additional revenue from Web page maintenance work.

Exhibit 8 shows the accountant's analysis of CyberWeb Services' outsourcing decision. Although the cost to hire an employee to perform the work in the company ($21,600) was less than the cost to contract the work to Ky, the opportunity cost of $4,000 from additional maintenance services influenced Simon's final decision to outsource the work to Ky. Fixed overhead costs were excluded from the analysis because none would be eliminated if Ky did the work. Simon decided to outsource the work to Ky so that he could expand the company's Web page maintenance services.

Because Simon wanted to ensure the quality and timely delivery of the outsourced work, he planned to measure Ky's performance. He would measure timeliness by tracking the number of times Ky did not deliver the Web pages on time, and

Exhibit 8. Incremental Analysis: Outsourcing Decision for a Nonmanufacturing Organization

CyberWeb Services
Outsourcing Decision
Incremental Analysis

	Hire a New Designer for the Company	Outsource Work to Ky To	Difference in Favor of Outsourcing
Cost to buy graphic design work		$21,600*	($21,600)
Cost to do graphic design work in-house			
Direct professional labor	$19,200†		19,200
Service overhead	1,200‡		1,200
Total costs	$20,400	$21,600	(1,200)
Opportunity costs	4,000		4,000
Totals	$24,400	$21,600	$ 2,800

Decision: Outsource the work to Ky To.

*$36 per design hour × 600 design hours.
†$32 per design hour × 600 design hours.
‡$2 per design hour × 600 design hours.

Exhibit 9. Incremental Analysis: Special Order Decision for a Nonmanufacturing Organization

	CyberWeb Services Special Order Decision Incremental Analysis		
	Without THC Order (10 Web Pages)	With THC Order (11 Web Pages)	Difference in Favor of Rejecting Order
Service revenue	$7,500	$7,900	($400)
Less variable costs			
Direct professional labor	6,000	6,420	420
Contribution margin	$1,500	$1,480	$20
Less fixed costs	1,000	1,000	-0-
Net income (loss)	$ 500	$ 480	$ 20

Decision: Reject special order.

he would measure quality by identifying the number of customer complaints related to Ky's work. Those performance measures would help Simon make a later decision about whether to continue outsourcing work to Ky To or to hire a new full-time designer.

Special Order Decisions   In September, a nonprofit organization, Toys for Homeless Children (THC), offered CyberWeb $400 to prepare a Custom Web Page to help the organization use the Internet to attract toy donations. The home page for the THC Web site was to include special animated graphics of toys and stuffed animals. Simon estimated that it would take 12.5 design labor hours at $32 per design hour and 2 installation labor hours at $10 per installation hour to complete the job. Fixed costs were already covered by regular business. The analysis is summarized in Exhibit 9. An alternative approach would be to compare the special order price to the incremental costs, as follows:

Special order price		$400
Incremental costs:		
Direct professional labor: design ($32 × 12.5)	$400	
Direct professional labor: install ($10 × 2)	20	420
Loss on special order		$(20)

Although the special order would reduce net income by $20, Simon decided to accept it because he wanted CyberWeb to donate services to help the community.

Segment Profitability Decisions   Simon became concerned about the profitability of his product lines. He believed that Custom Web Pages were providing only a small contribution to the company's net income from operations. The accountant prepared a segmented income statement for CyberWeb Service by separating the sales, variable costs, and direct fixed costs into segments for Basic Web Pages and Custom Web Pages. As shown in Exhibit 10, Custom Web Pages had a negative segment margin of $2,000. The revenues from those services were not sufficient to cover the related direct costs.

Simon needed to find out why Custom Web Page services were not profitable because he wanted to continue providing them. To help him identify the problem

Exhibit 10. Segmented Income Statement: Decision for a Nonmanufacturing Organization

CyberWeb Services
Segmented Income Statement
For the Year Ended December 31, 20x1

	Basic Web Pages (1,000 units)	Custom Web Pages (200 units)	Total Company
Service revenue			
Basic Web Pages	$200,000		$200,000
Custom Web Pages		$150,000	150,000
	$200,000	$150,000	$350,000
Less: Variable costs			
Direct professional labor: design	$ 32,000	$ 80,000	$112,000
Direct professional labor: install	30,000	4,000	34,000
Direct professional labor: maintain	15,000	36,000	51,000
Total variable costs	$ 77,000	$120,000	$197,000
Contribution margin	$123,000	$ 30,000	$153,000
Less: Direct fixed costs			
Depreciation on computer equipment	$ 6,000	$ 12,000	$ 18,000
Depreciation on servers	10,000	20,000	30,000
Total direct fixed costs	$ 16,000	$ 32,000	$ 48,000
Segment margin	$107,000	($ 2,000)	$105,000
Less: Common fixed costs			
Building rent			24,000
Supplies			1,000
Insurance			3,000
Telephone			1,500
Web site rental			500
Total fixed costs			$ 30,000
Net income			$ 75,000

Exhibit 11. Incremental Analysis: Segment Profitability Decision for a Nonmanufacturing Organization

CyberWeb Services
Segment Profitability Decision
Incremental Analysis

	Design	Install	Maintain	Total
Service revenue	$60,000	$25,000	$65,000	$150,000
Less variable costs	80,000	4,000	36,000	120,000
Contribution margin	($20,000)	$21,000	$29,000	$ 30,000
Less direct fixed costs	6,000	13,000	13,000	32,000
Segment margin	($26,000)	$ 8,000	$16,000	($ 2,000)

area, the accountant prepared a segment margin analysis for Custom Web Pages showing the three professional labor activities (design, install, and maintain). Exhibit 11 shows that the design activity has a negative segment margin of $26,000. This information helped Simon focus his attention on that activity. He will also want information about the time spent completing the design work and the wages paid to the designers to see if he can reduce labor costs. He may also want to increase the company's fees for Custom Web Page services, especially if the competition is charging higher fees for similar work.

Chapter Review

REVIEW OF LEARNING OBJECTIVES

1. **Discuss the role of cost information in short-run decision analysis and the management cycle.** Cost information is used for short-run decision analysis. Both quantitative and qualitative information are important. Such information should be relevant, timely, and presented in a format that is easy to use in decision making. In the planning stage of the management cycle, management estimates the cost and revenue information that will be useful for short-run decisions. Managers use this information during the executing stage to make decisions to accept a special order, examine the profitability of a segment, select the appropriate product mix given a resource constraint, contract with outside suppliers of goods and services, or sell a product as is or process it further. In the review stage, each decision is evaluated to determine if the forecasted results were obtained. Reporting occurs throughout the period to support the information selected, the decision made, and the impact of that decision on the organization.

2. **Identify the steps in the management decision cycle and discuss the role of relevant decision information and incremental analysis in short-run decision analysis.** The management decision cycle begins with discovery of a problem or need. Then alternative courses of action to solve the problem or meet the need are identified. Next, a complete analysis to determine the effects of each alternative on business operations is prepared. With those supporting data, the decision maker chooses the best alternative. After the decision has been carried out, the accountant conducts a postdecision review to see if the decision was correct or if other needs have arisen. Any data that relate to future costs, revenues, or uses of resources and that will differ among alternative courses of action are considered relevant decision information. Projected sales or estimated costs, such as direct materials or direct labor, that differ for each decision alternative are examples of relevant information. Incremental analysis helps managers compare alternatives by focusing on the differences in their projected revenues and costs. The accountant organizes relevant information to determine which alternative contributes the most to profits or incurs the lowest costs. Only data that differ for each alternative appear in the report.

3. **Prepare decision analyses in a manufacturing organization for (a) outsourcing decisions, (b) special order decisions, (c) segment profitability decisions, (d) product mix decisions involving constrained resources, and (e) sell or process-further decisions.** Outsourcing (also called make-or-buy) decision analysis helps managers decide whether to use suppliers from outside the organization to provide

services and/or goods that could be performed or produced internally. An incremental analysis of the expected costs and revenues for each alternative identifies the best alternative.

A special order decision is a decision about whether to accept or reject a special order at a price below the normal market price. One approach is to compare the special order price to the relevant costs to see if a profit can be generated. Another approach is to prepare a special order bid price by calculating a minimum selling price for the special order. Generally, fixed costs are irrelevant to a special order decision, since such costs were covered by regular sales activity.

Segment profitability decisions involve the review of segments of an organization, such as product lines, services, sales territories, divisions, or departments. Often managers must decide whether to add or drop a segment. A segment with a negative segment margin may be dropped. A segment margin is a segment's sales revenue minus its direct costs, which include variable costs and avoidable fixed costs.

Product mix decisions require the selection of the most profitable combination of product sales when a company makes more than one product using a common constrained resource. The product lines that generate the highest contribution margin per constrained resource are produced and sold first.

Sell or process-further decisions require managers to choose between selling a joint product at its split-off point or processing it into a more refined product. The accountant compares the incremental revenues and costs of the two alternatives. Joint processing costs are irrelevant to the decision, since they are identical for both alternatives. A product should be processed further only if the incremental revenues generated exceed the incremental costs incurred.

4. **Apply short-run decision analysis to nonmanufacturing organizations.** Short-run decision analysis applies to nonmanufacturing organizations as well as to manufacturing organizations. Typical short-run decisions in a service organization include whether to outsource a service, accept or bid for a special order, drop an unprofitable service, and provide one service before another because of limited labor hours. Retail operations must also make decisions about whether to add or drop a product line and what products should be displayed for sale when shelf and floor space are limited.

REVIEW OF CONCEPTS AND TERMINOLOGY

The following concepts and terms were introduced in this chapter:

LO 2   **Incremental analysis:** A technique used in decision analysis that compares alternatives by focusing on the differences in their projected revenues and costs.

LO 2   **Irrelevant costs:** Costs that may be either sunk costs or costs that do not differ among alternatives.

LO 3   **Joint products:** Two or more products, made from a common material or process, that cannot be identified as separate products during some or all of the production process.

LO 2   **Management decision cycle:** The five steps managers take in making decisions and following up on them.

LO 2   **Opportunity costs:** The revenues forfeited or lost when one alternative is chosen over another.

LO 3   **Outsourcing:** The use of suppliers outside the organization to perform services or produce goods that could be performed or produced internally.

LO 2   **Relevant costs:** Costs that differ among alternatives. Also called *avoidable costs*.

LO 2   **Relevant decision information:** Data about future costs, revenues, and resource usage that differ among the alternatives being evaluated.

LO 3   **Segment margin:** A segment's sales revenue minus its direct costs (direct variable costs and direct fixed costs traceable to the segment).

LO 3   **Sell or process-further decision:** A decision about whether to sell a joint product at the split-off point or sell it after further processing.

LO 3   **Special order decision:** A decision about whether to accept or reject a special product order at a price below the normal market price.

LO 3 **Split-off point:** A specific point in the production process at which two or more joint products become separate and identifiable. At that point, a company may choose to sell the product as is or to process it into another form for sale to a different market.

LO 2 **Sunk costs:** Costs incurred because of a previous decision that cannot be recovered through the current decision.

REVIEW PROBLEM
Short-Run Operating Decision Analysis

LO 4 Ten years ago, Dale Bandy formed Home Services, Inc., a company specializing in repair and maintenance services for the home and its surroundings. At present, Home Services has six offices in major cities across the country. Services are available to the home owner. During the past two years, the company's profitability has decreased, and Dale wants to determine which service lines are not meeting the company's profit targets. Once the unprofitable service lines have been identified, he will either eliminate them or set higher prices. If higher prices are set, all variable and fixed operating, selling, and general administration costs will be covered by the price structure. The data from the most recent year-end closing shown below were available for the analysis. Four service lines are under serious review.

Home Services, Inc.
Segmented Income Statement
For the Year Ended December 31, 20x2

	Auto Repair Service	Boat Repair Service	Tile Floor Repair Service	Tree Trimming Service	Total Company Impact
Net sales	$297,500	$114,300	$126,400	$97,600	$635,800
Less: Variable costs					
Direct labor	$119,000	$ 40,005	$ 44,240	$34,160	$237,405
Operating supplies	14,875	5,715	6,320	4,880	31,790
Small tools	11,900	4,572	5,056	7,808	29,336
Replacement parts	59,500	22,860	25,280	—	107,640
Truck costs	—	11,430	12,640	14,640	38,710
Selling costs	44,625	17,145	18,960	9,760	90,490
Other variable costs	5,950	2,286	2,528	1,952	12,716
Total	$255,850	$104,013	$115,024	$73,200	$548,087
Contribution margin	$ 41,650	$ 10,287	$ 11,376	$24,400	$ 87,713
Less direct fixed costs	35,800	16,300	24,100	5,200	81,400
Segment margin	$ 5,850	($ 6,013)	($ 12,724)	$19,200	$ 6,313
Less common fixed costs					32,100
Net income (loss)					($ 25,787)

REQUIRED

1. Analyze the performance of the four services being reviewed. Should Dale eliminate any of the service lines? Why?
2. Why might Dale want to continue providing unprofitable service lines?
3. Even though some of the unprofitable services can be eliminated, the company still has a net loss from its operations. Identify some possible causes for poor performance by the services. What actions do you recommend?

ANSWER TO REVIEW PROBLEM

1. When deciding whether to eliminate any of the four service lines, Dale should concentrate on the service lines that have a negative segment margin. If the revenues from a service line are less than the sum of its variable and direct fixed costs, then other service lines must cover some of the losing line's costs while carrying the burden of the common fixed costs.

   By looking at the segmented income statement, Dale can see that the company will improve its net income by $18,737 ($6,013 + $12,724) by eliminating the Boat Repair Service and the Tile Floor Repair Service, both of which have a negative segment margin. His decision can also be supported by the following analysis:

Home Services, Inc.
Segmented Profitability Decision
Incremental Analysis

	Keep Boat Repair and Tile Floor Repair	Eliminate Boat Repair and Tile Floor Repair	Difference in Favor of Dropping Boat Repair and Tile Floor Repair
Net sales	$635,800	$395,100	($240,700)
Less variable costs	548,087	329,050	219,037
Contribution margin	$ 87,713	$ 66,050	($ 21,663)
Less direct fixed costs	81,400	41,000	40,400
Segment margin	$ 6,313	$ 25,050	$ 18,737
Less common fixed costs	32,100	32,100	0
Net income (loss)	($ 25,787)	($ 7,050)	$ 18,737

2. Dale may want to continue offering the unprofitable service lines if their elimination would negatively affect the sale of auto repair or tree trimming services. Dale may also want to diversify into new markets by offering new services. Dale should be prepared to initially suffer some losses in order to enter the new markets.
3. Among the possible causes for poor performance by the four services are

   a. Service fees set too low
   b. Inadequate advertising
   c. High direct labor costs
   d. Other variable costs too high
   e. Poor management of fixed costs
   f. Excessive management costs

   To improve profitability, the organization can eliminate nonvalue-adding costs, increase service fees, or increase the volume of services provided to customers.

Chapter Assignments

BUILDING YOUR KNOWLEDGE FOUNDATION

Questions

1. List some common types of short-run decisions that can be made during the executing stage of the management cycle.
2. List qualitative factors that will influence a short-run decision.
3. What are the objectives of incremental analysis? What types of decision analyses depend on the incremental approach?
4. Illustrate and discuss some qualitative information included in decision analysis.
5. List the business activities that are outsourced more often than others. What makes them attractive for outsourcing?
6. How does one determine which data are relevant to a make-or-buy decision?
7. What is the objective of a special order decision?
8. Discuss two approaches to making a special order decision.
9. What justifies excluding fixed overhead costs from the analysis of a special order? Under what circumstances are fixed costs relevant to the analysis?
10. How does a manager decide whether to keep or drop an unprofitable segment?
11. What is a segment margin?
12. Give examples of resource constraints that could affect the order in which products are made.
13. What are the two steps in the analysis of a product mix decision?
14. What are joint products?
15. What is the split-off point?
16. Explain the sell or process-further decision analysis.
17. Explain the role of joint costs in sell or process-further decision analysis.
18. List the types of short-run decision analyses that can also be performed in a non-manufacturing organization.

Short Exercises

SE 1.

LO 1 *Qualitative and Quantitative Information in Short-Run Decision Analysis*

The owner of Le Chat Rouge, a French restaurant, is deciding whether to take Chicken Tarragon off the menu. Tell whether each of the following pieces of decision information is qualitative or quantitative. If quantitative, then specify whether financial or nonfinancial.

1. The time needed to prepare the chicken *Qty.-Nonfinancial*
2. The daily number of customers who order the chicken *Qty.- nonfinancial*
3. Whether competing French restaurants have this entrée on the menu *Qual.*
4. The labor cost of the chef who prepares the chicken *Qty.-financial-Stated in terms of $*
5. The fact that the president of a nearby company, who brings ten guests with him each week, always orders Chicken Tarragon *Qual.*

SE 2.

LO 2 *Using Incremental Analysis*

Forlands Corporation has assembled the following information related to the purchase of a new automated degreasing machine.

	Harvey Machine	Vogle Machine
Increase in revenue	$43,200	$49,300
Increase in annual operating costs		
Direct materials	12,200	12,200
Direct labor	10,200	10,600
Variable manufacturing overhead	24,500	26,900
Fixed manufacturing overhead (including depreciation)	12,400	12,400

Using incremental analysis and only relevant information, compute the difference in favor of the Vogle machine.

LO 3 *Make-or-Buy Decision*

SE 3. Zorich Company assembles products from a group of interconnecting parts. Some of the parts are produced by the company, and some are purchased from outside vendors. The vendor for Part 23X has just increased its price by 35 percent, to $10 per unit for the first 5,000 units and $9 per additional unit ordered each year. The company uses 7,500 units of Part 23X each year. Unit costs to make and sell the part are:

Direct materials	$3.50
Direct labor	1.75
Variable manufacturing overhead	4.25
Variable selling costs for the assembled product	3.75

[handwritten: will be the same with either option]

Should the company continue to purchase the part, or should it begin making the part?

LO 3 *Special Order Decision*

SE 4. Bixler Company has received a special order for Product YTZ at a selling price of $20 per unit. This order is over and above normal production, and budgeted production and sales targets for the year have already been exceeded. Capacity exists to satisfy the special order. No selling costs will be incurred in connection with this order. Unit costs to manufacture and sell Product YTZ are as follows: Direct materials, $7.60; direct labor, $3.75; variable manufacturing overhead, $9.25; fixed manufacturing costs, $4.85; variable selling costs, $2.75; and fixed general and administrative costs, $6.75. Should Bixler Company accept the order?

LO 3 *Decision to Eliminate Unprofitable Segment*

SE 5. Perez Company is evaluating its two divisions, West Division and East Division. Data for the West Division include sales of $530,000, variable costs of $290,000, and fixed costs of $260,000, 50 percent of which are traceable to the division. East Division's efforts for the same time period include sales of $610,000, variable costs of $340,000, and fixed costs of $290,000, 60 percent of which are traceable to the division. Should either of the divisions be considered for elimination? Is there any other problem that needs attention?

LO 3 *Product Mix Decision with Resource Constraints*

SE 6. Let It Snow, Inc., makes three kinds of snowboards, but it has a limited number of machine hours available to make them. Product line data are as follows:

	Wood	Plastic	Graphite
Machine hours per unit	1.25	1.0	1.5
Selling price per unit	$100	$120	$200
Variable manufacturing cost per unit	45	50	100
Variable selling costs per unit	15	26	36

In what order should the snowboard product lines be produced?

LO 3 *Sell or Process-Further Decision*

SE 7. Matsuki Industries produces three products from a single operation. Product A sells for $3 per unit, Product B sells for $6 per unit, and Product C sells for $9 per unit. When B is processed further, there are additional unit costs of $3, and its new selling price is $10 per unit. Each product is allocated $2 of joint costs from the initial production operation. Should Product B be processed further, or should it be sold at the end of the initial operation?

LO 4 *Dropping a Segment in a Service Organization*

SE 8. Dental Associates, Inc., is currently operating at less than capacity. The company thinks it could cut costs by outsourcing dental cleaning to an independent dental hygienist for $50 per cleaning. Currently, a dental hygienist is employed for $30 an hour. A dental cleaning usually takes one hour to perform and consumes $10 of dental supplies, $8 of variable overhead, and $16 of fixed overhead. Should Dental Associates, Inc., continue to perform dental cleanings, or should it begin to outsource them?

Exercises

LO 2 *Relevant Data and Incremental Analysis*

E 1. Henry Corrado, the business manager for Socorro Industries, must select a new computer and word processing package for his secretary. Rental of Model A, which is similar to the model now being used, is $2,200 per year. Model B is a deluxe computer that rents for $2,900 per year, but will require a new desk for the secretary. The annual desk rental charge is $750. The secretary's salary of $1,200 per month will not change. If Model B is rented, $280 in annual software training costs will be incurred. Model B has greater capacity and is expected to save $1,550 per year in part-time secretarial wages. Upkeep and operating costs will not differ between the two models.

1. Identify the relevant data in this problem.
2. Prepare an incremental analysis to aid the business manager in his decision.

LO 3 *Make-or-Buy Decision*

E 2. One component of a radio produced by Burns Audio Systems, Inc., is currently being purchased for $225 per 100 parts. Management is studying the possibility of manufacturing that component. Annual production (usage) at Burns is 70,000 units; fixed costs (all of which remain unchanged whether the part is made or purchased) are $38,500; and variable costs are $.95 per unit for direct materials, $.55 per unit for direct labor, and $.60 per unit for manufacturing overhead.

Using incremental decision analysis, decide whether Burns Audio Systems, Inc., should manufacture the part or continue to purchase it from an outside vendor.

LO 3 *Special Order Decision*

E 3. Littell Antiquities, Ltd., produces antique-looking lampshades. Management has just received a request for a special order for 1,000 shades and must decide whether to accept it. Lowe Furniture Company, the purchaser, is offering to pay $25.00 per shade, including $3.00 per shade for shipping costs.

The variable production costs per shade include $9.20 for direct materials, $4.00 for direct labor, and $3.80 for variable manufacturing overhead. The current year's production is 20,000 shades, and maximum capacity is 25,000 shades. Fixed costs, including manufacturing overhead, advertising, and selling and administrative costs, total $70,000. The usual selling price is $25.00 per shade. Shipping costs average $3.00 per shade.

Determine whether Littell Antiquities should accept the special order.

LO 3 *Elimination of Unprofitable Segment*

E 4. Skylar Glass, Inc., has three divisions: Otta, Payo, and Qeeto. The segmented income statement for 20x0 revealed the following:

	Otta Division	Payo Division	Qeeto Division	Total Company
Skylar Glass, Inc.				
Divisional Profit Summary and Decision Analysis				
Sales	$290,000	$533,000	$837,000	$1,660,000
Less variable costs	147,000	435,000	472,000	1,054,000
Contribution margin	$143,000	$ 98,000	$365,000	$ 606,000
Less direct fixed costs	124,000	106,000	139,000	369,000
Segment margin	$ 19,000	($ 8,000)	$226,000	$ 237,000
Less common fixed costs				168,000
Net income				$ 69,000

1. How will Skylar Glass, Inc., be affected if the Payo Division is dropped?
2. If the Payo Division is dropped, the sales of the Qeeto Division will decrease by 10 percent. How will Skylar Glass, Inc., be affected if the Payo Division is dropped?

LO 3 *Scarce-Resource Usage*

E 5. Brunner, Inc., manufactures two products that require both machine processing and labor operations. Although there is unlimited demand for both products, Brunner could devote all its capacities to a single product. Unit prices, cost data, and processing requirements are:

	Product A	Product M
Unit selling price	$80	$220
Unit variable costs	$40	$ 90
Machine hours per unit	.4	1.4
Labor hours per unit	2	6

In 20x2 the company will be limited to 160,000 machine hours and 120,000 labor hours.

1. Compute the most profitable combination of products to be produced in 20x2.
2. Prepare an income statement using the contribution margin format for the product volume computed in **1.**

LO 3 *Sell or Process-Further Decision*

E 6. The Meat Market, in an attempt to provide superb customer service, is considering the expansion of its product offerings from whole hams and turkeys to complete ham and turkey dinners. Each dinner would include a carved ham or turkey, two side dishes, and six rolls or cornbread. The store's accountant has compiled the following relevant information:

Product	Sales Revenue, No Additional Service	Sales Revenue If Processed Further	Additional Processing Costs
Ham	$30	$50	$15
Turkey	20	35	15

A cooked, uncarved ham costs the Meat Market $20 to produce. A cooked, uncarved turkey costs $15 to prepare. Use incremental analysis to determine which products the Meat Market should offer.

LO 4 *Special Order for a Service Organization*

E 7. Courtney Accounting Services is considering a special order that it received from one of its corporate clients. The special order calls for Courtney to prepare the individual tax returns of the corporation's four largest shareholders. The company has idle capacity that could be used to complete the special order. The following data have been gathered about the preparation of individual tax returns:

Material cost per page	$ 1
Average hourly labor rate	$60
Standard hours per return	4
Standard pages per return	10
Variable overhead cost per page	$ .50
Fixed overhead cost per page	$ .50

Courtney Accounting Services would be satisfied with a $40 gross profit per return. Compute the minimum bid price for the entire order.

Problems

LO 3 *Make-or-Buy Decision*

P 1. The Westwinds Furniture Company of Santa Fe, New Mexico, is famous for its dining room furniture. One full department is engaged in the production of the Cottonwood line, an elegant but affordable dining room set. To date, the company has been manufacturing all pieces of the set, including the six chairs.

Management has just received word that a company in Montevideo, Colorado, is willing to produce the chairs for Westwinds Furniture Company at a total purchase price of $2,688,000 for the annual demand. Company records show that the following costs have been incurred in the production of the chairs: wood materials, $2,250 per 100 chairs; cloth materials, $850 per 100 chairs; direct labor, 1.2 hours per chair at $14.00 per hour; variable manufacturing overhead, $7.00 per direct labor hour; fixed factory overhead, depreciation, $135,000; and fixed manufacturing overhead, other, $109,400. Fixed manufacturing overhead would continue whether or not the chairs are produced. Assume that idle facilities cannot be used for any other purpose and that annual usage is 56,000 chairs.

REQUIRED

1. Prepare an incremental analysis to determine whether the chairs should be made by the company or purchased from the outside supplier in Montevideo.
2. Compute the unit costs to make one chair and to buy one chair.

LO 3 *Special-Order Decision*

P 2. La Union Resorts, Ltd., has approached Star Technical Printers, Inc., with a special order to produce 300,000 two-page brochures. Most of Star Technical's work consists of recurring short-run orders. La Union Resorts is offering a one-time order, and Star Technical does have the capacity to handle the order over a two-month period.

La Union's management has stated that the company would be unwilling to pay more than $48 per 1,000 brochures. The following cost data were assembled by Star Technical's controller for this decision analysis: Direct materials (paper) would be $26.50 per 1,000 brochures. Direct labor costs would be $6.80 per 1,000 brochures. Direct materials (ink) would be $4.40 per 1,000 brochures. Variable production overhead would be $6.20 per 1,000 brochures. Machine maintenance (fixed cost) is $1.00 per direct labor dollar. Other fixed production overhead amounts to $2.40 per direct labor dollar. Variable packing costs would be $4.30 per 1,000 brochures. Also, the share of general and administrative expenses (fixed costs) to be allocated would be $5.25 per direct labor dollar.

REQUIRED

1. Prepare an analysis for Star Technical's management to use in deciding whether to accept or reject La Union Resorts' offer. What decision should be made?
2. What is the lowest possible price Star Technical can charge per thousand and still make a $6,000 profit on the order?

P 3.

LO 3 *Decision to Eliminate an Unprofitable Product*

Seven years ago, Singer & Lubbock Publishing Company produced its first book. Since then, the company has added four more books to its product list. Management is considering proposals for three more new books, but editorial capacity limits the company to producing only seven books. Before deciding which of the proposed books to publish, management wants you to evaluate the performance of its present book list. The revenue and cost data for the most recent year (each book is identified by the author) are given below.

Projected data for the proposed new books are Book P, sales, $450,000, segment margin, $45,000; Book Q, sales, $725,000, segment margin, ($25,200); and Book R, sales, $913,200, segment margin, $115,500.

Singer & Lubbock Publishing Company
Product Profit and Loss Summary
For the Year Ended December 31, 20x2

	Rico	Thompson	Halpern	Nieto	Yardley	Company Totals
Sales	$813,800	$782,000	$634,200	$944,100	$707,000	$3,881,100
Less variable costs						
Materials and binding	$325,520	$312,800	$190,260	$283,230	$212,100	$1,323,910
Editorial services	71,380	88,200	73,420	57,205	80,700	370,905
Author royalties	130,208	125,120	101,472	151,056	113,120	620,976
Sales commissions	162,760	156,400	95,130	141,615	141,400	697,305
Other selling costs	50,682	44,740	21,708	18,334	60,700	196,164
Total variable costs	$740,550	$727,260	$481,990	$651,440	$608,020	$3,209,260
Contribution margin	$ 73,250	$ 54,740	$152,210	$292,660	$ 98,980	$ 671,840
Less total fixed costs	97,250	81,240	89,610	100,460	82,680	451,240
Net income	($ 24,000)	($ 26,500)	$ 62,600	$192,200	$ 16,300	$ 220,600
Direct fixed costs included in total fixed costs above	$ 51,200	$ 55,100	$ 49,400	$ 69,100	$ 58,800	$ 283,600

REQUIRED

1. Analyze the performance of the five books currently being published.
2. Should the company eliminate any of its present products? If so, which one(s)?
3. Identify the new books you would use to replace those eliminated. Justify your answer. (**Hint:** Consider contribution margin as a percentage of sales on all books.)

LO 3   *Product Mix Analysis*

P 4. The vice president of finance for Salagi Machine Tool, Inc., is evaluating the profitability of the company's four product lines. During the current year, the company will operate at full machine-hour capacity. The following production data have been compiled for the vice president's use.

Product	Current Year's Production (Units)	Total Machine Hours Used
WR1	30,000	75,000
WR2	50,000	100,000
WR3	20,000	20,000
WR4	90,000	45,000

Sales and operating cost data are as follows:

	Product WR1	Product WR2	Product WR3	Product WR4
Selling price per unit	$20.00	$25.00	$30.00	$35.00
Unit variable manufacturing cost	8.00	17.00	21.00	29.00
Unit fixed manufacturing cost	4.00	3.00	2.50	2.00
Unit variable selling cost	2.00	2.00	4.50	3.25
Unit fixed administrative cost	3.00	2.00	3.00	1.75

REQUIRED

1. Compute the machine hours needed to produce one unit of each product type.
2. Determine the contribution margin per machine hour of each product type.
3. Which product line(s) should be pushed by the company's sales force? Why?

LO 4   *Service Mix Decision*

P 5. Dr. Robert Domingo, a doctor specializing in internal medicine, wants to analyze his service mix to find out how the time of his physician assistant, Rosa Gomez, can be used to generate the highest net income. Rosa sees patients in the office, consults with patients over the telephone, and conducts one daily weight loss support group attended by up to 50 patients. Statistics for the three daily services are:

	Office Visits	Phone Calls	Weight Loss Support Group
Maximum number of patient billings per day	20	40	50
Minutes per billing	15	6	60
Billing rate	$50	$25	$10
Variable costs	$25	$12	$ 5

Rosa works seven hours a day.

REQUIRED

1. Perform the two-step analysis to determine the best service mix. Rank the services in order of their profitability.
2. Based on the ranking in **1,** how much time should Rosa spend on each service in a day? (*Note:* Remember to consider the maximum number of patient billings per day.) What would be the daily total contribution margin generated by Rosa?
3. Dr. Domingo believes the ranking is incorrect. He knows that the daily weight loss support group has 50 patients and should continue to be performed. If the new ranking for the services is weight loss support group, phone calls, and office visits, how much time should Rosa spend on each service in a day? What would be the total contribution margin generated by Rosa, assuming the weight loss support group has the maximum number of patient billings?
4. Which ranking would you recommend? What additional amount of total contribution margin would be generated if your recommendation is accepted?

Alternate Problems

LO 3   *Sell or Process-Further Decision*

P 6. Bagels, Inc., produces and sells twenty types of bagels by the dozen. Bagels are priced at $6.00 per dozen and cost $.20 per unit to produce. The company is considering further processing the bagels into two products: bagels with cream cheese and bagel sandwiches. It would cost an additional $.50 per unit to produce bagels with cream cheese, but the new selling price would be $2.00 each. It would cost an additional $1.00 per sandwich to produce bagel sandwiches, but the new selling price would be $3.00 each.

1. Identify the relevant per unit costs and revenues for the alternatives.
2. Based on the information in **1,** should Bagels, Inc., expand its product offerings?
3. Suppose that Bagels, Inc., did expand its product line to include bagels with cream cheese and bagel sandwiches. Based on customer feedback, the company determined that it could further process those two products into bagels with fruit and cream cheese and bagel sandwiches with cheese. The company's accountant compiled the following information:

Product (per unit)	Sales Revenue If Sold with No Further Processing	Sales Revenue If Processed Further	Additional Processing Costs
Bagels with cream cheese	$2.00	$3.00	Fruit: $1.00
Bagel sandwiches	$3.00	$4.00	Cheese: $ .50

Perform an incremental analysis and determine if Bagels, Inc., should process its products further. Explain your findings.

P 7.

LO 3 *Segment Profitability Decision*

AllSports, Inc., is a nationwide distributor of sporting equipment. The company's home office is located in Dallas. The corporate president, Cleota Helmsley, is upset with overall corporate operating results, particularly those of the Bristol Branch, and has asked for more information. The controller prepared the following segmented income statement (in thousands of dollars) for the Bristol Branch.

AllSports, Inc., Bristol Branch
Segmented Income Statement
For the Year Ended December 31, 20x0
(Amounts in Thousands)

	Football	Baseball	Basketball	Bristol Branch
Sales	$3,500	$2,500	$2,059	$8,059
Less variable costs	2,900	2,395	1,800	7,095
Contribution margin	$ 600	$ 105	$ 259	$ 964
Less direct fixed costs	300	150	159	609
Segment margin	$ 300	($ 45)	$ 100	$ 355
Less common fixed costs				450
Net income (loss)				($ 95)

Cleota is considering adding a new product line, In-Line Skating. The controller estimates that adding this line to the Bristol Branch will increase sales by $300,000, variable costs by $150,000, and direct fixed costs by $20,000. The new product line will have no effect on common fixed costs.

1. What will be the impact on net income if the Baseball line is dropped?
2. What will be the impact on net income if the Baseball line is kept and an In-Line Skating line is added?
3. If the Baseball line is dropped and the In-Line Skating line is added, sales of the Football line will decrease by 10 percent and sales of the Basketball line will decrease by 5 percent. How will those changes affect net income?
4. What decision do you recommend? Explain.

P 8.

LO 3 *Special Order Decision*

On March 26, Rio Frio Industries received a special order request for 120 ten-foot aluminum fishing boats. Operating on a fiscal year ending May 31, the company already has orders that will allow it to produce at budget levels for the period. However, extra capacity exists to produce the 120 additional boats.

The terms of the special order call for a selling price of $625 per boat, and the customer will pay all shipping costs. No sales personnel were involved in soliciting the order.

The ten-foot fishing boat has the following cost estimates: direct materials, aluminum, two 4' × 8' sheets at $145 per sheet; direct labor, 14 hours at $14.50 per hour; variable manufacturing overhead, $5.75 per direct labor hour; fixed manufacturing overhead, $4.50 per direct labor hour; variable selling expenses, $46.50 per boat; and variable shipping expenses, $57.50 per boat.

REQUIRED

1. Prepare an analysis for management of Rio Frio Industries to use in deciding whether to accept or reject the special order. What decision should be made?
2. To make an $8,000 profit on this order, what would be the lowest possible price that Rio Frio Industries could charge per boat?

EXPANDING YOUR CRITICAL THINKING, COMMUNICATION, AND INTERPERSONAL SKILLS

Skills Development

CONCEPTUAL ANALYSIS

SD 1.

LO 2 *Management Decision Cycle*

Two weeks ago your cousin Rhonda moved from New York City to Houston. She has found that she needs a car to drive to work and to run errands. She has no experience in selecting a car, so she has asked for your help.

Using the management decision cycle presented in this chapter, write her a letter explaining how she can approach making this decision.

How would your response change if the president of your company asked you to help make a decision about acquiring a fleet of cars for use by sales personnel?

ETHICAL DILEMMA

SD 2.

LO 3 *Ethics of a Make-or-Buy Decision*

Tima Iski is the assistant controller for **Tagwell Corp.,** a leading producer of home appliances. Her friend Zack Marsh is the supervisor of the Cookware Department. Zack has the authority to decide whether parts are purchased from outside vendors or manufactured in his department. Tima recently conducted an internal audit of the parts being manufactured in the Cookware Department, including a comparison of the prices currently charged by vendors for similar parts. She found over a dozen parts that could be purchased for less than they cost the company to produce. When she approached Zack about the situation, he replied that if those parts were purchased from outside vendors, two automated machines would be idled for several hours a week. Increased machine

| Communication | Critical Thinking | Group Activity | Memo | Ethics | International | Spreadsheet | Managerial Technology | Internet |

idle time would have a negative effect on his performance evaluation and could reduce his yearly bonus. He reminded Tima that he was in charge of the decision to make or purchase those parts and asked her not to pursue the matter any further.

What should Tima do in this situation? Discuss her options.

RESEARCH ACTIVITY

SD 3.

LO 2 *Identifying Relevant Decision Information*

Assume you want to take a two-week vacation. Select two destinations for your vacation and gather information about them from brochures, magazines, travel agents, and people you know. Then list the relevant quantitative and qualitative information in its order of importance to your decision. Analyze the information and select a destination. What factors were the most important to your decision? Why? What factors were the least important to your decision? Why? How would the process of identifying relevant decision information differ if you were asked by the president of your company to prepare a budget for the next training meeting, to be held at a location of your choice?

Group Activity: Divide the class into groups and ask them to discuss this SD. Then debrief the entire class by asking one person from each group to summarize his or her group's findings.

DECISION-MAKING PRACTICE

SD 4.

LO 3 *Decision to Add a New Department*

Management at ***Transco Company*** is considering a proposal to install a third production department within its factory building. With the company's present production setup, direct materials are processed through the Mixing Department to produce Materials A and B in equal proportions. Material A is then processed through the Shaping Department to yield Product C. Material B is sold as is at $20.25 per pound. Product C has a selling price of $100.00 per pound. Current per-pound standard costs used by Transco Company are shown below.

	Mixing Department (Materials A or B)	Shaping Department (Product C)	(Material B)
Prior department's cost	—	$53.03[†]	$13.47[†]
Direct materials	$20.00	—	—
Direct labor	6.00	9.00	—
Variable manufacturing overhead	4.00	8.00	—
Fixed manufacturing overhead			
Traceable	2.25	2.25	—
Assigned	1.00	1.00	—
	$33.25[*]	$73.28	$13.47

[*]Cost to produce each A and B product.
[†]Mixing Department costs ($33.25 + $33.25) assigned based on relative sales value at split-off point:
$$\$66.50 \times 79.75\% = \underline{\underline{\$53.03}}$$
$$\$66.50 \times 20.25\% = \underline{\underline{\$13.47}}$$

The costs were developed by using an estimated production volume of 200,000 pounds of direct material. The company assigns Mixing Department costs to Materials A and B in proportion to their net sales values at the split-off point. Those values are computed by deducting subsequent production costs from sales prices. The $300,000 in common fixed overhead costs is assigned to the two producing departments on the basis of the space used by the departments.

There is a proposal to add a Baking Department to process Material B into Product D. It is expected that any quantity of Product D can be sold for $30 per pound. Costs per pound under this proposal were developed by using 200,000 pounds of direct material as the standard volume. Those costs are shown on the next page.

	Mixing Department (Materials A & B)	Shaping Department (Product C)	Baking Department (Product D)
Prior department's cost	—	$52.80	$13.20
Direct materials	$20.00	—	—
Direct labor	6.00	9.00	3.50
Variable manufacturing overhead	4.00	8.00	4.00
Fixed manufacturing overhead			
Traceable	2.25	2.25	1.80
Allocated ($\frac{1}{2}$, $\frac{1}{4}$, $\frac{1}{4}$)	.75	.75	.75
	$33.00	$72.80	$23.25

1. If (a) sales and production levels are expected to remain constant in the foreseeable future and (b) there are no foreseeable alternative uses for the factory space, should Transco Company add a Baking Department and produce Product D, if 100,000 pounds of D can be sold? Show calculations to support your answer.
2. List at least two qualitative reasons why Transco Company may *not* want to install a Baking Department and produce Product D, even if it appears that this decision is profitable.
3. List at least two qualitative reasons why Transco Company may want to install a Baking Department and produce Product D, even if it appears that this decision is *un*profitable.

(CMA adapted)

Managerial Reporting and Analysis

INTERPRETING MANAGEMENT REPORTS

MRA 1.

LO 3 *Special Order Decision*

Metallica Can Opener Company is a subsidiary of **Maltz Appliances, Inc.** The can opener Metallica produces is in strong demand. Sales during the present year, 20x0, are expected to hit 1,000,000 units. Full plant capacity is 1,150,000 units, but 1,000,000 units was considered normal capacity for the current year. The following unit price and cost breakdown is applicable in 20x0:

	Per Unit
Sales price	$22.50
Less: Manufacturing costs	
Direct materials	$ 6.00
Direct labor	2.50
Manufacturing overhead: Variable	3.50
Fixed	1.50
Total manufacturing costs	$13.50
Gross margin	$ 9.00
Less: Selling and administrative expenses	
Selling: Variable	$ 1.50
Fixed	1.00
Administrative, fixed	1.25
Packaging, variable*	.75
Total selling and administrative expenses	$ 4.50
Net income	$ 4.50

*Three types of packaging are available: deluxe, $.75 per unit; plain, $.50 per unit; and bulk pack, $.25 per unit.

During November, the company received three special-order requests from large chain-store companies. Those orders are not part of the budgeted 1,000,000-unit sales for 20x0, but company officials think that sufficient capacity exists for one order to be accepted. Orders received and their terms are:

> Order 1: 75,000 can openers @ $20.00 per unit, deluxe packaging
>
> Order 2: 90,000 can openers @ $18.00 per unit, plain packaging
>
> Order 3: 125,000 can openers @ $15.75 per unit, bulk packaging

Since the orders were placed directly with company officials, no variable selling costs will be incurred.

REQUIRED

1. Analyze the profitability of each of the three special orders.
2. Which special order should be accepted?

FORMULATING MANAGEMENT REPORTS

MRA 2.

LO 3 *Formulating a Segmented Income Statement*

Carmen Mendoza recently purchased the **Mesa Grande Country Club** in Tucson, Arizona. The club offers swimming, golfing, and tennis activities as well as dining services for its members. Carmen is unfamiliar with the actual operating activity of those areas. Because you are the controller for the country club's operations, Carmen has asked you to formulate a memo that shows how each activity or service contributed to the profitability of the country club for the year ended December 31, 20x1. The information you provide will assist Carmen in her decision to keep or eliminate one or more areas.

REQUIRED

1. In preparation for writing your memo, answer the following questions.
   a. What kinds of information about each area do you need?
   b. Why is this information relevant?
   c. Where would you find the information?
   d. When would you want to obtain the information?
2. Prepare a draft of your memo, omitting the actual numbers. Show only the headings and line items.
3. Assume that Carmen wants to increase the membership of the country club and will invest a large sum of money to promote membership sales. How would you structure the memo differently to address such a decision?

INTERNATIONAL COMPANY

MRA 3.

LO 2 *Define and Identify Relevant Information*

Bob's Burgers is a competitor in the fast-food restaurant business. One component of the company's marketing strategy is to increase sales by expanding its foreign markets. The company uses both financial and nonfinancial, quantitative and qualitative information when deciding whether to open restaurants in foreign markets.

Bob's decided to open a restaurant in Saudi Arabia five years ago. The following information helped the managers in making that decision.

Financial Quantitative Information
Operating information
    Estimated food, labor, and other operating costs (for example, taxes, insurance, utilities, and supplies)
    Estimated selling price for each food item
Capital investment information
    Cost of land, building, equipment, and furniture
    Financing options and amounts

Nonfinancial Quantitative Information
Estimated daily number of customers, hamburgers to be sold, employees to work
High-traffic time periods
Income of people living in the area
Ratio of population to number of restaurants in the market area
Traffic counts in front of similar restaurants in the area

Qualitative Information

Government regulations, taxes, duties, tariffs, political involvement in business operations
Property ownership restrictions
Site visibility
Accessibility of store location
Training process for local managers
Hiring process for employees
Local customs and practices

Bob's Burgers has hired you as a consultant and has given you an income statement comparing the net incomes of its five restaurants in the Middle East. You have noticed that the Saudi Arabian location is operating at a loss (including unallocated fixed costs) and must decide whether to recommend closing that restaurant.

REQUIRED

Review the information used to make the decision to open the restaurant. Identify the types of information that would also be relevant in deciding whether to close the restaurant. What period or periods of time should be reviewed in making your decision? What additional information would be relevant in making your decision?

MRA 4.

LO 4 *Sell or Process-Further Decision in a Nonmanufacturing Organization*

Maya Marketeers, Inc., has developed a promotional program for a large shopping center in Tempe, Arizona. After investing $360,000 in developing the original promotion campaign, the firm is ready to present its client with an add-on contract offer that includes the original promotion areas of (1) TV advertising program, (2) series of brochures for mass mailing, and (3) special rotating BIG SALE schedule for 10 of the 28 tenants in the shopping center. Following are the revenue terms from the original contract with the shopping center and the offer for an add-on contract, which extends the original contract terms.

	Contract Terms	
	Original Contract Terms	Extended Contract Including Add-On Terms
TV advertising program	$520,000	$ 580,000
Brochure package	210,000	230,000
Rotating BIG SALE schedule	170,000	190,000
Totals	$900,000	$1,000,000

Maya estimates that the following additional costs will be incurred by extending the contract.

	TV Program	Brochures	BIG SALE Schedule
Direct labor	$30,000	$ 9,000	$7,000
Variable overhead costs	22,000	14,000	6,000
Fixed overhead costs*	12,000	4,000	2,000

*80 percent are direct fixed costs applied to this contract.

REQUIRED

1. Using an Excel spreadsheet, compute the costs that will be incurred for each part of the add-on portion of the contract.
2. Should Maya Marketeers, Inc., offer the add-on contract, or should it ask for a final settlement check based on the original contract only? Defend your answer.
3. If management of the shopping center indicated the terms of the add-on contract were negotiable, how should Maya respond?

ENDNOTES

1. Data Warehousing Institute, *Data Warehousing: What Works?* Volume 4. Gaithersburg, Md.: Data Warehousing Institute, 1997, pp. 2–3.
2. Tim R. V. Davis and Bruce L. Darling, "ABC in a Virtual Corporation," *Management Accounting,* Institute of Management Accountants, October 1996, pp. 18–26.
3. Society of Management Accountants of Canada, *Management Accounting Guideline no. 23. Outsourcing Information Systems,* 1994.

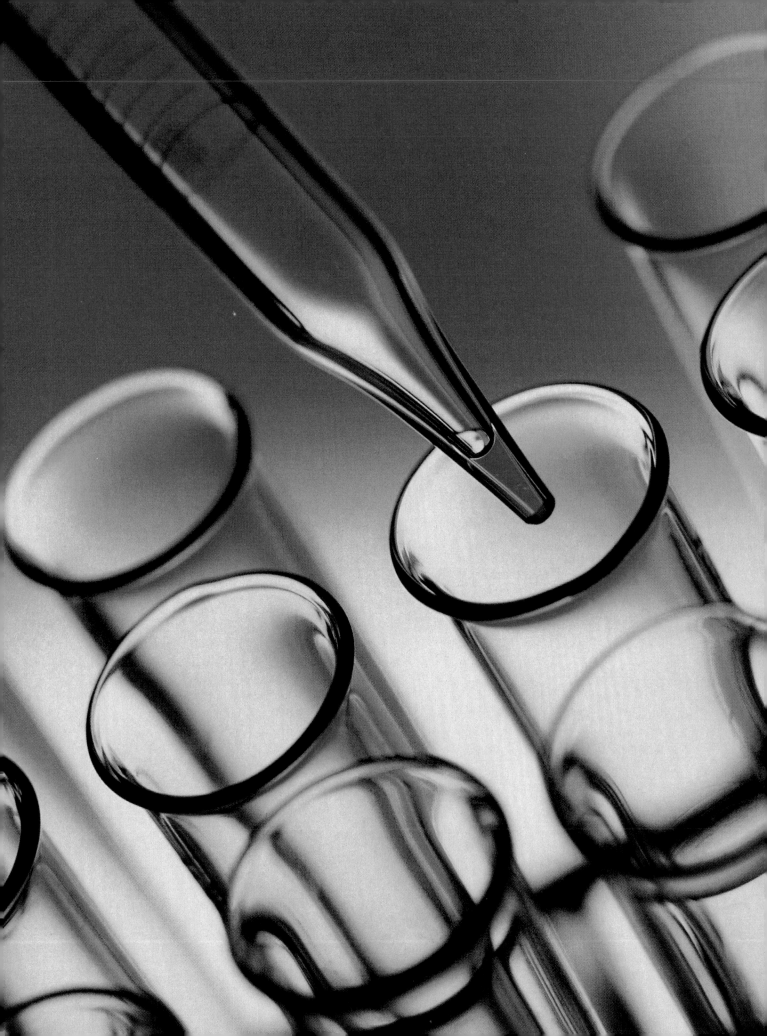

Capital Investment Analysis

1. Explain the capital investment decision cycle and describe the manager's role in the decision process.
2. State the purpose of the minimum desired rate of return and identify the methods used to arrive at this rate.
3. Identify the types of projected costs and revenues used to evaluate alternatives for capital investment.
4. Evaluate capital investment proposals using (a) the accounting rate-of-return method and (b) the payback period method.
5. Apply the concept of the time value of money.
6. Evaluate capital investment proposals using the net present value method.

DECISION POINT

CYTO TECHNOLOGIES

Cyto Technologies is a rapidly growing biotechnology company that specializes in seven product areas: enzymes, nucleic acid, molecular biology, cellular regulation, eukaryotic transcription, protein translation, and biochemical reagents.[1] These products are used as materials by life science researchers and by laboratories for DNA and food testing. Most products have short life spans, so generating new products is a primary concern of management. In the past, projects to develop new products were selected based only on approximate ideas of costs and revenues and rough projections of payback periods. However, increased competition and higher costs of capital had made the continued use of such a casual approach expensive and impractical. What changes needed to be made to improve the project-selection process?

The company created a project approval team (PAT) and developed a project development and approval process that consists of four phases: idea and initial screening, product design, product development, and launch. Idea and initial screening consists of two stages, idea generation and investigation. Funds are provided to test each idea, followed by a review and a go/no-go decision by the PAT. Product design consists of technological and marketing feasibility studies, followed by a review by the PAT. A positive review moves the project to the next phase. Product development consists of two stages, (1) specifications, including full product testing and complete financial analysis, and (2) final optimization, in which the first batch is made, regulatory compliance and quality assurance specifications are met, and the final design is approved. Launch occurs when a project is approved for full production.

With this new method of capital investment decision making in place, what is next for the PAT? Traditional overhead application procedures are still being used to assign overhead costs to the projects, and project managers are complaining that the approach causes cost inequities. The company is now considering the use of activity-based costing to further refine its capital investment approval process.

The Capital Investment Decision Process

OBJECTIVE 1

Explain the capital investment decision cycle and describe the manager's role in the decision process

Among the most significant decisions facing management are capital investment decisions, which are decisions about when and how much to spend on capital facilities. A capital facility might be machinery, systems, or processes; building additions, renovations, or new structures; or entire new divisions or product lines. Thus, decisions about installing new equipment, replacing old equipment, expanding the production area by adding to a building, buying or building a new factory, or acquiring another company are all examples of capital investment decisions. Spending on capital assets is expensive. A new factory or production system may cost millions of dollars and require several years to implement. Managers must make capital investment decisions carefully to select the alternative that contributes the most to profits.

Capital Budgeting: A Cooperative Venture

The process of making decisions about capital investments is called capital budgeting, or *capital investment decision analysis*. It consists of identifying the need for a capital investment, analyzing courses of action to meet the need, preparing reports for managers, choosing the best alternative, and dividing funds among competing needs. People in every part of the organization participate in capital budgeting. Financial analysts supply a target cost of capital or desired rate of return and an estimate of how much money can be spent annually on capital facilities. Marketing specialists predict sales trends and new product demands, which help in determining operations that need expansion or new equipment. Managers at all levels help identify facility needs and often prepare preliminary cost estimates of the desired capital investment. Then all work together to implement the project selected and to keep results within revenue and cost estimates.

The capital investment decision process involves the evaluation of alternative proposals for large capital investments, including considerations for financing the projects. Capital investment decision analyses affect both short-term and long-term planning. Figure 1 illustrates the time span of the capital expenditure planning process. Most companies have developed a long-term plan, a projection of operations for the next five or ten years. Large capital investments should be an integral part of the long-term plan. Anticipated additions or changes to product lines, replacements of equipment, and acquisitions of other companies are examples of items to be included in long-term capital investment plans. In addition, needs for capital investments may arise from changes in current operations.

One of the period budgets in the master budget is a capital investment budget. The capital investment budget must fit into the planning process and the capital investment decision process. Long-term plans are not very specific; they are expressed in broad, goal-oriented terms. Each annual budget must help accomplish the organization's long-term plans. Look again at Figure 1. In 2001, the company plans to purchase a large, special-purpose machine. When the ten-year plan was developed, it included only a broad statement about a plan to purchase the machine. Nothing was specified about the cost of the machine or the anticipated operating details and costs. Those details are contained in the annual master budget for 2001, and it is in 2001 that the capital investment decision analysis will occur. So,

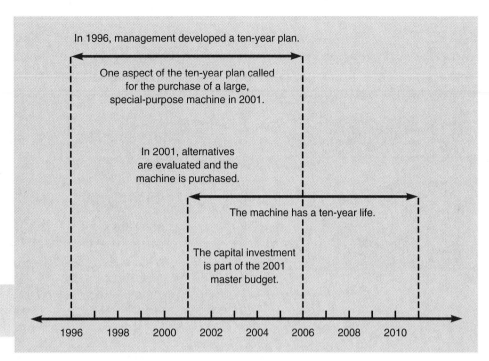

Figure 1
Time Span of the Capital Investment Planning Process

even though capital investment decisions that will affect the company for many years are discussed and estimates of future revenues and expenditures are made when the long-term plan is first developed, the capital investment decision analysis is performed in the period when the expenditure will be made. This point is often confusing and needs to be emphasized here so that the remainder of the chapter can be studied in the proper perspective.

The Capital Investment Decision Cycle

Evaluating capital investment proposals, deciding on projects to be authorized, and making capital investments are long, involved procedures. The complexity of capital investment decision making was illustrated in the Decision Point about Cyto Technologies. Because of the large dollar amounts usually connected with capital investments, any mistakes made in the decision process can be very costly to the company. Cyto Technologies adopted a capital investment decision process that was centered around a project approval team (PAT). Such a team approach is not necessary, but the decision process must include some method of project review and approval to be effective.

Thus far, we have discussed each topic of management accounting in terms of the management cycle. In this chapter, we will examine capital investment decisions in terms of a different cycle, the capital investment decision cycle. However, you will notice that underlying the capital investment decision cycle are the four stages of the management cycle. Most of the capital investment decision analysis occurs during the planning stage of the management cycle. The screening, evaluation, and funding activities that take place prior to a capital investment decision are all part of the planning stage. A decision is actually made during the executing stage of the management cycle. Postcompletion audits of prior decisions are conducted as part of the reviewing stage of the management cycle. Reports on the results of capital investment decisions are prepared and distributed within the organization during the reporting stage. Based on those reports, managers will decide

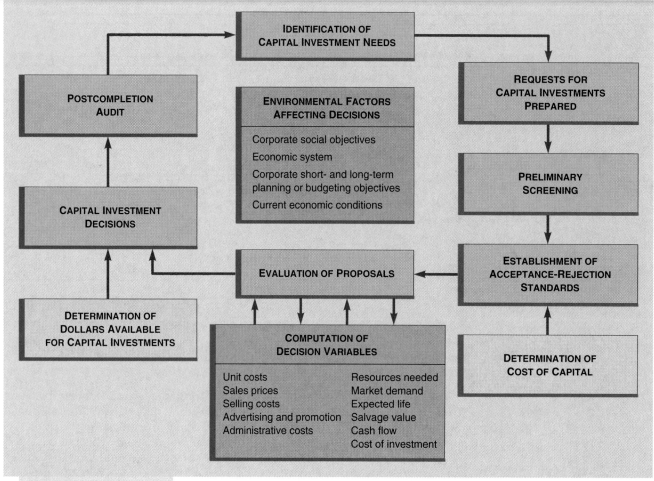

Figure 2
The Capital Investment
Decision Cycle

either that the initial problem has been solved and the capital investment decision process is complete or that the problem still exists and the process must begin again.

Figure 2 illustrates the capital investment decision cycle. Its parts are explained below.

Environmental Factors   The capital investment decision cycle occurs within a defined time period and under constraints imposed by economic policies, conditions, and objectives originating at organizational, industry, and/or national levels. Coordinating short- and long-term capital investment plans within this dynamic environment is the manager's responsibility, and it is vital to profitable operations.

Identification of Capital Investment Needs   Identifying the need for a new capital investment is the starting point of the decision process. Managers identify capital investment opportunities from past sales experience, changes in sources and quality of materials, subordinates' suggestions, production bottlenecks caused by obsolete equipment, new production or distribution methods, or customer complaints. In addition, capital investment needs are identified through proposals to

1. Add new products to the product line
2. Expand capacity in existing product lines

3. Reduce production costs of existing products without altering operating levels
4. Automate existing production processes

Request for Capital Investment   To facilitate control over capital investments, the appropriate manager prepares a formal request for a new capital investment. The request should include a complete description of the investment under review, the reasons a new investment is needed, the alternative means of satisfying the need, the estimated costs and related cost savings for each alternative, and the investment's engineering specifications, if necessary.

Preliminary Screening   Preliminary screening processes are used by organizations that have several branch plants and a highly developed program for capital investments. The objective of preliminary screening is to ensure that the only proposals that receive serious review are those that both meet company objectives and produce the minimum desired rate of return established by management.

Establishment of Acceptance-Rejection Standards   When there are many requests for capital investments and limited funds for such investments, an organization establishes an acceptance-rejection standard. Such a standard may be expressed as a minimum desired rate of return or as a minimum cash-flow payback period. As shown in Figure 2, acceptance-rejection standards are used in the screening process to identify projects that are expected to yield inadequate or marginal returns. This step also identifies proposed projects for which high product demand and high financial returns are expected. Cost of capital information is often used to establish minimum desired rates of return on investment. The development of such rates is discussed later in this chapter.

Evaluation of Proposals   Proposals are evaluated by verifying decision variables and applying established proposal evaluation methods. The management accountant is primarily responsible for such procedures. Figure 2 lists several variables that may be relevant to a capital expenditure request. Generally, the categories of variables in capital investment decisions are (1) expected life, (2) estimated cash flow, and (3) investment cost. Each variable in a proposal should be checked for accuracy. Methods used for proposal evaluation include the accounting rate-of-return method, the payback period method, and the net present value method. Using management's minimum acceptance-rejection standard as a cutoff point, the management accountant evaluates all proposals, using one or more evaluation methods. In addition to this quantitative analysis, management will also consider qualitative factors such as availability and training of employees, competition, anticipated future technological improvements, and impact on other operations of the company.

Capital Investment Decisions   The proposals that meet the standards of the evaluation process are given to the appropriate manager for final review. When deciding which requests to implement, the manager must consider the funds available for capital investments. The acceptable proposals are ranked in order of profitability or payback potential, and the highest-ranking proposals are funded first. Often there will not be enough money to fund all proposals. The final capital investment budget is then prepared by allocating funds to the selected proposals.

Postcompletion Audit   The decision process does not end when the new investment is completed. The accountant should perform a postcompletion audit for each project to evaluate the accuracy of forecasted results. Any weakness found in the decision process should be corrected to avoid the same problem in future decisions.

BUSINESS BULLETIN: TECHNOLOGY IN PRACTICE

Activity-based costing is useful only as a cost assignment tool, right? Wrong! ABC can also be a very useful source of decision-support information. Teletech Corporation of Denver, Colorado, used activity-based costing information to check the forecasted data supporting its decision to invest in a "cybermall."[2] A cybermall brings together sellers and buyers via the Internet in ways similar to the now commonplace television marketplace.

The company used ABC to generate decision-support data about business processes, activities, revenues, operating costs, and capital asset costs for the cybermall project. Using ABC data, management discovered that traditional forecasting methods had overestimated the projected business volume. As a result, forecasted revenues had to be lowered in the early years of the project. In addition, ABC estimates showed that capital investment needs had been underestimated by more than $10 million. The ABC decision-support data caused management to reverse its decision, and the company did not fund the cybermall project.

The postcompletion audit is a difficult step in the decision-making process. To isolate how a decision affects a company's overall operating results requires extensive analysis. Only when an entire new plant is constructed can one clearly isolate and identify relevant information and measure the investment's performance. The main problems in the postcompletion audit are that (1) long-term projects must be evaluated by concentrating on cash flows over the project's life, (2) a particular decision may influence the operations of existing facilities, and (3) profitability resulting from a decision may be difficult to isolate and identify.

Summary   The capital investment decision cycle is vital to the management of an organization. By making correct decisions about capital investments, managers provide for the continued existence of their organization. A series of incorrect decisions about capital investments could cause an organization to fail. The role of the manager in this very involved decision process is to identify and explain capital investment needs; the management accountant's role is to provide the information the manager must have to make sound capital investment decisions. In the remaining parts of this chapter, we look at the aspects of capital investment decision making that are the responsibility of the management accountant, including the development of a minimum desired rate of return on investment, proposal evaluation methods, and ranking of acceptable proposals.

Desired Rate of Return on Investment

OBJECTIVE 2

State the purpose of the minimum desired rate of return and identify the methods used to arrive at this rate

Most companies have a set minimum rate of return, and any capital expenditure proposal that fails to produce that rate of return is automatically refused. If none of the capital investment requests is expected to meet the minimum desired rate of return, all requests will be turned down.

Organizations set a minimum rate of return to guard their profitability. If the return from a capital investment falls below the minimum rate of return, the funds can be used more profitably in another part of the organization. Supporting proposals that produce poor returns will lower the organization's profitability later.

Choosing a minimum desired rate of return is not a simple task. Each measure that can be used to set a cutoff point has certain advantages. The most commonly used measures are (1) cost of capital, (2) corporate return on investment, (3) industry average return on investment, and (4) federal bank interest rates.

Cost of Capital Measures   Of all the possible measures of desired rates of return, cost of capital measures are the most widely used and discussed. To set a desired rate of return, an organization must find the cost of financing its activities. This is not easy because to finance its activities, an organization borrows funds and issues preferred and common stock. It also tries to produce goods or services that it can sell at a profit. Each of these sources of funds has a different cost rate. And each organization uses a different mix of these sources to finance current and future operations.

To set a desired cutoff rate of return, management can use cost of debt, cost of preferred stock, cost of equity capital, or cost of retained earnings. In many cases a company will average these costs to establish an average cost of capital. Sophisticated methods are used to compute these costs.[3] However, for the purposes of this discussion, we present only a brief description of each cost.

Cost of debt is the ratio of loan charges to net proceeds of the loan. The effects of income taxes and the present value of interest charges must be taken into account, but the rate is essentially the ratio of costs to loan proceeds. Cost of preferred stock is the stated dividend rate of the individual preferred stock issue. Tax effects are unimportant in this case because dividends, unlike interest charges, are a nondeductible expense. Cost of equity capital is the rate of return to the investor and is determined by calculating net income as a percentage of invested capital. It is not just the dividend rate to the stockholder because management can raise or lower the dividend rate almost at will. This concept is very complex, but it has sound authoritative financial support. Cost of retained earnings is the opportunity cost, or the dividends given up by the common stockholders. Such a cost is linked closely to the cost of equity capital.

A firm's average cost of capital can be complex to compute because it is the weighted average of the costs of many different methods of financing, and those costs themselves may be very complex to compute. Nonetheless, that average is the best estimate of an organization's minimum desired rate of return. Basically, average cost of capital is computed in four steps:

1. Identify the cost of each source of capital.
2. Compute the proportion (percentage) of the organization's total amount of debt and equity (that is, the organization's capital mix) that each source of capital represents.
3. Multiply each source's cost by its proportion of the capital mix.
4. Sum the weighted costs computed in Step **3.**

For example, assume the Pickett Company's financing structure is as follows:

Cost (Percentage)	Source of Capital	Amount	Proportion of Capital Mix (Percentage)
10	Debt financing	$150,000	30
8	Preferred stock	50,000	10
12	Common stock	200,000	40
14	Retained earnings	100,000	20
	Totals	$500,000	100

The weighted average cost of capital of 11.4 percent would be computed as follows:

Source of Capital	Cost	× Proportion of Capital Mix =	Weighted Cost
Debt financing	.10	.30	.030
Preferred stock	.08	.10	.008
Common stock	.12	.40	.048
Retained earnings	.14	.20	.028
Weighted average cost of capital			.114

Other Cutoff Measures   If cost of capital information is unavailable, management can use one of three less accurate but still useful amounts as the minimum desired rate of return. The first is average total corporate return on investment. The reasoning used to support such a measure is that any capital investment that produced a return lower than the amount earned historically by the company would negatively affect future operations. A second method is to use an industry's average cost of capital. Most sizable industry associations supply such information. As a last resort, a company might use the current bank lending rate. But because most companies are financed by both debt and equity, this rate seldom reflects an accurate rate of return.

OBJECTIVE 3

Identify the types of projected costs and revenues used to evaluate alternatives for capital investment

Cost and Revenue Measures Used in Capital Budgeting

When evaluating a proposed capital investment, the management accountant must predict how the new asset will perform and how it will benefit the company. Various measures of costs and revenues are used to estimate the benefits to be derived from these projects.

Net Income and Cash Flow   Each capital investment analysis must include a measure of the expected benefit from the investment project. The measure of expected benefit depends on the method of analyzing capital investment alternatives. One possible measure is net income, calculated in the usual way. Increases in net income resulting from the capital investment must be determined for each alternative. A more widely used measure of expected benefit is projected cash flows. Net cash inflow is the balance of increases in projected cash receipts over increases in projected cash payments resulting from a capital investment. In some cases, equipment replacement decisions involve alternatives that do not increase current revenue. In such cases, cost savings measure the benefits from the proposed capital investments. Either net cash flow or cost savings can be used as a basis for an evaluation, but one should not be confused with the other. If the analysis involves cash receipts, net cash flow is used. If the analysis involves only cash outlays, cost savings are used. All the investment alternatives must be measured and evaluated consistently.

Equal Versus Unequal Cash Flows   Projected cash flows may be the same for each year of an asset's life, or they may vary from year to year. Unequal cash flows are common and must be analyzed for each year of an asset's life. Proposed projects with equal annual cash flows require less detailed analysis. Both a project with equal cash flows and one with unequal cash flows are illustrated and explained later in this chapter.

Book Value of Assets   Book value is the undepreciated portion of the original cost of a fixed asset. When evaluating a decision to replace an asset, the book value of the old asset is irrelevant, since it is a past, or historical, cost and will not be altered by the decision. Net proceeds from the asset's sale or disposal are relevant, however, because the proceeds affect cash flows and may differ for each alternative.

Depreciation Expense   Since depreciation is a noncash expense requiring no cash outlay during the period, it is irrelevant to decision analyses based on cash flow. But, because depreciation expense reduces net income, it *is* relevant to income-based evaluations.

Disposal or Salvage Values   Proceeds from the sale of an old asset are current cash inflows and are relevant to evaluating a proposed capital investment. Projected disposal or salvage values of replacement equipment are also relevant because they represent future cash inflows and usually differ among alternatives. Remember, salvage values will be received at the end of the asset's estimated life.

Methods of Evaluating Capital Investments

Although many methods are used to evaluate capital expenditure proposals, the most common are (1) the accounting rate-of-return method, (2) the payback period method, and (3) the net present value method.

The Accounting Rate-of-Return Method

OBJECTIVE 4a

Evaluate capital investment proposals using the accounting rate-of-return method

The accounting rate-of-return method is a crude but easy way to measure the estimated performance of a capital investment. With this method, expected performance is measured using two variables: (1) estimated annual net income from the project and (2) average investment cost. The basic equation is as follows:

$$\text{Accounting Rate of Return} = \frac{\text{Project's Average Annual Net Income}}{\text{Average Investment Cost}}$$

To compute average annual net income, use the cost and revenue data prepared for evaluating the project. Average investment in a proposed capital facility is figured as follows:

$$\text{Average Investment Cost} = \left(\frac{\text{Total Investment} - \text{Salvage Value}}{2}\right) + \text{Salvage Value}$$

To see how this equation is used in evaluating a capital expenditure decision, assume the Gordon Company is interested in purchasing a new bottling machine. The company's management will consider only those projects that promise to yield more than a 16 percent return. Estimates for the proposal include revenue increases of $17,900 a year and operating cost increases of $11,696 a year (including depreciation and taxes). The cost of the machine is $51,000. Its salvage value is $3,000. To determine if the company should invest in the machine, compute the accounting rate of return as follows:

$$\text{Accounting Rate of Return} = \frac{\$17,900 - \$11,696}{\left(\dfrac{\$51,000 - \$3,000}{2}\right) + \$3,000}$$

$$= \frac{\$6,204}{\$27,000}$$

$$= 22.98\%$$

The projected rate of return is higher than the 16 percent minimum desired rate, so management should think seriously about making the investment.

The accounting rate-of-return method is widely used because it is easy to understand and apply. It does have several disadvantages, however. First, because net income is averaged over the life of the investment, it is not a reliable figure. Actual net income may vary considerably from the estimates. Second, the method is unreliable if estimated annual income differs from year to year. Third, cash flows are ignored. Finally, the time value of money is not considered in the computations. Thus, future and present dollars are treated as equal.

Cash Flow and the Payback Period Method

OBJECTIVE 4b

Evaluate capital investment proposals using the payback period method

Instead of measuring the rate of return, many managers estimate the cash flow generated by a capital investment. Their goal is to determine the minimum time it will take to recover the initial investment. If two investment alternatives are being studied, management should choose the investment that pays back its initial cost in the shortest time. That period of time is known as the payback period, and the method of evaluation is called the payback period method. The payback period is computed as follows.

$$\text{Payback Period} = \frac{\text{Cost of Investment}}{\text{Annual Net Cash Inflow}}$$

To apply the payback period method to the proposed capital investment of the Gordon Company, determine the net cash flow. To do so, first find and eliminate the effects of all noncash revenue and expense items included in the analysis of net income. In this case, the only noncash expense or revenue is machine depreciation. To calculate this amount, you must know the asset's life and the depreciation method. Suppose the Gordon Company uses the straight-line method of depreciation, and the new bottling machine will have a ten-year estimated service life. Using this information and the facts given earlier, the payback period is computed as follows.

$$\text{Annual Depreciation} = \frac{\text{Cost} - \text{Salvage Value}}{10 \text{ (years)}}$$

$$= \frac{\$51,000 - \$3,000}{10}$$

$$= \$4,800 \text{ per year}$$

$$\text{Payback Period} = \frac{\text{Cost of Machine}}{\text{Cash Revenue} - \text{Cash Expenses}}$$

$$= \frac{\$51,000}{\$17,900 - (\$11,696 - \$4,800)}$$

$$= \frac{\$51,000}{\$11,004}$$

$$= 4.635 \text{ years}$$

If the company's desired payback period is five years or less, this proposal would be approved.

If a proposed capital expenditure has unequal annual net cash inflows, the payback period is determined by subtracting each annual amount (in chronological order) from the cost of the capital facility. When a zero balance is reached, the payback period has been determined. This will often occur in the middle of a year. The portion of the final year is computed by dividing the amount needed to reach zero (the unrecovered portion of the investment) by the entire year's estimated cash inflow. The Review Problem at the end of the chapter illustrates this process.

Like the accounting rate of return method, the payback period method is widely used because it is easy to compute and understand. However, the disadvantages of this approach far outweigh its advantages. First, the payback method does not measure profitability. Second, it ignores differences in the present values of cash flows from different periods; thus it does not adjust cash flows for the time value of money. Finally, the payback period method emphasizes the time it takes to recover the investment rather than the long-run return on the investment.

The Time Value of Money

Today an organization has many options for investing capital besides buying fixed assets. Consequently, management expects an asset to yield a reasonable return during its useful life. Techniques of capital investment analysis that treat cash flows from different periods as if they have the same value in current dollars do not properly value the returns from an investment. As mentioned earlier, this is a shortcoming of both the accounting rate-of-return and the payback period methods.

Cash flows of equal dollar amounts separated by an interval of time have different values, a phenomenon known as the time value of money. The values differ because of the effect of compound interest. For example, assume that D. K. Shewman was awarded a $20,000 settlement in a lawsuit over damages from an automobile accident. The terms of the settlement dictate that the first payment of $10,000 is to be paid on December 31, 1999. The second $10,000 installment is due on December 31, 2003. What is the current (present) value of the total settlement on December 31, 1999? Assume that Shewman could earn 10 percent interest on her current funds. To compute the present value of the settlement, you must go to Table 3 in the appendix on future value and present value tables. There you will find the multiplier for four years at 10 percent, which is .683. The settlement's present value is computed as:

Present value of first payment on Dec. 31, 1999	$10,000
Present value of second payment, to be received on Dec. 31, 2003 ($10,000 × .683)	6,830
Present value of the total settlement	$16,830

If Shewman had to choose between (1) accepting the $20,000 settlement as offered or (2) receiving $16,830 today as total compensation for the lawsuit, she would be indifferent, because the amounts would be equal.

Because of the time value of money, the $10,000 to be received in four years is not worth $10,000 today. If those funds can be invested to earn 10 percent interest, then each $1 to be received in four years is worth only $.683 today. To prove that Shewman should be indifferent, look at the value of the total settlement on December 31, 2003, for each choice. In this analysis, Table 1 in the appendix on future value and present value tables is used because we are now dealing with future values based on compounding of interest.

1. Accept the $20,000 settlement as offered

December 31, 1999, payment after earning four years of interest income @ 10% annual rate ($10,000 × 1.464)	$14,640.00
December 31, 2003, payment	10,000.00
Total amount at December 31, 2003	$24,640.00

2. Receive $16,830 on December 31, 1999, as total compensation for the lawsuit

December 31, 1999, payment after earning four years of interest income @ 10% annual rate ($16,830 × 1.464)	$24,639.12*

*Difference due to rounding.

The preceding analysis was based on single payments received either today or on a future date. Now, assume that Bengt Sverige was just told that he won the lottery. His winnings are $1,000,000, to be received in a series of twenty $50,000 payments, made at the end of each of the next twenty years. If he could choose to receive the value of the winnings today and earn 9 percent interest on his savings, how much should he settle for? Since a series of payments is being dealt with, use Table 4 in the appendix on future value and present value tables to locate the applicable multiplier of 9.129, which represents the discounting of twenty future payments to the present at a 9 percent rate of return.

Present value of twenty annual future payments
 of $50,000 starting one year from now,
 assuming a 9% interest factor
 ($50,000 × 9.129) $456,450

In other words, Sverige would be indifferent if given the choice of (1) receiving $1,000,000 in twenty future annual installments of $50,000 each or (2) receiving $456,450 today. To prove this point, determine the future value of the two alternatives by using data from Tables 1 and 2 in the appendix on future value and present value tables. Such data are used because we are now dealing with a series of future payments and the compounding of interest on those payments.

1. Receive $1,000,000 in twenty future annual
   installments of $50,000 each (using Table 2:
   $50,000 × 51.16) $2,558,000.00

2. Receive $456,450 today, and invest it
   for twenty years at 9% interest (using Table 1:
   $456,450 × 5.604) $2,557,945.80 *

*Difference due to rounding.

   When dealing with the time value of money, use compounding to find the future value of an amount now held. To find the present value of an amount to be received, use discounting. When determining future values, refer to Tables 1 and 2 in the appendix on future value and present value tables. To determine present values of future amounts of money, use Tables 3 and 4 in the appendix on future value and present value tables. Also, remember that Tables 1 and 3 deal with a single payment or amount, whereas Tables 2 and 4 are used for a series of equal annual amounts.

The Net Present Value Method

OBJECTIVE 6

Evaluate capital investment proposals using the net present value method

The net present value method evaluates a capital investment by discounting its future cash flows to their present values. Under the net present value method, all future cash flows for each proposed project are discounted to their present value, and the amount of the initial investment is subtracted from the sum of those amounts. The projects with the highest positive net present value—the amount that exceeds the initial investment—are selected for implementation. The multipliers used to find the present values of future cash flows can be found in the appendix on future value and present value tables. Which multiplier to use is determined by connecting the minimum desired rate of return and the life of the asset or length of time for which the amount is being discounted. Each cash inflow and cash outflow to be realized over the life of the asset is discounted back to the present. If the present value of all expected future net cash inflows is greater than the amount of the current expenditure, the investment meets the minimum desired rate of return, and the project should be carried out.

   The method of calculating a project's net present value depends on whether annual cash flows are equal or unequal. If all annual net cash flows (inflows less outflows) are equal, the discount factor comes from Table 4 of the appendix on future value and present value tables. That table gives multipliers for the present value of $1 received each period for a given number of periods. One computation will cover the cash flows of all periods involved. If, however, expected cash inflows and outflows differ from one year to the next, each year's cash flow amount must be individually discounted to the present. Discount factors used in this kind of analysis are found in Table 3 of the appendix on future value and present value tables. Multipliers in that table are used to find the present value of $1 to be received (or paid out) at the end of a given number of periods.

The following example shows the difference in the present value analysis of investments with equal and unequal cash flows. Suppose the Janus Company is deciding which of two stamping machines to buy. The blue machine has equal expected annual net cash inflows and the black machine has unequal annual amounts.

	Blue Machine	Black Machine
Purchase price: January 1, 2000	$16,500	$16,500
Salvage value	—	—
Expected life	5 years	5 years
Estimated net cash inflows		
2000	$5,000	$6,000
2001	$5,000	$5,500
2002	$5,000	$5,000
2003	$5,000	$4,500
2004	$5,000	$4,000

The company's minimum desired rate of return is 16 percent. Which—if either—of the two alternatives should be chosen?

The evaluation process is shown in Exhibit 1. The analysis of the blue machine is easier to prepare because that machine generates equal annual cash flows. The present value of the net cash inflows for the five-year period for the blue machine is found by first locating the appropriate multiplier in Table 4 of the appendix on

---

Exhibit 1. Net Present Value Analysis: Equal Versus Unequal Cash Flows

**Janus Company
Capital Investment Analysis
2000**

Blue Machine	
Present value of cash inflows ($5,000 × 3.274)	$16,370.00
Less purchase price of machine	16,500.00
Negative net present value	($ 130.00)
Black Machine	
Present value of cash inflows	
2000 ($6,000 × .862)	$ 5,172.00
2001 ($5,500 × .743)	4,086.50
2002 ($5,000 × .641)	3,205.00
2003 ($4,500 × .552)	2,484.00
2004 ($4,000 × .476)	1,904.00
Total present value	$16,851.50
Less purchase price of machine	16,500.00
Positive net present value	$ 351.50

Note: If a piece of equipment has a salvage value at the end of its useful life, the present value of that amount needs to be computed to determine the present value of all future net cash inflows.

future value and present value tables. By matching the row for five years with the column for 16 percent, the factor 3.274 is found. Multiplying that factor by the $5,000 annual cash inflow yields $16,370, the present value of the total cash inflows from the blue machine. Comparing that figure with the machine's $16,500 purchase price results in a negative net present value of $130.

Analysis of the black machine gives a different result. Multipliers for this part of the analysis are found by using the same 16 percent rate. But five multipliers must be used, one for each year of the asset's life. Table 3 in the appendix on future value and present value tables applies here, since each annual amount must be discounted to the present. For the black machine, the $16,851.50 present value of the net cash inflows is more than the $16,500 purchase price of the machine. Thus, there is a positive net present value of $351.50.

A positive net present value means that the return on the asset exceeds the 16 percent minimum desired rate of return. A negative figure means that the rate of return is below the minimum cutoff point. In the Janus Company case, the right decision would be to purchase the black machine.

The incorporation of the time value of money into the evaluation of a proposed capital investment is the main advantage of the net present value method. This method also measures total cash flows from the investment over its estimated useful life, so total profitability can be brought into the analysis as well. The principal disadvantage of the net present value method is that its computations are more difficult than those made for the payback period and rate-of-return methods.

Tax Considerations in Capital Investment Decisions

In profit-oriented organizations, income taxes alter the amount and timing of cash flows of projects under consideration. To accurately assess the benefits of a capital investment, the management accountant must include the effects of taxes in the decision analysis. However, because of the complexity of the corporate tax tables and their impact on cash flow projections, a detailed discussion of the effects of income taxes on capital investment decisions has been left for a more advanced course.

Chapter Review

REVIEW OF LEARNING OBJECTIVES

1. **Explain the capital investment decision cycle and describe the manager's role in the decision process.** Capital investment decisions focus on when and how much to spend on capital facilities. The capital investment decision-making process, often referred to as capital budgeting, consists of identifying the need for a capital investment, analyzing courses of action to meet that need, preparing reports for management, choosing the best alternative, and dividing funds among competing resource needs.

   Underlying the capital investment decision cycle are all the parts of the management cycle. Most of the capital investment decision analysis occurs during the planning stage of the management cycle. The screening, evaluation, and funding activities that take place prior to a capital investment decision are all part of the planning stage of the cycle. A decision is actually made during the executing stage of the management cycle. Postcompletion audits are conducted as part of the reviewing stage of the management cycle. Reports on the results of capital investment decisions are prepared and distributed within the organization during the reporting stage. Based on those reports, managers will decide either that the initial problem has been solved and the capital investment decision process is complete or that the problem still exists and the process must begin again.

   The capital investment decision cycle begins when the need for a facility is identified. A proposal or request is then prepared and analyzed before being subjected to one or two screening processes, depending on the size of the organization. Based on various evaluation methods and a minimum desired rate of return, the proposal is determined to be either acceptable or unacceptable. If acceptable, the proposal is ranked with all other acceptable proposals. Total dollars available for capital investment are used to determine which of the ranked proposals to authorize and implement. The final step is a postcompletion audit to determine the accuracy of the forecasted data used in the decision cycle and to find out if some of the projections need correction.

   The role of the manager in this decision process is to identify and explain capital investment needs; the management accountant's role is to provide information that will help managers make sound capital investment decisions.

2. **State the purpose of the minimum desired rate of return and identify the methods used to arrive at this rate.** The minimum desired rate of return acts as a screening mechanism by eliminating from further consideration capital investment requests with anticipated low returns. With such an approach to decision making, many unprofitable requests are turned away or discouraged without a great deal of wasted executive time. The most common measures used to compute minimum desired rates of return include (1) cost of capital, (2) corporate return on investment, (3) industry's average return on investment, and (4) federal and bank interest rates. The weighted average cost of capital and the average return on investment are the most widely used measures.

3. **Identify the types of projected costs and revenues used to evaluate alternatives for capital investment.** The accounting rate-of-return method requires measures of net income. Other methods of evaluating capital investments evaluate net cash inflow or cash savings. The analysis process must take into consideration whether cash flows will be equal in each period or unequal. Book values and depreciation expense of assets awaiting replacement are irrelevant. Net proceeds from the sale of an old asset and estimated salvage value of a new facility represent future cash flows and must be part of the estimated benefit of a project. Depreciation expense on replacement equipment is relevant to income-based evaluations.

4. **Evaluate capital investment proposals using (a) the accounting rate-of-return method and (b) the payback period method.** When managers use the accounting rate-of-return method to evaluate two or more capital investment proposals, they select the alternative that yields the highest ratio of average annual net income to

average cost of investment. The payback period method of evaluating a capital invest-ment proposal focuses on the shortest time period needed to recover in cash the origi-nal amount of the investment.

5. **Apply the concept of the time value of money.** Cash flows of equal dollar amounts at different times have different values because of the effect of compound interest. This phenomenon is known as the time value of money. Of the evaluation methods discussed in this chapter, only the net present value method is based on the concept of the time value of money.

6. **Evaluate capital investment proposals using the net present value method.** The net present value method of evaluating capital investments depends on the time value of money. Present values of future cash flows are computed to see if their sum is greater than the current cost of the capital investment being evaluated.

REVIEW OF CONCEPTS AND TERMINOLOGY

The following concepts and terms were introduced in this chapter:

LO 4 **Accounting rate-of-return method:** A capital investment evaluation method designed to measure the estimated performance of a potential capital project. It is calculated by dividing the project's average annual net income by the average cost of the investment.

LO 2 **Average cost of capital:** A minimum desired rate of return on invested capital that is computed by taking an average of the cost of debt, the cost of preferred stock, the cost of equity capital, and the cost of retained earnings.

LO 3 **Book value:** The undepreciated portion of the original cost of a fixed asset.

LO 1 **Capital budgeting:** The process of making decisions about capital investments. It includes identifying the need for a capital investment, analyzing courses of action to meet that need, preparing reports for managers, choosing the best alternative, and rationing funds among competing needs. Also called *capital investment decision analysis*.

LO 1 **Capital investment decisions:** Management decisions about when and how much to spend on capital facilities for the organization.

LO 2 **Cost of debt:** A minimum desired rate of return on invested capital that is computed as the ratio of loan charges to net proceeds of the loan.

LO 2 **Cost of equity capital:** A minimum desired rate of return on invested capital that is determined by calculating net income as a percentage of invested capital.

LO 2 **Cost of preferred stock:** A minimum desired rate of return on invested capital that is the stated dividend rate of the individual preferred stock issue.

LO 2 **Cost of retained earnings:** A minimum desired rate of return on invested capital that is the opportunity cost, or the dividends given up by the common stockholders.

LO 3 **Net cash inflow:** The balance of increases in cash receipts over increases in cash pay-ments resulting from a proposed capital investment.

LO 6 **Net present value method:** A technique for evaluating capital investments in which all future cash flows for each proposed project are discounted to their present value, and the amount of the initial investment is subtracted from the sum of those amounts. Those projects with the highest positive net present value—the amount that exceeds the initial investment—are selected for implementation.

LO 3 **Noncash expense:** An expense that did not require a cash outlay during the period under review.

LO 4 **Payback period method:** A capital investment evaluation method that bases the deci-sion to invest in a capital project on the minimum length of time it will take to get back in cash the amount of the initial investment.

LO 5 **Time value of money:** The concept that cash flows of equal dollar amounts separated by an interval of time have different present values because of the effect of compound interest.

REVIEW PROBLEM

Capital Investment Decision Analysis

LO 3
LO 4
LO 5
LO 6

The Roland Construction Company specializes in developing large shopping centers. The company is considering the purchase of a new earth-moving machine and has gathered the following information:

Purchase price	$600,000
Salvage value	$100,000
Useful life	4 years
Depreciation method	Straight-line
Desired payback period	3 years
Minimum rate of return	15%

The cash flow estimates are as follows:

Year	Cash Inflows	Cash Outflows	Net Cash Inflow
1	$ 500,000	$260,000	$240,000
2	450,000	240,000	210,000
3	400,000	220,000	180,000
4	350,000	200,000	150,000
Totals	$1,700,000	$920,000	$780,000

REQUIRED

1. Analyze the Roland Construction Company's investment in the new earth-moving machine. In your analysis, use (a) the accounting rate-of-return method, (b) the payback period method, and (c) the net present value method.
2. Summarize your findings from **1** and recommend a course of action.

ANSWER TO REVIEW PROBLEM

1. The increase in net income is as follows:

Year	Net Cash Inflow	Depreciation	Projected Net Income
1	$240,000	$125,000	$115,000
2	210,000	125,000	85,000
3	180,000	125,000	55,000
4	150,000	125,000	25,000
Totals	$780,000	$500,000	$280,000

1a. Accounting rate-of-return method

$$\text{Accounting Rate of Return} = \frac{\text{Average Annual Net Income}}{\text{Average Investment Cost}}$$

$$= \frac{\$280,000 \div 4}{\left(\dfrac{\$600,000 - \$100,000}{2}\right) + \$100,000} = \frac{\$70,000}{\$350,000}$$

$$= 20\%$$

1b. Payback period method

Total cash investment		$600,000
Less cash-flow recovery		
Year 1	$240,000	
Year 2	210,000	
Year 3 (⅚ of $180,000)	150,000	(600,000)
Unrecovered investment		$ 0

Payback period: 2.833 (2⅚) years, or 2 years 10 months

1c. Net present value method (Multipliers are from Table 3 in the appendix on future value and present value tables.)

Year	Net Cash Inflow	Present-Value Multiplier	Present Value
1	$240,000	.870	$208,800
2	210,000	.756	158,760
3	180,000	.658	118,440
4	150,000	.572	85,800
4	100,000 (salvage)	.572	57,200
Total present value			$629,000
Less cost of original investment			600,000
Positive net present value			$ 29,000

2. Roland Construction Company: Summary of Decision Analysis

	Decision Measures	
	Desired	Predicted
Accounting rate of return	15%	20%
Payback period	3 years	2.833 years
Net present value	—	$29,000

Based on the calculations in **1,** the proposed investment in the earth-moving machine meets all company criteria for such investments. Given these results, the company should invest in the machine.

Chapter Assignments

BUILDING YOUR KNOWLEDGE FOUNDATION

Questions

1. What is a capital investment? Give examples of some capital investments.
2. Define *capital budgeting.*
3. Identify the connections between the management cycle and the capital investment decision cycle.
4. Describe the logical order of the following steps in the capital investment decision cycle:
   a. Methods of evaluation
   b. Determination of dollars available for capital investments
   c. Capital investment decisions
5. What difficulties may be encountered when trying to implement the postcompletion audit step of the capital investment decision cycle?
6. Identify some approaches companies use to determine a minimum desired rate of return for capital investment proposals.
7. Why is it important to know whether a capital investment will produce equal cash flows or unequal cash flows? Is such information relevant to the accounting rate-of-return method? The payback period method? The net present value method?
8. Of the three methods of capital investment analysis discussed in this chapter, which one is known as a crude but easy way to evaluate capital investments? List the advantages and disadvantages of this method.

9. What formula is used to determine payback period? Is this decision-making method very accurate? Defend your answer.

10. Distinguish between cost savings and net cash inflow.

11. Discuss the statement, "To treat all future income flows alike ignores the time value of money."

12. Explain the relationship of compound interest to the determination of future value and present value.

13. What is the objective of using discounted cash flows?

14. "In using the net present value method, the book value of an asset is irrelevant, whereas current and future salvage values are relevant." Is this statement valid? Why?

15. When evaluating equipment replacement proposals under the net present value method, why is depreciation of the old equipment ignored?

16. What is the role of the cost of capital when the net present value method is used to evaluate capital investment proposals?

Short Exercises

LO 1 *Manager's Role in Capital Investment Decisions*

SE 1. Joe Gooding, the supervisor of the Drilling Department, has suggested to Nina Habib, the plant manager, that a new machine costing $185,000 be purchased to improve drilling operations for the plant's newest product line. How should the plant manager proceed with this request?

LO 2 *Minimum Desired Rate of Return*

SE 2. Gutierrez Industries has three sources of funds for its planned $1 million plant expansion: a mortgage loan of $700,000 at 9 percent interest, a bank loan of $250,000 at 12 percent using existing machinery as collateral, and a second trust deed loan from a major stockholder of $50,000 at 14 percent interest. What is Gutierrez's average cost of capital for this investment?

LO 3 *Capital Budgeting Cost and Revenue Measures*

SE 3. Mah Corp. is analyzing a proposal to purchase a computer-integrated boring mill. The machine will be able to produce an entire product line in a single operation. Projected annual net cash inflow from the machine is $180,000, and projected net income is $120,000. Why is projected net income lower than projected net cash inflow? Identify possible causes for the $60,000 difference.

LO 4 *Capital Investment Decision: Payback Period Method*

SE 4. Joseph Communications, Inc., is considering the purchase of a new piece of computerized data transmission equipment. Estimated annual net cash inflow for the new equipment is $575,000. The equipment costs $2 million, it has a five-year life, and it will have no salvage value at the end of the five years. The company uses the following capital investment decision guidelines: maximum payback period of four years; minimum desired rate of return of 12 percent. Compute the payback period of the piece of equipment. Should the company purchase it?

LO 5 *Time Value of Money*

SE 5. Your Aunt Harriet recently inherited a trust fund from a distant relative. On January 2, the bank managing the trust fund notified Aunt Harriet that she has the option of receiving a lump-sum check for $175,500 or leaving the money in the trust fund and receiving an annual year-end check for $20,000 for each of the next twenty years. Aunt Harriet likes to earn at least an 8 percent return on her investments. What should Aunt Harriet do?

LO 6 *Capital Investment Decision: Net Present Value Method*

SE 6. Using the information about Joseph Communications, Inc., in **SE 4,** compute the net present value of the piece of equipment. Does this method yield a positive or negative response to the proposal to buy the equipment?

LO 6 *Salvage Value and the Net Present Value Method*

SE 7. JoAnne Jenkins is developing a capital investment decision analysis for her supervisor. The proposed capital investment has an estimated salvage value of $5,500 at the end of its five-year life. The company uses a 16 percent minimum desired rate of return. What is the present value of the salvage value?

Exercises

LO 1
Capital Investment Decision Cycle

E 1. Chris Hilt was just promoted to supervisor of building maintenance for the All-Star Theater complex. The complex consists of seventeen buildings. Lakes Entertainment, Inc., Hilt's employer, uses a companywide system for evaluating capital investment requests from its twenty-two supervisors. Hilt has approached you, the corporate controller, for advice on preparing her first proposal. She would also like to become familiar with the entire decision cycle.

1. What advice would you give Hilt before she prepares her first capital investment proposal?
2. Explain the capital investment decision cycle to Hilt.

LO 2
Minimum Desired Rate of Return

E 2. The controller of Harbor Corporation wants to establish a minimum desired rate of return and would like to use a weighted average cost of capital. Current data about the corporation's financing structure are as follows: debt financing, 40 percent; preferred stock, 30 percent; common stock, 20 percent; and retained earnings, 10 percent. The cost of debt is 9½ percent. Dividend rates on the preferred and common stock issues are 7½ and 12 percent, respectively. Cost of retained earnings is 12 percent.

Compute the weighted average cost of capital.

LO 3
Analysis of Relevant Information

E 3. Bazzetta & Co., a scrap-metal company, supplies area steel companies with recycled materials. The company collects scrap metal, sorts and cleans the material, and compresses it into one-ton blocks for easy handling. Increased demand for recycled metals has caused Mr. Bazzetta to decide to purchase an additional metal-compressing machine. He has narrowed the choice to two models. The company's management accountant has gathered the following information about each model.

	Model One	Model Two
Purchase price	$100,000	$120,000
Salvage value	12,000	20,000
Annual depreciation*	8,800	10,000
Resulting increases in annual sales	182,000	210,000
Annual operating costs		
Direct materials	70,000	80,000
Direct labor	40,000	40,000
Operating supplies	3,600	4,000
Indirect labor	24,000	36,000
Insurance and taxes	1,600	2,000
Plant rental	8,000	8,000
Electricity	1,000	1,120
Other overhead	5,000	5,680

*Computed using the straight-line method.

1. Identify the costs and revenues relevant to the decision.
2. Prepare a cash-flow analysis for year 1.

LO 4
Capital Investment Decision: Accounting Rate-of-Return Method

E 4. Heber Corporation manufactures metal hard hats for on-site construction workers. Recently, management has tried to raise productivity to meet the growing demand from the real estate industry. The company is now thinking about a new stamping machine. Management has decided that only capital investments that yield a 14 percent return will be accepted. The following projections for the proposal are given: The new machine will cost $325,000; revenue will increase $98,400 per year; the salvage value of the new machine will be $32,500; and operating cost increases (including depreciation) will be $74,600.

Using the accounting rate-of-return method, decide whether the company should invest in the machine. Show all computations to support your decision.

LO 4 *Capital Investment Decision: Payback Period Method*

E 5. Super Sounds, Inc., a manufacturer of stereo speakers, is thinking about adding a new injection molding machine. This machine can produce speaker parts that the company now buys from outsiders. The machine has an estimated useful life of fourteen years and will cost $425,000. Gross cash revenue from the machine will be about $400,000 per year, and related cash expenses should total $310,050. The payback period should be five years or less.

On the basis of the data given, use the payback period method to determine whether the company should invest in this new machine. Show your computations to support your answer.

LO 5 *Using the Present Value Tables*

E 6. For each of the following situations, identify the correct multiplier to use from the tables in the appendix on future value and present value tables. Also, compute the appropriate present value.

1. Annual net cash inflow of $35,000 for five years, discounted at 16%
2. An amount of $25,000 to be received at the end of ten years, discounted at 12%
3. The amount of $28,000 to be received at the end of two years, and $15,000 to be received at the end of years four, five, and six, discounted at 10%
4. Annual net cash inflow of $22,500 for twelve years, discounted at 14%
5. The following five years of cash inflows, discounted at 10%:

Year 1	$35,000
Year 2	20,000
Year 3	30,000
Year 4	40,000
Year 5	50,000

6. The amount of $70,000 to be received at the beginning of year 7, discounted at 14%

LO 6 *Present Value Computations*

E 7. Two machines—Machine K and Machine L—are being considered in a replacement decision. Both machines have about the same purchase price and an estimated ten-year life. The company uses a 12 percent minimum desired rate of return as its acceptance-rejection standard. Following are the estimated net cash inflows for each machine.

Year	Machine K	Machine L
1	$12,000	$17,500
2	12,000	17,500
3	14,000	17,500
4	19,000	17,500
5	20,000	17,500
6	22,000	17,500
7	23,000	17,500
8	24,000	17,500
9	25,000	17,500
10	20,000	17,500
Salvage value	14,000	12,000

1. Compute the present value of future cash flows for each machine.
2. Which machine should the company purchase, assuming they both involve the same capital investment?

LO 6 *Capital Investment Decision: Net Present Value Method*

E 8. Jamal and Associates wants to buy an automatic extruding machine. This piece of equipment would have a useful life of six years, would cost $219,500, and would increase annual net cash inflows by $57,000. Assume there is no salvage value at the end of six years. The company's minimum desired rate of return is 14 percent.

Using the net present value method, prepare an analysis to determine whether the company should purchase the machine.

Problems

P 1. Tom Trane, the controller of BSF Corporation, is developing his company's minimum desired rate of return for the year. This measure will be used as an acceptance-rejection standard in capital investment decision analyses during the coming year. As in the past, this rate will be based on the company's weighted average cost of capital. The capital mix and the respective costs for the previous twelve months were as follows:

	Percentage of Total Financing	Cost of Capital (Percentage)
Debt financing	20	9
Preferred stock	10	11
Common stock	50	10
Retained earnings	20	12

The company will soon convert one-fifth of its common stock financing into debt, increasing debt financing to 30 percent of total financing and decreasing common stock to 40 percent of total financing. Changes in the cost of capital are anticipated only in debt financing, where the rate is expected to increase to 12 percent.

Several capital investment proposals have been submitted for consideration for the current year. Those projects and their projected rates of return are as follows: Project A, 13 percent; Project B, 10 percent; Capital Equipment C, 15 percent; Project D, 9 percent; Capital Equipment E, 12 percent; and Project F, 14 percent.

REQUIRED

1. Using the anticipated adjustments to capital cost and mix, compute the weighted average cost of capital for the current year.
2. Identify the proposed capital investments that should be implemented on the basis of the minimum desired rate of return calculated in **1.**

P 2. Blue Island Corporation wants to buy a new stamping machine. The machine will provide the company with a new product line: pressed rubber food trays for kitchens. Two machines are being considered; the data applicable to each machine are as follows:

	Coupe Machine	Metro Machine
Estimated annual increase in revenue	$450,000	$500,000
Purchase price	280,000	300,000
Salvage value	28,000	30,000
Traceable annual costs		
Direct materials	161,670	157,500
Direct labor	65,250	92,300
Manufacturing overhead (excluding depreciation)	158,676	174,558
Estimated useful life in years	10	10

Depreciation is computed using the straight-line method net of salvage value. The company's minimum desired rate of return is 16 percent, and the maximum allowable payback period is 4.5 years.

REQUIRED

1. Compute how the company's net income will change under each alternative.
2. For each machine, compute the projected accounting rate of return.
3. Compute the payback period for each machine.
4. From the information generated in **2** and **3,** decide which machine should be purchased. Why?

P 3. Travel Entertainment, Ltd., operates a tour and sightseeing business in southern California. Its trademark is the use of trolley buses. Each vehicle has its own identity and is specially made for the company. Jenny, the oldest bus, was purchased fifteen years ago and has five years of its estimated useful life remaining. The company paid $25,000 for Jenny, and the bus has a current market value of $20,000. Jenny is expected to generate an average annual net cash inflow of $24,000 for the remainder of its estimated useful life.

Management wants to replace Jenny with a modern-looking vehicle called Sean. Sean has a purchase price of $140,000 and an estimated useful life of twenty years. Net cash inflows for Sean are projected as follows:

Years	Annual Net Cash Inflows
1–5	$40,000
6–10	45,000
11–20	30,000

Assume that (1) all cash flows occur at year end, (2) the company uses straight-line depreciation, (3) each vehicle's salvage value equals 10 percent of its purchase price, and (4) the minimum desired rate of return is 10 percent.

REQUIRED

1. Compute the net present value of the future cash flows from Jenny.
2. What would be the net present value of cash flows if Sean were purchased?
3. Should the company keep Jenny or purchase Sean?

P 4.

LO 6 *Net Present Value Method*

Mon Chateau is a famous restaurant in the New Orleans French Quarter. "Bouillabaisse Kathryn" is the house specialty. Management is currently considering the purchase of a machine that would prepare all the ingredients, mix them automatically, and cook the dish to the restaurant's specifications. The machine will function for an estimated twelve years, and the purchase price, including installation, is $250,000. Estimated salvage value is $25,000. This labor-saving device is expected to increase cash flows by an average of $42,000 per year during its estimated useful life. For purposes of capital investment decisions, the restaurant uses a 12 percent minimum desired rate of return.

REQUIRED

1. Using the net present value method, determine if the company should purchase the machine. Support your answer.
2. If management had decided on a minimum desired rate of return of 14 percent, should the machine be purchased? Show all computations to support your answer.

P 5.

LO 4 *Capital Investment*
LO 6 *Decision: Comprehensive*

The Pinetop Manufacturing Company, based in Pinetop, Colorado, is one of the fastest-growing companies in its industry. According to Mr. Bains, the company's production vice president, keeping up-to-date with technological changes is what makes the company successful.

Mr. Bains feels that a machine introduced recently would fill an important need. The machine has an estimated useful life of four years, a purchase price of $250,000, and a salvage value of $25,000. The company controller's estimated operating results, using the new machine, follow.

	Cash Flow Estimates	
Year	Cash Inflows	Cash Outflows
1	$325,000	$250,000
2	320,000	250,000
3	315,000	250,000
4	310,000	250,000

The company uses straight-line depreciation for all its machinery. Mr. Bains uses a 12 percent minimum desired rate of return and a three-year payback period for capital investment evaluation purposes.

REQUIRED

1. Analyze the data about the machine and decide if the company should purchase it. Use the following evaluation approaches in your analysis: (a) the accounting rate-of-return method, (b) the payback period method, and (c) the net present value method.
2. Summarize the information generated in **1** and make a recommendation to Mr. Bains.

Alternate Problems

P 6.

LO 4 *Accounting Rate-of-Return and Payback Period Methods*

The Coghill Company is expanding its production facilities to include a new product line, a sporty automotive tire rim. Using new computerized machinery, tire rims can now be produced with little labor cost. The controller has advised management about two such machines. The details about each machine are at the top of the next page.

The company uses the straight-line depreciation method. The minimum desired rate of return is 12 percent. The maximum payback period is six years. (Where necessary, round calculations to the nearest dollar.)

	Darcy Machine	Kypros Machine
Estimated annual increase in revenue	$280,000	$290,000
Purchase price	500,000	550,000
Salvage value	50,000	55,000
Traceable annual costs		
Direct materials	85,400	80,800
Direct labor	21,200	36,900
Manufacturing overhead (excluding depreciation)	82,185	82,130
Estimated useful life in years	8	10

REQUIRED

1. Compute the change in the company's net income from each alternative.
2. For each machine, compute the projected accounting rate of return.
3. Compute the payback period for each machine.
4. From the information generated in **2** and **3,** which machine should be purchased? Why?

P 7.

LO 6 *Net Present Value Method*

Barry and Dixon, Inc., owns and operates a group of apartment buildings. Management wants to sell one of its older four-family buildings and buy a new structure. The old building, which was purchased twenty-five years ago for $100,000, has a forty-year estimated useful life. The current market value is $80,000, and, if it is sold, the cash inflow will be $67,675. Annual net cash inflows on the old building are expected to average $16,000 for the remainder of its estimated useful life.

The new building being considered will cost $300,000. It has an estimated useful life of twenty-five years. Net cash inflows are expected to be $50,000 annually.

Assume that (1) all cash flows occur at year end, (2) the company uses straight-line depreciation, (3) the buildings will have a salvage value equal to 10 percent of their purchase price, and (4) the minimum desired rate of return is 14 percent.

REQUIRED

1. Compute the net present value of future cash flows from the old building.
2. What will be the net present value of cash flows if the new building is purchased?
3. Should the company keep the old building or purchase the new one?

P 8.

LO 6 *Net Present Value Method*

The management of Mega-Tuff Plastics has recently been looking at a proposal to purchase a new plastic injection-style molding machine. With the new machine, the company would not have to buy small plastic parts to use in production. The estimated useful life of the machine is fifteen years, and the purchase price, including all setup charges, is $400,000. Salvage value is estimated to be $40,000. The net addition to the company's cash inflow due to the savings from making the parts is estimated to be $70,000 a year. Mega-Tuff Plastics' management has decided on a minimum desired rate of return of 14 percent.

REQUIRED

1. Using the net present value method to evaluate this capital investment, determine whether the company should purchase the machine. Support your answer.
2. If management had decided on a minimum desired rate of return of 16 percent, should the machine be purchased? Show all computations to support your answer.

EXPANDING YOUR CRITICAL THINKING, COMMUNICATION, AND INTERPERSONAL SKILLS

Skills Development

CONCEPTUAL ANALYSIS

LO 1 *Capital Investments for Hazardous Waste*

SD 1. The ***Upjohn Company,*** a leading pharmaceutical company, uses thousands of chemicals considered to be hazardous.[5] The Superfund Amendments and Reauthorization Act of 1986 (SARA) requires companies to report their operating environmental discharges, and the Upjohn Company is in compliance. Assume that Chemical XOC, a hazardous material, requires a special building for its storage. In addition, the company must regularly monitor the chemical's condition and report it to government officials. (Some chemicals must be monitored for as long as thirty years.) In groups of three or four people, decide how to account for the cost of (1) the special building and (2) tracking the chemical's condition. Should these costs be capitalized or expensed in the period in which they are incurred? Can they be traced to specific products for costing purposes, or should they be included in manufacturing overhead and divided among all products? Select a spokesperson who will report the group's findings to the class and defend your position.

ETHICAL DILEMMA

LO 6 *Ethics, Capital Investment Decisions, and the New Globally Competitive Business Environment*

SD 2. Mark Jones is the controller of ***Bramer Corporation,*** a globally competitive producer of standard and custom-designed window units for the housing industry. As part of the corporation's move to become automated, Jones was asked to prepare a capital investment decision analysis for a robot-guided aluminum extruding and stamping machine. This machine would automate the entire window-casing manufacturing line. He had just returned from a national seminar on the subject of qualitative inputs into the capital investment decision process and was anxious to incorporate these new ideas into the decision analysis. In addition to the normal net present value analysis (which produced a significant negative result), Jones factored in figures for customer satisfaction, scrap reduction, reduced inventory needs, and quality reputation. With the additional information included, the analysis produced a positive response to the decision question.

When the chief financial officer finished reviewing Jones's work, he threw the papers on the floor and said, "What kind of garbage is this? You know it's impossible to quantify such things as customer satisfaction and quality reputation. How do you expect me to go to the board of directors and explain your work? I want you to redo the entire analysis and follow only the traditional approach to net present value. Get it back to me in two hours!"

What is Mark's dilemma? What ethical courses of action are available to Mark?

RESEARCH ACTIVITY

LO 1 *Capital Investment Decision Process*

SD 3. Computers are important in today's business world. Every business can benefit from computers' capabilities, which include rapid data processing, timely report generation, automated accounting systems, and the use of specialized software packages for such areas as payroll, accounts receivable, accounts payable, and tax return preparation. Make a trip to a local computer retailer. Inquire about the various types of computers available and identify one that would be useful to a local nursery selling landscape

| Communication | Critical Thinking | Group Activity | Memo | Ethics | International | Spreadsheet | Managerial Technology | Internet |

391

plants and gardening supplies and equipment. Find out the cost of this computer. Make notes of the model name, its special features and capabilities, and its cost. After gathering these data, identify the benefits that the nursery's controller would include in an analysis to justify the purchase of the computer. Describe the effect of each benefit on cash flow and profitability. Be prepared to discuss your findings in class.

 Group Activity: Assign teams to carry out the above assignments.

DECISION-MAKING PRACTICE

SD 4.

LO 6 *Using Net Present Value*

The **McCall Syndicate** owns four resort hotels in Europe. Because the Paris operation (Hotel 1) has been booming over the past five years, management has decided to build an addition to the hotel. This addition will increase the hotel's capacity by 20 percent. A construction company has offered to build the addition at a cost of $30,000,000. The building will have a salvage value of $3,000,000 and will be depreciated on a straight-line basis over its twenty-year life.

Erin McVan, the controller, has started an analysis of the net present value for the project. She has calculated the annual net cash inflow by subtracting the increase in cash operating expenses from the increase in cash inflows from room rentals. Her partially completed schedule follows.

Year	Annual Net Cash Inflows
1–7 (each year)	$ 3,809,700
8	4,007,700
9	4,535,700
10–20 (each year)	4,733,700

Capital investment projects must generate a 12 percent minimum rate of return to qualify for consideration.

Using net present value analysis, evaluate the proposal and make a recommendation to management.

Managerial Reporting and Analysis

INTERPRETING MANAGEMENT REPORTS

MRA 1.

LO 6 *Capital Investment Analysis*

Automatic teller machines (ATMs) have rapidly become a common element of the banking industry. **San Cimion Federal Bank** is planning to replace some old machines and has decided on the York Machine. Nora Chang, the controller, has prepared the decision analysis shown at the top of the next page. She has recommended the purchase of the machine based on the positive net present value shown in the analysis.

The York Machine has an estimated useful life of five years and an expected salvage value of $35,000. Its purchase price would be $385,000. Two existing ATMs, each having a book value of $25,000, would be sold for a total of $50,000 to a neighboring bank. Annual operating cash inflow is expected to increase in the following manner:

Year 1	$79,900
Year 2	76,600
Year 3	79,900
Year 4	83,200
Year 5	86,500

The bank uses straight-line depreciation. The minimum desired rate of return is 12 percent.

REQUIRED

1. Analyze the work of Ms. Chang. What changes need to be made in her capital investment decision analysis?
2. What would be your recommendation to bank management about the York Machine purchase?

San Cimion Federal Bank
Capital Investment Decision Analysis
Net Present Value Method
March 2, 20x1

Year	Net Cash Inflow	Present Value Multipliers	Present Value
1	$ 85,000	.909	$ 77,265
2	80,000	.826	66,080
3	85,000	.751	63,835
4	90,000	.683	61,470
5	95,000	.621	58,995
5 (salvage)	35,000	.621	21,735
Total Present Value			$349,380
Initial Investment	$385,000		
Less Proceeds from the Sale of Existing Teller Machines	50,000		
Net Capital Investment			(335,000)
Net Present Value			$ 14,380

FORMULATING MANAGEMENT REPORTS

MRA 2.

LO 3 *Evaluating a*
LO 4 *Capital Investment*
LO 6 *Proposal*

Quality work and timely output are the benchmarks upon which **Rock Photo, Inc.,** was organized. Rock Photo is a nationally franchised company with over fifty outlets located in the southern states. Part of the franchise agreement promises a centralized photo developing process with overnight delivery to the outlets.

Because of the tremendous increase in demand for its photo processing, Emma Dubois, the corporation's president, is considering the purchase of a new, deluxe processing machine by the end of this month. Dubois wants you to formulate a memo showing your evaluation. Your memo will be presented to the board of directors' meeting next week.

You have gathered the following information. The new machine will cost $320,000. The machine will function for an estimated five years and should have a $32,000 salvage value. All capital investments are expected to produce a 20 percent minimum rate of return, and the investment should be recovered in three years or less. All fixed assets are depreciated using the straight-line method. The forecasted increases in operating results of the new machine are as follows:

	Cash Flow Estimates	
Year	Cash Inflows	Cash Outflows
1	$310,000	$210,000
2	325,000	220,000
3	340,000	230,000
4	300,000	210,000
5	260,000	180,000

REQUIRED

1. In preparation for writing your memo, answer the following questions.
   a. What kinds of information do you need to prepare this memo?
   b. Why is the information relevant?
   c. Where would you find the information?
   d. When would you want to obtain the information?

2. Analyze the purchase of the machine and decide if the company should purchase it. Use (a) the accounting rate-of-return method; (b) the payback period method; and (c) the net present value method.

INTERNATIONAL COMPANY

MRA 3.

LO 1 *Evaluation of Capital Investment Decisions*

The board of directors of the ***Tanashi Corporation*** met to review a number of proposals involving the use of capital to improve the quality of company products. A proposal submitted by a production line manager requested the purchase of new computer-integrated machines to replace the older machines in one of the ten production departments at the Tokyo plant. Although the manager had presented quantitative information to support the purchase of the new machines, the board members asked the following important questions related to the proposal:

1. Why do we want to replace the old machines? Have they deteriorated? Are they obsolete?
2. Will the new machines require less cycle time?
3. Can we reduce inventory levels or save floor space by replacing the old machines?
4. How expensive is the software used with the new machines?
5. Will we be able to find highly skilled employees to maintain the new machines? Or can we find workers who are trainable? What would it cost to train those workers? Would the training disrupt the staff by causing relocations?
6. Would the implementation of the machines be delayed because of the time required to recruit new workers?
7. What impact would the new machines have on the other parts of the manufacturing systems? Would the company lose some of the flexibility in its manufacturing systems if it introduced the new machines?

The board members believe that the qualitative information needed to answer their questions could lead to the rejection of the project, even though it would have been accepted based on the quantitative information.

REQUIRED

1. Identify the questions that can be answered with quantitative information. Give an example of the quantitative information that could be used.
2. Identify the questions that can be answered with qualitative information. Explain why this information could negatively influence the capital investment decision even though the quantitative information suggests a positive outcome.

MRA 4.

LO 6 *Excel Analysis*

Harper Corporation is an international plumbing equipment and supply company located in southern California. The manager of the Pipe Extruding Division is considering the purchase of a computerized copper pipe extruding machine that costs $120,000. The machine has a six-year life, and its expected salvage value after six years of use will be 10 percent of its original cost. Cash revenue generated by the new machine is projected to be $50,000 in year 1 and will increase by $10,000 each year for the next five years. Variable cash operating costs will be materials and parts, 25 percent of revenue; machine labor, 5 percent of revenue; and manufacturing overhead, 15 percent of revenue. First-year sales and marketing cash outflows are expected to be $10,500 and will decrease by 10 percent each year over the life of the new machine. Anticipated cash administrative expenses will be $2,500 per year. The company uses a 15 percent minimum desired rate of return for all capital investment analyses.

REQUIRED

1. Prepare an Excel spreadsheet that will compute the net present value of the anticipated cash flows for the life of the proposed new extruding machine. Use the following format:

| | | Projected Cash Outflows | | | | | | | Present Value of |
Future Time Period	Projected Cash Revenue	Materials and Parts	Machine Labor	Manufacturing Overhead	Sales and Marketing	Administrative Expenses	Projected Net Cash Inflow	Present Value Multiplier	Future Cash Inflows

Should the company invest in the new machine?

2. After careful analysis, the controller has determined that the variable rate for materials and parts can be reduced to 22 percent of revenue. Will this reduction in cash outflow change the company's decision on investing in the new machine? Explain.

3. The marketing manager has determined that the initial estimate of sales and marketing cash expenses was too high and has reduced the initial estimate by $1,000. The 10 percent annual reductions are still expected to occur. Together with the change in **2,** will this reduction affect the initial investment decision? Explain your answer.

ENDNOTES

1. Suresh S. Kalagnanam and Suzanne K. Schmidt, "Analyzing Capital Investments in New Products," *Management Accounting,* Institute of Management Accountants, January 1996, pp. 31–36. The company's name has been changed at the request of its management.

2. Steve Coburn, Hugh Grove, and Tom Cook, "How ABC Was Used in Capital Budgeting," *Management Accounting,* Institute of Management Accountants, May 1997, pp. 38–46.

3. For specific information about the computation of cost of capital, see David F. Scott, Jr., John D. Martin, J. William Petty, and Arthur J. Keown, "Cost of Capital," *Basic Financial Management,* 7th Edition (Englewood Cliffs, N.J.: Prentice-Hall, 1996), pp. 424–471.

4. Wayne Arnold, "High-Tech Hopes in Asia May Be Laid Low," *The Wall Street Journal,* November 5, 1997, p. A15.

5. Gale E. Newell, Jerry G. Kreuze, and Stephen J. Newell, "Accounting for Hazardous Waste," *Management Accounting,* Institute of Management Accountants, May 1990, pp. 58–61.

CHAPTER 11

Pricing Decisions and Target Costing

LEARNING OBJECTIVES

1. Identify the objectives and rules used to establish prices of goods and services and relate pricing issues to the management cycle.
2. Describe traditional economic pricing concepts and identify the external and internal factors on which prices are based.
3. Use cost-based pricing methods to develop prices.
4. Describe target costing and use that concept to analyze pricing decisions.
5. Use target costing to evaluate a new product opportunity.
6. Define *transfer pricing,* distinguish between cost-based and market-based transfer prices, and develop a transfer price.

DECISION POINT

ITT Automotive is one of the world's largest suppliers of auto parts, including brake systems, wiper handling systems, fluid handling systems, electric motor switches, and headlamps. Competition for all of these product lines is very keen, and there is constant pressure to reduce prices to meet competition. Antilock brake systems are a good example: The system's current selling price is around $200, but it is expected to drop to $100 in the next decade.[1]

ITT AUTOMOTIVE

Several years ago, to remain competitive, the brake systems segment of the company began to use target costing to determine product prices. The segment's customers are all the major automobile manufacturers in the world, and price is usually determined by the customer. For example, Mercedes-Benz will offer to purchase a specified number of antilock brake systems from ITT Automotive for a stated price. This price was determined by Mercedes-Benz as it developed its target cost. Using the target costing approach, ITT managers subtract their target profit from the proposed amount to arrive at their target cost for the brake system. Is letting the customer determine a product's price a good business practice?

For ITT Automotive, letting the customer determine the price is the only way to stay in business. To ensure that the company makes a profit on such a transaction, a team of engineering, accounting, and sales managers analyzes each pricing proposal to verify that the product can be designed and produced to meet the target cost. ITT uses a process called tear-down analysis to make sure it is producing a top-quality product. To perform a tear-down analysis, company employees completely disassemble automobiles that use competitors' products in order to determine the quality levels of those products and to discover better methods of producing products so as to make them competitive. Through special target costing teams and such practices as tear-down analysis, ITT Automotive maintains its market superiority.

The Pricing Decision and the Manager

OBJECTIVE 1

Identify the objectives and rules used to establish prices of goods and services and relate pricing issues to the management cycle

The process of establishing a correct price is more an art than a science. There are many mechanical approaches to price setting. However, six different approaches to pricing the same product or service may very well produce six different prices. The art of price setting depends on a manager's ability to read the marketplace and anticipate customer reaction to a product and its price. Pricing methods do not provide a manager with the ability to react to the market. Market savvy is developed through experience in dealing with customers and products in an industry. Intuition also plays a major role in price setting.

Setting appropriate prices is one of a manager's most difficult day-to-day decisions. Such decisions affect the long-term survival of any profit-oriented enterprise. The long-run objectives of a company should include a pricing policy. Such a policy is one way to differentiate one company from another—for example, Mercedes-Benz from Ford or Neiman-Marcus from Kmart. All four companies are successful, but their pricing policies are quite different. Of primary importance in setting company pricing objectives is identifying the market being served and meeting the needs of that market. Possible pricing policy objectives include:

1. Identifying and adhering to both short-run and long-run pricing strategies
2. Maximizing profits
3. Maintaining or gaining market share
4. Setting socially responsible prices
5. Maintaining a minimum rate of return on investment targets
6. Being customer driven

Pricing strategies depend on many factors and conditions. Companies that produce standard items for a competitive marketplace will have different pricing strategies from firms that make custom-designed items. In a competitive market, companies can reduce prices in order to gain market share by winning sales away from competing companies. Continuous upgrading of a product or service can help in this area. A company making custom-designed items can be more conservative in its pricing strategy.

Maximizing profits has always been considered the underlying objective of any pricing policy. Maintaining or gaining market share is closely related to pricing strategies. However, market share is important only if sales are profitable. To increase market share by reducing prices below cost can be disastrous unless such a move is accompanied by other compensating objectives and goals.

Although still a dominant factor in price setting, profit maximization has been balanced in recent years by other, more socially acceptable concerns, such as environmental factors and the influence of an aging population. Prices have a social effect, and companies are concerned about their public image. We just mentioned Mercedes-Benz, Ford, Neiman-Marcus, and Kmart. Does not each company have an individual image in your mind? And are the prices not a part of that image? Other social concerns, such as legal constraints and ethical considerations, also affect many companies' pricing policies.

Other pricing policy objectives include maintaining a minimum return on investment and being customer-driven. Organizations look on each product as an investment. An organization will not invest in making a product unless that product will provide a minimum return. To maintain a minimum return on investment, an orga-

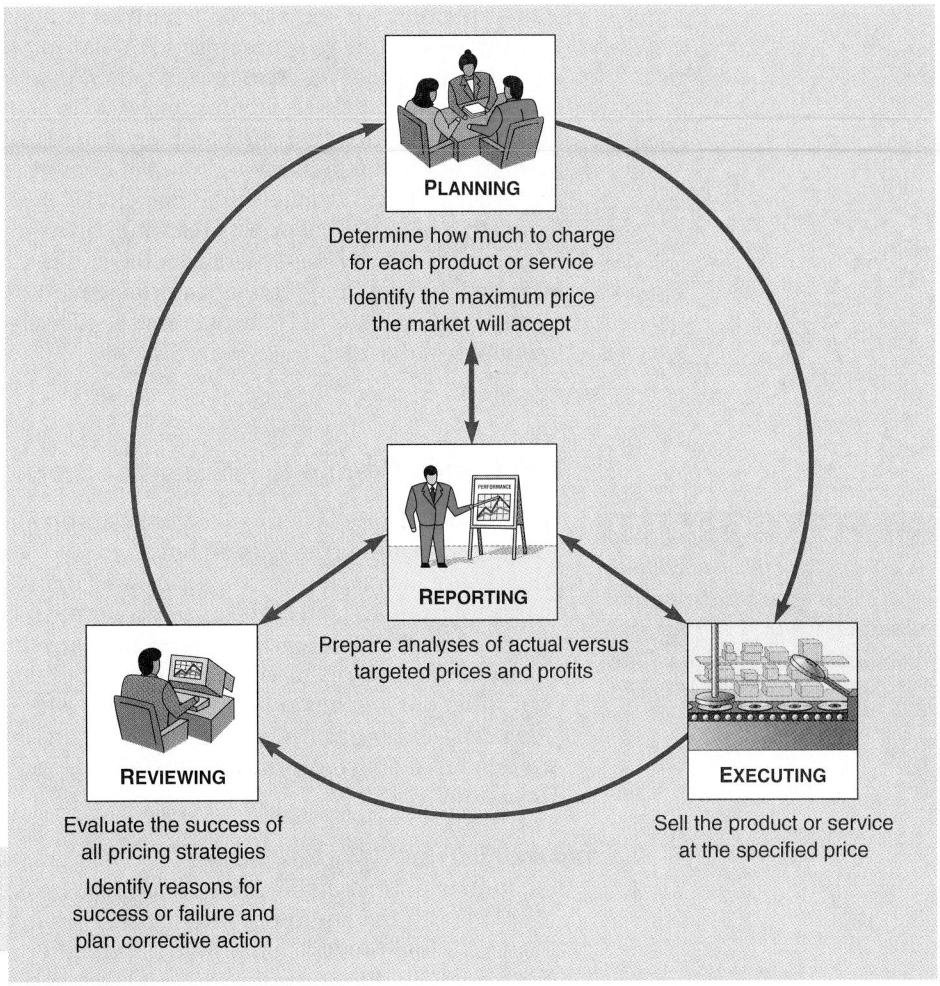

**Figure 1
Pricing and the
Management Cycle**

nization, when setting prices, adds a markup percentage to each product's costs of production. The markup percentage is closely related to the objective of profit maximization. Being customer-driven, which occurs when the needs of customers influence prices, is important for several reasons. First, sensitivity to customers is necessary to sustain sales growth. Second, customers' acceptance is crucial to success in a competitive market. Finally, prices should reflect the value that is added by the company, which is another way of saying that prices are customer-driven.

As illustrated in Figure 1, pricing issues are addressed at each stage of the management cycle. During the planning stage, managers must consider how much to charge for each product or service and identify the maximum price the market will accept. Those prices form the foundation for budgets and projections of profitability. During the executing stage, the products or services are sold at the specified prices. During the reviewing stage, managers evaluate sales to determine which pricing strategies were successful and which failed. At this stage, it is especially important to identify reasons for success or failure and plan corrective action. During the reporting stage, analyses of actual versus targeted prices and profits are prepared for use inside the organization. Those reports are used to assess past pricing strategies and plan future strategies.

For an organization to stay in business, its selling price must (1) be equal to or lower than the competition's price, (2) be acceptable to the customer, (3) recover all costs incurred in bringing the product or service to market, and (4) return a profit. If a manager deviates from any of these four selling rules, there must be a specific short-run objective that accounts for the change. Breaking these pricing rules for a long period will force a company into bankruptcy.

The methods discussed in this chapter illustrate the process of developing a specific price under defined circumstances or objectives. Some of the methods identify the minimum price that the company can charge and still make a profit. Others base prices on competition and market conditions. Still another approach is to set prices according to "whatever the market will bear," which will produce still another figure. In making a final pricing decision, managers must consider all those projected prices. The more data managers have, the more able they are to make a well-informed decision. But remember, pricing methods and approaches yield only support for decisions. The manager must still select the appropriate price and be evaluated on that decision.

Traditional Economic Pricing Concepts

OBJECTIVE 2

Describe traditional economic pricing concepts and identify the external and internal factors on which prices are based

The traditional approach to pricing is based on microeconomic theory. Pricing plays a strong role in the concepts underlying that theory as it is practiced at individual firms. Every firm is in business to maximize profits. Although each product has its own set of revenues and costs, microeconomic theory states that profit will be maximized when the difference between total revenue and total cost is the greatest. In breakeven analysis, a graphical representation is used to analyze each breakeven situation. A company will lose money when total costs exceed total revenues; it will realize a profit when total revenues are greater than total costs. But where is the point at which profits are maximized, and what is the role of pricing in this discussion?

Total Revenue and Total Cost Curves   In a graphic breakeven analysis, the representation of profits can be a bit misleading. The profit area can seem to increase significantly as more and more products are sold. Therefore, it may seem that if the company could produce an infinite number of products, it would realize the maximum profit. But this is not the case, and microeconomic theory explains why.

Figure 2A shows the economist's view of a breakeven chart. It contains two breakeven points, between which is a large space labeled *profit area*. Notice that the total revenue line is curved rather than straight. The curve is based on the theory that as a product is marketed, because of competition and other factors, price reductions will be necessary to sell additional units. Total revenue will continue to increase, but the rate of increase will diminish as more units are sold. Therefore, the total revenue line curves toward the right.

Costs react in an opposite fashion. Over the assumed relevant range, variable and fixed costs are fairly predictable, with fixed costs remaining constant and variable costs being the same per unit. The result is a straight line for total costs. Following microeconomic theory, costs per unit will increase as more units are sold, since fixed costs will change. As one moves into different relevant ranges, such fixed costs as supervision and depreciation increase, and competition causes marketing costs to rise. In addition, as the company pushes for more and more products from limited facilities, repair and maintenance costs increase. And as the push from management increases, total costs per unit rise at an accelerating rate. The result is that the total cost line in Figure 2A begins curving upward. The total revenue line and the total cost line then cross again, and beyond that point the company suffers a loss on additional sales.

Profits are maximized at the point at which the difference between total revenue and total cost is the greatest. In Figure 2A, this point is 7,000 units of sales. At that sales level, total revenue will be $210,000; total cost, $120,000; and profit, $90,000. In theory, if one additional unit is sold, profit per unit will drop, because total cost is rising at a faster rate than total revenues. As you can see, if the company sells 11,000

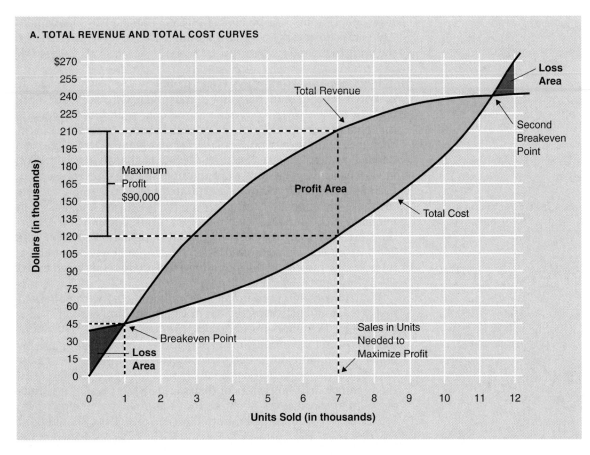

A. TOTAL REVENUE AND TOTAL COST CURVES

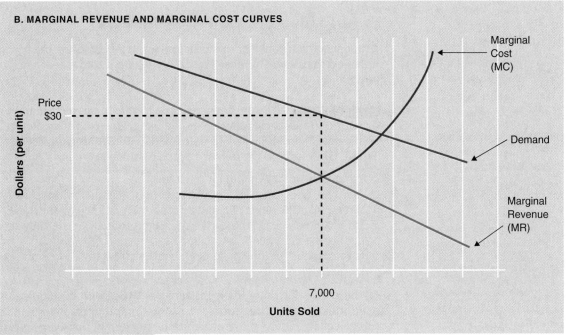

B. MARGINAL REVENUE AND MARGINAL COST CURVES

Figure 2
Microeconomic Pricing Theory

units, total profits will be almost entirely depleted by the rising costs. Therefore, 7,000 sales units is the optimal operating level, and the price charged at that level is the optimal price.

Marginal Revenue and Marginal Cost Curves   Economists use the concepts of marginal revenue and marginal cost to help determine the optimal price for a good or service. Marginal revenue is the change in total revenue caused by a one-unit change in output. Marginal cost is the change in total cost caused by a one-unit change in output. Graphic curves for marginal revenue and marginal cost are derived by measuring and plotting the rate of change in total revenue and total cost at various activity levels. If you computed marginal revenue and marginal cost for each unit sold in our example and plotted them on a graph, the lines would resemble those in Figure 2B. Notice that the marginal cost line crosses the marginal revenue line at 7,000 units. After that point, profit per unit will decrease as additional units are sold. Marginal cost will exceed marginal revenue for each unit sold over 7,000. Profit will be maximized when the marginal revenue and marginal cost lines intersect. By projecting this point onto the product's demand curve, you can locate the optimal price, which is $30 per unit.

If all information used in microeconomic theory were certain, picking the optimal price would be fairly easy. But most information used in such an analysis relies on projected amounts for unit sales, product costs, and revenues. Just computing total demand for a product or service from such data is difficult. And projections of repair and maintenance costs usually use unsupported estimates. Nevertheless, developing such an analysis usually makes the analyst aware of cost patterns and the unanticipated influences of demand. For this reason, it is important for management to consider the microeconomic approach to pricing when setting product prices. However, information from this type of analysis should not be the only data relied on.

Factors Influencing the Pricing Decision

A manager must consider many factors when determining the best price for a product or service. Some of those factors are external to the company; other factors are internal.

External Factors   Each product or service has a targeted market that determines demand. Strong consideration should be given to this market before choosing a final price. External factors to be considered in setting a price are summarized in Table 1. They include the following considerations:

1. What is the total demand for the item?
2. Are there one or several competing products in the marketplace?
3. What prices are being charged by others already selling the item?
4. Do customers want the least expensive product, or are they more interested in quality than in price?
5. Is the product unique or so new that the company is the only source in the marketplace?

All these questions should be answered by the person developing the price. If competition is keen and the quality of competing products is similar, market price will set the ceiling for any new entry into the market. If, however, a product is unique, a more flexible pricing environment exists. Customers' needs and desires are important for any new product. If quality is of primary importance, as is the case for top-of-the-line automobiles, then emphasis should be placed on using quality materials. The price will be adjusted upward accordingly.

It is important to know the marketplace, including customers' needs and the nature of the competition, before determining a final price.

Table 1. Factors to Consider When Setting a Price

External Factors
Total demand for product or service
Number of competing products or services
Quality of competing products or services
Current prices of competing products or services
Customers' preferences for quality versus price
Sole source versus heavy competition
Seasonal demand or continual demand
Life of product or service

Internal Factors
Cost of product or service
   Variable costs
   Full absorption costs
   Total costs
Price geared toward return on investment
Loss leader or main product
Quality of materials and labor
Labor-intensive or automated process
Markup percentage updated
Usage of scarce resources

Internal Factors   Several internal factors also influence the price of a good or service; they are summarized in Table 1 as well. Basic among those factors is an item's cost. What cost basis should be considered when determining price—variable costs, full absorption costs, or total costs? Should the price be based on a desired rate of return on assets? Is the product a loss leader, created to lure customers into considering additional, more expensive products? Where should one draw the line on the quality of materials and supplies? Is the product labor-intensive, or can it be produced using automated equipment? If markup percentages are used to establish prices, have they been updated to reflect current operating conditions? Are the company's scarce resources being overextended by introducing an additional product or service, and does the price reflect this use of scarce resources?

As with external factors, each of these questions should be answered before a manager establishes a price for a product or service. Underlying every pricing decision is the fact that all costs incurred must be recovered in the long run or the company will go out of business.

Cost-Based Pricing Methods

OBJECTIVE 3

Use cost-based pricing methods to develop prices

Many pricing methods are used in business. Although managers may depend on one or two traditional approaches, at some point they also deviate from those approaches and use their experience. A good starting point is to develop a price based on the cost of producing a good or service. Two pricing methods based on cost are gross margin pricing and return on assets pricing. Remember that in a competitive environment, market prices and conditions also influence price; however, if prices do not cover a company's costs, the company will eventually fail.

To illustrate the two methods of cost-based pricing, we will consider the Pearson Company, which buys parts from outside vendors and then assembles them into an electric car-wax buffer. Total costs and unit costs incurred in the previous accounting period to produce 14,750 wax buffers were as follows:

	Total Costs	Unit Costs
Variable production costs		
Direct materials and parts	$ 88,500	$ 6.00
Direct labor	66,375	4.50
Variable manufacturing overhead	44,250	3.00
Total variable production costs	$199,125	$13.50
Fixed manufacturing overhead	$154,875	$10.50
Selling, general, and administrative expenses		
Selling expenses	$ 73,750	$ 5.00
General expenses	36,875	2.50
Administrative expenses	22,125	1.50
Total selling, general, and administrative expenses	$132,750	$ 9.00
Total costs and expenses	$486,750	$33.00

No changes in unit costs are expected this period. The desired profit for the period is $110,625. The company uses assets totaling $921,875 in producing the wax buffers and expects a 12 percent return on those assets.

Gross Margin Pricing

One cost-based approach to determining a selling price is gross margin pricing. Gross margin is the difference between sales and the total production costs of those sales. Gross margin pricing is a cost-based pricing approach in which the price is computed using a markup percentage based on a product's total production costs. The markup percentage is designed to include all costs other than those used in the computation of gross margin. Therefore, the gross margin markup percentage is composed of selling, general, and administrative expenses and the desired profit. Because an accounting system often provides management with unit production cost data, both variable and fixed, this method of determining selling price can be easily applied. The formulas used are as follows:

$$\text{Markup Percentage} = \frac{\text{Desired Profit} + \text{Total Selling, General, and Administrative Expenses}}{\text{Total Production Costs}}$$

$$\text{Gross-Margin-Based Price} = \text{Total Production Costs per Unit} + (\text{Markup Percentage} \times \text{Total Production Costs per Unit})$$

For the Pearson Company, the markup percentage and selling price are computed as follows:

$$\text{Markup Percentage} = \frac{\$110,625 + \$132,750}{\$199,125 + \$154,875}$$

$$= \frac{\$243,375}{\$354,000}$$

$$= 68.75\%$$

$$\text{Gross-Margin-Based Price} = \$13.50 + \$10.50 + (68.75\% \times \$24.00)$$

$$= \$40.50$$

The numerator in the markup percentage formula is the sum of the desired profit ($110,625) and the total selling, general, and administrative expenses ($132,750). The denominator contains all production costs—variable costs of $199,125 and fixed production costs of $154,875. The gross margin markup is 68.75 percent of total production costs, or $16.50. Adding $16.50 to the total production costs per unit yields a selling price of $40.50.

Return on Assets Pricing

Return on assets pricing changes the objective of the price determination process. Earning a profit margin on total costs is replaced by earning a profit equal to a specified rate of return on assets employed in the operation. Since a business's primary objective should be to earn a minimum desired rate of return, the return on assets pricing approach has great appeal and support.

The following formula is used to calculate the return-on-assets-based price:

$$\text{Return-on-Assets-Based Price} = \text{Total Costs and Expenses per Unit} + [\text{Desired Rate of Return} \times (\text{Total Costs of Assets Employed} \div \text{Anticipated Units to Be Produced})]$$

To compute the return-on-assets-based price, the cost of the assets employed is divided by the projected number of units to be produced. The result is then multiplied by the rate of return to obtain desired earnings per unit. Desired earnings per unit plus total costs and expenses per unit yields the unit selling price.

Recall that the Pearson Company has an asset base of $921,875. It plans to produce 14,750 units and would like to earn a 12 percent return on assets. If the company uses return-on-assets-based pricing, the selling price per unit would be calculated as follows:

$$\begin{aligned} \text{Return-on-Assets-Based Price} &= \$13.50 + \$10.50 + \$9.00 \\ &\quad + [12\% \times (\$921,875 \div 14,750)] \\ &= \$40.50 \end{aligned}$$

Note that the desired profit amount used in gross margin pricing is replaced by an overall company rate of return on assets. By dividing cost of assets employed by projected units of output and multiplying the result by the minimum desired rate of return, a unit profit factor of $7.50 [12% × ($921,875 ÷ 14,750)] is obtained. Adding this profit factor to total unit costs and expenses gives the selling price of $40.50.

Summary of Cost-Based Pricing Methods

The two cost-based pricing methods are summarized in Figure 3. Although both methods yield the same selling price in our example, each could produce a different price. Companies select their methods based on their degree of trust in a cost base. The cost bases from which they can choose are (1) total product costs per unit or (2) total costs and expenses per unit. Often, total product costs per unit are readily available, which makes gross margin pricing a good way to compute selling prices. Return on assets pricing is also a good pricing method if the assets used to manufacture a product can be identified and a cost amount determined. If this is not the case, the method yields inaccurate results.

Pricing Services

Service businesses take a different approach to pricing. Although a service has no physical substance, it must still be priced and billed to the customer. Most service

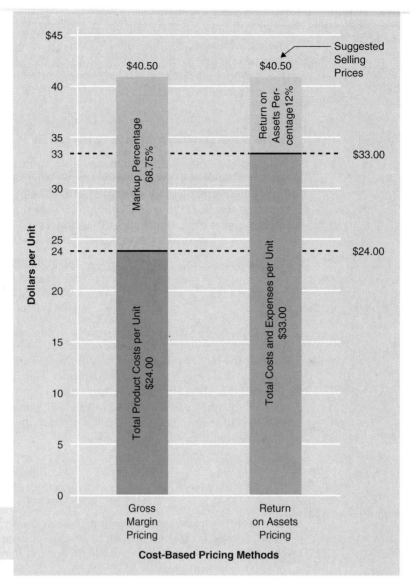

Figure 3
Cost-Based Pricing Methods:
Pearson Company

organizations use a form of time and materials pricing to arrive at the price of a service. Service companies, such as appliance repair shops, home-remodeling specialists, pool cleaners, and automobile repair businesses, arrive at prices by using two computations, one for direct labor and one for direct materials and parts. A markup percentage is added to the costs of materials and labor to cover the cost of overhead and provide a profit factor. If direct materials and parts are not a component of the service being performed, then only direct labor costs are used in developing the price. For professionals, such as attorneys, accountants, and consultants, a factor representing all overhead costs is applied to the base labor costs to establish a price for the services.

Pete's Auto Pampering just completed working on Heather Lamb's 1994 Jaguar XJS. The parts used to repair the vehicle cost $840. The company's 40 percent markup rate on parts covers parts-related overhead costs and profit. The repairs required four hours of labor by a Jaguar specialist, whose wages are $35 per hour. The company's overhead markup rate on labor is 80 percent. Pete will compute Heather's bill as follows:

BUSINESS BULLETIN: BUSINESS PRACTICE

Culp, Inc., is a textile manufacturer for the home furnishings industry. The company now uses the target costing approach in making pricing decisions. Prior to this change, the company's price-setting objective was to cover all costs and then add a profit factor. Why this shift in pricing methods? Because the aim of target costing is to reduce costs before they are incurred. According to John Brausch, the company's former cost accounting manager, "Target costing is a strategic management tool that seeks to reduce a product's cost over its lifetime. Target costing presumes interaction between cost accounting and the rest of the firm, well-executed long-range profit planning, and a commitment to continuous cost reduction. . . . It is used to understand costs better and to enhance long-term profitability."[2] Management at Culp, Inc., sees accurate product costing as necessary for accurate financial reporting but not as a tool for controlling costs. Target costing is not a product costing approach; it is a pricing method that emphasizes cost control. Cost control begins at the product design stage by placing cost limits on a product or service. Cost reduction is engineered into the product. Target costing represents a significant change in management philosophy as well. Managers at Culp, Inc., are now more interested in the long-run profitability of their products than in maximizing their quarterly net income.

Repair parts used	$840	
Overhead charges		
$840 × 40%	336	
Total parts charges		$1,176
Labor charges		
4 hours @ $35 per hour	$140	
Overhead charges		
$140 × 80%	112	
Total labor charges		252
Total billing		$1,428

Final Notes on Cost-Based Pricing Methods

Pricing is an art, not a science. Although a variety of methods may be used to mechanically compute a price, many factors external to the product or service require attention. Once the cost-based price has been determined, the decision maker must consider such factors as competitors' prices, customers' expectations, and the cost of substitute products and services. Pricing is a risky part of operating a business, and care must be taken when establishing that all-important selling price.

Pricing Based on Target Costing

OBJECTIVE 4

Describe target costing and use that concept to analyze pricing decisions

The Japanese developed target costing to enhance their ability to compete in the global marketplace. This approach to product pricing differs significantly from the cost-based methods just described. Instead of first determining the cost of a product or service and then adding a profit factor to arrive at its price, target costing reverses the procedure. Target costing is a pricing method that involves (1) identifying the price at which a product will be competitive in the marketplace, (2) defining

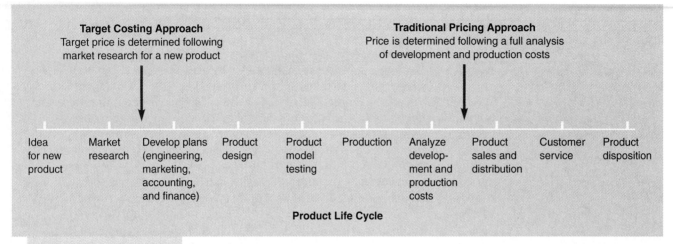

**Figure 4
Price Decision Timing
Comparison**

the desired profit to be made on the product, and (3) computing the target cost for the product by subtracting the desired profit from the competitive market price. The formula is

$$\text{Target Price} \ - \ \text{Desired Profit} \ = \ \text{Target Cost}$$

The target cost is then given to the engineers and product designers, who use it as the maximum cost to be incurred for the materials and other resources needed to design and manufacture the product. It is their responsibility to create the product at or below its target cost.

Pricing based on target costing may not seem revolutionary, but a detailed look at its underlying principles reveals its strategic superiority. Target costing gives managers the ability to control or dictate the costs of a new product beginning at the planning stage of the product's life cycle. Figure 4 compares the timing of a pricing decision using a traditional approach and using target costing. The stages of the product life cycle, from the generation of the product idea to its final disposition, are identified at the base of the figure. When traditional, cost-based pricing practices are used, prices cannot be set until production has taken place and costs have been incurred and analyzed. At that point, a profit factor is added to the product's cost and the product is ready to be offered to customers. In contrast, under target costing, the pricing decision takes place immediately after the market research for a new product. The market research not only reveals the potential demand for the product, but also identifies the maximum price a customer would be willing to pay. Once the price is determined, target costing enables the company's engineers to design the product with a fixed maximum target cost on which to base the product's features.

An example will help to differentiate cost-based pricing from pricing under the target costing concept. Ancient Company and Modern Company are about to enter the market with a new product, the Zip Gadget. Both companies have conducted market research and know that demand exists for the product. Ancient Company's strategy is to jump right into the planning phase, design the product, and get into production as soon as possible. The product's prototype model will be tested during the production phase. The company assumes that flaws will be found, so engineering change orders will be necessary and the production process will have to be redesigned to fit the design changes. Cost control will not be a part of this process. Only after the product has been produced successfully can a total unit cost be computed and a price determined.

The cost patterns associated with Ancient Company's new product are illustrated in Figure 5. Once the company makes the decision to produce a new product, new

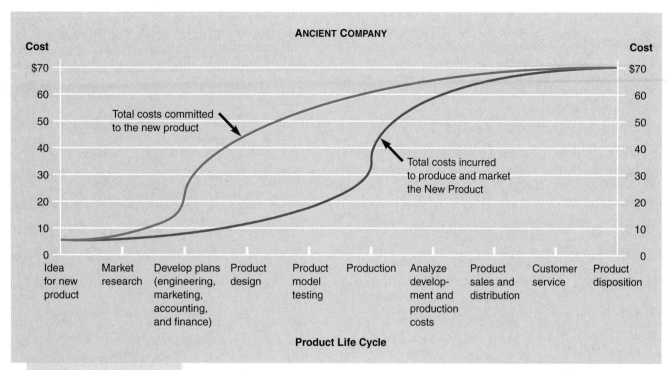

ANCIENT COMPANY

Figure 5
Traditional Cost-Based
Approach to Pricing: Committed
Versus Incurred Costs

costs are incurred at each stage in the product's life cycle. The patterns of two kinds of costs are shown. Committed costs are the costs of design, development, engineering, testing, and production that are engineered into a product or service at the design stage of development and should occur if all design specifications are followed during production. Incurred costs are the actual costs to make the product. When cost-based pricing is used, it is very difficult to control costs from the planning phase through the production phase. Management has no idea of targets or goals because the product is being made for the first time. Since customers are expected to pay whatever amount cost-based pricing identifies, the focus is on sales and not on the design and manufacture of the product. Cost control efforts will focus on incurred costs after the product has been introduced to the marketplace. In this example, Ancient Company's new product will cost around $70, so to yield 20 percent of target cost, the company will need to price the product at around $84.

Now let's take a look at Modern Company's target costing approach. Market research indicated that the product would be successful if it was priced at or below $48. Using the target costing formula, the following analysis was conducted:

$$\$48 \ - \ 20\% \text{ of Target Cost} \ = \ \text{Target Cost}$$
$$\$48 \ - \ .2X \ = \ X$$
$$1.2X \ = \ \$48$$
$$X \ = \ \underline{\underline{\$40}}$$

This analysis indicated that the product had to be produced for $40 or less if it was to be successful in the marketplace and profitable to the company. Engineers set about designing a product that would comply with this cost restriction. Production efforts were not started until the prototype model had met the requirements for both cost and quality. Figure 6 shows the patterns for the committed and incurred costs associated with Modern Company's new product. Because a $40 maximum cost was engineered into the design of the product, committed costs are set at that amount, much lower than the $70 committed costs for Ancient Company's product.

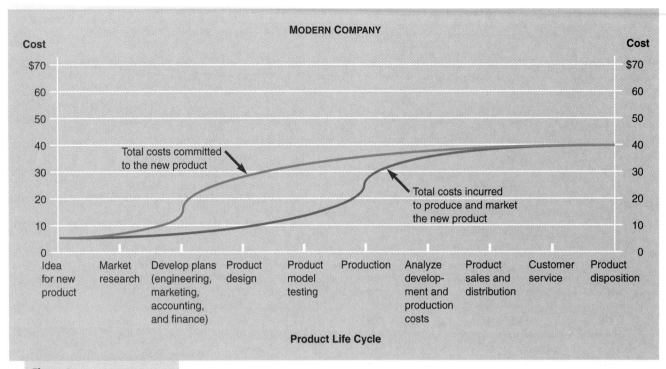

Figure 6
Target Costing Approach to Pricing: Committed Versus Incurred Costs

Two Zip Gadgets will now be marketed, one selling for $84 and the other selling for $48. If both are of equal quality, which one do you think will dominate the market-place?

Sometimes the engineers will determine that the product cannot be manufactured at or below its target cost. In that case, the product's design should be examined and attempts should be made to improve the approach to production. If the product still cannot be made at its target cost, the company must understand that its current facilities prevent it from competing in that particular market. The company should either invest in new equipment and procedures or abandon its plans to make and market the product.

One of the primary benefits of using target costing is the ability to design and build a product to a specific cost goal. The increased emphasis on product design allows the company to engineer the target cost into the product before manufacturing begins. A new product is designed only if its projected costs are equal to or lower than its target cost. Then, cost control efforts can focus on the committed cost curve, that is, on holding costs down in the planning and design stages, before the costs are actually committed and eventually incurred. Under the cost-based approach, concern about reducing costs begins only after the product has been produced. This often leads to random efforts to cut costs, which can reduce product quality and further erode the customer base.

In a highly competitive market, product quality and price determine which organizations will succeed. Customers will purchase the product that has the highest quality at the lowest price. The two variables—quality and price—go together; one cannot be sacrificed for the other. Target costing is a very useful pricing tool in such an environment because it allows an organization to critically analyze a product's potential for success before committing resources to its production. If an organization first manufactures a product and then finds out that its cost-based price is not competitive, the organization will lose the money it has already spent on the resources used to create the product. In most cases, the target costing approach can identify the potential success or failure of a product before many resources are spent on its creation.

Target costing should not be confused with the cost-based methods used for pricing decisions. In cost-based situations, if the product does not produce a desired profit, production procedures are analyzed to find areas in which costs can be cut and controlled. This approach is based on guesswork until the product hits the marketplace. A target cost is not an anticipated cost to be achieved by some midway point in a product's life cycle. The product is expected to produce a profit as soon as it is marketed. Cost-cutting improvements in a product's design and production methods can still be made, but profitability is built into the selling price from the beginning.

Even though management accountants are not directly involved in the process of designing a product to meet its target cost, they do supply cost information to the designers during a product's development. In addition, accountants are responsible for tracking the costs of a new product and advising the engineers of their success or failure to meet the target cost.

Illustrative Problem: Target Costing

OBJECTIVE 5

Use target costing to evaluate a new product opportunity

To see how target costing is implemented, consider the approach to new product decisions that is used by Burch Products Company. A salesperson has reported that a customer is seeking price quotations for two electronic components: a special-purpose battery charger (Product XA4) and a small transistorized machine computer (Product XC6). Competing for the customer's order are one German company and two Swedish companies. The current market price ranges for the two products are as follows:

Product XA4 $320–$380 per unit
Product XC6 $750–$850 per unit

The salesperson feels that if Burch could quote prices of $300 for Product XA4 and $725 for Product XC6, the company would get the order and gain a significant share of the global market for those goods. Burch's usual profit markup is 25 percent of total unit cost. The company's design engineers and accountants put together the following specifications and costs for the new products:

Activity-based cost rates

Materials handling activity	$1.30	per dollar of raw materials and purchased parts cost
Production activity	$3.50	per machine hour
Product delivery activity	$24.00	per unit of XA4
	$30.00	per unit of XC6

	Product XA4	Product XC6
Projected unit demand	26,000	18,000
Per unit data:		
Raw materials cost	$25.00	$65.00
Purchased parts cost	$15.00	$45.00
Manufacturing labor		
Hours	2.6	4.8
Hourly labor rate	$12.00	$15.00
Assembly labor		
Hours	3.4	8.2
Hourly labor rate	$14.00	$16.00
Machine hours	12.8	28.4

BUSINESS BULLETIN: INTERNATIONAL PRACTICE

In Japanese, *kaizen* means "continuous improvement." When this concept is applied to target costing, the result is a practice known as kaizen costing. As explained in the chapter, target costing involves first identifying the price at which a product will be competitive, then subtracting a profit factor to arrive at the item's target cost. That amount is used by design engineers to develop a product that satisfies the customers' requirements and yet can be produced at or below the target cost. Adding kaizen to this approach means that even after a product that meets the target cost has been designed, engineers, production personnel, marketing people, and the accounting staff must work continuously to find better ways to manufacture the product, reduce its cost, and improve its quality. When kaizen costing is used, the target cost is not the end result of the pricing strategy; it is the starting point that will be used to measure continuous improvement.

REQUIRED

1. Compute the target cost for each product.
2. Compute the projected total unit cost of production and delivery.
3. Use the target costing approach to determine if the company should produce the products.

SOLUTION

1. Target cost for each product:

$$\text{Product XA4} = \$300.00 \div 1.25 = \$240.00^*$$
$$\text{Product XC6} = \$725.00 \div 1.25 = \$580.00$$

*Target Price $-$ Desired Profit $=$ Target Cost
$$\$300.00 - .25X = X$$
$$\$300.00 = 1.25X$$
$$X = \frac{\$300.00}{1.25} = \underline{\$240.00}$$

2. Projected total unit cost of production and delivery:

	Product XA4	Product XC6
Raw materials cost	$ 25.00	$ 65.00
Purchased parts cost	15.00	45.00
Total cost of raw materials and parts	$ 40.00	$110.00
Manufacturing labor		
XA4 (2.6 hours × $12.00)	31.20	
XC6 (4.8 hours × $15.00)		72.00
Assembly labor		
XA4 (3.4 hours × $14.00)	47.60	
XC6 (8.2 hours × $16.00)		131.20
Activity-based costs		
Materials handling activity		
XA4 ($40.00 × $1.30)	52.00	
XC6 ($110.00 × $1.30)		143.00
Production activity		
XA4 (12.8 machine hours × $3.50)	44.80	
XC6 (28.4 machine hours × $3.50)		99.40
Product delivery activity		
XA4	24.00	
XC6		30.00
Projected total unit cost	$239.60	$585.60

3. Production decision:

	Product XA4	Product XC6
Target unit cost	$240.00	$580.00
Less projected unit cost	239.60	585.60
Difference	$ 0.40	($ 5.60)

Product XA4 can be produced below its target cost, so it should be produced. As currently designed, Product XC6 cannot be produced at or below its target cost; either it needs to be redesigned or the company should discontinue plans to produce it.

Transfer Pricing Decisions

OBJECTIVE 6

Define transfer pricing, distinguish between cost-based and market-based transfer prices, and develop a transfer price

A decentralized organization is an organization that has several operating segments; operating control of each segment's activities is the responsibility of the segment's manager. Cost/expense centers and profit centers are important to a decentralized organization because they alleviate some of the difficulty of controlling diverse operations. Responsibility for a center's functions is placed with its managers, and their performance is measured by comparing actual results with budgeted or projected results.

Profit measurement and return on investment are important gauges of performance in decentralized divisions. But in cost/expense centers, because only costs are involved, profitability is difficult to measure. The problem becomes more complicated when divisions within a company exchange goods or services and assume the role of customer or supplier to another division. In such cases, transfer prices are used. A transfer price is the price at which goods and services are charged and exchanged between a company's divisions or segments. Such prices allow intracompany transactions to be measured and accounted for and affect the revenues and costs of the divisions involved. Because a transfer price contains an estimated amount of profit, a cost/expense center manager's ability to meet a targeted profit can be measured. Although transfer prices are often called artificial or created prices, they and their related policies are closely connected with performance evaluation. Transfer pricing is somewhat controversial. Some people believe in the benefits of using transfer prices. Others believe transfer prices should never be used because they are not real prices.

Methods of Transfer Pricing

There are two primary approaches to developing a transfer price.

1. The price may be based on the cost of the item until its transfer to the next department or process.
2. A market value may be used if the item has an existing external market when transferred.

When no external markets are involved, division managers in a decentralized company may agree on a *cost-plus transfer price* or a *negotiated transfer price*. A cost-plus transfer price is the sum of costs incurred by the producing division plus an agreed-on profit percentage. The weakness of the cost-plus pricing method is that cost recovery is guaranteed to the selling division. Guaranteed cost recovery fails to detect inefficient operating conditions and excessive cost incurrence, and may even inappropriately reward inefficient divisions that incur excessive costs. This reduces overall company profitability and reduces shareholder value.

BUSINESS BULLETIN: ETHICS IN PRACTICE

Transfer prices are artificial prices created by managers to allow the internal segments of a company that supply goods and services to other company segments to be evaluated on the basis of profitability. However, there is an entirely different side of transfer pricing that is followed closely by local, national, and international government bodies. Governments raise their revenue by levying various taxes. Many types of corporate taxes are based on income. Let's assume that Big Bucks Company has divisions in both Taxing Jurisdiction A and Taxing Jurisdiction B. Taxing Jurisdiction A's corporate tax rate is 22 percent of income, whereas Taxing Jurisdiction B's corporate tax rate is 36 percent. Using low transfer prices, the corporation's Taxing Jurisdiction B division transfers (sells) goods to the division in Taxing Jurisdiction A, which in turn sells the goods to external customers. Most of the profit is recorded in Taxing Jurisdiction A, thereby minimizing Big Bucks Company's taxes. Since Taxing Jurisdiction B was cheated out of tax revenue, legislative action would be needed in this scenario. Corporate income should be computed based on the productive activities within a taxing jurisdiction, not based on an accounting practice that was designed for a completely different purpose.

A negotiated transfer price, on the other hand, is arrived at through bargaining between the managers of the buying and selling divisions or segments. Such a transfer price may be based on an agreement to use a standard cost plus a profit percentage. This approach emphasizes cost control through the use of standard costs while still allowing the selling division to return a profit even though it is a cost center. A negotiated transfer price may also be based on a market price that was reduced in the bargaining process.

A market transfer price is based on the price that could be charged if a segment could buy from or sell to an external party. Such prices are seldom used without negotiations between managers. Using market prices may cause the selling division to ignore negotiation attempts from the buying division manager and sell directly to outside customers. If this causes an internal shortage of materials and forces the buying division to purchase materials from the outside, overall company profits may be lowered even when the selling division makes a profit. Such use of market prices works against a company's overall operating objectives. Therefore, when market prices are used to develop transfer prices, they are normally used only as a basis for negotiation.

Developing a Transfer Price

To illustrate the application of the two approaches to the development of transfer prices, consider Kowalski Pulp Company, a company that makes cardboard boxes. This company has three divisions: the Pulp Division, the Cardboard Division, and the Box Division. Exhibit 1 shows the development of a transfer price for the Pulp Division, whose output is transferred to the Cardboard Division. The Pulp Division manager's computations supporting a cost-plus transfer price of $14.19 are shown. This one-year budget is based on the expectation that the Cardboard Division will require 480,000 pounds of pulp. Unit costs are stated in the right column. Notice that allocated corporate overhead is not included in the computation of the transfer price. Only costs related to the Pulp Division are included. The profit markup of 10 percent adds $1.29, producing the final transfer price of $14.19.

At this point, management could dictate that the $14.19 price be used. On the other hand, the manager of the Cardboard Division could bring the outside pur-

Exhibit 1. Transfer Price Computation

Kowalski Pulp Company
Pulp Division—Transfer Price Computation

Cost Categories	Budgeted Costs	Cost per Unit
Direct materials		
Wood	$1,584,000	$ 3.30
Scrap wood	336,000	0.70
Direct labor		
Shaving/cleaning	768,000	1.60
Pulverizing	1,152,000	2.40
Blending	912,000	1.90
Manufacturing overhead		
Variable	936,000	1.95
Fixed	504,000	1.05
Subtotals	$6,192,000	$12.90
Costs allocated from corporate office	144,000	
Target profit, 10% of division's costs	619,200	1.29
Total costs and profit	$6,955,200	
Cost-plus transfer price		$14.19

chase price of $14.10 per pound to the attention of management. Usually, such situations end up being negotiated to determine the final transfer price. Each side has a position and strong arguments to support a price. And each manager's performance will be compromised by adopting the other's price.

In this example, both managers brought their concerns to the attention of top management. A unique settlement was reached. Since internal profits must be erased before financial statements are prepared, management allowed the Pulp Division to use the $14.19 price and the Cardboard Division the $14.10 price for purposes of performance evaluation. Obviously, the company did not want the Cardboard Division to buy pulp from another company. At the same time, the Pulp Division had the right to a 10 percent profit.

Such approaches are often used to maintain harmony within an organization. In this case, it allowed top management to measure the managers' performance while avoiding behavioral issues. After the period was over, all fictitious profits were canceled by using adjusting entries before preparing end-of-year financial statements. The final product, in this case the boxes, had a profit factor that took into account all operations of the business.

Chapter Review

REVIEW OF LEARNING OBJECTIVES

1. **Identify the objectives and rules used to establish prices of goods and services and relate pricing issues to the management cycle.** The long-run objectives of a company should include statements on pricing policy. Possible pricing policy objectives include (a) identifying and adhering to both short-run and long-run pricing strategies, (b) maximizing profits, (c) maintaining or gaining market share, (d) setting socially responsible prices, (e) maintaining a minimum rate of return on investment targets, and (f) being customer-driven. For a company to stay in business, a product's or service's selling price must (a) be equal to or lower than the competition's price, (b) be acceptable to the customer, (c) recover all costs incurred in bringing the product or service to a marketable condition, and (d) return a profit. If a manager deviates from these four selling rules, there must be a specific short-run objective that accounts for the change. Breaking these pricing rules for a long period will force a company into bankruptcy.

   Pricing issues are addressed at each stage of the management cycle. During the planning stage, managers must consider how much to charge for each product or service and identify the maximum price the market will accept. During the executing stage, the products or services are sold at the specified prices. During the reviewing stage, managers evaluate sales to determine which pricing strategies were successful and which failed. During the reporting stage, analyses of actual versus targeted prices and profits are prepared for use inside the organization.

2. **Describe traditional economic pricing concepts and identify the external and internal factors on which prices are based.** The traditional approach to pricing is based on microeconomic theory. Microeconomic theory states that profits will be maximized when the difference between total revenue and total cost is greatest. Total revenue then increases more slowly, since as a product is marketed, price reductions are necessary to sell more units. Total cost increases when large quantities are produced because fixed costs change. To locate the point of maximum profit, marginal revenue and marginal cost must be computed and plotted. Profit is maximized at the point at which the marginal revenue and marginal cost curves intersect.

   Many factors influence the determination of a selling price. Factors external to a company include (a) total demand for the product or service, (b) number of competing products or services, (c) competitors' quality and price, (d) customer preference, (e) seasonal demand, and (f) life of the product. Internal factors are (a) costs of producing the product or service, (b) purpose and quality of the product, (c) type of process used—labor-intensive versus automated, (d) markup percentage updated, and (e) amount of scarce resources used.

3. **Use cost-based pricing methods to develop prices.** Cost-based pricing methods include gross margin pricing and return on assets pricing. A pricing method often used by service businesses is time and materials pricing. Although managers may depend on one or two traditional approaches to pricing, they often also factor in their own experience.

4. **Describe target costing and use that concept to analyze pricing decisions.** The concept of target costing was developed by the Japanese to enhance their ability to compete in the global marketplace. Instead of first determining the cost of a product or service and then adding a profit factor to arrive at its price, target costing reverses the procedure. Target costing involves (1) identifying the price at which a product will be competitive in the marketplace, (2) defining the desired profit to be made on the product, and (3) computing the target cost for the product by subtracting the desired profit from the competitive market price. Target costing gives managers the ability to control or dictate the costs of a new product beginning at the planning stage in the product's life cycle, whereas under a traditional pricing system, managers cannot control costs until after the product has been manufactured.

5. Use target costing to evaluate a new product opportunity. To identify a new product's target cost, the following formula is applied:

$$\text{Target Price} - \text{Desired Profit} = \text{Target Cost}$$

The target cost is then given to the engineers and product designers, who use it as a maximum cost to be incurred for materials and other resources needed to design and manufacture the product. It is their responsibility to create the product at or below its target cost. Sometimes the cost requirements cannot be met. In such a case, the organization should try to adjust the product's design and the approach to production. If those attempts fail, the organization should either invest in new equipment and procedures or abandon its plans to market the product.

6. Define *transfer pricing* and distinguish between cost-based and market-based transfer prices. A transfer price is the price at which goods and services are charged and exchanged between a company's divisions or segments. There are two primary approaches to developing transfer prices: (a) The price may be based on the cost of the item up to the point at which it is transferred to the next department or process, or (b) a market value may be used if the item has an existing external market. A cost-plus transfer price is the sum of costs incurred by the producing division plus an agreed-on profit percentage. A market-based transfer price is based on external market prices. In most cases, a negotiated transfer price is used, that is, a price that was reached through bargaining between the managers of the selling and buying divisions.

REVIEW OF CONCEPTS AND TERMINOLOGY

The following concepts and terms were introduced in this chapter:

LO 4 **Committed costs:** The costs of design, development, engineering, testing, and production that are engineered into a product or service at the design stage of development and should occur if all design specifications are followed during production.

LO 6 **Cost-plus transfer price:** A transfer price computed as the sum of the costs incurred by the producing division plus an agreed-on profit percentage.

LO 6 **Decentralized organization:** An organization that has several operating segments; operating control of each segment's activities is the responsibility of the segment's manager.

LO 3 **Gross margin pricing:** A cost-based pricing approach in which the price is computed using a markup percentage based on a product's total production costs.

LO 2 **Marginal cost:** The change in total cost caused by a one-unit change in output.

LO 2 **Marginal revenue:** The change in total revenue caused by a one-unit change in output.

LO 6 **Market transfer price:** A transfer price based on the price that could be charged if a segment could buy from or sell to an external party.

LO 6 **Negotiated transfer price:** A transfer price that is arrived at through bargaining between the managers of the buying and selling divisions or segments.

LO 3 **Return on assets pricing:** A pricing method in which the objective of price determination is to earn a profit equal to a specific rate of return on assets employed in the operation.

LO 4 **Target costing:** A pricing method that (1) identifies the price at which a product will be competitive in the marketplace, (2) defines the desired profit to be made on the product, and (3) computes the target cost for the product by subtracting the desired profit from the competitive market price.

LO 3 **Time and materials pricing:** An approach to pricing used by service businesses in which the total billing is composed of actual direct materials and parts cost and actual direct labor cost plus a percentage markup of each to cover overhead costs and a profit factor.

LO 6 **Transfer price:** The price at which goods and services are charged and exchanged between a company's divisions or segments.

REVIEW PROBLEM
Gross Margin Pricing

LO 3   The Timeless Toy Company makes a complete line of toy vehicles, including three types of trucks: a pickup, a dumpster, and a flatbed. The toy trucks are produced on an assembly line, beginning with the Stamping Department and continuing through the Welding, Painting, and Detailing departments. The projected costs of each toy truck and percentages for assigning fixed and common costs are as follows:

Cost Categories	Total Projected Costs	Toy Pickup Truck	Toy Dumpster Truck	Toy Flatbed Truck
Direct materials				
Metal	$137,000	$62,500	$29,000	$45,500
Axles	5,250	2,500	1,000	1,750
Wheels	9,250	3,750	2,000	3,500
Paint	70,500	30,000	16,000	24,500
Direct labor				
Stamping	53,750	22,500	12,000	19,250
Welding	94,000	42,500	20,000	31,500
Painting	107,500	45,000	24,000	38,500
Detailing	44,250	17,500	11,000	15,750
Indirect labor	173,000	77,500	36,000	59,500
Operating supplies	30,000	12,500	7,000	10,500
Variable production costs	90,500	40,000	19,000	31,500
Fixed production costs	120,000	45%	25%	30%
Distribution expenses	105,000	40%	20%	40%
Variable marketing expenses	$123,000	$55,000	$26,000	$42,000
Fixed marketing expenses	85,400	40%	25%	35%
General and administrative expenses	47,600	40%	25%	35%

Timeless Toy's policy is to earn a minimum of 30 percent over total cost on each type of toy produced. Expected sales for 20xx are: pickup, 50,000 units; dumpster, 20,000 units; and flatbed, 35,000 units. Assume no change in inventory levels, and round all answers to two decimal places.

REQUIRED

1. Using the gross margin pricing method, compute the selling price for each kind of toy truck.
2. The competition is selling a similar pickup truck for around $14.00. Should this influence Timeless Toy's pricing decision? Give reasons for your answer.

ANSWER TO REVIEW PROBLEM

Before the selling prices are computed, the cost analysis must be completed and restructured to supply the information needed for the pricing computations.

Cost Categories	Total Projected Costs	Toy Pickup Truck	Toy Dumpster Truck	Toy Flatbed Truck
Total direct materials	$ 222,000	$ 98,750	$ 48,000	$ 75,250
Total direct labor	299,500	127,500	67,000	105,000
Indirect labor	173,000	77,500	36,000	59,500
Operating supplies	30,000	12,500	7,000	10,500
Variable production costs	90,500	40,000	19,000	31,500
Fixed production costs	120,000	54,000	30,000	36,000
Total production costs	$ 935,000	$410,250	$207,000	$317,750
Distribution expenses	$ 105,000	$ 42,000	$ 21,000	$ 42,000
Variable marketing expenses	123,000	55,000	26,000	42,000
Fixed marketing expenses	85,400	34,160	21,350	29,890
General and administrative expenses	47,600	19,040	11,900	16,660
Total selling, general, and administrative expenses	$ 361,000	$150,200	$ 80,250	$130,550
Total costs	$1,296,000	$560,450	$287,250	$448,300
Desired profit	$ 388,800	$168,135	$ 86,175	$134,490

1. Pricing using the gross margin approach.

   Markup percentage formula:

   $$\text{Markup Percentage} = \frac{\text{Desired Profit} + \text{Total Selling, General, and Administrative Expenses}}{\text{Total Production Costs}}$$

   Gross margin pricing formula:

   Gross-Margin-Based Price = Total Production Costs per Unit + (Markup Percentage × Total Production Costs per Unit)

   Pickup truck:

   $$\text{Markup Percentage} = \frac{\$168,135 + \$150,200}{\$410,250} = 77.60\%$$

   Gross-Margin-Based Price = ($410,250 ÷ 50,000) + [($410,250 ÷ 50,000) × 77.6%] = $14.57

   Dumpster truck:

   $$\text{Markup Percentage} = \frac{\$86,175 + \$80,250}{\$207,000} = 80.40\%$$

   Gross-Margin-Based Price = ($207,000 ÷ 20,000) + [($207,000 ÷ 20,000) × 80.4%] = $18.67

   Flatbed truck:

   $$\text{Markup Percentage} = \frac{\$134,490 + \$130,550}{\$317,750} = 83.41\%$$

   Gross-Margin-Based Price = ($317,750 ÷ 35,000) + [($317,750 ÷ 35,000) × 83.41%] = $16.65

2. Competition's influence on price.

If the competition's toy pickup truck is similar in quality and design, Timeless Toy's management should consider reducing the price of Timeless's truck to the $14.00 range. At $14.58, Timeless has a 30 percent profit built into its price. The pickup truck's breakeven is at $11.22 ($14.58 ÷ 1.3). Therefore, the company could reduce its price below the competitor's price and still make a significant profit.

Chapter Assignments

BUILDING YOUR KNOWLEDGE FOUNDATION

Questions

1. Identify six possible pricing policy objectives. Discuss each one briefly.
2. If a manager's strategy is to price products so that total market share will increase, what considerations should go into selecting a price?
3. Do prices have a social effect? In what way?
4. How are pricing issues addressed at each stage of the management cycle?
5. Identify some factors decision makers must consider when setting the price of a product or service.
6. Discuss the concept of basing pricing decisions on "whatever the market will bear."
7. In traditional economic theory, what role does total revenue play in maximizing profit?
8. Why is profit maximized at the point where marginal revenue equals marginal cost?
9. List four external factors to consider when establishing the price of a good or service.
10. Identify four internal factors that affect the price of a good or service.
11. What is the gross margin pricing method? How is the markup percentage calculated under this method? How does the return on assets pricing method differ from the gross margin pricing approach?
12. In the pricing of services, what is meant by time and materials pricing?
13. Describe pricing based on target costing and state the formula used to compute a target cost.
14. Why is the target costing approach to pricing more useful in a competitive marketplace than the cost-based pricing methods are?
15. Explain how target costing affects the committed costs of a product.
16. What is a transfer price? Why are transfer prices usually associated with decentralized companies?
17. Why is a transfer price often referred to as an artificial or created price?
18. Describe the cost-plus approach to setting transfer prices.
19. How are market prices used to develop a transfer price? Under what circumstances are market prices relevant to the setting of a transfer price?
20. "Most transfer prices are negotiated prices." Explain this statement.

Short Exercises

SE 1.

LO 1 *Rules for Establishing Prices*

John Knot is planning to open a pizza restaurant next month in Athens, Alabama. He plans to sell his large pizzas for a base price of $18 plus $2 for each topping selected. When asked how he arrived at the base price, he said that his cousin developed that price for his pizza restaurant in New York City. What pricing rules has John not followed?

SE 2.

LO 2 *Traditional Economic Pricing Concept*

You are to decide the total demand for a particular product. Assume that the product you are evaluating has the total cost and total revenue curves pictured in Figure 2A in this chapter. Also assume that the difference between total revenue and total cost is the same at the 4,000 and 9,000 unit levels. If you had to choose between those two levels of activity as goals for total sales over the life of the product, which would you prefer? Why?

LO 2 *External Factors That Influence Prices*

SE 3. Your client is about to introduce a very high-quality product that will remove Spanish moss from trees in the southern United States. The Marketing Department has established a price of $37 per gallon, and the company controller has projected total production, selling, and distribution costs at $26 per gallon. What other factors should your client consider before introducing the product into the marketplace?

LO 3 *Cost-Based Price Setting*

SE 4. The Windgate Company has collected the following data for one of its product lines: total production costs, $300,000; total selling, general, and administrative expenses, $112,600; desired profit, $67,400; and production costs per unit, $50. Using the gross margin pricing method, compute a suggested selling price for this product that would yield the desired profit.

LO 3 *Pricing a Service*

SE 5. Tony Williams runs a home repair business. Recently he gathered the following cost information about the repair of a client's pool deck: replacement wood, $650; deck screws and supplies, $112; and labor, 12 hours at $14 per hour. Tony applies a 40 percent overhead rate to all direct costs of a job. Compute the total billing price for this job.

LO 4 *Committed Costs and Target Costing*

SE 6. Nancy Manzo is a design engineer for Dot Enterprises. In a discussion focusing on a proposed new product line, Nancy stated that the product's projected target cost was $6.50 below the committed costs identified by design estimates. Given this information, should the company proceed with the new product line? Explain your answer and include a definition of committed cost in your analysis.

LO 5 *Pricing Using Target Costing*

SE 7. Kang Furniture is considering a new product and must make a go-or-no-go decision before tomorrow's planning team meeting. Market research shows that the unit selling price agreeable to potential customers is $1,600, and the company's desired profit is 22 percent of target cost. The design engineer's preliminary estimate of the product's design, production, and distribution costs is $1,380 per unit. Using the target costing approach, determine whether the company should market the new product.

LO 6 *Decision to Use Transfer Prices*

SE 8. The production process at National Castings includes eight work cells, each of which is currently treated as a cost center with a specific set of operations to perform on each casting produced. Following the fourth work cell's operations, the rough castings have an external market. The fourth work cell must also supply the fifth work cell with its direct materials. Management wants to develop a new approach to measuring work cell performance. Is National a candidate for using transfer prices? Explain your answer.

LO 6 *Cost-Based Versus Market-Based Transfer Prices*

SE 9. Refer to the information in **SE 8**. Should National Castings use cost-based or market-based transfer prices?

LO 6 *Developing a Negotiated Transfer Price*

SE 10. The Molding Work Cell at Ridge Plastic Products has been treated as a cost center since the company was founded in 1968. Recently, management decided to change the performance evaluation approach and treat its work cells as profit centers. Each cell is expected to earn a 20 percent profit on its total production costs. One of Ridge's products is a plastic base for a tool storage chest. The Molding Work Cell supplies this base to the Cabinet Work Cell, and it also sells the base to another company. Molding's total production cost for the base is $27.40. It sells the base to the other company for $38.00. What should the transfer price for the plastic base be?

Exercises

LO 1 *Pricing Policy Objectives*

E 1. Ashton, Ltd., is an international clothing company that retails medium-priced goods. Retail outlets are located throughout the United States, France, Germany, and Great Britain. Management wants to maintain the company's image of providing the highest possible quality at the lowest possible prices. Selling prices are developed to draw customers away from competitors' stores. First-of-the-month sales are regularly held at all stores, and customers are accustomed to this practice. Company buyers are carefully trained to seek out quality goods at inexpensive prices. Sales are targeted to increase a minimum of 5 percent per year. All sales should yield a 15 percent return on assets. Sales personnel are expected to wear Ashton clothing while working, and all personnel can purchase clothing at 10 percent above cost. All stores are required to be clean and well organized. Competitors' prices are checked daily.

Identify the pricing policy objectives of Ashton, Ltd.

E 2.
LO 2 *Traditional Economic Pricing Theory*

Vail & Lauretta, a product design firm, has just completed a contract to develop a portable telephone. The telephone needs to be recharged only once a week and can be used up to one mile from the receiver. Initial fixed costs for this product are $4,000. The designers estimate that the product will break even at the $5,000/100-unit mark. Total revenues will again equal total costs at the $25,000/900-unit point. Marginal cost is expected to equal marginal revenue when 550 units are sold.

1. Sketch total revenue and total cost curves for this product. Mark the vertical axis at each $5,000 increment and the horizontal axis at each 100-unit increment.
2. Based on your total revenue and total cost curves in **1,** at what unit selling price will profits be maximized?

E 3.
LO 2 *External and Internal Pricing Factors*

Baird's Tire Outlet features more than a dozen brands of tires in many sizes. Two of the brands are Gripper and Roadster, both imports. The tire size 205/70-VR15 is available in both brands. The following information about the two brands was obtained:

	Gripper	**Roadster**
Selling price		
Single tire, installed	$125	$110
Set of four tires, installed	460	400
Cost per tire	90	60

As shown, selling prices include installation costs. Each Gripper and Roadster tire costs $20 to mount and balance.

1. Compute each brand's net unit selling price after installation *(excluding installation)* for both a single tire and a set of four.
2. Was cost the main consideration in setting those prices?
3. What other factors could have influenced those prices?

E 4.
LO 3 *Price Determination*

Theresa Industries has just patented a new product called "Luster," an automobile wax for lasting protection against the elements. Annual information developed by the company's controller for use in price determination meetings is as follows:

Variable production costs	$1,110,000
Fixed manufacturing overhead	540,000
Selling expenses	225,000
General and administrative expenses	350,000
Desired profit	250,000

Annual demand for the product is expected to be 250,000 cans.

1. Compute the projected unit cost for one can of Luster.
2. Using the gross margin pricing method, compute the markup percentage and selling price for one can.

E 5.
LO 3 *Pricing a Service*

The state of Montana has just passed a law making it mandatory to have every head of cattle inspected at least once a year for a variety of communicable diseases. Granger Enterprises is considering entering this inspection business. After extensive studies, Mr. Granger has developed the following annual projections.

Direct service labor	$525,000
Variable service overhead costs	250,000
Fixed service overhead costs	225,000
Selling expenses	142,500
General and administrative expenses	157,500
Minimum desired profit	120,000
Cost of assets employed	750,000

Mr. Granger believes his company would inspect 250,000 head of cattle per year. On average, the company now earns a 16 percent return on assets.

1. Compute the projected cost of inspecting each head of cattle.
2. Determine the price to charge for inspecting each head of cattle. Use the gross margin pricing method.
3. Using the return on assets method, compute the unit price to charge for this inspection service.

E 6.

LO 3 *Time and Materials Pricing*

Randall's Home Remodeling Service specializes in refurbishing older homes. Last week Randall was asked to bid on a remodeling job for the town's mayor. His list of materials and labor needed to complete the job is as follows:

Materials		Labor	
Lumber	$ 6,500	Carpenter	$2,000
Nails/bolts	160	Floor specialist	1,300
Paint	1,420	Painter	1,500
Glass	2,890	Supervisor	1,420
Doors	730	Helpers	1,680
Hardware	600	Total	$7,900
Supplies	400		
Total	$12,700		

The company uses an overhead markup percentage for both materials (60 percent) and labor (40 percent). Those markups cover all operating costs of the business. In addition, Randall expects to make at least a 25 percent profit on all jobs. Compute the price that Randall should quote for the mayor's job.

E 7.

LO 4 *Target Costing*
LO 5 *and Pricing*

Trevino Company has determined that its new fireplace heat shield would gain widespread customer acceptance if the company could price it at or under $80. Anticipated labor hours and costs for each unit of this new product are:

Direct materials cost	$15
Direct labor cost	
Manufacturing labor	
Hours	1.2
Hourly labor rate	$12
Assembly labor	
Hours	1.5
Hourly labor rate	$10
Machine hours	2

The company currently uses the following three activity-based cost rates:

Materials handling activity	$1.30 per dollar of direct materials
Production activity	$3.00 per machine hour
Product delivery activity	$5.50 per unit

The company's minimum desired profit is 25 percent over total production and delivery cost. Compute the target cost for this product and determine if the product should be marketed by the company.

E 8.

LO 5 *Target Costing*

Management at Milan Machine Tool Co. is considering the development of a new automated drill press called the AutoDrill. After conferring with the design engineers, the controller's staff assembled the following data about this product:

Target selling price	$7,500	per unit
Desired profit percentage	25%	of total unit cost
Projected unit demand	4,500	units
Activity-based cost rates		
Materials handling activity	5%	of raw materials and purchased parts cost
Engineering activity	$300	per unit for AutoDrill
Production and assembly activity	$50	per machine hour
Delivery activity	$570	per unit for AutoDrill
Marketing activity	$400	per unit for AutoDrill

Per unit data

Raw materials cost	$1,620
Purchased parts cost	$840
Manufacturing labor	
Hours	6 hours
Hourly labor rate	$14
Assembly labor	
Hours	10 hours
Hourly labor rate	$15
Machine hours	30 hours

1. Compute the product's target cost.
2. Compute the product's projected unit cost based on the design engineers' estimates.
3. Should management produce and market the AutoDrill? Defend your answer.

LO 6 *Transfer Price Comparison*

E 9. June Rector is developing a transfer price for the housing section of an automatic pool-cleaning device. The housing for the device is made in Department A. It is then passed on to Department D, where final assembly occurs. Unit costs for the housing are as follows:

Cost Categories	Unit Costs
Direct materials	$5.20
Direct labor	2.30
Variable manufacturing overhead	1.30
Fixed manufacturing overhead	2.60
Profit markup, 20% of cost	?

An outside vendor can supply the housing for $13.60 per unit.

1. Develop a cost-plus transfer price for the housing.
2. What should the transfer price be? Support your answer.

Problems

LO 3 *Pricing Decision*

P 1. Mogul & Company specializes in the assembly of home appliances. One division, Kevin Operations, focuses most of its efforts on assembling a standard bread toaster. Projected costs of this product for 20xx are as follows:

Cost Description	Budgeted Costs	unit costs
Toaster casings	$ 900,000	$ 1.50
Electrical components	2,220,000	3.70
Direct labor	3,600,000	6.00
Variable indirect assembly costs	780,000	1.30
Fixed indirect assembly costs	1,740,000	2.90 $15.40
Selling expenses	1,560,000	$ 2.60
General operating expenses	840,000	1.40
Administrative expenses	780,000	1.30 $5.30
	$ 12,420,000	$ 20.70

Annual demand is estimated at 600,000 toasters per year. The above budgeted amounts were geared to this demand. The company wants to make a $1,260,000 profit.

Competitors have just published their wholesale prices for the coming year. They range from $21.60 to $22.40 per toaster. The Mogul toaster is known for its high quality, and it competes with products at the top end of the price range. Even with its reputation, however, every $.20 increase above the top competitor's price causes a drop in demand of 60,000 units below the original estimate. Assume that all price changes are in $.20 increments.

REQUIRED

1. Use the gross margin pricing method to compute the anticipated selling price.
2. Based on competitors' prices, what should the Mogul toaster sell for in 20xx (assume a constant unit cost)? Defend your answer. (**Hint:** Determine the total profit at various sales levels.)
3. Would your pricing structure in **2** change if the company had only limited competition at its quality level? If so, in what direction? Explain why.

P 2.

LO 3   *Cost-Based Pricing*

Supremo Coffee Company produces special types of blended coffee. Its products are used in exclusive restaurants throughout the world. Quality is the primary objective of the company. A team of consultants is employed to continuously assess the blending procedures and the quality of the purchased coffee beans and other ingredients. The company's controller is in the process of determining prices for the coming year. Three blends are currently produced: Regular Blend, Mint Blend, and Choco Blend. The desired profit on each blend is 20 percent above costs. The expected production for 20xx is 360,000 pounds of Regular Blend, 150,000 pounds of Mint Blend, and 90,000 pounds of Choco Blend. The total anticipated costs and percentages of total costs per blend for 20xx follow.

	Percentage of Total Costs			Total Projected Costs
Cost Categories	Regular Blend	Mint Blend	Choco Blend	
Coffee beans	60%	25%	15%	$748,000
Chocolate	0	10	90	45,000
Mint leaf	10	80	10	32,000
Direct labor				
Cleaning	60	25	15	170,000
Blending	40	30	30	372,000
Roasting	60	25	15	288,000
Indirect labor	60	25	15	120,000
Supplies	30	40	30	36,500
Other variable manufacturing overhead	60	25	15	280,000
Fixed manufacturing overhead	60	25	15	166,000
Selling expenses	40	30	30	138,500
General and administrative expenses	34	33	33	146,000

REQUIRED

1. Use the gross margin pricing method to compute the selling price for each blend.
2. If the competition's selling price for a product like Choco Blend averaged $7.20 per pound, should this influence the controller's pricing decision? Explain.

P 3.

LO 3   *Time and Materials Pricing*

Augusta Construction Company specializes in custom additions to homes. Last week a potential customer called for a quote on a two-room addition to the family home. After visiting the site and taking all relevant measurements, Joe Palmeski returned to the office to work on drawings for the addition. As part of the process of preparing a bid, a total breakdown of costs is required.

The company follows the time and materials pricing system and uses data from the previous six months to compute markup percentages for overhead. Separate rates are used for direct materials and supplies and for direct labor. During the past six months, $35,750 of direct materials and supplies-related overhead was incurred and $143,000 of direct materials and supplies were billed. The direct labor cost for the six-month period was $341,600. Direct labor-related overhead was $170,800. A 20 percent markup is always added to cover the desired profit. According to Mr. Palmeski's design, the following direct materials, supplies, and direct labor are needed to complete the job.

Quantity	Materials	Unit Price		
150	2″ × 4″ × 8′ cedar	$ 1.50	× 150	$225.00
40	2″ × 6″ × 8′ cedar	3.00	× 40	120.00
14	2″ × 8″ × 8′ cedar	4.50	× 14	63.00
20	4′ × 8′ sheets, ½″ plywood	20.80	× 20	416.00
6	Framed windows	80.00	× 6	480.00
3	Framed doors	110.00	× 3	330.00
30	4′ × 8′ sheets, siding	24.00	× 30	720.00
	Supplies	65.00		6500
				$2419.00

Direct Labor		Hourly Rate
Hours		
120	Laborers/helpers	$12.50
80	Semiskilled carpenters	14.00
60	Carpenters	16.00

1. Compute a markup percentage for overhead and profit for (a) direct materials and supplies and (b) direct labor.
2. Prepare a complete billing for this job. Include itemized amounts for each type of direct materials, supplies, and direct labor. Follow the time and materials pricing approach and show the total price for the job.

P 4.

LO 5 *Pricing Using Target Costing*

Djuing Hi-Tech Corp. is considering marketing two new high-speed desk calculators and has named them Speed-Calc 4 and Speed-Calc 5. According to recent market research, the two products will surpass current competition in both speed and quality and would be welcomed into the market. Customers would be willing to pay $98 for Speed-Calc 4 and $110 for Speed-Calc 5, based on their projected design capabilities. Both products have many uses, but the primary market interest comes from the payroll activity of all types of businesses. Current production capacity exists for the manufacture and assembly of the two products. The company has a minimum desired profit of 25 percent above all costs for all of its products. Current activity-based cost rates are:

Materials/parts handling activity	$1.20 per dollar of raw materials and purchased parts cost
Production activity	$8.00 per machine hour
Marketing/delivery activity	$4.40 per unit of Speed-Calc 4
	$6.20 per unit of Speed-Calc 5

Design engineering and accounting estimates to produce the two new products follow:

	Speed-Calc 4	Speed-Calc 5
Projected unit demand	100,000	80,000
Per unit data		
Raw materials cost	$5.50 ⎞ 16.10	$7.50 ⎞ 19.20
Computer chip cost	$10.60 ⎠	$11.70 ⎠
Production labor		
Hours	1.2 ⎞ 19.20	1.3 ⎞ 20.80
Hourly labor rate	$16.00 ⎠	$16.00 ⎠
Assembly labor		
Hours	0.6 ⎞ 7.20	0.5 ⎞ 6.00
Hourly labor rate	$12.00 ⎠	$12.00 ⎠
Machine hours	1	1.2

1. Compute the target costs for each product.
2. Compute the projected total unit cost of production and delivery.
3. Using the target costing approach, decide whether the products should be produced.

P 5.

LO 6 *Developing Transfer Prices*

Kaetz Company has two divisions, Jean Division and Charles Division. For several years, Jean Division has manufactured a special glass container, which it sells to Charles Division at the prevailing market price of $20. Jean Division produces the glass containers only for Charles Division and does not sell the product to outside customers. Annual production and sales volume is 20,000 containers. A unit cost analysis for Jean Division showed the following.

Cost Categories	Costs per Container
Direct materials	$ 3.50
Direct labor, ¼ hour	2.30
Variable manufacturing overhead	7.50
Traceable fixed costs	
$30,000 ÷ 20,000	1.50
Corporate overhead, $18 per direct labor hour	4.50
Variable shipping costs	1.20
Unit cost	$20.50

Corporate overhead represents such allocated joint fixed costs of production as building depreciation, property taxes, fire insurance, and salaries of production executives. A profit markup of 20 percent is used in determining transfer prices.

REQUIRED

1. What would be the appropriate transfer price for Jean Division to use in billing its transactions with Charles Division?
2. If Jean Division decided to sell some containers to outside customers, would your answer to **1** change? Defend your response.

Alternate Problems

P 6.

LO 3 *Pricing Decision*

Walker & James, Ltd., designs and assembles handguns for police departments across the country. Only four other companies compete in this specialty market. The most popular police handgun is the W&J .357-Caliber Magnum, Model 87, made of stainless steel. Walker & James estimates that there will be 23,500 requests for this model in 20xx.

Estimated costs related to this product for 20xx are shown in the following table. The budget is based on the demand previously stated. The company wants to earn an $846,000 profit in 20xx.

Description	Budgeted Costs
Gun casing	$ 434,750
Ammunition chamber	542,850
Trigger mechanism	1,222,000
Direct labor	1,527,500
Variable indirect assembly costs	810,750
Fixed indirect assembly costs	317,250
Selling expenses	446,500
General operating expenses	206,800
Administrative expenses	150,400

Last week the four competitors released their wholesale prices for the next year.

Gunsmith A	$256.80
Gunsmith B	245.80
Gunsmith C	239.60
Gunsmith D	253.00

Walker & James handguns are known for their high quality. They compete with handguns at the top of the price range. Despite the guns' high quality, however, every $10 price increase above the top competitor's price causes a 5,500-unit drop in demand from what was originally estimated. (Assume all price changes occur in $10 increments.)

REQUIRED

1. Use the gross margin pricing method to compute the anticipated selling price.
2. Based on competitors' prices, what should the Walker & James handgun sell for in 20xx (assume a constant unit cost)? Defend your answer. (**Hint:** Determine the total profit at various sales levels.)
3. Would your pricing structure in **2** change if the company had only limited competition at this quality level? If so, in what direction? Explain why.

P 7.

LO 4 *Pricing Using*
LO 5 *Target Costing*

Molly Machine Tool Company designs and produces a line of high-quality machine tools and markets them throughout the world. The company's main competition comes from companies in France, Great Britain, and Korea. Two highly specialized machine tools, Y14 and Z33, have recently been introduced by five competing firms. The prices charged for Y14 range from $625 to $675 per tool, and the price range for Z33 is from $800 to $840 per tool. The company is contemplating entering the market for these two products. Market research has indicated that if Molly can sell Y14 for $650 per tool and Z33 for $750 per tool, the company will be successful in marketing the products worldwide. The company's profit markup is 25 percent over all costs to produce and deliver a product. Current activity-based cost rates are as follows on the next page:

Materials handling activity	$1.30 per dollar of raw materials and purchased parts cost	
Production activity	$4.40 per machine hour	
Product delivery activity	$34.00 per unit of Y14	
	$40.00 per unit of Z33	

Design engineering and accounting estimates for the production of the two new products are as follows:

	Product Y14	Product Z33
Projected unit demand	75,000	95,000
Per unit data		
Raw materials cost	$50.00	$60.00
Purchased parts cost	$65.00	$70.00
Manufacturing labor		
Hours	6.2	7.4
Hourly labor rate	$14.00	$14.00
Assembly labor		
Hours	4.6	9.2
Hourly labor rate	$12.00	$12.00
Machine hours	14	16

REQUIRED

1. Compute the target cost for each product.
2. Compute the total projected unit cost of production and delivery.
3. Using the target costing approach, decide whether the products should be produced.

P 8.

LO 6 *Developing Transfer Prices*

Seven years ago Lynn Salazar formed the Salazar Corporation and began producing sound equipment for home use. Because of the highly technical and competitive nature of the industry, Salazar established the Research and Development Division. That division is responsible for continually evaluating and updating critical electronic parts used in the corporation's products. The R & D staff has been very successful and has greatly contributed to the corporation's ranking as America's leader in the industry.

Two years ago, R & D took on the added responsibility of producing all microchip circuit boards for the company's sound equipment. One of Salazar's specialties is a sound dissemination board (SDB) used in videocassette recorders (VCRs). The SDB greatly enhances the sound quality of Salazar's VCRs.

Demand for the SDB has increased significantly in the past year. As a result, R & D has increased its production and assembly labor force. Three outside customers want to purchase the SDB for their sound products. To date, R & D has been producing SDBs for internal use only.

The controller of the R & D Division wants to create a transfer price for the SDBs that will apply to all intracompany transfers. The following data show cost projections for the next six months:

Direct materials and parts	$2,600,000
Direct labor	1,920,000
Supplies	100,000
Indirect labor	580,000
Other variable overhead costs	200,000
Fixed overhead, SDBs	1,840,000
Other fixed overhead, corporate	560,000
Variable selling expenses, SDBs	1,480,000
Fixed selling expenses, corporate	520,000
General corporate operating expenses	880,000
Corporate administrative expenses	680,000

A profit markup of at least 20 percent must be added to total unit cost for internal transfer purposes. Outside customers are willing to pay $35 for each SDB. Estimated demand over the next six months is 235,000 SDBs for internal use and 165,000 SDBs for external customers.

REQUIRED

1. Compute the cost of producing and distributing one SDB.
2. What transfer price should R & D use? Explain the factors that influenced your decision.

Skills Development

CONCEPTUAL ANALYSIS

LO 1
LO 2 *Product Differentiation and Pricing*

SD 1. **Maytag Corporation** can price its products higher than any other company in the home appliance industry and still maintain and even increase market share. How can the company do this? Are its costs higher, resulting in higher prices than those of its competitors? No. Will customers shop around for products with lower price tags? No. Will competitors single out Maytag products in comparative ad campaigns and try to exploit the higher prices? No. Think about the Maytag repairman television commercials that you have seen over the past ten years. They feature a very lonely person who never gets a call to repair a Maytag product. The ads say nothing about price. They do not attack competitors' products. But the commercials do inspire customers to purchase Maytag products through what is known in the marketing field as product differentiation. Prepare a one-page memo to your teacher explaining how Maytag Corporation has differentiated its products from the competition. Is product cost a factor in Maytag's pricing strategy?

ETHICAL DILEMMA

LO 1
LO 2 *Ethics in Pricing*

SD 2. **Barnes Company** has been doing business with mainland China for the last three years. The company produces leather handbags that are in great demand in the cities of China. On a recent trip to Hong Kong, Kwan Cho, the purchasing agent for Shen Enterprises, approached Barnes salesperson Frank Edwards to arrange for a purchase of 2,500 handbags. Barnes's usual price is $75 per bag. Kwan Cho wanted to purchase the handbags at $65 per bag. After an hour of haggling, the two people agreed to a final price of $68 per item. When Edwards returned to his hotel room after dinner, he found an envelope containing five new $100 bills and a note that said, "Thank you for agreeing to our order of 2,500 handbags at $68 per bag. My company's president wants you to have the enclosed gift for your fine service." Edwards later learned that Kwan Cho was following her company's normal business practice. What should Frank Edwards do? Is the gift his to keep? Be prepared to justify your opinion.

Group Activity: Break class into small groups and ask each group to decide what Frank should do. Assemble a panel consisting of one spokesperson from each group and debate Frank's position.

RESEARCH ACTIVITY

LO 6 *Transfer Pricing*

SD 3. One reason that companies use transfer prices is to allow cost/expense centers to function and be evaluated as profit centers. Transfer prices are fictitious prices charged to one department by another for internally manufactured parts and products that are used by the "purchasing" department. Transfer pricing policies and methods have generated much controversy in recent years. Using *The Accountant's Index*, the *Business Periodicals Index*, the *Wall Street Journal Index*, or the Needles Accounting Resource Center Web site at http://www.hmco.com/college/needles/home.html, locate an article about transfer prices. Prepare a one-page summary of the article and use it as the basis for a classroom presentation. Include in your summary the name and date of the publication, the article's title and author(s), a list of the issues being discussed, and a brief statement about the conclusions reached by the author(s).

Communication	Critical Thinking	Group Activity	Memo	Ethics	International	Spreadsheet	Managerial Technology	Internet

DECISION-MAKING PRACTICE

LO 3 *Pricing Decisions*

SD 4. The **Highlands Company** manufactures office equipment for retail stores. Carol McBride, the vice president of marketing, has proposed that Highlands introduce two new products: an electric stapler and an electric pencil sharpener.

McBride has requested that the Profit Planning Department develop preliminary selling prices for the two new products for her review. Profit Planning is to follow the company's standard policy for developing potential selling prices. It is to use all data available for each product. The data accumulated by Profit Planning are as follows:

	Electric Stapler	Electric Pencil Sharpener
Estimated annual demand in units	16,000	12,000
Estimated unit manufacturing costs	$14.00	$15.00
Estimated unit selling and administrative expenses	$3.00	Not available
Assets employed in manufacturing	$160,000	Not available

Highlands plans to use an average of $1,200,000 in assets to support operations in the current year. The condensed pro forma operating income statement that follows represents the planned costs and return on assets for the entire company for all products.

Highlands Company
Pro Forma Operating Income Statement
For the Year Ended May 31, 20xx
($000 omitted)

Revenue	$2,400
Cost of goods sold, manufacturing costs	1,440
Gross profit	$ 960
Selling and administrative expenses	720
Operating profit	$ 240

---

1. Calculate a potential selling price for the:
   a. electric stapler, using return on assets pricing
   b. electric pencil sharpener, using gross margin pricing
2. Could a selling price for the electric pencil sharpener be calculated using return on assets pricing? Explain your answer.
3. Which of the two pricing methods—return on assets pricing or gross margin pricing—is more appropriate for decision analysis? Explain your answer.
4. Discuss the additional steps Carol McBride is likely to take after she receives the potential selling prices for the two new products (as calculated in **1**) to set an actual selling price for each of the two products.

(CMA adapted)

Managerial Reporting and Analysis

INTERPRETING MANAGEMENT REPORTS

MRA 1.

LO 6 *Transfer Pricing*

Two major operating divisions, the Cabinet Division and the Electronics Division, make up **Cirrus Industries, Inc.** The company's main products are deluxe console television sets. The TV cabinets are manufactured by the Cabinet Division, and the Electronics Division produces all electronic components and assembles the sets. The company uses a decentralized organizational structure.

The Cabinet Division not only supplies cabinets to the Electronics Division, but also sells cabinets to other TV manufacturers. Based on a typical sales order of 40 cabinets, the following unit cost breakdown for a deluxe television cabinet was developed.

Direct materials	$ 32.00
Direct labor	15.00
Variable manufacturing overhead	12.00
Fixed manufacturing overhead	18.00
Variable selling expenses	9.00
Fixed selling expenses	6.00
Fixed general and administrative expenses	8.00
Total unit cost	$100.00

The Cabinet Division's usual profit margin is 20 percent, and the regular selling price of a deluxe cabinet is $120. Divisional management recently decided that $120 will also be the transfer price for all intracompany transactions.

Managers at the Electronics Division are unhappy with that decision. They claim that the Cabinet Division will show superior performance at the expense of the Electronics Division. Competition recently forced the company to lower its prices. Because of the newly established transfer price for the cabinet, the Electronics Divisions portion of the profit margin on deluxe television sets was lowered to 18 percent. To counteract the new intracompany transfer price, management at the Electronics Division announced that, effective immediately, all cabinets will be purchased from an outside supplier. They will be purchased in lots of 200 cabinets at a unit price of $110 per cabinet.

The company president, Jerry Hermann, has called a meeting of both divisions to negotiate a fair intracompany transfer price. The following prices were listed as possible alternatives.

Current market price	$120 per cabinet
Current outside purchase price (This price is based on a large-quantity purchase discount. It will cause increased storage costs for the Electronics Division.)	$110 per cabinet
Total unit manufacturing costs plus a 20 percent profit margin: $77.00 + $15.40	$92.40 per cabinet
Total unit costs, excluding variable selling expenses, plus a 20 percent profit margin: $91.00 + $18.20	$109.20 per cabinet

REQUIRED

1. What price should be established for intracompany transactions? Defend your answer by showing the shortcomings of each alternative.
2. If there were an outside market for all units produced by the Cabinet Division at the $120 price, would you change your answer to **1**? Why?

FORMULATING MANAGEMENT REPORTS

MRA 2

LO 6 *Transfer Prices and Performance Evaluation*

"That Pinehurst Division is robbing us blind!" This statement by the director of the Carmel Division was heard during the board of directors meeting at **Handy-Brell Company.** The company produces umbrellas in a two-step process. The Pinehurst Division prepares the fabric tops and transfers them to the Carmel Division. The Carmel Division produces the ribs and handles, secures the tops, and packs all finished umbrellas for shipment.

Because of the director's concern, the company controller gathered data for the past year, as shown in the table at the top of the next page.

	Pinehurst Division	Carmel Division	Company Totals
Sales			
Regular	$700,000	$1,720,000	$2,420,000
Deluxe	900,000	3,300,000	4,200,000
Materials			
Fabric tops (from Pinehurst Division)	—	1,600,000	1,600,000
Cloth	360,000	—	360,000
Aluminum	—	660,000	660,000
Closing mechanisms	—	1,560,000	1,560,000
Direct labor	480,000	540,000	1,020,000
Variable manufacturing overhead	90,000	240,000	330,000
Fixed divisional overhead	150,000	210,000	360,000
Selling and general operating expenses	132,000	372,000	504,000
Company administrative expenses	84,000	108,000	192,000

During the year, 200,000 regular umbrellas and 150,000 deluxe umbrellas were completed and transferred or shipped by the two divisions. Transfer prices used by the Pinehurst Division were:

Regular $3.50
Deluxe   6.00

The regular umbrella wholesales for $8.60; the deluxe model, for $22.00. Company administrative costs are allocated to divisions by a predetermined formula.

Management has indicated that the transfer price should include a 20 percent profit factor on total division costs.

REQUIRED

1. Prepare a performance report on the Pinehurst Division.
2. Prepare a performance report on the Carmel Division.
3. Compute each division's rate of return on controllable costs and on total division costs.
4. Do you agree with the director's statement?
5. What procedures would you recommend to the board of directors?

INTERNATIONAL COMPANY

MRA 3.

LO 3   *Product Pricing*
LO 4   *in a Foreign*
LO 5   *Market*

Borner, Inc., is an international corporation that manufactures and sells home care products. Today, a meeting is being held at corporate headquarters in New York City. The purpose of the meeting is to discuss changing the price of the laundry detergent the company manufactures and sells in Brazil. During the meeting, a conflict develops between Carl Dickson, the corporate sales manager, and Jose Cabral, the Brazilian Division's sales manager.

Dickson insists that the selling price of the laundry detergent should be increased to the equivalent of $3 U.S. This increase is necessary because the Brazilian Division's costs are higher than those of other international divisions. The Brazilian Division is paying high interest rates on notes payable for the acquisition of the new manufacturing plant. In addition, a stronger, more expensive ingredient has been introduced into the laundry detergent, which has caused the product cost to increase by $.20.

Cabral believes that the laundry detergent's selling price should remain at $2.50 for several reasons. Cabral argues that the market for laundry detergent in Brazil is highly competitive. Labor costs are low and the costs of distribution are small since the target market is the Rio de Janeiro metropolitan area. Inflation is extremely high in Brazil, and the Brazilian government continues to impose a policy to control inflation. Because of these controls, Cabral insists that the buyers will resist any price hikes.

REQUIRED

1. What selling price do you believe Borner, Inc., should set for the laundry detergent? Explain your answer. Do you believe Borner, Inc., should let the Brazilian Division set the selling price for laundry detergent in the future? When should corporate headquarters set prices?
2. Based on the information given above, should cost-based pricing or target costing be used to set the selling price for laundry detergent in Brazil? Explain your answer.

EXCEL ANALYSIS

MRA 4.

LO 4   *Target Costing*
LO 5

Gilcrist Electronics, Inc., produces circuit boards for flexible manufacturing systems (FMS) that are made by more than a dozen customers. Competition among the producers of circuit boards is keen, with over thirty companies bidding on every job request from those FMS producers. The circuit boards can vary widely in their complexity, and their unit prices can range from $250 to more than $500,000.

Gilcrist's controller is concerned about the analysis just completed by the engineering design people. The cost planning projection for a new complex circuit board, the CX35, was almost 6 percent above its target cost. The controller has asked the design engineers to review their design and projections and come up with alternatives that will bring the proposed product's costs to equal or below the target cost.

The following information was used to develop the initial cost projections:

Target selling price	$590.00	per unit
Desired profit percentage	25%	of total unit cost
Projected unit demand	13,600	units
Per unit data		
Raw materials cost	$56.00	
Purchased parts cost	$37.00	
Manufacturing labor		
Hours	4.5	hours
Hourly labor rate	$14.00	
Assembly labor		
Hours	5.2	hours
Hourly labor rate	$15.00	
Machine hours	26	hours
Activity-based cost rates		
Materials handling activity	10%	of raw materials and purchased parts cost
Engineering activity	$13.50	per unit for CX35
Production activity	$8.20	per machine hour
Product delivery activity	$24.00	per unit for CX35
Marketing activity	$6.00	per unit for CX35

REQUIRED

1. Compute the product's target cost.
2. Compute the product cost of the original estimate to verify that the controller's calculations were correct.
3. Rework the product cost calculations for each of the following changes recommended by the design engineers:
   a. Cut product quality, which will reduce raw materials cost by 20 percent and purchased parts cost by 15 percent.
   b. Increase raw materials quality, which will increase raw materials cost by 20 percent but will reduce machine hours by 10 percent, manufacturing labor hours by 16 percent, and assembly labor hours by 20 percent.
4. What decision should the management of Gilcrist Electronics, Inc., make about the new product? Defend your answer.

ENDNOTES

1. George Schmelze, Rolf Geier, and Thomas E. Buttross, "Target Costing at ITT Automotive," *Management Accounting*, Institute of Management Accountants, December 1996, pp. 26–30.
2. John M. Brausch, "Beyond ABC: Target Costing for Profit Enhancement," *Management Accounting*, Institute of Management Accountants, November 1994, pp. 45–49.

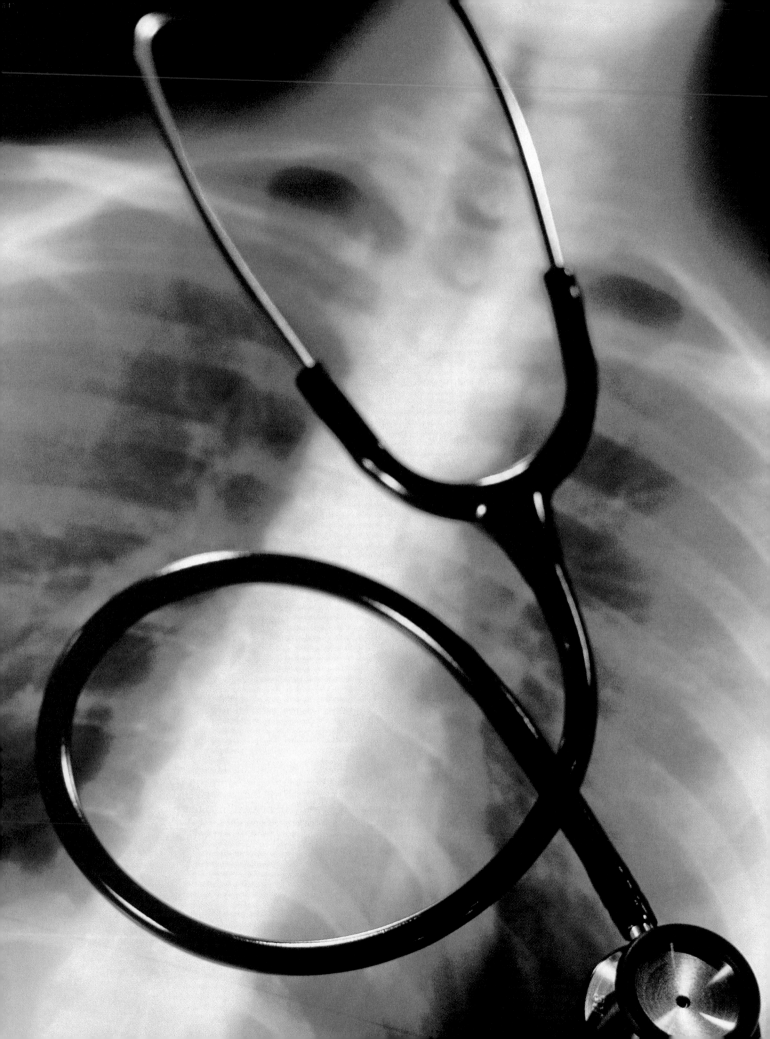

CHAPTER 12

Cost Management, Measures of Quality, and Performance Measurement

1. Define *cost management,* describe a cost management system, and explain how the management cycle is used to implement a cost management system.

2. Define *total quality management* and identify and compute the costs of quality for products and services.

3. Use nonfinancial measures of quality to evaluate operating performance.

4. Describe performance measurement and state the issues that accompany management's ability to measure performance.

5. Define *full cost profit margin* and identify the advantages of this measure of performance.

DECISION POINT

Group Health Cooperative (GHC)of Puget Sound is a health maintenance organization (HMO) headquartered in Seattle that serves over 480,000 people in the state of Washington. GHC's original cost management system had been primarily designed to meet financial reporting needs and had been used for several decades without being updated. GHC's managers found, however, that to remain profitable in the heavy competition of the HMO industry, they needed significantly more information of various kinds. In response, in 1989, the organization began the ongoing process of redesigning its cost management system. Using the principles of total quality management, it developed an extensive cost management database that captures as much data as possible about business operations.[1]

Since GHC is a service organization, the new cost management system focuses on the costs of delivering health care services. It enables management to identify the full cost of operating its delivery system, including both the direct costs of delivering health care to patients and the overhead costs of administering the program. The new cost management system allows management accountants to analyze costs by (1) treatment patterns, such as uses of specific services, (2) treatment differences, such as uses of in-patient versus outpatient hospital care, (3) patient diagnosis, (4) manner of payment, such as users of Medicare, and (5) service location. Why did

GROUP HEALTH COOPERATIVE OF PUGET SOUND

competition pressure GHC to redesign its cost management system? How has the role of the cost management system changed for the managers of GHC?

To perform their jobs effectively in today's highly competitive environment, managers need more than just after-the-fact financial results. They need detailed, timely information, both financial and nonfinancial, about every aspect of the organization's operation. For such information, they depend on the cost management system. When the cost management system is well constructed and uses the latest database technology, it becomes the focal point for all operating information. It is no longer merely a source of financial data.

This chapter presents some of the newer techniques of managerial accounting that have been developed to provide managers with more timely and relevant information. These techniques include managing costs for particular objectives, using financial and nonfinancial measures to evaluate quality and performance, and using the balanced scorecard approach to reflect broadened organizational perspectives.

Cost Management Systems

OBJECTIVE 1

Define cost management, describe a cost management system, and explain how the management cycle is used to implement a cost management system

Many traditional management accounting techniques and practices do not produce meaningful results in today's globally competitive business environment. Companies that have adopted just-in-time and activity-based accounting and management approaches have found that traditional cost assignment and product costing practices generate incorrect unit cost information. Computerized facilities and computer-aided processes enable the accountant to trace more types of costs directly to work cells or products. Traditional management accounting practices were not designed to identify and help eliminate nonvalue-adding activities. Those practices do not trace costs adequately, they do not isolate the costs of unnecessary activities, they do not penalize for overproduction, and they do not quantify measures that help in achieving product or service quality, process flexibility, and reduced throughput time. Their focus is on costs, not on the activities that generate those costs.

Such concerns have led to the creation of cost management systems (CMS). According to James Brimson, a partner in Coopers & Lybrand, Deloitte, United Kingdom, cost management is the management and control of *activities* to determine accurate product costs, to improve business processes, to eliminate waste, to identify cost drivers, to plan operations, and to set business strategies.[2] A cost management system (CMS) is a management accounting and reporting system that identifies, monitors, and maintains continuous, detailed analyses of a company's activities and provides managers with timely measures of operating results. A CMS is designed to support new management philosophies, including just-in-time (JIT) operations, activity-based costing (ABC) and activity-based management (ABM), and total quality management (TQM).

Rather than take a historical approach to cost control, as most accounting systems do, a cost management system is on-line and reflects current management strategies and decisions. A CMS plays a major role in planning, managing, and reducing costs. Cost cutting is not accomplished merely by slashing the amount of resources a department can use to make a product, as happens in a traditional costing system. A CMS relies on the concept of continuous improvement to reduce costs while still increasing product quality. Continuous improvement means that design engineers are always looking for ways to improve the product while still cutting its cost; the production process is constantly watched to find ways to increase efficiency and reduce costs; and nonvalue-adding activities are continuously monitored to find activities or resource usage that can be reduced or eliminated. In cost management systems, the primary focus is on the management of activities, not costs, for both product costing and cost control. CMS advocates believe that when activities are managed effectively, a natural consequence is the effective use of money and other resources.

Another trait of a cost management system is the use of target costing. Target costing involves setting a unit cost that must be achieved by subtracting a desired profit from a competitive selling price. The product is then designed to be produced at the target cost. When continuous improvement is employed, a company first designs a product so that its target cost is achieved. It can then increase profits by making ongoing improvements to reduce costs further. Finally, cost assignment within a cost management system is far superior to that within traditional costing systems. When costs are accumulated by activities and the usage of these activities is traced to specific products or product types, costs can be assigned easily and accurately.

By focusing on activities, a CMS provides managers with improved knowledge of the processes for which they are responsible. Activity-related information needed to trim process cycle time or product throughput time is readily available. More accurate product costs lead to improved pricing decisions. Nonvalue-adding activities are highlighted, and managers can work to reduce or eliminate them. In addition to providing information about product profitability, a CMS can analyze the profitability of individual customers by looking at the costs of servicing customers. Overall, the CMS pinpoints resource usage and cost for each activity and fosters managerial decisions that lead to continuous improvement throughout the organization.

Figure 1 illustrates the management cycle for planning and implementing a new cost management system. During the planning stage, managers consider which new management approaches to implement. They may choose a single approach or combine aspects of several different approaches. They then create a new cost management system that will support their choice. For example, all of today's new approaches to management include the goal of continuous improvement. Thus, any new cost management system must supply the information managers need to continuously improve all aspects of the operating environment.

During the executing stage of the management cycle, managers activate the processes that will implement the new cost management system. This includes training personnel to function within the new system.

During the reviewing stage, managers develop and implement new performance measures for evaluating product quality, process quality and flexibility, effectiveness of distribution, and customer satisfaction. They also analyze information to identify possible bottlenecks and other problems caused by the new processes.

Finally, during the reporting stage, managers develop reports of the new performance measures, identify who will receive the reports, and determine how often reports are prepared. A new approach to reporting called the *balanced scorecard* is especially effective in today's new operating environments. It is discussed later in this chapter.

Accounting for Product and Service Quality

OBJECTIVE 2

Define total quality management *and identify and compute the costs of quality for products and services*

In the past, U.S. manufacturers often sacrificed or ignored quality in an attempt to lower prices to meet world competition. At the same time, Japan and other countries increased the quality of their goods while lowering prices. To survive in global markets, U.S. companies must produce quality products and services at competitive prices. Quality, however, is not something that a company can simply add at some point in the production process or assume will happen automatically. Inspections can detect bad products, but they do not ensure quality. Managers need reliable

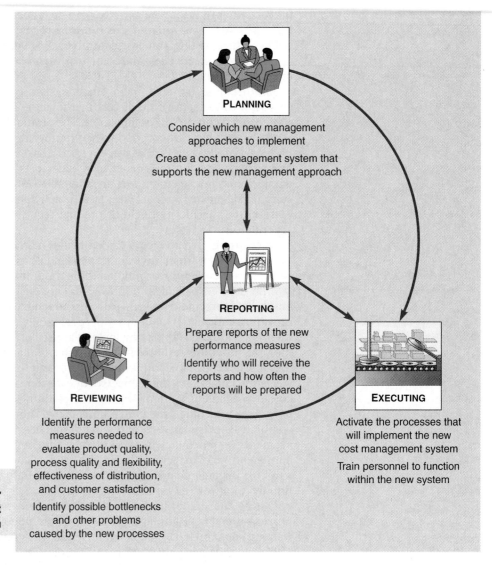

measures of quality to help them meet the goal of producing high-quality, reasonably priced products or services. They need to create a total quality management environment. Total quality management (TQM) is an organizational environment in which all business functions work together to build quality into the firm's products or services. From a management accounting perspective, the first step toward a TQM environment is to identify and manage the costs of quality. The second step is to analyze operating performance using nonfinancial measures and to require that all operating processes and products be improved continuously.

Financial Measures of Quality[3]

To the average person, quality means that one product or service is better than another—possibly because of design, durability, or some other attribute. In a business setting, however, quality is an operating environment in which a company's product or service meets or conforms to a customer's specifications the first time it is produced or delivered. The costs of quality are the costs specifically associated with the achievement or nonachievement of product or service quality. Total costs of quality include (1) costs of good quality incurred to ensure the successful development of a product or service and (2) costs of poor quality incurred to transform a faulty product or service into one that is acceptable to the customer.

The costs of quality make up a significant portion of a product's or service's total cost. In his book *Thriving on Chaos*, Tom Peters states that the costs of poor quality consume 25 percent of all labor and assets in manufacturing firms; in service firms, they can run as high as 40 percent of labor and asset costs.[4] Therefore, controlling the costs of quality has a sizable impact on profitability. Today's managers should be able to identify the activities associated with improving quality and should be aware of the cost of resources used to achieve high quality.

The costs of quality have two components: the costs of conformance, which are the costs incurred to produce a quality product or service, and the costs of nonconformance, which are the costs incurred to correct defects in a product or service. Costs of conformance are made up of prevention costs and appraisal costs. Prevention costs are the costs associated with the prevention of defects and failures in products and services. Appraisal costs are the costs of activities that measure, evaluate, or audit products, processes, or services to ensure conformance to quality standards and performance requirements.

The costs of nonconformance include internal failure costs and external failure costs. Internal failure costs are the costs incurred when defects are discovered before a product or service is delivered to a customer. Costs incurred after the delivery of a defective product or service are called external failure costs. Examples of each cost category are shown in Table 1. Note that there is a trade-off between the two major categories: If a company spends money on the costs of conformance, the costs of nonconformance should be reduced. However, if little attention is paid to the costs of conformance, then the costs of nonconformance may escalate.

The management accountant is responsible for supplying the information that managers need if they are to control the costs of quality. The overall objective is to

BUSINESS BULLETIN: BUSINESS PRACTICE

Self-directed work teams (SDWTs) are an important element of today's work environment. "A SDWT is a group of employees who have day-to-day responsibilities for managing themselves and a whole work process that delivers a service or a product."[5] Managing such a group of people requires a radical switch from traditional autocratic methods. A successful SDWT manager must play the following roles:

Leader—Holds an inspiring and motivating vision to which team members can make personal commitments.

Role model—"Walks the walk," demonstrating the desired behaviors.

Coach—Teaches and helps team members to realize their potential, ensures accountability, and maintains authority.

Business analyzer—Brings the big picture perspective to the team, and translates changes in the business environment into opportunities for the team.

Advocate—Opens doors for the team, manages senior support, and challenges the status quo and artificial barriers that limit team performance.

Facilitator—Brings together resources, information, and technologies and does whatever it takes to allow the team to be successful.

Customer advocate—Keeps close to the customers, understands their needs, and brings the customer perspective to the team.

Table 1. Financial Measures of Quality

Costs of Conformance to Customer Standards

Prevention Costs

Quality training of employees	Design and development of
Design review	quality equipment
Quality planning activities	Quality improvement projects
Quality engineering	On-line statistical process
Preventive maintenance	control

Appraisal Costs

Sample preparation	Vendor audits and sample testing
All inspection activities	Maintenance of test equipment
Setup for testing	Quality audits
Product simulation and	Maintenance of equipment used
development	for quality enhancement

Costs of Nonconformance to Customer Standards

Internal Failure Costs

Scrap and rework	Failure analysis
Reinspection of rework	Inventory control and scheduling
Quality-related downtime	costs
Losses caused by vendor scrap	Downgrading because of defects

External Failure Costs

Loss of goodwill and future	Returned goods
orders	Investigation of defects
Warranty claims and adjustments	Product recalls
Customer complaint processing	Product liability suits
Customer service	

Measures of Quality

Total costs of quality as a percentage of net sales
Ratio of costs of conformance to total costs of quality
Ratio of costs of nonconformance to total costs of quality
Costs of nonconformance as a percentage of net sales

avoid costs of nonconformance because internal and external failures affect customers' satisfaction as well as the company's profitability. High initial costs of conformance are justified when they minimize the total costs of quality over the life of a product or service. The cost-based measures of quality listed at the bottom of Table 1 are used and explained in the illustrative problem that follows in a few pages.

Nonfinancial Measures of Quality

OBJECTIVE 3
Use nonfinancial measures of quality to evaluate operating performance

By measuring the costs of quality, a company learns how much it has spent in its efforts to improve product or service quality. But critics say that tracking historical data to account for quality performance does little to help production and engineering personnel enhance quality. What managers need is a measurement and evaluation system that signals poor quality early enough in the process so they can correct problems before a defective product reaches the customer. Implementing a policy of continuous improvement satisfies this need and is the second stage of total quality management.

Nonfinancial measures of operating performance, identified and reported to engineering and production managers in a timely manner, are used to augment cost-based measures. Although cost control is still an important consideration, a commitment to ongoing product improvement encourages activities that enhance product quality, from design to delivery. As explained earlier, those activities, or cost drivers, cause costs. By controlling the nonfinancial performance measures of production activities, managers can ultimately maximize the financial return from operations.

Measures of Product Design Quality   Problems with quality often are the result of poor design. Most automated production operations utilize computer-aided design (CAD), a computer-based engineering system with a built-in program to detect product design flaws. Such computer programs automatically identify faultily designed parts or manufacturing processes so that engineers can correct them before actual production begins. The management accountant is not directly involved in this process but should be aware of the existence and use of product design control measures.

Measures of High-Quality Raw Materials   One of the most significant changes for a company that is converting to a JIT operating environment occurs in the company's relationship with suppliers of raw materials and parts. Instead of dealing with dozens of suppliers, looking for the lowest cost, JIT companies analyze their vendors to determine which are most reliable, deal in high-quality goods, have a record of timely deliveries, and charge competitive prices. Once such vendors are identified, they become an integral part of the production team. A JIT company works closely with its vendors to ensure a continuing supply of high-quality raw materials and parts. Vendors may even contribute to product design to ensure that the correct materials and parts are being used. The management accountant should conduct the necessary analyses to identify and monitor reliable vendors so that high-quality, reasonably priced materials are available when they are needed.

Measures of In-Process and Delivery Controls   Automated machinery linked into a manufacturing system can easily be programmed with in-process product control mechanisms. Product quality problems are detected by computer-programmed control techniques, and corrective action is taken when a problem is detected. No longer is it necessary to wait for a specified inspection point to detect a product flaw. In-process controls form a continuous inspection system that highlights trouble spots, significantly reduces scrap, cuts overall product rework machine time, and eliminates the nonvalue-adding product costs of traditional inspection activities. Although management accountants are not expected to develop and program in-process quality controls, they should understand the control points, maintain records, and prepare reports of the rates of defective parts produced. Because product delivery is part of overall quality, the cost management system should maintain records of on-time deliveries to track the performance of the firm's delivery systems.

Measures of Customer Acceptance   The sale and shipment of a product no longer marks the end of performance measurement. Customer follow-up helps in evaluating total customer satisfaction. Accounting measures used to determine the degree of customer acceptance include (1) the percentage of shipments returned by customers (or the percentage of shipments accepted by customers), (2) the number and types of customer complaints, and (3) an analysis of the number and causes of warranty claims. Several companies have developed their own customer satisfaction indexes from these measures so they can compare different product lines over different time periods.

Table 2. Nonfinancial Measures of Quality	
Measures of High-Quality Raw Materials	
Vendor quality analysis	An analysis of the quality of materials and parts received; prepared for each vendor used
Vendor delivery analysis	An analysis of timely vendor deliveries; prepared for each vendor used
Measures of In-Process and Delivery Controls	
Production quality level	Defective parts per million; usually tracked by product line
Percentage of on-time deliveries	Percentage of total shipments received by the promised date
Measures of Customer Acceptance	
Returned-order percentage	Number of shipments returned by customers as a percentage of total shipments
Customer complaints	An analysis of the number and types of customer complaints
Customer acceptance percentage	Number of shipments accepted as a percentage of total shipments; computed for each customer
Warranty claims	An analysis of the number and causes of warranty claims

Table 2 contains a summary of the nonfinancial measures of quality discussed above. This is only a sample of the many nonfinancial measures used to monitor quality. These measures help a company move toward its goals of continuously seeking to produce higher-quality products, to improve production processes, and to reduce throughput time and costs.

Illustrative Problem: Measuring Quality

Using many of the examples of the costs of quality identified in Table 1 and the non-financial measures of quality listed in Table 2, the following situations demonstrate how a company's progress toward its goal of achieving total quality management is measured and evaluated.

Evaluating the Costs of Quality   As shown in Part A of Exhibit 1, three companies, Able, Baker, and Cane, have taken different approaches to achieving product quality. All three companies are the same size, each generating $15 million in sales last year.

Evaluate each company's approach to quality enhancement by analyzing the costs of quality and by answering the following questions.

Which company is more likely to remain competitive in the global marketplace?

Which company has serious problems with its products' quality?

What do you think will happen to the total costs of quality for each company over the next five years? Why?

Exhibit 1. Measures of Quality—Data for Analysis

A. Costs of Quality

	Able Co.	Baker Co.	Cane Co.
Annual Sales	$15,000,000	$15,000,000	$15,000,000

Costs of Conformance to Customer Standards

Prevention Costs

	Able Co.	Baker Co.	Cane Co.
Quality training of employees	$ 210,000	$ 73,500	$ 136,500
Quality engineering	262,500	115,500	189,000
Design review	105,000	42,000	84,000
Preventive maintenance	157,500	84,000	115,500

Appraisal Costs

Setup for testing	$ 126,000	$ 63,000	$ 73,500
Product simulation and development	199,500	31,500	115,500
Quality audits	84,000	21,000	42,000
Vendor audits and sample testing	112,500	52,500	63,000

Costs of Nonconformance to Customer Standards

Internal Failure Costs

Scrap and rework	$ 21,000	$ 189,000	$ 126,000
Reinspection of rework	15,750	126,000	73,500
Quality-related downtime	42,000	231,000	178,500
Losses caused by vendor scrap	26,250	84,000	52,500

External Failure Costs

Warranty claims	$ 47,250	$ 94,500	$ 84,000
Returned goods	15,750	68,250	36,750
Investigation of defects	26,250	78,750	57,750
Customer service	120,750	178,500	126,000

B. Nonfinancial Measures of Quality

	Able Co.	Baker Co.	Cane Co.
Vendor Quality Analysis			
20x3	98.20%	94.40%	95.20%
20x4	98.40%	93.20%	95.30%
20x5	98.60%	93.10%	95.20%
Production Quality Level (product defects per million)			
20x3	1,400	4,120	2,710
20x4	1,340	4,236	2,720
20x5	1,210	4,340	2,680
Percentage of On-Time Deliveries			
20x3	94.20%	76.20%	84.10%
20x4	94.60%	75.40%	84.00%
20x5	95.40%	73.10%	83.90%
Order-Return Percentage			
20x3	1.30%	6.90%	4.20%
20x4	1.10%	7.20%	4.10%
20x5	0.80%	7.60%	4.00%
Number of Customer Complaints			
20x3	22	189	52
20x4	18	194	50
20x5	12	206	46

BUSINESS BULLETIN: INTERNATIONAL PRACTICE

Although the value of human resources is never shown on a balance sheet, they are a company's most important asset. Because intellectual capital is intangible, it is very difficult to measure, so accountants have shied away from quantifying and reporting its value. But that is changing. The Swedish firm Skandia AFS (Assurance and Financial Services) is one of many companies around the world that are beginning to measure and report the value of their human capital. Skandia created a top management position entitled Director of Intellectual Capital and now publishes a supplement to its annual report presenting measures of this valuable asset. Among the new measures are annual comparisons of (1) information technology investments as a percentage of total expenses, (2) information technology employees as a percentage of all employees, (3) innovative business development expenses as a percentage of total expenses, and (4) the amount of production from newly launched projects. Also tracked is the amount of gross insurance premiums per employee, a bottom-line measure of the impact of human resource utilization and refined business practices on the amount of new business.[6]

SOLUTION

The costs of quality have been summarized and analyzed in Exhibit 2. The analysis shows that each company spent between 10.22 and 10.48 percent of its sales dollars on costs of quality. The following statements are based on that analysis.

Which company is more likely to remain competitive in the global marketplace? Able Co. spent the most money on costs of quality. More important, however, 80 percent of the money was spent on costs of conformance. Those dollars spent now will bring benefits in years to come. The company's focus on the costs of conformance means that only a small amount had to be spent on internal and external failure costs. The resulting high-quality products would lead to high customer satisfaction.

Which company has serious problems with its products' quality? Baker Co. spent the least on costs of quality, but that's not the reason the company is in serious trouble. Over 68 percent of its costs of quality ($1,050,000 of a total of $1,533,000) was spent on internal and external failure costs. Scrap costs, reinspection costs, the cost of downtime, warranty costs, and customer service costs were all high. Baker's products are very low in quality, which will mean hard times in future years.

What do you think will happen to the total costs of quality for each company over the next five years? Why? When money is spent on costs of conformance early in a product's life cycle, quality is integrated into the development and production processes. Once a high level of quality has been established, total costs of quality should be lower in future years. Able Co. seems to be in that position today.

Baker's costs of conformance will have to increase significantly if the company expects to stay in business. Seven percent of its sales revenue is being spent on internal and external failure costs. Because its products are not being accepted by the marketplace, the company is vulnerable to its competitors. It is in a weak position to face competition on a global scale.

Cane Co. is taking a middle road. It is spending a little more than half (53 percent) of its cost-of-quality dollars on conformance, so product quality should be increasing. But the company is still incurring high internal and external failure costs. Cane's managers must learn to prevent such costs if they expect to remain competitive.

Exhibit 2. Analysis of the Costs of Quality

	Able Co.	Baker Co.	Cane Co.
Annual Sales	$15,000,000	$15,000,000	$15,000,000
Costs of Conformance to Customer Standards			
Prevention Costs			
Quality training of employees	$ 210,000	$ 73,500	$ 136,500
Quality engineering	262,500	115,500	189,000
Design review	105,000	42,000	84,000
Preventive maintenance	157,500	84,000	115,500
Subtotal	$ 735,000	$ 315,000	$ 525,000
Appraisal Costs			
Setup for testing	$ 126,000	$ 63,000	$ 73,500
Product simulation and development	199,500	31,500	115,500
Quality audits	84,000	21,000	42,000
Vendor audits and sample testing	112,500	52,500	63,000
Subtotal	$ 522,000	$ 168,000	$ 294,000
Total Costs of Conformance	$ 1,257,000	$ 483,000	$ 819,000
Costs of Nonconformance to Customer Standards			
Internal Failure Costs			
Scrap and rework	$ 21,000	$ 189,000	$ 126,000
Reinspection of rework	15,750	126,000	73,500
Quality-related downtime	42,000	231,000	178,500
Losses caused by vendor scrap	26,250	84,000	52,500
Subtotal	$ 105,000	$ 630,000	$ 430,500
External Failure Costs			
Warranty claims	$ 47,250	$ 94,500	$ 84,000
Returned goods	15,750	68,250	36,750
Investigation of defects	26,250	78,750	57,750
Customer service	120,750	178,500	126,000
Subtotal	$ 210,000	$ 420,000	$ 304,500
Total Costs of Nonconformance	$ 315,000	$ 1,050,000	$ 735,000
Total Costs of Quality	$ 1,572,000	$ 1,533,000	$ 1,554,000
Total costs of quality as a percentage of sales	10.48%	10.22%	10.36%
Ratio of costs of conformance to total costs of quality	.80 to 1	.32 to 1	.53 to 1
Ratio of costs of nonconformance to total costs of quality	.20 to 1	.68 to 1	.47 to 1
Costs of nonconformance as a percentage of sales	2.10%	7.00%	4.90%

Evaluating Nonfinancial Measures of Quality   From the information presented in Part B of Exhibit 1, evaluate each company's experience in its pursuit of total quality management.

SOLUTION

The nonfinancial measures presented in Exhibit 1 identify trends for each company for three years—20x3, 20x4, and 20x5. Those data tend to support the findings in the analysis of the costs of quality.

> *Able Co.*   For Able Co. in 20x5, 98.6 percent of the raw materials and parts received from suppliers have been of high quality, and the quality over the three

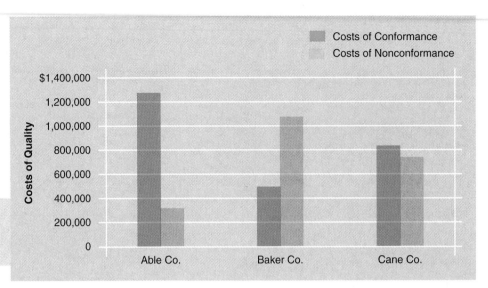

Figure 2
Comparison of Costs of Quality:
Conformance Versus
Nonconformance

years has been increasing. The product defect rate, measured in number of defects per million, has been decreasing rapidly, proof that the costs of conformance are having a positive effect. The percentage of on-time deliveries has been increasing, and both the order-return percentage and the number of customer complaints have been decreasing, which means that customer acceptance and satisfaction have been increasing.

Baker Co. Baker Co.'s experience is not encouraging. The number of high-quality shipments of materials and parts from vendors has been decreasing; the product defect rate has been increasing (it seems to be out of control); on-time deliveries were bad to begin with and have been getting worse; more goods have been returned each year; and customer complaints have been on the rise. All those signs reflect the company's high costs of nonconformance.

Cane Co. Cane Co. is making progress toward higher quality standards, but that progress is very slow. Most of the nonfinancial measures show a very slight positive trend. More money needs to be spent on the costs of conformance.

A graphical comparative analysis can be very useful when a manager is evaluating the performance of several operating units. Mere columns of numbers do not always adequately depict differences in operating performance and may be difficult to interpret. In such cases, a chart or graph can help managers picture what the data are saying. For example, the bar graph in Figure 2 illustrates the amounts that Able, Baker, and Cane are spending on costs of quality. It clearly shows that Able Co. is focusing on costs of conformance and has low costs of nonconformance. Baker Co., in contrast, is paying over $1,000,000 in costs of nonconformance because it has not tried to increase spending on prevention and appraisal. Cane Co. spends slightly more on costs of conformance than on costs of nonconformance, but, like Baker Co., it is spending too much on failure costs.

Measuring Service Quality

The quality of services rendered can be measured and analyzed. Many of the costs of product conformance and nonconformance also apply to the development and delivery of a service. Flaws in service design lead to poor-quality services. Timely service delivery is as important as timely product shipments. Customer satisfaction in a service business can be measured by services accepted or rejected, the number of complaints, and the number of returning customers. Poor service development leads to internal and external failure costs. Many of the costs-of-quality categories and several of the nonfinancial measures of quality can be applied directly to services and can be adopted by any type of service company. For example, the service departments of Mercedes-Benz dealers ask customers to complete a short, three-question form when they pay their bills. Chubb Insurance Company sends a brief questionnaire to customers after every claim. PBS has an Internet address where viewers can record their comments about programming.

Performance Measurement

OBJECTIVE 4

Describe performance measurement and state the issues that accompany management's ability to measure performance

One of the biggest changes to take place within the field of management accounting in the last decade has been the realization that as a company's management philosophy changes, so must the accompanying management accounting system. In addition, companies no longer rely on financial information as the sole basis for evaluating operating performance. So far in this text, we have discussed three new approaches to management: activity-based management, just-in-time operations, and total quality management. Each new management approach requires the development of new measures to evaluate operating performance. Without an effective performance measurement system, a company is unable to identify how well it is doing, where it is going, and what improvements are necessary if it is to become more profitable.

If a system of performance measurement is to succeed, managers must be able to distinguish between what is being measured and the actual measures used to monitor performance. For instance, product quality is not a performance measure. It is part of a management strategy: Management wants to produce the highest-quality product possible, given the resources available. Product quality is what management wants to measure. To measure product quality, the accountant must collaborate with production managers to develop a group of measures that will identify changes in product quality. The costs of quality can often be used for that purpose. Increases in prevention and appraisal costs tend to improve product quality, whereas increases in internal and external failure costs point to a reduction in product quality. However, these measures do not help production personnel determine what needs to be done to actually improve product quality.

So what performance measures can be used to direct production personnel to areas that need improvement? How do we monitor the level of product quality? Should we also monitor the production process to identify areas that need improvement or that are currently lowering product quality? These are all issues that must be dealt with when developing a set of performance measures. Examples of possible nonfinancial measures of product quality include number of defective units per million items produced, number of units scrapped, number of units of raw materials rejected when received, hours of employee training, and number of employee suggestions for process improvement implemented.

Product quality is not the only goal that is often mistaken for a performance measure. Machine and work cell flexibility is also a strategy or goal, not a performance measure. Specific measures must be developed to assess flexibility. One possibility is the time taken to reset machinery when changing from one product line to another. Customer satisfaction is also a goal or strategy that requires specific measures to monitor performance. Performance measures might include the number of products returned because of defects and the number of customers who place repeat orders.

We will now examine four additional areas that require specific performance measures. As you study those areas, keep in mind that every organization has many activities that require constant monitoring. Although we cannot cover every possibility in this chapter, all can be evaluated.

Inventory Control Performance

Within a JIT environment, the objective is to reduce inventory to a very low level or to zero. Therefore the management accountant must emphasize zero inventory balances and concentrate on measures that detect why inventory exists, not on measures that lead to accurate inventory valuation. Because inventory storage is often a nonvalue-adding activity, it should be reduced or eliminated.

Inventory control measures in a competitive operating environment are designed to reduce or eliminate inventory balances and related nonvalue-adding product costs. Old control measures such as those that focus on the appropriate size and timing of orders are no longer as useful; now the emphasis is on reducing the amount of space used to store materials, work in process, and finished goods. Measures that detect possible product obsolescence are very important. Inventory turnover measures such as the ratio of inventory to total sales have become more important because the number of turnovers during a year may double or triple with the adoption of JIT.

The inventory area remains critical to company profitability in a competitive operating environment. But there is heavy emphasis on nonfinancial measures to minimize the cost incurred in handling and storing inventory. The management accountant must develop measures that identify unreliable vendors because using fewer vendors who supply high-quality, timely raw material inputs is an objective. Another objective is to determine the amount of production time wasted because of engineering change orders and highlight the causes for management. The same approach must be applied to production schedule changes because time wasted here can be significant. Maintaining accurate records of required machine maintenance is an important control measure. Cutting the downtime resulting from machine breakdowns reduces the need for inventory. Every company's production process and inventory needs are different. When a set of inventory control measures is being developed, each must be tailored to a particular set of operating circumstances. Although most of these measures are nonfinancial, they are critical to gaining market share and remaining profitable.

Materials Cost and Scrap Control Performance

In a traditional situation, controlling the cost of materials meant seeking the lowest possible price while maintaining some minimum level of quality. Responsibility for this transaction was given to the Purchasing Department. Performance was measured by analyzing the materials price variance (the difference between the standard price and the actual price of the materials purchased). Today, emphasis is on the quality of materials, timeliness of delivery, and reasonableness of price. Because materials cost is often the largest single cost element, control in this area is extremely important.

Control of scrap also takes on a different focus in a competitive operating environment. The JIT and TQM objective is to incur no scrap in the production process; this is a significant difference from the traditional approach, which developed a normal scrap level or tolerance at or below which no corrective action was taken. The factory of the future sees scrap as a nonvalue-added series of costs. Each defective product has already cost the company materials costs, labor costs, and materials handling and manufacturing overhead costs. In the new competitive operating environment, specific records of scrap, rework, and defective units are kept. Machine operators are expected to detect flaws in the production process and to suggest possible corrective action on the spot. When a flaw is detected, the work cell should be stopped, and a solution should be developed immediately. Personnel should work continuously to eradicate bad or defective output.

The management accountant is responsible for developing a set of control measures for the scrap area. Although financial data about the cost of scrap are important and should be computed, nonfinancial measures should also be developed and maintained. Answers to questions such as the following should be analyzed and reported.

1. Where was the scrap detected?
2. How often does a product flaw occur at each of those locations?
3. Was the flaw detected at the point of machine or product failure, or at a later point in the manufacturing process?
4. Who is responsible for providing information about scrap incurrence to the management accountant?
5. Who should the scrap control reports go to, and how often should the reports be prepared?

Machine Management Performance

One of the most challenging areas for the management accountant in the JIT setting is keeping records of machine maintenance and downtime. Automated equipment requires large capital expenditures. For a company today, the largest item on the balance sheet is often automated machinery and equipment. Each piece of equipment has a specific capability, above which continuous operation is threatened. The machine management measures should have two objectives:

1. Evaluate performance of each piece of equipment in relation to its capacity.
2. Evaluate performance of maintenance personnel to keep to a prescribed maintenance program.

Machines must operate within specified tolerances, or damage and downtime could result. Keeping track of proper machine operation is not easy, but electronic surveillance is possible because of the computer network connecting all of the machines in a JIT cell. These controls should be programmed into the system and tracked as a regular part of the operation. The accountant should help prepare the reporting format for this function and analyze and report the findings to appropriate production personnel.

Because automated equipment requires a heavy investment and unanticipated machine downtime is not tolerated in a JIT environment, machine maintenance is critical. Minor maintenance tasks are part of the machine operator's duties. When the operating cell does not have an order to process, the operator is expected to perform routine maintenance. A regular program of extensive maintenance should also be implemented. Timing can be flexible, based on work orders, but extensive maintenance cannot be ignored. Detailed records of machine maintenance should be maintained, similar to the maintenance records required for commercial aircraft.

Total Product Delivery Performance

Beside emphasizing product quality and customer satisfaction, a company is also interested in product delivery. The delivery cycle time is the time period between acceptance of the order and final delivery of the product. It is important for a salesperson to be able to promise an accurate delivery schedule at the time a sales order is gained; the goal is for product delivery to be 100 percent on time and for each order to be filled 100 percent of the time. To meet this goal, a company must establish and maintain consistency and reliability within its manufacturing process.

JIT companies place heavy importance on the delivery cycle. One company cut its delivery cycle from more than six months to less than five weeks; another company cut its four-week delivery cycle to less than five days. Such reductions in delivery time have a significant impact on income from operations. The delivery cycle consists of the purchase order lead time (the time it takes for raw materials and parts to be ordered and received so that production can begin) production cycle time (the time it takes for the production personnel to make the product available for shipment to the customer), and delivery time (the time period between product completion and customer receipt of the item).

The management accountant should establish and maintain several control measures that help management minimize the delivery cycle. The accountant should provide managers with records and reports that monitor each product's purchase order lead time, production cycle time, delivery time, and total delivery cycle time. Trends should be highlighted, and the reports should be made available on a daily or weekly basis. Other measures designed to monitor the delivery cycle include an on-time delivery performance record and a daily or weekly report showing percentage of orders filled.

Examples of Performance Measures

Table 3 shows examples of control measures used in a globally competitive operating environment. Successful inventory performance may be identified through such measures as turnover rates and space reduction. Materials cost and scrap control performance are measured by incoming materials inspection results, materials as a percentage of total cost, actual scrap loss, and scrap as a percentage of total cost. Machine management performance is revealed through machine maintenance records, available time and downtime duration, and equipment capacity utilization information. Total product delivery performance is shown by on-time delivery data,

---

Table 3. Performance Measures in a Globally Competitive Operating Environment

Inventory Control Performance
  Turnover rates by product
  Turnover rates by location
  Space reduction
  Number of inventoried items

Materials Cost and Scrap Control Performance
  Quality of incoming goods
  Materials cost as a percentage
    of total cost
  Scrap loss by part, product, and
    operation
  Scrap loss as a percentage of total cost

Machine Management Performance
  Machine availability
  Amount of machine downtime
  Machine maintenance
  Equipment capacity utilization

Total Product Delivery Performance
  Order fulfillment rate
  On-time deliveries
  Production backlog
  Setup time
  Lead time (order to shipment)
  Cycle time (materials receipt to
    product shipment)
  Waste time (lead time less
    processing time)

production backlog information, and production lead time, cycle time, and waste time data.

Full Cost Profit Margin

OBJECTIVE 5

Define full cost profit margin *and identify the advantages of this measure of performance*

The new competitive operating environment has yet another dimension that must be analyzed when measuring performance. For years, management accountants have praised the usefulness of contribution margin as a performance measure. This number focuses only on revenue and the costs that are variable in relation to the products being sold. Fixed costs are excluded from the analysis so that they will not cloud the measurement of the performance of a division or a product.

Today, more and more companies are moving in the direction of computer-integrated manufacturing (CIM) systems, in which most manufacturing operations are coordinated by computer. In such systems, direct labor hours are mostly replaced by machine hours, and very little direct labor cost is incurred. A major part of the traditional variable product cost is replaced by expensive machinery, a fixed cost. As a result, contribution margins get larger and less meaningful.

Today, management accountants are turning to full cost profit margins to help measure the performance of a division or a product line. Full costing has always been an alternative for performance evaluation, but the approach was considered inaccurate because fixed costs had to be assigned to the product. Full cost profit margins are more appropriate in a capital-intensive environment. Full cost profit margin is the difference between total revenue and total costs traceable to a work cell or product. Computers have enabled the accountant to more easily trace costs to work cells. A CIM system can provide data that permit most costs to be treated as direct costs of the work cells. If direct traceability is not possible, new cost drivers have been established to more closely link indirect costs with cost objects, such as work cells or products. Only building occupancy costs remain as nontraceable costs to be assigned using a base such as machine hours or square footage occupied. Full cost profit margin, therefore, is a meaningful figure for performance evaluation as well as for decision analyses of new product lines.

An example points out the differences between contribution margin and full cost profit margin as measures of performance. Exhibit 3 shows operating data for three product lines of the Montvale Manufacturing Company. First, the cost data are summarized as they were before full cost profit margin was adopted. Next, the data have been reclassified to reflect the increased traceability of a CIM environment using full cost profit margin. The bottom portion of Exhibit 3 contains computations for contribution margins prior to the installation of the CIM system and for full cost profit margins following its adoption.

The Montvale Manufacturing Company example illustrates what is likely to happen when an organization switches from the contribution margin to the full cost profit margin approach to performance evaluation. Better methods of tracing costs and the identification of more direct costs provide a more complete picture of which product lines are most profitable. In our example, before the full cost profit margin was used, the most profitable product was 162. Product 214 was the second most profitable, and Product 305 generated the lowest profit. The order of product profitability remains the same after the full cost profit margin is adopted, but note the percentages of revenue for the contribution margins and the full cost profit margins: Costs have generally shifted from Products 162 and 305 to Product 214. Such a shift often occurs when activity-based costing is introduced, as more direct cost relationships are uncovered and better cost tracing is made possible. Under the traditional costing methods, Product 214 had an inflated profit structure, which could have led to some bad decisions on the part of Montvale's management. With full cost profit margins, management receives more accurate decision support and information for price determination.

Exhibit 3. Before and After Adopting Full Cost Profit Margin

Montvale Manufacturing Company
Product Performance Evaluation

	Product 162	Product 214	Product 305
Total revenue	$2,340,000	$2,400,000	$1,560,000
Before adopting full cost profit margin			
Variable costs			
Direct materials	$ 450,000	$ 560,000	$ 270,000
Direct labor	660,000	600,000	420,000
Variable manufacturing overhead	240,000	240,000	150,000
Variable selling expenses	90,000	80,000	60,000
Variable distribution costs	120,000	200,000	180,000
Total variable costs	$1,560,000	$1,680,000	$1,080,000
Assigned costs			
Fixed manufacturing overhead	$ 210,000	$ 360,000	$ 240,000
Fixed selling expenses	60,000	40,000	90,000
Fixed distribution costs	150,000	128,000	135,000
Total fixed costs	$ 420,000	$ 528,000	$ 465,000
After adopting full cost profit margin			
Traceable costs			
Direct materials	$ 450,000	$ 560,000	$ 270,000
Materials-related overhead	72,000	88,000	54,000
Direct labor	90,000	128,000	84,000
Indirect labor	108,000	112,000	90,000
Setup labor	66,000	104,000	66,000
Electrical power	54,000	80,000	48,000
Supervision	96,000	120,000	96,000
Repairs and maintenance	78,000	96,000	78,000
Operating supplies/lubricants	36,000	56,000	42,000
Other traceable indirect costs	114,000	168,000	120,000
Traceable selling expenses	102,000	104,000	72,000
Traceable distribution costs	156,000	284,000	204,000
Total traceable costs	$1,422,000	$1,900,000	$1,224,000
Assigned costs			
Nontraceable manufacturing overhead	$ 126,000	$ 244,000	$ 132,000
Nontraceable selling and distribution costs	96,000	112,000	108,000
Total nontraceable costs	$ 222,000	$ 356,000	$ 240,000

(continued)

Exhibit 3. Before and After Adopting Full Cost Profit Margin *(continued)*

	Product 162	Product 214	Product 305
Product Performance Measures			
Before adopting full cost profit margin			
Contribution margin			
Total revenue	$2,340,000	$2,400,000	$1,560,000
Less variable costs	1,560,000	1,680,000	1,080,000
Contribution margin	$ 780,000	$ 720,000	$ 480,000
Less total fixed costs	420,000	528,000	465,000
Operating profit	$ 360,000	$ 192,000	$ 15,000
Contribution margin as a percentage of revenue	33.33%	30.00%	30.77%
Operating profit as a percentage of revenue	15.38%	8.00%	.96%
After adopting full cost profit margin			
Full cost profit margin			
Total revenues	$2,340,000	$2,400,000	$1,560,000
Less total traceable costs	1,422,000	1,900,000	1,224,000
Full cost profit margin	$ 918,000	$ 500,000	$ 336,000
Less total nontraceable costs	222,000	356,000	240,000
Operating profit	$ 696,000	$ 144,000	$ 96,000
Full cost profit margin as a percentage of revenue	39.23%	20.83%	21.54%
Operating profit as a percentage of revenue	29.74%	6.00%	6.15%

Chapter Review

REVIEW OF LEARNING OBJECTIVES

1. **Define *cost management*, describe a cost management system, and explain how the management cycle is used to implement a cost management system.** Cost management is the management and control of activities to determine accurate product costs, to improve business processes, to eliminate waste, to identify cost drivers, to plan operations, and to set business strategies. In a cost management system (CMS), the primary focus is on the management of activities, not costs, for both product costing and cost control. A CMS plays a key role in planning, managing, and reducing costs. Cost cutting is not accomplished merely by slashing the amount of resources a department can use to make a product, as happens in a traditional costing system. A CMS relies on the concept of continuous improvement to reduce costs while still increasing product quality. When continuous improvement is employed, a company first designs a product so that its target cost is achieved and then can increase profits by making ongoing improvements to reduce costs further. Finally, cost assignment within a cost management system is far superior to that in traditional cost systems.

By focusing on activities, a CMS provides managers with improved knowledge of the processes for which they are responsible. The CMS pinpoints resource usage for each activity and fosters managerial decisions that lead to continuous improvement throughout the organization.

The management cycle is used to plan and implement a new cost management system. During the planning stage, managers consider which new management approaches to implement, then create a new cost management system to support their choice. During the executing stage, managers activate the processes that will implement the new system. During the reviewing stage, managers develop and implement new performance measures for evaluating product quality, process quality and flexibility, effectiveness of distribution, and customer satisfaction. Finally, during the reporting stage, managers develop reports of the various performance measures, identify who gets the reports, and determine how often reports are prepared.

2. **Define *total quality management* and identify and compute the costs of quality for products and services.** Total quality management is an organizational environment in which all business functions work together to build quality into a firm's products or services. The costs of quality are measures of costs specifically related to the achievement or nonachievement of product or service quality. The costs of quality have two components. One is the cost of conforming to a customer's product or service standards by preventing defects and failures and by appraising quality and performance. The other is the cost of nonconformance—the costs incurred when defects are discovered before a product is shipped and the costs incurred after a defective product or faulty service is delivered.

The objective is to reduce or eliminate the costs of nonconformance, the internal and external failure costs that are associated with customer dissatisfaction. To this end, management can justify high initial costs of conformance if they minimize the total costs of quality over the product's or service's life cycle.

3. **Use nonfinancial measures of quality to evaluate operating performance.** Nonfinancial measures of quality are related to product design, raw materials input, in-process and delivery control, and customer acceptance. Those measures, together with the costs of quality, help a firm meet its goal of continuously improving product or service quality and the production process.

4. **Describe performance measurement and state the issues that accompany management's ability to measure performance.** Companies no longer rely on financial information as the sole basis for evaluating operating performance. Without an effective performance measurement system, a company is unable to identify how well it is doing, where it is going, and what improvements are necessary to become more profitable. Each new management approach requires the development of new measures to evaluate operating performance. Many of those measures are nonfinancial in nature.

If a system of performance measurement is to succeed, managers must be able to distinguish between what is being measured and the actual measures used to monitor performance. They must also consider exactly what kind of performance they want to measure and select the most effective performance measures for accomplishing their goals.

5. **Define *full cost profit margin* and identify the advantages of this measure of performance.** Full cost profit margin is the difference between total revenue and total costs traceable to a work cell or product. This measure is more meaningful than contribution margin because additional costs are brought into the analysis. Full cost profit margin is also a more accurate measure of profitability.

REVIEW OF CONCEPTS AND TERMINOLOGY

The following concepts and terms were introduced in this chapter:

LO 2   **Appraisal costs:** The costs of activities that measure, evaluate, or audit products, processes, or services to ensure conformance to quality standards and performance requirements; a cost of conformance.

LO 3   **Computer-aided design (CAD):** A computer-based engineering system with a built-in program to detect product design flaws.

LO 5   **Computer-integrated manufacturing (CIM) system:** A system in which most manufacturing activities are coordinated by computer.

LO 1 Cost management: The management and control of activities to determine accurate product costs, to improve business processes, to eliminate waste, to identify cost drivers, to plan operations, and to set business strategies.

LO 1 Cost management system (CMS): A management accounting and reporting system that identifies, monitors, and maintains continuous, detailed analyses of a company's activities and provides managers with timely measures of operating results.

LO 2 Costs of conformance: The costs incurred to produce a quality product or service.

LO 2 Costs of nonconformance: The costs incurred to correct defects in a product or service.

LO 2 Costs of quality: The costs specifically associated with the achievement or nonachievement of product or service quality.

LO 4 Delivery cycle time: The time period between acceptance of an order and final delivery of the product.

LO 4 Delivery time: The time period between product completion and customer receipt of the item.

LO 2 External failure costs: The costs incurred after the delivery of a defective product or service; a cost of nonconformance.

LO 5 Full cost profit margin: The difference between total revenue and total costs traceable to a work cell or product.

LO 2 Internal failure costs: The costs incurred when a defect is discovered before a product or service is delivered to a customer; a cost of nonconformance.

LO 2 Prevention costs: The costs associated with the prevention of defects and failures in products and services; a cost of conformance.

LO 4 Production cycle time: The time it takes for production personnel to make the product available for shipment to the customer.

LO 4 Purchase order lead time: The time it takes for raw materials and parts to be ordered and received so that production can begin.

LO 2 Quality: An operating environment in which a company's product or service meets or conforms to a customer's specifications the first time it is produced or delivered.

LO 2 Total quality management (TQM): An organizational environment in which all business functions work together to build quality into the firm's products or services.

REVIEW PROBLEM
Analysis of Nonfinancial Data—Linda Products, Inc.

LO 2
LO 3
LO 4
The Cooper Motor Division of Linda Products, Inc., has been in operation for six years. Three months ago a new manufacturing system was installed in the small motors department. A just-in-time approach is followed for everything from ordering materials and parts to product shipment and delivery. The division's superintendent is very interested in the initial results of the venture. The following data have been collected for your analysis.

	Weeks							
	1	**2**	**3**	**4**	**5**	**6**	**7**	**8**
Warranty claims	2	4	1	1	0	5	7	11
Average setup time (hours)	.3	.25	.25	.3	.25	.2	.2	.15
Average lead time (hours)	2.4	2.3	2.2	2.3	2.35	2.4	2.4	2.5
Average cycle time (hours)	2.1	2.05	1.95	2	2	2.1	2.2	2.3
Average process time (hours)	1.9	1.9	1.85	1.8	1.9	1.95	1.95	1.9
Number of inventoried items	2,450	2,390	2,380	2,410	2,430	2,460	2,610	2,720
Customer complaints	12	12	10	8	9	7	6	4
Times inventory turnover	4.5	4.4	4.4	4.35	4.3	4.25	4.25	4.35
Production backlog (units)	9,210	9,350	9,370	9,420	9,410	8,730	8,310	7,950
Machine downtime (hours)	86.5	83.1	76.5	80.1	90.4	100.6	120.2	124.9
Parts scrapped (units)	112	126	134	118	96	89	78	64
Equipment utilization rate (%)	98.2	98.6	98.9	98.5	98.1	97.3	96.6	95.7
On-time deliveries (%)	93.2	94.1	96.5	95.4	92.1	90.5	88.4	89.3
Machine maintenance time (hours)	34.6	32.2	28.5	22.1	18.5	12.6	19.7	26.4

1. Analyze the performance of the Cooper Motor Division for the eight-week period. Focus on the following areas of performance:
   a. Product quality
   b. Total product delivery
   c. Inventory control
   d. Materials cost and scrap control
   e. Machine management
2. Summarize your findings in a report to the division's superintendent.

ANSWER TO REVIEW PROBLEM

The data given were reorganized in the following manner, and two additional pieces of information, average waste time and estimated number of units sold, were calculated from the given information.

1. Analysis of performance

	Weeks								Weekly
	1	2	3	4	5	6	7	8	Average
Product quality performance									
Customer complaints	12	12	10	8	9	7	6	4	8.5 complaints
Warranty claims	2	4	1	1	0	5	7	11	3.875 claims
Total product delivery performance									
On-time deliveries (%)	93.2	94.1	96.5	95.4	92.1	90.5	88.4	89.3	92.44 %
Average setup time (hours) (a)	.3	.25	.25	.3	.25	.2	.2	.15	.238 hours
Average lead time (hours)	2.4	2.3	2.2	2.3	2.4	2.4	2.4	2.5	2.356 hours
Average cycle time (hours)	2.1	2.1	2.0	2.0	2.0	2.1	2.2	2.3	2.088 hours
Average process time (hours) (b)	1.9	1.9	1.85	1.8	1.9	1.95	1.95	1.9	1.894 hours
Production backlog (units)	9,210	9,350	9,370	9,420	9,410	8,730	8,310	7,950	8,969 units
Average waste time (hours) (average lead time less average process time) (a-b)	.5	.4	.35	.5	.45	.45	.45	.6	.463 hours
Inventory control performance									
Number of inventoried items (units) (c)	2,450	2,390	2,380	2,410	2,430	2,460	2,610	2,720	2,481 units
Times inventory turnover (d)	4.5	4.4	4.4	4.35	4.3	4.25	4.25	4.35	4.35 times
Estimated number of units sold (c × d)	11,025	10,516	10,472	10,484	10,449	10,455	11,093	11,832	10,791 units
Materials cost and scrap control performance									
Parts scrapped (units)	112	126	134	118	96	89	78	64	102.125 units
Machine management performance									
Machine downtime (hours)	86.5	83.1	76.5	80.1	90.4	100.6	120.2	124.9	95.288 hours
Equipment utilization rate (%)	98.2	98.6	98.9	98.5	98.1	97.3	96.6	95.7	97.74 %
Machine maintenance time (hours)	34.6	32.2	28.5	22.1	18.5	12.6	19.7	26.4	24.325 hours

2. Memorandum to division superintendent.

My analysis of the operating data for the Cooper Motor Division for the last eight weeks revealed the following:

Product quality performance
Product quality seems to be improving, with the number of complaints decreasing rapidly. However, warranty claims have risen significantly in the past three weeks, which may be a signal of quality problems.

Total product delivery performance
Although the averages for the product delivery measures seem great when compared to our old standards, we are having trouble maintaining the averages established eight weeks ago. Waste time is increasing, which is contrary to our goals. Backlogged orders are decreasing, which is a good sign from a JIT viewpoint but could spell problems in the future. On-time deliveries percentages are slipping. On the positive side, setup time seems to be under control. Emphasis needs to be placed on reducing lead time, cycle time, and process time.

Inventory control performance
This area spells trouble. Inventory size is increasing, and the number of inventory turns is decreasing. The results are increased storage costs and decreased units sold. The last two weeks do show signs of improvement.

Materials cost and scrap control performance
The incidence of scrap has decreased significantly, which is very good. We had to increase cycle time to correct our manufacturing problems, which accounts for the increases in that area. With the scrap problem under control, process and cycle times may improve in the future.

Machine management performance
Machine downtime is increasing, which is consistent with the scrap report. Also, the equipment utilization rate is down. Machine maintenance time had also decreased, but has increased in the past two weeks. Department managers should be made aware of these pending problem areas.

Overall, we can see good signs from the new equipment, but we need to stay on top of all pending problem areas.

Chapter Assignments

BUILDING YOUR KNOWLEDGE FOUNDATION

Questions

1. Define *cost management* and describe a cost management system.
2. What is total quality management?
3. How can the management accountant help a company achieve total quality management?
4. How is *quality* defined in business? What are the costs of quality?
5. Identify and describe the categories of costs of quality.
6. Name five nonfinancial measures of quality and tell what each is designed to measure.
7. Identify the four types of nonfinancial analyses used to measure product quality performance. Describe the kind of data used in each analysis.
8. Why is customer satisfaction emphasized in a competitive operating environment? How is this attention related to profitability?
9. In a competitive operating environment, "inventory controls are designed to eliminate inventory balances and nonvalue-adding costs connected with inventory storage and maintenance." Do you agree? Why is there so much interest in eliminating inventories?

10. In a JIT operating environment, formal inspection activities are eliminated, but product quality controls are given high priority. How is this accomplished?

11. Why are accurate records of machine maintenance so critical in an operating environment that utilizes work cells and a continuous production flow?

12. Define *full cost profit margin* and contrast it with contribution margin. Why is full cost profit margin a better measure of product line profitability than contribution margin?

Short Exercises

SE 1.

LO 1 *Traits of a Cost Management System*

Identify three traits of cost management systems that differentiate them from traditional systems. Explain how each trait helps control costs.

SE 2.

LO 1 *Continuous Improvement*

Maxine Gianner is the controller for Dixon Industries. She has been asked to develop a plan for installing a continuous improvement environment in her company. The president has already approved the concept and has given Maxine the go-ahead. What steps should Maxine plan on taking in each stage of the management cycle?

SE 3.

LO 2 *Costs of Quality in a Service Business*

Sharkey-Elam Insurance Agency incurred the following activity costs related to service quality. Identify those that are costs of conformance (CC) and those that are costs of nonconformance (CN).

Policy processing improvements	$76,400
Customer complaints response	34,100
Policy writer training	12,300
Policy error losses	82,700
Policy proofing	39,500

SE 4.

LO 2 *Measures of*
LO 3 *Quality*

Internal reports on quality at the Debneth Publishing Company generated the following information for the College Division for the first three months of the year:

Total sales	$60,000,000
Costs of quality:	
Prevention	523,000
Appraisal	477,000
Internal failure	1,360,000
External failure	640,000

Compute:

a. Total costs of quality as a percentage of sales
b. Ratio of costs of conformance to total costs of quality
c. Ratio of costs of nonconformance to total costs of quality
d. Costs of nonconformance as a percentage of total sales

SE 5.

LO 3 *Nonfinancial Measures of Quality*

For a fast-food restaurant that specializes in deluxe cheeseburgers, identify two nonfinancial measures of good product quality and two nonfinancial measures of poor product quality.

SE 6.

LO 4 *Total Product Delivery Performance Evaluation*

Quality Cosmetics, Inc., has developed a set of nonfinancial measures to evaluate on-time total product delivery performance for one of its best-selling cosmetics. The following data have been generated for the past four weeks.

Week	Purchase Order Lead Time	Production Cycle Time	Delivery Time
1	2.4 days	3.5 days	4.0 days
2	2.3 days	3.5 days	3.5 days
3	2.4 days	3.3 days	3.4 days
4	2.5 days	3.2 days	3.3 days

Compute total delivery cycle time for each week. Evaluate the total product delivery performance. Is there an area that needs management's attention?

SE 7.

LO 5 *Full Cost Profit Margin*

Maples Company hired a consultant to refine its cost management system. One of the changes implemented was a shift in division performance indicators from contribution margin to full cost profit margin. The Egglund Division generated the information summarized below for the last two quarters of the year.

Month	Revenue	Variable Costs	Traceable Fixed Costs
July–September	$1,400,000	$450,000	$630,000
October–December	2,550,000	980,000	680,000

Evaluate the performance of the division by computing the contribution margin and the full cost profit margin for each quarter. Also compute the percentages of each to total revenue. How is the division performing?

Exercises

E 1.

LO 1 *Adapting to Changing Information Needs*

The management of Stepanov Software Company feels that it must make changes in the company's operating environment. What outside factors might influence management to make changes? What changes can management make within the company? Identify the new information the management accounting system would need to provide for each of the following changes.

1. Management wants to reduce the size of inventories.
2. Management wants to focus on reducing the throughput time of its operations.

E 2.

LO 2 *Costs of Quality*
LO 3

Konstantinos Corp. produces and supplies automotive manufacturers with the mechanisms used to adjust the seat positions of front seating units. Several new competitors have recently entered the marketplace, and management is concerned that the quality of the company's current products may be surpassed by these competitors. The controller was asked to conduct an analysis of the current efforts to improve product quality. His analysis generated the following quality costs for January 20xx.

Training of employees	$22,400	Returned goods	$98,700
Customer service	13,600	Preventive maintenance	26,500
Reinspection of rework	28,000	Quality engineering	18,700
Quality audits	31,300	Setup for testing new products	42,100
Design review	27,500	Scrap and rework	76,500
Warranty claims	67,100	Losses caused by vendor scrap	65,800
Sample testing of materials	27,400	Product simulation	28,400

1. Prepare a detailed analysis of the costs of quality.
2. Comment on the company's current efforts to improve product quality.

E 3.

LO 2 *Measuring Costs of*
LO 3 *Quality*

Ahn Corporation operates using two departments that produce two separate product lines. The company has been implementing a total quality management operating philosophy over the past year. Revenue and costs of quality data for that year are presented below.

	Dept. A	Dept. B	Totals
Annual Sales	$9,200,000	$11,000,000	$20,200,000
Costs of Quality			
Prevention costs	$ 186,000	$ 124,500	$ 310,500
Appraisal costs	136,000	68,000	204,000
Internal failure costs	94,000	197,500	291,500
External failure costs	44,000	160,000	204,000
Totals	$ 460,000	$ 550,000	$ 1,010,000

Which department is taking the most serious approach to implementing TQM? Base your answer on the following computations:

a. Total costs of quality as a percentage of sales
b. Ratio of costs of conformance to total costs of quality
c. Ratio of costs of nonconformance to total costs of quality
d. Costs of nonconformance as a percentage of sales

LO 3 *Nonfinancial Measures of Quality and TQM*

E 4. "A satisfied customer is the most important goal of this company!" was the opening remark of the corporate president, Lester Tepper, at the monthly executive committee meeting of Wickenkamp Company. The company manufactures piping products for customers in sixteen western states. Four divisions, each producing a different type of piping material, make up the company's organizational structure. Tepper, a proponent of total quality management, was reacting to the latest measures of quality data from the four divisions. The data are presented below.

	Brass Division	Plastics Division	Aluminum Division	Copper Division	Company Averages
Vendor on-time delivery	97.20%	91.40%	98.10%	88.20%	93.73%
Production quality rates (defective parts per million)	1,440	2,720	1,370	4,470	2,500
On-time shipments	89.20%	78.40%	91.80%	75.60%	83.75%
Returned orders	1.10%	4.60%	.80%	6.90%	3.35%
Number of customer complaints	24	56	10	62	38
Number of warranty claims	7	12	4	14	9.3[*]

[*]Rounded.

Why was Tepper upset? Which division or divisions do not appear to have satisfied customers? What criteria did you use to make your decision?

LO 4 *Nonfinancial Data Analysis*

E 5. Nomura Company makes racing bicycles. Its Lightning model is considered the top of the line within the industry. Three months ago the company purchased and installed a computer-integrated manufacturing system for the Lightning line, with emphasis on improving quality and reducing production time. Management is interested in cutting time in all phases of the delivery cycle.

Following are data the controller's office gathered for the past four-week period.

	Weeks			
	1	2	3	4
Average process time (hours)	24.6	24.4	23.8	23.2
Average setup time (hours)	1.4	1.3	1.2	1.1
Customer complaints	7	6	8	9
Delivery time (hours)	34.8	35.2	36.4	38.2
On-time deliveries (%)	98.1	97.7	97.2	96.3
Production backlog (units)	8,230	8,340	8,320	8,430
Production cycle time (hours)	28.5	27.9	27.2	26.4
Purchase order lead time (hours)	38.5	36.2	35.5	34.1
Warranty claims	2	3	3	2

Analyze the performance of the Lightning model for the four-week period, focusing specifically on product quality and product delivery.

LO 5 *Full Cost Profit Margin*

E 6. Burnett Enterprises produces all-purpose sports vehicles. The company recently installed a computer-integrated manufacturing system for its AJ-25 product line. The accounting system has been recast to reflect the new operating process using full cost profit margin. Following are monthly operating data for periods before and after the new installation.

	Product AJ-25
Average monthly revenue	$1,350,000
Total operating costs	
For month before new installation and adoption of full cost profit margin:	
Direct materials	$ 320,720
Direct labor	444,740
Variable manufacturing overhead	134,020
Variable selling expenses	51,340
Variable distribution costs	55,120
Fixed manufacturing overhead	456,200
Fixed selling expenses	132,300
Fixed distribution costs	189,700
For month after new installation and adoption of full cost profit margin:	
Direct materials	$ 320,720
Materials-related overhead	58,230
Direct labor	62,010
Indirect labor	99,216
Setup labor	56,144
Electrical power	34,804
Supervision	35,828
Repairs and maintenance	46,852
Operating supplies and lubricants	11,024
Other traceable indirect costs	20,316
Traceable selling expenses	62,364
Traceable distribution costs	57,876
Nontraceable manufacturing overhead	245,300
Nontraceable selling and distribution costs	178,200

Using the data after the new installation and adoption of full cost profit margin, compute the full cost profit margin for product AJ-25. Include full cost profit margin as a percentage of revenue and operating profit as a percentage of revenue in your answer.

LO 5 *Margin and Performance Measurement*

E 7. Robolini Products, Ltd., specializes in winter sports equipment and has four main product lines. Recently, the controller's staff installed an activity-based costing system and began tracing many of the fixed costs to the four product lines. The following income statement information was generated during the first quarter of the current year.

	Product Line 1	Product Line 2	Product Line 3	Product Line 4	Company Totals
Total sales	$12,500,000	$16,300,000	$18,800,000	$14,200,000	$61,800,000
Contribution margin	3,125,000	3,260,000	6,580,000	4,260,000	17,225,000
Full cost profit margin	1,875,000	2,934,000	5,076,000	3,692,000	13,577,000
Total nontraceable costs					8,520,000
Net income					5,057,000

Management has asked the controller to interpret this information to see if there have been any significant changes in the profitability of the four product lines. Analyze the data to see if profitability has shifted because of the ABC costing system. (**Hint:** Transform the data into percentages of total sales.) Did profitability shift between product lines? Which products increased in profitability? Which ones declined in profitability?

Problems

P 1.

LO 2 *Costs and*
LO 3 *Nonfinancial*
Measures of Quality

The Abrams Company operates as three autonomous divisions. Each division has a general manager in charge of product development, production, and distribution. Management recently adopted total quality management, and the divisions now track, record, and analyze their costs and nonfinancial measures of quality. All three divisions are operating in a global, highly competitive marketplace. Sales and quality-related data for April are summarized below.

	East Division	Central Division	West Division
Annual sales	$8,500,000	$9,500,000	$13,000,000
Costs of quality			
Setup for testing	$ 51,600	$ 112,800	$ 183,950
Quality audits	17,200	79,100	109,650
Failure analysis	103,100	14,700	92,700
Quality training of employees	60,200	188,000	167,700
Scrap and rework	151,000	18,800	154,800
Quality planning activities	34,400	94,000	108,200
Preventive maintenance	65,800	148,000	141,900
Warranty claims	107,500	42,300	106,050
Customer service	151,500	108,100	154,800
Quality engineering	94,600	235,000	232,200
Product simulation and development	24,700	178,600	141,900
Losses caused by vendor scrap	77,400	23,500	64,500
Returned goods	152,500	16,200	45,150
Product recalls	64,500	32,900	64,500
Total costs of quality	$1,156,000	$1,292,000	$ 1,768,000
Nonfinancial measures of quality			
Defective parts per million	3,410	1,104	1,940
Returned orders	7.40%	1.10%	3.20%
Customer complaints	62	12	30
Number of warranty claims	74	16	52

REQUIRED

1. Prepare an analysis of the costs of quality of the three divisions. Categorize the costs as (a) costs of conformance with subsets of prevention costs and appraisal costs or (b) costs of nonconformance with subsets of internal failure costs and external failure costs. Compute the total costs for each category for each division.
2. Compute the percentage of sales of each cost-of-quality total for each division.
3. Interpret the cost-of-quality data for each division. Is each division's product of high or low quality? Explain your answers. Are the divisions headed in the right direction to be globally competitive?
4. Evaluate the nonfinancial measures of quality in terms of customer satisfaction. Are the results consistent with your analysis in **3**? Explain your answers.

P 2.

LO 2 *Interpreting*
LO 3 *Measures*
LO 4 *of Quality*

Carr Corporation supplies electronic circuitry to major appliance manufacturers in all parts of the world. Producing a high-quality product in each of the company's four divisions is the mission of management. Each division is required to record and report its efforts to achieve quality in all of its primary product lines. The information on the next page was submitted to the company's chief financial officer for the most recent three-month period.

	Anchor Division		Bravo Division		Carter Division		Dano Division	
	Amount	% of Revenue	Amount	% of Revenue	Amount	% of Revenue	Amount	% of Revenue
Costs of Quality								
Costs of conformance								
Prevention costs:								
Quality training for employees	$ 23,600		$15,600		$ 4,400		$ 8,900	
Quality engineering	45,900		19,700		3,100		9,400	
Preventive machine maintenance	13,800		14,400		5,800		11,100	
Total prevention costs	$ 83,300	5.55%	$49,700	3.11%	$ 13,300	0.95%	$ 29,400	1.73%
Appraisal costs:								
Product simulation	$ 21,400		$19,500		$ 3,500		$ 6,900	
Setups for product testing	17,600		11,900		6,100		8,700	
Vendor audits	9,800		10,100		4,100		7,300	
Total appraisal costs	$ 48,800	3.25%	$41,500	2.59%	$ 13,700	0.98%	$ 22,900	1.35%
Total costs of conformance	$132,100	8.81%	$91,200	5.70%	$ 27,000	1.93%	$ 52,300	3.08%
Costs of nonconformance								
Internal failure costs:								
Quality-related downtime	$ 6,500		$ 8,300		$ 26,800		$ 22,600	
Scrap and rework	7,800		9,100		17,500		16,200	
Losses caused by vendor scrap	3,600		7,200		31,200		19,900	
Total internal failure costs	$ 17,900	1.19%	$24,600	1.54%	$ 75,500	5.39%	$ 58,700	3.45%
External failure costs:								
Warranty claims	$ 2,500		$ 4,400		$ 22,600		$ 17,100	
Customer service	6,400		8,100		31,600		22,300	
Returned goods	3,100		5,600		29,900		19,800	
Total external failure costs	$ 12,000	0.80%	$18,100	1.13%	$ 84,100	6.01%	$ 59,200	3.48%
Total costs of nonconformance	$ 29,900	1.99%	$42,700	2.67%	$159,600	11.40%	$117,900	6.94%
Total costs of quality	$162,000	10.80%	$133,900	8.37%	$186,600	13.33%	$170,200	10.02%
Ratios of nonfinancial measures:								
Number of sales to number of warranty claims	996 to 1		372 to 1		168 to 1		225 to 1	
Number of products produced to number of products reworked	6,430 to 1		3,257 to 1		1,420 to 1		2,140 to 1	
Change in throughput time (positive amount means time reduction)	5.600%		2.163%		−4.615%		−1.241%	
Total number of deliveries to number of late deliveries	290 to 1		168 to 1		86 to 1		128 to 1	

REQUIRED

1. Rank the divisions in order of their apparent product quality.
2. What three measures were most important in your rankings in 1? Why?
3. Which division is most successful in its bid to improve quality? What measures illustrate its high quality rating?
4. Consider the two divisions producing the lowest-quality products. What actions would you recommend to the management of each division? Where should their quality dollars be spent?

P 3.

LO 2 *Analysis of*
LO 3 *Nonfinancial Data*
LO 4

Dimitrio Electronics Company was formed in 1969. Over the years the company has become known for its high-quality electronics products and its on-time delivery. Six months ago management decided to install a computer-integrated manufacturing system for its Sensitive Components Department. The new equipment produces the entire component so the finished product is ready to be shipped when needed. The controller's staff gathered the data on the next page during the past eight-week period.

				Weeks				
	1	**2**	**3**	**4**	**5**	**6**	**7**	**8**
Average process time (hours)	10.9	11.1	10.6	10.8	11.2	11.8	12.2	13.6
Average setup time (hours)	2.5	2.6	2.6	2.8	2.7	2.4	2.2	2.2
Customer complaints	11	10	23	15	9	7	5	6
Delivery time (hours)	26.2	26.4	26.1	25.9	26.2	26.6	27.1	26.4
Equipment utilization rate (%)	96.2	96.1	96.3	97.2	97.4	96.2	96.4	95.3
Machine downtime (hours)	106.4	108.1	120.2	110.4	112.8	102.2	124.6	136.2
Machine maintenance time (hours)	64.8	66.7	72.6	74.2	76.8	66.6	80.4	88.2
Number of inventoried items	3,450	3,510	3,680	3,790	3,620	3,490	3,560	3,260
On-time deliveries (%)	97.2	97.5	97.6	98.2	98.4	96.4	94.8	92.6
Parts scrapped	243	268	279	245	256	280	290	314
Production backlog (units)	10,246	10,288	10,450	10,680	10,880	11,280	11,350	12,100
Production cycle time (hours)	16.5	16.4	16.3	16.1	16.3	17.6	19.8	21.8
Purchase order lead time (hours)	15.2	15.1	14.9	14.6	14.6	13.2	12.4	12.6
Times inventory turnover	2.1	2.3	2.2	2.4	2.2	2.1	2.1	1.9
Warranty claims	4	8	2	1	6	4	2	3

REQUIRED

1. Analyze the performance of the Sensitive Components Department for the eight-week period. Focus on performance in the following areas:
   a. Product quality
   b. Total product delivery
   c. Inventory control
   d. Materials cost and scrap control
   e. Machine management
2. Summarize your findings in a report to the department's superintendent.

P 4.

LO 5 *Full Cost Profit Margin*

St. Cloud Molded Products Company produces three main products, identified as B4, C10, and F17. Two months ago, the company installed three fully automated computer-integrated manufacturing systems for the product lines. At the same time, the company added an activity-based costing system that allows for more tracing of costs to cost centers. The controller is anxious to see how the machinery affects operating costs for the three products. Product C10 has been a low performer for the company and is being out-priced on the market. The line may have to be dropped.

Monthly operating data for before and after the new installation appear at the top of the next page:

REQUIRED

1. Recast the information about the three products into an analysis that reveals total traceable and total nontraceable costs (a) before and (b) after the new systems were installed and the full cost profit margin was adopted.
2. Describe and differentiate between full cost profit margin and contribution margin.
3. Using the before-installation and full cost profit margin data, prepare an analysis that presents contribution margin, operating profit, contribution margin as a percentage of revenue, and operating profit as a percentage of revenue.
4. Using the after-installation and full cost profit margin data, prepare an analysis that presents full cost profit margin, operating profit, full cost profit margin as a percentage of revenue, and operating profit as a percentage of revenue.
5. Should the company drop the C10 product line? Defend your answer.

St. Cloud Molded Products Company
Product Performance Evaluation

	Assembly B4	Assembly C10	Assembly F17
Total revenue	$4,700,000	$5,250,000	$3,500,000
Total operating costs			
Before new installation and adoption of full cost profit margin:			
Direct materials	$1,201,600	$1,446,800	$ 874,400
Direct labor	1,414,700	1,661,200	885,600
Variable manufacturing overhead	313,100	159,000	58,400
Variable selling expenses	237,700	255,400	223,200
Variable distribution costs	183,600	310,800	193,600
Fixed manufacturing overhead	456,200	654,200	432,600
Fixed selling expenses	132,300	103,290	196,700
Fixed distribution costs	189,700	304,520	291,800
After new installation and adoption of full cost profit margin:			
Direct materials	$1,201,600	$1,446,800	$ 874,400
Materials-related overhead	160,650	150,220	112,640
Direct labor	206,550	227,920	147,840
Indirect labor	330,480	331,520	260,480
Setup labor	120,320	117,560	54,880
Electrical power	92,620	103,240	66,320
Supervision	119,340	145,040	91,520
Repairs and maintenance	156,060	160,580	130,240
Operating supplies/lubricants	26,720	36,620	18,160
Other traceable indirect costs	100,980	108,780	84,480
Traceable selling expenses	174,420	170,940	133,760
Traceable distribution costs	192,780	202,020	154,880
Nontraceable manufacturing overhead	245,300	323,100	241,100
Nontraceable selling and distribution costs	178,200	231,400	198,760

Alternate Problems

LO 2 *Costs and*
LO 3 *Nonfinancial*
Measures of Quality

P 5. Rennie Enterprises, Inc., operates as three autonomous companies. Each company has a chief executive officer who oversees its operations. At a recent corporate meeting, the company CEOs agreed to adopt total quality management for their operations and to track, record, and analyze their costs and nonfinancial measures of quality. All three companies are operating in a highly competitive global market. Sales and quality-related data for September are summarized at the top of the next page.

REQUIRED

1. Prepare an analysis of the costs of quality for the three companies. Categorize the costs as (a) costs of conformance, with subsets of prevention costs and appraisal costs or (b) costs of nonconformance, with subsets of internal failure costs and external failure costs. Compute the total costs for each category for each of the three companies.
2. Compute the percentage of sales for each cost-of-quality total for each company.

	Currence Company	Aspen Company	Prescott Company
Annual sales	$11,600,000	$13,300,000	$10,800,000
Costs of quality			
Sample preparation	$ 69,000	$ 184,800	$ 130,800
Quality audits	58,900	115,550	141,700
Failure analysis	188,500	92,400	16,350
Design review	80,500	176,700	218,000
Scrap and rework	207,000	160,800	21,200
Quality planning activities	49,200	105,600	231,600
Preventive maintenance	92,000	158,400	163,500
Warranty adjustments	149,550	105,600	49,050
Customer service	201,250	198,000	80,050
Quality training of employees	149,500	237,600	272,500
Product simulation and development	34,500	145,200	202,700
Reinspection of rework	126,500	66,000	27,250
Returned goods	212,750	72,600	16,350
Customer complaint processing	109,250	162,450	38,150
Total costs of quality	$ 1,728,400	$ 1,981,700	$ 1,609,200
Nonfinancial measures of quality			
Number of warranty claims	61	36	12
Customer complaints	107	52	18
Defective parts per million	4,610	2,190	1,012
Returned orders	9.20%	4.10%	.90%

3. Interpret the cost-of-quality data for each company. Is the company's product of high or low quality? Why? Is each company headed in the right direction to be globally competitive?
4. Evaluate the nonfinancial measures of quality in terms of customer satisfaction. Are the results consistent with your analysis in **3**? Explain your answer.

P 6.

LO 2
LO 3
LO 4

Analysis of Nonfinancial Data

Karlson Enterprises, Inc., manufactures several lines of small machinery. Before automated equipment was installed, the total delivery cycle for the Federal machine models averaged about three weeks. Last year management decided to purchase a new computer-integrated manufacturing system for the Federal line. The cost was over $17,500,000 and included twelve separate work stations producing the four components needed to assemble a finished product. Each machine is linked to the next via an automated conveyor system. Assembly of the four parts, including the machine's entire electrical system, now takes only two hours. Following is a summary of operating data for the past eight weeks for the Federal line.

	Weeks							
	1	2	3	4	5	6	7	8
Average process time (hours)	7.2	7.2	7.1	7.4	7.6	7.2	6.8	6.6
Average setup time (hours)	2.2	2.2	2.1	1.9	1.9	1.8	2.0	1.9
Customer complaints	5	6	4	7	6	8	9	9
Delivery time (hours)	36.2	37.4	37.2	36.4	35.9	35.8	34.8	34.2
Equipment utilization rate (%)	98.1	98.2	98.4	98.1	97.8	97.6	97.8	97.8
Machine downtime (hours)	82.3	84.2	85.9	84.3	83.4	82.2	82.8	80.4
Machine maintenance time (hours)	50.4	52.8	49.5	46.4	47.2	45.8	44.8	42.9
Number of inventoried items	5,642	5,820	5,690	5,780	5,630	5,510	5,280	5,080
On-time deliveries (%)	92.4	92.5	93.2	94.2	94.4	94.1	95.8	94.6
Parts scrapped	98.0	96.0	102.0	104.0	100.0	98.2	98.6	100.6
Production backlog (units)	15,230	15,440	15,200	16,100	14,890	13,560	13,980	13,440
Production cycle time (hours)	12.2	12.6	11.9	11.8	12.2	11.6	11.2	10.6
Purchase order lead time (hours)	26.2	26.8	26.5	25.9	25.7	25.3	24.8	24.2
Times inventory turnover	3.2	3.4	3.4	3.6	3.8	3.8	4.2	4.4
Warranty claims	2	2	3	2	3	4	3	3

1. Analyze the performance of the Federal machine line for the eight-week period. Focus on performance in the following areas:
   a. Product quality
   b. Total product delivery
   c. Inventory control
   d. Materials cost and scrap control
   e. Machine management

2. Summarize your findings in a report to the company's management.

EXPANDING YOUR CRITICAL THINKING, COMMUNICATION, AND INTERPERSONAL SKILLS

Skills Development

CONCEPTUAL ANALYSIS

LO 2 *Total Quality Management and Employee Attitudes*

SD 1. For the total quality management philosophy to work, everyone in the organization must "buy in" to the concept. Homer Lordon has just been told that he needs to attend four two-hour training sessions about his company's new "Quality or Else" approach to operations. Homer has been with Bayer Industries for twenty-five years and is currently managing one of its JIT work cells. Homer's response to the training program was: "Who needs it? I know this operation better than anyone in the organization. My work cell out-produces all other work cells in this division. Give the training to the new people, especially those new MBAs in middle management who are still wet behind the ears." You are Homer's supervisor. Write a memo to Homer explaining why everyone in the company needs to go through a special training program to learn about the TQM approach to management.

ETHICAL DILEMMA

LO 1 *Cost Management and Ethics*

SD 2. Three months ago, **Maxwell Enterprises** hired a consultant, Stacy Slone, to assist in the design and installation of a new cost management system for the company. Mike Carns, one of Maxwell's product/systems design engineers, was assigned to work with Slone on the project. During the three-month period, Slone and Carns met six times and developed a tentative design and installation plan for the CMS. Before the plan was to be unveiled to top management, Carns asked his supervisor, Todd Bowman, to look it over and comment on the design.

Included in the plan is the consolidation of three engineering functions into one. Both of the current supervisors of the other two functions have seniority over Bowman, so he believed that the design would lead to his losing his management position. He communicated this to Carns and ended his comments with the following statement: "If you don't redesign the system to accommodate all three of the existing engineering functions, I will see to it that you are given an unsatisfactory performance evaluation for this year!"

How should Carns respond to Bowman's assertion? Should he handle the problem alone, keeping it inside the company, or communicate the comment to Slone? Outline Carns's options and be prepared to discuss them in class.

Communication	Critical Thinking	Group Activity	Memo	Ethics	International	Spreadsheet	Managerial Technology	Internet

Group Activity: Divide the class into groups. Have each group present its recommended course of action. Have groups debate when different recommendations are made.

RESEARCH ACTIVITY

SD 3. Many large multinational companies have recently installed automated just-in-time production processes to improve product quality and to compete for new domestic and foreign business. Locate an article about a company that has recently installed a JIT system to help improve product quality. Conduct your search using the company annual reports in your campus library, the business section of your local newspaper, *The Wall Street Journal*, or the Needles Accounting Resource Center Web site at http//www.hmco.com/college/needles/home.html.

Choose a source that describes the changes the company made within its plant to increase product quality and to compete as a world-class manufacturer. Prepare a one-page description of those changes. Include in your report the name of the company, its geographic location, the name of the chief executive officer and/or president, and the dollar amount of the company's total sales for the most recent year, if stated. Be prepared to present your findings to your classmates.

DECISION-MAKING PRACTICE

LO 4   *Evaluating*
        Performance Measures

SD 4. Ahern Company and Siedle Company compete in the same industry. Each company is located in a large midwestern city, and each employs between 300 and 350 people. Both companies have adopted a total quality management approach, and both want to improve their ability to compete in the marketplace. They have installed common performance measures to help track their quest for quality and a competitive advantage. The following data were generated by the companies during the most recent three-month period:

Performance Measures	Ahern Company Financial	Ahern Company Nonfinancial	Siedle Company Financial	Siedle Company Nonfinancial
Product quality performance				
Customer complaints		28		24
Scrap and rework costs	$14,390		$13,680	
Field service costs	9,240		7,700	
Inventory control performance				
Average turnover rate		4.8 times		5.2 times
Percentage of inventory change		−10.4%		−16.2%
Materials cost and scrap performance				
Materials cost as a percentage of total cost		22.0%		28.0%
Scrap as a percentage of total cost		3.0%		2.0%
Machine management performance				
Equipment utilization percentage		89.4%		92.1%
Amount of machine downtime in machine hours		720		490
Total product delivery performance				
Percentage of on-time deliveries		92.1%		96.5%
Average lead time		17 hours		18 hours
Average cycle time		14 hours		16 hours
Average waste time		3 hours		2 hours

1. For each measure, indicate which company has the better performance.
2. Which company is more successful in achieving a total quality environment and an improved competitive position? Explain.

Managerial Reporting and Analysis

INTERPRETING MANAGEMENT REPORTS

MRA 1.

LO 2   *Costs of Quality*

Pete Malarek has been appointed chief accountant for *Gary Industries.* The business has three divisions that manufacture oil well depth gauges. The business is very competitive, and Gary Industries has lost market share in each of the last four years. Three years ago, management announced a companywide restructuring and the adoption of total quality management. Since that time, each of the divisions has been allowed to chart its own path toward TQM. Mr. Malarek is new to the company and has asked to see a summary of the costs of quality for each of the divisions. The following data for the past six months were presented to him:

	Gary Industries Costs of Quality Report For the six months ended June 30, 20xx			
	Illinois Division	Indiana Division	Ohio Division	Company Totals
Sales	$1,849,400	$1,773,450	$1,757,400	$5,380,250
Prevention costs	$ 32,680	$ 48,120	$ 15,880	$ 96,680
Appraisal costs	42,340	32,210	17,980	92,530
Internal failure costs	24,100	21,450	41,780	87,330
External failure costs	32,980	16,450	45,560	94,990
Total Costs of Quality	$ 132,100	$ 118,230	$ 121,200	$ 371,530

Evaluate the three divisions' quality control programs by first computing the costs of conformance and the costs of nonconformance for each division. Also compute quality costs as a percentage of sales for each division. Identify the division that is developing the strongest quality program. What division has been the slowest to react to the management directive? Be prepared to explain your answers.

FORMULATING MANAGEMENT REPORTS

MRA 2.

LO 2   *Reporting Quality*
LO 3   *Data*

Jason Morgon is chief executive officer of *Dundee Machinery, Inc.* The company adopted a JIT operating environment about five years ago. Since then, each segment of the company has been converted, and a complete computer-integrated manufacturing system operates in all parts of the company's five plants. Processing of Dundee's products now averages less than four days once the materials have been placed into production. Morgon is worried about customer satisfaction and has asked you, as the controller, for some advice and help. He also asked the Marketing Department to perform a quick survey of customers to determine weak areas in customer relations. Here is a summary of four customers' replies.

Customer A
Customer for five years; waits an average of six weeks for delivery; located 1,200 miles from plant; returns an average of 3 percent of products; receives 90 percent on-time deliveries; never hears from salesperson after placing order; likes quality or would go with competitor.

Customer B

Customer for seven years; waits an average of five weeks for delivery; orders usually sit in backlog for at least three weeks; located 50 miles from plant; returns about 5 percent of products; receives 95 percent on-time deliveries; has great rapport with salesperson; salesperson is reason why this customer is loyal.

Customer C

Customer for twelve years; waits an average of seven weeks for delivery; located 1,500 miles from plant; returns about 4 percent of products; receives 92 percent on-time deliveries; salesperson is available but of little help in getting faster delivery; customer is thinking about dealing with another source for its product needs.

Customer D

Customer for fifteen years; very pleased with company's product; waits almost five weeks for delivery; located 120 miles from plant; returns only 2 percent of goods received; rapport with salesperson is very good; follow-up service of salesperson is excellent; would like delivery cycle time reduced to equal that of competitors; usually deals with three-week backlog.

REQUIRED

1. Identify the areas of concern and give at least three examples of reports that will help managers improve the company's response to customer needs.
2. Assume you are asked to write a report that will provide information about product quality. In preparation, answer the following questions.
   a. What kinds of information do you need to prepare this report?
   b. Why is this information relevant?
   c. Where would you find this information (sources)?
   d. When would you want to obtain this information?

INTERNATIONAL COMPANY

MRA 3.

LO 5 *Full Cost Profit Margin Analysis*

Tecnologico Instituto is a technology research company headquartered in Mexico City. The company's chief financial officer, Gloria Enriquez, has just finished installing a new activity-based costing system and is anxious to begin using the new information in her reports to management. One of the new performance measures generated by the ABC system is full cost profit margin. Management has used contribution margin to evaluate its divisions for several years. Ms. Enriquez is concerned that management will not trust the new measure because tracing of fixed costs is involved.

REQUIRED

1. Identify the differences between contribution margin and full cost profit margin.
2. Prepare a memo from Ms. Enriquez to the company president, Oscar Rivera, explaining the new performance measure and provide an abbreviated example of the report form.

EXCEL SPREADSHEET ANALYSIS

MRA 4.

LO 2 *Interpreting*
LO 3 *Measures of*
LO 4 *Quality*

Travis Corporation has five divisions, each manufacturing a product line that competes in the global marketplace. The company is planning to compete for the Baldrige Award, a national quality award, so management requires that each division record and report its efforts to achieve quality in its product line. The information on the next page was submitted to the company's controller for the most recent six-month period:

	Division A	Division B	Division C	Division D	Division E
Total revenue	$886,000	$1,040,000	$956,000	$1,225,000	$1,540,000
Costs of quality					
Customer service	$ 10,400	$ 12,600	$ 12,300	$ 10,100	$ 15,600
Scrap and rework	26,800	13,500	38,700	11,900	34,800
Setup for testing	13,600	28,400	6,300	25,600	11,700
Returned goods	18,700	11,400	38,400	11,300	36,000
Warranty claims	21,100	6,400	36,200	6,500	42,600
Employee training	8,900	12,600	4,600	11,400	4,200
Preventive maintenance	11,300	18,700	8,300	13,600	6,300
Process failure	34,800	9,800	46,900	10,200	56,900
Product simulation	12,500	18,700	7,800	17,500	5,600
Nonfinancial measures					
Number of warranty claims versus	22	12	46	12	62
number of sales	6,500	8,900	7,200	9,800	9,600
Number of products reworked versus	150	140	870	70	900
number of products manufactured	325,000	456,000	365,000	450,000	315,600
Throughput time in hours versus	6.2	8.5	6.8	9.2	11.6
throughput time at beginning of period	6.2	8.6	6.5	9.8	10.8
Number of late deliveries versus	450	260	760	80	1,500
total number of deliveries	8,600	12,400	9,200	12,600	12,800

REQUIRED

1. Prepare an analysis of the costs of quality for each division. Categorize the costs as costs of conformance or costs of nonconformance.
2. For each division, compute the percentage of total revenue for each of the four cost of quality categories and the ratios for the nonfinancial data.
3. Rank the divisions in order of their apparent product quality.
4. What three measures were most important in your rankings in **3**? Why?
5. Which division is most successful in its bid to improve quality? What measures illustrate its high quality rating?
6. Consider the two divisions producing the lowest-quality products. What actions would you recommend to the management of each division? Where should their quality dollars be spent?

ENDNOTES

1. John Y. Lee and Pauline Nefcy, "The Anatomy of an Effective HMO Cost Management System," *Management Accounting,* Institute of Management Accountants, January 1997, pp. 49–54.
2. James A. Brimson, *Activity Accounting* (New York: John Wiley & Sons, 1991).
3. Many of the thoughts in this section come from John Hawley Atkinson, Jr., Gregory Hohner, Barry Mundt, Richard B. Troxel, and William Winchell, *Current Trends in Cost of Quality: Linking the Cost of Quality and Continuous Improvement,* a joint study of the Institute of Management Accountants, KPMG Peat Marwick, and William Winchell (Montvale, N.J., 1991).
4. Tom Peters, *Thriving on Chaos* (New York: Alfred A. Knopf, 1987), p. 91.
5. Don Irwin and Victor Rocine, "Self-Directed Work Teams," *CMA Magazine,* September 1994, pp. 10–15. Used by permission of The Society of Management Accountants of Canada.
6. Thomas A. Stewart, "Your Company's Most Valuable Asset: Intellectual Capital," *Fortune,* October 3, 1994, pp. 68–74.

CHAPTER 13

The Statement of Cash Flows

1. Describe the statement of cash flows, and define *cash* and *cash equivalents.*
2. State the principal purposes and uses of the statement of cash flows.
3. Identify the principal components of the classifications of cash flows, and state the significance of noncash investing and financing transactions.
4. Analyze the statement of cash flows.
5. Use the indirect method to determine cash flows from operating activities.
6. Determine cash flows from (a) investing activities and (b) financing activities.
7. Use the indirect method to prepare a statement of cash flows.

8. Prepare a work sheet for the statement of cash flows.
9. Use the direct method to determine cash flows from operating activities and prepare a statement of cash flows.

DECISION POINT

MARRIOTT INTERNATIONAL, INC.

Marriott International, Inc., is a world leader in lodging and contract services. The balance sheet, income statement, and statement of stockholders' equity presented in the company's annual report give an excellent picture of management's philosophy and performance.

Those three financial statements are essential to the evaluation of a company, but they do not tell the entire story. Some information that they do not contain is presented in a fourth statement, the statement of cash flows, as shown in the Financial Highlights on the next page.[1] This statement shows how much cash was generated by the company's operations during the past three years and how much was used in or came from investing and financing activities. Marriott feels that maintaining adequate cash flows is important to the future of the company. In fact, Marriott's emphasis on cash flows is reflected in its executive compensation plan for its chief executive officer and senior executive officers. A review of the plan indicates that a measure of cash flows, at the firm or business group level, is the financial measure given the highest weight in determining compensation. Why would Marriott emphasize cash flows to such an extent?

Strong cash flows are essential to management's key goal of liquidity. If cash flows exceed the amount needed for operations and expansion, the

Financial Highlights: Consolidated Statement of Cash Flows

Marriott International, Inc. and Subsidiaries

Fiscal years ended January 3, 1996, December 29, 1995, and December 30, 1994	1996	1995	1994
	(in millions)		
Operating Activities			
Net income	**$306**	$247	$200
Adjustments to reconcile to cash from operations:			
Depreciation and amortization	**156**	129	117
Income taxes	**65**	42	23
Timeshare activity, net	**(95)**	(192)	(44)
Other	**62**	57	70
Working capital changes:			
Accounts receivable	**(52)**	(36)	(38)
Inventories	**14**	(7)	—
Other current assets	**3**	(10)	(4)
Accounts payable and accruals	**143**	139	73
Cash from operations	**602**	369	397
Investing Activities			
Capital expenditures	**(326)**	(153)	(115)
Acquisitions	**(331)**	(254)	—
Dispositions of property and equipment	**65**	42	—
Loans to Host Marriott Corporation	**(16)**	(210)	(48)
Loan repayments from Host Marriott Corporation	**141**	250	30
Other	**(82)**	(232)	(49)
Cash used in investing activities	**(549)**	(557)	(182)
Financing Activities			
Issuances of long-term debt	**—**	556	255
Repayments of long-term debt	**(137)**	(341)	(309)
Issuance of convertible subordinated debt	**288**	—	—
Issuances of common stock	**43**	40	29
Dividends paid	**(40)**	(35)	(35)
Purchases of treasury stock	**(158)**	(17)	(189)
Cash provided by (used in) financing activities	**(4)**	203	(249)
Increase/(Decrease) in Cash and Equivalents	**49**	15	(34)
Cash and Equivalents, beginning of year	**219**	204	238
Cash and Equivalents, end of year	**$268**	$219	$204

company will not have to borrow additional funds. The excess cash flows will be available to reduce the company's debt and improve its financial position by lowering its debt to equity ratio. Another reason for the emphasis on cash flows may be the belief that strong cash flows from operations create shareholder value or increase the market value of the company's stock.

The statement of cash flows demonstrates management's commitments for the company in ways that are not readily apparent in the other financial statements. For example, the statement of cash flows can show whether management's focus is on the short term or the long term. This statement is required by the FASB[2] and satisfies the FASB's long-held position that a primary objective of financial statements is to provide investors and creditors with information about a company's cash flows.[3]

Overview of the Statement of Cash Flows

OBJECTIVE 1

Describe the statement of cash flows, and define **cash** *and* **cash equivalents**

The statement of cash flows shows how a company's operating, investing, and financing activities have affected cash during an accounting period. It explains the net increase (or decrease) in cash during the accounting period. For purposes of preparing this statement, cash is defined to include both cash and cash equivalents. Cash equivalents are defined by the FASB as short-term, highly liquid investments, including money market accounts, commercial paper, and U.S. Treasury bills. A company maintains cash equivalents to earn interest on cash that would otherwise remain unused temporarily. Suppose, for example, that a company has $1,000,000 that it will not need for thirty days. To earn a return on this amount, the company may place the cash in an account that earns interest (such as a money market account); it may loan the cash to another corporation by purchasing that corporation's short-term note (commercial paper); or it may purchase a short-term obligation of the U.S. government (a Treasury bill). In this context, short-term refers to original maturities of ninety days or less. Since cash and cash equivalents are considered the same, transfers between the Cash account and cash equivalents are not treated as cash receipts or cash payments. In effect, cash equivalents are combined with the Cash account on the statement of cash flows.

Cash equivalents should not be confused with short-term investments or marketable securities, which are not combined with the Cash account on the statement of cash flows. Purchases of marketable securities are treated as cash outflows and sales of marketable securities as cash inflows on the statement of cash flows. In this chapter, cash will be assumed to include cash and cash equivalents.

Purposes of the Statement of Cash Flows

OBJECTIVE 2

State the principal purposes and uses of the statement of cash flows

The primary purpose of the statement of cash flows is to provide information about a company's cash receipts and cash payments during an accounting period. A secondary purpose of the statement is to provide information about a company's operating, investing, and financing activities during the accounting period. Some information about those activities may be inferred by examining other financial statements, but it is on the statement of cash flows that all the transactions affecting cash are summarized.

Internal and External Uses of the Statement of Cash Flows

The statement of cash flows is useful internally to management and externally to investors and creditors. Management uses the statement to assess liquidity, to determine dividend policy, and to evaluate the effects of major policy decisions involving investments and financing. In other words, management may use the statement to determine if short-term financing is needed to pay current liabilities, to decide whether to raise or lower dividends, and to plan for investing and financing needs.

Investors and creditors will find the statement useful in assessing the company's ability to manage cash flows, to generate positive future cash flows, to pay its liabilities, to pay dividends and interest, and to anticipate its need for additional financing. Also, they may use the statement to explain the differences between net income on the income statement and the net cash flows generated from operations. In addition, the statement shows both the cash and the noncash effects of investing and financing activities during the accounting period.

Classification of Cash Flows

OBJECTIVE 3

Identify the principal components of the classifications of cash flows, and state the significance of noncash investing and financing transactions

The statement of cash flows classifies cash receipts and cash payments into the categories of operating, investing, and financing activities. The components of these activities are illustrated in Figure 1 and summarized below.

1. Operating activities include the cash effects of transactions and other events that enter into the determination of net income. Included in this category as cash inflows are cash receipts from customers for goods and services, interest and dividends received on loans and investments, and sales of trading securities. Included as cash outflows are cash payments for wages, goods and services, expenses, interest, taxes, and purchases of trading securities. In effect, the income statement is changed from an accrual to a cash basis.

2. Investing activities include the acquiring and selling of long-term assets, the acquiring and selling of marketable securities other than trading securities or cash equivalents, and the making and collecting of loans. Cash inflows include the cash received from selling long-term assets and marketable securities and from collecting loans. Cash outflows include the cash expended for purchases of long-term assets and marketable securities and the cash loaned to borrowers.

3. Financing activities include obtaining resources from or returning resources to owners and providing them with a return on their investment, and obtaining resources from creditors and repaying the amounts borrowed or otherwise settling the obligations. Cash inflows include the proceeds from issues of stocks and from short-term and long-term borrowing. Cash outflows include the repayments of loans (excluding interest) and payments to owners, including cash dividends. Treasury stock transactions are also considered financing activities. Repayments of accounts payable or accrued liabilities are not considered repayments of loans under financing activities, but are classified as cash outflows under operating activities.

A company will occasionally engage in significant noncash investing and financing transactions involving only long-term assets, long-term liabilities, or stockholders' equity, such as the exchange of a long-term asset for a long-term liability or the settlement of a debt by issuing capital stock. For instance, a company might take out a long-term mortgage for the purchase of land and a building. Or it might convert long-term bonds into common stock. Such transactions represent significant investing and financing activities, but they would not be reflected on the statement of cash flows because they do not involve either cash inflows or cash outflows. However, since one purpose of the statement of cash flows is to show investing and financing activities, and since such transactions will affect future cash flows, the FASB has determined that they should be disclosed in a separate schedule as part of the statement of cash flows. In this way, the reader of the statement will see the company's investing and financing activities more clearly.

Format of the Statement of Cash Flows

The statement of cash flows, as shown in the Financial Highlights for Marriott International on page 474, is divided into three sections. The first section, cash flows

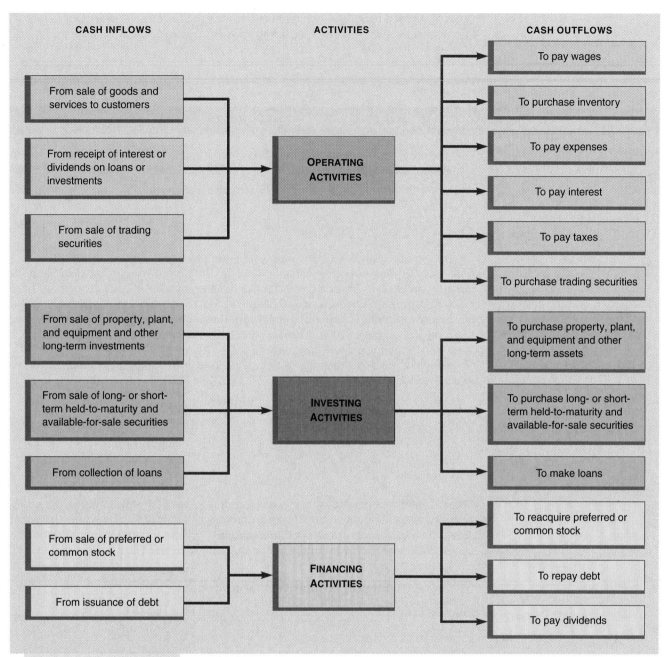

CASH INFLOWS

- From sale of goods and services to customers
- From receipt of interest or dividends on loans or investments
- From sale of trading securities

- From sale of property, plant, and equipment and other long-term investments
- From sale of long- or short-term held-to-maturity and available-for-sale securities
- From collection of loans

- From sale of preferred or common stock
- From issuance of debt

ACTIVITIES

- **OPERATING ACTIVITIES**
- **INVESTING ACTIVITIES**
- **FINANCING ACTIVITIES**

CASH OUTFLOWS

- To pay wages
- To purchase inventory
- To pay expenses
- To pay interest
- To pay taxes
- To purchase trading securities

- To purchase property, plant, and equipment and other long-term assets
- To purchase long- or short-term held-to-maturity and available-for-sale securities
- To make loans

- To reacquire preferred or common stock
- To repay debt
- To pay dividends

Figure 1
Classification of Cash Inflows and Cash Outflows

from operating activities, is presented using the indirect method. This is the most common method and is explained in learning objective 5 of this chapter. The other two sections of the statement of cash flows are the cash flows from investing activities and the cash flows from financing activities. The individual cash inflows and outflows from investing and financing activities are shown separately in their respective categories. Normally, cash outflows for the purchase of plant assets are shown separately from cash inflows from the disposal of plant assets. However, some companies follow the practice of combining these two lines to show the net amount of outflow, because the inflows are not usually material.

A reconciliation of the beginning and ending balances of cash is shown near the bottom of the statement. It shows that Marriott International had a net increase in cash of $49 million in 1996, which together with the beginning balance of $219 million results in $268 million of cash and cash equivalents on hand at the end of the year.

Analyzing the Statement of Cash Flows

OBJECTIVE 4

Analyze the statement of cash flows

Like the other financial statements, the statement of cash flows can be analyzed to reveal significant relationships. Two areas analysts examine when studying a company are cash-generating efficiency and free cash flow.

Cash-Generating Efficiency

Cash-generating efficiency is the ability of a company to generate cash from its current or continuing operations. Three ratios are helpful in measuring cash-generating efficiency: cash flow yield, cash flows to sales, and cash flows to assets. These ratios are computed and discussed below for Marriott International for 1996.[4] Data for the computations are obtained from the Financial Highlights for Marriott International on page 474 and below; all dollar amounts used to compute the ratios are stated in millions.

Cash flow yield is the ratio of net cash flows from operating activities to net income, as follows:

$$\text{Cash Flow Yield} = \frac{\text{Net Cash Flows from Operating Activities}}{\text{Net Income}}$$

$$= \frac{\$602}{\$306}$$

$$= 2.0 \text{ times}$$

Marriott International provides a good cash flow yield of 2.0 times; that is, operating activities are generating about 100 percent more cash flow than net income. If special items, such as discontinued operations, appear on the income statement and are material, income from continuing operations should be used as the denominator.

Financial Highlights for Marriott International

(In millions of dollars)

	1996	1995	1994
Net Sales	$10,172	$8,961	$8,415
Total Assets	5,075	4,018	3,207

Cash flows to sales is the ratio of net cash flows from operating activities to sales.

$$\text{Cash Flows to Sales} = \frac{\text{Net Cash Flows from Operating Activities}}{\text{Net Sales}}$$

$$= \frac{\$602}{\$10,172}$$

$$= 5.9\%$$

Marriott generates cash flows to sales of 5.9 percent. The company generated a positive but relatively small percentage of net cash from sales.

Cash flows to assets is the ratio of net cash flows from operating activities to average total assets, as follows:

$$\text{Cash Flows to Assets} = \frac{\text{Net Cash Flows from Operating Activities}}{\text{Average Total Assets}}$$

$$= \frac{\$602}{(\$5,075 + \$4,018)/2}$$

$$= 13.2\%$$

The cash flows to assets is much higher than cash flows to sales because Marriott has an excellent asset turnover ratio (sales ÷ average total assets) of about 2.2 times. Cash flows to sales and cash flows to assets are closely related to the profitability measures profit margin and return on assets. They exceed those measures by the amount of the cash flow yield ratio because cash flow yield is the ratio of net cash flows from operating activities to net income.

Although Marriott's cash flow yield and cash flows to assets are relatively good, its efficiency at generating cash flows from operating activities, as measured by cash flows to sales, could be improved.

Free Cash Flow

It would seem logical for the analysis to move along to investing and financing activities. For example, in 1996 there is a net cash outflow of $549 million in the investing activities section, which could indicate that the company is expanding. However, that figure mixes capital expenditures for plant assets, which reflect management's expansion of operations, with the acquisition of another hotel chain and loans to and repayments from Host Marriott Corporation. Also, cash flows from financing activities were a negative $4 million, but that figure combines financing activities associated with long-term debt and stocks with dividends paid to stockholders. While something can be learned by looking at those broad categories, many analysts find it more informative to go beyond them and focus on a computation called free cash flow.

Free cash flow is the amount of cash that remains after deducting the funds the company must commit to continue operating at its planned level. The commitments must cover current or continuing operations, interest, income taxes, dividends, and net capital expenditures. Cash requirements for current or continuing operations, interest, and income taxes must be paid or the company's creditors and the government can take legal action. Although the payment of dividends is not strictly required, dividends normally represent a commitment to stockholders. If these payments are reduced or eliminated, stockholders will be unhappy and the price of the company's stock will fall. Net capital expenditures represent management's plans for the future.

If free cash flow is positive, it means that the company has met all of its planned cash commitments and has cash available to reduce debt or expand. A negative free cash flow means that the company will have to sell investments, borrow money, or issue stock in the short term to continue at its planned levels. If free cash flow remains negative for several years, a company may not be able to raise cash by selling investments or issuing stock or bonds.

Since cash commitments for current or continuing operations, interest, and income taxes are incorporated in cash flows from current operations, free cash flow for Marriott is computed as follows (in millions):

$$
\begin{aligned}
\text{Free Cash Flow} &= \text{Net Cash Flows from Operating Activities} \; - \; \text{Dividends} \\
&\quad - \; \text{Purchases of Plant Assets} \; + \; \text{Sales of Plant Assets} \\
&= \$602 \; - \; \$40 \; - \; \$326 \; + \; \$65 \\
&= \$301
\end{aligned}
$$

Purchases and sales of plant assets appear in the investing activities section of the statement of cash flows. Marriott reports both capital expenditures and dispositions of property and equipment. Dividends are found in the financing activities section. Marriott has positive free cash flow of $301 million and can use this cash to partially fund its business acquisitions. Looking at the financing activities section, it may be seen that the company repaid long-term debt of $137 million while issuing new debt of $288 million. Marriott also issued common stock in the amount of $43 million and purchased treasury stock for $158 million. The result is that financing activities, with net cash used of only $4 million, had little overall effect.

Cash flows can vary from year to year, so it is best to look at trends in cash flow measures over several years when analyzing a company's cash flows. For example, Marriott International's 1995 cash flow yield was only 1.5 times ($369 million ÷ $247 million). This is because, although net income rose about 24 percent in 1996, cash

BUSINESS BULLETIN: BUSINESS PRACTICE

Because the statement of cash flows has been around for only a decade, no generally accepted analyses have yet been developed. For example, the term *free cash flow* is commonly used in the business press, but there is no agreement on its definition. An article in *Forbes* defines free cash flow as "cash available after paying out capital expenditures and dividends, *but before taxes and interest*"[6] [emphasis added]. In *The Wall Street Journal,* free cash flow was defined as "operating income less maintenance-level capital expenditures."[7] The definition with which we are most in agreement is the one used in *Business Week,* which is net cash flows from operating activities less net capital expenditures and dividends. This "measures truly discretionary funds—company money that an owner could pocket without harming the business."[8]

flows from operations increased 63 percent. Management sums up in the annual report:

> **Cash from Operations**
> The company's operations generate substantial amounts of cash with only limited reinvestment requirements.[9]

In fact, all the cash flow measures improved from 1995 to 1996 as a result of this increase in cash flows from operations.

The Indirect Method of Preparing the Statement of Cash Flows

OBJECTIVE 5

Use the indirect method to determine cash flows from operating activities

To demonstrate the preparation of the statement of cash flows, we will work through an example step by step. The data for this example are presented in Exhibits 1 and 2. Those two exhibits present Ryan Corporation's balance sheets for December 31, 20x1 and 20x0, and its 20x1 income statement. Since the changes in the balance sheet accounts will be used for analysis, those changes are shown in Exhibit 1. Whether the change in each account is an increase or a decrease is also shown. In addition, Exhibit 2 contains data about transactions that affected noncurrent accounts. Those transactions would be identified by the company's accountants from the records.

There are four steps in preparing the statement of cash flows:

1. Determine cash flows from operating activities.
2. Determine cash flows from investing activities.
3. Determine cash flows from financing activities.
4. Use the information obtained in the first three steps to compile the statement of cash flows.

Determining Cash Flows from Operating Activities

The first step in preparing the statement of cash flows is to determine cash flows from operating activities. The income statement indicates a business's success or failure in earning an income from its operating activities, but it does not reflect the inflow and outflow of cash from those activities. The reason is that the income statement is prepared on an accrual basis. Revenues are recorded even though the cash for them may not have been received, and expenses are recorded even though the cash for them may not have been expended. As a result, to arrive at cash flows from operations, the figures on the income statement must be converted from an accrual basis to a cash basis.

There are two methods of converting the income statement from an accrual basis to a cash basis: the direct method and the indirect method. Under the direct method, each item in the income statement is adjusted from the accrual basis to the cash basis. The result is a statement that begins with cash receipts from sales and interest and deducts cash payments for purchases, operating expenses, interest payments, and income taxes to arrive at net cash flows from operating activities. The indirect method on the other hand, does not require the individual adjustment of each item in the income statement, but lists only those adjustments necessary to convert net income to cash flows from operations. Because the indirect method is more common, it will be used to illustrate the conversion of the income statement to a cash basis in the sections that follow. The direct method is presented in a supplemental objective at the end of the chapter.

Exhibit 1. Comparative Balance Sheets with Changes in Accounts Indicated for Ryan Corporation

Ryan Corporation
Comparative Balance Sheets
December 31, 20x1 and 20x0

	20x1	20x0	Change	Increase or Decrease
Assets				
Current Assets				
Cash	$ 46,000	$ 15,000	$ 31,000	Increase
Accounts Receivable (net)	47,000	55,000	(8,000)	Decrease
Inventory	144,000	110,000	34,000	Increase
Prepaid Expenses	1,000	5,000	(4,000)	Decrease
Total Current Assets	$238,000	$185,000	$ 53,000	
Investments Available for Sale	$115,000	$127,000	($ 12,000)	Decrease
Plant Assets				
Plant Assets	$715,000	$505,000	$210,000	Increase
Accumulated Depreciation	(103,000)	(68,000)	(35,000)	Increase
Total Plant Assets	$612,000	$437,000	$175,000	
Total Assets	$965,000	$749,000	$216,000	
Liabilities				
Current Liabilities				
Accounts Payable	$ 50,000	$ 43,000	$ 7,000	Increase
Accrued Liabilities	12,000	9,000	3,000	Increase
Income Taxes Payable	3,000	5,000	(2,000)	Decrease
Total Current Liabilities	$ 65,000	$ 57,000	$ 8,000	
Long-Term Liabilities				
Bonds Payable	295,000	245,000	50,000	Increase
Total Liabilities	$360,000	$302,000	$ 58,000	
Stockholders' Equity				
Common Stock, $5 par value	$276,000	$200,000	$ 76,000	Increase
Paid-in Capital in Excess of Par Value, Common	189,000	115,000	74,000	Increase
Retained Earnings	140,000	132,000	8,000	Increase
Total Stockholders' Equity	$605,000	$447,000	$158,000	
Total Liabilities and Stockholders' Equity	$965,000	$749,000	$216,000	

The indirect method, as illustrated in Figure 2, focuses on items from the income statement that must be adjusted to reconcile net income to net cash flows from operating activities. The items that require attention are those that affect net income but not net cash flows from operating activities, such as depreciation and amortization, gains and losses, and changes in the balances of current asset and current liability accounts. The reconciliation of Ryan Corporation's net income to net cash flows from operating activities is shown in Exhibit 3. Each adjustment is discussed in the following sections.

Exhibit 2. Income Statement and Other Information on Noncurrent Accounts for Ryan Corporation

Ryan Corporation
Income Statement
For the Year Ended December 31, 20x1

Net Sales		$698,000
Cost of Goods Sold		520,000
Gross Margin		$178,000
Operating Expenses (including Depreciation Expense of $37,000)		147,000
Operating Income		$ 31,000
Other Income (Expenses)		
Interest Expense	($23,000)	
Interest Income	6,000	
Gain on Sale of Investments	12,000	
Loss on Sale of Plant Assets	(3,000)	(8,000)
Income Before Income Taxes		$ 23,000
Income Taxes		7,000
Net Income		$ 16,000

Other transactions affecting noncurrent accounts during 20x1:

1. Purchased investments in the amount of $78,000.
2. Sold investments for $102,000 that cost $90,000.
3. Purchased plant assets in the amount of $120,000.
4. Sold plant assets that cost $10,000 with accumulated depreciation of $2,000 for $5,000.
5. Issued $100,000 of bonds at face value in a noncash exchange for plant assets.
6. Repaid $50,000 of bonds at face value at maturity.
7. Issued 15,200 shares of $5 par value common stock for $150,000.
8. Paid cash dividends in the amount of $8,000.

Depreciation   Cash payments for plant assets, intangibles, and natural resources occur when the assets are purchased and are reflected as investing activities on the statement of cash flows at that time. When depreciation expense, amortization expense, and depletion expense appear on the income statement, they simply indicate allocations of the costs of the original purchases to the current accounting period; they do not affect net cash flows in the current period. The amount of such

**Figure 2
Indirect Method of
Determining Net Cash Flows
from Operating Activities**

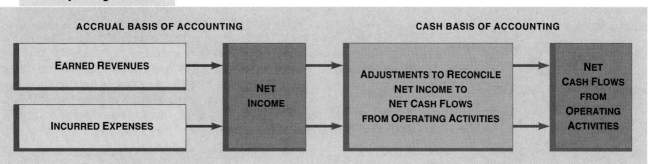

Exhibit 3. Schedule of Cash Flows from Operating Activities: Indirect Method

Ryan Corporation
Schedule of Cash Flows from Operating Activities
For the Year Ended December 31, 20x1

Cash Flows from Operating Activities		
Net Income		$16,000
Adjustments to Reconcile Net Income to Net		
Cash Flows from Operating Activities		
Depreciation	$37,000	
Gain on Sale of Investments	(12,000)	
Loss on Sale of Plant Assets	3,000	
Changes in Current Assets and Current Liabilities		
Decrease in Accounts Receivable	8,000	
Increase in Inventory	(34,000)	
Decrease in Prepaid Expenses	4,000	
Increase in Accounts Payable	7,000	
Increase in Accrued Liabilities	3,000	
Decrease in Income Taxes Payable	(2,000)	14,000
Net Cash Flows from Operating Activities		$30,000

expenses can usually be found by referring to the income statement or a note to the financial statements.

For Ryan Corporation, the income statement reveals depreciation expense of $37,000, which would have been recorded as follows:

$A = L + OE$

Depreciation Expense	37,000	
Accumulated Depreciation		37,000
To record annual depreciation on plant assets		

The recording of depreciation involved no outlay of cash. Thus, as cash flow was not affected, an adjustment for depreciation is needed to increase net income by the amount of depreciation recorded.

Gains and Losses   Gains and losses that appear on the income statement also do not affect cash flows from operating activities and need to be removed from this section of the statement of cash flows. The cash receipts generated from the disposal of the assets that resulted in the gains or losses are shown in the investing section of the statement of cash flows. Therefore, gains and losses are removed from net income to reconcile net income to cash flows from operating activities. For example, on the income statement, Ryan Corporation showed a $12,000 gain on the sale of investments, and this is subtracted from net income to reconcile net income to net cash flows from operating activities. Also, Ryan Corporation showed a $3,000 loss on the sale of plant assets, and this is added to net income to reconcile net income to net cash flows from operating activities.

DECISION POINT

SURVEY OF LARGE COMPANIES

The direct method and the indirect method of determining cash flows from operating activities produce the same results. Although it will accept either method, the FASB recommends that the direct method be used. If the direct method of reporting net cash flows from operating activities is used, reconciliation of net income to net cash flows from operating activities must be provided in a separate schedule (the indirect method). Despite the FASB's recommendation, a survey of large companies showed that an overwhelming majority, 98 percent, chose to use the indirect method. Of six hundred companies, only eleven chose the direct approach.[10] Why did so many choose the indirect approach?

The reasons for choosing the indirect method may vary, but chief financial officers tend to prefer it because it is easier and less expensive to prepare. Moreover, because the FASB requires the reconciliation of net income (accrual) to cash flow (operations) as a supplemental schedule, the indirect method has to be implemented anyway.

A knowledge of the direct method helps managers and the readers of financial statements perceive the underlying causes for the differences between reported net income and cash flows from operations. The indirect method is a practical way of presenting the differences. Both methods have advantages.

Changes in Current Assets Decreases in current assets other than cash have positive effects on cash flows, and increases in current assets have negative effects on cash flows. For example, refer to the balance sheets and income statement for Ryan Corporation in Exhibits 1 and 2. Note that net sales in 20x1 were $698,000 and that Accounts Receivable decreased by $8,000. Thus, cash received from sales was $706,000, calculated as follows:

$$\$706,000 \ = \ \$698,000 \ + \ \$8,000$$

Collections were $8,000 more than sales recorded for the year. This relationship may be illustrated as follows:

Accounts Receivable

Sales to Customers			
Beg. Bal.	55,000	706,000 →	Cash Receipts from Customers
→	698,000		
End. Bal.	47,000		

Thus, to reconcile net income to net cash flows from operating activities, the $8,000 decrease in Accounts Receivable is added to net income.

Inventory may be analyzed in the same way. For example, Exhibit 1 shows that Inventory increased by $34,000 from 20x0 to 20x1. This means that Ryan Corporation expended $34,000 more in cash for purchases than was included in cost of goods sold on the income statement. As a result of this expenditure, net income is higher than the net cash flows from operating activities, so $34,000 must be deducted from net income.

Using the same logic, the decrease of $4,000 in Prepaid Expenses is added to net income to reconcile net income to net cash flows from operations.

Changes in Current Liabilities   Changes in current liabilities have the opposite effects on cash flows from those of changes in current assets. Increases in current liabilities are added to net income, and decreases in current liabilities are deducted from net income to reconcile net income to net cash flows from operating activities. For example, note from Exhibit 1 that Ryan Corporation had a $7,000 increase in Accounts Payable from 20x0 to 20x1. This means that Ryan Corporation paid $7,000 less to creditors than what appears as purchases on the income statement. This relationship may be visualized as follows:

Accounts Payable

Cash Payments to Suppliers	← 547,000	Beg. Bal.	43,000		
			554,000* ←	Purchases	
		End. Bal.	50,000		

*Purchases = Cost of Goods Sold ($520,000) + Increase in Inventory ($34,000).

As a result, $7,000 is added to net income to reconcile net income to net cash flows from operating activities.

Using this same logic, the increase of $3,000 in Accrued Liabilities is added to net income and the decrease of $2,000 in Income Taxes Payable is deducted from net income to reconcile net income to net cash flows from operating activities.

Schedule of Cash Flows from Operating Activities   In summary, Exhibit 3 shows that by using the indirect method, net income of $16,000 has been adjusted by reconciling items totaling $14,000 to arrive at net cash flows from operating activities of $30,000. This means that although net income was $16,000, Ryan Corporation actually had net cash flows available from operating activities of $30,000 to use for purchasing assets, reducing debts, or paying dividends.

Summary of Adjustments   The effects of items on the income statement that do not affect cash flows may be summarized as follows:

	Add to or Deduct from Net Income
Depreciation Expense	Add
Amortization Expense	Add
Depletion Expense	Add
Losses	Add
Gains	Deduct

The adjustments for increases and decreases in current assets and current liabilities may be summarized as follows.

	Add to Net Income	Deduct from Net Income
Current Assets		
Accounts Receivable (net)	Decrease	Increase
Inventory	Decrease	Increase
Prepaid Expenses	Decrease	Increase
Current Liabilities		
Accounts Payable	Increase	Decrease
Accrued Liabilities	Increase	Decrease
Income Taxes Payable	Increase	Decrease

Determining Cash Flows from Investing Activities

OBJECTIVE 6 a

Determine cash flows from investing activities

The second step in preparing the statement of cash flows is to determine cash flows from investing activities. Each account involving cash receipts and cash payments from investing activities is examined individually. The objective is to explain the change in each account balance from one year to the next.

Investing activities center on the long-term assets shown on the balance sheet, but they also include transactions affecting short-term investments from the current assets section of the balance sheet and investment gains and losses from the income statement. The balance sheets in Exhibit 1 show that Ryan Corporation has long-term assets of investments and plant assets, but no short-term investments. The income statement in Exhibit 2 shows that Ryan has investment-related items in the form of a gain on the sale of investments and a loss on the sale of plant assets. The schedule at the bottom of Exhibit 2 lists the following five items pertaining to investing activities in 20x1:

1. Purchased investments in the amount of $78,000.
2. Sold investments for $102,000 that cost $90,000.
3. Purchased plant assets in the amount of $120,000.
4. Sold plant assets that cost $10,000 with accumulated depreciation of $2,000 for $5,000.
5. Issued $100,000 of bonds at face value in a noncash exchange for plant assets.

The following paragraphs analyze the accounts related to investing activities to determine their effects on Ryan Corporation's cash flows.

Investments   The objective here is to explain the corporation's $12,000 decrease in investments, all of which are classified as available-for-sale securities. This is accomplished by analyzing the increases and decreases in the Investments account to determine the effects on the Cash account. Purchases increase investments, and sales decrease investments. Item **1** in Ryan's list of investing activities shows purchases of $78,000 during 20x1. The transaction is recorded as follows:

A = L + OE
+
−

Investments	78,000	
Cash		78,000
Purchase of investments		

The entry shows that the effect of this transaction is a $78,000 decrease in cash flows.

Item **2** in the list shows a sale of investments for $102,000 that cost $90,000, which results in a gain of $12,000. This transaction was recorded as follows:

A = L + OE
+   +
−

Cash	102,000	
Investments		90,000
Gain on Sale of Investments		12,000
Sale of investments for a gain		

The effect of this transaction is a $102,000 increase in cash flows. Note that the gain on sale of investments is included in the $102,000. This is the reason it was excluded earlier in computing cash flows from operations. If it had been included in that section, it would have been counted twice.

The $12,000 decrease in the Investments account during 20x1 has now been explained, as seen in the following T account.

Investments			
Beg. Bal.	127,000	Sales	90,000
Purchases	78,000		
End. Bal.	115,000		

The cash flow effects from these transactions are shown in the Cash Flows from Investing Activities section on the statement of cash flows as follows:

Purchase of Investments	($ 78,000)
Sale of Investments	102,000

Notice that purchases and sales are listed separately as cash outflows and cash inflows to give readers of the statement a complete view of investing activity. Some companies prefer to combine them into a single net amount.

If Ryan Corporation had short-term investments or marketable securities, the analysis of cash flows would be the same.

Plant Assets   In the case of plant assets, it is necessary to explain the changes in both the asset account and the related accumulated depreciation account. According to Exhibit 1, Plant Assets increased by $210,000 and Accumulated Depreciation increased by $35,000. Purchases increase plant assets, and sales decrease plant assets. Accumulated depreciation is increased by the amount of depreciation expense and decreased by the removal of the accumulated depreciation associated with plant assets that are sold. Three items listed in Exhibit 2 affect plant assets. Item **3** in the list on the previous page indicates that Ryan Corporation purchased plant assets totaling $120,000 during 20x1, as shown by this entry:

A = L + OE
+
–

Plant Assets	120,000	
Cash		120,000
Purchase of plant assets		

This transaction results in a cash outflow of $120,000.

Item **4** states that Ryan Corporation took plant assets that had cost $10,000 and had accumulated depreciation of $2,000, and sold them for $5,000, which resulted in a loss of $3,000. The entry to record this transaction is as follows:

A = L + OE
+
+
–

Cash	5,000	
Accumulated Depreciation	2,000	
Loss on Sale of Plant Assets	3,000	
Plant Assets		10,000
Sale of plant assets at a loss		

Note that in this transaction the positive cash flow is equal to the amount of cash received, or $5,000. The loss on the sale of plant assets is included here and excluded from the operating activities section by adjusting net income for the amount of the loss. The amount of a loss or gain on the sale of an asset is determined by the amount of cash received and does not represent a cash outflow or inflow.

The disclosure of these two transactions in the investing activities section of the statement of cash flows is as follows:

Purchase of Plant Assets	($120,000)
Sale of Plant Assets	5,000

As with investments, cash outflows and cash inflows are not combined here, but are sometimes combined into a single net amount.

Item **5** on the list of Ryan's investing activities is a noncash exchange that affects two long-term accounts, Plant Assets and Bonds Payable. It was recorded as follows:

A = L + OE
+ +

Plant Assets	100,000	
Bonds Payable		100,000
Issued bonds at face value for plant assets		

Although this transaction does not involve an inflow or outflow of cash, it is a significant transaction involving both an investing activity (the purchase of plant assets) and a financing activity (the issue of bonds payable). Because one purpose of the statement of cash flows is to show important investing and financing activities, the transaction is listed in a separate schedule, either at the bottom of the statement of cash flows or accompanying the statement, as follows:

Schedule of Noncash Investing and Financing Transactions

Issue of Bonds Payable for Plant Assets $100,000

Through our analysis of the preceding transactions and the depreciation expense for plant assets of $37,000, all the changes in the plant assets accounts have now been accounted for, as shown in the following T accounts:

Plant Assets

Beg. Bal.	505,000	Sale	10,000
Cash Purchase	120,000		
Noncash Purchase	100,000		
End. Bal.	715,000		

Accumulated Depreciation

Sale	2,000	Beg. Bal.	68,000
		Dep. Exp.	37,000
		End. Bal.	103,000

If the balance sheet had included specific plant asset accounts, such as Buildings and Equipment and their related accumulated depreciation accounts, or other long-term asset accounts, such as intangibles or natural resources, the analysis would have been the same.

Determining Cash Flows from Financing Activities

OBJECTIVE 6b
Determine cash flows from financing activities

The third step in preparing the statement of cash flows is to determine cash flows from financing activities. The procedure is similar to the analysis of investing activities, including treatment of related gains or losses. The only difference is that the accounts to be analyzed are the short-term borrowings, long-term liabilities, and stockholders' equity accounts. Cash dividends from the statement of stockholders' equity must also be considered. Since Ryan Corporation does not have short-term borrowings, only long-term liabilities and stockholders' equity accounts are considered here. The following items from Exhibit 2 pertain to Ryan Corporation's financing activities in 20x1:

5. Issued $100,000 of bonds at face value in a noncash exchange for plant assets.
6. Repaid $50,000 of bonds at face value at maturity.
7. Issued 15,200 shares of $5 par value common stock for $150,000.
8. Paid cash dividends in the amount of $8,000.

Bonds Payable   Exhibit 1 shows that Bonds Payable increased by $50,000 in 20x1. This account is affected by items **5** and **6.** Item **5** was analyzed in connection with plant assets. It is reported on the schedule of noncash investing and financing transactions (see Exhibit 4 on page 492), but it must be remembered here in preparing the T account for Bonds Payable. Item **6** results in a cash outflow, which can be seen in the following transaction.

A = L + OE
–   –

Bonds Payable	50,000	
Cash		50,000

    Repayment of bonds at face value
    at maturity

This cash outflow is shown in the financing activities section of the statement of cash flows as follows:

Repayment of Bonds   ($50,000)

From these transactions, the change in the Bonds Payable account can be explained as follows:

Bonds Payable

Repayment	50,000	Beg. Bal.	245,000
		Noncash Issue	100,000
		End. Bal.	295,000

If Ryan Corporation had notes payable, either short-term or long-term, the analysis would be the same.

Common Stock   As with plant assets, related stockholders' equity accounts should be analyzed together. For example, Paid-in Capital in Excess of Par Value, Common should be examined with Common Stock. In 20x1 Ryan Corporation's Common Stock account increased by $76,000 and Paid-in Capital in Excess of Par Value, Common increased by $74,000. Those increases are explained by item **7,** which states that Ryan Corporation issued 15,200 shares of stock for $150,000. The entry to record the cash inflow was as follows:

A = L + OE
+   +
**   +**

Cash	150,000	
Common Stock		76,000
Paid-in Capital in Excess of Par Value, Common		74,000

    Issued 15,200 shares of $5 par value common stock

The cash inflow is shown in the financing activities section of the statement of cash flows as follows:

Issue of Common Stock $150,000

The analysis of this transaction is all that is needed to explain the changes in the two accounts during 20x1, as follows:

Common Stock			**Paid-in Capital in Excess of Par Value, Common**		
	Beg. Bal.	200,000		Beg. Bal.	115,000
	Issue	76,000		Issue	74,000
	End. Bal.	276,000		End. Bal.	189,000

Retained Earnings   At this point in the analysis, several items that affect retained earnings have already been dealt with. For instance, in the case of Ryan Corporation, net income was used as part of the analysis of cash flows from operating activities. The only other item affecting the retained earnings of Ryan

Corporation is the payment of $8,000 in cash dividends (item **8** on the list on page 489), as reflected by the following transaction.

A = L + OE
−   −

Retained Earnings	8,000	
Cash		8,000
Cash dividends for 20x1		

Ryan Corporation would have declared the dividend before paying it and therefore would have debited the Cash Dividends Declared account instead of Retained Earnings, but after paying the dividend and closing the Cash Dividends Declared account to Retained Earnings, the effect is as shown. Cash dividends are displayed in the financing activities section of the statement of cash flows:

Dividends Paid   ($8,000)

The following T account shows the change in the Retained Earnings account.

Retained Earnings

Dividends	8,000	Beg. Bal.	132,000
		Net Income	16,000
		End. Bal.	**140,000**

Compiling the Statement of Cash Flows

At this point in the analysis, all income statement items have been analyzed, all balance sheet changes have been explained, and all additional information has been taken into account. The resulting information may now be assembled into a statement of cash flows for Ryan Corporation, as presented in Exhibit 4. The Schedule of Noncash Investing and Financing Transactions is presented at the bottom of the statement.

Preparing the Work Sheet

Previous sections illustrated the preparation of the statement of cash flows for Ryan Corporation, a relatively simple company. To assist in preparing the statement of cash flows for more complex companies, accountants have developed a work sheet approach. The work sheet approach employs a special format that allows for the systematic analysis of all the changes in the balance sheet accounts to arrive at the statement of cash flows. In this section, the work sheet approach is demonstrated using the statement of cash flows for Ryan Corporation. The work sheet approach uses the indirect method of determining cash flows from operating activities because of its basis in changes in the balance sheet accounts.

Procedures in Preparing the Work Sheet

The work sheet for Ryan Corporation is presented in Exhibit 5. The work sheet has four columns, labeled as follows:

Column A: Description
Column B: Account balances for the end of the prior year (20x0)
Column C: Analysis of transactions for the current year
Column D: Account balances for the end of the current year (20x1)

Exhibit 4. Statement of Cash Flows: Indirect Method

Ryan Corporation
Statement of Cash Flows
For the Year Ended December 31, 20x1

Cash Flows from Operating Activities

Net Income		$ 16,000
Adjustments to Reconcile Net Income to Net		
Cash Flows from Operating Activities		
Depreciation	$ 37,000	
Gain on Sale of Investments	(12,000)	
Loss on Sale of Plant Assets	3,000	
Changes in Current Assets and Current Liabilities		
Decrease in Accounts Receivable	8,000	
Increase in Inventory	(34,000)	
Decrease in Prepaid Expenses	4,000	
Increase in Accounts Payable	7,000	
Increase in Accrued Liabilities	3,000	
Decrease in Income Taxes Payable	(2,000)	14,000
Net Cash Flows from Operating Activities		$ 30,000

Cash Flows from Investing Activities

Purchase of Investments	($ 78,000)	
Sale of Investments	102,000	
Purchase of Plant Assets	(120,000)	
Sale of Plant Assets	5,000	
Net Cash Flows from Investing Activities		(91,000)

Cash Flows from Financing Activities

Repayment of Bonds	($ 50,000)	
Issue of Common Stock	150,000	
Dividends Paid	(8,000)	
Net Cash Flows from Financing Activities		92,000
Net Increase (Decrease) in Cash		$ 31,000
Cash at Beginning of Year		15,000
Cash at End of Year		$ 46,000

Schedule of Noncash Investing and Financing Transactions

Issue of Bonds Payable for Plant Assets		$100,000

Five steps are followed in preparing the work sheet. As you read each one, refer to Exhibit 5.

1. Enter the account names from the balance sheets (Exhibit 1) in column A. Note that all accounts with debit balances are listed first, followed by all accounts with credit balances.
2. Enter the account balances for 20x0 in column B and the account balances for 20x1 in column D. In each column, total the debits and the credits. The total debits should equal the total credits in each column. (This is a check of whether all accounts were correctly transferred from the balance sheets.)

Exhibit 5. Work Sheet for the Statement of Cash Flows

Ryan Corporation
Work Sheet for Statement of Cash Flows
For the Year Ended December 31, 20x1

Description	Account Balances 12/31/x0	Analysis of Transactions				Account Balances 12/31/x1
			Debit		Credit	
Debits						
Cash	15,000	(x)	31,000			46,000
Accounts Receivable (net)	55,000			(b)	8,000	47,000
Inventory	110,000	(c)	34,000			144,000
Prepaid Expenses	5,000			(d)	4,000	1,000
Investments Available for Sale	127,000	(h)	78,000	(i)	90,000	115,000
Plant Assets	505,000	(j)	120,000	(k)	10,000	715,000
		(l)	100,000			
Total Debits	817,000					1,068,000
Credits						
Accumulated Depreciation	68,000	(k)	2,000	(m)	37,000	103,000
Accounts Payable	43,000			(e)	7,000	50,000
Accrued Liabilities	9,000			(f)	3,000	12,000
Income Taxes Payable	5,000	(g)	2,000			3,000
Bonds Payable	245,000	(n)	50,000	(l)	100,000	295,000
Common Stock	200,000			(o)	76,000	276,000
Paid-in Capital	115,000			(o)	74,000	189,000
Retained Earnings	132,000	(p)	8,000	(a)	16,000	140,000
Total Credits	817,000		425,000		425,000	1,068,000
Cash Flows from Operating Activities						
Net Income		(a)	16,000			
Decrease in Accounts Receivable		(b)	8,000			
Increase in Inventory				(c)	34,000	
Decrease in Prepaid Expenses		(d)	4,000			
Increase in Accounts Payable		(e)	7,000			
Increase in Accrued Liabilities		(f)	3,000			
Decrease in Income Taxes Payable				(g)	2,000	
Gain on Sale of Investments				(i)	12,000	
Loss on Sale of Plant Assets		(k)	3,000			
Depreciation Expense		(m)	37,000			
Cash Flows from Investing Activities						
Purchase of Investments				(h)	78,000	
Sale of Investments		(i)	102,000			
Purchase of Plant Assets				(j)	120,000	
Sale of Plant Assets		(k)	5,000			
Cash Flows from Financing Activities						
Repayment of Bonds				(n)	50,000	
Issue of Common Stock		(o)	150,000			
Dividends Paid				(p)	8,000	
			335,000		304,000	
Net Increase in Cash				(x)	31,000	
			335,000		335,000	

3. Below the data entered in step **2,** insert the headings Cash Flows from Operating Activities, Cash Flows from Investing Activities, and Cash Flows from Financing Activities, leaving several lines of space between each one. As you do the analysis in step **4,** write the results in the appropriate categories.

4. Analyze the changes in each balance sheet account, using information from both the income statement (see Exhibit 2) and other transactions affecting noncurrent accounts during 20x1. (The procedures for this analysis are presented in the next section.) Enter the results in the debit and credit columns. Identify each item with a letter. On the first line, identify the change in cash with an (x). In a complex situation, these letters will refer to a list of explanations on another working paper.

5. When all the changes in the balance sheet accounts have been explained, add the debit and credit columns in both the top and the bottom portions of column C. The debit and credit columns in the top portion should equal each other. They should *not* be equal in the bottom portion. If no errors have been made, the difference between columns in the bottom portion should equal the increase or decrease in the Cash account, identified with an (x) on the first line of the work sheet. Add this difference to the lesser of the two columns, and identify it as either an increase or a decrease in cash. Label the change with an (x) and compare it with the change in Cash on the first line of the work sheet, also labeled (x). The amounts should be equal, as they are in Exhibit 5, where the net increase in cash is $31,000. Also, the new totals from the debit and credit columns should be equal.

When the work sheet is complete, the statement of cash flows may be prepared using the information in the lower half of the work sheet.

Analyzing the Changes in Balance Sheet Accounts

The most important step in preparing the work sheet is the analysis of the changes in the balance sheet accounts (step **4**). Although a number of transactions and reclassifications must be analyzed and recorded, the overall procedure is systematic and not overly complicated. It is as follows:

1. Record net income.
2. Account for changes in current assets and current liabilities.
3. Use the information about other transactions to account for changes in noncurrent accounts.
4. Reclassify any other income and expense items not already dealt with.

In the following explanations, the identification letters refer to the corresponding transactions and reclassifications in the work sheet.

a. *Net Income*   Net income results in an increase in Retained Earnings. Under the indirect method, it is the starting point for determining cash flows from operating activities. Under this method, additions and deductions are made to net income to arrive at cash flows from operating activities. Work sheet entry **a** is as follows:

(a) Cash Flows from Operating Activities: Net Income   16,000
      Retained Earnings   16,000

b–g. *Changes in Current Assets and Current Liabilities*   Entries **b** to **g** record the effects on cash flows of the changes in current assets and current liabilities. In each case, there is a debit or credit to the current asset or current liability to account for the change from year to year and a corresponding debit or credit in the operating activities section of the work sheet. For example, work sheet entry **b** records the decrease in Accounts Receivable as a credit (decrease) to Accounts Receivable and as a debit in the operating activities section because the decrease has a positive effect on cash flows, as follows:

(b) Cash Flows from Operating Activities:
    Decrease in Accounts Receivable   8,000
      Accounts Receivable   8,000

Work sheet entries **c–g** reflect the effects on cash flows from operating activities of the changes in the other current assets and current liabilities. As you study these entries, note how the effects of each entry on cash flows are automatically determined by debits or credits reflecting changes in the balance sheet accounts.

(c) Inventory   34,000
    Cash Flows from Operating Activities:
      Increase in Inventory   34,000

(d) Cash Flows from Operating Activities:
    Decrease in Prepaid Expenses   4,000
      Prepaid Expenses   4,000

(e) Cash Flows from Operating Activities:
    Increase in Accounts Payable   7,000
      Accounts Payable   7,000

(f) Cash Flows from Operating Activities:
    Increase in Accrued Liabilities   3,000
      Accrued Liabilities   3,000

(g) Income Taxes Payable   2,000
    Cash Flows from Operating Activities:
      Decrease in Income Taxes Payable   2,000

h–i. Investments   Among the other transactions affecting noncurrent accounts during 20x1 (see Exhibit 2), two pertain to investments. One is the purchase for $78,000, and the other is the sale at $102,000. The purchase is recorded on the work sheet as a cash flow in the investing activities section, as follows:

(h) Investments   78,000
    Cash Flows from Investing Activities:
      Purchase of Investments   78,000

Note that instead of a credit to Cash, a credit entry with the appropriate designation is made in the appropriate section in the lower half of the work sheet. The sale transaction is more complicated because it involves a gain that appears on the income statement and is included in net income. The work sheet entry shows this gain as follows:

(i) Cash Flows from Investing Activities:
    Sale of Investments   102,000
      Investments   90,000
      Cash Flows from Operating Activities:
        Gain on Sale of Investments   12,000

This entry records the cash inflow in the investing activities section, accounts for the remaining difference in the Investments account, and removes the gain on sale of investments from net income.

j–m. Plant Assets and Accumulated Depreciation   The four transactions that affect plant assets and the related accumulated depreciation are the purchase of plant assets, the sale of plant assets at a loss, the noncash exchange of bonds for plant assets, and the depreciation expense for the year. Because these transactions may appear complicated, it is important to work through them systematically when preparing the work sheet. First, the purchase of plant assets for $120,000 is entered (entry **j**) in the same way the purchase of investments was entered in entry **h:**

(j) Plant Assets   120,000
    Cash Flows from Investing Activities:
      Purchase of Plant Assets   120,000

Second, the sale of plant assets is similar to the sale of investments, except that a loss is involved, as follows:

(k) Cash Flows from Investing Activities:
    Sale of Plant Assets   5,000
    Cash Flows from Operating Activities:
    Loss on Sale of Plant Assets   3,000
    Accumulated Depreciation   2,000
      Plant Assets   10,000

The cash inflow from this transaction is $5,000. The rest of the entry is necessary in order to add the loss back into net income in the operating activities section of the statement of cash flows (since it was deducted to arrive at net income and no cash outflow resulted) and to record the effects on plant assets and accumulated depreciation.

The third transaction (entry **l**) is the noncash issue of bonds for the purchase of plant assets, as follows:

(l) Plant Assets   100,000
    Bonds Payable   100,000

Note that this transaction does not affect Cash. Still, it needs to be recorded because the objective is to account for all changes in the balance sheet accounts. It is listed at the end of the statement of cash flows (Exhibit 4) in the schedule of noncash investing and financing transactions.

At this point, the increase of $210,000 ($715,000 − $505,000) in plant assets has been explained by the two purchases less the sale ($120,000 + $100,000 − $10,000 = $210,000), but the change in Accumulated Depreciation has not been completely explained. The depreciation expense for the year needs to be entered, as follows:

(m) Cash Flows from Operating Activities:
    Depreciation Expense   37,000
      Accumulated Depreciation   37,000

The debit is to the operating activities section of the work sheet because, as explained earlier in the chapter, no current cash outflow is required for depreciation expense. The effect of this debit is to add the amount for depreciation expense back into net income. The $35,000 increase in Accumulated Depreciation has now been explained by the sale transaction and the depreciation expense (−$2,000 + $37,000 = $35,000).

n. Bonds Payable   Part of the change in Bonds Payable was explained in entry **l** when a noncash transaction, a $100,000 issue of bonds in exchange for plant assets, was entered. All that remains to be entered is the repayment, as follows:

(n) Bonds Payable   50,000
    Cash Flows from Financing Activities:
      Repayment of Bonds   50,000

o. Common Stock and Paid-in Capital in Excess of Par Value, Common   One transaction affects both these accounts. It is an issue of 15,200 shares of $5 par value common stock for a total of $150,000. The work sheet entry follows.

(o) Cash Flows from Financing Activities:

Issue of Common Stock	150,000	
Common Stock		76,000
Paid-in Capital in Excess of Par Value, Common		74,000

p. Retained Earnings Part of the change in Retained Earnings was recognized when net income was entered (entry **a**). The only remaining effect to be recognized is the $8,000 in cash dividends paid during the year, as follows:

(p) Retained Earnings	8,000	
Cash Flows from Financing Activities:		
Dividends Paid		8,000

x. Cash The final step is to total the debit and credit columns in the top and bottom portions of the work sheet and then to enter the net change in cash at the bottom of the work sheet. The columns in the upper half equal $425,000. In the lower half, the debit column totals $335,000 and the credit column totals $304,000. The credit difference of $31,000 (entry **x**) equals the debit change in cash on the first line of the work sheet.

The Direct Method of Preparing the Statement of Cash Flows

To this point in the chapter, the indirect method of preparing the statement of cash flows has been used. In this section, the direct method is presented. First, the use of the direct method to determine net cash flows from operating activities is covered. Then the statement of cash flows under the direct method is illustrated.

Determining Cash Flows from Operating Activities

The principal difference between the indirect and the direct methods appears in the cash flows from operating activities section of the statement of cash flows. As you have seen, the indirect method starts with net income from the income statement and converts it to net cash flows from operating activities by adding or subtracting items that do not affect net cash flows. The direct method takes a different approach. It converts each item on the income statement to its cash equivalent, as illustrated in Figure 3. For instance, sales are converted to cash receipts from sales, and purchases are converted to cash payments for purchases. Exhibit 6 shows the schedule of cash flows from operating activities under the direct method for Ryan Corporation. The conversion of the components of Ryan Corporation's income statement to those figures is explained in the following paragraphs.

**Figure 3
Direct Method of
Determining Net Cash Flows
from Operating Activities**

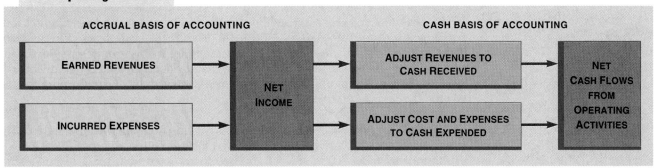

Exhibit 6. Schedule of Cash Flows from Operating Activities: Direct Method

Ryan Corporation
Schedule of Cash Flows from Operating Activities
For the Year Ended December 31, 20x1

Cash Flows from Operating Activities		
Cash Receipts from		
Sales	$706,000	
Interest Received	6,000	$712,000
Cash Payments for		
Purchases	$547,000	
Operating Expenses	103,000	
Interest	23,000	
Income Taxes	9,000	682,000
Net Cash Flows from Operating Activities		$ 30,000

Cash Receipts from Sales   Sales result in a positive cash flow for a company. Cash sales are direct cash inflows. Credit sales are not, because they are originally recorded as accounts receivable. When they are collected, they become cash inflows. You cannot, however, assume that credit sales are automatically inflows of cash, because the collections of accounts receivable in any one accounting period are not likely to equal credit sales. Receivables may be uncollectible, sales from a prior period may be collected in the current period, or sales from the current period may be collected in the next period. For example, if accounts receivable increase from one accounting period to the next, cash receipts from sales will not be as great as sales. On the other hand, if accounts receivable decrease from one accounting period to the next, cash receipts from sales will exceed sales.

The relationships among sales, changes in accounts receivable, and cash receipts from sales are reflected in the following formula:

$$\text{Cash Receipts from Sales} = \text{Sales} \begin{cases} + \text{ Decrease in Accounts Receivable} \\ \text{or} \\ - \text{ Increase in Accounts Receivable} \end{cases}$$

Refer to the balance sheets and income statement for Ryan Corporation in Exhibits 1 and 2. Note that sales were $698,000 in 20x1 and that accounts receivable decreased by $8,000. Thus, cash received from sales is $706,000:

$$\$706,000 = \$698,000 + \$8,000$$

Collections were $8,000 more than sales recorded for the year.

Cash Receipts from Interest and Dividends   Although interest and dividends received are most closely associated with investment activity and are often called investment income, the FASB has decided to classify the cash received from these items as operating activities. To simplify the examples in this text, it is assumed that interest income equals interest received and that dividend income equals dividends received. Thus, based on Exhibit 2, interest received by Ryan Corporation is assumed to equal $6,000, which is the amount of interest income.

Cash Payments for Purchases   Cost of goods sold (from the income statement) must be adjusted for changes in two balance sheet accounts to arrive at cash payments for purchases. First, cost of goods sold must be adjusted for changes in inventory to arrive at net purchases. Then, net purchases must be adjusted for the change in accounts payable to arrive at cash payments for purchases. If inventory has increased from one accounting period to another, net purchases will be greater than cost of goods sold because net purchases during the period have exceeded the dollar amount of the items sold during the period. If inventory has decreased, net purchases will be less than cost of goods sold. Conversely, if accounts payable have increased, cash payments for purchases will be less than net purchases; if accounts payable have decreased, cash payments for purchases will be greater than net purchases.

These relationships may be stated in equation form as follows:

$$\text{Cash Payments for Purchases} = \text{Cost of Goods Sold} \begin{Bmatrix} +\ \text{Increase in Inventory} \\ \text{or} \\ -\ \text{Decrease in Inventory} \end{Bmatrix} \begin{Bmatrix} +\ \text{Decrease in Accounts Payable} \\ \text{or} \\ -\ \text{Increase in Accounts Payable} \end{Bmatrix}$$

From Exhibits 1 and 2, cost of goods sold is $520,000, inventory increased by $34,000, and accounts payable increased by $7,000. Thus, cash payments for purchases is $547,000, as the following calculation shows:

$$\$547{,}000 = \$520{,}000 + 34{,}000 - \$7{,}000$$

In this example, Ryan Corporation purchased $34,000 more inventory than it sold and paid out $7,000 less in cash than it made in purchases. The net result is that cash payments for purchases exceeded cost of goods sold by $27,000 ($547,000 − $520,000).

Cash Payments for Operating Expenses   Just as cost of goods sold does not represent the amount of cash paid for purchases during an accounting period, operating expenses do not match the amount of cash paid to employees, suppliers, and others for goods and services. Three adjustments must be made to operating expenses to arrive at the cash outflows. The first adjustment is for changes in prepaid expenses, such as prepaid insurance or prepaid rent. If prepaid assets increase during the accounting period, more cash will have been paid out than appears on the income statement as expenses. If prepaid assets decrease, the expenses shown on the income statement will exceed the cash spent.

The second adjustment is for changes in liabilities resulting from accrued expenses, such as wages payable and payroll taxes payable. If accrued liabilities increase during the accounting period, operating expenses on the income statement will exceed the cash spent. And if accrued liabilities decrease, operating expenses will fall short of cash spent.

The third adjustment is made because certain expenses do not require a current outlay of cash; those expenses must be subtracted from operating expenses to arrive at cash payments for operating expenses. The most common expenses in this category are depreciation expense, amortization expense, and depletion expense. For example, Ryan Corporation recorded 20x1 depreciation expense of $37,000. No cash payment was made in this transaction. Therefore, to the extent that operating expenses include depreciation and similar items, an adjustment is needed to reduce operating expenses to the amount of cash expended.

The three adjustments to operating expenses are summarized in the equations that follow.

$$\text{Cash Payments for Operating Expenses} = \text{Operating Expenses} \begin{Bmatrix} +\ \text{Increase in Prepaid Expenses} \\ \text{or} \\ -\ \text{Decrease in Prepaid Expenses} \end{Bmatrix} \begin{Bmatrix} +\ \text{Decrease in Accrued Liabilities} \\ \text{or} \\ -\ \text{Increase in Accrued Liabilities} \end{Bmatrix} \begin{Bmatrix} -\ \text{Depreciation and Other Noncash Expenses} \end{Bmatrix}$$

According to Exhibits 1 and 2, Ryan's operating expenses (including depreciation of $37,000) were $147,000, prepaid expenses decreased by $4,000, and accrued liabilities increased by $3,000. As a result, Ryan Corporation's cash payments for operating expenses are $103,000, computed as follows:

$$\$103,000 \; = \; \$147,000 \; - \; \$4,000 \; - \; \$3,000 \; - \; \$37,000$$

If there are prepaid expenses and accrued liabilities that are *not* related to specific operating expenses, they are not included in these computations. One example is income taxes payable, which is the accrued liability related to income taxes expense. The cash payment for income taxes will be discussed shortly.

Cash Payments for Interest   The FASB classifies cash payments for interest as operating activities, although some authorities argue that they should be considered financing activities because of their association with loans incurred to finance the business. The FASB feels that interest expense is a cost of operating a business, and this is the position followed in this text. Also, for the sake of simplicity, all examples in this text assume that interest payments are equal to interest expense on the income statement. Thus, based on Exhibit 2, Ryan Corporation's interest payments are assumed to be $23,000 in 20x1.

Cash Payments for Income Taxes   The amount of income taxes expense that appears on the income statement rarely equals the amount of income taxes actually paid during the year. To determine cash payments for income taxes, income taxes (from the income statement) is adjusted by the change in Income Taxes Payable. If Income Taxes Payable increased during the accounting period, cash payments for taxes will be less than the expense shown on the income statement. If Income Taxes Payable decreased, cash payments for taxes will exceed income taxes on the income statement. In other words, the following equation is applicable:

$$\begin{array}{l}\text{Cash Payments} \\ \text{for Income Taxes}\end{array} = \begin{array}{l}\text{Income} \\ \text{Taxes}\end{array} \left\{ \begin{array}{l} + \text{ Decrease in Income Taxes Payable} \\ \qquad\qquad\qquad \text{or} \\ - \text{ Increase in Income Taxes Payable} \end{array} \right.$$

In 20x1, Ryan Corporation showed income taxes of $7,000 on its income statement and a decrease of $2,000 in Income Taxes Payable on its balance sheets (see Exhibits 1 and 2). As a result, cash payments for income taxes during 20x1 were $9,000, calculated as follows:

$$\$9,000 \; = \; \$7,000 \; + \; \$2,000$$

Compiling the Statement of Cash Flows

The Ryan Corporation's statement of cash flows under the direct method is presented in Exhibit 7. The only differences between that statement of cash flows and the one based on the indirect method shown in Exhibit 4 occur in the first and last sections. The middle sections, which present cash flows from investing activities and financing activities, net increases or decreases in cash, and the schedule of noncash investing and financing activities, are the same under both methods.

The first section of the statement in Exhibit 7 shows the net cash flows from operating activities on a direct basis, as presented in Exhibit 6. The last section is the same as the cash flows from operating activities section of the statement of cash flows under the indirect method (see Exhibit 4). The FASB believes that when the direct method is used, a schedule must be provided that reconciles net income to net cash flows from operating activities. Thus, the statement of cash flows under the direct method includes a section that accommodates the main difference between it and the indirect method.

Exhibit 7. Statement of Cash Flows: Direct Method

Ryan Corporation
Statement of Cash Flows
For the Year Ended December 31, 20x1

Cash Flows from Operating Activities

Cash Receipts from		
Sales	$706,000	
Interest Received	6,000	$712,000
Cash Payments for		
Purchases	$547,000	
Operating Expenses	103,000	
Interest	23,000	
Income Taxes	9,000	682,000
Net Cash Flows from Operating Activities		$ 30,000

Cash Flows from Investing Activities

Purchase of Investments	($ 78,000)	
Sale of Investments	102,000	
Purchase of Plant Assets	(120,000)	
Sale of Plant Assets	5,000	
Net Cash Flows from Investing Activities		(91,000)

Cash Flows from Financing Activities

Repayment of Bonds	($ 50,000)	
Issue of Common Stock	150,000	
Dividends Paid	(8,000)	
Net Cash Flows from Financing Activities		92,000
Net Increase (Decrease) in Cash		$ 31,000
Cash at Beginning of Year		15,000
Cash at End of Year		$ 46,000

Schedule of Noncash Investing and Financing Transactions

Issue of Bonds Payable for Plant Assets	$100,000

Reconciliation of Net Income to Net Cash Flows from Operating Activities

Net Income		$ 16,000
Adjustments to Reconcile Net Income to Net Cash Flows from Operating Activities		
Depreciation	$ 37,000	
Gain on Sale of Investments	(12,000)	
Loss on Sale of Plant Assets	3,000	
Changes in Current Assets and Current Liabilities		
Decrease in Accounts Receivable	8,000	
Increase in Inventory	(34,000)	
Decrease in Prepaid Expenses	4,000	
Increase in Accounts Payable	7,000	
Increase in Accrued Liabilities	3,000	
Decrease in Income Taxes Payable	(2,000)	14,000
Net Cash Flows from Operating Activities		$ 30,000

Chapter Review

REVIEW OF LEARNING OBJECTIVES

1. Describe the statement of cash flows, and define *cash and cash equivalents.* The statement of cash flows explains the changes in cash and cash equivalents from one accounting period to the next by showing cash inflows and cash outflows from the operating, investing, and financing activities of a company for an accounting period. For purposes of preparing the statement of cash flows, *cash* is defined to include cash and cash equivalents. *Cash equivalents* are short-term (ninety days or less), highly liquid investments, including money market accounts, commercial paper, and U.S. Treasury bills.

2. State the principal purposes and uses of the statement of cash flows. The primary purpose of the statement of cash flows is to provide information about a company's cash receipts and cash payments during an accounting period. Its secondary purpose is to provide information about a company's operating, investing, and financing activities. The statement is useful to management as well as to investors and creditors in assessing the liquidity of a business, including its ability to generate future cash flows and to pay debts and dividends.

3. Identify the principal components of the classifications of cash flows, and state the significance of noncash investing and financing transactions. Cash flows may be classified as stemming from (1) operating activities, which include the cash effects of transactions and other events that enter into the determination of net income; (2) investing activities, which include the acquiring and selling of long- and short-term marketable securities and property, plant, and equipment, and the making and collecting of loans, excluding interest; or (3) financing activities, which include the obtaining and returning or repaying of resources, excluding interest, to owners and creditors. Noncash investing and financing transactions are also important because they are exchanges of assets and/or liabilities that are of interest to investors and creditors when evaluating the financing and investing activities of a business.

4. Analyze the statement of cash flows. In analyzing a company's statement of cash flows, analysts tend to focus on cash-generating efficiency and free cash flow. Cash-generating efficiency is a company's ability to generate cash from its current or continuing operations. Three ratios used in measuring cash-generating efficiency are cash flow yield, cash flows to sales, and cash flows to assets. Free cash flow is the cash that remains after deducting funds a company must commit to continue operating at its planned level. Such commitments must cover current or continuing operations, interest, income taxes, dividends, and net capital expenditures.

5. Use the indirect method to determine cash flows from operating activities. Under the indirect method, net income is adjusted for all noncash effects and for items that need to be converted from an accrual to a cash basis to arrive at a cash flow basis, as follows:

Cash Flows from Operating Activities		
Net Income		xxx
Adjustments to Reconcile Net Income to Net Cash		
Flows from Operating Activities		
(List of individual items)	xxx	xxx
Net Cash Flows from Operating Activities		xxx

6. Determine cash flows from (a) investing activities and (b) financing activities. Cash flows from investing activities are determined by identifying the cash flow effects of the transactions that affect each account relevant to investing activities. Such accounts include all long-term assets and short-term marketable securities. The same procedure is followed for financing activities, except that the accounts involved are short-term borrowings, long-term liabilities, and stockholders' equity. The effects of gains and losses reported on the income statement must also be considered. After the changes in the balance sheet accounts from one accounting period to the next have been explained, all the cash flow effects should have been identified.

7. **Use the indirect method to prepare a statement of cash flows.** The statement of cash flows lists cash flows from operating activities, investing activities, and financing activities, in that order. The sections on investing and financing activities are prepared by examining individual accounts involving cash receipts and cash payments from investing and financing activities to explain year-to-year changes in the account balances. Significant noncash transactions are included in a schedule of noncash investing and financing transactions that accompanies the statement of cash flows.

Supplemental Objectives

8. **Prepare a work sheet for the statement of cash flows.** A work sheet is useful in preparing the statement of cash flows for complex companies. The basic procedures are to analyze the changes in the balance sheet accounts for their effects on cash flows (in the top portion of the work sheet) and to classify those effects according to the format of the statement of cash flows (in the lower portion of the work sheet). When all changes in the balance sheet accounts have been explained and entered on the work sheet, the change in the Cash account will also be explained, and all necessary information will be available to prepare the statement of cash flows. The work sheet approach lends itself to the indirect method of preparing the statement of cash flows.

9. **Use the direct method to determine cash flows from operating activities and prepare a statement of cash flows.** The principal difference between a statement of cash flows prepared under the direct method and one prepared under the indirect method appears in the cash flows from operating activities section. Instead of beginning with net income and making additions and subtractions, as is done with the indirect method, the direct method converts each item on the income statement to its cash equivalent by adjusting for changes in the related current asset or current liability accounts and for other items such as depreciation. The rest of the statement of cash flows is the same under the direct method, except that a schedule that reconciles net income to net cash flows from operating activities must be included.

REVIEW OF CONCEPTS AND TERMINOLOGY

The following concepts and terms were introduced in this chapter.

LO 1   **Cash:** For purposes of the statement of cash flows, both cash and cash equivalents.

LO 1   **Cash equivalents:** Short-term (ninety days or less), highly liquid investments, including money market accounts, commercial paper, and U.S. Treasury bills.

LO 4   **Cash flows to assets:** The ratio of net cash flows from operating activities to average total assets.

LO 4   **Cash flows to sales:** The ratio of net cash flows from operating activities to sales.

LO 4   **Cash flow yield:** The ratio of net cash flows from operating activities to net income.

LO 4   **Cash-generating efficiency:** The ability of a company to generate cash from its current or continuing operations.

LO 5   **Direct method:** The procedure for converting the income statement from an accrual basis to a cash basis by separately adjusting each item in the income statement.

LO 3   **Financing activities:** Business activities that involve obtaining resources from or returning resources to owners and providing them with a return on their investment, and obtaining resources from creditors and repaying any amounts borrowed or otherwise settling the obligations.

LO 4   **Free cash flow:** The amount of cash that remains after deducting the funds a company must commit to continue operating at its planned level; net cash flows from operating activities minus dividends minus net capital expenditures.

LO 5 **Indirect method:** The procedure for converting the income statement from an accrual basis to a cash basis by adjusting net income for items that do not affect cash flows, including depreciation, amortization, depletion, gains, losses, and changes in current assets and current liabilities.

LO 3 **Investing activities:** Business activities that involve the acquiring and selling of long-term assets, the acquiring and selling of marketable securities other than trading securities or cash equivalents, and the making and collecting of loans.

LO 3 **Noncash investing and financing transactions:** Significant investing and financing transactions that do not involve an actual cash inflow or outflow but involve only long-term assets, long-term liabilities, or stockholders' equity, such as the exchange of a long-term asset for a long-term liability or the settlement of a debt by issuing capital stock.

LO 3 **Operating activities:** Business activities that involve the cash effects of transactions and other events that enter into the determination of net income.

LO 1 **Statement of cash flows:** A primary financial statement that shows how a company's operating, investing, and financing activities have affected cash during an accounting period.

REVIEW PROBLEM

The Statement of Cash Flows

LO 4
LO 5 The 20x2 income statement for Northwest Corporation is presented below and the comparative balance sheets for the years 20x2 and 20x1 are shown on the next page.
LO 6
LO 7
SO 9

Northwest Corporation
Income Statement
For the Year Ended December 31, 20x2

Net Sales		$1,650,000
Cost of Goods Sold		920,000
Gross Margin		$ 730,000
Operating Expenses (including Depreciation Expense of $12,000 on Buildings and $23,100 on Equipment, and Amortization Expense of $4,800)		470,000
Operating Income		$ 260,000
Other Income (Expenses)		
Interest Expense	($55,000)	
Dividend Income	3,400	
Gain on Sale of Investments	12,500	
Loss on Disposal of Equipment	(2,300)	(41,400)
Income Before Income Taxes		$ 218,600
Income Taxes		52,200
Net Income		$ 166,400

Northwest Corporation
Comparative Balance Sheets
December 31, 20x2 and 20x1

	20x2	20x1	Change	Increase or Decrease
Assets				
Cash	$ 115,850	$ 121,850	($ 6,000)	Decrease
Accounts Receivable (net)	296,000	314,500	(18,500)	Decrease
Inventory	322,000	301,000	21,000	Increase
Prepaid Expenses	7,800	5,800	2,000	Increase
Long-Term Investments	36,000	86,000	(50,000)	Decrease
Land	150,000	125,000	25,000	Increase
Buildings	462,000	462,000	—	—
Accumulated Depreciation, Buildings	(91,000)	(79,000)	(12,000)	Increase
Equipment	159,730	167,230	(7,500)	Decrease
Accumulated Depreciation, Equipment	(43,400)	(45,600)	2,200	Decrease
Intangible Assets	19,200	24,000	(4,800)	Decrease
Total Assets	$1,434,180	$1,482,780	($ 48,600)	
Liabilities and Stockholders' Equity				
Accounts Payable	$ 133,750	$ 233,750	($100,000)	Decrease
Notes Payable (current)	75,700	145,700	(70,000)	Decrease
Accrued Liabilities	5,000	—	5,000	Increase
Income Taxes Payable	20,000	—	20,000	Increase
Bonds Payable	210,000	310,000	(100,000)	Decrease
Mortgage Payable	330,000	350,000	(20,000)	Decrease
Common Stock, $10 par value	360,000	300,000	60,000	Increase
Paid-in Capital in Excess of Par Value	90,000	50,000	40,000	Increase
Retained Earnings	209,730	93,330	116,400	Increase
Total Liabilities and Stockholders' Equity	$1,434,180	$1,482,780	($ 48,600)	

The following additional information was taken from the company's records:

a. Long-term investments (available-for-sale securities) that cost $70,000 were sold at a gain of $12,500; additional long-term investments were made in the amount of $20,000.

b. Five acres of land were purchased for $25,000 to build a parking lot.

c. Equipment that cost $37,500 with accumulated depreciation of $25,300 was sold at a loss of $2,300; new equipment costing $30,000 was purchased.

d. Notes payable in the amount of $100,000 were repaid; an additional $30,000 was borrowed by signing notes payable.

e. Bonds payable in the amount of $100,000 were converted into 6,000 shares of common stock.

f. The Mortgage Payable account was reduced by $20,000 during the year.

g. Cash dividends declared and paid were $50,000.

REQUIRED

1. Prepare a schedule of cash flows from operating activities using the (a) indirect method and (b) direct method.
2. Prepare a statement of cash flows using the indirect method.
3. Compute cash flow yield, cash flows to sales, cash flows to assets, and free cash flow for 20x2.

ANSWER TO REVIEW PROBLEM

1. (a) Prepare a schedule of cash flows from operating activities using the indirect method.

Northwest Corporation
Schedule of Cash Flows from Operating Activities
For the Year Ended December 31, 20x2

Cash Flows from Operating Activities		
Net Income		$166,400
Adjustments to Reconcile Net Income to		
Net Cash Flows from Operating Activities		
Depreciation Expense, Buildings	$ 12,000	
Depreciation Expense, Equipment	23,100	
Amortization Expense, Intangible Assets	4,800	
Gain on Sale of Investments	(12,500)	
Loss on Disposal of Equipment	2,300	
Changes in Current Assets		
and Current Liabilities		
Decrease in Accounts Receivable	18,500	
Increase in Inventory	(21,000)	
Increase in Prepaid Expenses	(2,000)	
Decrease in Accounts Payable	(100,000)	
Increase in Accrued Liabilities	5,000	
Increase in Income Taxes Payable	20,000	(49,800)
Net Cash Flows from Operating Activities		$116,600

1. (b) Prepare a schedule of cash flows from operating activities using the direct method.

Northwest Corporation
Schedule of Cash Flows from Operating Activities
For the Year Ended December 31, 20x2

Cash Flows from Operating Activities		
Cash Receipts from		
Sales	$1,668,500[1]	
Dividends Received	3,400	$1,671,900
Cash Payments for		
Purchases	$1,041,000[2]	
Operating Expenses	427,100[3]	
Interest	55,000	
Income Taxes	32,200[4]	1,555,300
Net Cash Flows from Operating Activities		$ 116,600

1. $1,650,000 + $18,500 = $1,668,500
2. $920,000 + $100,000 + $21,000 = $1,041,000
3. $470,000 + $2,000 − $5,000 − ($12,000 + $23,100 + $4,800) = $427,100
4. $52,200 − $20,000 = $32,200

2. Prepare a statement of cash flows using the indirect method.

Northwest Corporation
Statement of Cash Flows
For the Year Ended December 31, 20x2

Cash Flows from Operating Activities

Net Income		$166,400
Adjustments to Reconcile Net Income to		
Net Cash Flows from Operating Activities		
Depreciation Expense, Buildings	$ 12,000	
Depreciation Expense, Equipment	23,100	
Amortization Expense, Intangible Assets	4,800	
Gain on Sale of Investments	(12,500)	
Loss on Disposal of Equipment	2,300	
Changes in Current Assets and		
Current Liabilities		
Decrease in Accounts Receivable	18,500	
Increase in Inventory	(21,000)	
Increase in Prepaid Expenses	(2,000)	
Decrease in Accounts Payable	(100,000)	
Increase in Accrued Liabilities	5,000	
Increase in Income Taxes Payable	20,000	(49,800)
Net Cash Flows from Operating Activities		$116,600

Cash Flows from Investing Activities

Sale of Long-Term Investments	$ 82,500[1]	
Purchase of Long-Term Investments	(20,000)	
Purchase of Land	(25,000)	
Sale of Equipment	9,900[2]	
Purchase of Equipment	(30,000)	
Net Cash Flows from Investing Activities		17,400

Cash Flows from Financing Activities

Repayment of Notes Payable	($100,000)	
Issuance of Notes Payable	30,000	
Reduction in Mortgage	(20,000)	
Dividends Paid	(50,000)	
Net Cash Flows from Financing Activities		(140,000)

Net Increase (Decrease) in Cash		($ 6,000)
Cash at Beginning of Year		121,850
Cash at End of Year		$115,850

Schedule of Noncash Investing and Financing Transactions

Conversion of Bonds Payable into Common Stock	$100,000

---

1. $70,000 + $12,500 (gain) = $82,500
2. $37,500 − $25,300 = $12,200 (book value) − $2,300 (loss) = $9,900

3. Compute cash flow yield, cash flows to sales, cash flows to assets, and free cash flow for 20x2.

$$\text{Cash Flow Yield} = \frac{\$116,600}{\$166,400} = .7 \text{ times}$$

$$\text{Cash Flows to Sales} = \frac{\$116,600}{\$1,650,000} = 7.1\%$$

$$\text{Cash Flows to Assets} = \frac{\$116,600}{(\$1,434,180 + \$1,482,780)/2} = 8.0\%$$

$$\text{Free Cash Flow} = \$116,600 - \$50,000 - \$25,000 - \$30,000 + \$9,900$$
$$= \$21,500$$

Chapter Assignments

BUILDING YOUR KNOWLEDGE FOUNDATION

Questions

1. In the statement of cash flows, what is the term *cash* understood to include?
2. To earn a return on cash on hand during 20x3, Sallas Corporation transferred $45,000 from its checking account to a money market account, purchased a $25,000 Treasury bill, and invested $35,000 in common stocks. How will each of these transactions affect the statement of cash flows?
3. What are the purposes of the statement of cash flows?
4. Why is the statement of cash flows needed when most of the information in it is available from a company's comparative balance sheets and income statement?
5. What are the three classifications of cash flows? Give some examples of each.
6. Why is it important to disclose certain noncash transactions? How should they be disclosed?
7. Define *cash-generating efficiency* and identify three ratios that measure cash-generating efficiency.
8. Define *free cash flow* and identify its components. What does it mean to have a positive or a negative free cash flow?
9. What are the essential differences between the direct method and the indirect method of determining cash flows from operations?
10. In determining net cash flows from operating activities (assuming the indirect method is used), what are the effects on cash generated of the following items: (a) an increase in accounts receivable, (b) a decrease in inventory, (c) an increase in accounts payable, (d) a decrease in wages payable, (e) depreciation expense, and (f) amortization of patents?
11. Cell-Borne Corporation had a net loss of $12,000 in 20x1 but had positive cash flows from operations of $9,000. What conditions may have caused this situation?
12. What is the proper treatment on the statement of cash flows of a transaction in which a building that cost $50,000 with accumulated depreciation of $32,000 is sold at a loss of $5,000?
13. What is the proper treatment on the statement of cash flows of (a) a transaction in which buildings and land are purchased by the issuance of a mortgage for $234,000 and (b) a conversion of $50,000 in bonds payable into 2,500 shares of $6 par value common stock?
14. Why is the work sheet approach considered to be more compatible with the indirect method than with the direct method of determining cash flows from operations?
15. Assuming in each of the following independent cases that only one transaction occurred, what transactions would be likely to cause (a) a decrease in investments

and (b) an increase in common stock? How would each case be treated on the work sheet for the statement of cash flows?

16. Glen Corporation has the following other income and expense items: interest expense, $12,000; interest income, $3,000; dividend income, $5,000; and loss on the retirement of bonds, $6,000. How does each of these items appear on or affect the statement of cash flows, assuming the direct method is used?

Short Exercises

SE 1.
LO 3 *Classification of Cash Flow Transactions*

Tosca Corporation engaged in the transactions below. Identify each as (a) an operating activity, (b) an investing activity, (c) a financing activity, (d) a noncash transaction, or (e) none of the above.

1. Sold land for a gain.
2. Declared and paid a cash dividend.
3. Paid interest.
4. Issued common stock for plant assets.
5. Issued preferred stock.
6. Borrowed cash on a bank loan.

SE 2.
LO 4 *Cash-Generating Efficiency Ratios and Free Cash Flow*

In 20x2, Wu Corporation had year-end assets of $550,000, net sales of $790,000, net income of $90,000, net cash flows from operating activities of $180,000, purchases of plant assets of $120,000, sales of plant assets of $20,000, and paid dividends of $40,000. In 20x1, year-end assets were $500,000. Calculate the cash-generating efficiency ratios of cash flow yield, cash flows to sales, and cash flows to assets. Also calculate free cash flow.

SE 3.
LO 4 *Cash Flow Efficiency and Free Cash Flow*

Examine the cash flow measures in **3** of the review problem on page 508. Discuss the meaning of these ratios.

SE 4.
LO 5 *Computing Cash Flows from Operating Activities: Indirect Method*

Specialty Products Corporation had a net income of $33,000 during 20x1. During the year the company had depreciation expense of $14,000. Accounts receivable increased by $11,000, and accounts payable increased by $5,000. Those were the company's only current assets and current liabilities. Use the indirect method to determine cash flows from operating activities.

SE 5.
LO 5 *Computing Cash Flows from Operating Activities: Indirect Method*

During 20x1, Ayzarian Corporation had a net income of $72,000. Included on the income statement was depreciation expense of $8,000 and amortization expense of $900. During the year, accounts receivable decreased by $4,100, inventories increased by $2,700, prepaid expenses decreased by $500, accounts payable decreased by $7,000, and accrued liabilities decreased by $850. Use the indirect method to determine cash flows from operating activities.

SE 6.
LO 6 *Cash Flows from Investing Activities and Noncash Transactions*

During 20x1, Rhode Island Company purchased land for $750,000. It paid $250,000 in cash and signed a $500,000 mortgage for the rest. The company also sold a building that had originally cost $180,000, on which it had $140,000 of accumulated depreciation, for $190,000 cash and a gain of $150,000. Prepare the cash flows from investing activities and schedule of noncash investing and financing transactions sections of the statement of cash flows.

SE 7.
LO 6 *Cash Flows from Financing Activities*

During 20x1, South Carolina Company issued $1,000,000 in long-term bonds at 96, repaid $150,000 of bonds at face value, paid interest of $80,000, and paid dividends of $50,000. Prepare the cash flows from the financing activities section of the statement of cash flows.

SE 8.
LO 7 *Identifying Components of the Statement of Cash Flows*

Assuming the indirect method is used to prepare the statement of cash flows, tell whether each item below would appear (a) in cash flows from operating activities, (b) in cash flows from investing activities, (c) in cash flows from financing activities, (d) in the schedule of noncash investing and financing transactions, or (e) not on the statement of cash flows at all.

1. Dividends paid
2. Cash receipts from sales
3. Decrease in accounts receivable
4. Sale of plant assets
5. Gain on sale of investment
6. Issue of stock for plant assets
7. Issue of common stock
8. Net income

SE 9.
SO 9
Cash Receipts from Sales and Cash Payments for Purchases: Direct Method

During 20x2, Nebraska Wheat Company, a marketer of whole-grain products, had sales of $426,500. The ending balance of Accounts Receivable was $127,400 in 20x1 and $96,200 in 20x2. Also, during 20x2, Nebraska Wheat Company had cost of goods sold of $294,200. The ending balance of inventory was $36,400 in 20x1 and $44,800 in 20x2. The ending balance of Accounts Payable was $28,100 in 20x1 and $25,900 in 20x2. Using the direct method, calculate cash receipts from sales and cash payments for purchases in 20x2.

SE 10.
SO 9
Cash Payments for Operating Expenses and Income Taxes: Direct Method

During 20x2, Nebraska Wheat Company had operating expenses of $79,000 and income taxes expense of $12,500. Depreciation expense of $20,000 for 20x2 was included in operating expenses. The ending balance of Prepaid Expenses was $3,600 in 20x1 and $2,300 in 20x2. The ending balance of Accrued Liabilities (excluding Income Taxes Payable) was $3,000 in 20x1 and $2,000 in 20x2. The ending balance of Income Taxes Payable was $4,100 in 20x1 and $3,500 in 20x2. Calculate cash payments for operating expenses and income taxes in 20x2 using the direct method.

Exercises

E 1.
LO 1
LO 3
Classification of Cash Flow Transactions

Horizon Corporation engaged in the following transactions. Identify each as (a) an operating activity, (b) an investing activity, (c) a financing activity, (d) a noncash transaction, or (e) not on statement of cash flow.

1. Declared and paid a cash dividend.
2. Purchased a long-term investment.
3. Received cash from customers.
4. Paid interest.
5. Sold equipment at a loss.
6. Issued long-term bonds for plant assets.
7. Received dividends on securities held.
8. Issued common stock.
9. Declared and issued a stock dividend.
10. Repaid notes payable.
11. Paid employees their wages.
12. Purchased a 60-day Treasury bill.
13. Purchased land.

E 2.
LO 4
Cash-Generating Efficiency Ratios and Free Cash Flow

In 20x5, Black Wolf Corporation had year-end assets of $4,800,000, net sales of $6,600,000, net income of $560,000, net cash flows from operating activities of $780,000, dividends of $240,000, and net capital expenditures of $820,000. In 20x4, year-end assets were $4,200,000. Calculate the cash-generating efficiency ratios of cash flow yield, cash flows to sales, and cash flows to assets. Also calculate free cash flow.

E 3.
LO 5
Cash Flows from Operating Activities: Indirect Method

The condensed single-step income statement of Union Chemical Company, a distributor of farm fertilizers and herbicides, appears as follows:

Sales		$6,500,000
Less: Cost of Goods Sold	$3,800,000	
Operating Expenses (including depreciation of $410,000)	1,900,000	
Income Taxes	200,000	5,900,000
Net Income		$ 600,000

Selected accounts from the company's balance sheets for 20x2 and 20x1 are as follows:

	20x2	20x1
Accounts Receivable	$1,200,000	$850,000
Inventory	420,000	510,000
Prepaid Expenses	130,000	90,000
Accounts Payable	480,000	360,000
Accrued Liabilities	30,000	50,000
Income Taxes Payable	70,000	60,000

Present in good form a schedule of cash flows from operating activities using the indirect method.

E 4.

LO 5 *Computing Cash Flows from Operating Activities: Indirect Method*

During 20x1, Mayfair Corporation had a net income of $41,000. Included on the income statement was depreciation expense of $2,300 and amortization expense of $300. During the year, accounts receivable increased by $3,400, inventories decreased by $1,900, prepaid expenses decreased by $200, accounts payable increased by $5,000, and accrued liabilities decreased by $450. Determine cash flows from operating activities using the indirect method.

E 5.

LO 5 *Preparing a Schedule of Cash Flows from Operating Activities: Indirect Method*

For the year ended June 30, 20xx, net income for Dedam Corporation was $7,400. The following is additional information: (a) Depreciation expense was $2,000; (b) accounts receivable increased by $4,400 during the year; (c) inventories increased by $7,000, and accounts payable increased by $14,000 during the year; (d) prepaid rent decreased by $1,400, and salaries payable increased by $1,000; and (e) income taxes payable decreased by $600 during the year. Use the indirect method to prepare a schedule of cash flows from operating activities.

E 6.

LO 6 *Computing Cash Flows from Investing Activities: Investments*

Krieger Company's T account for long-term available-for-sale investments at the end of 20x3 is as follows:

Investments			
Beg. Bal.	38,500	Sales	39,000
Purchases	58,000		
End. Bal.	57,500		

In addition, Krieger's income statement shows a loss on the sale of investments of $6,500. Compute the amounts to be shown as cash flows from investing activities and show how they are to appear on the statement of cash flows.

E 7.

LO 6 *Computing Cash Flows from Investing Activities: Plant Assets*

The T accounts for plant assets and accumulated depreciation for Krieger Company at the end of 20x3 are as follows:

Plant Assets					Accumulated Depreciation			
Beg. Bal.	65,000	Disposals	23,000		Disposals	14,700	Beg. Bal.	34,500
Purchases	33,600						Depreciation	10,200
End. Bal.	75,600						End. Bal.	30,000

In addition, Krieger Company's income statement shows a gain on sale of plant assets of $4,400. Compute the amounts to be shown as cash flows from investing activities and show how they are to appear on the statement of cash flows.

E 8.

LO 6 *Determining Cash Flows from Investing and Financing Activities*

All transactions involving Notes Payable and related accounts engaged in by Krieger Company during 20x3 are as follows:

Cash	18,000	
Notes Payable		18,000
Bank loan		
Patent	30,000	
Notes Payable		30,000
Purchase of patent by issuing note payable		
Notes Payable	5,000	
Interest Expense	500	
Cash		5,500
Repayment of note payable at maturity		

Determine the amounts of the transactions affecting financing activities and show how they are to appear in the statement of cash flows for 20x3.

LO 7 *Preparing the Statement of Cash Flows: Indirect Method*

E 9. Bradbury Corporation's 20x2 income statement and its comparative balance sheets for June 30, 20x2 and 20x1, follow.

Bradbury Corporation
Income Statement
For the Year Ended June 30, 20x2

Sales	$468,000
Cost of Goods Sold	312,000
Gross Margin	$156,000
Operating Expenses	90,000
Operating Income	$ 66,000
Interest Expense	5,600
Income Before Income Taxes	$ 60,400
Income Taxes	24,600
Net Income	$ 35,800

Bradbury Corporation
Comparative Balance Sheets
June 30, 20x2 and 20x1

	20x2	20x1
Assets		
Cash	$139,800	$ 25,000
Accounts Receivable (net)	42,000	52,000
Inventory	86,800	96,800
Prepaid Expenses	6,400	5,200
Furniture	110,000	120,000
Accumulated Depreciation, Furniture	(18,000)	(10,000)
Total Assets	$367,000	$289,000
Liabilities and Stockholders' Equity		
Accounts Payable	$ 26,000	$ 28,000
Income Taxes Payable	2,400	3,600
Notes Payable (long-term)	74,000	70,000
Common Stock, $10 par value	230,000	180,000
Retained Earnings	34,600	7,400
Total Liabilities and Stockholders' Equity	$367,000	$289,000

Additional information: (a) Issued $44,000 note payable for purchase of furniture; (b) sold furniture that cost $54,000 with accumulated depreciation of $30,600 at carrying value; (c) recorded depreciation on the furniture during the year, $38,600; (d) repaid a note in the amount of $40,000; (e) issued $50,000 of common stock at par value; and (f) declared and paid dividends of $8,600. Without using a work sheet, prepare a statement of cash flows for 20x2 using the indirect method.

E 10.

LO 7   *Preparing a Work Sheet*
SO 8   *for the Statement of Cash Flows: Indirect Method*

Using the information in **E 9,** prepare a work sheet for the statement of cash flows for Bradbury Corporation for 20x2. From the work sheet, prepare a statement of cash flows using the indirect method.

E 11.

SO 9   *Computing Cash Flows from Operating Activities: Direct Method*

Europa Corporation engaged in the following transactions in 20x2. Using the direct method, compute the various cash flows from operating activities as required.

a. During 20x2, Europa Corporation had cash sales of $41,300 and sales on credit of $123,000. During the same year, accounts receivable decreased by $18,000. Determine the cash receipts from sales during 20x2.

b. During 20x2, Europa Corporation's cost of goods sold was $119,000. During the same year, merchandise inventory increased by $12,500 and accounts payable decreased by $4,300. Determine the cash payments for purchases during 20x2.

c. During 20x2, Europa Corporation had operating expenses of $45,000, including depreciation of $15,600. Also during 20x2, related prepaid expenses decreased by $3,100 and relevant accrued liabilities increased by $1,200. Determine the cash payments for operating expenses to suppliers of goods and services during 20x2.

d. Europa Corporation's income taxes expense for 20x2 was $4,300. Income taxes payable decreased by $230 that year. Determine the cash payments for income taxes during 20x2.

E 12.

SO 9   *Preparing a Schedule of Cash Flows from Operating Activities: Direct Method*

The income statement for the Karsko Corporation follows.

Karsko Corporation
Income Statement
For the Year Ended June 30, 20xx

Sales		$122,000
Cost of Goods Sold		60,000
Gross Margin		$ 62,000
Operating Expenses		
Salaries Expense	$32,000	
Rent Expense	16,800	
Depreciation Expense	2,000	50,800
Income Before Income Taxes		$ 11,200
Income Taxes		2,400
Net Income		$ 8,800

Additional information: (a) Accounts receivable increased by $4,400 during the year; (b) inventories increased by $7,000, and accounts payable increased by $14,000 during the year; (c) prepaid rent decreased by $1,400, while salaries payable increased by $1,000; and (d) income taxes payable decreased by $600 during the year. Using the direct method, prepare a schedule of cash flows from operating activities as illustrated in Exhibit 6.

Problems

LO 1 *Classification of*
LO 3 *Transactions*

P 1. Analyze each transaction below and place *X*'s in the appropriate columns to indicate its classification and its effect on cash flows using the indirect method.

Transaction	Cash Flow Classification				Effect on Cash		
	Operating Activity	Investing Activity	Financing Activity	Noncash Transaction	Increase	Decrease	No Effect
1. Earned a net income.							
2. Declared and paid cash dividend.							
3. Issued stock for cash.							
4. Retired long-term debt by issuing stock.							
5. Paid accounts payable.							
6. Purchased inventory with cash.							
7. Purchased a one-year insurance policy with cash.							
8. Purchased a long-term investment with cash.							
9. Sold trading securities at a gain.							
10. Sold a machine at a loss.							
11. Retired fully depreciated equipment.							
12. Paid interest on debt.							
13. Purchased available-for-sale securities (long-term).							
14. Received dividend income.							
15. Received cash on account.							
16. Converted bonds to common stock.							
17. Purchased ninety-day Treasury bill.							

LO 4 *The Statement of Cash*
LO 7 *Flows: Indirect Method*

P 2. The comparative balance sheets for Mateo Fabrics, Inc., for December 31, 20x3 and 20x2, appear on the next page. Additional information about Mateo Fabrics's operations during 20x3: (a) Net income, $56,000; (b) building and equipment depreciation expense amounts, $30,000 and $6,000, respectively; (c) equipment that cost $27,000 with accumulated depreciation of $25,000 sold at a gain of $10,600; (d) equipment purchases, $25,000; (e) patent amortization, $6,000; purchase of patent, $2,000; (f) funds borrowed by issuing notes payable, $50,000; notes payable repaid, $30,000; (g) land and building purchased for $324,000 by signing a mortgage for the total cost; (h) 3,000 shares of $20 par value common stock issued for a total of $100,000; and (i) cash dividend, $18,000.

Mateo Fabrics, Inc.
Comparative Balance Sheets
December 31, 20x3 and 20x2

	20x3	20x2
Assets		
Cash	$189,120	$ 54,720
Accounts Receivable (net)	204,860	150,860
Inventory	225,780	275,780
Prepaid Expenses	—	40,000
Land	50,000	—
Building	274,000	—
Accumulated Depreciation, Building	(30,000)	—
Equipment	66,000	68,000
Accumulated Depreciation, Equipment	(29,000)	(48,000)
Patents	8,000	12,000
Total Assets	$958,760	$553,360
Liabilities and Stockholders' Equity		
Accounts Payable	$ 21,500	$ 73,500
Notes Payable	20,000	—
Accrued Liabilities (current)	—	24,600
Mortgage Payable	324,000	—
Common Stock, $20 par value	360,000	300,000
Paid-in Capital in Excess of Par Value	114,400	74,400
Retained Earnings	118,860	80,860
Total Liabilities and Stockholders' Equity	$958,760	$553,360

REQUIRED

1. Using the indirect method, prepare a statement of cash flows for Mateo Fabrics, Inc. (Do not use a work sheet.)
2. Why did Mateo Fabrics have an increase in cash of $134,400 when it recorded net income of $56,000? Discuss and interpret.
3. Compute and assess cash flow yield and free cash flow for 20x3.

P 3.
LO 4   *Statement of Cash Flows:*
LO 7   *Indirect Method*

The comparative balance sheets for Bausch Ceramics, Inc., for December 31, 20x3 and 20x2, appear on the next page. The following is additional information about Bausch Ceramics' operations during 20x3: (a) Net income was $96,000; (b) building and equipment depreciation expense amounts were $80,000 and $60,000, respectively; (c) intangible assets were amortized in the amount of $20,000; (d) investments in the amount of $116,000 were purchased; (e) investments were sold for $150,000, on which a gain of $34,000 was recorded; (f) the company issued $240,000 in long-term bonds at face value; (g) a small warehouse building with the accompanying land was purchased through the issue of a $320,000 mortgage; (h) the company paid $40,000 to reduce mortgage payable during 20x3; (i) the company borrowed funds in the amount of $60,000 by issuing notes payable and repaid notes payable in the amount of $180,000; and (j) cash dividends in the amount of $36,000 were declared and paid.

REQUIRED

1. Using the indirect method, prepare a statement of cash flows for Bausch Ceramics. (Do not use a work sheet.)
2. Why did Bausch Ceramics experience a decrease in cash in a year in which it had a net income of $96,000? Discuss and interpret.
3. Compute and assess cash flow yield and free cash flow for 20x3.

Bausch Ceramics, Inc. Comparative Balance Sheets December 31, 20x3 and 20x2		
	20x3	**20x2**
Assets		
Cash	$ 277,600	$ 305,600
Accounts Receivable (net)	738,800	758,800
Inventory	960,000	800,000
Prepaid Expenses	14,800	26,800
Long-Term Investments	440,000	440,000
Land	361,200	321,200
Building	1,200,000	920,000
Accumulated Depreciation, Building	(240,000)	(160,000)
Equipment	480,000	480,000
Accumulated Depreciation, Equipment	(116,000)	(56,000)
Intangible Assets	20,000	40,000
Total Assets	$4,136,400	$3,876,400
Liabilities and Stockholders' Equity		
Accounts Payable	$ 470,800	$ 660,800
Notes Payable (current)	40,000	160,000
Accrued Liabilities	10,800	20,800
Mortgage Payable	1,080,000	800,000
Bonds Payable	1,000,000	760,000
Common Stock	1,200,000	1,200,000
Paid-in Capital in Excess of Par Value	80,000	80,000
Retained Earnings	254,800	194,800
Total Liabilities and Stockholders' Equity	$4,136,400	$3,876,400

P 4.

LO 4 *The Work Sheet and the*
LO 7 *Statement of Cash Flows:*
SO 8 *Indirect Method*

Use the information for Bausch Ceramics, Inc., given in **P 3** to complete the following requirements.

REQUIRED

1. Prepare a work sheet for the statement of cash flows for Bausch Ceramics, Inc.
2. Answer requirements **1, 2,** and **3** in **P 3** if that problem was not assigned.

P 5.

SO 9 *Cash Flows from*
Operating Activities:
Direct Method

The income statement for Broadwell Clothing Store is at the top of the next page. The following is additional information: (a) Other sales and administrative expenses include depreciation expense of $104,000 and amortization expense of $36,000; (b) accrued liabilities for salaries were $24,000 less than the previous year, and prepaid expenses were $40,000 more than the previous year; and (c) during the year accounts receivable (net) increased by $288,000, accounts payable increased by $228,000, and income taxes payable decreased by $14,400.

Broadwell Clothing Store
Income Statement
For the Year Ended June 30, 20xx

Net Sales		$4,900,000
Cost of Goods Sold		
Beginning Inventory	$1,240,000	
Net Cost of Purchases	3,040,000	
Goods Available for Sale	$4,280,000	
Ending Inventory	1,400,000	
Cost of Goods Sold		2,880,000
Gross Margin		$2,020,000
Operating Expenses		
Sales and Administrative Salaries Expense	$1,112,000	
Other Sales and Administrative Expenses	624,000	
Total Operating Expenses		1,736,000
Income Before Income Taxes		$ 284,000
Income Taxes		78,000
Net Income		$ 206,000

REQUIRED

Using the direct method, prepare a schedule of cash flows from operating activities as illustrated in Exhibit 6.

P 6.
LO 4   *Statement of Cash Flows:*
SO 9   *Direct Method*

Gutierrez Corporation's 20x2 income statement and its comparative balance sheets as of June 30, 20x2 and 20x1 appear as follows:

Gutierrez Corporation
Income Statement
For the Year Ended June 30, 20x2

Sales		$2,081,800
Cost of Goods Sold		1,312,600
Gross Margin		$ 769,200
Operating Expenses (including Depreciation		
Expense of $120,000)		378,400
Income from Operations		$ 390,800
Other Income (Expenses)		
Loss on Disposal of Equipment	($ 8,000)	
Interest Expense	(75,200)	(83,200)
Income Before Income Taxes		$ 307,600
Income Taxes		68,400
Net Income		$ 239,200

Gutierrez Corporation
Comparative Balance Sheets
June 30, 20x2 and 20x1

	20x2	20x1
Assets		
Cash	$ 334,000	$ 40,000
Accounts Receivable (net)	200,000	240,000
Inventory	360,000	440,000
Prepaid Expenses	1,200	2,000
Property, Plant, and Equipment	1,256,000	1,104,000
Accumulated Depreciation, Property, Plant, and Equipment	(366,000)	(280,000)
Total Assets	$1,785,200	$1,546,000
Liabilities and Stockholders' Equity		
Accounts Payable	$ 128,000	$ 84,000
Notes Payable (due in 90 days)	60,000	160,000
Income Taxes Payable	52,000	36,000
Mortgage Payable	720,000	560,000
Common Stock, $5 par value	400,000	400,000
Retained Earnings	425,200	306,000
Total Liabilities and Stockholders' Equity	$1,785,200	$1,546,000

The following is additional information about 20x2: (a) equipment that cost $48,000 with accumulated depreciation of $34,000 was sold at a loss of $8,000; (b) land and building were purchased in the amount of $200,000 through an increase of $200,000 in the mortgage payable; (c) a $40,000 payment was made on the mortgage; (d) the notes were repaid, but the company borrowed an additional $60,000 through the issuance of a new note payable; and (e) a $120,000 cash dividend was declared and paid.

REQUIRED

1. Use the direct method to prepare a statement of cash flows. Include a supporting schedule of noncash investing and financing transactions. Do not use a work sheet, and do not include a reconciliation of net income to net cash flows from operating activities.
2. What are the primary reasons for Gutierrez Corporation's large increase in cash from 20x1 to 20x2?
3. Compute and assess cash flow yield and free cash flow for 20x2.

Alternate Problems

LO 1 *Classification of*
LO 3 *Transactions*

P 7. Analyze each transaction below and place *X*'s in the appropriate columns to indicate its classification and its effect on cash flows using the indirect method.

	Cash Flow Classification				Effect on Cash		
Transaction	**Operating Activity**	**Investing Activity**	**Financing Activity**	**Noncash Transaction**	**Increase**	**Decrease**	**No Effect**
1. Incurred a net loss.							
2. Declared and issued a stock dividend.							
3. Paid a cash dividend.							
4. Collected accounts receivable.							
5. Purchased inventory with cash.							
6. Retired long-term debt with cash.							
7. Sold available-for-sale securities at a loss.							
8. Issued stock for equipment.							
9. Purchased a one-year insurance policy with cash.							
10. Purchased treasury stock with cash.							
11. Retired a fully depreciated truck (no gain or loss).							
12. Paid interest on note.							
13. Received cash dividend on investment.							
14. Sold treasury stock.							
15. Paid income taxes.							
16. Transferred cash to money market account.							
17. Purchased land and building with a mortgage.							

P 8.

LO 4 *The Statement of Cash*
LO 7 *Flows: Indirect Method*

P 8. Meridian Corporation's comparative balance sheets as of December 31, 20x2 and 20x1, and its income statement for the year ended December 31, 20x2, follow.

Meridian Corporation
Comparative Balance Sheets
December 31, 20x2 and 20x1

	20x2	20x1
Assets		
Cash	$ 82,400	$ 25,000
Accounts Receivable (net)	82,600	100,000
Inventory	175,000	225,000
Prepaid Rent	1,000	1,500
Furniture and Fixtures	74,000	72,000
Accumulated Depreciation, Furniture and Fixtures	(21,000)	(12,000)
Total Assets	$394,000	$411,500
Liabilities and Stockholders' Equity		
Accounts Payable	$ 71,700	$100,200
Income Taxes Payable	700	2,200
Notes Payable (long-term)	20,000	10,000
Bonds Payable	50,000	100,000
Common Stock, $10 par value	120,000	100,000
Paid-in Capital in Excess of Par Value	90,720	60,720
Retained Earnings	40,880	38,380
Total Liabilities and Stockholders' Equity	$394,000	$411,500

Meridian Corporation
Income Statement
For the Year Ended December 31, 20x2

Net Sales		$804,500
Cost of Goods Sold		563,900
Gross Margin		$240,600
Operating Expenses (including Depreciation Expense of $23,400)		224,700
Income from Operations		$ 15,900
Other Income (Expenses)		
Gain on Disposal of Furniture and Fixtures	$ 3,500	
Interest Expense	(11,600)	(8,100)
Income Before Income Taxes		$ 7,800
Income Taxes		2,300
Net Income		$ 5,500

The following is additional information about 20x2: (a) Furniture and fixtures that cost $17,800 with accumulated depreciation of $14,400 were sold at a gain of $3,500; (b) furniture and fixtures were purchased in the amount of $19,800; (c) a $10,000 note payable was paid and $20,000 was borrowed on a new note; (d) bonds payable in the amount of $50,000 were converted into 2,000 shares of common stock; and (e) $3,000 in cash dividends were declared and paid.

REQUIRED

1. Using the indirect method, prepare a statement of cash flows. Include a supporting schedule of noncash investing and financing transactions. (Do not use a work sheet.)
2. What are the primary reasons for Meridian Corporation's large increase in cash from 20x1 to 20x2, despite its low net income?
3. Compute and assess cash flow yield and free cash flow for 20x2.

P 9.
LO 4 *The Work Sheet and the*
LO 7 *Statement of Cash Flows:*
SO 8 *Indirect Method*

Use the information for Meridian Corporation given in **P 8** to answer the following requirements.

REQUIRED

1. Prepare a work sheet to gather information for the preparation of the statement of cash flows.
2. Answer requirements **1, 2,** and **3** if that problem was not assigned.

EXPANDING YOUR CRITICAL THINKING, COMMUNICATION, AND INTERPERSONAL SKILLS

Skills Development

CONCEPTUAL ANALYSIS

SD 1.
LO 5 *Direct Versus Indirect Method*

AST Research, Inc., a computer company, uses the direct method of presenting cash flows from operating activities in its statement of cash flows. As noted in the text, 98 percent of large companies use the indirect method.[11] Explain the difference between the direct and indirect methods of presenting cash flows from operating activities. Then choose either the direct or the indirect method and tell why it is the best way of presenting cash flows from operations. Be prepared to discuss your opinion in class.

ETHICAL DILEMMA

SD 2.
LO 3 *Ethics and Cash Flow Classifications*

Chemical Waste Treatment, Inc., is a fast-growing company that disposes of chemical wastes. The company has an $800,000 line of credit at its bank. One section in the loan agreement says that the ratio of cash flows from operations to interest expense must exceed 3.0. If this ratio falls below 3.0, the company must reduce the balance outstanding on its line of credit to one-half the total line if the funds borrowed against the line of credit exceed that amount. After the end of the fiscal year, the controller informs the president: "We will not meet the ratio requirements on our line of credit in 20x2 because interest expense was $1.2 million and cash flows from operations were $3.2 million. Also, we have borrowed 100 percent of our line of credit. We do not have the cash to reduce the credit line by $400,000." The president says, "This is a serious situation. To pay our ongoing bills, we need our bank to increase our line of credit, not decrease it. What can

Communication | Critical Thinking | Group Activity | Memo | Ethics | International | Spreadsheet | General Ledger | CD-ROM | Internet

we do?" "Do you recall the $500,000 two-year note payable for equipment?" replied the controller. "It is now classified as 'Proceeds from Notes Payable' in cash flows provided from financing activities in the statement of cash flows. If we move it to cash flows from operations and call it 'Increase in Payables,' it would increase cash flows from operations to $3.7 million and put us over the limit." "Well, do it," ordered the president. "It surely doesn't make any difference where it is on the statement. It is an increase in both places. It would be much worse for our company in the long term if we failed to meet this ratio requirement." What is your opinion of the president's reasoning? Is the president's order ethical? Who benefits and who is harmed if the controller follows the president's order? What are management's alternatives? What would you do?

RESEARCH ACTIVITY

SD 3.

LO 3
LO 4

Basic Research Skills

Select the annual reports of three corporations, using one or more of the following sources: your library, the Fingraph® Financial Analyst™ CD-ROM software that accompanies this text, or the Needles Accounting Resource Center Web site at http://www.hmco. com/college/needles/home.html. You may choose them from the same industry or at random, at the direction of your instructor. (If you did a related exercise in a previous chapter, use the same three companies.) Prepare a table with a column for each corporation. Then, for any year covered by the statement of cash flows, answer the following questions: Does the company use the direct or the indirect approach? Is net income more or less than net cash flows from operating activities? What are the major causes of differences between net income and net cash flows from operating activities? Compute cash flow efficiency ratios and free cash flow. Does the dividend appear secure? Did the company make significant capital expenditures during the year? How were the expenditures financed? Do you notice anything unusual about the investing and financing activities of your companies? Do the investing and financing activities provide any insights into management's plan for each company? If so, what are they? Be prepared to discuss your findings in class.

DECISION-MAKING PRACTICE

SD 4.

LO 4
LO 7

Analysis of Cash Flow Difficulty

May Hashimi, president of **Hashimi Print Gallery, Inc.,** is examining the following income statement, which has just been handed to her by her accountant, Lou Klein, CPA.

Hashimi Print Gallery, Inc.
Income Statement
For the Year Ended December 31, 20x2

Net Sales	$884,000
Cost of Goods Sold	508,000
Gross Margin	$376,000
Operating Expenses (including Depreciation Expense of $20,000)	204,000
Operating Income	$172,000
Interest Expense	24,000
Income Before Income Taxes	$148,000
Income Taxes	28,000
Net Income	$120,000

After looking at the statement, Hashimi said to Klein, "Lou, the statement seems to be well done, but what I need to know is why I don't have enough cash to pay my bills this month. You show that I earned $120,000 in 20x2, but I have only $24,000 in the bank. I know I bought a building on a mortgage and paid a cash dividend of $48,000, but what else is going on?" Klein replied, "To answer your question, we have to look at comparative balance sheets and prepare another type of statement. Take a look at these balance sheets." The statements handed to Hashimi follow.

Hashimi Print Gallery, Inc.
Comparative Balance Sheets
December 31, 20x2 and 20x1

	20x2	20x1
Assets		
Cash	$ 24,000	$ 40,000
Accounts Receivable (net)	178,000	146,000
Inventory	240,000	180,000
Prepaid Expenses	10,000	14,000
Building	400,000	—
Accumulated Depreciation	(20,000)	—
Total Assets	$832,000	$380,000
Liabilities and Stockholders' Equity		
Accounts Payable	$ 74,000	$ 96,000
Income Taxes Payable	6,000	4,000
Mortgage Payable	400,000	—
Common Stock	200,000	200,000
Retained Earnings	152,000	80,000
Total Liabilities and Stockholders' Equity	$832,000	$380,000

1. To what statement is Klein referring? From the information given, prepare the additional statement using the indirect method.
2. Hashimi Print Gallery, Inc., has a cash problem despite profitable operations. Why?

Financial Reporting and Analysis

INTERPRETING FINANCIAL REPORTS

FRA 1.

LO 4 *Cash-Generating Efficiency and Free Cash Flow*

The statement of cash flows for **Tandy Corporation,** the owner of Radio Shack and other retail store chains, appears on the next page. For the two years shown, compute the cash-generating efficiency ratios of cash flow yield, cash flows to sales, and cash flows to assets. Also compute free cash flow for the two years. Assume that you report to an investment analyst who has asked you to analyze Tandy's statement of cash flows for 1995 and 1996. Prepare a memorandum to the investment analyst that assesses Tandy's cash-generating efficiency and evaluates its available free cash flow in light of its financing activities. Are there any special operating circumstances that should be taken into consideration? Refer to your computations and to Tandy's Statement of Cash Flows as attachments. The following data come from Tandy's annual report (in thousands):[12]

	1996	1995	1994
Net Sales	$6,285.5	$5,839.1	$4,943.7
Total Assets	2,583.4	2,722.1	3,243.8

Tandy Corporation
Statement of Cash Flows
For the Years Ended December 31, 1996 and 1995

(In millions)	1996	1995
Cash flows from operating activities:		
Net income (loss)	$ (91.6)	$211.9
Adjustments to reconcile net income (loss) to net cash provided by operating activities:		
Impairment of long-lived assets	112.8	—
Provision for restructuring cost and other charges	253.5	1.1
Gain on sale of extended service contracts	—	—
Gain on sale of credit card portfolios	—	—
Depreciation and amortization	108.6	92.0
Deferred income taxes and other items	(127.8)	20.1
Provision for credit losses and bad debts	2.8	15.7
Changes in operating assets and liabilities:		
Sale of credit card portfolios	—	342.8
Receivables	8.0	167.4
Inventories	(0.1)	(23.3)
Other current assets	3.2	3.2
Accounts payable, accrued expenses and income taxes	38.1	(157.9)
Net cash provided by operating activities	307.5	673.0
Investing activities:		
Additions to property, plant and equipment	(174.8)	(226.5)
Proceeds from sale of property, plant and equipment	2.8	42.0
Proceeds from sale of divested operations	—	—
Payment on AST note	60.0	6.7
Other investing activities	(0.9)	(2.5)
Net cash (used) provided by investing activities	(112.9)	(180.3)
Financing activities:		
Purchases of treasury stock	(232.9)	(502.2)
Sales of treasury stock to employee stock purchase program	39.4	44.6
Proceeds from exercise of stock options	7.4	18.2
Dividends paid, net of taxes	(52.5)	(63.0)
Changes in short-term borrowings, net	40.9	(1.8)
Additions to long-term borrowings	8.0	10.3
Repayments of long-term borrowings	(26.9)	(60.9)
Net cash used by financing activities	(216.6)	(554.8)
Decrease in cash and cash equivalents	(22.0)	(62.1)
Cash and cash equivalents, at the beginning of the year	143.5	205.6
Cash and cash equivalents, at the end of the year	$121.5	$143.5

INTERNATIONAL COMPANY

FRA 2.

LO 3   *Format and*
LO 4   *Interpretation of*
     Statement of Cash Flows

The format of the statement of cash flows can differ from country to country. One of the more interesting presentations, as shown below, is that of *Guinness PLC,* a large British liquor company that distributes Johnny Walker Scotch and many other products.[13] (The word *group* means the same as *consolidated* in the United States.) What differences can you identify between this British statement of cash flows and the one used in the United States? In what ways do you find the Guinness format more useful than the format used in the United States? Assume that net cash flows from operating activities are computed similarly in both countries, except for the items shown.

Guinness PLC
Group Cash Flow Statement
For the Years Ended 31 December 1996 and 1995

	1996 £m	1995 £m
Cash flow from operating activities	**1,020**	**989**
Interest received	25	33
Interest paid	(178)	(153)
Dividends paid to minority shareholders in subsidiary undertakings	(34)	(22)
Returns on investments and servicing of finance	**(187)**	**(142)**
United Kingdom corporation tax paid	(194)	(127)
Overseas tax paid	(61)	(81)
Taxation	**(255)**	**(208)**
Purchase of tangible fixed assets:		
Spirits	(58)	(56)
Brewing	(134)	(123)
Sale of tangible fixed assets	22	24
Capital expenditure and financial investment	**(170)**	**(155)**
Free cash flow before dividends	**408**	**484**
Purchase of subsidiary undertakings	(38)	(15)
Purchase of long term investments	(4)	(16)
Disposals	5	90
Acquisitions and disposals	**(37)**	**59**
Equity dividends paid	(294)	(285)
Cash inflow before use of liquid resources and financing	**77**	**258**
Decrease/(increase) in liquid resources	390	(231)
Financing:		
Issue of ordinary share capital (employee share schemes)	23	26
Repurchase of shares	(466)	—
Increase/(decrease) in debt	32	(40)
Increase in cash in the period	**56**	**13**

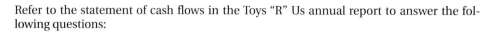

TOYS "R" US ANNUAL REPORT

FRA 3.

LO 4 *Analysis of the Statement of Cash Flows*

Refer to the statement of cash flows in the Toys "R" Us annual report to answer the following questions:

1. Does Toys "R" Us use the direct or the indirect method of reporting cash flows from operating activities? Other than net earnings, what are the most important factors affecting cash flows from operating activities? Explain the trend of each.

2. Based on the cash flows from investing activities, would you say that Toys "R" Us is a contracting or an expanding company?

3. Calculate the cash flow yield, cash flows to sales, cash flows to assets, and free cash flow for the last three years for Toys "R" Us. How would you evaluate the company's cash-generating efficiency? Does Toys "R" Us need external financing? If so, where has it come from?

FINGRAPH® FINANCIAL ANALYST™

FRA 4.

LO 3
LO 4 *Cash Flow Analysis*

Choose any two companies from the same industry in the Fingraph® Financial Analyst™ CD-ROM software.

1. In the annual reports for the companies you have selected, identify the statement of cash flows. Do the companies use the direct or indirect form of the statement?

2. Display and print in tabular and graphical form the Statement of Cash Flows: Operating Activities Analysis page. Prepare a table that compares the cash flow yield, cash flows to sales, and cash flows to assets for both companies for two years. Are the ratios moving in the same or opposite directions? Study the operating activities sections of the statements to determine the main causes of differences between the net income and cash flows from operations. How do the companies compare?

3. Display and print in tabular and graphical form the Statement of Cash Flows: Investing and Financing Activities Analysis page. Prepare a table that compares the free cash flow for both companies for two years. How do the companies compare? Are the companies growing or contracting? Study the investing and financing activities sections of the statements to determine the main causes of differences between the companies.

4. Find and read references to cash flows in the liquidity analysis section of management's discussion and analysis in each annual report.

5. Write a one-page executive summary that reports your findings from parts **1–4,** including your assessment of the companies' comparative liquidity. Include the Fingraph® pages and your tables as attachments to your report.

ENDNOTES

1. Marriott International, Inc., *Annual Report,* 1996.

2. *Statement of Financial Accounting Standards No. 95,* "Statement of Cash Flows" (Norwalk, Conn.: Financial Accounting Standards Board, 1987).

3. *Statement of Financial Accounting Concepts No. 1,* "Objectives of Financial Reporting for Business Enterprises" (Norwalk, Conn.: Financial Accounting Standards Board, 1978), par. 37–39.

4. Marriott International, Inc., *Annual Report,* 1996.

5. Melville Corporation, *Annual Report,* 1995.

6. Gary Slutsker, "Look at the Birdie and Say: 'Cash Flow,'" *Forbes,* October 25, 1993.

7. Jonathan Clements, "Yacktman Fund Is Bloodied but Unbowed," *The Wall Street Journal,* November 8, 1993.

8. Jeffrey Laderman, "Earnings, Schmearnings—Look at the Cash," *Business Week,* July 24, 1989.

9. Marriott International, Inc., *Annual Report,* 1996.

10. American Institute of Certified Public Accountants, *Accounting Trends & Techniques* (New York: AICPA, 1997), p. 461.

11. American Institute of Certified Public Accountants, *Accounting Trends & Techniques* (New York: AICPA, 1997), p. 461.

12. Tandy Corporation, *Annual Report,* 1996.

13. Adapted from Guinness PLC, *Annual Report,* 1996.

Financial Statement Analysis

1. Describe and discuss the objectives of financial statement analysis.
2. Describe and discuss the standards for financial statement analysis.
3. State the sources of information for financial statement analysis.
4. Apply horizontal analysis, trend analysis, and vertical analysis to financial statements.
5. Apply ratio analysis to financial statements in a comprehensive evaluation of a company's financial situation.

DECISION POINT

MOODY'S INVESTORS SERVICE, INC.

Moody's Investors Service, Inc., rates the bonds and other indebtedness of companies on the basis of safety—that is, the likelihood of repayment. Investors rely on this service when making investments in bonds and other long-term company debt. *The Wall Street Journal* reported on February 26, 1997, that Moody's had downgraded $1.1 billion in Apple Computer, Inc.'s, long-term debt. This downgrade was one of a series that have occurred in the last few years because of Apple's declining sales and net losses. Moody's lowered the rating on Apple's senior unsecured debt to B3 from B1 and its subordinated debt to Caa from B3. Bonds with a B rating or lower are considered speculative. On what basis would Moody's decide to upgrade or lower the bond rating of a company? According to *The Wall Street Journal* "Moody's said it expected Apple's market share to continue to decline against PC's using Microsoft Corp.'s Windows operating system. That will result in deteriorating operating performance and erosion of support from independent software makers."[1]

This case demonstrates several features of the evaluation of a company's financial prospects. First, the analysis is rooted in the financial statements (for example, sales, profits, and cash flows). Second, it is directed toward the future (for example, expected erosion in Apple's market share). Third, the operating environment must be taken into consideration (for example, strong competition). Fourth, judgment is involved (for example, after its first debt rating downgrade, Moody's determined that subsequent downgrades of Apple's long-term debt were needed).

Objectives of Financial Statement Analysis

Financial statement analysis comprises all the techniques employed by users of financial statements to show important relationships in the financial statements. Users of financial statements fall into two broad categories: internal and external. Management is the main internal user. However, because the people who run a company have inside information on operations, other techniques are available to them. The main focus here is on the external users of financial statements and the analytical techniques they employ.

Creditors make loans in the form of trade accounts, notes, or bonds. They expect them to be repaid according to specified terms and receive interest on the notes and bonds payable. Investors buy capital stock, from which they hope to receive dividends and an increase in value. Both groups face risks. The creditor faces the risk that the debtor will fail to pay back the loan. The investor faces the risks that dividends will be reduced or not paid and that the market price of the stock will drop. For both groups, the goal is to achieve a return that makes up for the risk. In general, the greater the risk taken, the greater the return required as compensation.

Any one loan or any one investment can turn out badly. As a result, most creditors and investors put their funds into a portfolio or a group of loans or investments. The portfolio allows them to average both the returns and the risks. Nevertheless, individual decisions about the loans and stock in the portfolio must still be made. It is in making those individual decisions that financial statement analysis is most useful. Creditors and investors use financial statement analysis in two general ways: (1) to judge past performance and current position and (2) to judge future potential and the risk connected with that potential.

Assessment of Past Performance and Current Position

Past performance is often a good indicator of future performance. Therefore, an investor or creditor looks at the trend of past sales, expenses, net income, cash flow, and return on investment not only as a means for judging management's past performance but also as a possible indicator of future performance. In addition, an analysis of current position will tell, for example, what assets the business owns and what liabilities must be paid. It will also tell what the cash position is, how much debt the company has in relation to equity, and what levels of inventories and receivables exist. Knowing a company's past performance and current position is often important in achieving the second general objective of financial analysis.

Assessment of Future Potential and Related Risk

Information about the past and present is useful only to the extent that it bears on decisions about the future. An investor judges the potential earning ability of a company because that ability will affect the market price of the company's stock and the amount of dividends the company will pay. A creditor judges the potential debt-paying ability of the company.

The riskiness of an investment or loan depends on how easy it is to predict future profitability or liquidity. If an investor can predict with confidence that a company's earnings per share will be between $2.50 and $2.60 in the next year, the investment is less risky than if the earnings per share are expected to fall between $2.00 and $3.00. For example, the potential associated with an investment in an established and stable electric utility, or a loan to it, is relatively easy to predict on the basis of the company's past performance and current position. The potential associated with a small microcomputer manufacturer, on the other hand, may be much harder to predict. For this reason, the investment in or loan to the electric utility carries less risk than the investment in or loan to the small microcomputer company.

Often, in return for taking a greater risk, an investor in the microcomputer company will demand a higher expected return (increase in market price plus dividends) than will an investor in the utility company. Also, a creditor of the microcomputer company will demand a higher interest rate and possibly more assurance of repayment (a secured loan, for instance) than a creditor of the utility company. The higher interest rate reimburses the creditor for assuming a higher risk.

Standards for Financial Statement Analysis

OBJECTIVE 2
Describe and discuss the standards for financial statement analysis

When analyzing financial statements, decision makers must judge whether the relationships they have found are favorable or unfavorable. Three commonly used standards of comparison are (1) rule-of-thumb measures, (2) past performance of the company, and (3) industry norms.

Rule-of-Thumb Measures

Many financial analysts, investors, and lenders employ ideal, or rule-of-thumb, measures for key financial ratios. For example, it has long been thought that a current ratio (current assets divided by current liabilities) of 2:1 is acceptable. The credit-rating firm of Dun & Bradstreet, in its *Industry Norms and Key Business Ratios,* offers such rules of thumb as the following:

Current debt to tangible net worth. Ordinarily, a business begins to pile up trouble when this relationship exceeds 80%.

Inventory to net working capital. Ordinarily, this relationship should not exceed 80%.

Although such measures may suggest areas that need further investigation, there is no proof that the specified levels are the best for any company. A company with a current ratio higher than 2:1 may have a poor credit policy (resulting in accounts receivable being too large), too much inventory, or poor cash management. Another company may have a ratio that is lower than 2:1 as a result of excellent management in all three of those areas. Thus, rule-of-thumb measures must be used with great care.

Past Performance of the Company

An improvement over rule-of-thumb measures is the comparison of financial measures or ratios of the same company over a period of time. This standard will give the analyst at least some basis for judging whether the measure or ratio is getting better or worse. It may also be helpful in showing possible future trends. However, since trends reverse at times, such projections must be made with care. Another problem with trend analysis is that the past may not be a useful measure of adequacy. In other words, past performance may not be enough to meet present needs. For example, even if return on total investment improved from 3 percent one year to 4 percent the next, the 4 percent return may in fact not be adequate.

PEPSICO, INC.

Most people think of PepsiCo, Inc., as a maker of soft drinks. In fact, the company is also involved in snack foods (Frito-Lay) and restaurants (Pizza Hut, Taco Bell, and KFC). The overall success of PepsiCo as reflected in its financial statements is affected by the relative amounts of investment and

earnings in each of its very different businesses. How should a financial analyst assess the impact of each of these three segments on the company's overall financial performance?

In accordance with FASB *Statement No. 131*, PepsiCo reports key information about its three segments in a note to the financial statements in its annual report (see Exhibit 1). The analyst can learn a lot about the company from this information. For example, net sales and operating profit for each segment are shown for the past three years. Note that for the combined segments, net sales have grown each year, but operating profit has declined. On January 23, 1997, PepsiCo, in an effort to focus on its more profitable segments, announced plans to spin off its restaurant segment, and before year-end 1997, PepsiCo had spun off its restaurants as Tricom Corporation. From the operating profit data in Exhibit 1, the restaurant segment was less profitable than beverages and snack foods. In 1996, beverages experienced lower operating profits because of problems with international operations. Identifiable assets, capital spending, and depreciation and amortization expense of each segment are also indicated in the note. Segment information allows the analyst to see the profitability of each business and to identify where management is investing most for the future. The information about net sales, segment operating profits, and identifiable assets by geographic area is also useful. It is interesting to note, for instance, that although PepsiCo's net sales in Europe are increasing, its operating profits in this region are declining.

Industry Norms

One way of making up for the limitations of using past performance as a standard is to use industry norms. Such norms will tell how the company being analyzed compares with the average of other companies in the same industry. For example, suppose that other companies in an industry have an average rate of return on total investment of 8 percent. In such a case, 3 and 4 percent returns are probably not adequate. Industry norms can also be used to judge trends. Suppose that a company's profit margin dropped from 12 to 10 percent because of a downward turn in the economy. A finding that other companies in the same industry had experienced an average drop in profit margin from 12 to 4 percent would indicate that the first company being analyzed did relatively well. Sometimes, instead of industry averages, data for the industry leader or a specific competitor are used for analysis.

Exhibit 1. Segment Information for PepsiCo, Inc.

INDUSTRY SEGMENTS

	1996	1995	1994
NET SALES			
Beverages	$10,524	$10,382	$ 9,566
Snack Foods	9,680	8,545	8,264
Restaurants	11,441	11,328	10,521
	$31,645	$30,255	$28,351
OPERATING PROFIT (b)			
Beverages	$ 890	$ 1,309	$ 1,217
Snack Foods	1,608	1,432	1,377
Restaurants	511	430	730
Combined Segments	3,009	3,171	3,324
Equity (Loss) Income	(266)	(3)	38
Unallocated Expenses, net	(197)	(181)	(161)
Operating Profit	$ 2,546	$ 2,987	$ 3,201
Depreciation Expense			
Beverages	$ 440	$ 445	$ 385
Snack Foods	346	304	297
Restaurants	546	579	539
Corporate	7	7	7
	$ 1,339	$ 1,335	$ 1,228
Amortization of Intangible Assets			
Beverages	$ 164	$ 166	$ 165
Snack Foods	41	41	42
Restaurants	96	109	105
	$ 301	$ 316	$ 312

	1996	1995	1994
Capital Spending (a)			
Beverages	$ 650	$ 566	$ 677
Snack Foods	973	769	532
Restaurants	665	750	1,072
Corporate	9	34	7
	$ 2,297	$ 2,119	$ 2,288
United States	$ 1,613	$ 1,496	$ 1,492
International	684	623	796
	$ 2,297	$ 2,119	$ 2,288
Acquisitions and Investments in Unconsolidated Affiliates (c)			
Beverages	$ 75	$ 323	$ 195
Snack Foods	–	82	12
Restaurants	1	70	148
	$ 76	$ 475	$ 355
United States	$ 16	$ 73	$ 88
International	60	402	267
	$ 76	$ 475	$ 355
Identifiable Assets			
Beverages	$ 9,816	$10,032	$ 9,566
Snack Foods	6,279	5,451	5,044
Restaurants	6,435	6,759	7,203
Investments in Unconsolidated Affiliates	1,375	1,635	1,295
Corporate	607	1,555	1,684
	$24,512	$25,432	$24,792

GEOGRAPHIC AREAS (d)

	Net Sales			Segment Operating Profit (Loss)			Identifiable Assets		
	1996	1995	1994	1996(e)	1995(e)	1994	1996	1995	1994
Europe	$ 2,865	$ 2,783	$ 2,177	$ (90)	$ (65)	$ 17	$ 3,159	$ 3,127	$ 3,062
Canada	1,340	1,299	1,244	134	86	82	1,354	1,344	1,342
Mexico	1,334	1,228	2,023	116	80	261	661	637	995
Other	3,658	3,437	2,782	(73)	342	258	2,628	2,629	2,196
Total International	9,197	8,747	8,226	87	443	618	7,802	7,737	7,595
United States	22,448	21,508	20,125	2,922	2,728	2,706	14,728	14,505	14,218
Combined Segments	$31,645	$30,255	$28,351	$3,009	$3,171	$3,324	22,530	22,242	21,813
Investments in Unconsolidated Affiliates							1,375	1,635	1,295
Corporate							607	1,555	1,684
							$24,512	$25,432	$24,792

(a) Included immaterial, noncash amounts related to capital leases, largely in the restaurants segment.

(b) See Items Affecting Comparability on page 43.

(c) Included immaterial noncash amounts related to treasury stock and debt issued.

(d) The results of centralized concentrate manufacturing operations in Puerto Rico and Ireland have been allocated based upon sales to the respective geographic areas.

(e) The unusual impairment, disposal and other charges reduced combined segment operating profit by $822 (United States - $246, Europe - $69, Mexico - $4, Other - $503) in 1996 and $503 (United States - $302, Europe - $119, Mexico - $21, Canada - $30, Other - $31) in 1995 (see Items Affecting Comparability on page 43).

Source: PepsiCo, Inc., *Annual Report*, 1996, p. 44.

There are three limitations to using industry norms as standards. First, two companies that seem to be in the same industry may not be strictly comparable. Consider two companies said to be in the oil industry. The main business of one may be purchasing oil products and marketing them through service stations. The other, an international company, may discover, produce, refine, and market its own oil products. The operations of these two companies cannot be compared because they are different.

Second, most large companies today operate in more than one industry. Some of these diversified companies or *conglomerates,* operate in many unrelated industries. The individual segments of a diversified company generally have different rates of profitability and different degrees of risk. In analyzing the consolidated financial statements of such companies, it is often impossible to use industry norms as standards. There are simply no other companies that are similar enough. A requirement by the Financial Accounting Standards Board, presented in *Statement No. 131,* provides a partial solution to this problem. It states that diversified companies must report segment profit or loss, certain revenue and expense items, and segment assets for each of their operating segments. Depending on how the company is organized for resource allocation in assessing performance, segment information may be reported for operations in different industries or in different geographical areas, or for major customers.[2]

The third limitation of industry norms is that companies in the same industry with similar operations may use different acceptable accounting procedures. That is, different methods may be used to value inventories, or different methods may be used to depreciate similar assets. Even so, if little information about a company's prior performance is available, industry norms probably offer the best available standards for judging current performance—as long as they are used with care.

Sources of Information

OBJECTIVE 3

State the sources of information for financial statement analysis

The external analyst is often limited to using publicly available information about a company. The major sources of information about publicly held corporations are reports published by the company, SEC reports, business periodicals, and credit and investment advisory services.

Reports Published by the Company

The annual report of a publicly held corporation is an important source of financial information. The main parts of an annual report are (1) management's analysis of the past year's operations, (2) the financial statements, (3) the notes to the statements, including the principal accounting procedures used by the company, (4) the auditors' report, and (5) a summary of operations for a five- or ten-year period. Most publicly held companies also publish interim financial statements each quarter. Those reports present limited information in the form of condensed financial statements, which need not be subjected to a full audit by the independent auditor. The interim statements are watched closely by the financial community for early signs of important changes in a company's earnings trend.

SEC Reports

Publicly held corporations must file annual reports, quarterly reports, and current reports with the Securities and Exchange Commission (SEC). All such reports are available to the public at a small charge. The SEC calls for a standard form for the annual report (Form 10-K) that contains more information than the published annual report. For that reason, Form 10-K is a valuable source of information. It is available free of charge to stockholders of the company. The quarterly report (Form 10-Q) presents important facts about interim financial performance. The current report (Form 8-K) must be filed within a few days of the date of certain significant events, such as the sale or purchase of a division of the company or a change in auditors. This report is often the first indicator of important changes that may affect the company's financial performance in the future. Many company reports that are filed with the Securities and Exchange Commission are now available on the Internet at http://www.sec.gov/edgarhp.htm.

Business Periodicals and Credit and Investment Advisory Services

Financial analysts must keep up with current events in the financial world. Probably the best source of financial news is *The Wall Street Journal,* which is published every business day and is the most complete financial newspaper in the United States. Some helpful magazines, published every week or every two weeks, are *Forbes, Barron's, Fortune,* and the *Commercial and Financial Chronicle.*

For further details about the financial history of companies, the publications of such services as Moody's Investors Service, Inc., and Standard & Poor's are useful. Data on industry norms, average ratios and relationships, and credit ratings are available from such agencies as The Dun & Bradstreet Corp. In its *Industry Norms and Key Business Ratios,* Dun & Bradstreet offers an annual analysis giving fourteen ratios for each of 125 industry groups, classified as retailing, wholesaling, manufacturing, and construction. *Annual Statement Studies,* published by Robert Morris Associates, presents many facts and ratios for 223 different industries. A number of private services are also available for a yearly fee.

An example of specialized financial reporting that is readily available to the public is Moody's *Handbook of Dividend Achievers,* which profiles companies that have increased their dividends consistently over the past ten years. A sample listing from that publication—for PepsiCo, Inc.—is shown in Exhibit 2. A wealth of information about the company is summarized on one page: the market action of its stock; summaries of its business operations, recent developments, and prospects; earnings and dividend data; annual financial data for the past six or seven years; and other information. From the data contained in those summaries, it is possible to do many of the trend analyses and calculate the ratios explained in this chapter.

BUSINESS BULLETIN: TECHNOLOGY IN PRACTICE

Performance reports and other financial information, stock quotes, reference data, and news about companies and markets are available instantaneously to individuals on the Internet through such services as Prodigy, CompuServe, and America Online. The Internet is an international web of computer-driven communications systems that links tens of millions of homes and businesses through telephone, cable, and computer networks. Combined with the services of brokers like Charles Schwab & Co., Inc., that allow customers to use their own computers to buy and sell stock and other securities, individuals have access to resources equivalent to those used by many professional analysts.

Exhibit 2. Sample Listing from Moody's *Handbook of Dividend Achievers*

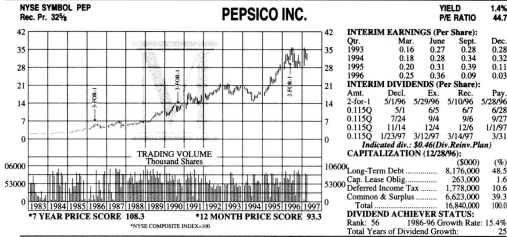

NYSE SYMBOL PEP
Rec. Pr. 32⅝

PEPSICO INC.

YIELD 1.4%
P/E RATIO 44.7

TRADING VOLUME Thousand Shares

| | 1983 | 1984 | 1985 | 1986 | 1987 | 1988 | 1989 | 1990 | 1991 | 1992 | 1993 | 1994 | 1995 | 1996 | 1997 |

*7 YEAR PRICE SCORE 108.3   *12 MONTH PRICE SCORE 93.3
*NYSE COMPOSITE INDEX=100

INTERIM EARNINGS (Per Share):

Qtr.	Mar.	June	Sept.	Dec.
1993	0.16	0.27	0.28	0.28
1994	0.18	0.28	0.34	0.32
1995	0.20	0.31	0.39	0.11
1996	0.25	0.36	0.09	0.03

INTERIM DIVIDENDS (Per Share):

Amt.	Decl.	Ex.	Rec.	Pay.
2-for-1	5/1/96	5/29/96	5/10/96	5/28/96
0.115Q	5/1	6/5	6/7	6/28
0.115Q	7/24	9/4	9/6	9/27
0.115Q	11/14	12/4	12/6	1/1/97
0.115Q	1/23/97	3/12/97	3/14/97	3/31

Indicated div.: $0.46(Div.Reinv.Plan)

CAPITALIZATION (12/28/96):

	($000)	(%)
Long-Term Debt	8,176,000	48.5
Cap. Lease Oblig.	263,000	1.6
Deferred Income Tax	1,778,000	10.6
Common & Surplus	6,623,000	39.3
Total	16,840,000	100.0

DIVIDEND ACHIEVER STATUS:
Rank: 56   1986-96 Growth Rate: 15.4%
Total Years of Dividend Growth: 25

RECENT DEVELOPMENTS: For the year ended 12/28/96, net income was $1.15 billion compared with $1.61 billion a year earlier. The 1996 and 1995 results include nonrecurring charges of $716.0 million and $384.0 million, respectively. Sales rose 4.6% to $31.65 billion. Operating results were dampened by lower results at Pizza Hut and Taco Bell and dramatic losses from PEP's international beverage businesses. Results from North American beverages, global snacks, international restaurants and KFC were improved.

PROSPECTS: On 1/23/97, PEP announced that it plans to spin off its restaurant businesses to shareholders of the Company by the end of 1997. The spin-off will include the operations of Pizza Hut, Taco Bell and KFC, consisting of approximately 29,000 restaurants and more that $20.00 billion in annual retail sales as of 12/28/96. The spin-off will allow the Company to sharpen its focus on its core businesses, which will consist of its snack foods and beverage operations. Also, PEP is examining the sale of its Pepsico Food Systems unit.

BUSINESS

PEPSICO, INC. operates on a worldwide basis within three distinct business segments: soft drinks, snack-foods and restaurants. The soft drinks segment, which accounted for 33% of sales in 1996 (21% of operating profit), manufactures concentrates, and markets Pepsi-Cola, Diet Pepsi, Mountain Dew, Slice and allied brands worldwide, and 7-up internationally. This segment also operates soft drink bottling businesses principally in the United States. Snack Foods, 31% (60%), manufactures and markets snack chips through Frito-Lay Inc. Well-known brands include: Doritos, Ruffles and Lays. The Restaurant segment, 36% (19%), consists of Pizza Hut, Taco Bell and KFC.

ANNUAL EARNINGS AND DIVIDENDS PER SHARE

	12/28/96	12/30/95	12/31/94	12/25/93	12/26/92	12/28/91	12/29/90
Earnings Per Share	0.72	1.00	1.11	0.98	0.81	0.68	0.69
Dividends Per Share	0.43	0.38	0.34	0.29	0.25	0.22	0.184
Dividend Payout %	59.7	38.0	30.6	29.6	30.9	32.4	26.7

ANNUAL FINANCIAL DATA

RECORD OF EARNINGS (IN MILLIONS):

Total Revenues	31,645.0	30,421.0	28,472.4	25,020.7	21,970.0	19,607.9	17,802.7
Costs and Expenses	28,798.0	27,118.0	24,959.0	21,810.5	19,332.9	17,276.3	15,558.0
Depreciation & Amort	1,719.0	1,740.0	1,576.5	1,444.2	1,214.9	1,034.5	884.0
Operating Profit	2,546.0	2,987.0	3,201.2	2,906.5	2,371.2	2,122.9	2,055.6
Inc Fr Cont Opers Bef Income Taxes	2,047.0	2,432.0	2,664.4	2,422.5	1,898.8	1,670.3	1,667.4
Income Taxes	898.0	826.0	880.4	834.6	597.1	590.1	576.8
Net Income	1,149.0	1,606.0	①1,784.0	1,587.9	②1,301.7	1,080.2	③1,090.6
Aver. Shs. Outstg. (000)	1,606,000	1,608,000	1,607,200	1,620,200	1,613,400	1,605,000	1,597,400

① Before acctg. change dr$32,000,000. ② Before acctg. change dr$927,400,000. ③ Before disc. op. dr$13,700,000.

BALANCE SHEET (IN MILLIONS):

Cash and Cash Equivalents	786.0	1,498.0	1,488.1	1,856.2	2,058.4	2,036.0	1,815.7
Receivables, Net	2,516.0	2,407.0	2,050.9	1,883.4	1,588.5	1,481.7	1,414.7
Inventories	1,038.0	1,051.0	970.0	924.7	768.8	661.5	585.8
Gross Property	17,840.0	16,751.0	16,130.1	14,250.0	12,095.2	10,501.7	8,977.7
Accumulated Depreciation	7,649.0	6,881.0	6,247.3	5,394.4	4,653.2	3,907.0	3,266.8
Long-Term Debt	8,176.0	8,215.0	8,542.3	7,442.6	7,964.8	7,806.2	5,600.1
Capital Lease Obligations	263.0	294.0	298.2	...	...	...	...
Net Stockholders' Equity	6,623.0	7,313.0	6,856.1	6,338.7	5,355.7	5,545.4	4,904.2
Total Assets	24,512.0	25,432.0	24,792.0	23,705.8	20,951.2	18,775.1	17,143.4
Total Current Assets	5,139.0	5,546.0	5,072.2	5,164.1	4,842.3	4,566.1	4,081.4
Total Current Liabilities	5,139.0	5,230.0	5,270.4	6,574.9	4,324.4	3,722.1	4,770.5
Net Working Capital	...	316.0	d198.2	d1,410.8	517.9	844.0	d689.1
Year End Shs Outstg (000)	1,545,000	1,576,000	1,579,800	1,597,600	1,597,600	1,578,200	1,576,780

STATISTICAL RECORD:

Operating Profit Margin %	8.0	9.8	11.2	11.6	10.8	10.8	11.5
Return on Equity %	17.3	22.0	26.0	25.1	24.3	19.5	22.2
Return on Assets %	4.7	6.3	7.2	6.7	6.2	5.8	6.4
Average Yield %	1.4	1.6	2.0	1.5	1.4	1.5	1.6
P/E Ratio	49.8-37.8	29.4-17.0	18.6-13.2	22.3-17.6	26.9-18.8	26.8-17.3	20.3-13.0
Price Range	35⅞-27¼	29⅜-17	20⅝-14⅝	21⅞-17¼	21¾-15¼	18¼-11¾	14-9

Statistics are as originally reported.

OFFICERS:
R.A. Enrico, Chmn. & C.E.O.
K.M. von der Heyden, Vice Chm. & C.F.O.
E.V. Lahey, Jr., Sr. V.P., Gen. Coun. & Sec.

INCORPORATED: NC, Dec., 1986

PRINCIPAL OFFICE: 700 Anderson Hill Rd., Purchase, NY 10577-1444

TELEPHONE NUMBER: (914) 253-2000
FAX: (914) 253-2070
NO. OF EMPLOYEES: 486,000
ANNUAL MEETING: In May
SHAREHOLDERS: 207,000
INSTITUTIONAL HOLDINGS:
No. of Institutions: 1,452
Shares Held: 844,281,498

REGISTRAR(S): Bank of Boston, Boston, MA

TRANSFER AGENT(S): Bank of Boston, Boston, MA

Tools and Techniques of Financial Analysis

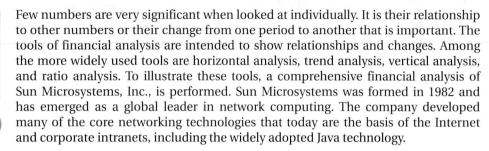

OBJECTIVE 4

Apply horizontal analysis, trend analysis, and vertical analysis to financial statements

Few numbers are very significant when looked at individually. It is their relationship to other numbers or their change from one period to another that is important. The tools of financial analysis are intended to show relationships and changes. Among the more widely used tools are horizontal analysis, trend analysis, vertical analysis, and ratio analysis. To illustrate these tools, a comprehensive financial analysis of Sun Microsystems, Inc., is performed. Sun Microsystems was formed in 1982 and has emerged as a global leader in network computing. The company developed many of the core networking technologies that today are the basis of the Internet and corporate intranets, including the widely adopted Java technology.

Horizontal Analysis

Generally accepted accounting principles require the presentation of comparative financial statements that give financial information for the current year and the previous year. A common starting point for studying such statements is horizontal analysis, which begins with the computation of changes from the previous year to the current year in both dollar amounts and percentages. The percentage change must be computed to relate the size of the change to the size of the dollar amounts involved. A change of $1 million in sales is not as impressive as a change of $1 million in net income, because sales is a larger amount than net income.

Exhibits 3 and 4 present the comparative balance sheets and income statements, respectively, for Sun Microsystems, Inc., with the dollar and percentage changes shown. The percentage change is computed as follows:

$$\text{Percentage Change} = 100 \times \left(\frac{\text{Amount of Change}}{\text{Base Year Amount}}\right)$$

The base year in any set of data is always the first year being studied. For example, from 1996 to 1997, Sun Microsystems' total current assets increased by $695 million, from approximately $3,034 million to $3,728 million, or by 22.9 percent. This is computed as follows:

$$\text{Percentage Change} = 100 \times \left(\frac{\$695 \text{ million}}{\$3,034 \text{ million}}\right) = 22.9\%$$

An examination of the components of current assets in the comparative balance sheet shows many changes from 1996 to 1997. For example, there were the large increases in deferred tax assets and accounts receivables of 61.5 percent and 38.1 percent, respectively. Also, cash and cash equivalents increased 24.8 percent, and other current assets increased 12.8 percent. However, it is important to consider the changes in dollars as well as in percentages. Consider again the changes in deferred tax assets and accounts receivable. In dollar terms, the increase in accounts receivable, $460 million, is more than four times the increase in deferred tax assets, $109 million. The increase in accounts receivable is in fact the primary reason for the increase in current assets. Overall, this and other increases far outweighed the decreases in short-term investments and inventories from 1996 to 1997. Further, net property, plant, and equipment increased 49.8 percent, or $266 million. With such a large increase in total assets, one expects to see growth in liabilities and equity. The comparative balance sheets show substantial growth in both these areas.

From the income statements in Exhibit 4, the most important result is that net revenues increased by $1,504 million, or 21.2 percent, while total costs and expenses increased by only $1,152 million, or 17.9 percent. Cost of sales and research and development increased 10.2 percent and 26.5 percent, respectively. The result of these favorable relationships is that operating income increased by $352 million, or 52.1 percent, and net income increased by $286 million, or 60.0 percent.

Exhibit 3. Comparative Balance Sheets with Horizontal Analysis

Sun Microsystems, Inc.
Consolidated Balance Sheets
June 30, 1997 and 1996

(In thousands)	1997	1996	Increase (Decrease) Amount	Increase (Decrease) Percentage
Assets				
Current Assets				
Cash and Cash Equivalents	$ 660,170	$ 528,854	$131,316	24.8
Short-Term Investments	452,590	460,743	(8,153)	(1.8)
Accounts Receivable, Net of Allowances of $196,091 in 1997 and $100,730 in 1996	1,666,523	1,206,612	459,911	38.1
Inventories	437,978	460,914	(22,936)	(5.0)
Deferred Tax Assets	286,720	177,554	109,166	61.5
Other Current Assets	224,469	199,059	25,410	12.8
Total Current Assets	$3,728,450	$3,033,736	$694,714	22.9
Property, Plant and Equipment	$1,658,341	$1,282,384	$375,957	29.3
Accumulated Depreciation and Amortization	(858,448)	(748,535)	109,913	14.7
Net Property, Plant and Equipment	$ 799,893	$ 533,849	$266,044	49.8
Other Assets, Net	168,931	233,324	(64,393)	(27.6)
Total Assets	$4,697,274	$3,800,909	$896,365	23.6
Liabilities and Stockholders' Equity				
Current Liabilities				
Short-Term Borrowings	$ 100,930	$ 49,161	$ 51,769	105.3
Accounts Payable	468,912	325,067	143,845	44.3
Accrued Payroll-Related Liabilities	337,412	282,778	54,634	19.3
Accrued Liabilities and Other	625,600	518,772	106,828	20.6
Deferred Service Revenues	197,616	140,157	57,459	41.0
Income Taxes Payable	118,568	134,934	(16,366)	(12.1)
Current Portion of Long-Term Debt	—	38,400	(38,400)	(100.0)
Total Current Liabilities	$1,849,038	$1,489,269	$359,769	24.2
Long-Term Debt and Other Obligations	106,299	60,154	46,145	76.7
Total Stockholders' Equity	2,741,937	2,251,486	490,451	21.8
Total Liabilities and Stockholders' Equity	$4,697,274	$3,800,909	$896,365	23.6

Source: Sun Microsystems, Inc., *Annual Report*, 1997.

Trend Analysis

A variation of horizontal analysis is trend analysis, in which percentage changes are calculated for several successive years instead of for two years. Trend analysis, with its long-run view, is important because it may point to basic changes in the nature of a business. In addition to comparative financial statements, most companies present a summary of operations and data about other key indicators for five or more years. Domestic and international net revenues from Sun Microsystems' summary of operations together with a trend analysis are presented in Exhibit 5.

Exhibit 4. Comparative Income Statements with Horizontal Analysis

Sun Microsystems, Inc.
Consolidated Income Statements
For the Years Ended June 30, 1997 and 1996

			Increase (Decrease)	
(In thousands, except per share amounts)	1997	1996	Amount	Percentage
Net Revenues	$8,598,346	$7,094,751	$1,503,595	21.2
Costs and Expenses				
Cost of Sales	$4,320,460	$3,921,228	$ 399,232	10.2
Research and Development	825,968	653,044	172,924	26.5
Selling, General and Administrative	2,402,442	1,787,567	614,875	34.4
Nonrecurring Charges	22,958	57,900	(34,942)	(60.3)
Total Costs and Expenses	$7,571,828	$6,419,739	$1,152,089	17.9
Operating Income	$1,026,518	$ 675,012	$ 351,506	52.1
Gain on Sale of Equity Investment	62,245	—	62,245	NA
Interest Income	39,899	42,976	(3,077)	(7.2)
Interest Expense	(7,455)	(9,114)	1,659	18.2
Income Before Income Taxes	$1,121,207	$ 708,874	$ 412,333	58.2
Provision for Income Taxes	358,787	232,486	126,301	54.3
Net Income	$ 762,420	$ 476,388	$ 286,032	60.0
Net Income per Common and Common-Equivalent Share	$ 1.96	$ 1.21	$ .75	62.0
Common and Common-Equivalent Shares Used in the Calculation of Net Income per Share	388,967	393,380	(4,413)	(1.1)

Source: Sun Microsystems, Inc., *Annual Report,* 1997.

Exhibit 5. Trend Analysis

Sun Microsystems, Inc.
Net Revenues and Operating Income
Trend Analysis

	1997	1996	1995	1994	1993
Dollar Values (in millions)					
Net Revenues	$8,598	$7,095	$5,902	$4,690	$4,309
Operating Income	1,027	675	500	277	241
Trend Analysis (in percentages)					
Net Revenues	199.5	164.7	137.0	108.8	100.0
Operating Income	426.1	280.1	207.5	114.9	100.0

Source: Sun Microsystems, Inc., *Annual Report,* 1997.

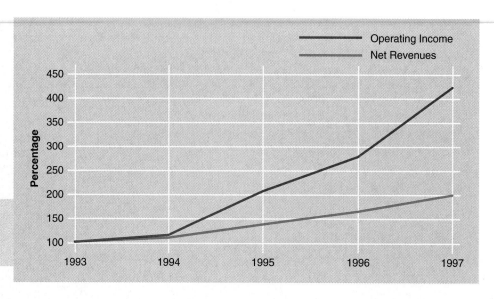

Figure 1
Trend Analysis Presented Graphically for Sun Microsystems, Inc.

Trend analysis uses an index number to show changes in related items over a period of time. For index numbers, the base year is equal to 100 percent. Other years are measured in relation to that amount. For example, the 1997 index for net revenues was figured as follows (dollar amounts in millions):

$$\text{Index} = 100 \times \left(\frac{\text{Index Year Amount}}{\text{Base Year Amount}} \right) = 100 \times \left(\frac{\$8,598}{\$4,309} \right) = 199.5$$

A study of the trend analysis in Exhibit 5 clearly shows that operating income has grown faster than net revenues at Sun Microsystems. However, both net revenues and operating income have shown increases every year. These trends may be seen visually in Figure 1.

Vertical Analysis

In vertical analysis, percentages are used to show the relationship of the different parts to a total in a single statement. The accountant sets a total figure in the statement equal to 100 percent and computes each component's percentage of that total. (The figure would be total assets or total liabilities and stockholders' equity on the balance sheet, and net revenues or net sales on the income statement.) The resulting statement of percentages is called a common-size statement. Common-size balance sheets and income statements for Sun Microsystems are shown in pie-chart form in Figures 2 and 3, and in financial statement form in Exhibits 6 and 7.

Vertical analysis is useful for comparing the importance of specific components in the operation of a business. Also, comparative common-size statements can be used to identify important changes in the components from one year to the next. For Sun Microsystems, the composition of assets in Exhibit 6, illustrated in Figure 2, shifted from other assets toward net property, plant, and equipment, whereas liabilities showed a small shift to long-term liabilities from stockholders' equity. The main conclusion that can be drawn from this analysis of Sun Microsystems is that current assets and current liabilities make up a large portion of the company and that the company's financial structure has little long-term debt.

The common-size income statements in Exhibit 7, illustrated in Figure 3, show that Sun Microsystems improved its cost of sales from 1996 to 1997 by 5.1 percent of revenues (55.3 – 50.2). This improvement resulted in increased gross margin, operating income, and net income as a percentage of net revenues. Selling, general, and

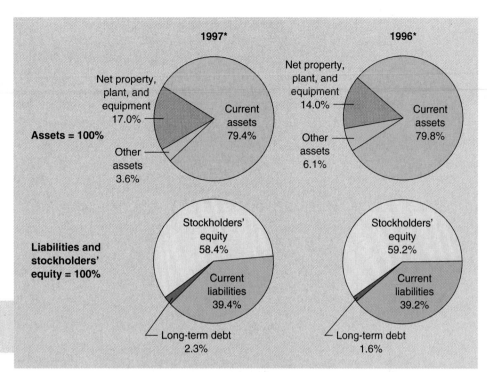

Figure 2
Common-Size Balance Sheets Presented Graphically

* Rounding causes some additions not to total precisely.

administrative expenses increased 2.7 percent of net revenues, which is the primary reason why total costs and expenses decreased only 2.4 percent of net revenues. Also, the company continued to invest over 9 percent of its net revenues in research and development.

Common-size statements are often used to make comparisons between companies. They allow an analyst to compare the operating and financing characteristics of two companies of different size in the same industry. For example, the analyst might want to compare Sun Microsystems with other companies in terms of

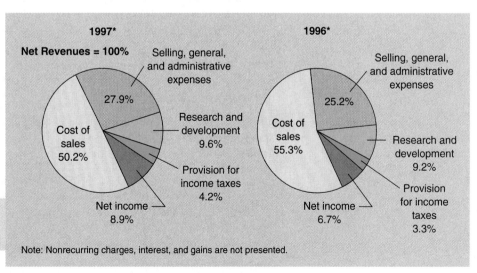

Figure 3
Common-Size Income Statements Presented Graphically

Note: Nonrecurring charges, interest, and gains are not presented.

* Rounding causes some additions not to total precisely.

Exhibit 6. Common-Size Balance Sheets

Sun Microsystems, Inc.
Common-Size Balance Sheets
June 30, 1997 and 1996

	1997*	1996*
Assets		
Current Assets	79.4%	79.8%
Net Property, Plant, and Equipment	17.0	14.0
Other Assets, Net	3.6	6.1
Total Assets	100.0%	100.0%
Liabilities and Stockholders' Equity		
Current Liabilities	39.4%	39.2%
Long-Term Debt and Other Obligations	2.3	1.6
Total Liabilities	41.6%	40.8%
Total Stockholders' Equity	58.4	59.2
Total Liabilities and Stockholders' Equity	100.0%	100.0%

*Amounts do not precisely total 100 percent in all cases due to rounding.
Source: Sun Microsystems, Inc., *Annual Report*, 1997.

Exhibit 7. Common-Size Income Statements

Sun Microsystems, Inc.
Common-Size Income Statements
For the Years Ended June 30, 1997 and 1996

	1997*	1996*
Net Revenues	100.0%	100.0%
Costs and Expenses		
Cost of Sales	50.2%	55.3%
Research and Development	9.6	9.2
Selling, General and Administrative	27.9	25.2
Nonrecurring Charges	.3	.8
Total Costs and Expenses	88.1%	90.5%
Operating Income	11.9%	9.5%
Gain on Sale of Equity Investment	.8	—
Interest, Net	.4	.5
Income Before Income Taxes	13.1%	10.0%
Provision for Income Taxes	4.2	3.3
Net Income	8.9%	6.7%

*Rounding causes some additions and subtractions not to total precisely.
Source: Sun Microsystems, Inc., *Annual Report*, 1997.

percentage of total assets financed by debt or in terms of selling, general, and administrative expenses as a percentage of net revenues. Common-size statements would show those and other relationships.

Ratio Analysis

Ratio analysis is an important way to state meaningful relationships between the components of the financial statements. To be most meaningful, the interpretation of ratios must include a study of the underlying data. Ratios are guides or shortcuts that are useful in evaluating a company's financial position and operations and making comparisons with results in previous years or with other companies. The primary purpose of ratios is to point out areas needing further investigation. They should be used in connection with a general understanding of the company and its environment. Ratios may be expressed in several ways. For example, a ratio of net income of $100,000 to sales of $1,000,000 may be stated as (1) net income is 1/10 or 10 percent of sales; (2) the ratio of sales to net income is 10 to 1 (10:1), or sales are 10 times net income; or (3) for every dollar of sales, the company has an average net income of 10 cents.

Comprehensive Illustration of Ratio Analysis

OBJECTIVE 5

Apply ratio analysis to financial statements in a comprehensive evaluation of a company's financial situation

The management's discussion and analysis section of Sun Microsystems' annual report states, "The company's financial condition strengthened as of fiscal 1997 year end when compared with fiscal 1996."[3] To verify this statement, a comprehensive ratio analysis is used to compare Sun Microsystems' performance for the years 1996 and 1997 with regard to the following objectives: (1) liquidity, (2) profitability, (3) long-term solvency, (4) cash flow adequacy, and (5) market strength. Most data for the analyses come from the financial statements presented in Exhibits 3 and 4. Other data are presented as needed.

Evaluating Liquidity

Liquidity is a company's ability to pay bills when they are due and to meet unexpected needs for cash. All the ratios that relate to liquidity involve working capital or some part of it, because it is out of working capital that debts are paid. The objective of liquidity is also closely related to the cash flow ratios.

The liquidity ratios from 1996 to 1997 for Sun Microsystems are presented in Exhibit 8. The current ratio and the quick ratio are measures of short-term debt-paying ability. The principal difference between the two is that the numerator of the current ratio includes inventories and prepaid expenses. Inventories take longer to convert to cash than do the current assets included in the numerator of the quick ratio. Both ratios remained constant from 1996 to 1997. The current ratio was 2.0 times, and the quick ratio was 1.5 times. The primary reason for the consistent results is that current assets and current liabilities grew at similar rates.

Analysis of two major components of current assets, receivables and inventory, shows contrasting trends. The major change in this category of ratios is in the receivable turnover. The relative size of the accounts receivable and the effectiveness of credit policies are measured by the receivable turnover, which fell from 6.3 times in 1996 to 6.0 times in 1997. The related ratio of average days' sales uncollected increased by almost three days, from 57.9 days in 1996 to 60.8 days in 1997. The inventory turnover, which measures the relative size of inventories, also worsened. Inventory turnover declined from 10.0 times in 1996 to 9.6 times in 1997. This

Exhibit 8. Liquidity Ratios of Sun Microsystems, Inc.

(Dollar amounts in thousands)	1997	1996

Current ratio: Measure of short-term debt-paying ability

$$\frac{\text{Current Assets}}{\text{Current Liabilities}} \qquad \frac{\$3,728,450}{\$1,849,038} = 2.0 \text{ times} \qquad \frac{\$3,033,736}{\$1,489,269} = 2.0 \text{ times}$$

Quick ratio: Measure of short-term debt-paying ability

$$\frac{\text{Cash + Marketable Securities + Receivables}}{\text{Current Liabilities}} \qquad \frac{\$660,170 + \$452,590 + \$1,666,523}{\$1,849,038} \qquad \frac{\$528,854 + \$460,743 + \$1,206,612}{\$1,489,269}$$

$$= \frac{\$2,779,283}{\$1,849,038} = 1.5 \text{ times} \qquad = \frac{\$2,196,209}{\$1,489,269} = 1.5 \text{ times}$$

Receivable turnover: Measure of relative size of accounts receivable balance and effectiveness of credit policies

$$\frac{\text{Net Sales}}{\text{Average Accounts Receivable*}} \qquad \frac{\$8,598,346}{(\$1,666,523 + \$1,206,612)/2} \qquad \frac{\$7,094,751}{(\$1,206,612 + \$1,046,374)/2}$$

$$= \frac{\$8,598,346}{\$1,436,568} = 6.0 \text{ times} \qquad = \frac{\$7,094,751}{\$1,126,493} = 6.3 \text{ times}$$

Average days' sales uncollected: Measure of average time taken to collect receivables

$$\frac{\text{Days in Year}}{\text{Receivable Turnover}} \qquad \frac{365 \text{ days}}{6.0 \text{ times}} = 60.8 \text{ days} \qquad \frac{365 \text{ days}}{6.3 \text{ times}} = 57.9 \text{ days}$$

Inventory turnover: Measure of relative size of inventory

$$\frac{\text{Cost of Goods Sold}}{\text{Average Inventory*}} \qquad \frac{\$4,320,460}{(\$437,978 + \$460,914)/2} \qquad \frac{\$3,921,228}{(\$460,914 + \$325,172)/2}$$

$$= \frac{\$4,320,460}{\$449,446} = 9.6 \text{ times} \qquad = \frac{\$3,921,228}{\$393,043} = 10.0 \text{ times}$$

Average days' inventory on hand: Measure of average days taken to sell inventory

$$\frac{\text{Days in Year}}{\text{Inventory Turnover}} \qquad \frac{365 \text{ days}}{9.6 \text{ times}} = 38.0 \text{ days} \qquad \frac{365 \text{ days}}{10.0 \text{ times}} = 36.5 \text{ days}$$

*1995 figures are derived from the statement of cash flows in Sun Microsystems' annual report.
Source: Sun Microsystems, Inc., *Annual Report*, 1997.

results in an unfavorable increase in average days' inventory on hand from 36.5 days in 1996 to 38.0 days in 1997. When taken together, this means that Sun Microsystems, operating cycle, or the time it takes to sell products and collect for them, increased from 94.4 days in 1996 (57.9 days + 36.5 days) to 98.8 days in 1997 (60.8 days + 38.0 days). This increase represents a small decline in liquidity. Overall, Sun Microsystems' liquidity remains strong.

Evaluating Profitability

The objective of profitability relates to a company's ability to earn a satisfactory income so that investors and stockholders will continue to provide capital to the company. A company's profitability is also closely linked to its liquidity because

Exhibit 9. Profitability Ratios of Sun Microsystems, Inc.

(Dollar amounts in thousands)	1997	1996

Profit margin: Measure of net income produced by each dollar of sales

$$\frac{\text{Net Income*}}{\text{Net Sales}} \qquad \frac{\$762,420}{\$8,598,346} = 8.9\% \qquad \frac{\$476,388}{\$7,094,751} = 6.7\%$$

Asset turnover: Measure of how efficiently assets are used to produce sales

$$\frac{\text{Net Sales}}{\text{Average Total Assets}^\dagger} \qquad \frac{\$8,598,346}{(\$4,697,274 + \$3,800,909)/2} \qquad \frac{\$7,094,751}{(\$3,800,909 + \$3,545,000)/2}$$

$$= \frac{\$8,598,346}{\$4,249,092} = 2.0 \text{ times} \qquad = \frac{\$7,094,751}{\$3,672,955} = 1.9 \text{ times}$$

Return on assets: Measure of overall earning power or profitability

$$\frac{\text{Net Income}}{\text{Average Total Assets}^\dagger} \qquad \frac{\$762,420}{\$4,249,092} = 17.9\% \qquad \frac{\$476,388}{\$3,672,955} = 13.0\%$$

Return on equity: Measure of the profitability of stockholders' investments

$$\frac{\text{Net Income}}{\text{Average Stockholders' Equity}^\dagger} \qquad \frac{\$762,420}{(\$2,741,937 + \$2,251,486)/2} \qquad \frac{\$476,388}{(\$2,251,486 + \$2,122,595)/2}$$

$$= \frac{\$762,420}{\$2,496,712} = 30.5\% \qquad = \frac{\$476,388}{\$2,187,041} = 21.8\%$$

*In comparing companies in an industry, some analysts use income before income taxes as the numerator to eliminate the effect of differing tax rates among firms.

†1995 figures are from the eleven-year financial history or the statements of stockholders' equity in Sun Microsystems' annual report.

Source: Sun Microsystems, Inc., *Annual Report*, 1997.

earnings ultimately produce cash flow. For this reason, evaluating profitability is important to both investors and creditors. The profitability ratios of Sun Microsystems, Inc., are shown in Exhibit 9.

All measures of Sun Microsystems' profitability improved from 1996 to 1997, primarily because of the large increase in net income. The reasons for the increase were discussed in the sections on horizontal and vertical analysis. Profit margin, which measures the net income produced by each dollar of sales, increased from 6.7 to 8.9 percent, and asset turnover, which measures how efficiently assets are used to produce sales, increased from 1.9 to 2.0 times. The result is an improvement in the overall earning power of the company, or return on assets, from 13.0 to 17.9 percent. These relationships may be illustrated as follows:

Profit Margin		Asset Turnover		Return on Assets
$\dfrac{\text{Net Income}}{\text{Net Sales}}$	$\times$	$\dfrac{\text{Net Sales}}{\text{Average Total Assets}}$	$=$	$\dfrac{\text{Net Income}}{\text{Average Total Assets}}$
1997 8.9%	$\times$	2.0	$=$	17.8%
1996 6.7%	$\times$	1.9	$=$	12.7%

The slight difference in the two sets of return on assets figures results from the rounding of the ratios used in the above computation. Finally, the profitability of stockholders' investments, or return on equity, became more favorable, increasing from 21.8 percent to 30.5 percent.

Exhibit 10. Long-Term Solvency Ratios of Sun Microsystems, Inc.		
(Dollar amounts in thousands)	1997	1996

Debt to equity ratio: Measure of capital structure and leverage

$$\frac{\text{Total Liabilities}}{\text{Stockholders' Equity}} \qquad \frac{\$1,955,337}{\$2,741,937} = .7 \text{ times} \qquad \frac{\$1,549,423}{\$2,251,486} = .7 \text{ times}$$

Interest coverage ratio: Measure of creditors' protection from default on interest payments

$$\frac{\text{Income Before Income}}{\text{Taxes + Interest Expense}} \qquad \frac{\$1,121,207 + \$7,455}{\$7,455} \qquad \frac{\$708,874 + \$9,114}{\$9,114}$$
$$\text{Interest Expense} \qquad = 151.4 \text{ times} \qquad = 78.8 \text{ times}$$

Source: Sun Microsystems, Inc., *Annual Report,* 1997.

Evaluating Long-Term Solvency

Long-term solvency has to do with a company's ability to survive for many years. The aim of long-term solvency analysis is to detect early signs that a company is on the road to bankruptcy. Studies have indicated that accounting ratios can show as much as five years in advance that a company may fail.[4] Declining profitability and liquidity ratios are key indicators of possible business failure. Two other ratios that analysts often consider when assessing long-term solvency are debt to equity and interest coverage. Long-term solvency ratios are shown in Exhibit 10.

Increasing amounts of debt in a company's capital structure mean that the company is becoming more heavily leveraged. This condition negatively affects long-term solvency because it represents increasing legal obligations to pay interest periodically and the principal at maturity. Failure to make those payments can result in bankruptcy. The debt to equity ratio measures capital structure and leverage by showing the amount of a company's assets provided by creditors in relation to the amount provided by stockholders. Sun Microsystems' debt to equity ratio was only .7 times in both 1996 and 1997. It is noteworthy to recall from Exhibit 3 that the company has primarily short-term debt and little long-term debt and that the company has ample current assets as reflected by the current ratio and the quick ratio. All of these are positive factors for the company's long-term solvency. As to the future, "The Company believes the level of financial resources is a significant competitive factor in its industry, and it may choose at any time to raise additional capital through debt or equity financing to strengthen its financial position, facilitate growth, and provide the Company with additional flexibility to take advantage of business opportunities that may arise."[5]

If debt is risky, why have any? The answer is that the level of debt is a matter of balance. Despite its riskiness, debt is a flexible means of financing certain business operations. Sun Microsystems is using debt to finance what management plans to be a temporary increase in inventory. The interest paid on that debt is deductible for income tax purposes, whereas dividends on stock are not. Because debt usually carries a fixed interest charge, the cost of financing can be limited and leverage can be used to advantage. If the company is able to earn a return on assets greater than the cost of interest, it makes an overall profit.[6] However, the company runs the risk of not earning a return on assets equal to the cost of financing those assets, thereby incurring a loss.

The interest coverage ratio measures the degree of protection creditors have from a default on interest payments. Because of its small amount of long-term debt, Sun

Exhibit 11. Cash Flow Adequacy Ratios of Sun Microsystems, Inc.

(Dollar amounts in thousands)	1997	1996

Cash flow yield: Measure of a company's ability to generate operating cash flows in relation to net income

$$\frac{\text{Net Cash Flows from Operating Activities*}}{\text{Net Income}} \qquad \frac{\$1,105,088}{\$762,420} = 1.4 \text{ times} \qquad \frac{\$688,314}{\$476,388} = 1.4 \text{ times}$$

Cash flows to sales: Measure of the ability of sales to generate operating cash flows

$$\frac{\text{Net Cash Flows from Operating Activities*}}{\text{Net Sales}} \qquad \frac{\$1,105,088}{\$8,598,346} = 12.9\% \qquad \frac{\$688,314}{\$7,094,751} = 9.7\%$$

Cash flows to assets: Measure of the ability of assets to generate operating cash flows

$$\frac{\text{Net Cash Flows from Operating Activities*}}{\text{Average Total Assets}^\dagger} \qquad \frac{\$1,105,088}{(\$4,697,274 + \$3,800,909)/2} \qquad \frac{\$688,314}{(\$3,800,909 + \$3,545,000)/2}$$

$$= \frac{\$1,105,088}{\$4,249,092} = 26.0\% \qquad = \frac{\$688,314}{\$3,672,955} = 18.7\%$$

Free cash flow: Measure of cash generated or cash deficiency after providing for commitments

Net Cash Flows from Operating Activities* − Dividends − Net Capital Expenditures*

$$\$1,105,088 - \$0 - \$554,018 \qquad \$688,314 - \$0 - \$295,638$$
$$= \$551,070 \qquad = \$392,676$$

*These figures are from the statements of cash flows in Sun Microsystems' annual report.
†The 1995 figure is from the eleven-year financial history in Sun Microsystems' annual report.
Source: Sun Microsystems, Inc., *Annual Report*, 1997.

Microsystems has large interest coverage ratios of 78.8 times in 1996 and 151.4 times in 1997. Interest coverage is not a problem for the company.

Evaluating Cash Flow Adequacy

Because cash flows are needed to pay debts when they are due, cash flow measures are closely related to the objectives of liquidity and long-term solvency. Sun Microsystems' cash flow adequacy ratios are presented in Exhibit 11. By most measures, the company's ability to generate positive operating cash flows showed improvement from 1996 to 1997. Key to those increases is the fact that net cash flows from operating activities had a large increase, from $688 million in 1996 to $1,105 million in 1997, while net income, net sales, and average total assets increased by lesser percentages. Cash flow yield, or the relationship of cash flows from operating activities to net income, remained unchanged at 1.4 times. Cash flows to sales, or the ability of sales to generate operating cash flows, increased from 9.7 percent to 12.9 percent. Cash flows to assets, or the ability of assets to generate operating cash flows, increased from 18.7 percent to 26.0 percent.

Free cash flow, the cash generated after providing for commitments, also increased and remains very positive primarily because capital expenditures were increased by a smaller amount than the increase in net cash flows from operating activities and because the company pays no dividends. Management's comment with regard to cash flows in the future is, "The Company believes that the liquidity provided by existing cash and short-term investment balances and the borrowing

Exhibit 12. Market Strength Ratios of Sun Microsystems, Inc.

	1997	1996
Price/earnings ratio: Measure of investor confidence in a company		

$$\frac{\text{Market Price per Share*}}{\text{Earnings per Share}} \qquad \frac{\$37.2190}{\$1.96} = 19.0 \text{ times} \qquad \frac{\$29.4375}{\$1.21} = 24.3 \text{ times}$$

Dividends yield: Measure of the current return to an investor in a stock

$$\frac{\text{Dividends per Share}}{\text{Market Price per Share}} \qquad \text{Sun Microsystems does not pay a dividend.}$$

*Market price is from Sun Microsystems' annual report.
Source: Sun Microsystems, Inc., *Annual Report*, 1997.

arrangements . . . may have to be supplemented with additional resources to provide sufficient capital to meet the Company's capital requirements through fiscal 1998."[7]

Evaluating Market Strength

The market price of a company's stock is of interest to the analyst because it represents what investors as a whole think of the company at a point in time. Market price is the price at which the stock is bought and sold. It provides information about how investors view the potential return and risk connected with owning the company's stock. Market price by itself is not very informative for this purpose, however. Companies differ in number of outstanding shares and amount of underlying earnings and dividends. Thus, market price must be related to earnings by considering the price/earnings ratio and the dividends yield. Those ratios for Sun Microsystems appear in Exhibit 12 and have been computed using the market price for Sun Microsystems' stock at the end of 1996 and 1997.

The price/earnings (P/E) ratio, which measures investor confidence in a company, is the ratio of the market price per share to earnings per share. The P/E ratio is useful in comparing the relative values placed on the earnings of different companies and in comparing the value placed on a company's shares in relation to the overall market. With a lower P/E ratio, the investor obtains more underlying earnings per dollar invested. However, Sun Microsystems' P/E ratio decreased from 24.3 times in 1996 to 19.0 times in 1997. In effect, investors probably do not believe that the more than 60 percent increase in earnings per share is sustainable in future years. It does not signal a lack of confidence by investors in Sun Microsystems. It is an indication that investors think the company will continue to increase earnings in future years. The dividends yield measures a stock's current return to an investor in the form of dividends. Because Sun Microsystems pays no dividend, it may be concluded that investors expect their return from owning the company's stock to come from increases in its market value.

Summary of the Financial Analysis of Sun Microsystems, Inc.

This ratio analysis clearly shows that Sun Microsystems' financial condition is strong, as measured by its liquidity, long-term solvency, and cash flow adequacy ratios. The company's profitability is excellent and increased from 1996 to 1997, as measured by its profitability ratios. This performance has been rewarded by a higher market price per share.

Chapter Review

REVIEW OF LEARNING OBJECTIVES

1. **Describe and discuss the objectives of financial statement analysis.** Creditors and investors, as well as managers, use financial statement analysis to judge the past performance and current position of a company, and also to judge its future potential and the risk associated with it. Creditors use the information gained from their analysis to make reliable loans that will be repaid with interest. Investors use the information to make investments that will provide a return that is worth the risk.

2. **Describe and discuss the standards for financial statement analysis.** Three commonly used standards for financial statement analysis are rule-of-thumb measures, the company's past performance, and industry norms. Rule-of-thumb measures are weak because of the lack of evidence that they can be widely applied. The past performance of a company can offer a guideline for measuring improvement but is not helpful in judging performance relative to other companies. Although the use of industry norms overcomes this last problem, its disadvantage is that firms are not always comparable, even in the same industry.

3. **State the sources of information for financial statement analysis.** The main sources of information about publicly held corporations are company-published reports, such as annual reports and interim financial statements; SEC reports; business periodicals; and credit and investment advisory services.

4. **Apply horizontal analysis, trend analysis, and vertical analysis to financial statements.** Horizontal analysis involves the computation of changes in both dollar amounts and percentages from year to year. Trend analysis is an extension of horizontal analysis in that percentage changes are calculated for several years. The changes are usually computed by setting a base year equal to 100 and calculating the results for subsequent years as percentages of that base year. Vertical analysis uses percentages to show the relationship of the component parts to a total in a single statement. The resulting financial statements, which are expressed entirely in percentages, are called common-size statements.

5. **Apply ratio analysis to financial statements in a comprehensive evaluation of a company's financial situation.** A comprehensive ratio analysis includes the evaluation of a company's liquidity, profitability, long-term solvency, cash flow adequacy, and market strength. The ratios for measuring these characteristics are found in Exhibits 8 to 12.

REVIEW OF CONCEPTS AND TERMINOLOGY

The following concepts and terms were introduced in this chapter.

LO 5   **Asset turnover:** Net sales divided by average total assets. Used to measure how efficiently assets are used to produce sales.

LO 5   **Average days' inventory on hand:** Days in the year divided by inventory turnover. Shows the average number of days taken to sell inventory.

LO 5   **Average days' sales uncollected:** Days in the year divided by receivable turnover. Shows the speed at which receivables are turned over—literally, the number of days, on average, that a company must wait to receive payment for credit sales.

LO 4   **Base year:** In financial analysis, the first year to be considered in any set of data.

LO 5   **Cash flows to assets:** Net cash flows from operating activities divided by average total assets. Used to measure the ability of assets to generate operating cash flows.

LO 5   **Cash flows to sales:** Net cash flows from operating activities divided by net sales. Used to measure the ability of sales to generate operating cash flows.

LO 5   **Cash flow yield:** Net cash flows from operating activities divided by net income. Used to measure the ability of a company to generate operating cash flows in relation to net income.

LO 4   **Common-size statement:** A financial statement in which the components of a total figure are stated in terms of percentages of that total.

LO 5   **Current ratio:** Current assets divided by current liabilities. Used as an indicator of a company's liquidity and short-term debt-paying ability.

LO 5   **Debt to equity ratio:** Total liabilities divided by stockholders' equity. Used to measure the relationship of debt financing to equity financing, or the extent to which a company is leveraged.

LO 2   **Diversified companies:** Companies that operate in more than one industry; also called *conglomerates*.

LO 5   **Dividends yield:** Dividends per share divided by market price per share. Used as a measure of the current return to an investor in a stock.

LO 1   **Financial statement analysis:** All the techniques used to show important relationships among amounts in financial statements.

LO 5   **Free cash flow:** Net cash flows from operating activities minus dividends minus net capital expenditures. Used to measure cash generated after providing for commitments.

LO 4   **Horizontal analysis:** A technique for analyzing financial statements that involves the computation of changes in both dollar amounts and percentages from the previous to the current year.

LO 4   **Index number:** In trend analysis, a number from which changes in related items over a period of time are measured. Calculated by setting the base year equal to 100 percent.

LO 5   **Interest coverage ratio:** Income before income taxes plus interest expense divided by interest expense. Used as a measure of the degree of protection creditors have from a default on interest payments.

LO 3   **Interim financial statements:** Financial statements issued for a period of less than one year, usually a quarter or a month.

LO 5   **Inventory turnover:** The cost of goods sold divided by average inventory. Used to measure the relative size of inventory.

LO 5   **Operating cycle:** The time it takes to sell products and collect for them; average days' inventory on hand plus average days' sales uncollected.

LO 1   **Portfolio:** A group of loans or investments designed to average the returns and risks of a creditor or investor.

LO 5   **Price/earnings (P/E) ratio:** Market price per share divided by earnings per share. Used as a measure of investor confidence in a company and as a means of comparison among stocks.

LO 5   **Profit margin:** Net income divided by net sales. Used to measure the percentage of each revenue dollar that contributes to net income.

LO 5   **Quick ratio:** The more liquid current assets—cash, marketable securities or short-term investments, and receivables—divided by current liabilities. Used as a measure of short-term debt-paying ability.

LO 4   **Ratio analysis:** A technique of financial analysis in which meaningful relationships are shown between the components of the financial statements.

LO 5   **Receivable turnover:** Net sales divided by average accounts receivable. Used as a measure of the relative size of a company's accounts receivable and the success of its credit and collection policies; shows how many times, on average, receivables were turned into cash during the period.

LO 5   **Return on assets:** Net income divided by average total assets. Used to measure the amount earned on each dollar of assets invested. A measure of overall earning power, or profitability.

LO 5   **Return on equity:** Net income divided by average stockholders' equity. Used to measure how much income was earned on each dollar invested by stockholders.

LO 4   **Trend analysis:** A type of horizontal analysis in which percentage changes are calculated for several successive years instead of for two years.

LO 4   **Vertical analysis:** A technique for analyzing financial statements that uses percentages to show the relationships of the different parts to the total in a single statement.

REVIEW PROBLEM
Comparative Analysis of Two Companies

LO 5 Maggie Washington is considering an investment in one of two fast-food restaurant chains because she believes the trend toward eating out more often will continue. Her choices have been narrowed to Quik Burger and Big Steak, whose balance sheets and income statements appear below.

Balance Sheets
December 31, 20xx
(in thousands)

	Quik Burger	Big Steak
Assets		
Cash	$ 2,000	$ 4,500
Accounts Receivable (net)	2,000	6,500
Inventory	2,000	5,000
Property, Plant, and Equipment (net)	20,000	35,000
Other Assets	4,000	5,000
Total Assets	$30,000	$56,000
Liabilities and Stockholders' Equity		
Accounts Payable	$ 2,500	$ 3,000
Notes Payable	1,500	4,000
Bonds Payable	10,000	30,000
Common Stock, $1 par value	1,000	3,000
Paid-in Capital in Excess of Par Value, Common	9,000	9,000
Retained Earnings	6,000	7,000
Total Liabilities and Stockholders' Equity	$30,000	$56,000

Income Statements
For the Year Ended December 31, 20xx
(in thousands, except per share amounts)

	Quik Burger	Big Steak
Net Sales	$53,000	$86,000
Costs and Expenses		
Cost of Goods Sold	$37,000	$61,000
Selling Expenses	7,000	10,000
Administrative Expenses	4,000	5,000
Total Costs and Expenses	$48,000	$76,000
Income from Operations	$ 5,000	$10,000
Interest Expense	1,400	3,200
Income Before Income Taxes	$ 3,600	$ 6,800
Income Taxes	1,800	3,400
Net Income	$ 1,800	$ 3,400
Earnings per Share	$ 1.80	$ 1.13

The statements of cash flows show that net cash flows from operations were $2,200,000 for Quik Burger and $3,000,000 for Big Steak. Net capital expenditures were $2,100,000 for Quik Burger and $1,800,000 for Big Steak. Dividends of $500,000 were paid by Quik Burger and $600,000 by Big Steak. The market prices of the stocks of Quik Burger and Big Steak were $30 and $20, respectively. Financial information pertaining to prior years is not readily available to Maggie Washington. Assume that all notes payable are current liabilities and that all bonds payable are long-term liabilities.

REQUIRED

Conduct a comprehensive ratio analysis of Quik Burger and Big Steak and compare the results. The analysis should be performed using the following steps (use end-of-year balances for averages and round all ratios and percentages to one decimal place):

1. Prepare an analysis of liquidity.
2. Prepare an analysis of profitability.
3. Prepare an analysis of long-term solvency.
4. Prepare an analysis of cash flow adequacy.
5. Prepare an analysis of market strength.
6. Compare the two companies by inserting the ratio calculations from the preceding five steps in a table with the following column headings: Ratio Name, Quik Burger, Big Steak, and Company with More Favorable Ratio. Indicate in the last column the company that apparently had the more favorable ratio in each case. (Consider differences of .1 or less to be neutral.)
7. In what ways would having access to prior years' information aid this analysis?

ANSWER TO REVIEW PROBLEM

Ratio Name	Quik Burger	Big Steak
1. Liquidity analysis		

a. Current ratio

$$\frac{\$2,000 + \$2,000 + \$2,000}{\$2,500 + \$1,500}$$
$$= \frac{\$6,000}{\$4,000} = 1.5 \text{ times}$$

$$\frac{\$4,500 + \$6,500 + \$5,000}{\$3,000 + \$4,000}$$
$$= \frac{\$16,000}{\$7,000} = 2.3 \text{ times}$$

b. Quick ratio

$$\frac{\$2,000 + \$2,000}{\$2,500 + \$1,500}$$
$$= \frac{\$4,000}{\$4,000} = 1.0 \text{ times}$$

$$\frac{\$4,500 + \$6,500}{\$3,000 + \$4,000}$$
$$= \frac{\$11,000}{\$7,000} = 1.6 \text{ times}$$

c. Receivable turnover

$$\frac{\$53,000}{\$2,000} = 26.5 \text{ times}$$

$$\frac{\$86,000}{\$6,500} = 13.2 \text{ times}$$

d. Average days' sales uncollected

$$\frac{365}{26.5} = 13.8 \text{ days}$$

$$\frac{365}{13.2} = 27.7 \text{ days}$$

e. Inventory turnover

$$\frac{\$37,000}{\$2,000} = 18.5 \text{ times}$$

$$\frac{\$61,000}{\$5,000} = 12.2 \text{ times}$$

f. Average days' inventory on hand

$$\frac{365}{18.5} = 19.7 \text{ days}$$

$$\frac{365}{12.2} = 29.9 \text{ days}$$

Ratio Name	Quik Burger	Big Steak
2. Profitability analysis		

a. Profit margin

$$\frac{\$1,800}{\$53,000} = 3.4\% \qquad\qquad \frac{\$3,400}{\$86,000} = 4.0\%$$

b. Asset turnover

$$\frac{\$53,000}{\$30,000} = 1.8 \text{ times} \qquad\qquad \frac{\$86,000}{\$56,000} = 1.5 \text{ times}$$

c. Return on assets

$$\frac{\$1,800}{\$30,000} = 6.0\% \qquad\qquad \frac{\$3,400}{\$56,000} = 6.1\%$$

d. Return on equity

$$\frac{\$1,800}{\$1,000 \;+\; \$9,000 \;+\; \$6,000} \qquad\qquad \frac{\$3,400}{\$3,000 \;+\; \$9,000 \;+\; \$7,000}$$

$$= \frac{\$1,800}{\$16,000} = 11.3\% \qquad\qquad = \frac{\$3,400}{\$19,000} = 17.9\%$$

3. Long-term solvency analysis

a. Debt to equity ratio

$$\frac{\$2,500 \;+\; \$1,500 \;+\; \$10,000}{\$1,000 \;+\; \$9,000 \;+\; \$6,000} \qquad\qquad \frac{\$3,000 \;+\; \$4,000 \;+\; \$30,000}{\$3,000 \;+\; \$9,000 \;+\; \$7,000}$$

$$= \frac{\$14,000}{\$16,000} = .9 \text{ times} \qquad\qquad = \frac{\$37,000}{\$19,000} = 1.9 \text{ times}$$

b. Interest coverage ratio

$$\frac{\$3,600 \;+\; \$1,400}{\$1,400} \qquad\qquad \frac{\$6,800 \;+\; \$3,200}{\$3,200}$$

$$= \frac{\$5,000}{\$1,400} = 3.6 \text{ times} \qquad\qquad = \frac{\$10,000}{\$3,200} = 3.1 \text{ times}$$

4. Cash flow adequacy analysis

a. Cash flow yield

$$\frac{\$2,200}{\$1,800} = 1.2 \text{ times} \qquad\qquad \frac{\$3,000}{\$3,400} = .9 \text{ times}$$

b. Cash flows to sales

$$\frac{\$2,200}{\$53,000} = 4.2\% \qquad\qquad \frac{\$3,000}{\$86,000} = 3.5\%$$

c. Cash flows to assets

$$\frac{\$2,200}{\$30,000} = 7.3\% \qquad\qquad \frac{\$3,000}{\$56,000} = 5.4\%$$

d. Free cash flow

$$\$2,200 - \$500 - \$2,100 \qquad\qquad \$3,000 - \$600 - \$1,800$$

$$= (400) \qquad\qquad = \$600$$

5. Market strength analysis

a. Price/earnings ratio

$$\frac{\$30}{\$1.80} = 16.7 \text{ times} \qquad\qquad \frac{\$20}{\$1.13} = 17.7 \text{ times}$$

b. Dividends yield

$$\frac{\$500,000/1,000,000}{\$30} = 1.7\% \qquad\qquad \frac{\$600,000/3,000,000}{\$20} = 1.0\%$$

6. **Comparative analysis**

Ratio Name	Quik Burger	Big Steak	Company with More Favorable Ratio*
1. Liquidity analysis			
a. Current ratio	1.5 times	2.3 times	Big Steak
b. Quick ratio	1.0 times	1.6 times	Big Steak
c. Receivable turnover	26.5 times	13.2 times	Quik Burger
d. Average days' sales uncollected	13.8 days	27.7 days	Quik Burger
e. Inventory turnover	18.5 times	12.2 times	Quik Burger
f. Average days' inventory on hand	19.7 days	29.9 days	Quik Burger
2. Profitability analysis			
a. Profit margin	3.4%	4.0%	Big Steak
b. Asset turnover	1.8 times	1.5 times	Quik Burger
c. Return on assets	6.0%	6.1%	Neutral
d. Return on equity	11.3%	17.9%	Big Steak
3. Long-term solvency analysis			
a. Debt to equity ratio	.9 times	1.9 times	Quik Burger
b. Interest coverage ratio	3.6 times	3.1 times	Quik Burger
4. Cash flow adequacy analysis			
a. Cash flow yield	1.2 times	.9 times	Quik Burger
b. Cash flows to sales	4.2%	3.5%	Quik Burger
c. Cash flows to assets	7.3%	5.4%	Quik Burger
d. Free cash flow	($400)	$600	Big Steak
5. Market strength analysis			
a. Price/earnings ratio	16.7 times	17.7 times	Big Steak
b. Dividends yield	1.7%	1.0%	Quik Burger

*This analysis indicates the company with the apparently more favorable ratio. Class discussion may focus on conditions under which different conclusions may be drawn.

7. **Usefulness of prior years' information**
Prior years' information would be helpful in two ways. First, turnover, return, and cash flows to assets ratios could be based on average amounts. Second, a trend analysis could be performed for each company.

Chapter Assignments

BUILDING YOUR KNOWLEDGE FOUNDATION

Questions

1. What are the differences and similarities in the objectives of investors and creditors in using financial statement analysis?
2. What role does risk play in making loans and investments?
3. What standards of comparison are commonly used to evaluate financial statements, and what are their relative merits?
4. Why would a financial analyst compare the ratios of Steelco, a steel company, with the ratios of other companies in the steel industry? What factors might invalidate such a comparison?

5. Where may an investor look for information about a publicly held company in which he or she is thinking of investing?

6. Why would an investor want to see both horizontal and trend analyses of a company's financial statements?

7. What does the following sentence mean: "Based on 1980 equaling 100, net income increased from 240 in 1996 to 260 in 1997"?

8. What is the difference between horizontal and vertical analysis?

9. What is the purpose of ratio analysis?

10. Under what circumstances would a current ratio of 3:1 be good? Under what circumstances would it be bad?

11. In a period of high interest rates, why are receivable turnover and inventory turnover especially important?

12. The following statements were made on page 35 of the November 6, 1978, issue of *Fortune* magazine: "Supermarket executives are beginning to look back with some nostalgia on the days when the standard profit margin was 1 percent of sales. Last year the industry overall margin came to a thin 0.72 percent." How could a supermarket earn a satisfactory return on assets with such a small profit margin?

13. Company A and Company B both have net incomes of $1,000,000. Is it possible to say that these companies are equally successful? Why or why not?

14. Circo Company has a return on assets of 12 percent and a debt to equity ratio of .5. Would you expect return on equity to be more or less than 12 percent?

15. What amount is common to all cash flow adequacy ratios? To what other groups of ratios are the cash flow adequacy ratios most closely related?

16. The market price of Company J's stock is the same as that of Company Q's. How might you determine whether investors are equally confident about the future of these companies?

Short Exercises

SE 1.

LO 1 *Objectives and Standards*
LO 2 *of Financial Statement*
         Analysis

Indicate whether each of the following items is (a) an objective or (b) a standard of comparison of financial statement analysis.

1. Industry norms
2. Assessment of the company's past performance
3. The company's past performance
4. Assessment of future potential and related risk
5. Rule-of-thumb measures

SE 2.

LO 3 *Sources of Information*

For each piece of information listed below, indicate whether the *best* source would be (a) reports published by the company, (b) SEC reports, (c) business periodicals, or (d) credit and investment advisory services.

1. Current market value of a company's stock
2. Management's analysis of the past year's operations
3. Objective assessment of a company's financial performance
4. Most complete body of financial disclosures
5. Current events affecting the company

SE 3.

LO 4 *Trend Analysis*

Using 2000 as the base year, prepare a trend analysis for the following data, and tell whether the results suggest a favorable or unfavorable trend. (Round your answers to one decimal place.)

	20x2	20x1	20x0
Net sales	$158,000	$136,000	$112,000
Accounts receivable (net)	43,000	32,000	21,000

LO 4   *Horizontal Analysis*

SE 4. Compute the amount and percentage changes for the income statements that appear below, and comment on the changes from 20x0 to 20x1. (Round the percentage changes to one decimal place.)

SiteWorks, Inc.
Comparative Income Statements
For the Years Ended December 31, 20x1 and 20x0

	20x1	20x0
Net Sales	$180,000	$145,000
Cost of Goods Sold	112,000	88,000
Gross Margin	$ 68,000	$ 57,000
Operating Expenses	40,000	30,000
Operating Income	$ 28,000	$ 27,000
Interest Expense	7,000	5,000
Income Before Income Taxes	$ 21,000	$ 22,000
Income Taxes	7,000	8,000
Net Income	$ 14,000	$ 14,000
Earnings per Share	$ 1.40	$ 1.40

LO 4   *Vertical Analysis*

SE 5. Express the comparative balance sheets that follow as common-size statements, and comment on the changes from 20x0 to 20x1. (Round computations to one decimal place.)

SiteWorks, Inc.
Comparative Balance Sheets
December 31, 20x1 and 20x0

	20x1	20x0
Assets		
Current Assets	$ 24,000	$ 20,000
Property, Plant, and Equipment (net)	130,000	100,000
Total Assets	$154,000	$120,000
Liabilities and Stockholders' Equity		
Current Liabilities	$ 18,000	$ 22,000
Long-Term Liabilities	90,000	60,000
Stockholders' Equity	46,000	38,000
Total Liabilities and Stockholders' Equity	$154,000	$120,000

LO 5   *Liquidity Analysis*

SE 6. Using the information for SiteWorks, Inc., in **SE 4** and **SE 5,** compute the current ratio, quick ratio, receivable turnover, average days' sales uncollected, inventory turnover, and average days' inventory on hand for 20x0 and 20x1. Inventories were $4,000 in 19x9 $5,000 in 20x0, and $7,000 in 20x1. Accounts Receivable were $6,000 in 19x9, $8,000 in

20x0, and $10,000 in 20x1. There were no marketable securities or prepaid assets. Comment on the results. (Round computations to one decimal place.)

SE 7.
LO 5 *Profitability Analysis*

Using the information for SiteWorks, Inc., in **SE 4** and **SE 5,** compute the profit margin, asset turnover, return on assets, and return on equity for 20x0 and 20x1. In 19x9, total assets were $100,000 and total stockholders' equity was $30,000. Comment on the results. (Round computations to one decimal place.)

SE 8.
LO 5 *Long-Term Solvency Analysis*

Using the information for SiteWorks, Inc., in **SE 4** and **SE 5,** compute the debt to equity and interest coverage ratios for 20x0 and 20x1. Comment on the results. (Round computations to one decimal place.)

SE 9.
LO 5 *Cash Flow Adequacy Analysis*

Using the information for SiteWorks, Inc., in **SE 4, SE 5,** and **SE 7,** compute the cash flow yield, cash flows to sales, cash flows to assets, and free cash flow for 20x0 and 20x1. Net cash flows from operating activities were $21,000 in 20x0 and $16,000 in 20x1. Net capital expenditures were $30,000 in 20x0 and $40,000 in 20x1. Cash dividends were $6,000 in both years. Comment on the results. (Round computations to one decimal place.)

SE 10.
LO 5 *Market Strength Analysis*

Using the information for SiteWorks, Inc., in **SE 4, SE 5,** and **SE 9,** compute the price/earnings and dividends yield ratios for 20x0 and 20x1. The company had 10,000 shares of common stock outstanding in both years. The price of SiteWorks' common stock was $30 in 20x0 and $20 in 20x1. Comment on the results. (Round computations to one decimal place.)

Exercises

E 1.
LO 1 *Objectives, Standards,*
LO 2 *and Sources of*
LO 3 *Information for Financial Statement Analysis*

Identify each of the following as (a) an objective of financial statement analysis, (b) a standard for financial statement analysis, or (c) a source of information for financial statement analysis:

1. Average ratios of other companies in the same industry
2. Assessment of the future potential of an investment
3. Interim financial statements
4. Past ratios of the company
5. SEC Form 10-K
6. Assessment of risk
7. A company's annual report

E 2.
LO 4 *Horizontal Analysis*

Compute the amount and percentage changes for the following balance sheets, and comment on the changes from 20x1 to 20x2. (Round the percentage changes to one decimal place.)

Lindquist Company
Comparative Balance Sheets
December 31, 20x2 and 20x1

	20x2	20x1
Assets		
Current Assets	$ 37,200	$ 25,600
Property, Plant, and Equipment (net)	218,928	194,400
Total Assets	$256,128	$220,000
Liabilities and Stockholders' Equity		
Current Liabilities	$ 22,400	$ 6,400
Long-Term Liabilities	70,000	80,000
Stockholders' Equity	163,728	133,600
Total Liabilities and Stockholders' Equity	$256,128	$220,000

LO 4 *Trend Analysis*

E 3. Using 20x1 as the base year, prepare a trend analysis of the following data, and tell whether the situation shown by the trends is favorable or unfavorable. (Round your answers to one decimal place.)

	20x5	20x4	20x3	20x2	20x1
Net sales	$25,520	$23,980	$24,200	$22,880	$22,000
Cost of goods sold	17,220	15,400	15,540	14,700	14,000
General and administrative expenses	5,280	5,184	5,088	4,896	4,800
Operating income	3,020	3,396	3,572	3,284	3,200

LO 4 *Vertical Analysis*

E 4. Express the comparative income statements that follow as common-size statements, and comment on the changes from 20x1 to 20x2. (Round computations to one decimal place.)

Lindquist Company
Comparative Income Statements
For the Years Ended December 31, 20x2 and 20x1

	20x2	20x1
Net Sales	$424,000	$368,000
Cost of Goods Sold	254,400	239,200
Gross Margin	$169,600	$128,800
Selling Expenses	$106,000	$ 73,600
General Expenses	50,880	36,800
Total Operating Expenses	$156,880	$110,400
Net Operating Income	$ 12,720	$ 18,400

LO 5 *Liquidity Analysis*

E 5. Partial comparative balance sheet and income statement information for Lum Company follows.

	20x2	20x1
Cash	$ 6,800	$ 5,200
Marketable Securities	3,600	8,600
Accounts Receivable (net)	22,400	17,800
Inventory	27,200	24,800
Total Current Assets	$ 60,000	$ 56,400
Current Liabilities	$ 20,000	$ 14,100
Net Sales	$161,280	$110,360
Cost of Goods Sold	$108,800	101,680
Gross Margin	$ 52,480	$ 8,680

The year-end balances for Accounts Receivable and Inventory were $16,200 and $25,600, respectively, in 20x0. Compute the current ratio, quick ratio, receivable turnover, average days' sales uncollected, inventory turnover, and average days' inventory on hand for each year. (Round computations to one decimal place.) Comment on the change in the company's liquidity position from 20x1 to 20x2.

E 6.

LO 5 *Turnover Analysis*

Alberto's Men's Shop has been in business for four years. Because the company has recently had a cash flow problem, management wonders whether there is a problem with receivables or inventories. Here are selected figures from the company's financial statements (in thousands):

	20x4	20x3	20x2	20x1
Net sales	$288	$224	$192	$160
Cost of goods sold	180	144	120	96
Accounts receivable (net)	48	40	32	24
Merchandise inventory	56	44	32	20

Compute receivable turnover and inventory turnover for each of the four years, and comment on the results relative to the cash flow problem that Alberto's Men's Shop has been experiencing. Round computations to one decimal place.

E 7.

LO 5 *Profitability Analysis*

At year end, Canzoneri Company had total assets of $640,000 in 20x0, $680,000 in 20x1, and $760,000 in 20x2. Its debt to equity ratio was .67 in all three years. In 20x1, the company had net income of $77,112 on revenues of $1,224,000. In 20x2, the company had net income of $98,952 on revenues of $1,596,000. Compute the profit margin, asset turnover, return on assets, and return on equity for 20x1 and 20x2. Comment on the apparent cause of the increase or decrease in profitability. (Round the percentages and other ratios to one decimal place.)

E 8.

LO 5 *Long-Term Solvency and Market Strength Ratios*

An investor is considering investing in the long-term bonds and common stock of Companies X and Y. Both companies operate in the same industry. In addition, both companies pay a dividend per share of $4, and a yield of 10 percent on their long-term bonds. Other data for the two companies follow:

	Company X	Company Y
Total assets	$2,400,000	$1,080,000
Total liabilities	1,080,000	594,000
Income before income taxes	288,000	129,600
Interest expense	97,200	53,460
Earnings per share	3.20	5.00
Market price of common stock	40	47.50

Compute the debt to equity, interest coverage, price/earnings (P/E), and dividends yield ratios, and comment on the results. (Round computations to one decimal place.)

E 9.

LO 5 *Cash Flow Adequacy Analysis*

Using the data below, taken from the financial statements of Liarano, Inc., compute the cash flow yield, cash flows to sales, cash flows to assets, and free cash flow. (Round computations to one decimal place.)

Net sales	$6,400,000
Net income	704,000
Net cash flows from operating activities	912,000
Total assets, beginning of year	5,780,000
Total assets, end of year	6,240,000
Cash dividends	240,000
Net capital expenditures	596,000

E 10.

LO 5 *Preparation of Statements from Ratios and Incomplete Data*

On the next page are the income statement and balance sheet of Pandit Corporation, with most of the amounts missing. Pandit's only interest expense is on long-term debt. Its debt to equity ratio is .5, its current ratio 3:1, its quick ratio 2:1, the receivable turnover 4.5, and its inventory turnover 4.0. The return on assets is 10 percent. All ratios are based on the current year's information. Complete the financial statements using the information presented. Show supporting computations.

Pandit Corporation
Income Statement
For the Year Ended December 31, 20x1
(in thousands of dollars)

Net Sales		$18,000
Cost of Goods Sold		(a)
Gross Margin		$ (b)
Operating Expenses		
Selling Expenses	$ (c)	
Administrative Expenses	234	
Total Operating Expenses		(d)
Income from Operations		(e)
Interest Expense		162
Income Before Income Taxes		(f)
Income Taxes		620
Net Income		$ (g)

Pandit Corporation
Balance Sheet
December 31, 20x1
(in thousands of dollars)

Assets

Cash	$ (h)	
Accounts Receivable (net)	(i)	
Inventories	(j)	
Total Current Assets		$ (k)
Property, Plant, and Equipment (net)		5,400
Total Assets		$ (l)

Liabilities and Stockholders' Equity

Current Liabilities	$ (m)	
Bonds Payable, 9% interest	(n)	
Total Liabilities		$ (o)
Common Stock, $20 par value	$3,000	
Paid-in Capital in Excess of Par Value, Common	2,600	
Retained Earnings	4,000	
Total Stockholders' Equity		9,600
Total Liabilities and Stockholders' Equity		$ (p)

Problems

P 1.
LO 4 *Horizontal and Vertical Analysis*

The condensed comparative income statements and balance sheets of Mariano Corporation follow. All figures are given in thousands of dollars.

Mariano Corporation
Comparative Income Statements
For the Years Ended December 31, 20x2 and 20x1

	20x2	20x1
Net Sales	$3,276,800	$3,146,400
Cost of Goods Sold	2,088,800	2,008,400
Gross Margin	$1,188,000	$1,138,000
Operating Expenses		
Selling Expenses	$ 476,800	$ 518,000
Administrative Expenses	447,200	423,200
Total Operating Expenses	$ 924,000	$ 941,200
Income from Operations	$ 264,000	$ 196,800
Interest Expense	65,600	39,200
Income Before Income Taxes	$ 198,400	$ 157,600
Income Taxes	62,400	56,800
Net Income	$ 136,000	$ 100,800
Earnings per Share	$ 3.40	$ 2.52

Mariano Corporation
Comparative Balance Sheets
December 31, 20x2 and 20x1

	20x2	20x1
Assets		
Cash	$ 81,200	$ 40,800
Accounts Receivable (net)	235,600	229,200
Inventory	574,800	594,800
Property, Plant, and Equipment (net)	750,000	720,000
Total Assets	$1,641,600	$1,584,800
Liabilities and Stockholders' Equity		
Accounts Payable	$ 267,600	$ 477,200
Notes Payable (short-term)	200,000	400,000
Bonds Payable	400,000	—
Common Stock, $10 par value	400,000	400,000
Retained Earnings	374,000	307,600
Total Liabilities and Stockholders' Equity	$1,641,600	$1,584,800

Perform the following analyses. Round all ratios and percentages to one decimal place.

1. Prepare schedules showing the amount and percentage changes from 20x1 to 20x2 for Mariano's comparative income statements and balance sheets.
2. Prepare common-size income statements and balance sheets for 20x1 and 20x2.
3. Comment on the results in **1** and **2** by identifying favorable and unfavorable changes in the components and composition of the statements.

P 2.

LO 5 *Analyzing the Effects of Transactions on Ratios*

Rader Corporation engaged in the transactions listed in the first column of the following table. Opposite each transaction is a ratio and space to indicate the effect of each transaction on the ratio.

		Effect		
Transaction	Ratio	Increase	Decrease	None
a. Sold merchandise on account.	Current ratio			
b. Sold merchandise on account.	Inventory turnover			
c. Collected on accounts receivable.	Quick ratio			
d. Wrote off an uncollectible account.	Receivable turnover			
e. Paid on accounts payable.	Current ratio			
f. Declared cash dividend.	Return on equity			
g. Incurred advertising expense.	Profit margin			
h. Issued stock dividend.	Debt to equity ratio			
i. Issued bond payable.	Asset turnover			
j. Accrued interest expense.	Current ratio			
k. Paid previously declared cash dividend.	Dividends yield			
l. Purchased treasury stock.	Return on assets			
m. Recorded depreciation expense.	Cash flow yield			

Place an *X* in the appropriate column to show whether the transaction increased, decreased, or had no effect on the indicated ratio.

P 3.

LO 5 *Ratio Analysis*

Additional data for Mariano Corporation in 20x2 and 20x1 follow. This information should be used in conjunction with the data in **P 1.**

	20x2	**20x1**
Net cash flows from operating activities	($196,000,000)	$144,000,000
Net capital expenditures	$ 40,000,000	$ 65,000,000
Dividends paid	$ 44,000,000	$ 34,400,000
Number of common shares	40,000,000	40,000,000
Market price per share	$18	$30

Selected balances at the end of 20x0 were Accounts Receivable (net), $206,800; Inventory, $547,200; Total Assets, $1,465,600; and Stockholders' Equity, $641,200. All of Mariano's notes payable were current liabilities; all of the bonds payable were long-term liabilities.

Perform the following analyses. Round all answers to one decimal place, and consider changes of .1 or less to be neutral. After making the calculations, indicate whether each ratio improved or deteriorated from 20x1 to 20x2 by writing *F* for favorable or *U* for unfavorable.

1. Prepare a liquidity analysis by calculating for each year the (a) current ratio, (b) quick ratio, (c) receivable turnover, (d) average days' sales uncollected, (e) inventory turnover, and (f) average days' inventory on hand.
2. Prepare a profitability analysis by calculating for each year the (a) profit margin, (b) asset turnover, (c) return on assets, and (d) return on equity.
3. Prepare a long-term solvency analysis by calculating for each year the (a) debt to equity ratio and (b) interest coverage ratio.
4. Prepare a cash flow adequacy analysis by calculating for each year the (a) cash flow yield, (b) cash flows to sales, (c) cash flows to assets, and (d) free cash flows.
5. Prepare a market strength analysis by calculating for each year the (a) price/earnings ratio, and (b) dividends yield.

P 4.

LO 5 *Comprehensive Ratio Analysis of Two Companies*

Willis Rowe is considering an investment in the common stock of a chain of retail department stores. He has narrowed his choice to two retail companies, Allison Corporation and Marker Corporation, whose income statements and balance sheets are shown below and on the next page. During the year, Allison Corporation paid a total of $50,000 in dividends. The market price per share of its stock is currently $30. In comparison, Marker Corporation paid a total of $114,000 in dividends, and the current market price of its stock is $38 per share. Allison Corporation had net cash flows from operations of $271,500 and net capital expenditures of $625,000. Marker Corporation had net cash flows from operations of $492,500 and net capital expenditures of $1,050,000. Information for prior years is not readily available. Assume that all notes payable are current liabilities and all bonds payable are long-term liabilities.

	Allison Corporation	Marker Corporation
Assets		
Cash	$ 80,000	$ 192,400
Marketable Securities	203,400	84,600
Accounts Receivable (net)	552,800	985,400
Inventories	629,800	1,253,400
Prepaid Expenses	54,400	114,000
Property, Plant, and Equipment (net)	2,913,600	6,552,000
Intangibles and Other Assets	553,200	144,800
Total Assets	$4,987,200	$9,326,600
Liabilities and Stockholders' Equity		
Accounts Payable	$ 344,000	$ 572,600
Notes Payable	150,000	400,000
Income Taxes Payable	50,200	73,400
Bonds Payable	2,000,000	2,000,000
Common Stock, $10 par value	1,000,000	600,000
Paid-in Capital in Excess of Par Value, Common	609,800	3,568,600
Retained Earnings	833,200	2,112,000
Total Liabilities and Stockholders' Equity	$4,987,200	$9,326,600

	Allison Corporation	Marker Corporation
Net Sales	$12,560,000	$25,210,000
Costs and Expenses		
Cost of Goods Sold	$ 6,142,000	$14,834,000
Selling Expenses	4,822,600	7,108,200
Administrative Expenses	986,000	2,434,000
Total Costs and Expenses	$11,950,600	$24,376,200
Income from Operations	$ 609,400	$ 833,800
Interest Expense	194,000	228,000
Income Before Income Taxes	$ 415,400	$ 605,800
Income Taxes	200,000	300,000
Net Income	$ 215,400	$ 305,800
Earnings per Share	$ 2.15	$ 5.10

REQUIRED

Conduct a comprehensive ratio analysis for each company, using the available information. Compare the results. Round percentages and ratios to one decimal place, and consider changes of .1 or less to be indeterminate. This analysis should be done in the following steps:

1. Prepare an analysis of liquidity by calculating for each company the (a) current ratio, (b) quick ratio, (c) receivable turnover, (d) average days' sales uncollected, (e) inventory turnover, and (f) average days' inventory on hand.
2. Prepare an analysis of profitability by calculating for each company the (a) profit margin, (b) asset turnover, (c) return on assets, and (d) return on equity.
3. Prepare an analysis of long-term solvency by calculating for each company the (a) debt to equity ratio and (b) interest coverage ratio.
4. Prepare an analysis of cash flow adequacy by calculating for each company the (a) cash flow yield, (b) cash flows to sales, (c) cash flows to assets, and (d) free cash flow.
5. Prepare an analysis of market strength by calculating for each company the (a) price/earnings ratio and (b) dividends yield.
6. Compare the two companies by inserting the ratio calculations from **1** through **5** in a table with the following column headings: Ratio Name, Allison Corporation, Marker Corporation, and Company with More Favorable Ratio. Indicate in the right-hand column which company had the more favorable ratio in each case.
7. How could the analysis be improved if information from prior years were available?

Alternate Problems

P 5.

LO 5 *Analyzing the Effects of Transactions on Ratios*

Estevez Corporation engaged in the transactions listed in the first column of the table on the next page. Opposite each transaction is a ratio and space to mark the effect of each transaction on the ratio.

		Effect		
Transaction	**Ratio**	**Increase**	**Decrease**	**None**
a. Issued common stock for cash.	Asset turnover			
b. Declared cash dividend.	Current ratio			
c. Sold treasury stock.	Return on equity			
d. Borrowed cash by issuing note payable.	Debt to equity ratio			
e. Paid salaries expense.	Inventory turnover			
f. Purchased merchandise for cash.	Current ratio			
g. Sold equipment for cash.	Receivable turnover			
h. Sold merchandise on account.	Quick ratio			
i. Paid current portion of long-term debt.	Return on assets			
j. Gave sales discount.	Profit margin			
k. Purchased marketable securities for cash.	Quick ratio			
l. Declared 5% stock dividend.	Current ratio			
m. Purchased a building.	Free cash flow			

REQUIRED   Place an *X* in the appropriate column to show whether the transaction increased, decreased, or had no effect on the indicated ratio.

LO 5   *Ratio Analysis*

P 6.   The condensed comparative income statements and balance sheets of Schumacker Corporation appear below and on the next page. All figures are given in thousands of dollars, except earnings per share.

Schumacker Corporation
Comparative Income Statements
For the Years Ended December 31, 20x6 and 20x5

	20x6	20x5
Net Sales	$1,638,400	$1,573,200
Costs and Expenses		
Cost of Goods Sold	$1,044,400	$1,004,200
Selling Expenses	238,400	259,000
Administrative Expenses	223,600	211,600
Total Costs and Expenses	$1,506,400	$1,474,800
Income from Operations	$ 132,000	$ 98,400
Interest Expense	32,800	19,600
Income Before Income Taxes	$ 99,200	$ 78,800
Income Taxes	31,200	28,400
Net Income	$ 68,000	$ 50,400
Earnings per Share	$ 1.70	$ 1.26

Schumacker Corporation
Comparative Balance Sheets
December 31, 20x6 and 20x5

	20x6	20x5
Assets		
Cash	$ 40,600	$ 20,400
Accounts Receivable (net)	117,800	114,600
Inventory	287,400	297,400
Property, Plant, and Equipment (net)	375,000	360,000
Total Assets	$820,800	$792,400
Liabilities and Stockholders' Equity		
Accounts Payable	$133,800	$238,600
Notes Payable	100,000	200,000
Bonds Payable	200,000	—
Common Stock, $5 par value	200,000	200,000
Retained Earnings	187,000	153,800
Total Liabilities and Stockholders' Equity	$820,800	$792,400

Additional data for Schumacker Corporation in 20x6 and 20x5 follow.

	20x6	20x5
Net cash flows from operating activities	$106,500,000	$86,250,000
Net capital expenditures	$22,500,000	$16,000,000
Dividends paid	$22,000,000	$17,200,000
Number of common shares	40,000,000	40,000,000
Market price per share	$9	$15

Selected balances (in thousands) at the end of 20x4 were Accounts Receivable (net), $103,400; Inventory, $273,600; Total Assets, $732,800; and Stockholders' Equity, $320,600. All of Schumacker's notes payable were current liabilities; all of the bonds payable were long-term liabilities.

REQUIRED

Perform the following analyses. Round percentages and ratios to one decimal place, and consider changes of .1 or less to be neutral. After making the calculations, indicate whether each ratio had a favorable (F) or unfavorable (U) change from 20x5 to 20x6.

1. Conduct a liquidity analysis by calculating for each year the (a) current ratio, (b) quick ratio, (c) receivable turnover, (d) average days' sales uncollected, (e) inventory turnover, and (f) average days' inventory on hand.
2. Conduct a profitability analysis by calculating for each year the (a) profit margin, (b) asset turnover, (c) return on assets, and (d) return on equity.
3. Conduct a long-term solvency analysis by calculating for each year the (a) debt to equity ratio and (b) interest coverage ratio.
4. Conduct a cash flow adequacy analysis by calculating for each year the (a) cash flow yield, (b) cash flows to sales, (c) cash flows to assets, and (d) free cash flow.
5. Conduct a market strength analysis by calculating for each year the (a) price/earnings ratio and (b) dividends yield.

LO 5 *Comprehensive Ratio Analysis of Two Companies*

P 7. José Trevás has decided to invest some of his savings in common stock. He feels that the chemical industry has good growth prospects and has narrowed his choice to two companies in that industry. As a final step in making the choice, he has decided to perform a comprehensive ratio analysis of the two companies, Emax and Savlow. Income statement and balance sheet data for the two companies appear below.

	Emax	Savlow
Net Sales	$9,486,200	$27,287,300
Costs and Expenses		
Cost of Goods Sold	$5,812,200	$18,372,400
Selling Expenses	1,194,000	1,955,700
Administrative Expenses	1,217,400	4,126,000
Total Costs and Expenses	$8,223,600	$24,454,100
Income from Operations	$1,262,600	$ 2,833,200
Interest Expense	270,000	1,360,000
Income Before Income Taxes	$ 992,600	$ 1,473,200
Income Taxes	450,000	600,000
Net Income	$ 542,600	$ 873,200
Earnings per Share	$ 1.55	$ .87

	Emax	Savlow
Assets		
Cash	$ 126,100	$ 514,300
Marketable Securities (at cost)	117,500	1,200,000
Accounts Receivable (net)	456,700	2,600,000
Inventories	1,880,000	4,956,000
Prepaid Expenses	72,600	156,600
Property, Plant, and Equipment (net)	5,342,200	19,356,000
Intangibles and Other Assets	217,000	580,000
Total Assets	$8,212,100	$29,362,900
Liabilities and Stockholders' Equity		
Accounts Payable	$ 517,400	$ 2,342,000
Notes Payable	1,000,000	2,000,000
Income Taxes Payable	85,200	117,900
Bonds Payable	2,000,000	15,000,000
Common Stock, $1 par value	350,000	1,000,000
Paid-in Capital in Excess of Par Value, Common	1,747,300	5,433,300
Retained Earnings	2,512,200	3,469,700
Total Liabilities and Stockholders' Equity	$8,212,100	$29,362,900

During the year, Emax paid a total of $140,000 in dividends, and its current market price per share is $20. Savlow paid a total of $600,000 in dividends during the year, and its current market price per share is $9. Emax had net cash flows from operations of $771,500 and net capital expenditures of $450,000. Savlow had net cash flows from operations of $843,000 and net capital expenditures of $1,550,000. Information pertaining to prior years is not readily available. Assume that all notes payable are current liabilities and that all bonds payable are long-term liabilities.

REQUIRED

Conduct a comprehensive ratio analysis of Emax and of Savlow, using the current end-of-year data. Compare the results. Round all ratios and percentages to one decimal place. This analysis should be done in the following steps:

1. Prepare an analysis of liquidity by calculating for each company the (a) current ratio, (b) quick ratio, (c) receivable turnover, (d) average days' sales uncollected, (e) inventory turnover, and (f) average days' inventory on hand.
2. Prepare an analysis of profitability by calculating for each company the (a) profit margin, (b) asset turnover, (c) return on assets, and (d) return on equity.
3. Prepare an analysis of long-term solvency by calculating for each company the (a) debt to equity ratio and (b) interest coverage ratio.
4. Prepare an analysis of cash flow adequacy by calculating for each company the (a) cash flow yield, (b) cash flows to sales, (c) cash flows to assets, and (d) free cash flow.
5. Prepare an analysis of market strength by calculating for each company the (a) price/earnings ratio and (b) dividends yield.
6. Compare the two companies by inserting the ratio calculations from **1** through **5** in a table with the following column headings: Ratio Name, Emax, Savlow, and Company with More Favorable Ratio. Indicate in the right-hand column of the table which company had the more favorable ratio in each case.
7. How could the analysis be improved if information from prior years were available?

EXPANDING YOUR CRITICAL THINKING, COMMUNICATION, AND INTERPERSONAL SKILLS

Skills Development

CONCEPTUAL ANALYSIS

SD 1.

LO 2 *Standards for Financial*
LO 5 *Analysis*

Helene Curtis, a well-known, publicly owned corporation, became a take-over candidate and sold out in the 1990s after years of poor profit performance. "By almost any standard, Chicago-based Helene Curtis rates as one of America's worst-managed personal care companies. In recent years its return on equity has hovered between 10% and 13%, well below the industry average of 18% to 19%. Net profit margins of 2% to 3% are half that of competitors. . . . As a result, while leading names like Revlon and Avon are trading at three and four times book value, Curtis trades at less than two-thirds book value."[8] Considering that many companies in other industries are happy with a return on equity of 10 percent to 13 percent, why is this analysis so critical of Curtis's performance? Assuming that Curtis could double its profit margin, what other information would be

| Communication | Critical Thinking | Group Activity | Memo | Ethics | International | Spreadsheet | General Ledger | CD-ROM | Internet |

necessary to project the resulting return on stockholders' investment? Why are Revlon's and Avon's stocks trading for more than Curtis's? Be prepared to discuss your answers to these questions in class.

SD 2.
LO 3   *Use of Investors Service*

Refer to Exhibits 1 and 2, which contain the segment information for **PepsiCo, Inc.,** and its listing in Moody's *Handbook of Dividend Achievers.* Assume that an investor has asked you to assess PepsiCo's recent history and prospects. Write a memorandum to the investor that addresses the following points:

1. PepsiCo's business segments and their relative importance. (In what three business segments does PepsiCo, Inc., operate, and what is the relative size of each in terms of their sales and operating income? Which business segment appears to be the most profitable?)
2. PepsiCo's earnings history. (What generally has been the relationship between PepsiCo's return on assets and its return on equity over the years 1990 to 1996? What does this tell you about the way the company is financed? What figures back up your conclusion?)
3. The trend of PepsiCo's stock price and price/earnings ratio for the seven years shown.
4. PepsiCo's prospects, including developments that are likely to affect the future of the company.

ETHICAL DILEMMA

SD 3.
LO 3   *Management of Earnings*

In 1993, *The Wall Street Journal* reported that **H. J. Heinz Co.,** the famous maker of catsup and many other food products, earned a quarterly income of $.75 per share, which included a gain on sale of assets of $.24 per share. Income from continuing operations was only $.51 per share, or 16 percent below the previous year's figure. The paper was critical of Heinz's use of a one-time gain to increase earnings: "In recent years, H. J. Heinz Co. has been spicing up its earnings with special items. The latest quarter is no exception." An analyst was quoted as saying that Heinz had not admitted the slump in its business but had "started including nonrecurring items in the results they were showing. That created an artificially high base of earnings that they can no longer match."[9] Do you think it is unethical for a company's management to increase earnings periodically through the use of one-time transactions, such as sales of assets, on which it has a profit? What potential long-term negative effects might this practice have for Heinz?

RESEARCH ACTIVITY

SD 4.
LO 3   *Use of Investors Services*

Find *Moody's Investors Service* or *Standard & Poor's Industry Guide* using one or more of the following sources: your library, the Fingraph® Financial Analyst™ CD-ROM that accompanies this text, or the Needles Accounting Resource Center Web site at http://www.hmco.com/college/needles/home.html. Locate the reports on three corporations. You may choose the corporations at random or choose them from the same industry, if directed to do so by your instructor. (If you did a related exercise in a previous chapter, use the same three companies.) Write a summary of what you learned about each company's financial performance and its prospects for the future, and be prepared to discuss your findings in class.

DECISION-MAKING PRACTICE

SD 5.
LO 4   *Effect of One-Time Item*
LO 5   *on Loan Decision*

Apple a Day, Inc., and **Unforgettable Edibles, Inc.,** both operate food catering businesses in the metropolitan area. Their customers include *Fortune* 500 companies, regional firms, and individuals. The two firms reported similar profit margins for the current year, and both determine bonuses for managers based on reaching a target profit margin and return on equity. Each firm has submitted a loan request to you as a loan officer for City National Bank.

	Apple a Day	Unforgettable Edibles
Net Sales	$625,348	$717,900
Cost of Goods Sold	225,125	287,080
Gross Margin	$400,223	$430,820
Operating Expenses	281,300	371,565
Operating Income	$118,923	$ 59,255
Gain on Sale of Real Estate		81,923
Interest Expense	(9,333)	(15,338)
Income Before Income Taxes	$109,590	$125,840
Income Taxes	25,990	29,525
Net Income	$ 83,600	$ 96,315
Average Stockholders' Equity	$312,700	$390,560

REQUIRED

1. Perform a vertical analysis and prepare a common-size income statement for each firm. Compute profit margin and return on equity.
2. Discuss these results, the bonus plan for management, and loan considerations. Make a recommendation as to which company is a better risk for receiving the loan.

Financial Reporting and Analysis

INTERPRETING FINANCIAL REPORTS

FRA 1.

LO 4 *Trend Analysis*

H. J. Heinz Company is a global company engaged in several lines of business, including food service, infant foods, condiments, pet foods, tuna, and weight control food products. Below is a five-year summary of operations and other related data for Heinz.

Five-Year Summary of Operations and Other Related Data
H.J. Heinz Company and Subsidiaries

	1996	1995	1994	1993	1992
	(Dollars in thousands, except per share data)				
Summary of Operations					
Sales	$9,112,265	$8,086,794	$7,046,738	$7,103,374	$6,581,867
Cost of products sold	5,775,357	5,119,597	4,381,745	4,530,563	4,102,816
Interest expense	277,411	210,585	149,243	146,491	134,948
Provision for income taxes	364,342	346,982	319,442	185,838	346,050
Income before cumulative effect of accounting change	659,319	591,025	602,944	529,943	638,295
Cumulative effect of FAS No. 106 adoption	—	—	—	(133,630)	—
Net income	659,319	591,025	602,944	396,313	638,295
Other Related Data					
Dividends paid:					
Common	381,871	345,358	325,887	297,009	270,512
Preferred	56	64	71	78	86
Total assets	8,623,691	8,247,188	6,381,146	6,821,321	5,931,901
Total debt	3,363,828	3,401,076	2,166,703	2,613,736	1,902,483
Shareholders' equity	2,706,757	2,472,869	2,338,551	2,320,996	2,367,398

REQUIRED

Prepare a trend analysis for Heinz and discuss. Identify important trends and tell whether the trends are favorable or unfavorable. Discuss significant relationships among the trends.

INTERNATIONAL COMPANY

FRA 2.

LO 5 *Analyzing Non-U.S. Financial Statements*

When dealing with non-U.S. companies, the analyst is often faced with financial statements that do not follow the same format as the statements of U.S. companies. The 1996 balance sheet and the profit and loss account (income statement) for *Granada Group*,[10] a leading British hotel, restaurant, and media company, present such a situation. The statements are below and on the next page.

Show that you can read these British financial statements by computing as many of the following ratios as you can: (a) current ratio, (b) receivable turnover, (c) inventory turnover, (d) profit margin, (e) asset turnover, (f) return on assets, (g) return on equity,

Granada Group
Balance Sheet

At 28 September 1996	£m	1996 £m
Fixed assets:		
Tangible assets		4,834.5
Investments		462.0
		5,296.5
Current assets:		
Stocks	190.9	
Debtors: amounts falling due within one year	664.4	
Debtors: amounts falling due after more than one year	267.5	
Cash, short term deposits and liquid investments	428.1	
	1,550.9	
Creditors: amounts falling due within one year:		
Borrowings	382.0	
Other creditors	1,685.0	
	2,067.0	
Net current (liabilities)/assets		(516.1)
Total assets less current liabilities		4,780.4
Creditors: amounts falling due after more than one year:		
Borrowings	3,561.5	
Other creditors	70.9	
		3,632.4
Provisions for liabilities and charges		55.8
Net assets		1,092.2
Capital and reserves:		
Called up share capital		231.0
Share premium account		82.5
Revaluation reserve		163.3
Merger reserve		(134.2)
Profit and loss account		645.2
Shareholders' funds		987.8
Minority interests		104.4
		1,092.2

Granada Group
Profit and Loss Account

For the 52 weeks ended 28 September 1996	1996 £ m
Turnover:	3,816.9
Depreciation on tangible assets	184.6
Staff costs	928.6
Net other operating costs	2,104.0
	3,217.2
Operating profit:	599.7
Profit on disposal of businesses	1.6
Profit before interest and taxation	601.3
Net interest	196.5
Profit on ordinary activities before taxation	404.8
Tax on profit on ordinary activities	108.3
Profit on ordinary activities after taxation	296.5
Minority interests	2.1
Profit for the financial period	294.4
Dividends on shares	121.6
Amount transferred to reserves	172.8
Earnings per share (basic)	37.0p
Earnings per share (fully diluted)	35.6p

---

and (h) debt to equity. Use year-end figures to compute ratios that normally require averages. Indicate what data are missing for any ratio you are not able to compute. What terms or accounts did you have trouble interpreting? How do you evaluate the usefulness of the formats of the British financial statements compared to the formats of U.S. financial statements?

Group Activity: Assign groups to prepare an analysis of Granada. Allow one week for this project to be completed.

Toys "R" Us Annual Report

FRA 3.
LO 5 *Comprehensive Ratio Analysis*

Refer to the Toys "R" Us annual report, and conduct a comprehensive ratio analysis that compares data from 1997 and 1996. If you have been computing ratios for Toys "R" Us in previous chapters, you may prepare a table that summarizes the ratios for 1997 and 1996 and show calculations only for the ratios not previously calculated. If this is the first time you are doing a ratio analysis for Toys "R" Us, show all your computations. In either case, after each group of ratios, comment on the performance of Toys "R" Us. Round your calculations to one decimal place. Prepare and comment on the following categories of ratios:

> Liquidity analysis: Current ratio, quick ratio, receivable turnover, average days' sales uncollected, inventory turnover, and average days' inventory on hand

Profitability analysis: Profit margin, asset turnover, return on assets, and return on equity (Comment on the effect of the restructuring in 1996 on the company's profitability.)

Long-term solvency analysis: Debt to equity ratio and interest coverage ratio

Cash flow adequacy analysis: Cash flow yield, cash flows to sales, cash flows to assets, and free cash flow

Market strength analysis: Price/earnings ratio and dividends yield

FINGRAPH® FINANCIAL ANALYST™

FRA 4.

LO 5 *Comprehensive Financial Statement Analysis*

Choose any company in the Fingraph® Financial Analyst™ CD-ROM software database.

1. Display and print for the company you have selected the following pages:
   a. Balance Sheet Analysis
   b. Current Assets and Current Liabilities Analysis
   c. Liquidity and Asset Utilization Analysis
   d. Income from Operations Analysis
   e. Statement of Cash Flows: Operating Activities Analysis
   f. Statement of Cash Flows: Investing and Financing Activities Analysis
   g. Market Strength Analysis
2. Prepare an executive summary that describes the financial condition and performance of your company for the past two years. Attach the pages you printed above in support of your analysis.

ENDNOTES

1. "Credit Ratings," *The Wall Street Journal*, February 26, 1997.
2. *Statement of Financial Accounting Standards No. 131*, "Segment Disclosures" (Norwalk, Conn.: Financial Accounting Standards Board, 1997).
3. Sun Microsystems, Inc., *Annual Report*, 1997.
4. William H. Beaver, "Alternative Accounting Measures as Indicators of Failure," *Accounting Review*, January 1968; and Edward Altman, "Financial Ratios, Discriminant Analysis and the Prediction of Corporate Bankruptcy," *Journal of Finance*, September 1968.
5. Sun Microsystems, Inc., "Management's Discussion and Analysis," *Annual Report*, 1997.
6. In addition, there are advantages to being a debtor in periods of inflation because the debt, which is fixed in dollar amount, may be repaid with cheaper dollars.
7. Sun Microsystems, Inc., "Management's Discussion and Analysis," *Annual Report*, 1997.
8. *Forbes*, November 13, 1978, p. 154.
9. "Heinz's 25% Jump in 2nd-Period Profit Masks Weakness," *The Wall Street Journal*, December 8, 1993.
10. Granada Group, *Annual Report*, 1996.

The Time Value of Money

Simple Interest and Compound Interest

Interest is the cost associated with the use of money for a specific period of time. Because interest is a cost associated with time, and "time is money," it is also an important consideration in any business decision. *Simple interest* is the interest cost for one or more periods, under the assumption that the amount on which the interest is computed stays the same from period to period. *Compound interest* is the interest cost for two or more periods, under the assumption that after each period the interest of that period is added to the amount on which interest is computed in future periods. In other words, compound interest is interest earned on a principal sum that is increased at the end of each period by the interest for that period.

Example: Simple Interest   Joe Sanchez accepts an 8 percent, $30,000 note due in ninety days. How much will he receive in total at that time? Remember that the formula for calculating simple interest is as follows:

$$
\begin{aligned}
\text{Interest} &= \text{Principal} \times \text{Rate} \times \text{Time} \\
&= \$30,000 \times 8/100 \times 90/360 \\
&= \$600
\end{aligned}
$$

Therefore, the total that Sanchez will receive is calculated as follows:

$$
\begin{aligned}
\text{Total} &= \text{Principal} + \text{Interest} \\
&= \$30,000 + \$600 \\
&= \$30,600
\end{aligned}
$$

Example: Compound Interest   Ann Clary deposits $5,000 in a savings account that pays 6 percent interest. She expects to leave the principal and accumulated interest in the account for three years. How much will her account total at the end of three years? Assume that the interest is paid at the end of the year and is added to the principal at that time, and that this total in turn earns interest. The amount at the end of three years is computed as follows:

(1) Year	(2) Principal Amount at Beginning of Year	(3) Annual Amount of Interest (Col. 2 × 6%)	(4) Accumulated Amount at End of Year (Col. 2 + Col. 3)
1	$5,000.00	$300.00	$5,300.00
2	5,300.00	318.00	5,618.00
3	5,618.00	337.08	5,955.08

At the end of three years, Clary will have $5,955.08 in her savings account. Note that the annual amount of interest increases each year by the interest rate times the interest of the previous year. For example, between year 1 and year 2, the interest increased by $18 ($318 − $300), which exactly equals 6 percent times $300.

Table 1. Future Value of $1 after a Given Number of Time Periods

Periods	1%	2%	3%	4%	5%	6%	7%	8%	9%	10%	12%	14%	15%
1	1.010	1.020	1.030	1.040	1.050	1.060	1.070	1.080	1.090	1.100	1.120	1.140	1.150
2	1.020	1.040	1.061	1.082	1.103	1.124	1.145	1.166	1.188	1.210	1.254	1.300	1.323
3	1.030	1.061	1.093	1.125	1.158	1.191	1.225	1.260	1.295	1.331	1.405	1.482	1.521
4	1.041	1.082	1.126	1.170	1.216	1.262	1.311	1.360	1.412	1.464	1.574	1.689	1.749
5	1.051	1.104	1.159	1.217	1.276	1.338	1.403	1.469	1.539	1.611	1.762	1.925	2.011
6	1.062	1.126	1.194	1.265	1.340	1.419	1.501	1.587	1.677	1.772	1.974	2.195	2.313
7	1.072	1.149	1.230	1.316	1.407	1.504	1.606	1.714	1.828	1.949	2.211	2.502	2.660
8	1.083	1.172	1.267	1.369	1.477	1.594	1.718	1.851	1.993	2.144	2.476	2.853	3.059
9	1.094	1.195	1.305	1.423	1.551	1.689	1.838	1.999	2.172	2.358	2.773	3.252	3.518
10	1.105	1.219	1.344	1.480	1.629	1.791	1.967	2.159	2.367	2.594	3.106	3.707	4.046

Source: Excerpt from Table 1 in the appendix on future value and present value tables.

Future Value of a Single Invested Sum at Compound Interest

Another way to ask the question in the example of compound interest above is, What is the future value of a single sum ($5,000) at compound interest (6 percent) for three years? *Future value* is the amount that an investment will be worth at a future date if invested at compound interest. A businessperson often wants to know future value, but the method of computing the future value illustrated above is too time-consuming in practice. Imagine how tedious the calculation would be if the example were ten years instead of three. Fortunately, there are tables that simplify solving problems involving compound interest. Table 1, showing the future value of $1 after a given number of time periods, is an example. It is actually part of a larger table, Table 1 in the appendix on future value and present value tables. Suppose that we want to solve the problem of Clary's savings account above. We simply look down the 6 percent column in Table 1 until we reach the line for 3 periods and find the factor 1.191. This factor, when multiplied by $1, gives the future value of that $1 at compound interest of 6 percent for three periods (years in this case). Thus, we solve the problem as follows:

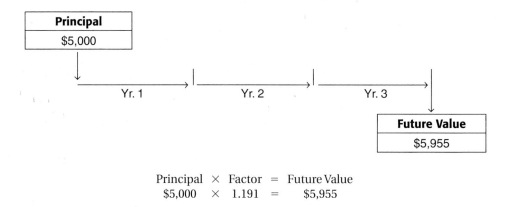

Principal × Factor = Future Value
$5,000 × 1.191 = $5,955

Except for a rounding difference of $.08, the answer is exactly the same as that calculated earlier.

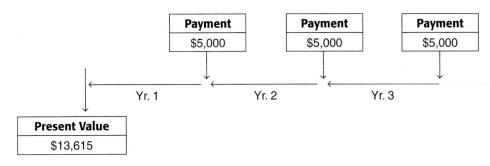

$$\begin{array}{ccccc}
\text{Periodic Payment} & \times & \text{Factor} & = & \text{Present Value} \\
\$5{,}000 & \times & 2.723 & = & \$13{,}615
\end{array}$$

This result is the same as the one computed earlier.

Time Periods

In all of the previous examples, and in most other cases, the compounding period is one year, and the interest rate is stated on an annual basis. However, in each of the four tables, the left-hand column refers not to years but to periods. This wording is intended to accommodate compounding periods of less than one year. Savings accounts that record interest quarterly and bonds that pay interest semiannually are cases in which the compounding period is less than one year. To use the tables in such cases, it is necessary to (1) divide the annual interest rate by the number of periods in the year, and (2) multiply the number of periods in one year by the number of years.

For example, assume that a $6,000 note is to be paid in two years and carries an annual interest rate of 8 percent. Compute the maturity (future) value of the note, assuming that the compounding period is semiannual. Before using the table, it is necessary to compute the interest rate that applies to each compounding period and the total number of compounding periods. First, the interest rate to use is 4 percent (8% annual rate ÷ 2 periods per year). Second, the total number of compounding periods is 4 (2 periods per year × 2 years). From Table 1, therefore, the maturity value of the note is computed as follows:

$$\begin{array}{ccccc}
\text{Principal} & \times & \text{Factor} & = & \text{Future Value} \\
\$6{,}000 & \times & 1.170 & = & \$7{,}020
\end{array}$$

The note will be worth $7,020 in two years.

This procedure for determining the interest rate and the number of periods when the compounding period is less than one year may be used with all four tables.

Applications of Present Value to Accounting

The concept of present value is widely applicable in the discipline of accounting. Here, the purpose is to demonstrate its usefulness in some simple applications. In-depth study of present value is deferred to more advanced courses.

Imputing Interest on Non-Interest-Bearing Notes

Clearly there is no such thing as an interest-free debt, regardless of whether the interest rate is explicitly stated. The Accounting Principles Board has declared that when a long-term note does not explicitly state an interest rate (or if the interest rate is unreasonably low), a rate based on the normal interest cost of the company in question should be assigned, or imputed.[1]

The following example applies this principle. On January 1, 20x0, Gato purchased merchandise from Haines by issuing an $8,000 non-interest-bearing note due in two years. Gato can borrow money from the bank at 9 percent interest. Gato paid the note in full after two years.

Note that the $8,000 note represents partly a payment for merchandise and partly a payment of interest for two years. In recording the purchase and sale, it is necessary to use Table 3 to determine the present value of the note. The calculation follows.

Future Payment × Present Value Factor (9%, 2 years) = Present Value
$8,000 × .842 = $6,736

The imputed interest cost is $1,264 ($8,000 − $6,736) and is recorded as a discount on notes payable in Gato's records and as a discount on notes receivable in Haines's records. The entries necessary to record the purchase in the Gato records and the sale in the Haines records are as follows:

Gato Journal

A = L + OE
− +
+

Purchases — 6,736
Discount on Notes Payable — 1,264
  Notes Payable — 8,000

Haines Journal

Notes Receivable — 8,000
  Discount on Notes Receivable — 1,264
  Sales — 6,736

A = L + OE
+ +
−

On December 31, 20x0, the adjustments to recognize the interest expense and interest income are as follows:

Gato Journal

A = L + OE
+ −

Interest Expense — 606.24
  Discount on Notes Payable — 606.24

Haines Journal

Discount on Notes Receivable — 606.24
  Interest Income — 606.24

A = L + OE
+ +

The interest is calculated by multiplying the amount of the original purchase by the interest rate for one year ($6,736.00 × .09 = $606.24). When payment is made on December 31, 20x0, the following entries are made in the respective journals.

Gato Journal

A = L + OE
− + −

Interest Expense — 657.76
Notes Payable — 8,000.00
  Discount on Notes Payable — 657.76
  Cash — 8,000.00

Haines Journal

Discount on Notes Receivable — 657.76
Cash — 8,000.00
  Interest Income — 657.76
  Notes Receivable — 8,000.00

A = L + OE
+ +
+
−

The interest entries represent the remaining interest to be expensed or realized ($1,264 − $606.24 = $657.76). This amount approximates (because of rounding differences in the table) the interest for one year on the purchase plus last year's interest [($6,736 + $606.24) × .09 = $660.80].

Valuing an Asset

An asset is recorded because it will provide future benefits to the company that owns it. These future benefits are the basis for the definition of an asset. Usually, the purchase price of the asset represents the present value of these future benefits. It is possible to evaluate a proposed purchase price for an asset by comparing that price with the present value of the asset to the company.

For example, Sam Hurst is thinking of buying a new machine that will reduce his annual labor cost by $700 per year. The machine will last eight years. The interest rate that Hurst assumes for making managerial decisions is 10 percent. What is the maximum amount (present value) that Hurst should pay for the machine?

The present value of the machine to Hurst is equal to the present value of an ordinary annuity of $700 per year for eight years at compound interest of 10 percent. Using the factor from Table 4, we compute the value as follows:

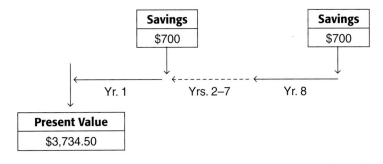

Periodic Savings × Factor = Present Value
$700.00 × 5.335 = $3,734.50

Hurst should not pay more than $3,734.50 for the new machine because this amount equals the present value of the benefits that will be received from owning the machine.

Deferred Payment

A seller will sometimes agree to defer payment for a sale in order to encourage the buyer to make the purchase. This practice is common, for example, in the farm implement industry, where the farmer needs the equipment in the spring but cannot pay for it until the fall crop is in. Assume that Plains Implement Corporation sells a tractor to Dana Washington for $50,000 on February 1, agreeing to take payment ten months later, on December 1. When this type of agreement is made, the future payment includes not only the sales price of the tractor but also an implied (imputed) interest cost. If the prevailing annual interest rate for such transactions is 12 percent compounded monthly, the actual sale (purchase) price of the tractor would be the present value of the future payment, computed using the factor from Table 3 (10 periods, 1 percent), as follows:

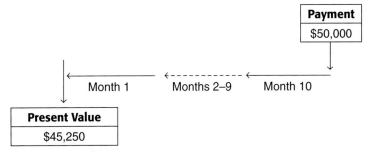

Future Payment × Factor = Present Value
$50,000 × .905 = $45,250

The purchase in Washington's records and the sale in Plains's records are recorded at the present value, $45,250. The balance consists of interest expense or interest income. The entries necessary to record the purchase in Washington's records and the sale in Plains's records are as follows:

Washington Journal

Plains Journal

A = L + OE   Feb. 1   Tractor   45,250   Accounts Receivable   45,250   A = L + OE
+   +   Accounts Payable   45,250   Sales   45,250   +   +
         Purchase of tractor   Sale of tractor

When Washington pays for the tractor, the entries are as follows:

Washington Journal

Plains Journal

A = L + OE   Dec. 1   Accounts Payable   45,250   Cash   50,000   A = L + OE
−   −   −   Interest Expense   4,750   Accounts Receivable   45,250   +   +
         Cash   50,000   Interest Income   4,750   −
          Payment on account,   Receipt on account from
          including imputed   Washington, including
          interest expense   imputed interest earned

Investment of Idle Cash

Childware Corporation, a toy manufacturer, has just completed a successful fall selling season and has $10,000,000 in cash to invest for six months. The company places the cash in a money market account that is expected to pay 12 percent annual interest. Interest is compounded monthly and credited to the company's account each month. How much cash will the company have at the end of six months, and what entries will be made to record the investment and the monthly interest? The future value factor from Table 1 is based on six monthly periods of 1 percent (12 percent divided by 12 months), and the future value is computed as follows:

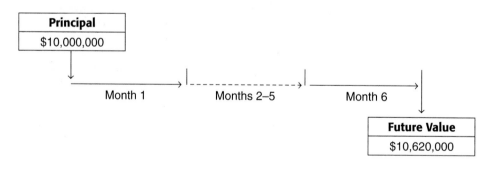

Investment × Factor = Future Value
$10,000,000 × 1.062 = $10,620,000

When the investment is made, the following entry is made:

A = L + OE   Short-Term Investments   10,000,000
+   Cash   10,000,000
−   Investment of cash

After the first month, the interest is recorded by increasing the Short-Term Investments account.

A = L + OE   Short-Term Investments   100,000
+   +   Interest Income   100,000
                            One month's interest income
                            $10,000,000 × .01 = $100,000

After the second month, the interest is earned on the new balance of the Short-Term Investments account.

A = L + OE   Short-Term Investments   101,000
+   +   Interest Income   101,000
                            One month's interest income
                            $10,100,000 × .01 = $101,000

Entries would continue in a similar manner for four more months, at which time the balance of Short-Term Investments would be about $10,620,000. The actual amount accumulated may vary from this total because the interest rate paid on money market accounts can vary over time as a result of changes in market conditions.

Accumulation of a Fund

When a company owes a large fixed amount due in several years, management would be wise to accumulate a fund with which to pay off the debt at maturity. Sometimes creditors, when they agree to provide a loan, require that such a fund be established. In establishing the fund, management must determine how much cash to set aside each period in order to pay the debt. The amount will depend on the estimated rate of interest the investments will earn. Assume that Vason Corporation agrees with a creditor to set aside cash at the end of each year to accumulate enough to pay off a $100,000 note due in five years. Since the first contribution to the fund will be made in one year, five annual contributions will be made by the time the note is due. Assume also that the fund is projected to earn 8 percent, compounded annually. The amount of each annual payment is calculated using Table 2 (5 periods, 8 percent), as follows:

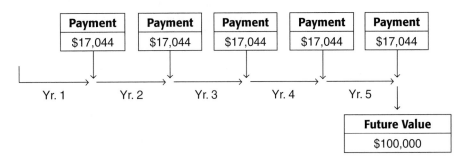

Future Value of Fund ÷ Factor = Annual Investment
$100,000 ÷ 5.867 = $17,044 (rounded)

Each year's contribution to the fund is $17,044. This contribution is recorded as follows:

A = L + OE   Loan Repayment Fund   17,044
+   Cash   17,044
–   Annual contribution to loan repayment fund

Other Accounting Applications

There are many other applications of present value in accounting, including accounting for installment notes, valuing a bond, and recording lease obligations. Present value is also applied in such areas as pension obligations; premium and discount on debt; depreciation of property, plant, and equipment; capital expenditure decisions; and generally any problem in which time is a factor.

Exercises

Tables 1 to 4 in the appendix on future value and present value tables may be used where appropriate to solve these exercises.

Future Value Calculations

E 1. Wieland receives a one-year note for $3,000 that carries a 12 percent annual interest rate for the sale of a used car.

Compute the maturity value under each of the following assumptions: (1) The interest is simple interest. (2) The interest is compounded semiannually. (3) The interest is compounded quarterly. (4) The interest is compounded monthly.

Future Value Calculations

E 2. Find the future value of (1) a single payment of $20,000 at 7 percent for ten years, (2) ten annual payments of $2,000 at 7 percent, (3) a single payment of $6,000 at 9 percent for seven years, and (4) seven annual payments of $6,000 at 9 percent.

Future Value Calculations

E 3. Assume that $40,000 is invested today. Compute the amount that would accumulate at the end of seven years when the interest rate is (1) 8 percent compounded annually, (2) 8 percent compounded semiannually, and (3) 8 percent compounded quarterly.

Future Value Calculations

E 4. Calculate the accumulation of periodic payments of $1,000 made at the end of each of four years, assuming (1) 10 percent annual interest compounded annually, (2) 10 percent annual interest compounded semiannually, (3) 4 percent annual interest compounded annually, and (4) 16 percent annual interest compounded quarterly.

Future Value Applications

E 5. a. Two parents have $20,000 to invest for their child's college tuition, which they estimate will cost $40,000 when the child enters college twelve years from now.

Calculate the approximate rate of annual interest that the investment must earn to reach the $40,000 goal in twelve years. (**Hint:** Make a calculation; then use Table 1 in the appendix on future value and present value tables.)

b. Ted Pruitt is saving to purchase a summer home that will cost about $64,000. He has $40,000 now, on which he can earn 7 percent annual interest.

Calculate the approximate length of time he will have to wait to purchase the summer home. (**Hint:** Make a calculation; then use Table 1 in the appendix on future value and present value tables.)

Working Backward from a Future Value

E 6. Gloria Faraquez has a debt of $90,000 due in four years. She wants to save enough money to pay it off by making annual deposits in an investment account that earns 8 percent annual interest.

Calculate the amount she must deposit each year to reach her goal. (**Hint:** Use Table 2 in the appendix on future value and present value tables; then make a calculation.)

Determining an Advance Payment

E 7. Ellen Saber is contemplating paying five years' rent in advance. Her annual rent is $9,600. Calculate the single sum that would have to be paid now for the advance rent, if we assume compound interest of 8 percent.

Present Value Calculations

E 8. Find the present value of (1) a single payment of $24,000 at 6 percent for twelve years, (2) twelve annual payments of $2,000 at 6 percent, (3) a single payment of $5,000 at 9 percent for five years, and (4) five annual payments of $5,000 at 9 percent.

Present Value of a Lump-Sum Contract

E 9. A contract calls for a lump-sum payment of $60,000. Find the present value of the contract, assuming that (1) the payment is due in five years, and the current interest rate is 9 percent; (2) the payment is due in ten years, and the current interest rate is 9 percent; (3) the payment is due in five years, and the current interest rate is 5 percent; and (4) the payment is due in ten years, and the current interest rate is 5 percent.

E 10. *Present Value of an Annuity Contract*	A contract calls for annual payments of $1,200. Find the present value of the contract, assuming that (1) the number of payments is seven, and the current interest rate is 6 percent; (2) the number of payments is fourteen, and the current interest rate is 6 percent; (3) the number of payments is seven, and the current interest rate is 8 percent; and (4) the number of payments is fourteen, and the current interest rate is 8 percent.
E 11. *Non-interest-Bearing Note*	On January 1, 20x0, Pendleton purchased a machine from Leyland by signing a two-year, non-interest-bearing $32,000 note. Pendleton currently pays 12 percent interest to borrow money at the bank. Prepare entries in Pendleton's and Leyland's journals to (1) record the purchase and the note, (2) adjust the accounts after one year, and (3) record payment of the note after two years (on December 31, 20x2).
E 12. *Valuing an Asset for the Purpose of Making a Purchasing Decision*	Oscaro owns a service station and has the opportunity to purchase a car wash machine for $30,000. After carefully studying projected costs and revenues, Oscaro estimates that the car wash machine will produce a net cash flow of $5,200 annually and will last for eight years. Oscaro feels that an interest rate of 14 percent is adequate for his business. Calculate the present value of the machine to Oscaro. Does the purchase appear to be a correct business decision?
E 13. *Deferred Payment*	Johnson Equipment Corporation sold a precision tool machine with computer controls to Borst Corporation for $800,000 on January 1, agreeing to take payment nine months later, on October 1. Assuming that the prevailing annual interest rate for such a transaction is 16 percent compounded quarterly, what is the actual sale (purchase) price of the machine tool, and what journal entries will be made at the time of the purchase (sale) and at the time of the payment (receipt) on the records of both Borst and Johnson?
E 14. *Investment of Idle Cash*	Scientific Publishing Company, a publisher of college books, has just completed a successful fall selling season and has $5,000,000 in cash to invest for nine months, beginning on January 1. The company placed the cash in a money market account that is expected to pay 12 percent annual interest compounded monthly. Interest is credited to the company's account each month. How much cash will the company have at the end of nine months, and what entries are made to record the investment and the first two monthly (February 1 and March 1) interest amounts?
E 15. *Accumulation of a Fund*	Laferia Corporation borrowed $3,000,000 from an insurance company on a five-year note. Management agreed to set aside enough cash at the end of each year to accumulate the amount needed to pay off the note at maturity. Since the first contribution to the fund will be made in one year, four annual contributions are needed. Assuming that the fund will earn 10 percent compounded annually, how much will the annual contribution to the fund be (round to nearest dollar), and what will be the journal entry for the first contribution?
E 16. *Negotiating the Sale of a Business*	Horace Raftson is attempting to sell his business to Ernando Ruiz. The company has assets of $900,000, liabilities of $800,000, and owner's equity of $100,000. Both parties agree that the proper rate of return to expect is 12 percent; however, they differ on other assumptions. Raftson believes that the business will generate at least $100,000 per year of cash flows for twenty years. Ruiz thinks that $80,000 in cash flows per year is more reasonable and that only ten years in the future should be considered. Using Table 4 in the appendix on future value and present value tables, determine the range for negotiation by computing the present value of Raftson's offer to sell and of Ruiz's offer to buy.

ENDNOTE

1. Accounting Principles Board, *Opinion No. 21*, "Interest on Receivables and Payables" (New York: American Institute of Certified Public Accountants, 1971), par. 13.

APPENDIX

Future Value and Present Value Tables

Table 1 provides the multipliers necessary to compute the future value of a *single* cash deposit made at the *beginning* of year 1. Three factors must be known before the future value can be computed: (1) the time period in years, (2) the stated annual rate of interest to be earned, and (3) the dollar amount invested or deposited.

Table 1. Future Value of $1 After a Given Number of Time Periods

Periods	1%	2%	3%	4%	5%	6%	7%	8%	9%	10%	12%	14%	15%
1	1.010	1.020	1.030	1.040	1.050	1.060	1.070	1.080	1.090	1.100	1.120	1.140	1.150
2	1.020	1.040	1.061	1.082	1.103	1.124	1.145	1.166	1.188	1.210	1.254	1.300	1.323
3	1.030	1.061	1.093	1.125	1.158	1.191	1.225	1.260	1.295	1.331	1.405	1.482	1.521
4	1.041	1.082	1.126	1.170	1.216	1.262	1.311	1.360	1.412	1.464	1.574	1.689	1.749
5	1.051	1.104	1.159	1.217	1.276	1.338	1.403	1.469	1.539	1.611	1.762	1.925	2.011
6	1.062	1.126	1.194	1.265	1.340	1.419	1.501	1.587	1.677	1.772	1.974	2.195	2.313
7	1.072	1.149	1.230	1.316	1.407	1.504	1.606	1.714	1.828	1.949	2.211	2.502	2.660
8	1.083	1.172	1.267	1.369	1.477	1.594	1.718	1.851	1.993	2.144	2.476	2.853	3.059
9	1.094	1.195	1.305	1.423	1.551	1.689	1.838	1.999	2.172	2.358	2.773	3.252	3.518
10	1.105	1.219	1.344	1.480	1.629	1.791	1.967	2.159	2.367	2.594	3.106	3.707	4.046
11	1.116	1.243	1.384	1.539	1.710	1.898	2.105	2.332	2.580	2.853	3.479	4.226	4.652
12	1.127	1.268	1.426	1.601	1.796	2.012	2.252	2.518	2.813	3.138	3.896	4.818	5.350
13	1.138	1.294	1.469	1.665	1.886	2.133	2.410	2.720	3.066	3.452	4.363	5.492	6.153
14	1.149	1.319	1.513	1.732	1.980	2.261	2.579	2.937	3.342	3.798	4.887	6.261	7.076
15	1.161	1.346	1.558	1.801	2.079	2.397	2.759	3.172	3.642	4.177	5.474	7.138	8.137
16	1.173	1.373	1.605	1.873	2.183	2.540	2.952	3.426	3.970	4.595	6.130	8.137	9.358
17	1.184	1.400	1.653	1.948	2.292	2.693	3.159	3.700	4.328	5.054	6.866	9.276	10.76
18	1.196	1.428	1.702	2.026	2.407	2.854	3.380	3.996	4.717	5.560	7.690	10.58	12.38
19	1.208	1.457	1.754	2.107	2.527	3.026	3.617	4.316	5.142	6.116	8.613	12.06	14.23
20	1.220	1.486	1.806	2.191	2.653	3.207	3.870	4.661	5.604	6.728	9.646	13.74	16.37
21	1.232	1.516	1.860	2.279	2.786	3.400	4.141	5.034	6.109	7.400	10.80	15.67	18.82
22	1.245	1.546	1.916	2.370	2.925	3.604	4.430	5.437	6.659	8.140	12.10	17.86	21.64
23	1.257	1.577	1.974	2.465	3.072	3.820	4.741	5.871	7.258	8.954	13.55	20.36	24.89
24	1.270	1.608	2.033	2.563	3.225	4.049	5.072	6.341	7.911	9.850	15.18	23.21	28.63
25	1.282	1.641	2.094	2.666	3.386	4.292	5.427	6.848	8.623	10.83	17.00	26.46	32.92
26	1.295	1.673	2.157	2.772	3.556	4.549	5.807	7.396	9.399	11.92	19.04	30.17	37.86
27	1.308	1.707	2.221	2.883	3.733	4.822	6.214	7.988	10.25	13.11	21.32	34.39	43.54
28	1.321	1.741	2.288	2.999	3.920	5.112	6.649	8.627	11.17	14.42	23.88	39.20	50.07
29	1.335	1.776	2.357	3.119	4.116	5.418	7.114	9.317	12.17	15.86	26.75	44.69	57.58
30	1.348	1.811	2.427	3.243	4.322	5.743	7.612	10.06	13.27	17.45	29.96	50.95	66.21
40	1.489	2.208	3.262	4.801	7.040	10.29	14.97	21.72	31.41	45.26	93.05	188.9	267.9
50	1.645	2.692	4.384	7.107	11.47	18.42	29.46	46.90	74.36	117.4	289.0	700.2	1,084

Example—Table 1   Determine the future value of $5,000 deposited now that will earn 9 percent interest compounded annually for five years. From Table 1, the necessary multiplier for five years at 9 percent is 1.539, and the answer is

$$\$5,000 \times 1.539 = \$7,695$$

Where r is the interest rate and n is the number of periods, the factor values for Table 1 are

$$\text{FV Factor} = (1 + r)^n$$

Situations requiring the use of Table 2 are similar to those requiring the use of Table 1 except that Table 2 is used to compute the future value of a *series* of *equal* deposits made at the end of each period.

Table 2. Future Value of $1 Paid in Each Period for a Given Number of Time Periods

Periods	1%	2%	3%	4%	5%	6%	7%	8%	9%	10%	12%	14%	15%
1	1.000	1.000	1.000	1.000	1.000	1.000	1.000	1.000	1.000	1.000	1.000	1.000	1.000
2	2.010	2.020	2.030	2.040	2.050	2.060	2.070	2.080	2.090	2.100	2.120	2.140	2.150
3	3.030	3.060	3.091	3.122	3.153	3.184	3.215	3.246	3.278	3.310	3.374	3.440	3.473
4	4.060	4.122	4.184	4.246	4.310	4.375	4.440	4.506	4.573	4.641	4.779	4.921	4.993
5	5.101	5.204	5.309	5.416	5.526	5.637	5.751	5.867	5.985	6.105	6.353	6.610	6.742
6	6.152	6.308	6.468	6.633	6.802	6.975	7.153	7.336	7.523	7.716	8.115	8.536	8.754
7	7.214	7.434	7.662	7.898	8.142	8.394	8.654	8.923	9.200	9.487	10.09	10.73	11.07
8	8.286	8.583	8.892	9.214	9.549	9.897	10.26	10.64	11.03	11.44	12.30	13.23	13.73
9	9.369	9.755	10.16	10.58	11.03	11.49	11.98	12.49	13.02	13.58	14.78	16.09	16.79
10	10.46	10.95	11.46	12.01	12.58	13.18	13.82	14.49	15.19	15.94	17.55	19.34	20.30
11	11.57	12.17	12.81	13.49	14.21	14.97	15.78	16.65	17.56	18.53	20.65	23.04	24.35
12	12.68	13.41	14.19	15.03	15.92	16.87	17.89	18.98	20.14	21.38	24.13	27.27	29.00
13	13.81	14.68	15.62	16.63	17.71	18.88	20.14	21.50	22.95	24.52	28.03	32.09	34.35
14	14.95	15.97	17.09	18.29	19.60	21.02	22.55	24.21	26.02	27.98	32.39	37.58	40.50
15	16.10	17.29	18.60	20.02	21.58	23.28	25.13	27.15	29.36	31.77	37.28	43.84	47.58
16	17.26	18.64	20.16	21.82	23.66	25.67	27.89	30.32	33.00	35.95	42.75	50.98	55.72
17	18.43	20.01	21.76	23.70	25.84	28.21	30.84	33.75	36.97	40.54	48.88	59.12	65.08
18	19.61	21.41	23.41	25.65	28.13	30.91	34.00	37.45	41.30	45.60	55.75	68.39	75.84
19	20.81	22.84	25.12	27.67	30.54	33.76	37.38	41.45	46.02	51.16	63.44	78.97	88.21
20	22.02	24.30	26.87	29.78	33.07	36.79	41.00	45.76	51.16	57.28	72.05	91.02	102.4
21	23.24	25.78	28.68	31.97	35.72	39.99	44.87	50.42	56.76	64.00	81.70	104.8	118.8
22	24.47	27.30	30.54	34.25	38.51	43.39	49.01	55.46	62.87	71.40	92.50	120.4	137.6
23	25.72	28.85	32.45	36.62	41.43	47.00	53.44	60.89	69.53	79.54	104.6	138.3	159.3
24	26.97	30.42	34.43	39.08	44.50	50.82	58.18	66.76	76.79	88.50	118.2	158.7	184.2
25	28.24	32.03	36.46	41.65	47.73	54.86	63.25	73.11	84.70	98.35	133.3	181.9	212.8
26	29.53	33.67	38.55	44.31	51.11	59.16	68.68	79.95	93.32	109.2	150.3	208.3	245.7
27	30.82	35.34	40.71	47.08	54.67	63.71	74.48	87.35	102.7	121.1	169.4	238.5	283.6
28	32.13	37.05	42.93	49.97	58.40	68.53	80.70	95.34	113.0	134.2	190.7	272.9	327.1
29	33.45	38.79	45.22	52.97	62.32	73.64	87.35	104.0	124.1	148.6	214.6	312.1	377.2
30	34.78	40.57	47.58	56.08	66.44	79.06	94.46	113.3	136.3	164.5	241.3	356.8	434.7
40	48.89	60.40	75.40	95.03	120.8	154.8	199.6	259.1	337.9	442.6	767.1	1,342	1,779
50	64.46	84.58	112.8	152.7	209.3	290.3	406.5	573.8	815.1	1,164	2,400	4,995	7,218

Table 3. Present Value of $1 to Be Received at the End of a Given Number of Time Periods

Periods	1%	2%	3%	4%	5%	6%	7%	8%	9%	10%	12%
1	0.990	0.980	0.971	0.962	0.952	0.943	0.935	0.926	0.917	0.909	0.893
2	0.980	0.961	0.943	0.925	0.907	0.890	0.873	0.857	0.842	0.826	0.797
3	0.971	0.942	0.915	0.889	0.864	0.840	0.816	0.794	0.772	0.751	0.712
4	0.961	0.924	0.888	0.855	0.823	0.792	0.763	0.735	0.708	0.683	0.636
5	0.951	0.906	0.883	0.822	0.784	0.747	0.713	0.681	0.650	0.621	0.567
6	0.942	0.888	0.837	0.790	0.746	0.705	0.666	0.630	0.596	0.564	0.507
7	0.933	0.871	0.813	0.760	0.711	0.665	0.623	0.583	0.547	0.513	0.452
8	0.923	0.853	0.789	0.731	0.677	0.627	0.582	0.540	0.502	0.467	0.404
9	0.914	0.837	0.766	0.703	0.645	0.592	0.544	0.500	0.460	0.424	0.361
10	0.905	0.820	0.744	0.676	0.614	0.558	0.508	0.463	0.422	0.386	0.322
11	0.896	0.804	0.722	0.650	0.585	0.527	0.475	0.429	0.388	0.350	0.287
12	0.887	0.788	0.701	0.625	0.557	0.497	0.444	0.397	0.356	0.319	0.257
13	0.879	0.773	0.681	0.601	0.530	0.469	0.415	0.368	0.326	0.290	0.229
14	0.870	0.758	0.661	0.577	0.505	0.442	0.388	0.340	0.299	0.263	0.205
15	0.861	0.743	0.642	0.555	0.481	0.417	0.362	0.315	0.275	0.239	0.183
16	0.853	0.728	0.623	0.534	0.458	0.394	0.339	0.292	0.252	0.218	0.163
17	0.844	0.714	0.605	0.513	0.436	0.371	0.317	0.270	0.231	0.198	0.146
18	0.836	0.700	0.587	0.494	0.416	0.350	0.296	0.250	0.212	0.180	0.130
19	0.828	0.686	0.570	0.475	0.396	0.331	0.277	0.232	0.194	0.164	0.116
20	0.820	0.673	0.554	0.456	0.377	0.312	0.258	0.215	0.178	0.149	0.104
21	0.811	0.660	0.538	0.439	0.359	0.294	0.242	0.199	0.164	0.135	0.093
22	0.803	0.647	0.522	0.422	0.342	0.278	0.226	0.184	0.150	0.123	0.083
23	0.795	0.634	0.507	0.406	0.326	0.262	0.211	0.170	0.138	0.112	0.074
24	0.788	0.622	0.492	0.390	0.310	0.247	0.197	0.158	0.126	0.102	0.066
25	0.780	0.610	0.478	0.375	0.295	0.233	0.184	0.146	0.116	0.092	0.059
26	0.772	0.598	0.464	0.361	0.281	0.220	0.172	0.135	0.106	0.084	0.053
27	0.764	0.586	0.450	0.347	0.268	0.207	0.161	0.125	0.098	0.076	0.047
28	0.757	0.574	0.437	0.333	0.255	0.196	0.150	0.116	0.090	0.069	0.042
29	0.749	0.563	0.424	0.321	0.243	0.185	0.141	0.107	0.082	0.063	0.037
30	0.742	0.552	0.412	0.308	0.231	0.174	0.131	0.099	0.075	0.057	0.033
40	0.672	0.453	0.307	0.208	0.142	0.097	0.067	0.046	0.032	0.022	0.011
50	0.608	0.372	0.228	0.141	0.087	0.054	0.034	0.021	0.013	0.009	0.003

Example—Table 2 What will be the future value at the end of thirty years if $1,000 is deposited each year on January 1, beginning in one year, assuming 12 percent interest compounded annually? The required multiplier from Table 2 is 241.3, and the answer is

$$\$1,000 \times 241.3 = \$241,300$$

The factor values for Table 2 are

$$\text{FVa Factor} = \frac{(1 + r)^n - 1}{r}$$

Table 3 is used to compute the value today of a *single* amount of cash to be received sometime in the future. To use Table 3, you must first know: (1) the time period in years until funds will be received, (2) the stated annual rate of interest, and (3) the dollar amount to be received at the end of the time period.

Table 3. (*continued*)

14%	15%	16%	18%	20%	25%	30%	35%	40%	45%	50%	Periods
0.877	0.870	0.862	0.847	0.833	0.800	0.769	0.741	0.714	0.690	0.667	1
0.769	0.756	0.743	0.718	0.694	0.640	0.592	0.549	0.510	0.476	0.444	2
0.675	0.658	0.641	0.609	0.579	0.512	0.455	0.406	0.364	0.328	0.296	3
0.592	0.572	0.552	0.516	0.482	0.410	0.350	0.301	0.260	0.226	0.198	4
0.519	0.497	0.476	0.437	0.402	0.328	0.269	0.223	0.186	0.156	0.132	5
0.456	0.432	0.410	0.370	0.335	0.262	0.207	0.165	0.133	0.108	0.088	6
0.400	0.376	0.354	0.314	0.279	0.210	0.159	0.122	0.095	0.074	0.059	7
0.351	0.327	0.305	0.266	0.233	0.168	0.123	0.091	0.068	0.051	0.039	8
0.308	0.284	0.263	0.225	0.194	0.134	0.094	0.067	0.048	0.035	0.026	9
0.270	0.247	0.227	0.191	0.162	0.107	0.073	0.050	0.035	0.024	0.017	10
0.237	0.215	0.195	0.162	0.135	0.086	0.056	0.037	0.025	0.017	0.012	11
0.208	0.187	0.168	0.137	0.112	0.069	0.043	0.027	0.018	0.012	0.008	12
0.182	0.163	0.145	0.116	0.093	0.055	0.033	0.020	0.013	0.008	0.005	13
0.160	0.141	0.125	0.099	0.078	0.044	0.025	0.015	0.009	0.006	0.003	14
0.140	0.123	0.108	0.084	0.065	0.035	0.020	0.011	0.006	0.004	0.002	15
0.123	0.107	0.093	0.071	0.054	0.028	0.015	0.008	0.005	0.003	0.002	16
0.108	0.093	0.080	0.060	0.045	0.023	0.012	0.006	0.003	0.002	0.001	17
0.095	0.081	0.069	0.051	0.038	0.018	0.009	0.005	0.002	0.001	0.001	18
0.083	0.070	0.060	0.043	0.031	0.014	0.007	0.003	0.002	0.001		19
0.073	0.061	0.051	0.037	0.026	0.012	0.005	0.002	0.001	0.001		20
0.064	0.053	0.044	0.031	0.022	0.009	0.004	0.002	0.001			21
0.056	0.046	0.038	0.026	0.018	0.007	0.003	0.001	0.001			22
0.049	0.040	0.033	0.022	0.015	0.006	0.002	0.001				23
0.043	0.035	0.028	0.019	0.013	0.005	0.002	0.001				24
0.038	0.030	0.024	0.016	0.010	0.004	0.001	0.001				25
0.033	0.026	0.021	0.014	0.009	0.003	0.001					26
0.029	0.023	0.018	0.011	0.007	0.002	0.001					27
0.026	0.020	0.016	0.010	0.006	0.002	0.001					28
0.022	0.017	0.014	0.008	0.005	0.002						29
0.020	0.015	0.012	0.007	0.004	0.001						30
0.005	0.004	0.003	0.001	0.001							40
0.001	0.001	0.001									50

Example—Table 3   What is the present value of $30,000 to be received twenty-five years from now, assuming a 14 percent interest rate? From Table 3, the required multiplier is .038, and the answer is

$$\$30,000 \times .038 = \$1,140$$

The factor values for Table 3 are

$$\text{PV Factor} = (1 + r)^{-n}$$

Table 3 is the reciprocal of Table 1.

Table 4 is used to compute the present value of a *series* of *equal* periodic cash flows.

Table 4. Present Value of $1 Received Each Period for a Given Number of Time Periods

Periods	1%	2%	3%	4%	5%	6%	7%	8%	9%	10%	12%
1	0.990	0.980	0.971	0.962	0.952	0.943	0.935	0.926	0.917	0.909	0.893
2	1.970	1.942	1.913	1.886	1.859	1.833	1.808	1.783	1.759	1.736	1.690
3	2.941	2.884	2.829	2.775	2.723	2.673	2.624	2.577	2.531	2.487	2.402
4	3.902	3.808	3.717	3.630	3.546	3.465	3.387	3.312	3.240	3.170	3.037
5	4.853	4.713	4.580	4.452	4.329	4.212	4.100	3.993	3.890	3.791	3.605
6	5.795	5.601	5.417	5.242	5.076	4.917	4.767	4.623	4.486	4.355	4.111
7	6.728	6.472	6.230	6.002	5.786	5.582	5.389	5.206	5.033	4.868	4.564
8	7.652	7.325	7.020	6.733	6.463	6.210	5.971	5.747	5.535	5.335	4.968
9	8.566	8.162	7.786	7.435	7.108	6.802	6.515	6.247	5.995	5.759	5.328
10	9.471	8.983	8.530	8.111	7.722	7.360	7.024	6.710	6.418	6.145	5.650
11	10.368	9.787	9.253	8.760	8.306	7.887	7.499	7.139	6.805	6.495	5.938
12	11.255	10.575	9.954	9.385	8.863	8.384	7.943	7.536	7.161	6.814	6.194
13	12.134	11.348	10.635	9.986	9.394	8.853	8.358	7.904	7.487	7.103	6.424
14	13.004	12.106	11.296	10.563	9.899	9.295	8.745	8.244	7.786	7.367	6.628
15	13.865	12.849	11.938	11.118	10.380	9.712	9.108	8.559	8.061	7.606	6.811
16	14.718	13.578	12.561	11.652	10.838	10.106	9.447	8.851	8.313	7.824	6.974
17	15.562	14.292	13.166	12.166	11.274	10.477	9.763	9.122	8.544	8.022	7.120
18	16.398	14.992	13.754	12.659	11.690	10.828	10.059	9.372	8.756	8.201	7.250
19	17.226	15.678	14.324	13.134	12.085	11.158	10.336	9.604	8.950	8.365	7.366
20	18.046	16.351	14.878	13.590	12.462	11.470	10.594	9.818	9.129	8.514	7.469
21	18.857	17.011	15.415	14.029	12.821	11.764	10.836	10.017	9.292	8.649	7.562
22	19.660	17.658	15.937	14.451	13.163	12.042	11.061	10.201	9.442	8.772	7.645
23	20.456	18.292	16.444	14.857	13.489	12.303	11.272	10.371	9.580	8.883	7.718
24	21.243	18.914	16.936	15.247	13.799	12.550	11.469	10.529	9.707	8.985	7.784
25	22.023	19.523	17.413	15.622	14.094	12.783	11.654	10.675	9.823	9.077	7.843
26	22.795	20.121	17.877	15.983	14.375	13.003	11.826	10.810	9.929	9.161	7.896
27	23.560	20.707	18.327	16.330	14.643	13.211	11.987	10.935	10.027	9.237	7.943
28	24.316	21.281	18.764	16.663	14.898	13.406	12.137	11.051	10.116	9.307	7.984
29	25.066	21.844	19.189	16.984	15.141	13.591	12.278	11.158	10.198	9.370	8.022
30	25.808	22.396	19.600	17.292	15.373	13.765	12.409	11.258	10.274	9.427	8.055
40	32.835	27.355	23.115	19.793	17.159	15.046	13.332	11.925	10.757	9.779	8.244
50	39.196	31.424	25.730	21.482	18.256	15.762	13.801	12.234	10.962	9.915	8.305

Example—Table 4   Arthur Howard won a contest on January 1, 20x8, in which the prize was $30,000, payable in fifteen annual installments of $2,000 every December 31, beginning in 20x8. Assuming a 9 percent interest rate, what is the present value of Mr. Howard's prize on January 1, 20x8? From Table 4, the required multiplier is 8.061, and the answer is

$$\$2,000 \times 8.061 = \$16,122$$

The factor values for Table 4 are

$$\text{PVa Factor} = \frac{1 - (1 + r)^{-n}}{r}$$

Table 4 is the columnar sum of Table 3.

Table 4. (continued)

14%	15%	16%	18%	20%	25%	30%	35%	40%	45%	50%	Periods
0.877	0.870	0.862	0.847	0.833	0.800	0.769	0.741	0.714	0.690	0.667	1
1.647	1.626	1.605	1.566	1.528	1.440	1.361	1.289	1.224	1.165	1.111	2
2.322	2.283	2.246	2.174	2.106	1.952	1.816	1.696	1.589	1.493	1.407	3
2.914	2.855	2.798	2.690	2.589	2.362	2.166	1.997	1.849	1.720	1.605	4
3.433	3.352	3.274	3.127	2.991	2.689	2.436	2.220	2.035	1.876	1.737	5
3.889	3.784	3.685	3.498	3.326	2.951	2.643	2.385	2.168	1.983	1.824	6
4.288	4.160	4.039	3.812	3.605	3.161	2.802	2.508	2.263	2.057	1.883	7
4.639	4.487	4.344	4.078	3.837	3.329	2.925	2.598	2.331	2.109	1.922	8
4.946	4.772	4.607	4.303	4.031	3.463	3.019	2.665	2.379	2.144	1.948	9
5.216	5.019	4.833	4.494	4.192	3.571	3.092	2.715	2.414	2.168	1.965	10
5.453	5.234	5.029	4.656	4.327	3.656	3.147	2.752	2.438	2.185	1.977	11
5.660	5.421	5.197	4.793	4.439	3.725	3.190	2.779	2.456	2.197	1.985	12
5.842	5.583	5.342	4.910	4.533	3.780	3.223	2.799	2.469	2.204	1.990	13
6.002	5.724	5.468	5.008	4.611	3.824	3.249	2.814	2.478	2.210	1.993	14
6.142	5.847	5.575	5.092	4.675	3.859	3.268	2.825	2.484	2.214	1.995	15
6.265	5.954	5.669	5.162	4.730	3.887	3.283	2.834	2.489	2.216	1.997	16
6.373	6.047	5.749	5.222	4.775	3.910	3.295	2.840	2.492	2.218	1.998	17
6.467	6.128	5.818	5.273	4.812	3.928	3.304	2.844	2.494	2.219	1.999	18
6.550	6.198	5.877	5.316	4.844	3.942	3.311	2.848	2.496	2.220	1.999	19
6.623	6.259	5.929	5.353	4.870	3.954	3.316	2.850	2.497	2.221	1.999	20
6.687	6.312	5.973	5.384	4.891	3.963	3.320	2.852	2.498	2.221	2.000	21
6.743	6.359	6.011	5.410	4.909	3.970	3.323	2.853	2.498	2.222	2.000	22
6.792	6.399	6.044	5.432	4.925	3.976	3.325	2.854	2.499	2.222	2.000	23
6.835	6.434	6.073	5.451	4.937	3.981	3.327	2.855	2.499	2.222	2.000	24
6.873	6.464	6.097	5.467	4.948	3.985	3.329	2.856	2.499	2.222	2.000	25
6.906	6.491	6.118	5.480	4.956	3.988	3.330	2.856	2.500	2.222	2.000	26
6.935	6.514	6.136	5.492	4.964	3.990	3.331	2.856	2.500	2.222	2.000	27
6.961	6.534	6.152	5.502	4.970	3.992	3.331	2.857	2.500	2.222	2.000	28
6.983	6.551	6.166	5.510	4.975	3.994	3.332	2.857	2.500	2.222	2.000	29
7.003	6.566	6.177	5.517	4.979	3.995	3.332	2.857	2.500	2.222	2.000	30
7.105	6.642	6.234	5.548	4.997	3.999	3.333	2.857	2.500	2.222	2.000	40
7.133	6.661	6.246	5.554	4.999	4.000	3.333	2.857	2.500	2.222	2.000	50

Table 4 applies to *ordinary annuities,* in which the first cash flow occurs one time period beyond the date for which the present value is to be computed. An *annuity due* is a series of equal cash flows for N time periods with the first payment occurring immediately. The present value of the first payment equals the face value of the cash flow; Table 4 then is used to measure the present value of $N - 1$ remaining cash flows.

Example—Table 4   Determine the present value on January 1, 20x8, of twenty lease payments; each payment of $10,000 is due on January 1, beginning in 20x8. Assume an interest rate of 8 percent.

$$\text{Present Value} = \text{Immediate Payment} + \begin{cases} \text{Present Value of 19 Subsequent} \\ \text{Payments at 8\%} \end{cases}$$

$$= \$10,000 + (\$10,000 \times 9.604) = \$106,040$$

Company Name Index

Subject Index

Note: **Boldface** type indicates key terms.

ABC, *see* Activity-based costing (ABC)
ABM, *see* Activity-based management (ABM)
Absorption approach, for income statement preparation, 18
Accounting
   international, *see* International accounting
   responsibility, 258, 260–261
Accounting Principles Board (APB), on imputed interest, 582
Accounting rate-of-return method, 375
Accumulated Depreciation account, changes in, analyzing, 495–496
Activity-based costing (ABC), 9, 60–65, **61**
   cost allocation using, 62–65, 63(fig.), 64(table)
   implementing, 169–172
   process costing and, 132(fig.), 132–134, 133(exh.)
   for selling and administrative activities, 172, 173(exh.)
Activity-based management (ABM), 9, 163, 163–172
   activity-based costing and, 169–172
   just-in-time compared with, 181(table), 181–182
   process value analysis and, 167
   in service organizations, 165, 166(fig.), 167–168, 168(table)
   supply chains and value chains and, 163–165, 164(fig.)
   value-adding and nonvalue-adding activities and, 166–168, 168t
Activity-based systems, 159–183, 161
   in management cycle, 161–163, 162(fig.)
Actual costing, 46, 46–47
Administrative activities, activity-based costing for, 172, 173(exh.)
Annual reports, 534
Annual Statement Studies, 535

Annuities, ordinary, present value of, 580(table), 580–581
APB (Accounting Principles Board), on imputed interest, 582
Appraisal costs, 439
Asset(s)
   cash flows to, 479, 547
   current, 485–486, 494–495
   depreciation of, *see* Depreciation
   fixed, 488–489, 495–496
   operating, 488–489, 495–496
   present value for valuing, 583
   return on, 545
Asset turnover, 545
Audits, postcompetition, capital investment decisions and, 371–372
Average costing approach, 123
   process costing using, 135–137
Average cost of capital, 373
Average days' inventory on hand, 544
Average days' sales uncollected, 543

Backflush costing, 178, 178–181
   cost flows in traditional and backflush costing and, 178–181, 179(fig.), 180(fig.)
Balance sheet
   common-size, 541(fig.), 542(exh.)
   consolidated, 534–539
Balance Sheet accounts, changes in, analyzing, 494–497
Barron's magazine, 535
Base year, 537
Batch-level activities, 169
Beginning inventory, cost flows in job order costing system and, 94
Beginning work in process inventory
   equivalent production with, 128(exh.), 128–129, 135–137, 136(exh.)
   equivalent production without, 126–127, 127(exh.), 135
Bills of activities, 170, 170(exh.), 171–172
Bonds payable, cash flows from financing activities and, 490

Bonds Payable account, changes in, analyzing, 496
Book value, 374
   capital budgeting and, 374
Breakeven point, 210, 210–211, 211(fig.)
Budget(s), 237
   capital expenditures, 254
   cash, 254(table), 254–256
   cost of goods manufactured, 251, 252(exh.), 253
   direct labor, 250, 250(exh.)
   direct materials purchases, 248–249, 249(exh.)
   flexible (variable), 299–302, 299–302(exh.)
   manufacturing overhead, 250–251, 251(exh.)
   master, *see* Master budget
   production, 247(exh.), 247–248, 248(exh.)
   sales, 246, 247
   selling and administrative expense, 251, 252(exh.)
Budgeted income statement, 253, 253(exh.)
Budget information, 239, 239–240
Budgeting, 235–264, 237
   long-range goals of, 241
   management cycle and, 239(fig.), 239–241
   process of, 237, 238(exh.), 239–242
   short-range goals and strategies of, 241–242
Business organizations, *see* Management; Manufacturing businesses; Merchandising businesses; Service businesses

CAD (computer-aided design), 441
Capacity, operating, 202–203
Capital
   cost of, 373
   human, 443
Capital budgeting, 368, 368–369, 369(fig.)
   cost and revenue measures used in, 374–375